Google·pedia ™

The Ultimate Google Resource

Michael Miller

Book Search · Pack · AdSense · Maps

que®

800 East 96th Street
Indianapolis, Indiana 46240

Googlepedia: The Ultimate Google Resource

International Standard Book Number: 0-7897-3639-X

Printed in the United States of America

First Printing: July 2006

09   08   07   06   4   3

Trademarks

All terms mentioned in this book that are known to be trademarks or service marks have been appropriately capitalized. Que Publishing cannot attest to the accuracy of this information. Use of a term in this book should not be regarded as affecting the validity of any trademark or service mark.

Warning and Disclaimer

Every effort has been made to make this book as complete and as accurate as possible, but no warranty or fitness is implied. The information provided is on an "as is" basis. The author and the publisher shall have neither liability nor responsibility to any person or entity with respect to any loss or damages arising from the information contained in this book.

Bulk Sales

Que Publishing offers excellent discounts on this book when ordered in quantity for bulk purchases or special sales. For more information, please contact

U.S. Corporate and Government Sales
1-800-382-3419
corpsales@pearsontechgroup.com

For sales outside of the U.S., please contact

International Sales
international@pearsoned.com

This Book Is Safari Enabled

The Safari® Enabled icon on the cover of your favorite technology book means the book is available through Safari Bookshelf. When you buy this book, you get free access to the online edition for 45 days.

Safari Bookshelf is an electronic reference library that lets you easily search thousands of technical books, find code samples, download chapters, and access technical information whenever and wherever you need it.

To gain 45-day Safari Enabled access to this book:

- Go to http://www.quepublishing.com/safarienabled
- Complete the brief registration form
- Enter the coupon code MAQB-KALQ-WL5L-Q5PU-5WA1

If you have difficulty registering on Safari Bookshelf or accessing the online edition, please e-mail customer-service@safaribooksonline.com.

Library of Congress Cataloging-in-Publication Data

Miller, Michael, 1958-
  Googlepedia : the ultimate Google resource / Michael Miller.
    p. cm.
  ISBN 0-7897-3639-X (pbk.)
  1. Google. 2. Internet searching. 3. Web search engines. I. Title.
TK5105.885.G66M55 2007
025.04--dc22
                      2006019448

Associate Publisher
Greg Wiegand

Acquisitions Editor
Stephanie J. McComb

Development Editors
Rick Kughen
Todd Brakke

Managing Editor
Patrick Kanouse

Project Editor
Mandie Frank

Indexer
Heather McNeill

Proofreader
Jessica McCarty

Technical Editor
Marc Charney

Publishing Coordinator
Cindy Teeters

Book Designer
Anne Jones

Page Layout
Bronkella Publishing LLC

Contents at a Glance

Introduction

Part I: Basic Searches

1   Inside Google

2   Searching the Web

3   Searching the Google Directory

Part II: Specialized Searches

4   Searching for People and Phone Numbers

5   Searching for Financial Information

6   Searching Blogs and Blog Postings

7   Searching for Scholarly Information

8   Searching for University, Technical, and Government Information

9   Searching for Words and Definitions

10 Searching for Other Special Information

Part III: Additional Search Features

11 Customizing Google and the Google Home Page

12 Making Google Safe for Kids

13 Using Google in Other Languages

14 Using Google as a Calculator and Converter

15 Keeping Updated with Google Alerts

Part IV: Shopping and Product Searches

16 Searching for Bargains with Froogle and Google Catalogs

17 Buying and Selling—Online and Locally—with Google Base

Part V: Maps and Directions

18 Using Google Maps

19 Using and Creating Google Map Mashups

20 Using Google Earth

Part VI: Communications Services

21 Using Gmail

22 Instant Messaging with Google Talk and Gmail Chat

23 Using Blogger

Part VII: Multimedia

24 Searching Google Images

25 Downloading Entertainment from Google Video

Part VIII: Other Google Services

26 Using Google Answers

27 Using Google Book Search

28   Using Google Groups

29   Using Google News

30   Using Google Mobile Services

Part IX: Google Software Tools

31   Using the Google Toolbar

32   Using Google Desktop

33   Using Google Calendar

34   Using Picasa

35   Using Google Pack

Part X: Google for Businesses

36   Submitting Your Site—and Increasing Your Ranking

37   Making Money with Google AdSense and AdWords

38   Using Google Within Your Organization

Part XI: Google for Developers

39   Adding Google to Your Website

40   Creating Custom Search Applications

41   Creating Google Map Mashups

Part XII: Into the Future

42   Exploring Google Labs

43   Beyond Search: What's Next for Google

Appendixes

A   Google's Site Directory

B   Google's Country-Specific Sites

C   Google's Advanced Search Operators

Index

Table of Contents

Introduction 1

What's in This Book 2

Who Can Use This Book 4

How to Use This Book 4

Get Ready to Google! 5

Part I: Basic Searches

1   Inside Google 9

Getting to Know Google, Inc. 10

Google's Mission 10

Google's History 11

Google's Revenues 13

Is Google a Search Company or an Advertising Company? 14

Life at the Googleplex 15

How Google Works 17

How a Typical Search Works 17

How Google Builds Its Database—And Assembles Its Index 18

How Google Ranks Its Results 20

The Bottom Line 22

2   Searching the Web 23

Conducting a Basic Search 23

Navigating Google's Home Page 24

Entering Your Query 24

Feeling Lucky? 25

How Google Displays Its Results 25

Omitted Results 27

Extending Your Search 28

Conducting a More Refined Search 29

Don't Worry About Capitalization... 29

...But Do Worry About Word Order 29

"And" Is Assumed 32

Search for One or Another Word 32

Common Words Are Automatically Excluded 33

Always Include Stop Words 33

Exclude Words from Results 34

Take Advantage of Automatic Word Stemming 34
Search for Similar Words 34
Search for an Exact Phrase 35
Use Wildcards to Search for Missing Words in an Exact Phrase 36
Search for Words That Don't Appear Together 36
Narrow Your Search to Specific File Types 37
Narrow Your Search to a Specific Domain or Website 38
Narrow Your Search to Words in the Page's Title 39
Narrow Your Search to Words in the Page's URL 39
Narrow Your Search to Words in the Page's Body Text 40
Narrow Your Search to Words in the Page's Link Text 40
Search for a Range of Numbers 41
Travel Way Back in Time for Your Search 41
List Pages That Link to a Specific Page 42
List Similar Pages 42
Find Out More About a Specific Page 43
Highlight Keywords 43

Using the Advanced Search Page 44

Narrowing Your Search Results with URL Parameters 46
Understanding Google's URLs 46
Displaying the Most Recent Results 47
Displaying More (or Fewer) Results 48
Restricting Results to a Specific Filetype 48

Other Ways to Query Google 48

Tips for More Effective Searches 51
Use the Correct Methodology 51
Use the Right Keywords in Your Query 51
Save Your Results 53

The Bottom Line 53

3   Searching the Google Directory 55

What the Google Directory Is—And What It Isn't 56
Why a Directory Isn't a Search Engine, and Vice Versa 56
How the Google Directory Is Assembled 58
Why You'd Want to Use the Google Directory Instead of Google's
Web Search 60

Navigating the Google Directory 61
  Searching Directory Listings 61
  Browsing Directory Categories 62
  Searching Within a Category 64
The Bottom Line 66

Part II: Specialized Searches

4   Searching for People and Phone Numbers 69
Searching for People by Name 69
Searching for People by Phone Number 74
Searching for Personal Information—And Home Pages 75
Googling Yourself 76
The Bottom Line 78

5   Searching for Financial Information 79
Searching via the Standard Search Box 79
Using Google Finance 80
  Accessing General Financial Information 81
  Accessing Specific Stock and Company Information 83
  Viewing Interactive Financial Charts 87
  Tracking Your Portfolio 89
Discussing Finances in Google Finance Groups 91
  Finding Google Finance Discussions 92
  Reading and Rating Messages 92
  Creating a Google Finance Profile 93
  Replying to Messages 94
  Starting a New Discussion 94
The Bottom Line 96

6   Searching Blogs and Blog Postings 97
How Google Blog Search Works 98
How to List Your Blog with Google Blog Search 99
Searching for Blogs—And Blog Posts 99
  Four Ways to Search 100
  Evaluating Blog Search Results 102

Fine-Tuning Your Blog Search Query 103
　　Using Advanced Search Operators 103
　　Using the Advanced Search Page 103
　　Advanced Searching from Blogger 105

Subscribing to Blog Search Results 106

Reading Blog Feeds with Google Reader 108
　　Search for Feeds 109
　　Enter the Site's URL 110
　　Enter the Feed URL 111
　　Import Feeds from Other Readers 112
　　Editing Your Subscriptions 112
　　Sharing Your Favorite Postings 113
　　Putting Your Favorite Feeds on Your Own Web Page 115

The Bottom Line 116

7　Searching for Scholarly Information 117

How Google Scholar Works 118
　　Identifying Scholarly Content 119
　　Searching Beyond the Public Internet 119
　　Including Print-Only Content 120

Understanding Google Scholar Search Results 121
　　Different Types of Results 121
　　Listing Information 123
　　How to Use Google Scholar Results 123

Searching Google Scholar 124
　　Conducting a Basic Search 124
　　Using Advanced Search Operators 124
　　Using the Advanced Scholar Search Page 125

Linking to Information at Your Library 126

Expanding Google Scholar 128
　　Add Google Scholar to Your Website 128
　　Google Scholar for Libraries 129
　　Google Scholar for Publishers 130

The Bottom Line 130

8　Searching for University, Technical, and Government Information 131

Using Google's University Search 132

Using Google's Special Technology Searches 134

Using Google U.S. Government Search 136
The Bottom Line 137

9 Searching for Words and Definitions 139
Using a "What Is" Search 139
Using the Google Glossary 141
Finding Similar Words with Google Sets 143
The Bottom Line 145

10 Searching for Other Special Information 147
Searching for Facts 148
Searching for Weather Information 149
Searching for Travel Information 149
    Viewing Airport Conditions 149
    Tracking Flight Status 150
Searching for Numbers 152
Searching for Movies 153
Searching for Music 156
The Bottom Line 158

Part III: Additional Search Features

11 Customizing Google and the Google Home Page 161
Setting Google Search Preferences 161
    Display Google in a Different Language 162
    Search in a Different Language 163
    Search Safely 163
    Display More Results Per Page 163
    Open a New Results Window 163
Creating Your Own Personalized Homepage 164
    Personalizing Start Page Content 165
    Adding RSS Feeds 166
    Customizing Individual Content Modules 167
    Rearranging Content Modules 169
    Deleting Content Modules 169
    Adding Even More Content 169
    Your Final Personalized Homepage 171

Making Google Your Home Page 172

The Bottom Line 173

12 Making Google Safe for Kids 175

How SafeSearch Filtering Works 176

Enabling the SafeSearch Filter 176

SafeSearch Filtering from the Preferences Page 177

SafeSearch Filtering from the Advanced Search Page 177

SafeSearch Filtering from the Standard Search Box 177

SafeSearch Filtering by Editing the Search Results URL 178

When Not to Use SafeSearch 179

The Bottom Line 180

13 Using Google in Other Languages 181

Searching for Language- and Country-Specific Pages 181

Changing Your Default Language Search 182

Conducting a Language-Specific Search 182

Conducting a Country-Specific Search 183

Displaying Google in Another Language 184

Using Country-Specific Google Sites 186

Translating Text and Web Pages from One Language to
Another 187

Languages Translated 188

Translating Text Passages 189

Translating Web Pages 190

Translating from Google's Search Results 192

Translating Web Pages from the Google Toolbar 192

Translating Words from the Google Toolbar 192

The Bottom Line 194

14 Using Google As a Calculator and Converter 195

Performing Basic Calculations from the Google Search Box 195

Performing Advanced Calculations 198

Looking Up the Values of Constants 199

Converting Units of Measure 202

An Easier Way to Calculate 208

The Bottom Line 210

15   Keeping Updated with Google Alerts 211

    Different Kinds of Alerts 211

    Signing Up for Alerts 213

    Customizing and Editing Your Alerts 215

    Deleting Google Alerts 216

    The Bottom Line 217

Part IV: Shopping and Product Searches

16   Searching for Bargains with Froogle and Google Catalogs 221

    Froogle: It's Different from Other Price Comparison Sites 222

        How Most Price Comparison Sites Work 222

        How Froogle Works 222

    Searching for the Lowest Prices 223

        Basic Searching 223

        Understanding Froogle's Search Results 224

        Getting the Most from the Product Detail Page 225

        Advanced Searching 226

        Using Advanced Search Operators 228

        Getting Ready to Buy 228

    Shopping for Local Bargains 229

        Local Bargains from the Main Froogle Search Box 230

        Local Bargains from the Search Results Page 230

    Using Froogle's Merchant Reviews 232

    Creating Your Own Froogle Shopping List 235

        Adding an Item to Your Shopping List 235

        Viewing and Managing Your Shopping List 235

        Creating a Wish List 236

    Shopping Online with Google Catalogs 237

        Searching for Specific Catalogs 238

        Browsing by Product Category 239

        Viewing Catalogs Online 239

    The Bottom Line 243

17   Buying and Selling—Online and Locally—with Google Base 245

    Understanding Google Base 246

    What's Not Permitted on Google Base 247

Finding Items on Google Base 248
        Searching for Items 248
        Browsing for Items 251
        Buying Items with Google Payments 253
    Selling Items on Google Base 256
        Submitting Google Base Listings 256
        Accepting Google Payments 259
    Uploading Bulk Items 261
        Creating and Submitting a Bulk Upload File 262
        Using Google Base to Submit Store Inventory to Froogle 262
        Using Google Base to Submit Business Location Data to
            Google Maps 262
    The Bottom Line 264

Part V: Maps and Directions

    18   Using Google Maps 267
    Introducing Google Maps 267
    Searching for Maps 269
        Searching by Address 269
        Searching by Landmark 271
        Displaying Google Maps by Entering a URL 272
        Displaying Street Maps from a Google Web Search 273
    Navigating a Google Map 274
    Displaying Satellite Images 276
        The View from Above 276
        Displaying Hybrid Satellite Maps 278
    Sharing Maps 279
        Linking to a Specific Map 279
        Emailing a Map 279
        Printing a Map 280
    Displaying Driving Directions 280
        Generating Turn-by-Turn Directions 280
        Following Directions 282
        Getting Back Home Again 283
        Printing Your Directions 285
    Setting Your Default Location 287
    Finding Nearby Businesses 288
        Adding Your Business to Google Maps 290

Using Google Maps on Your Cell Phone 291
   Sending Map Info to Your Cell Phone 291
   Querying Google Maps via Text Message 292
   Using Google Maps for Mobile 292
The Bottom Line 294

19 Using Google Map Mashups 295
Finding Google Map Mashups 296
News and Weather Mashups 297
Local Information and Services 299
Housing 301
Food, Dining, and Entertainment 302
Transportation 303
WiFi and Cellular 305
Demographic Information 306
Colleges and Universities 307
Photo Maps 308
Sports and Training 309
Games 311
Celebrity Sightings 312
Other Fun—And Informative—Mashups 314
The Bottom Line 316

20 Using Google Earth 317
Which Version Is for You? 317
Introducing Google Earth 318
Navigating Google Earth 319
   Navigating with the Onscreen Navigation Controls 320
   Navigating with the Mouse 321
   Navigating with the Keyboard 322
Taking a Quick Tour of Google Earth 323
Making Google Earth More Three-Dimensional 328
Configuring View Options 332
   Setting View Preferences 332
   Using Full-Screen Mode 333
   Displaying a Latitude/Longitude Grid 333
   Displaying the Overview Map 333

Saving and Printing a View 335

Searching for Locations to View 335

Displaying Driving Directions 336

Getting Directions 336

Touring Your Route 337

Printing and Saving Directions 337

Displaying and Using Layers 338

Displaying Points of Interest 342

Creating Custom Placemarks 343

Measuring Distance Along a Path 345

Using Google Earth with GPS Devices 347

The Bottom Line 347

Part VI: Communications Services

21   Sending and Receiving Email with Gmail 351

What Makes Gmail Unique 352

Signing Up (It's Free!) 354

Getting to Know the Gmail Interface 355

Sending and Receiving Email 356

Reading Messages 356

Viewing Conversations 356

Replying to Messages 358

Forwarding Messages 359

Composing and Sending New Messages 360

Attaching Files 361

Opening or Viewing Attached Files 362

Deleting Messages 363

Searching Your Inbox 363

Basic Search 364

Searching with Search Options 364

Searching with Advanced Operators 365

Other Ways of Organizing Your Email Messages 367

Starring Important Messages 367

Applying Labels 367

Archiving Old Messages 368

Filtering Incoming Mail 369

Dealing with Spam and Viruses 370
  Blocking Spam Messages 371
  Scanning Your Attachments for Viruses 371
Working with Contacts 371
  Adding a New Contact 372
  Importing Contacts from Another Program 374
  Displaying Contacts 374
  Searching for Contacts 375
  Using Contact Groups 375
  Sending a Message to a Contact or Contact Group 377
Using Gmail with Other Email Programs and Accounts 377
  Reading Gmail in Another Email Program 378
  Forwarding Gmail to Another Account 379
Putting Gmail into Vacation Mode 379
Viewing RSS Feeds in Gmail 380
Adding a Signature to Your Messages 382
Getting Notified of New Gmail Messages 383
  Using the Gmail Notifier 383
  Using the Google Toolbar 384
The Bottom Line 385

22 Instant Messaging with Google Talk and Gmail Chat 387
Instant Messaging with Google Talk 387
  Finding Someone to Talk To 388
  Initiating a Text-Based Chat 388
  Blocking Other Users 390
  Saving Your Chat History 390
  Changing Your Status—And Signing Out 391
  Initiating a Voice-Based Chat 391
  Customizing Google Talk 391
Chatting via Gmail with Gmail Chat 393
  Initiating a Chat 393
  Changing Your Status—And Ending Your Chat Session 394
Using Google Talk with Other IM Networks .396
The Bottom Line 399

23 Using Blogger 401
How Blogs Are Organized 402
Getting to Know Blogger 404

Creating a Blog 405

Viewing Your Blog 408

Posting New Blog Entries 409

Blogging from the Google Toolbar 411

Editing Your Posts 412

Managing Comments—And Fighting Spam 414
    Limiting Comments 414
    Moderating Comments 414
    Fighting Comment Spam 414

Syndicating Your Blog 416

Making Money from Your Blog 417

Changing Where Your Blog Is Hosted 419

Changing Templates 421
    Choosing a Different Template 421
    Using Third-Party Templates 421

Modifying Blogger Templates with HTML and Blogger Tags 424
    Understanding Essential Codes 425
    Understanding Blogger Tags 425
    Using Other HTML Tags 429

How Popular Is Your Blog? 431

The Bottom Line 431

Part VII: Multimedia

24   Searching Google Images 435

Searching for Images 435
    Basic Searching 436
    Advanced Searching 436

Viewing Image Search Results 438

Saving and Printing Images 439

Filtering Out Dirty Pictures 440

Removing Your Images from Image Search 441

The Bottom Line 442

25   Downloading Video Entertainment from Google Video 443

Searching for and Downloading Videos 444
    Browsing by Category 444
    Changing the Thumbnail Display 445

Basic Video Searching 447
Searching by Title 447
Viewing the Top 100 Videos 447
Viewing Google Picks Videos 448
Viewing Past Picks (and More) at the Google Video Blog 448

Viewing Videos 450
Previewing Videos 450
Understanding Google Video Viewing Options 451
Playing Streaming Videos on the Google Video Web Page 452
Downloading Videos 453

Watching Videos You've Downloaded 454
Using the Google Video Player for Playback .454
Playing Downloaded Videos on Another Video Player 456
Playing Purchased Videos on Another Computer 456

Downloading Videos to Portable Devices 457
Downloading to an Apple Video iPod 457
Downloading to a Sony Playstation Portable .458

Distributing Your Own Videos via the Google Video Upload
Program 458
Understanding Upload File Guidelines 459
Uploading Videos 459
Charging for Your Video 459

The Bottom Line 462

Part VIII: Other Google Services

26   Using Google Answers 465

Understanding Google Answers 465
What Kinds of Questions Can You Ask? 466
Who Answers Your Questions? 466
How Much Should You Pay for Answers? 467

Asking Questions—and Viewing Answers 467
Viewing Previously-Answered Questions 467
Adding Your Comments to a Question 470
Asking a New Question 470
Getting the Answer 472

Clarifying Your Question—And Your Answers 473

Ratings, Refunds, and Reposts 474

The Bottom Line 474

27 Using Google Book Search 475

  The Story Behind Google Book Search 476
    Google Books Partner Program 476
    Google Books Library Project 477

  Searching—And Viewing—Book Content 477
    Searching from the Standard Web Search Page 477
    Searching from Google Book Search 478
    Conducting an Advanced Book Search 478
    Viewing Book Content 479
    Getting More Information 484

  The Bottom Line 487

28 Using Google Groups 489

  The History of Usenet and Google Groups 490
    How Newsgroups Work 490
    Understanding Newsgroup Hierarchies 490
    Google Groups: Archiving Usenet Articles 492

  Searching the Newsgroups 492
    Searching for Groups 492
    Browsing Through the Groups 493
    Searching Across All Groups 494
    Using Advanced Search Operators 495
    Performing an Advanced Search 496

  Participating in Google Groups 497
    Visiting Groups and Reading Messages 497
    Subscribing to a Group 498
    Posting to a Group 499
    Creating a New Message Thread 500

  Creating Your Own Google Group 501
    Setting Up the Group 501
    Inviting Members to Your Group 503
    Managing Your Group 504

  The Bottom Line 506

29 Using Google News 507

  Viewing the Latest Headlines and Stories 508

  Viewing International News 510

  Personalizing Google News 512

Searching for News Articles 513

Reading Google News Feeds 514

Signing Up for News Alerts 515

Getting News on the Go 516

The Bottom Line 517

30 Using Google Mobile Services 519

Searching Google on Your Web-Enabled Mobile Phone 520

    Using Google Web Search 520

    Conducting Specialized Web Searches 521

    Using Google Mobile Web Search 521

    Using Google Image Search 522

    Using Google Local Search 522

Searching Google via Text Messaging 523

Downloading Google Maps and Directions on Your
    Mobile Phone 524

Viewing Google News on Your Mobile Phone 525

Sending and Receiving Gmail on Your Mobile Phone 525

Searching Froogle on Your Mobile Phone 526

Personalizing Your Google Mobile Home Page 526

The Bottom Line 527

Part IX: Google Software Tools

31 Using the Google Toolbar 531

Getting to Know the Google Toolbar 531

Using Google Toolbar's Default Buttons 532

    Enhanced Search Box 532

    Google News 534

    Google Desktop 534

    Weather 534

    Gmail 535

    Bookmarks 535

    PageRank 536

    Pop-up Blocker 536

    SpellCheck 536

    AutoLink 536

    AutoFill 537

Send To 538
Highlight 539
Word Find 539

Customizing the Google Toolbar 539
Adding and Removing Buttons 540
Using the Optional Toolbar Buttons .541
Adding Custom Buttons to the Toolbar 541

Other Ways to Search Google from Your Web Browser 542
Making Google Your Default Search Engine in Internet Explorer 542
Installing Google Browser Buttons 544

The Bottom Line 545

32   Using Google Desktop 547

Welcome to the Google Desktop 548

Searching Your Hard Disk 550
Conducting a Basic Search 550
Viewing Your Results 550
Filtering Your Results 552
Conducting an Advanced Desktop Search 553
Viewing Items in Timeline View 554
Viewing the Contents of Your Index 554

Searching within Microsoft Outlook .556

Searching Other Computers on Your Network 556

Searching the Web from Google Desktop 558
Searching from the Google Desktop Window 558
Searching from the Sidebar 559
Searching from the Quick Search Box .559

Using the Google Desktop Sidebar 561
Different Ways to Display the Sidebar .561
Working with Sidebar Gadgets 562

The Bottom Line 565

33   Using Google Calendar 567

All About Google Calendar 567

Setting Up Your Google Calendar 570
Setting Up a Basic Calendar 570
Setting Up Multiple Calendars 570
Setting Up Other Types of Calendars .570

Viewing Your Calendar 572
    Using Different Views 572
    Viewing Multiple Calendars 575
    Viewing Your Calendar from Other Calendar Applications 575
Working with Events 577
    Adding an Event to Your Calendar 577
    Adding an Event via Quick Add 579
    Adding an Event from Gmail 579
    Importing Events from Other Applications 579
    Inviting Others to an Event 581
Creating a Public Calendar 583
Searching Your Calendar—And Public Calenders 584
    Searching Your Private Calendars 584
    Searching Public Calendars 584
The Bottom Line 584

34 Using Picasa 585
Installing and Configuring the Program 585
Getting to Know the Picasa Desktop 587
Organizing Your Photos 589
    Moving Photos 589
    Renaming Photos 590
Fixing Common Photo Problems 590
    Fixing a Dark (or Light) Picture 591
    Fixing an Off-Color Picture 592
    Fixing Red Eye 594
    Cropping a Picture 595
    Applying Special Effects 596
Saving Your Changes 598
    Saving an Edited File 598
    Resizing a Photo for the Web 598
Printing and Sharing Your Photos 599
    Printing Photos on Your Personal Printer 599
    Printing Photos via an Online Print Service 599
    Sharing Your Photos with Picasa Web Albums 601
    Sharing Your Photos with Hello 601
    Emailing Photos 602
    Burning Photos to a Picture CD or DVD 604
The Bottom Line 605

35 Using Google Pack 607

What's in Google Pack? 607

Installing Google Pack—And Keeping It Up-to-Date 608

Using the Google Pack Screensaver 610

Using the Third-Party Software in Google Pack 612
  Surfing the Web with Mozilla Firefox 612
  Fighting Viruses with Norton Antivirus 2005 Special Edition 613
  Fighting Spyware with Ad-Aware SE Personal 613
  Viewing PDF Files with Adobe Reader 614
  Playing Music and Videos with RealPlayer 614
  Viewing GalleryPlayer HD Images 614

The Bottom Line 616

Part X: Google for Businesses

36 Submitting Your Site—And Increasing Your Ranking 619

How to Submit Your Site to the Google Index—The Easy Way ...620

How to Remove Your Site from the Google Index 621

How to Submit a Complete Sitemap 621
  Basic Site Submittal 622
  Submitting a Complete Sitemap 623
  Creating and Submitting Your Sitemap 623
  Using Sitemap Generator Tools 624
  Viewing Sitemap Diagnostics and Statistics 625

How to Optimize Your Site's Ranking 627
  Increase the Number of Links to Your Site 627
  Create a Clear Organization and Hierarchy 628
  Include Appropriate Keywords 628
  Put the Most Important Information First 629
  Make the Most Important Information Look Important 629
  Use Text Instead of Images 629
  Link via Text 629
  Incorporate <META> Tags 630
  Make Good Use of the <TITLE> Tag 631
  Use Heading Tags Instead of CSS 631
  Update Your Code Frequently 631
  Use RSS Feeds for Dynamic Content 632
  Use an OPML File 632

How Not to Optimize Your Site's Ranking 632
Site Design Problems to Avoid 633
Deliberate Practices to Avoid 634
Using Search Engine Optimizers 636
SEO Software 636
SEO Services 636
The Bottom Line 638

37   Making Money with Google AdSense and AdWords 639
Adding Advertising to Your Website with Google AdSense 640
Understanding Google AdSense for Content 640
Understanding Google AdSense for Search .641
How to Profit from AdSense 642
Joining the AdSense Program 643
Adding AdSense Ads to Your Website 644
Adding a Google Search Box to Your Site 647
Making More Money with AdSense Referrals 650
Monitoring Your AdSense Performance 653
Ten Tips for Improving Your AdSense Earnings 654
Advertising on Google with Google AdWords 658
Where Google AdWords Advertises 659
Determining Your Costs—And Choosing a Payment Option 660
Creating an AdWords Ad 660
Monitoring Your Ads' Performance 664
The Bottom Line 665

38   Using Google Within Your Organization 667
Searching the Corporate Network with the Google Toolbar
for Enterprise 667
Searching the Corporate Network with Google Desktop
for Enterprise 668
Searching Small Business Data with the Google Mini 669
Adding Enterprise-wide Search with the Google Search
Appliance 670
Creating Geo Data with Google Earth Enterprise 671
Creating 3D Models with Google SketchUp .671
The Bottom Line 672

Part XI: Google for Developers

39 Adding Google to Your Website 675

Adding Google Free WebSearch 675

Adding Google Free SafeSearch 676

Adding Google Free WebSearch with SiteSearch 677

Adding Customizable Google Free WebSearch 678

Adding Site-Flavored Google Search 681

The Bottom Line 682

40 Creating Custom Search Applications 683

Developing Your Own Google-Based Applications 684

Programming with the Google Webs API 685

Types of Google-Based Applications 686

Using the Google Webs API 687

The Bottom Line 689

41 Creating Google Map Mashups 691

Creating Mashups—The Easy Way 692

Programming with the Google Maps API 693

Using the Google Maps API 693

Creating a Basic Map 693

Adding Map Controls 696

Adding an Info Window 696

Creating an Animated Map 697

Adding a Marker to Your Map 698

Adding Multiple Markers from Your Own Database 698

And Even More... 699

The Bottom Line 700

Part XII: Into the Future

42 Exploring Google Labs 703

Projects That Started in the Labs 703

What's Cooking in Google Labs Today 704

Google Trends 704

Google Co-op 706

Google Notebook 706

Google Reader 707

Google Related Links 709

Google Sets 709

Google Page Creator 710

Google Mars 710

Google Ride Finder 711

Google Transit 711

Froogle for Mobile 711

Google Suggest 712

Google Dashboard Widgets for Mac 712

Google Extensions for Firefox 712

Google Web Accelerator 713

Google Spreadsheets 713

Other Upcoming Google Projects 714

Google Health 714

Google Music 714

Google Write 715

Orkut 715

The Bottom Line 716

43   Beyond Search: What's Next for Google 717

Google vs. Microsoft: Developing Competition 717

Google vs. Yahoo!: Even More Competition 719

What Does Google Want to Be When It Grows Up? 719

The Bottom Line 723

Part XIII: Appendixes

A   Google's Site Directory 727

B   Google's Country-Specific Sites 731

C   Google's Advanced Search Operators 737

Index 741

About the Author

Michael Miller has written more than 75 non-fiction how-to books since 1989, including Que's *Absolute Beginner's Guide to Computer Basics, Absolute Beginner's Guide to eBay,* and *How Home Theater and HDTV Work.* His 1999 book, *The Complete Idiot's Guide to Online Search Secrets,* was one of the first books to cover Google (then in beta testing).

Mr. Miller has established a reputation for clearly explaining technical topics to non-technical readers, and for offering useful real-world advice about complicated topics. More information can be found at the author's website, located at www.molehillgroup.com.

Dedication

To Sherry—my search is over.

Acknowledgments

Thanks to the usual suspects at Que, including but not limited to Greg Wiegand, Stephanie McComb, Todd Brakke, Rick Kughen, Mandie Frank, and Marc Charney.

We Want to Hear from You!

As the reader of this book, *you* are our most important critic and commentator. We value your opinion and want to know what we're doing right, what we could do better, what areas you'd like to see us publish in, and any other words of wisdom you're willing to pass our way.

As an associate publisher for Que Publishing, I welcome your comments. You can email or write me directly to let me know what you did or didn't like about this book—as well as what we can do to make our books better.

Please note that I cannot help you with technical problems related to the topic of this book. We do have a User Services group, however, where I will forward specific technical questions related to the book.

When you write, please be sure to include this book's title and author as well as your name, email address, and phone number. I will carefully review your comments and share them with the author and editors who worked on the book.

Email: feedback@quepublishing.com

Mail: Greg Wiegand
Associate Publisher
Que Publishing
800 East 96th Street
Indianapolis, IN 46240 USA

Reader Services

Visit our website and register this book at www.quepublishing.com/register for convenient access to any updates, downloads, or errata that might be available for this book.

Introduction

en-cy-clo-pe-di-a *noun* A comprehensive reference work containing articles on a wide range of subjects or on numerous aspects of a particular field.

Goo-gle-pe-di-a *noun* A comprehensive reference work containing articles on numerous aspects of Google, the largest and most popular search engine on the Web.

I use Google every day. I've been using it every day since it first launched—before it launched, actually, when it still had the word "beta" on its home page. I use Google because it's easy to use, and because it delivers quality results.

I'm not unusual, of course. Google is the most-used search site on the Web, and most people choose it for the same reason I do—ease-of-use and effectiveness. That's not news.

What is news, for a lot of users, anyway, is that Google is more than just simple search. Most users don't know that they can fine-tune their search in a number of interesting ways, or that they can use Google to find pictures and news articles and compact discs, or that they can use the Google search box to perform mathematical calculations and conversions, or that Google can function as a spell checker or dictionary.

It's also news to most users that Google offers a variety of products and services that have little or nothing to with web search. Google runs the largest blogging community on the Web, hosts an archive of Usenet news articles, distributes a top-notch picture-editing program, and provides free web-based email services. You might not get all this from looking at Google's attractively austere search page, but it's there, nonetheless.

All these "hidden" features are what makes Google so interesting, at least to me, and are why I wrote this book. I wanted to show other users all the cool and useful stuff I've discovered in the Google family of sites, and to share some of the tips and tricks I've developed over the years for getting the most out of Google's various products and services.

That's what *Googlepedia* is—a guide to everything that Google has to offer. It's not just web search (although I cover that, in much depth); *Googlepedia* also covers Gmail and Picasa and Blogger and every other application and service that has come out of Google's headquarters. There's plenty of how-to information, of course, but also a lot of tricks and advice that even the most experienced user will appreciate.

I should note, however, that while I know a lot about what Google does and how it works, I'm not a Google insider. I don't work for Google, and had no official contact with Google while writing this book. That means I don't always take the company line; I'll tell you, as honestly as possible, when Google gets it right, when Google needs improvement, and when Google just plain sucks. (The company isn't perfect.) I'm not obligated to put on a positive face, which means you'll get the straight poop, good or bad.

What's in This Book

Google isn't just web search; the company offers a lot of different products and services, all of which I discuss somewhere in this book. Because of everything that Google does, this is a long book—43 chapters in all, organized into 12 major sections:

- **Part I: Basic Searches** provides an inside look at Google (the company and the technology), and then shows you the best ways to use Google web search and the Google Directory.

- **Part II: Specialized Searches** discusses all the many narrow searches Google lets you conduct, from phone number lookup and blog searches to searches for scholarly information and word definitions.

- **Part III: Additional Search Features** shows you how to customize Google and the Google Personalized Homepage, use SafeSearch content filtering, use Google in different languages, and use Google as a calculator and a converter (really!).

- **Part IV: Shopping and Product Searches** guides you through using Froogle, Google Catalogs, and Google Base to search for bargains on the Web.

- **Part V: Maps and Directions** is all about Google Maps, Google Earth, and finding the coolest and most useful Google Maps mashups online.

- **Part VI: Communications Services**shows you why Google isn't just about search; we'll discuss emailing with Gmail, instant messaging with Google Talk, and blogging with Blogger.

- **Part VII: Multimedia** is all about pictures and videos, courtesy of Google Images and Google Video.

- **Part VIII: Other Google Services** discusses a variety of Google's search-related and non-search services, including Google Answers, Google Book Search, Google Groups, Google News, and Google Mobile Services.

- **Part IX: Google Software Tools** presents Google's software and web-based applications, including Google Toolbar, Google Desktop, Google Calendar, Picasa, and Google Pack.

- **Part X: Google for Businesses** discusses Google's business-oriented tools and services, including how to improve your site's PageRank, how to make money with Google AdWords and AdSense, and how to employ Google search in your organization.

- **Part XI: Google for Developers** shows you how to add Google search to your website, create custom search applications, and produce your own Google Maps mashups.

- **Part XII: Into the Future** shows you what new applications are percolating inside Google Labs, and discusses Google's future directions.

There are also three appendixes that present useful reference information. Appendix A is the Google Site Directory (a complete listing of URLs for all of Google's websites), Appendix B present's Google's country-specific sites, and Appendix C lists Google's advanced search operators. Handy references, all.

Who Can Use This Book

Googlepedia can be used by any level of user; you don't have to be a search expert or application developer to find something of value within these pages. That said, I think this book has particular appeal to more experienced or interested users, as a lot of advanced features are presented. Still, even if you've never used Google (or Gmail or Google Maps or whatever) before, you'll find a lot of useful information here.

How to Use This Book

I hope that this book is easy enough to read that you don't need instructions. That said, there are a few elements that bear explaining.

First, there are several special elements in this book, presented in what we in the publishing business call "margin notes." There are different types of margin notes for different types of information, as you see here.

note This is a note that presents information of interest, even if it isn't wholly relevant to the discussion in the main text.

tip This is a tip that might prove useful for whatever it is you're in the process of doing.

caution This is a caution that something you might accidentally do might have undesirable results.

In most chapters you'll also find some personal commentary, presented in the form of a sidebar. These sections are meant to be read separately, as they exist "outside" the main text. And remember—these sidebars are my opinions only, so feel free to agree or disagree as you like.

Obviously, there are lots of web page addresses in the book, like this one: www.google.com. When you see one of these addresses (also known as a URL), you can go to that web page by entering the URL into the address box in your web browser. I've made every effort to ensure the accuracy of the Web addresses presented here, but given the ever-changing nature of the web, don't be surprised if you run across an address or two that's changed. I apologize in advance.

The other thing you'll find in various places throughout this book is HTML code. A snippet of code might look like this:

```
<p>
This is a line of text.
</p>
<img src="URL">
```

When part of the code is italics (such as the *URL* in the previous example), this means that you need to replace the italicized code with your own individual information. In the previous example, you would replace *URL* with the full URL and filename of an image file you want to include in your auction template.

If you're a web page developer, you'll know what to do with this code. If you're not, you might want to skip over those sections. (You don't have to be a developer to use Google, of course.)

Get Ready to Google!

With all these preliminaries out of the way, it's now time to get started. While I recommend reading the book in consecutive order, that isn't completely necessary, as each part of Google exists independently of the other parts; just as it's okay to skip around through Google's various products and services, it's also okay to skip around through the various chapters in this book.

In addition, I urge you to move outside the Google universe from time to time and visit my personal website, located at www.molehillgroup.com. Here you'll find more information on this book and other books I've written—including an errata page for this book, in the inevitable event that an error or two creeps into this text. (Hey, nobody's perfect!)

Finally, you need to know that writing about Google is like shooting at a moving target—the folks at the Googleplex are always adding new features and services. To that end, it's a given that there will be new information about Google available by the time you read these words. (That's life in cyberspace.) That's why I suggest you check out the e-Books online at www.quepublishing. com, where you'll find a number of short online books about Google's very latest features. These e-Books are the best way to supplement the information found in this book—and stay up-to-date on everything that Google has to offer.

So get ready to turn the page and learn more about using the Google family of sites. I know you'll discover features you haven't noticed before, and hopefully become a more effective searcher.

Basic Searches

1 Inside Google

2 Searching the Web

3 Searching the Google Directory

Inside Google

You probably know Google as a web search engine—*the* web search engine, perhaps. But Google is a lot more than just a simple search engine. It's a collection of technologies (most of which are search related, to be fair) that helps users find and use all manner of information, both on the Internet and on their own computers.

Google is also the company behind the technology. It might surprise you to know that Google actually makes very little money from its search technologies. What Google does to make money is sell advertising based on its search results. When you look at its income statement, Google doesn't look much like a technology company; instead, it looks quite a bit like an advertising company.

So if you only know Google for its famous search page, you have a lot of catching up to do. Read on to learn more about what Google really is—and what it does.

1

Getting to Know Google, Inc.

Google the website is just one product of Google, Inc., the company. It's the primary product, to be sure, but it's just one facet of a multifaceted organization.

Google's Mission

If Google is about more than simple web searching, just what is it that the company does? Well, we can get a clue by examining Google's mission statement:

Google's mission is to organize the world's information and make it universally accessible and useful.

As mission statements go, this one is properly high-minded and vague. But it's also somewhat descriptive of what the company actually does on a day-by-day basis. By using its proprietary search technology, Google does help to organize information and make it both more accessible and more useful.

Note, however, that the mission statement actually doesn't use the word "search." Instead, Google says it wants to "organize" information. It just so happens that the way it chooses to organize this information is via searching. So, in terms of Google's business, organizing data is the mission; searching is the chosen strategy to achieve this mission.

COMMENTARY

GOOGLE'S BUSINESS MODEL

You may have noticed that Google's mission statement is a little vague about how the company expects to make money at this endeavor. In fact, a "a little vague" is an understatement; Google doesn't say one word about how it plans to generate revenues and income.

As we'll learn later in this chapter, Google doesn't make any money from its main search site or technology—at least, not directly. Google generates all its revenues from selling advertising, which is something you wouldn't guess by reading its mission statement. After all, the mission statement doesn't say anything about "selling advertising based on search results" or "generating revenue from the sale of advertising links" or the like.

I guess the folks at Google are allowed to take a little license with their own mission statement; there's no law that says you have to lay out all your goals and strategies for the public (and competitors) to see. But I feel it's important for us as consumers of Google's products to realize how the company is monetizing its technology. It's also important if you're thinking about investing in Google stock; you need to know that the number of site visitors or web pages indexed has no direct bearing on the company's revenues or profits—save for the fact that the more visitors to its site, the more advertising revenues it can generate from its *real* customers.

Google's History

How did Google get to be Google? It all started at a 5,000-watt radio station in Fresno, California....

Okay, not really. But it did start small, and it did start in California.

Google was the brainchild of two Stanford University graduate students. Larry Page, 24 years old at the time, had just graduated from the University of Michigan, and was visiting Stanford on a campus tour. Sergey Brin, then 23, was one of the students assigned to show the potential students around. Legend has it that when they first met on that weekend in 1995, they didn't get along. That changed, however, as they both entered Stanford's computer science grad program and began to collaborate. (The two happy fellas in Figure 1.1 are Larry and Sergey as they look today.)

FIGURE 1.1

The brains behind Google: Larry Page (left) and Sergey Brin. (Photo courtesy of Google, Inc.)

Their first collaboration, in January of 1996, was a simple search engine they called BackRub. It was unique in that it based its search results on the number of "back links" pointing to a given website— more or less the same approach later used by the Google search engine.

BackRub was also unique in that it was designed to work on a network of low-end PCs, instead of the expensive mainframes used by the major search engines of the day.

> **note** The word "google" is a play on the word "googol," the mathematical term for the number represented by a 1 followed by 100 zeros. The term was coined by Milton Sirotta, and popularized in the book *Mathematics and the Imagination* by Edward Kasner (Sirotta's uncle) and James Newman.

Larry and Sergey grew their search capacity by adding more and more consumer PCs to the network that was housed in Larry's dorm room.

By 1998, Larry and Sergey were trying to sell their technology to Yahoo! and other search portals, but had no takers. Instead, they moved out of the dorm, wrote up a business plan, and found an angel investor in the form of Andy Bechtolsheim, one of the founders of Sun Microsystems. Bechtolsheim wrote Larry and Sergey a check for $100,000, and Google, Inc. was born.

Additional investors followed (mainly family and friends), and the company soon had an initial investment of close to $1 million. That was enough to rent an office (actually, the garage of a friend) in Menlo Park, California, which is what they did in September 1998. The company stayed in the garage until February 1999, when they moved to a real office in Palo Alto. At that time, Google had a whole eight employees.

By then, the Google.com website was up and running and handling more than a half-million queries a day. (Figure 1.2 shows the original Google website from December 1998; it doesn't look a whole lot different from Google's current site!) Users loved what they found, which helped them garner a lot of press attention, which in turned helped to increase site traffic, which in turn garnered more press, and so on and so on. The increased traffic and increased press also helped to attract additional investors, which helped to finance the hiring of more employees and the purchasing of additional hardware.

Google was a hit.

As time went by, Google continuously expanded the size of its website index, as well as introduced additional features and services. By the turn of the millennium, Google was competing for the titles of both biggest search index and most popular search engine—and continued to grow.

FIGURE 1.2

Google's original home page, circa December 1998.

Amazingly, Google was able to finance this growth with nothing more than venture capital money, resisting the urge to go public during the late 1990s dot-com boom and resulting early 2000s dot-com bust. But the pressure to go public kept building, and on August 19, 2004, Google issued its initial public offering, listed on NASDAQ under the GOOG symbol. Like all things Google, the IPO had its unique qualities; the initial stock was offered through a little-used Dutch auction process, designed to attract a broader range of small investors than what you find with a normal IPO.

Today, Google continues to grow (and its stock continues to rise—from an initial price of $100/share to a high of close to $500/share in early 2006. (It's since dropped a bit from then, but still remains significantly higher than the initial price; Figure 1.3 shows a graph of Google's stock price through March 2006.) Google is one of the five most popular sites on the Web, and ranks as the number-one search engine in the U.S, the U.K., Canada, Australia, and numerous other countries. The Google site attracts close to 400 million unique users every month. (And the number of employees has risen from the initial two—Larry and Sergey—to 5,680, at the end of 2005.)

Google's Revenues

Google not only attracts a lot of visitors to its website, it also generates a lot of money. How much money? Table 1.1 details Google's revenues and profits for the years 2002 through 2005:

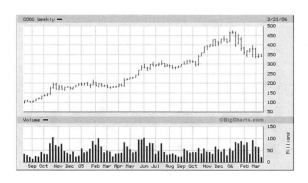

FIGURE 1.3

Google's LTD stock price, from 2004 through March 2006. (Courtesy www.bigcharts.com)

Table 1.1 Google Revenues and Profits 2002–2005				
	2002	**2003**	**2004**	**2005**
Advertising revenues	$410,915,000	$1,420,663,000	$3,143,288,000	$6,065,003,000
Licensing and other revenues	$28,593,000	$45,271,000	$45,935,000	$73,558,000
TOTAL REVENUES	**$439,508,000**	**$1,465,934,000**	**$3,189,223,000**	**$6,138,569,000**
Net income	$99,656,000	$105,648,000	$399,119,000	$1,465,397,000
Income as % of revenues	23%	7%	13%	24%

That's right, in 2005 Google generated more than six billion dollars in revenue, and close to one and a half billion dollars in profit. *One and a half billion dollars profit.* That's not bad. Not bad at all.

Is Google a Search Company or an Advertising Company?

Let's take another look at Table 1.1, and focus on how Google's revenues were generated. In 2005, Google generated $6 billion in *advertising revenues* versus just $73 million in licensing and other revenues. In other words, Google generated just 1.2% of its revenues from direct technology-related activities. Fully 98.8% of its revenues came from selling advertising.

What's that, you say? What is a technology company like Google doing selling advertising?

Well, my friend, it's all about monetizing the technology—and when it comes to search technology, you monetize it with ads. Since you can't charge users for searching, you charge advertisers for placing their ads (or "sponsored listings") on the search results pages. So while Google appears to be a company focused on search services and technologies, it's really a highly targeted advertising company.

What does that mean to you, a loyal Google user? Maybe nothing. Or maybe it's possible that Google focuses at least as much on how to increase advertising revenues as it does on improving search results. Or maybe the two activities go hand in hand.

After all, Google's advertising-based revenue model is not unlike what you find in the magazine business. Magazines may charge you a bit on the newsstand, but they generate the bulk of their revenues from advertisers. And the more copies of the magazine they sell, the more they can charge their advertisers for a full-page ad.

It's the same with Google. The more eyeballs they can deliver to their advertisers, the more they can charge for those "sponsored links." So whatever they can do to increase the number of site visitors—which benefits us as users, of course—they end up making more money from their advertisers. Make the experience better for users, they attract more users, they charge more for advertising, they make more money. That's the formula.

And how, exactly, does Google run its advertising business? There are actually two components to the business, *Google AdWords* and *Google AdSense*.

- AdWords sells targeted keywords to advertisers; when someone searches Google using one of those keywords, the advertiser's "sponsored listing" is displayed. Google gets paid (a penny or so) whenever someone clicks on the advertiser's listing.

- AdSense is the flip side of AdWords. The AdSense program places small ads on non-Google websites. (So if you run your own website, you can sign up for the AdSense program to put ads on your site's pages.) Google generates an appropriate ad based on the page's content; when a visitor clicks the ad, both Google and the site owner get paid.

Life at the Googleplex

So Google is a technology company that makes money from selling advertising. This kind of split personality is evident in Google's many offices around the world—some of which are strictly technology based, others of which are strictly sales based.

note There's a lot more to say about the AdWords and AdSense programs. To learn more, turn to Chapter 37, "Making Money with Google AdSense and AdWords."

Google's world headquarters in Mountain View, California, is called the Googleplex. The Googleplex combines both technology offices and sales offices, although it has a decidedly Silicon Valley flavor.

note The Googleplex is located at 1600 Amphitheatre Parkway, Mountain View, CA, 94043. The main telephone number is 650-253-0000.

The Googleplex has been described as "a joint founded by geeks and run by geeks." I've never been there, myself, but I've been told that it has a decidedly nonhierarchical feel, kind of an anticorporate atmosphere, where employees move from project to project regularly and frequently. Walk down the hallway and you'll see everything from lava lamps to large rubber exercise balls; the typical office is a "high-density cluster," like the one in Figure 1.4, where three or four staffers share couches and computers. During lunch, employees of all levels socialize at the Google Café, and there's a workout room, massage room, washers and dryers, video games, a pool table, and a baby grand piano available for anyone's use. Google's a big company, but the Googleplex still has a small company feel.

FIGURE 1.4

A typical employee "cluster" at the Googleplex. (Photo courtesy Google, Inc.)

Of course, the Googleplex isn't the only Google office. Google has offices all around the world, including a handful of technology-only offices (several in India), considerably more sales-only offices, and a few offices that, like the Googleplex, combine technology and ad sales. The different types of offices emphasize the technology/sales dichotomy that drives the company; here's a list:

- **Technology-only offices.** Pittsburgh, PA; Bangalore, India; Delhi, India; Hyderabad, India; Mumbai, India
- **Sales-only offices.** Atlanta, GA; Boston, MA; Chicago, IL; Dallas, TX; Denver, CO; Detroit, MI; Irvine, CA; Seattle, WA; Melbourne, Australia; Toronto, Canada; Copenhagen, Denmark; Manchester, England; Paris, France; Hamburg, Germany; Milan, Italy; Amsterdam, Netherlands; Seoul, South Korea; Madrid, Spain; Stockholm, Sweden
- **Technology and sales offices.** Mountain View, CA (world headquarters); Kirkland, WA; New York, NY; Phoenix, AZ; Santa Monica, CA; Sydney, Australia; Sao Paulo, Brazil; London, England; Dublin, Ireland; Tokyo, Japan; Mexico City, Mexico; Zurich, Switzerland; Istanbul, Turkey

How Google Works

Now that you have a better idea of what Google is and what it does, let's take a look at how it does what it does—in particular, how a Google search works. There's a lot of sophisticated technology behind even the most simple search.

How a Typical Search Works

The typical Google search takes less than half a second to complete. That's because all the searching takes place on Google's own web servers. That's right; you may think you're searching the Web, but in effect you're searching a huge index of websites stored on Google's servers. That index was created previously, over a period of time; because you're only searching a server, not the entire Web, your searches can be completed in the blink of an eye.

So what happens when you enter a query into the Google search box? It's a process that looks something like this:

1. When you click the Google Search button, your query is transmitted over the Internet to Google's web server.

note Google's servers are actually midpriced personal computers, just like the kind you have on your desktop. Google uses approximately 10,000 of these PCs, all of which run the Linux operating system. Google uses three types of servers: *web servers* (which host Google's public website), *index servers* (which hold the searchable index to the bigger document database), and *document servers* (which house copies of all the individual web pages in Google's database).

2. Google's web server sends your query to the company's array of index servers. These computers hold a searchable index to Google's database of web pages.

3. Your query is matched to listings in the Google index—that is, the index servers determine which actual web pages contain words that match your query.

4. Google now passes your query to the document servers, which store all the assembled web listings (documents) in the Google database.

5. The document servers assemble the results page for your query by pasting together snippets of the appropriate stored documents.

6. The document servers send the assembled results page back to the main web server.

7. Google's web server sends the results page across the Internet to your web browser, where you view it.

Of course, you're unaware of all this behind-the-scenes activity. You simply type your query into the search box on Google's main web page, click the Google Search button, and then view the search results page when it appears. All the shuffling of data from server to server is invisible to you.

How Google Builds Its Database—And Assembles Its Index

At the heart of Google's search system is the database of web pages stored on Google's document servers. These servers hold literally billions of individual web pages—not the entire Web, but a good portion of it.

How does Google determine which web pages to index and store on its servers? It's a complex process with several components.

First and foremost, most of the pages in the Google database are found by Google's special spider software. This is software that automatically crawls the Web, looking for new and updated web pages. Google's crawler, known as GoogleBot, not only searches for new web pages (by exploring links to other pages on the pages it already knows about), it also re-crawls pages already in the database, checking for changes and updates. A complete re-crawling of the web pages in the Google database takes place every few weeks, so no individual page is more than a few weeks out of date.

The GoogleBot crawler reads each page it encounters, much like a web browser does. It follows every link on every page until all the links have been followed. This is how new pages are added to the Google database, by following those links GoogleBot hasn't seen before.

> **note** GoogleBot is smart about how it updates the Google database. Web pages that are known to be frequently updated are crawled more frequently than other pages. For example, pages on a news site might be crawled hourly.

The pages discovered by GoogleBot are copied verbatim onto Google's document servers—and copied over each time they're updated. These web pages are used to compile the page summaries that appear on search results pages; they can also be viewed in their entirety when you click the Cached link in the search results. (These cached pages are a good way to view older versions of pages that have recently changed or been deleted.)

COMMENTARY

WHAT GOOGLE *ISN'T* GOOD AT

As big as Google's database is, there are still lots of web pages that don't make it into the database. In particular, Google doesn't do a good job of searching the "deep web," those web pages generated on the fly from big database-driven websites. Google also doesn't always find pages served by the big news sites, pages housed on web forums and discussion groups, blog pages, and the like.

These are all web pages with "dynamic" content that change frequently and don't always have a fixed URL; the URL—and the page itself—is generated on the fly, typically as a result of a search within the site itself.

This lack of a permanent URL makes these pages difficult, if not impossible, for GoogleBot to find. That's because GoogleBot, unlike a human being, can't enter a query into a site's search box and click the Search button. It has to take those pages that it finds, typically the site's fixed home page. The dynamically generated pages slip through the cracks, so to speak.

This is why it's possible to search for a page that you know exists (you've seen it yourself!) and not find it listed in Google's search results. It's not a trivial problem; more and more of the Web is moving to dynamically generated content, leaving at least half the Internet beyond the capability of Google's crawler. Google has technicians working on this challenge, but it's a big enough challenge that you shouldn't expect big improvements anytime soon.

In order to search the Google database, Google creates an index to all the stored web pages. This search engine index is much like the index found in the back of this book; it contains a list of all the important words used on every stored web page in the database. Once the index has been compiled, it's easy enough to search for a particular word, and have returned a list of all the web pages on which that word appears.

And that's exactly how the Google index and database work to serve your search queries. You enter one or more words in your query, Google searches its index for those words, and then those web pages that contain those words are returned as search results. Fairly simple in concept, but much more complex in execution—especially since Google is indexing all the words on several billion web pages.

How Google Ranks Its Results

Searching the Google index for all occurrences of a given word isn't all that difficult, especially with the computing power of 10,000 PCs driving things. What is difficult is returning the results in a format that is usable by and relevant to the person doing the searching. You can't just list the matching web pages in random order, nor is alphabetical or chronological order all that useful. No, Google has to return its search results with the most important or relevant pages listed first; it has to rank the results for its users.

How does Google determine which web pages are the best match to a given query? I wish I could give you all the details behind the scheme, but Google keeps this core methodology under lock and key; this methodology is what makes Google the most effective search engine on the Web today.

Even with all this secrecy, Google does provide some hints as to how its ranking system works. There are three components to the ranking:

- **Text analysis.** Google looks not only for matching words on a web page, but also for how those words are used. That means examining font size, usage, proximity, and more than a hundred other factors to help determine relevance. Google also analyzes the content of neighboring pages on the same website to ensure that the selected page is the best match.

- **Links and link text.** Google then looks at the links (and the text for those links) on the web page, making sure that they link to pages that are relevant to the searcher's query.

- **PageRank.** Finally, Google relies on its own proprietary PageRank technology to give an objective measurement of web page importance and popularity. PageRank determines a page's importance by counting the number of other pages that link to that page. The more pages that link to a page, the higher that page's PageRank—and the higher it will appear in the search results. The PageRank is a numerical ranking from 0 to 10, expressed as PR0, PR1, PR2, and so forth—the higher the better.

Although the other factors are important, PageRank is the secret sauce behind Google's page rankings. The theory is that the more popular a page is, the higher that page's ultimate value. While this sounds a little like a popularity contest (and it is), it's surprising how often this approach delivers high-quality results.

The actual formula used by PageRank (called the *PageRank Algorithm*) is super-duper top-secret classified, but by all accounts it's calculated using a combination of quantity and quality of the links pointing to a particular web page. In essence, the PageRank Algorithm considers the importance of each page that initiates a link, figuring (rightly so) that some pages have greater value than others. The higher the PageRank of the pages pointing to a given page, the higher the PageRank will be of the linked-to page. It's entirely possible that a page with fewer, higher-ranked pages linking to it will have a higher PageRank than a similar page with more (but lower-ranked) pages linking to it.

The PageRank factor on the linking page is also affected by the number of total outbound links on that page. That is, a page with a lot of outbound links will contribute a lower PageRank to each of its linked-to pages than will a page with just a few outbound links. As an example, a page with PageRank of PR8 that has 100 outbound links will boost a linked-to page's PageRank less than a similar PR8 page with just 10 outbound links.

It's important to note that Google's determination of a page's rank is completely automated. There is no human subjectivity involved, and no person or company can pay to increase the ranking of their listings. It's all about the math.

> **note** PageRank is page specific, not site specific. This means that the PageRank of the individual pages on a website can (and probably will) vary from page to page.

The Bottom Line

Google's one of those tech companies that started small (literally in a dorm room) and grew exponentially over the years. It's success is due to a focus on simplicity—a simple home page, a simple search process, and simple (yet relevant) results. There's a lot of complex technology behind the simplicity, of course, but however Google does it, it works.

And, to Google's credit, they've discovered how to make money (and lots of it) off what is essentially a free service. The searching may be free, but Google turns a profit by selling targeted ads (those "sponsored links") connected to specific search terms. Google makes money from its advertising customers without alienating its consumer customers—a very neat trick.

note If you run a commercial website, it's in your best interest to optimize your site in whatever ways are necessary to maximize your Google PageRank. In fact, an entire website optimization industry has sprung up to help sites improve their PageRank scores. To learn more about manipulating Google's PageRank, see Chapter 36, "Submitting Your Site—and Increasing Your Ranking."

Searching the Web

Of all the products and services that Google offers, none is more popular than its original web search engine. Last chapter you discovered how a Google web search works, from a behind-the-scenes perspective; in this chapter you'll learn how to conduct an effective—and efficient—search, using Google's basic search page, powerful advanced search operators, and the relatively easy-to-use Advanced Search page.

Conducting a Basic Search

One of the things that has made Google so popular is its ease of use. From the Spartan nature of the main Google search page to the ease-of-use of the search feature, a Google search is so effortless than just about anyone can do it, without a lot of effort or instruction.

Behind the simplicity, however, is a powerful search engine capable of providing highly refined results. That said, you have to know a little more than "query and enter" to gain benefit from all this power. Read on to learn more.

Navigating Google's Home Page

We'll start our examination of a basic Google search with Google's home page, located at www.google.com. Google's home page, shown in Figure 2.1, is almost shocking in its simplicity. Unlike what you find with Yahoo! and other web search portals, Google's home page has no category listings, no news headlines, no stock tickers, no weather reports, and no blatant advertisements. All you see is the Google logo, the search box, two search buttons (Google Search and I'm Feeling Lucky), and some links to additional search services. It's clean, it's simple, and it's fast.

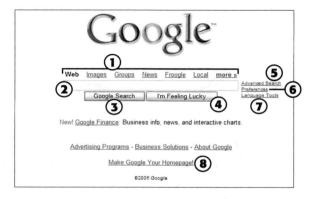

1. Top links to specialized searches
2. Search box
3. Click to search
4. Click to retrieve a single result
5. Link to Advanced Search
6. Click to set search preferences
7. Link to Google's language tools
8. Click to set Google as your browser home page

FIGURE 2.1

Google's main search page.

Entering Your Query

Initiating a basic search is incredibly easy. All you have to do is follow these steps:

1. Enter your query, consisting of one or more keywords, into the search box.

2. Click the Google Search button.

That's all there is to it. Enter your query, click the Search button, and wait for the search results page to display.

Feeling Lucky?

Google is so sure of its capability to generate high-quality results that it puts an I'm
Feeling Lucky button on its home page,
right next to the Google Search button.
Click this button and you skip the standard
search results page and go directly (and
blindly!) to the page that is the number-one match to your query. (Do I personally use the I'm Feeling Lucky button? Not often, I confess—because I seldom want to see just a single result.)

tip You can also initiate a
basic search from the
Google Toolbar, which installs in
any web browser. Learn more
about the Toolbar in Chapter 31,
"Using the Google Toolbar."

How Google Displays Its Results

After you click the Google Search button, Google searches its index for all the web
pages that match your query, and then displays the results on a search results
page, like the one in Figure 2.2. We'll look at each part of this page separately:

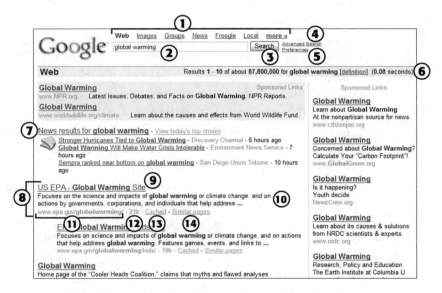

1. Top links to specialized searches
2. Search box
3. Search button
4. Link to advanced search
5. Click to configure preferences
6. Statistics bar
7. OneBox specialized results
8. Top-ranking result
9. Page title
10. Page excerpt
11. URL
12. Size
13. Link to cached version of page
14. Link to similar pages

FIGURE 2.2

A Google search results page.

- **Top links.** These links take you to other specialized Google searches— Web (the default Google search), Images (pictures only), Groups (Usenet newsgroup postings), News (current news headlines), Froogle (products for sale online), Local (local businesses), and More (other Google searches and services).

> **note** Depending on your query, Google might also display a short list of image results before the first regular result.

- **Search box.** This is where you enter your search query.

- **Search button.** Click here, after you've entered your query, to initiate the search.

- **Advanced Search.** This links to Google's Advanced Search page, which you can use to conduct more sophisticated, more targeted searches.

- **Preferences.** Click this link to determine which language you want to use, how many results you want to display per page, and to turn on or off Google's SafeSearch content filtering (great for shielding children from inappropriate content).

- **Statistics bar.** This bar displays how many results were returned for your query, and how long it took to display those results.

- **OneBox specialized results.** On some searches, Google will display a short list of specialized search results—news stories, maps, and the like. These are displayed before the main search results.

- **Sponsored Links.** These are links paid for by Google's advertisers. You should not confuse these links with the main search results; they may have only indirect relevance to your query.

- **Page title.** For each search result, Google displays the title of the page. The title is a clickable link; click it to view the linked-to page.

- **Page excerpt.** Below the page title is a short excerpt from the associated web page. This may be the first few sentences of text on the page, a summary of page contents, or something similar.

> **tip** Viewing a cached page is particularly valuable if, for some reason, the "live" version of the page is down or otherwise inaccessible. You can also use the cached page to examine recent changes to the page in question, as the cached page is likely a few days or weeks older than the current version of the page.

- **URL.** This is the full web address of the selected web page. It is *not* a clickable link; you have to click the page title to jump to the page.

- **Size.** The size (in kilobytes) of the selected page.

- **Cached.** Click this link to see the version of the page stored on Google's document servers. Note that the cached page may be slightly older than the current version of the page.

- **Similar pages.** These are pages that Google thinks have a lot in common with the listed page.

- **Other relevant pages.** In some instances, other relevant pages from the same site are listed (and indented) beneath the primary page listing.

> **caution**
>
> Google's legitimate search results are clearly separated from links paid for by advertisers. Paid links are set off the rest of the search results by a shaded box or separate column, and clearly identified as "Sponsored Links."

Omitted Results

There's one other thing to watch for on the search results page—in particular, on the very last search results page. When you get to the last of the page listings, you're likely to see a message like that shown in Figure 2.3. This message tells you that Google has omitted some results that are similar to those already listed. In other words, Google is trying to simplify your life by not displaying what it feels are duplicate results.

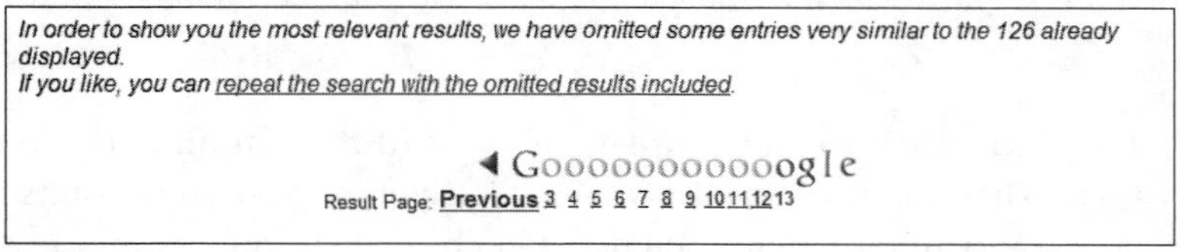

In order to show you the most relevant results, we have omitted some entries very similar to the 126 already displayed.
If you like, you can repeat the search with the omitted results included.

◀ Gooooooooooogle
Result Page: **Previous** 3 4 5 6 7 8 9 10 11 12 13

FIGURE 2.3

Google sometimes omits duplicate results.

In most cases, this is fine; you don't need to see results that essentially duplicate results you've already seen. But every now and then Google gets it wrong, and actually omits results that you might find useful. If you suspect this is the case, click the Repeat the Search with the Omitted Results Included link. This will repeat the search and display *all* results, even those that may (or may not) be duplicates.

Extending Your Search

For many searches, you can find what you want simply by clicking a few page titles on the first search results page. But you may want to see more results—which, of course, Google lets you do.

First things first. Don't assume that the only relevant results will appear on the first search results page. Some queries return literally thousands (if not *millions*) of matching pages, and even though the most relevant results are supposed to be listed first, it's possible to find much useful information buried deeper in the results. For this reason, make it a habit to at least browse a few pages deeper in the search results, which is easy enough to do by scrolling to the bottom of the search results page and clicking the Next link. You can also go directly to a specific page in the search results by clicking a page number, as shown in Figure 2.4. And if you want to view a page beyond the first ten listed, just click on the page 10 link and you'll see another 10 page numbers listed. Keep clicking to the right to view more and more pages of results.

FIGURE 2.4

The bottom of a typical search results page; click a page number to jump to that page of results.

There's another useful feature to be found at the bottom of the search results page. The Search Within Results link lets you narrow your results by refining your query and applying the new search solely to the original results. Here's how it works:

1. Simply click the Search Within Results link at the bottom of the search results page.

2. When the Search Within Results page appears, as shown in Figure 2.5, enter a new query into the search box.

3. Click the Search Within Results button.

Google now searches the existing results, using your new query. The new, refined results appear on a subsequent search results page.

FIGURE 2.5
Refine your query on the Search Within Results page.

Conducting a More Refined Search

Most users enter a keyword or two into Google's search box, click the Search button, and are satisfied with the results. This is a rather brute force method of searching, however, and typically generates a ton of (mostly unwanted) results.

There is a better way to search, however, one that generates a smaller, more targeted list of results. To generate fewer, better results, you have to refine your query—using a defined series of search operators.

Don't Worry About Capitalization...

First, let's expose the fact that Google's searches are not case-sensitive. It doesn't matter whether you search for **California** or **california**, the results will be the same—so don't worry about applying proper capitalization. (See Figures 2.6 and 2.7 to see for yourself.)

note An *operator* is a symbol or word that causes a search engine to do something special with the word directly following the symbol.

...But Do Worry About Word Order

In a Google query, the order of your keywords matters. Google weights the importance of your keywords in order of appearance, so that the first keyword is considered most important, the second keyword the second most important, and so on. You'll get slightly different results for **hdtv retailers chicago** (shown in Figure 2.8) than you will for **chicago retailers hdtv** (shown in Figure 2.9).

note To be fair, in many cases the very top results will be the same no matter what the word order. The difference tends to come as you move deeper into the result listings.

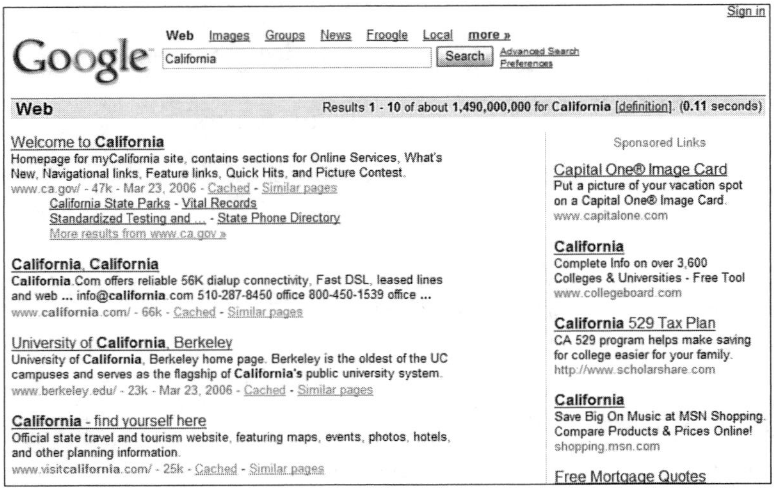

FIGURE 2.6

*The results of a search for the capitalized word **California**...*

FIGURE 2.7

*...are identical to the results for the all-lowercase **california**.*

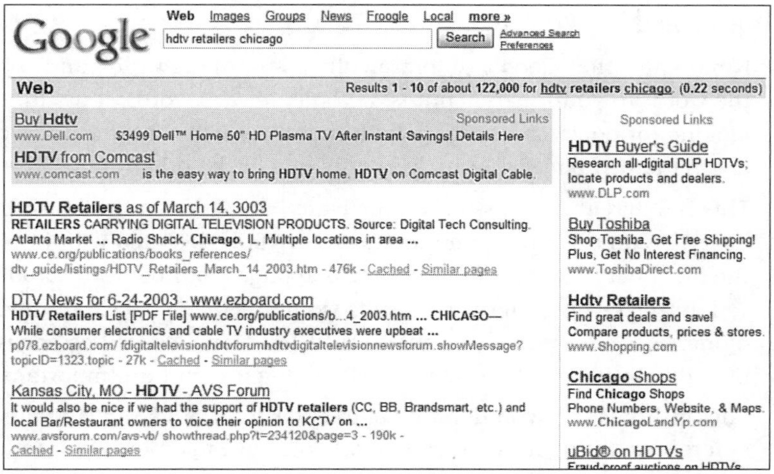

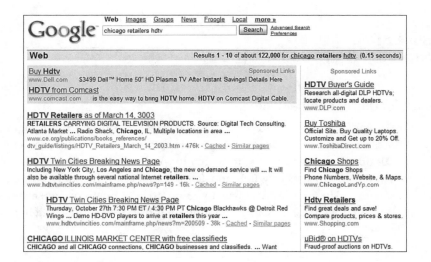

FIGURE 2.8

*The results of a search for **hdtv retailers chicago**...*

FIGURE 2.9

*...compared to a search for **chicago retailers hdtv**—the first result is the same, but all the others are different.*

"And" Is Assumed

Next, know that Google automatically assumes the word "and" between all the words in your query. That is, if you enter two words, it assumes you're looking for pages that include both those words—word one *and* word two. It doesn't return pages that include only one or the other of the words.

This is different from assuming the word "or" between the words in your query. As an example, compare the query **bob AND ted** with **bob OR ted**. In the first query, the results would include pages that mentioned both Bob and Ted. In the second query, the results would include pages that mentioned Bob alone, as well as pages that mentioned Ted alone, as well as pages that mentioned both Bob and Ted. It's a subtle difference, but an important one.

The upshot is that you don't have to enter the word "and" in your query. If you're searching for Bob and Ted, all you have to enter is **bob ted**, as shown in Figure 2.10. Google assumes the "and," and automatically includes it in its internal index search.

FIGURE 2.10

When you enter two keywords, an "and" is assumed between the two.

Search for One or Another Word

Similarly, if you want to conduct an "or" search—to search for pages that include one word or another word, but not necessarily both—you can use the **OR** operator. For example, to search for pages that talk about either Bob or Ted (but not necessarily Bob and Ted together), use the query **bob OR ted**, as shown in Figure 2.11. And when you use the **OR** operator, make sure to insert it in all uppercase, or Google will ignore it as a stop word—which we'll discuss next.

FIGURE 2.11

To search for pages that contain either one word or another, enter an OR between the two keywords.

Common Words Are Automatically Excluded

Speaking of the words "and" and "or," Google automatically ignores these and other small, common words in your queries. These are called *stop words*, and include "and," "the," "where," "how," "what," "or" (in all lowercase), and other similar words—along with certain single digits and single letters (such as "a").

> **note** The **OR** operator is the only Boolean operator accepted by the Google search engine. (Boolean operators come from Boolean logic and mathematics.) The Boolean **AND** operator is assumed in all Google searches; the Boolean **NOT** operator is replaced by the Google - operator, discussed a little later in this chapter.

Including a stop word in a search normally does nothing but slow the search down, which is why Google excises them. As an example, Google takes the query **how a toaster works**, removes the words "how" and "a," and creates the new, shorter query **toaster works**, as shown in Figure 2.12.

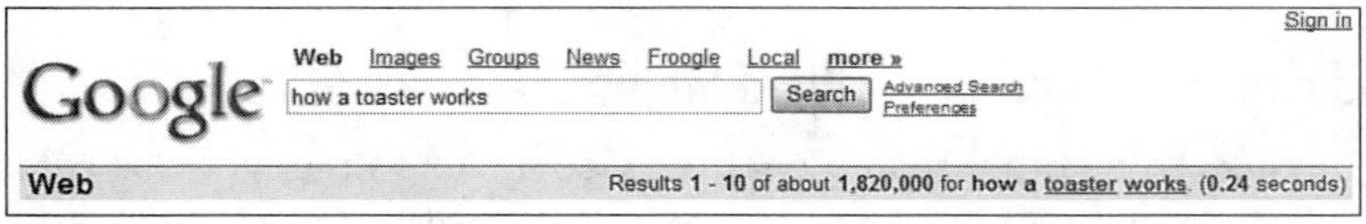

Sign in

Web   Images   Groups   News   Froogle   Local   **more »**

Google | how a toaster works | Search | Advanced Search
                                                           Preferences

Web   Results 1 - 10 of about **1,820,000** for **how a toaster works**. (0.24 seconds)

FIGURE 2.12

*Take a look at the statistics bar—Google simplified the query **how a toaster works** to just **toaster works**.*

If you want these common words included in your query, you have two options. You can automatically include them by using the + operator (discussed next), or you can include the common words within a phrase by enclosing the entire phrase within quotation marks (discussed a little later).

Always Include Stop Words

You can override the stop word exclusion by telling Google that it *must* include specific words in the query. You do this with the + operator, in front of the otherwise excluded word. For example, to include the word "how" in your query, you'd enter **+how**, as shown in Figure 2.13. Be sure to include a space before the + sign, but not after it.

| +how a toaster works | Search |

FIGURE 2.13

Enter the + operator before any stop word you want to include in your query.

Exclude Words from Results

Sometimes you want to refine your results by excluding pages that include a specific word. You can exclude words from your search by using the - operator; any word in your query preceded by the - sign is automatically excluded from the search results. Remember to always include a space before the - sign, and none after.

For example, if you search for **bass**, you could get pages about the type of male singer or about the type of fish. If you want to search for the type of singer only, enter a query that looks like this: **bass –fish** (as shown in Figure 2.14).

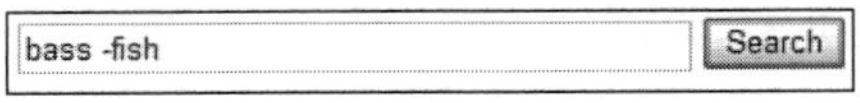

bass -fish	Search

FIGURE 2.14

Use the - operator to exclude a word from your search results.

Take Advantage of Automatic Word Stemming

Unlike some other search engines, Google doesn't let you use wildcards to indicate the variable ends of words. Wildcards, as used elsewhere, let you search for all words that include the first part of a keyword; for example, a search for **book*** (with the * wildcard) would typically return results for "books," "bookstore," "bookkeeper," and so on.

Instead, Google incorporates *automatic word stemming*, which is a fancy way of saying that Google automatically searches for all possible word variations. This is a great way to search for both singular and plural forms of a word, as well as different tenses and forms.

For example, a search for the word **monster** will return both "monster" (singular) and "monsters" (plural). A search for **rain** will return "rain" (current tense), "rained" (past tense), and "rains" (active form). And the word stemming works in the opposite direction, too; a search for **rains** will return both the words "rains" and "rain."

Search for Similar Words

Not sure you're thinking of the right word for a query? Do you worry that some web pages might use alternative words to describe what you're thinking of?

Fortunately, Google lets you search for similar words by using the ~ operator. Just include the ~ character before the word in question, and Google will search for all pages that include that word and all appropriate synonyms.

For example, to search for words that are like the word "elderly," enter the query **~elderly**, as shown in Figure 2.15. This will find pages that include not just the word "elderly," but also the words "senior," "older," "aged," and so on.

> **tip** To list *only* synonyms, without returning a ton of matches for the original word, combine the ~ operator with the - operator, like this: **~keyword -keyword**. This excludes the original word from the synonymous results. Using the previous example, to list only synonyms for the word "elderly," enter **~elderly -elderly**.

FIGURE 2.15
Use the ~ operator to include synonyms in your search.

Search for an Exact Phrase

When you're searching for an exact phrase, you won't get the best results simply by entering all the words in the phrase as your query. Google *might* return results including the phrase, but it will also return results that include all those words—but not necessarily in that exact order.

When you want to search for an exact phrase, you should enclose the entire phrase in quotation marks. This tells Google to search for the precise keywords in the prescribed order.

For example, if you're searching for Monty Python, you *could* enter **monty python** as your query, and you'd get acceptable results; the results will include pages that include both the words "monty" and "python." But these results will include not only pages about the British comedy troupe, but also pages about snakes named Monty, and guys named Monty who have snakes for pets, and any other pages where the words "monty" and "python" occur—anywhere in the page, even if they don't appear adjacent to one another. To limit the results just to pages about the Monty Python troupe, you want to search for pages that include the two words in that precise order as a phrase. So you should enter the query **"monty python"**—making sure to surround the phrase with the quotation marks, as shown in Figure 2.16. This way if the word "monty" occurs at the top of a page and "python" occurs at the bottom, it won't be listed in the search results.

FIGURE 2.16

To search for an exact phrase, include it in quotation marks.

Use Wildcards to Search for Missing Words in an Exact Phrase

I noted previously that Google doesn't use wildcards to complete missing letters in keywords. However, Google *does* let you use whole-word wildcards
within a phrase search. That is, you can search for a complete phrase even if
you're not sure of all the words in the phrase. You let the * wildcard character
stand in for those words you don't know.

Here's an example. Let's say you want to search for pages that discuss Martin
Luther King's famous "I have a dream" speech, but you're not sure whether he
has, had, or have that dream. So you use the * wildcard to stand in for the
word in question, and enter the following query: "**i * a dream**" (as shown in
Figure 2.17).

FIGURE 2.17

*Use the * wildcard to search for missing words in a phrase.*

You can even use multiple wildcards within a single phrase, within reason.
While "*** * a dream**" might return acceptable results, "*** * * dream**" is a fairly
useless query.

Search for Words That Don't Appear Together

Here's another usage of the * whole-word wildcard. If you want to search for
documents where two words *don't* appear side-by-side, insert the * operator
between the two keywords in your query—while still surrounding both keywords by quotation marks. This searches for instances where the two keywords
are separated by one or more words.

For example, to search for pages where the words "happy" and "holidays"
aren't adjacent, enter this query: "**happy * holidays**" (as shown in Figure
2.18).

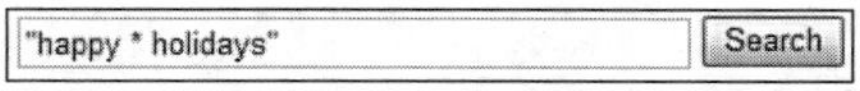

"happy * holidays"   Search

FIGURE 2.18

*You can also use the * wildcard to search for words that aren't adjacent.*

Narrow Your Search to Specific File Types

Google can search for information contained in all sorts of documents—not just HTML web pages. In particular, Google searches for the following file types and extensions, in addition to normal web pages:

- Adobe Portable Document Format (PDF)
- Adobe PostScript (PS)
- Lotus 1-2-3 (WK1, WK2, WK3, WK4, WK5, WKI, WKS, WKU)
- Lotus WordPro (LWP)
- MacWrite (MW)
- Microsoft Excel (XLS)
- Microsoft PowerPoint (PPT)
- Microsoft Word (DOC)
- Microsoft Works (WDB, WKS, WPS)
- Microsoft Write (WRI)
- Rich Text Format (RTF)
- Shockwave Flash (SWF)
- Text (ANS, TXT)

If you want to restrict your results to a specific file type, use the **filetype:** operator followed by the file extension, in this format: **filetype:***filetype*. For example, if you want to search only for Microsoft Word documents, enter **filetype:doc** along with the rest of your query (as shown in Figure 2.19).

To eliminate a particular file type from your search results, use the **filetype:** operator preceded by the - operator and followed by the file extension, like this: **-filetype:***filetype*. For example, if you want to elminate PDF files from your results, enter **-filetype:pdf**.

By the way, when you view a non-HTML document (something other than a web page, such as an Acrobat PDF or Word DOC file), Google displays a View As HTML link in the page listing, as shown in Figure 2.20. Clicking this link translates the original document into web page format—which often displays faster in your browser.

FIGURE 2.19

*Use the **filetype:** operator to limit your search to specific types of documents.*

FIGURE 2.20

Click the View As HTML link to translate the document file to web page format.

Narrow Your Search to a Specific Domain or Website

Maybe you want to search only those sites within a specific top-level web domain, such as .com or .org or .edu—or, perhaps, within a specific country's domain, such as .uk (United Kingdom) or .ca (Canada). Google lets you do this by using the **site:** operator. Just enter the operator followed by the domain name, like this: **site:.*domain*.**

For example, to search only those sites within the .edu domain, you'd enter **site:.edu** along with the rest of your query (as shown in Figure 2.21). To search only Canadian sites, enter **site:.ca**. Remember to put the "dot" before the domain.

FIGURE 2.21

*Use the **site:** operator to limit your search to a specific top-level domain.*

The **site:** operator can also be used to restrict your search to a specific website. In this instance, you enter the entire top-level URL, like this: **site:www.*website.domain*.** For example, to search only within my personal Molehill Group website (www.molehillgroup.com), enter **site:www.molehillgroup.com** (as shown in Figure 2.22). Your results will include only pages listed within the specified website.

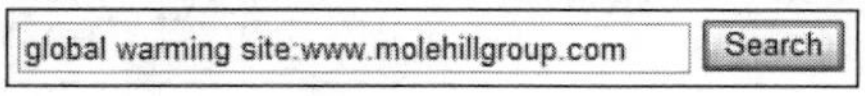

global warming site:www.molehillgroup.com   Search

FIGURE 2.22

*You can also use the **site:** operator to restrict your search to pages on a specific website.*

Narrow Your Search to Words in the Page's Title

Google offers two methods for restricting your search to the titles of web pages, ignoring the pages' body text. If your query contains a single word, use the **intitle:** operator. If your query contains multiple words, use the **allintitle:** operator.

For example, if you want to look for pages with the word "Honda" in the title, use the **intitle:** operator and enter this query: **intitle:honda** (as shown in Figure 2.23). Make sure not to leave a space between the **intitle:** operator and the keyword.

If you want to look for pages with both the words "Honda" and "Element" in the title, use the **allintitle:** operator and enter this query: **allintitle: honda element**. Notice that when you use the **allintitle:** operator, all the keywords after the operator are searched for; you separate the keywords with spaces.

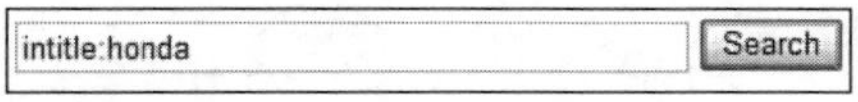

intitle:honda   Search

FIGURE 2.23

*Use the **intitle:** operator to restrict your search to web page titles only.*

Narrow Your Search to Words in the Page's URL

Similar to the **intitle:** and **allintitle:** operators are the **inurl:** and **allinurl:** operators. These operators let you restrict your search to words that appear in web page addresses (URLs). You use these operators in the same fashion—**inurl:** to search for single words and **allinurl:** to search for multiple words.

For example, to search for sites that have the word "molehill" in their URLs, enter this query: **inurl:molehill** (as shown in Figure 2.24). Make sure not to leave a space between the **inurl:** operator and the keyword.

caution If you enter **intitle:honda element**, Google will only search for the word "Honda" in the page titles; it will conduct a normal full-page search for the word "Element." This is why you want to use the **allintitle:** operator if you have multiple keywords in your query.

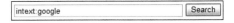

> inurl:molehill   Search

FIGURE 2.24

*Use the **inurl:** operator to restrict your search to web page adddresses.*

To search for sites that have both the words "molehill" and "group," enter this query: **allinurl:molehill group**. As with the **allintitle:** operator, all the keywords you enter after the **allinurl:** operator are searched for; you separate the keywords with spaces.

Narrow Your Search to Words in the Page's Body Text

For all this fuss about searching titles and URLs, it's more likely that you'll want to search the body text of web pages. You can restrict your search to body text only (excluding the page title, URL, and link text), by using the **intext:** and **allintext:** operators. The syntax is the same as the previous operators; use **intext:** to search for single words and **allintext:** to search for multiple words.

For example, to search for pages that include the word "Google" in their body text, enter the query **intext:google** (as shown in Figure 2.25). Make sure to leave a space between the **intext:** operator and the keyword.

> intext:google   Search

FIGURE 2.25

*Use the **intext:** operator to restrict your search to just the body of web pages.*

To search for pages that include both the words "Google" and "search" in the body text, enter the query **allintext:google search**.

Narrow Your Search to Words in the Page's Link Text

There are two more operators similar to the previous batch. The **inanchor:** operator lets you restrict your search to words in the link, or anchor, text on a web page. (This is the text that accompanies a hypertext link—the underlined text on the page.) The **allinanchor:** variation lets you search for multiple words in the anchor text.

For example, to search for links that reference the word "goose," you'd enter **inanchor:goose** (as shown in Figure 2.26). Make sure not to leave a space between the **inanchor:** operator and the keyword.

FIGURE 2.26
*Use the **inanchor:** operator to search for links that reference the given keyword.*

To search for links that reference the words "goose" and "duck," enter the query **allinanchor:goose duck**.

Search for a Range of Numbers

What if you want to search for pages that contain items for sale within a certain price range? Or selected back issues of a magazine?

For these tasks, use Google's ... operator. All you have to do is enter the lower number in the range, followed by the ... operator, followed by the higher number in the range. For example, when you enter **100...150** (as shown in Figure 2.27), you search for pages that include the numbers 100, 101, 102, and so forth on up to 150.

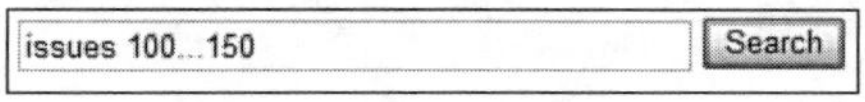

FIGURE 2.27
Searching for a range of numbers with the ... operator.

Travel Way Back in Time for Your Search

When you want to search for pages created between two specific dates, you can use Google's **daterange:** operator—assuming you can live with its quirks.

When you use the **daterange:** operator, Google restricts its search to web pages that match the dates you enter. Know, however, that Google dates the pages in its index based on when it indexed them—*not* when the pages were actually created. So if a page was created sometime back in 2001 but Google didn't get around to indexing it until May 12, 2002, it will be dated May 12, 2002. It's an imperfect way to approach this issue, but it's the only one that Google offers.

There's another catch to using the **daterange:** operator—and this is the killer, for most users. To use the **daterange:** operator, you have to express the date as a Julian date, not our standard month-day-year format. Julian chronology is a continuous count of dates since January 1, 4713 BC, so that July 8, 2002 is Julian date 2452463.5. There isn't really a good reason for the enforcement of Julian dates, other than that it's the simplest brute force method from a mathematics perspective. It's obviously much easier to calculate a single number than a series of three numbers (day/month/year).

If you insist on using the **daterange:** operator, your query syntax should look like this: **daterange:*startdate-enddate***. I won't bother with an example.

> **tip** To calculate Julian dates, go to the Julian Date Calculator at the U.S. Naval Observatory website (aa.usno. navy.mil/data/docs/JulianDate. html).

List Pages That Link to a Specific Page

Want to know which other web pages are linking to a specific page? Because Google works by tracking page links, this is easy to find out. All you have to do is use the **link:** operator, like this: **link:*URL***. For example, to see the thousands of pages that link to Microsoft's website, enter **link:www.microsoft.com** (as shown in Figure 2.28).

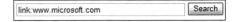

FIGURE 2.28

*Use the **link:** operator to find all pages that link to a specific page.*

List Similar Pages

Have you ever found a web page you really like, and then wondered if there were any more like it? Wonder no more; you can use Google's **related:** operator to display pages that are in some way similar to the specified page. For example, if you really like the news stories on CNET's News.com website (www.news.com), you can find similar pages by entering **related:www. news.com** (as shown in Figure 2.29).

FIGURE 2.29

*Use the **related:** operator to search for pages that are somehow like a given page.*

Find Out More About a Specific Page

Google collects a variety of information about the web pages it indexes. In particular, Google can tell you which pages link to that page (see the **link:** operator, discussed previously), which pages that page links to, which pages are similar to that page (the **related:** operator), and which pages contain that page's URL. To get links to all this information on a single page (plus a link to Google's cached version of that page), use Google's **info:** operator. This displays a set of links, like those shown in Figure 2.30, that you can click to obtain the desired page info.

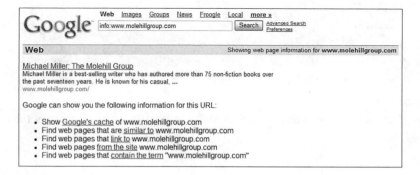

FIGURE 2.30

*The results of applying the **info:** operator to the author's www.molehillgroup.com website.*

Highlight Keywords

If you want to highlight all the instances of the keywords you searched for in a document, use the **cache:** operator, followed by the site's URL. This displays the cached version of the web page, with the keywords in your query highlighted in yellow, as shown in Figure 2.31.

For example, to highlight all instances of the keyword "windows" on the www.microsoft.com website, enter this query: **cache:www.microsoft.com windows.**

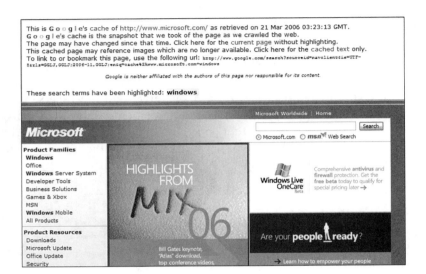

FIGURE 2.31

*Highlighting search keywords with the **cache**: operator. (Note the summary at the top of the cached page.)*

Using the Advanced Search Page

Not comfortable learning all those complicated search operators, but still want to fine-tune your search beyond the basic keyword query? Then you want to use Google's Advanced Search page, which performs most of these same advanced search functions, via a series of simple pull-down menus and checkboxes.

You can access the Advanced Search page, shown in Figure 2.32, by clicking the Advanced Search link on Google's home page. The Advanced Search page contains a number of options you can use to fine-tune your searches, without having to learn all those advanced operators. All you have to to is make the appropriate selections on the page and Google will do all the fine-tuning for you.

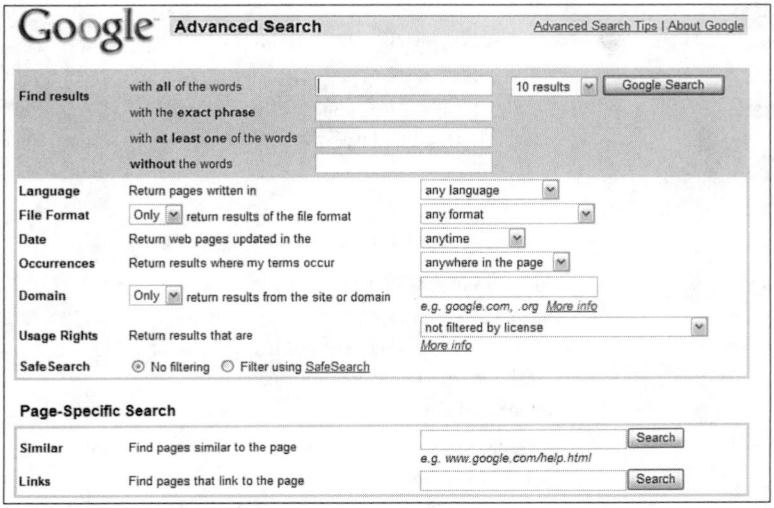

FIGURE 2.32

Google's Advanced Search page.

What options are available on the Advanced Search page? Table 2.1 provides the details:

Table 2.1   Options on Google's Advanced Search Page

Option	Description	Same As This Operator
Results (list)	Selects how many listings are displayed on the search results page	N/A
Find results with *all* of the words	Google's default search mode	N/A
Find results with the *exact phrase*	Searches for the exact phrase entered	""
Find results with *at least one* of the words	Searches for either one word or another	OR
Find results *without* the words	Excludes pages that contain the specified word(s)	-
Language	Searches for pages written in a specific language	N/A
File Format	Limits search to specific file types	**filetype:** and **-filetype:**
Date	Limits search to web pages created/updated in the past 3, 6, or 12 months	**date:**

Table 2.1   Continued

Option	Description	Same As This Operator
Occurrences	Restricts the query to specified parts of the web page: title, text, URL, links, or anywhere	**intitle:** and **allintitle:** **intext:** and **allintext:** **inurl:** and **allinurl:** **inanchor:** and **allinanchor:**
Domain	Restricts the search to the specified website or domain	**site:**
Usage Rights	For media files, returns pages/files that are not filtered by a license; free to use or share; free to use or share, even commercially; free to use, share, or modify; or free to use, share, or modify, even commercially	N/A
SafeSearch	Activates SafeSearch content filter for this particular search	**safesearch:**
Similar	Finds pages similar to the specified web page	**related:**
Links	Lists all pages that link to the specified web page	**link:**

For many users, it's easier to use the Advanced Search page than it is to learn and enter Google's advanced operators into a standard search query. When you need to fine-tune the occasional search, this is the page to use!

Narrowing Your Search Results with URL Parameters

There's one more way to tweak your Google results—not your queries, mind you, but rather the results that get returned. You can do this by modifying the URL of any search results page, via the addition of what the techno-wizards call URL parameters.

Understanding Google's URLs

What is a URL parameter? It's a technical modifier that appears at the end of a URL; it's essentially the internal code used to generate a particular page of search results. For example, do a basic Google search for **tweeter**, and then look at the URL for the ensuing search results page. As you can see in Figure 2.33, the URL looks like this: http://www.google.com/search?hl=en&q=tweeter. Everything after the www.google.com part of the URL are the URL parameters.

FIGURE 2.33
The URL of a Google search results page; note the URL parameters after the www.google.com.

Using our **tweeter** example, you can see that the first parameter is search?, which tells Google that you're conducting a search. The next parameter is hl=en, which sets the language for the search results to English. The final parameter is q=tweeter, which tells Google that your query is the single keyword, **tweeter**.

Now, it's not important that you learn all these URL parameters; they're essential to Google's internal search function, but not to you. However, if you know a few of these URL parameters, you can use them to manipulate the results that Google returns from a standard web search. Let's look at a few of the most useful of these parameters.

Displaying the Most Recent Results

If you want to filter your search results to include only those pages created within the past few months, you can add the &as_qdr=m# parameter to any search results URL. With this parameter, replace the # with the number of months back you want to search; for example, &as_qdr=m3 refines your results to pages created within the past three months. (You can search back between 1 and 12 months.)

How does this work? It's pretty simple, really. Just follow these steps:

1. Enter your query into the Google search box as normal, and then click the search button.

2. When the search results page appears, move your cursor to the end of the URL in your web browser's address box.

3. Add the following to the end of the URL: &as_qdr=m#, replacing # with a number between 1 and 12, as shown in Figure 2.34.

> **tip** You can also use the URL of a search results page as a bookmark for future searches. Just copy the URL into your favorites list, email it to a friend, or whatever. When you enter the full URL into your web browser, you'll jump to the same search results page, without having to re-enter the original search query.

4. Press the Enter key on your keyboard or click the Go button in your web browser.

FIGURE 2.34

A search results URL modified with the &as_qdr=m# *parameter.*

Google now reruns your search, this time filtering the results to include only those pages created within the past *x* number of months.

Displaying More (or Fewer) Results

Now let's look at expanding the number of results displayed on a page. While this is something you can manipulate from the Advanced Search page, you can also do this by adding the &num=*x* parameter to the end of any search results URL. Just replace *x* with the number of results you want to display on a page, and then rerun the search with the modified URL.

Restricting Results to a Specific Filetype

We'll look at one last URL parameter—this one is also available from the Advanced Search page but easily duplicable in the search results URL. If you want to narrow your results to documents of a certain type of file, just add the &as_filetype=*xxx* parameter to the end of the search results URL. Replace *xxx* with the file extension (doc, jpg, pdf, and so forth), and then rerun the search with the modified URL. It's that easy.

Other Ways to Query Google

While I think Google offers a very easy-to-use search interface, not everyone finds it quite as easy to work with Google's advanced search operators, even when they're using the Advanced Search page. To that end, several third-party developers have created their own front ends to the Google search engine. These sites let you create advanced queries without learning all of Google's advanced search operators, or slogging your way through the Advanced Search page. You may want to give them a try, especially if you do a lot of advanced searching.

First out of the box is the Google Ultimate Interface (www.faganfinder.com/google.html). As you can see in Figure 2.35, this page offers many of the same search parameters as found on Google's Advanced Search page, but organized in a way that makes a little more sense to a lot of users. You enter your keywords into the search boxes at the top left corner of the page, and then select the other search parameters you want applied. Click the Search button and your modified query is sent to Google, and the appropriate results returned.

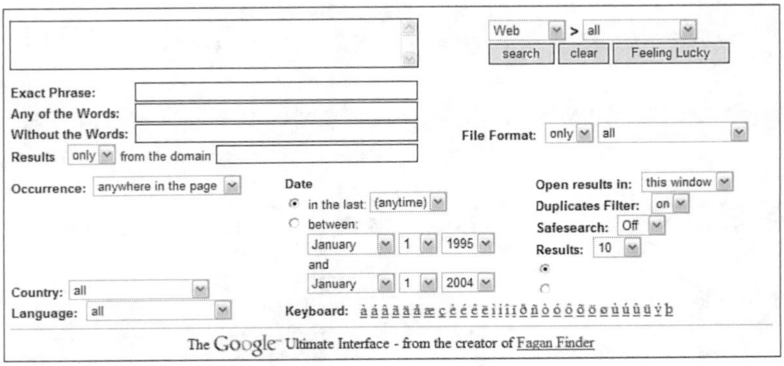

FIGURE 2.35

Google Ultimate Interface: An alternative advanced search form.

Next, consider Soople (www.soople.com), shown in Figure 2.36. Soople is a front-end to Google that offers specific search boxes tailor-made for many of Google's specialized searches. There are search boxes for music, movies, books, videos, images, and the like, as well as for searches constrained by various parameters. It's a lot easier to enter a query into a Soople box than it is to construct the query on the Google site using advanced search operators. As with the Google Ultimate Interface, your queries are modified with the appropriate search operators and passed onto Google proper, and the ensuing search results returned to you.

While neither of these sites is affiliated with Google, they both forward your queries to the Google search engine—modified, of course, behind-the-scenes with the appropriate operators as determined by the type of search you select. They're worth checking out.

2

FIGURE 2.36

Soople: Specialized Google searching made easy.

Tips for More Effective Searches

All the advanced operators aside, most people use Google in a very inefficient and often ineffective manner. If all you do is enter a few keywords and click the search button, you're one of those users who doesn't get as much out of Google as you could. Read on to learn how to make your searches more effective, and more efficient.

Use the Correct Methodology

Whether you're conducting a basic or an advanced Google search, there is a certain methodology you should employ. Follow the proper method and you'll get very targeted results; ignore this advice and you'll either get a ton of irrelevant results or a dearth of relevant ones.

While there are many different (and equally valid) approaches to web searching, I guarantee that this particular approach will generate excellent results. It's a six-step process that looks like this:

1. Start by thinking about what you want to find. What words best describe the information or concept you're looking for? What alternative words might some use instead? Are there any words that can be excluded from your search to better define your query?

2. Construct your query. Use as many keywords as you need, the more the better. If at all possible, try to refine your search with the appropriate search operators—or, if your prefer, Advanced Search page.

3. Click the Search button to perform the search.

4. Evaluate the matches on the search results page. If the initial results are not to your liking, refine your query and search again—or refine your search by altering switch to a more appropriate search site.

5. Select those matching pages that you wish to view and begin clicking through to those pages.

6. Save the information that best meets your needs.

In other words, it pays to think before you search—and to continue to refine your search after you obtain the initial results. The extra effort is slight, and well worth it.

Use the Right Keywords in Your Query

When you construct your query, you do so by using one or more keywords. The keywords you enter are compared to Google's index of web documents; the more keywords found on a web page, the better the match.

You should choose keywords that best describe the information you're looking for—using as many keywords as you need. Don't be afraid of using too many keywords; in fact, using too few keywords is a common fault of many novice searchers. The more words you use, the better idea Google has of what you're looking for. Think of it as describing something to a friend—the more descriptive you are (that is, the more words you use), the better the picture your friend has of what you're talking about.

> **note** The individual words that you enter into a search box are called *keywords*. Collectively, all your keywords (and the operators between the words) combine to form a *query*. Just remember that a query is composed of keywords, not the other way around, and you'll have it straight.

It's the same way when you "talk" to the Google search engine.

If you're looking for a thing or a place, choose keywords that describe that thing or place in as much detail as possible. For example, if you're looking for a car, one of your first keywords would, of course, be **car**. But you probably know what general type of car you're looking for—let's say that it's a sports car—so you might enhance your query to read **sports car**. You may even know that you want to find a foreign sports car, so you change your query to read **foreign sports car**. And if you're looking for a classic model, your query could be expanded to **classic foreign sports car**. As you can see, the better your description (using more keywords), the better Google can "understand" what you're searching for.

If you're looking for a concept or an idea, you should choose keywords that best help people understand that concept or idea. This often means using additional keywords that help to impart the meaning of the concept. Suppose you want to search for information about senior citizens; your initial query would be **senior citizens**. What other words could you use to describe the concept of senior citizens? How about words such as elderly, old, or retired? If these words help to describe your concept, add them to your search—like this: **senior citizens elderly old retired**. Adding keywords like these results in more targeted searches and higher-quality

> **tip** It's possible to include too many keywords in your query. Google searches only the first 32 words of your query, so anything more than that is just wasted. Enter a 33-word query (such as **she wore yellow polka dot bikini drove little red corvette around dead man's curve going surfing usa frankie annette muscle beach party southern california hot rod endless summer wipeout tan lotion sand castle**), and that 33rd word ("castle," if you're counting) won't be included in the actual search.

results. (Additionally, you can use Google's ~ operator to include synonyms of any selected word, as discussed previously.)

While we're on the subject of keywords, try to limit your keywords to nouns only. That's because many verbs and conjunctions are ignored by Google as stop words, or are simply too common to be useful. The key thing to remember is that you're searching for specific things; name those things in your query.

Save Your Results

If you manage to execute a search that results in a perfect set of matches, you probably want to save your results so you can access them again in the future. If you use Internet Explorer as your web browser, you should save the first results page of your search as a Favorite. (Select Favorites, Add to Favorites.) If you use another browser, learn how to save the page as a bookmark. This way, you can click the bookmark or favorite and return to that ideal page of results, without the need to replicate the query from scratch.

tip Of course, using Google's standard web page search isn't the only way to find information online. Google also offers the editor-compiled Google Directory (discussed in Chapter 3, "Searching the Google Directory"), the picture-oriented Google Image Search (Chapter 24, "Searching Google Images"), the Usenet newsgroup Google Groups search (Chapter 28, "Using Google Groups"), the news headline Google News search (Chapter 29, "Using Google News"), the Froogle online shopping search (Chapter 16, "Searching for Bargains with Froogle and Google Catalogs"), and many, many more specialized search options. If one search doesn't find what you're looking for, you can always try another!

The Bottom Line

Google's basic web search is a quick and easy way to search the web. However, you can produce better results by using a variety of search operators, or by using Google's Advanced Search page. Refining your search with these tools puts you one leg up on just about everyone else doing the Google thing; too few users know about or use these effective search tools.

Searching the Google Directory

oogle indexes billions and billions of web pages in its search database. That's both good and bad. The huge volume of pages virtually guarantees that you'll find something useful, while all that volume sometimes makes it difficult to separate that one useful page from the thousands (or millions) of less useful ones. It's kind of a needle and haystack problem.

By indexing literally billions of web pages, the Google search engine adopts a brute force approach. You get plenty of quantity, but the quality of results isn't always up to par.

When the quality of results matters, it's sometimes better to view a list of pages that have been personally selected for their content and appropriateness. (As opposed to letting the GoogleBot and PageRank Algorithm do the gathering and selecting for you, that is.) So if it's handpicked results you want, you want a web directory, not an automated search engine.

Not surprisingly, Google offers just this type of human-edited directory—
called, also not surprisingly, the Google Directory.

What the Google Directory Is—And What It Isn't

The Google Directory, shown in Figure 3.1, is a relatively small database of
web page listings. (Small compared to the main Google database, that is.)
Each listing in the Google Directory is handpicked by a team of human editors; the listings are then annotated and organized into relevant topic categories. You can browse the directory via category, or search for specific terms.

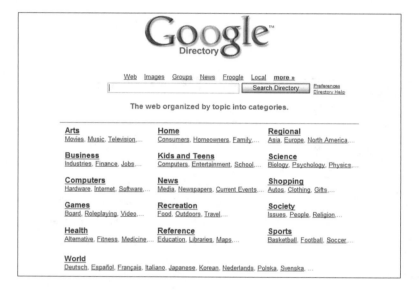

FIGURE 3.1

The Google Directory—ready to browse (by category) or search.

To access the Google Directory, click the More link on the Google home page
and then select Directory on the following page. Alternatively, you can go
directly to the Google Directory by entering **directory.google.com** in your web
browser.

Why a Directory Isn't a Search Engine, and Vice Versa

Most users don't know the difference between a search engine and a directory.
After all, both directories and search engines contain lots of web page listings,
and both are searchable. What's the diff?

The difference between a directory and a search engine is in how the listings are compiled. As you learned in Chapter 1, "Inside Google," Google's search engine works by sending automated GoogleBot software out to crawl the Web, and then uses a proprietary formula to match the pages to users' search queries. This process guarantees a huge number of results for most queries, but it's all very sterile and automated. There's no good way to truly judge the content or quality of a page; it's all about numbers.

In contrast, a directory is assembled by a team of human editors. That's right, human beings—not machines. The human beings find and evaluate pages on the Web, annotate the page listings, and organize them into relevant categories. Unlike computers, human beings can make qualitative judgments about a page's content, and can evaluate the actual meaning of the page. It's not about numbers; it's about content.

All of which means that a directory is likely to have higher-quality results than a search engine. It's also likely to have fewer results (far fewer, when compared to Google's gargantuan search index) because of the need to closely examine each individual page before it's added to the directory. Where the Google search index includes billions of listings, the Google Directory contains just 5 million listings—less than 1/10th of 1% of what's in the search index.

It's the difference between casting a wide net (in the case of Google's search engine) and taking everything that's caught inside, and dropping a single fishing line in the water (in the case of the Google Directory) with the intent of catching a particular type of fish. You get lots of fish with the wide net approach, but you get the fish you want by using a rod and reel.

The other big difference between a directory and a search engine is organization. A search index has none; those billions of pages are dumped into one big database, with no sense of order. A directory, on the other hand, is all about order; the human editors not only pick the web pages to be included, they also organize the sites into logical categories. So where you can't browse a search index, you *can* browse a directory, simply by clicking through the hierarchy of categories and subcategories.

Since they look at every page included in the directory, the directory's human editors also have the opportunity to annotate those pages. Browse through a directory's category listings and you're likely to see summaries, reviews, and comments about the web pages listed. These annotations are *not* automatically generated from the page's content; they're added by the editors, in what amounts to a very human touch.

A directory's human editors also provide one other important function—they continually check for and remove dead links. This is something that search engines don't always do well; a human being is going to be more diligent about keeping the listings updated.

So what are the final differences between a search engine and a directory? Table 3.1 summarizes them:

Table 3.1   Search Engines versus Directories

	Search Engine	Directory
Size (number of listings)	Large (billions)	Small (millions)
Organization	None	By category
Comments/annotations	None	Yes
Manually remove dead links	No	Yes
Assembled by	Computers	Human editors

How the Google Directory Is Assembled

The Google Directory works like most other web directories, such as the Yahoo! Directory (dir.yahoo.com), LookSmart (www.looksmart.com), or Best of the Web (www.botw.org). Thousands of human editors sort through sites submitted by users, as well as do their own web browsing, to find the sites included in the directory. Once a web page has been accepted for inclusion, the editors write a brief review/overview of the page, and assign it to a topic category. It's a totally manual process; there are no bots crawling the Web or linguistic programs excerpting page contents. All the work is done by hand.

But here's the thing. Google doesn't assemble it's own directory. No, the Google Directory is actually a customized version of a third-party directory called the Open Directory Project. (Figure 3.2 shows the Open Directory home page—look familiar?)

Google takes the Open Directory listings and grafts the Google interface and search engine on top of them. So, while the listings in the directory are assembled by Open Directory editors, they're ranked using Google's PageRank technology. If you compare a category in the Google Directory with the same category in the Open Directory, the listings will be the same, but arranged differently.

note You can access the Open Directory directly at www.dmoz.org. (DMOZ is an acronym for Directory Mozilla, which reflects the directory's loose association with Netscape's Mozilla web browser.)

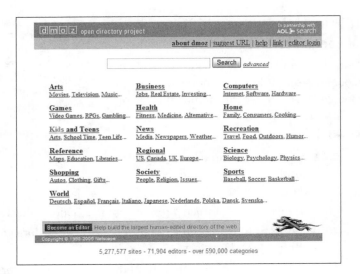

FIGURE 3.2
The Open Directory—the basis for the Google Directory.

The good thing about Google using the Open Directory is that it's perhaps the largest and highest-quality web directory available. The Open Directory Project is a huge undertaking, hosted and administered by Netscape (part of America Online), with more than 70,000 volunteer editors submitting reviews and rankings of websites and pages. Google made a good choice in partnering with the Open Directory; the combination of Open Directory listings with Google's interface and PageRank rankings makes the Google Directory the easiest-to-use and most useful directory on the Web.

It's the use of Google's PageRank technology that makes the Google Directory so easy to use. Instead of just browsing through the category listings (which you can do if you want), Google's search technology lets you search the directory listings the same way you search Google's search index. The listings in the directory—and thus the results of your query—are ranked according to relevance, thanks to the use of PageRank. The most relevant sites always appear near the top of the listings, which they don't necessarily do if you access the raw Open Directory listings.

> **tip** To submit a web page for possible inclusion in the Open Directory/Google Directory, follow the instructions at www.dmoz.org/add.html. To volunteer your services as an Open Directory editor, navigate to any category in the directory that interests you, and then click on the Become an Editor link at the bottom of the page and follow the onscreen instructions from there.

Why You'd Want to Use the Google Directory Instead of Google's Web Search

Now that you know the difference between Google's standard search engine and the Google Directory, which should you use for your searching?

Here are some tips:

tip You don't have to worry about the Google Directory containing results that don't appear in a standard Google web search. Google's search index includes all the entries in the Google Directory, in addition to the pages added by the GoogleBot crawler.

- If you want the maximum number of results, use the Google search engine.

- If you want more targeted results, use the Google Directory.

- If you want to read a little about a page or site before you jump to it, use the Google Directory.

- If you want to browse through all the pages in a category, rather than using the search function, use the Google Directory.

- If you want the "big picture" about a particular topic, use the Google Directory.

The bottom line is that if you want a lot of results, and don't mind wading through the chaff to find a little wheat, use the standard Google search engine. But if you're tired of search results that aren't quite what you're looking for and want more qualified results, consider using the Google Directory. In other words, if you want quantity, use the standard Google search engine. If you want quality—or a good category overview—use the Google Directory, instead.

COMMENTARY

AN UNDERUSED RESOURCE

I admit that I am not a big user of the Google Directory. I tend to be a wide-net kind of searcher, and am happy with the profusion of results returned by the main Google web search engine.

That said, I think I'm cheating myself. In doing the research for this chapter, I was reminded just how useful the Google Directory really is. Yes, I like having a large number of results to sort through, but sometimes the sheer number of results from a Google web search can be overwhelming. The Google Directory provides much more targeted results, which—depending on what you're looking for—can signifi-cantly reduce your total research time. I might have to click through a dozen links to find the most appropriate page in a Google web search; with the Google Directory, the best page is almost guaranteed to be in the top two or three pages listed. It's a real time-saver, and I should be using it more.

Here's another area where I've found the Google Directory to be indis-pensable. When you're searching for information about a popular product, the normal Google web search inundates you with results from online retailers selling that product. The Google Directory, on the other hand, skips a lot of the online sales offers and is more heavily weighted toward pure informational content. Take, for example, a search for information about a drug like Lipitor or Viagra; where the standard Google search results are full of low-priced sales offers (mil-lions of them, in both cases), the Google Directory results cut out a lot of this dross and present a higher percentage of informational sites. In terms of useful results, it's like night and day.

Bottom line, I'm making a vow right now to start using the Google Directory more often. You should consider doing the same.

Navigating the Google Directory

Now that you know how the Google Directory gets its listings, let's spend some time using the thing. It's a lot like using Google's regular search feature—with the ability to browse the listings thrown in.

Searching Directory Listings

Most users opt to use the Google Directory much as they do the regular Google search page—that is, by searching the directory, rather than browsing it. To search the Google Directory, follow these steps:

1. Go to the Google Directory home page (directory.google.com)—*not* the regular Google home page.

2. Enter one or more keywords into the search box at the top of the page.

3. Click the Google Search button.

> **tip** When searching the Google Directory, you can refine your search by using any of the search operators dis-cussed in Chapter 2, "Searching the Web."

Google now displays a search results page like the one in Figure 3.3. This page looks a lot like a standard web search results page, with the addition of a list of related categories at the top. Each result listing also features a link to the category in which it is included. Click a category link to view all the pages listed in that category.

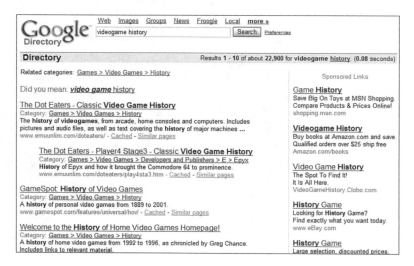

FIGURE 3.3

A Google Directory search results page—note the Related Categories link at the top of the page.

Browsing Directory Categories

If you're accustomed to using Google to search for information, the concept of browsing might be new to you. It's really quite simple; it all hinges on the concept of hierarchical organization of information into topic categories and subcategories.

You start at the Google Directory home page, where 16 different categories (and a handful of subcategories) are listed. Here are the major categories:

- Arts
- Business
- Computers
- Games
- Health

- Home
- Kids and Teens
- News
- Recreation
- Reference
- Science
- Shopping
- Society
- Sports
- World

You start your browsing by clicking a category that matches your interest. This displays a major category page, like the one in Figure 3.4, that lists all the subcategories within the major category. (Sometimes a few related categories are listed, also.) For example, The Home category lists 25 subcategories, such as Apartment Living, Consumer Information, Cooking, and the like.

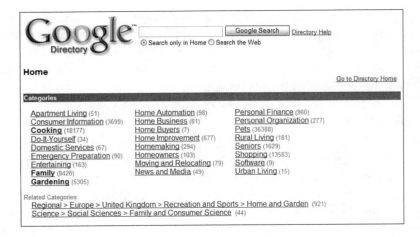

FIGURE 3.4

All the subcategories of a given major category—click one to keep browsing.

Click a subcategory link and you'll see a subcategory page, like the one in Figure 3.5. Some subcategories include even more subcategories (sub-subcategories?), which are listed at the top of the page. You'll also find a list of related categories; then you'll see the list of pages within the subcategory.

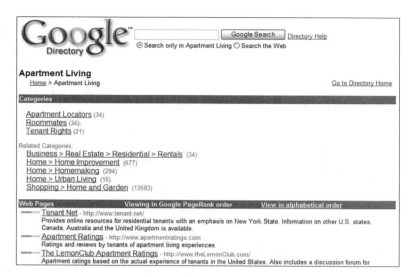

FIGURE 3.5
More subcategories within a subcategory, as well as pages listed in the subcategory.

These pages are ranked (using Google's PageRank technology) in order of relevance. The green bar to the left of each page listing visually indicates the relevance; the bigger the green bar, the more relevant the result. Each listing also includes the title of the page (click to jump to the page), the page's URL, and the editor's description of the page.

Searching Within a Category

When you stumble across a big category, one with lots of pages listed, it may be difficult to find exactly the page you want. To that end, Google lets you search for pages within a category. All you have to do is navigate to a category or subcategory page, enter your query in the search box at the top of the page, check the Search Only in *Category* option, and then click the Google Search button. Google now searches the current category—and only the current category—for the keywords you entered, and displays the results on a separate search results page.

Searching within a category can be particularly useful in restricting your search to a particular topic. For example, if you search the entire Google Directory for **lions**, Google might return pages about lions (the animal), Lions (the football team), Lions

> **tip** If you'd rather view the listings within a category alphabetically instead of by relevance, click the View in Alphabetical Order link at the top of the listings.

(the public service organization), or any number of other lion-related subjects, as shown in Figure 3.6. But if you first navigate to the Sports, Football, **American, NFL** category and *then* search for **lions**, you'll see only results related to the Detroit Lions football team, as shown in Figure 3.7.

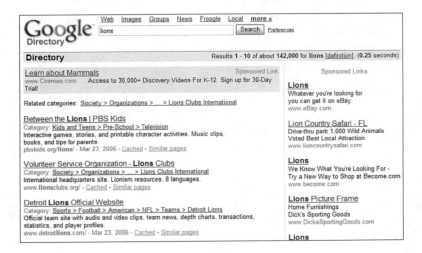

FIGURE 3.6
*The results of searching for **lions** across all Google Directory categories.*

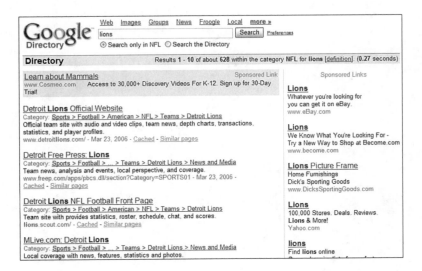

FIGURE 3.7
*The results of searching for **lions** in the Sports, Football, American, NFL category only—a much more targeted search.*

The Bottom Line

The Google Directory is a useful alternative to searching the massive Google web page index. Google Directory results are more focused and of uniformly higher quality than what you find in the larger search index, and also help you to get a feel of what's available in any given category. Plus, you get the advantage of browsing by category instead of searching, if that's your style. Kudos to Google for adapting the Open Directory to the Google site, and offering users the best of both worlds.

3

Specialized Searches

4 Searching for People and Phone Numbers

5 Searching for Financial Information

6 Searching Blogs and Blog Postings

7 Searching for Scholarly Information

8 Searching for University, Technical, and Government Information

9 Searching for Words and Definitions

10 Searching for Other Special Information

Searching for People and Phone Numbers

I f you're like me, every now and then you need (or want) to look up information about a particular person. I'm not talking about famous personages here, but rather normal people whose address or phone number I can't remember.

As far as Google is concerned, a person's name, address, or phone number is just another piece of information stored in the database. The techniques to retrieve this information, however, are a little different from normal web search techniques. Read on to learn how to search Google for information about people and places—and the occasional business.

Searching for People by Name

As part of its massive database of information, Google now includes listings for millions of U.S. households in what it calls the Google PhoneBook. You search the PhoneBook listings from the main Google search box, using specific query parameters.

There are six ways you can search for a person or household in the Google PhoneBook. Table 4.1 details each of these methods, along with an example for each.

Table 4.1   Ways to Search for People and Households

Query	Example
First name (or initial), last name, city	john smith minneapolis
First name (or initial), last name, state	john smith mn
First name (or initial), last name, city, state	john smith minneapolis mn
First name (or initial), last name, ZIP Code	john smith 55909
Last name, city, state	smith minneapolis mn
Last name, ZIP Code	smith 55909

As you might suspect, the more details you provide, the more targeted your results will be. Searching for all the Smiths in Minneapolis will produce a higher number of results (most of them unwanted) than searching for all the John Smiths; searching for all the John Smiths in a particular ZIP Code will be much more efficient than searching for all the John Smiths in an entire state.

When you enter your query using one of these methods, Google returns a search result page with a PhoneBook Results item at the top of the results list, as shown in Figure 4.1. The top matching names are listed here, along with the following information:

FIGURE 4.1

The results of a Google PhoneBook search.

- First and last name
- Phone number
- Street address
- City
- State
- ZIP Code

caution Because it takes so long to get change of address information into the system, Google PhoneBook listings may not always be up-to-date. In addition, Google can only display names that are publicly available. If a person's phone number is unlisted, it won't be displayed.

■ Links to maps of this address via Google Maps, Yahoo! Maps, and MapQuest

Probably the neatest thing here is the ability to quickly map each address. Just click one of the map links (I prefer Google Maps), and find out exactly where that person lives. (Figure 4.2 shows an address mapped with Google Maps.)

FIGURE 4.2

A PhoneBook address mapped with Google Maps.

The two or three names listed on the results page aren't the only matches in the Google PhoneBook, however. To see the other matching names, click the Phonebook Results link on the search results page. This displays a full page of PhoneBook listings, as shown in Figure 4.3.

Again, these listings include the full name, address, phone number, and map links for each listing. The names are segregated into business and residential listings; the business listings are typically for professionals like lawyers, doctors, and the like.

FIGURE 4.3
Residential and business results from the Google PhoneBook.

And, as you've no doubt noticed, even this page only lists a handful of the available results—five each of the residential and business listings. To see more listings, click the More Residential Listings link at the bottom of the page.

COMMENTARY

BETTER PEOPLE FINDERS

Let's be honest. Google is not the only place to search for people on the Internet—and it's far from the best. Better results can be found at one of the many sites that offer dedicated white pages directories, such as InfoSpace (www.infospace.com), Switchboard (www.switch-board.com), and White Pages.com (www.whitepages.com). Also good is The Ultimates (www.theultimates.com), a metasearch engine that queries multiple white pages directories from a single page, and Argali White & Yellow (www.argali.com), which also aggregates results from multiple directories and search engines.

These people finder sites let you search by full name (or any variation thereof), and refine your search by state, city, ZIP Code, and the like. The results from these sites display full name, address, and telephone number, and sometimes a link to a map of that person's neighbor-hood. Some people finders also let you do reverse phone-number lookups, like Google purports to do—but these sites offer much larger directories of numbers than does Google.

Beyond standard white pages directories, I have a special fondness for ZoomInfo (www.zoominfo.com), which is a search engine like Google, but specialized for people searching (see Figure 4.4). When you search for a person's name, ZoomInfo automatically creates a summary page for that person, based on all the references to that person found on the Web. It's kind of like an automatic biography generator, and it works pretty well. (See the figure for the summary page it generated for me—not totally accurate, but close.) In any case, if you do any amount of people searching, ZoomInfo is worth adding to your favorites list.

FIGURE 4.4
A typical ZoomInfo profile.

As much as I like Google, it isn't always the best tool for particular types of searches. Searching for people just happens to be one of those areas.

Searching for People by Phone Number

Once Google has captured name, address, and phone number information in the PhoneBook, it's an easy enough task to search that information in a variety of ways. One such approach is to do a reverse phone number lookup, where you enter a phone number and Google tells you who the number belongs to.

tip If you'd rather not have your phone number available for everyone on the Web to Google, you can have your phone information removed from Google's database by following the instructions at www.google.com/help/pbremoval.html.

To conduct a reverse phone number search, all you have to do is enter the full phone number, including area code, into the standard Google search box, as shown in Figure 4.5. You can enter all 10 numbers in a row, without hyphens (like this: **1234567890**), or use the standard hyphenated form (like this: **123-456-7890**); Google accepts either method. When you click the Search button, Google displays a single matching PhoneBook result, as shown in Figure 4.6.

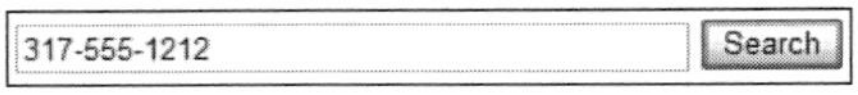

FIGURE 4.5

Searching to see who belongs to a specific phone number.

Phonebook results for 317-
Michael L Miller, (317)   Dr, Carmel, IN 46032
Google Maps Yahoo! Maps MapQuest

FIGURE 4.6

The very specific result of a reverse phone number lookup query.

Notice that when you search for a phone number, you get the PhoneBook result plus Google's standard web search results. To limit your search to the PhoneBook only, use Google's **phonebook:** operator. Just enter the operator followed by the phone number, like this: **phonebook:123-456-7890**. (Alternatively, you can limit your search to the residential PhoneBook by using the **rphonebook:** operator.) The page that's returned by this method is shown in Figure 4.7.

By the way, you can also use the **phonebook:** and **rphonebook:** operators to search for phone numbers by a person's name, address, or state, although the PhoneBook results are identical to entering the same information in the standard search box. What's different is that you get *only* PhoneBook results, as shown in Figure 4.8, without any web search results.

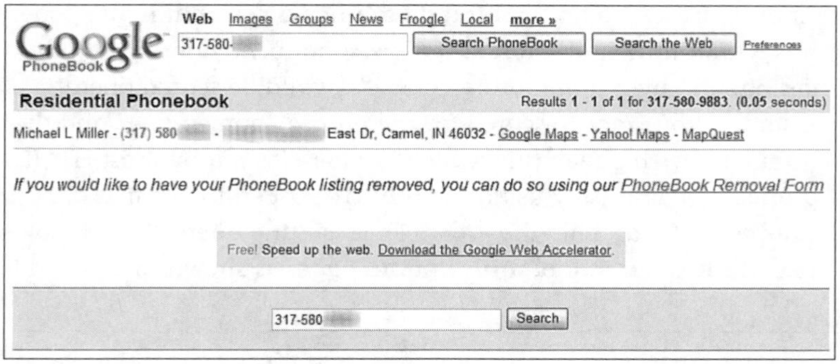

FIGURE 4.7
The results of a reverse phone number lookup.

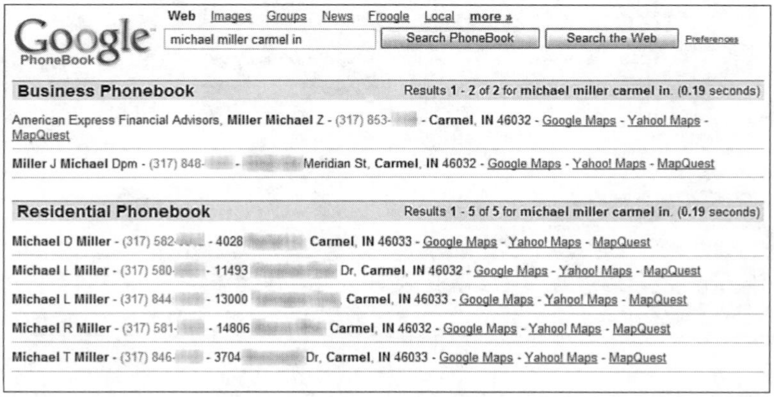

FIGURE 4.8
*The results of a standard phone number search using the **phonebook:** operator.*

Searching for Personal Information—And Home Pages

When you're looking for information about a particular person, you probably want more than just an address and phone number. This is where a standard Google web search on that person's name makes sense; if anything has been publicly written about or by that person online, Google will know. Just make sure you use the exact phrase operator by enclosing the person's name in quotation marks, like this: **"michael miller"**. You may also want to search for variations on the person's name, such as **"mike miller"** or **"m miller"**.

Another trick is to find out if a person has a personal home page. You can do this with a little understanding of personal behavior and standard web design, and by manipulating Google's available search operators. In this instance, you want to search for the phrase "home page" and the person's name in a web page's title, which is where it's put by most HTML editing programs. You do this by using the **allintitle:** operator, as first discussed in Chapter 2, "Searching the Web." The resulting query should look something like **allintitle: michael miller home page**, as shown in Figure 4.9.

FIGURE 4.9

*Searching for a person's personal home page with the **allintitle:** operator.*

Googling Yourself

In this Internet age, one of the most popular time wasters is searching for information about yourself on the Web—Googling yourself, in the common parlance. While this may seem to be a particularly useless and self-indulgent endeavor, there's more to it than meets the eye.

Yes, it's fun to enter your name into the Google search box and see what comes up. You never know who's saying what about you, especially if you have a little bit of a public presence.

The real value in self-Googling, however, comes when you discover how much of your personal information is—or hopefully isn't—available for public viewing on the Web. Googling yourself is a great way to find out just how private or public your phone number, email address, and street address are; you can also find out if any of your credit card or Social Security numbers are floating around the Web. (If they are, it's a sure sign you've been a victim of identity theft.)

To do a full-bore personal security check on your personal information, enter the following items into the Google search box (one at a time, of course), and see what results come up:

- First and last name
- Street address
- Phone number
- Email address
- Social security number
- Credit card numbers
- Bank account numbers

The first item, of course, is relatively innocuous; if you've ever posted any comments on a web forum or blog, your name is probably going to be in Google's database. Even your street address and phone number aren't much to worry about, especially if the results come primarily from the Google PhoneBook. (This just means that your address and phone number are public information, as published in your local white pages telephone directory.)

Discovering that your email address is public knowledge, however, is a bit of a bigger deal. Again, Google is likely to know your email address if you've ever placed a forum or blog posting, or created a web page with a link to your email address. The problem with having an easily Googleable email address is that if you can Google it, so can email spammers. In fact, Googling for email addresses is one of the most common ways for spammers to get your email address. A spammer might search for all email addresses within a given domain; if your address appears in the results, you're added to the spammer's mailing list. Sorry.

The worst possible situation is if you Google your financial information and get a match. This means that someone, somewhere has stolen your personal info, and made it available on the Web for others to use. If you find credit card or bank account info on the Web, contact your credit card company or bank immediately to put a hold on your account and check for fraudulent use.

If it's your Social Security number that you find online, you should contact the Federal Trade Commission at www.consumer.gov/idtheft/ or 1-877-438-4338. If you think someone is using your Social Security number for work purposes (which would be apparent by examining the Social Security Statement the government sends you each year), contact the Social Security Administration at 1-800-772-1213.

The Bottom Line

Google might not be the best people finder on the Internet, but it's not a bad place to start. It's easy enough to enter someone's name and location into the Google search box and see what comes up. Plus, the reverse phone number lookup feature is a nice way to find out just who it was who wrote their phone number on a napkin at that party last week.

More seriously, Google is also a good way to find out just how much information about you is out there on the Internet. Remember, if you can find it, everyone else can, too—including potential employers. While there might not be anything you can do about it, it's better to know what's out there than to be blindsided at a later date.

4

Searching for Financial Information

hile Google is primarily a search engine, not a financial information site, that's starting to change. Google has always let you search for financial information from its main search page, and now is offering even more financial information via the Google Finance site. While I'm not completely sure that Google Finance can replace a big full-service financial information site, such as Bloomberg.com (www.bloomberg.com) or MarketWatch (www.marketwatch.com), it offers more than enough information for the casual investor—and serves as a gateway to even more information on the Web.

Searching via the Standard Search Box

When you're looking for information about a particular stock or mutual fund, there are a number of ways to search Google for that information. The easiest way is to simply enter the stock or fund symbol into Google's search box, without any additional keywords, as shown in Figure 5.1.

FIGURE 5.1

Searching for stock information from the Google search box.

You can also use the **stocks:** operator to signify that the keywords following are ticker symbols. This method is recommended if you're looking up multiple stocks at one time. Just enter the **stocks:** operator followed by one or more stock symbols, with each symbol separated by a space. For example, to look up information on Boeing (BA), Google (GOOG), IBM (IBM), and Microsoft (MSFT), you'd enter the following query: **stocks: ba goog ibm msft**.

At the top of the search results page is a section devoted to the stock you entered, as shown in Figure 5.2. This section includes a graph of the current day's stock performance; the current stock price; opening, high, and low prices; volume and average volume; and market capitalization (market cap). There are also links to full coverage of the company's stock at Google Finance, Yahoo! Finance, MSN Money, MarketWatch, CNN Money, and Reuters. You can click any of these links for more information.

FIGURE 5.2

Basic stock information resulting from a standard Google search.

Using Google Finance

We just discussed how you can display basic stock info by searching for that stock from the standard Google search box. The resulting information is rather basic, but there's more info available. All you have to do is use the Google Finance site.

Google Finance is a somewhat full-featured financial information site. You can access Google Finance by going directly to finance.google.com, or by clicking the Google Finance link on the stock search results page.

Like other financial information sites, Google Finance offers a combination of general market news plus in-depth financial

> **tip**
> You can also get to the Google Finance page by clicking the stock symbol link or the intra-day chart.

information on specific stocks, mutual funds, and public and private companies. The information offered by Google Finance comes from a variety of financial data providers, as well as content obtained by the GoogleBot crawler and stored in Google's main search database.

> **tip** Stock quotes from Google Finance can also be delivered to your cell phone or PDA via SMS text messaging. Learn more in Chapter 30, "Using Google Mobile Services."

Accessing General Financial Information

The main Google Finance page, shown in Figure 5.3, offers a variety of general financial news and information. Here's what you'll find:

FIGURE 5.3

The main Google Finance page.

- **Market Summary.** This section displays the latest Nasdaq, Dow, S&P 500, and NYSE levels, as well as an intra-day graph of the Dow Jones Industrial Index. Click any exchange link to view detailed trading data and news. (The dedicated Dow Jones page is shown in Figure 5.4.)

> **caution** Google Finance isn't quite as full-featured as some other financial information sites. In particular, Google Finance does *not* offer information on stock options or bonds. It also offers information only on U.S. companies, although it does offer general news and information from selected international markets (Amsterdam, Brussels, Lisbon, Paris, and Toronto).

5

■ **Today's Headlines.** The top financial headlines, as reported from a
variety of news sites; click any
headline to read the entire story. To
view additional headlines, scroll

note Learn more about
Google News in
Chapter 29, "Using Google News."

down to the bottom of the Today's Headlines section and click the More
Headlines link. This displays the Business page from Google News, as
shown in Figure 5.5.

■ **Recent Quotes.** This is a list of stocks/companies you've recently
searched for, accompanied by the current stock price.

■ **Related News.** This is a list of news headlines for the companies listed
in the Recent Quotes section.

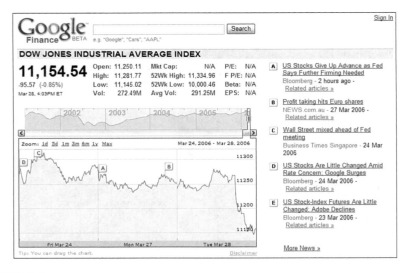

FIGURE 5.4

The detail page for the Dow Jones Industrial Average Index—news stories on the right.

Then, of course, there's the ubiquitous Google search box at the top of the
page. This isn't a standard Google search box, however; you use this search
box to search Google Finance for specific company and stock information.
Just enter a stock symbol or company name, and the matching company
page will be displayed.

FIGURE 5.5
More financial news, as displayed on the Google News site.

Accessing Specific Stock and Company Information

General financial information is good; more detailed information on specific companies, stocks, or mutual funds is even better. To that end, Google Finance offers dedicated pages for companies and securities, complete with all sorts of useful news and data.

To view a company/security-specific page, you can click the security's name anywhere it's displayed on the Google Finance site or in general Google search results. Alternatively, you can search for that company or security using the search box at the top of the Google Finance main page; instead of a list of search results, Google will display the dedicated company/security page.

As you can see in Figure 5.6, a dedicated company/security page includes a plethora of financial information. Here are the major sections you'll find:

- **Key metrics.** Located in the top-left corner of the page, these include the company/fund name, ticker symbol, current price, dollar/percentage change, open/high/low prices, trading volume and average volume, market cap, 52-week high and low prices, price/earnings (P/E) ratio, forward price/earnings (F P/E) ratio), beta, and earnings per share (EPS).

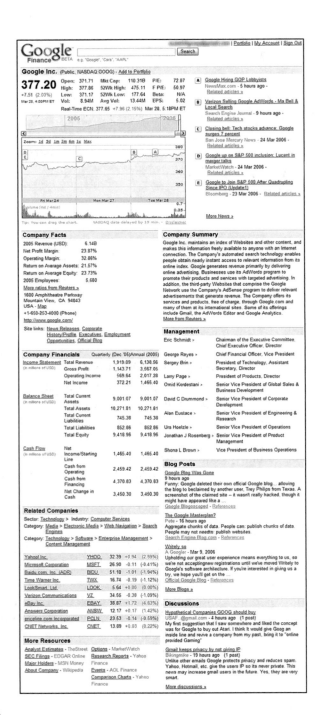

FIGURE 5.6

View detailed information about a company, stock, or mutual fund.

- **1-week stock chart.** This chart tracks the price of the stock over the past week. Key events are noted on the chart by letters; each letter corresponds to one of the news stories displayed to the right of the chart. (Read more about how to use these interactive charts later in this chapter.)

> **note** Learn more about Google Blog Search in Chapter 6, "Searching Blogs and Blog Postings."

- **Recent stories.** These numbered headlines correspond to the numbered events on the 1-week stock chart. Click any headline to read the complete story.

- **Company summary.** A brief description of what the company is and what it does.

- **Management.** The names and titles of the company's key officers and senior management.

- **Company facts.** More data about the company, including most recent yearly revenue, net profit margin, operating margin, return on average assets, return on average equity, number of employees, company address and phone number, website, and links to additional information.

- **Company financials.** Key financial data from the company's most recent annual report, including income statement, balance sheet, and cash flow numbers.

- **Related companies.** A list of market sectors and companies that are similar to the company in question. Click any company link to view that company's dedicated Google Finance page.

- **Blog posts.** From Google Blog Search, blog postings from around the blogosphere that discuss the company and its stock. Click a posting title to read more, or click the More Blogs link to view more related posts.

- **Discussions.** A list of posts discussing the company in the Google Finance Groups. (Learn more about Google Finance Groups later in this chapter.)

- **More resources.** Links to additional information about the company, in the form of SEC filings, analyst estimates, research reports, and the like. Click any link to learn more.

5

FINANCIAL METRICS

To the uninitiated, the various financial metrics displayed by Google Finance amount to nothing more than acronym soup. To the savvy investor, however, these metrics are key to evaluating the risk and potential reward for any investment.

So what do these metrics mean? Here's a short primer:

Trading volume: The number of shares traded on the most recent trading day. Important only when compared to the average volume.

Average volume: The total number of shares traded for the previous three months, divided by the number of total trading days in that period. Compare this number to the daily trading volume to see if investor interest in the stock has increased or decreased. For example, if the daily trading volume is higher than the average volume for the past three months, that means that more shares are being traded now than is usual for that stock; the increased investor interest, however, could mean almost anything.

Market capitalization (market cap). The company's market capitalization, calculated by multiplying the current stock price with the number of shares outstanding. For example, if a company's stock is trading at $10 per share and there are 1 million shares outstanding, then the company's market cap is $10 million.

52-week high. The highest price that this security has traded over the past year.

52-week low. The lowest price that this security has traded over the past year.

Revenue. The total sales generated by the company. Typically reported quarterly and yearly.

Operating income. The company's revenue minus all day-to-day operating expenses. It excludes financial-related items, such as interest income, dividend income, and interest expense, as well as taxes.

Operating margin. The company's operating income divided by revenue, expressed as a percentage.

Net income (profit, earnings). The amount of money left over after the company subtracts *all* its costs and expenses (including interest income, dividend income, and the like) from its revenue.

Net profit margin. The company's total net income divided by revenue, expressed as a percentage.

Earnings per share. The company's profits divided by the number of shares outstanding—in other words, the amount of profit earned by each share of stock.

Price/earnings ratio (P/E). The current stock price divided by the company's most recent earnings per share. You use P/E to compare the earnings power of different companies.

Forward price/earnings ratio (F P/E). The current stock price divided by the company's estimated future earnings per share. Some investors think this is a more accurate way to compare the future earnings potential of different companies than standard P/E analysis.

Return on average assets. The ratio of net income divided by average total assets. This is a financial measurement of the efficiency with which a company uses its assets.

Return on average equity (return on equity). The ratio of net income divided by average equity. This is a financial measurement of how effective a business has been in investing its net worth.

Beta. For mutual funds, this is a measure of the fund's volatility relative to the market, typically compared to the performance of the S&P 500. A beta of 1.0 indicates that the fund is more volatile than the market; a beta of less than 1.0 indicates that the fund is less volatile than the market.

Viewing Interactive Financial Charts

The stock chart displayed on the company/stock Google Finance page, like the one in Figure 5.7, is more informative than it might first appear. That's because this is an interactive chart that you can manipulate to display a variety of different information. You can click the chart to display more or different information.

First of all, you can change the date range displayed on the chart—in several different ways. Quick view zooming is accomplished by clicking the 1d (1-day), 5d (5-day), 1m (1-month), 6m (6-month), 1y (1-year), or

note To fully display Google Finance charts, your computer needs to be running Microsoft Windows 2000, Windows XP, Windows Vista, Mac OS, or Linux. You also need to be using a current version of the Internet Explorer, Firefox, Opera, or Safari web browsers, and have Macromedia Flash Player 7.0 or higher installed. (The charts themselves are displayed using Flash technology.)

Max (life-to-date) links. You can also click and drag the chart to the left or right to display a different range of dates; just hover your cursor anywhere on the chart, hold down the left mouse button, and drag.

In addition, the overview graph just above the main graph displays the stock's price over the life of the stock, with the currently selected range for the main chart displayed as a small slice of the life-to-date chart. To enlarge or shrink the time span displayed in the main chart, click and drag the left positioning handle in this "window" on the subsidiary chart. Alternatively, you can drag the positioning button below this "window" to display a different date range, as shown in Figure 5.8.

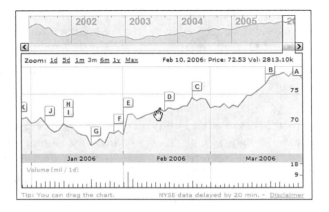

FIGURE 5.7

A Google Finance interactive stock chart.

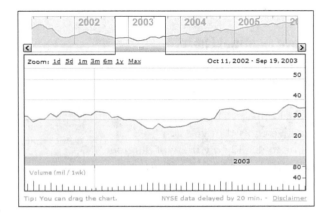

FIGURE 5.8

A different—and larger—date range displayed by manipulating the "window" in the upper overview graph.

Another fun thing about these interactive charts is the ability to display price information at a specific time. All you have to do is hover your cursor over a specific spot on the trend line, which highlights a specific date and time of day. The price and volume information for that point in time is displayed at the top of the chart.

And, as discussed previously, key news stories about the company are pin-pointed on the chart by a series of letter buttons (A, B, C, and so on). Click a letter and the corresponding news story is highlighted in the section to the right of the graph. Click the headline to read the full story.

Tracking Your Portfolio

There's one other section on the Google Finance site that you might find use-ful. I'm talking about the Portfolio section, shown in Figure 5.9. You access your portfolio by clicking the Portfolio link at the top of the main Google Finance page. (This feature is visible only if you have a Google Account and if you're signed in at the time.)

FIGURE 5.9

Tracking your personal portfolio with Google Finance.

Your Google Finance Portfolio is how you track the performance of a selected group of stocks and mutual funds, right from the main Google Finance page. This list can be those stocks in your actual portfolio, or simply a group of stocks in which you have interest. In any case, it's a good way to put the financial information you're most interested in front and center on the Google Finance page.

note To create a Google Account, go to www.google.com/accounts/ and follow the onscreen instructions. A Google Account is completely free, and is necessary to use the Google Finance Portfolio feature, as well as Gmail, Google Alerts, and other personalized Google features.

What information is included on the Google Finance Portfolio page? For each stock, you'll see the following:

- Symbol
- Company or fund name (click either the symbol or name link to view the detailed Google Finance page for that security)
- Last trade (current price)
- Change (dollar and percentage change from previous day price)
- Buy price (the price you paid for these shares, if entered)
- Shares (the number of shares you own, if entered)
- Investment (your total investment in this security, if you entered price and share information)
- Current value (the current value of your investment in this security, based on the current share price, if you entered price and share information)
- Gain/loss (your current gain or loss on this security, if you entered price and share information)

To create your portfolio, make sure you have a Google Account and that you're signed in before you access the Google Finance page. (Alternatively, you can click the Sign In link at the top of the Google Finance page.) Once you're signed in, you can then create your Google Finance Portfolio. Just follow these steps:

1. Click the Portfolio link at the top of the Google Finance page.
2. When the Portfolio pages appears, as shown in Figure 5.10, enter the stock symbol you want to track.
3. If you want to track performance versus cost, you should also enter the price you paid and how many shares you own (both optional).
4. Click the Add to Portfolio button.
5. Repeat steps 2-4 to add additional stocks to your portfolio.
6. When you're done adding stocks, click the Google Finance logo to return to the main Google Finance page.

You can add new stocks to your portfolio at any time by entering the Symbol, Price, and Shares information and clicking the Add to Portfolio button. You can also

tip To track a security with multiple shares purchased at different prices, you'll need to enter each purchase of the security separately.

change your portfolio information by clicking the Edit Portfolio button, and then changing the Buy Price and Shares information for any listed security. To delete any security from your portfolio, click the Delete link next to the security.

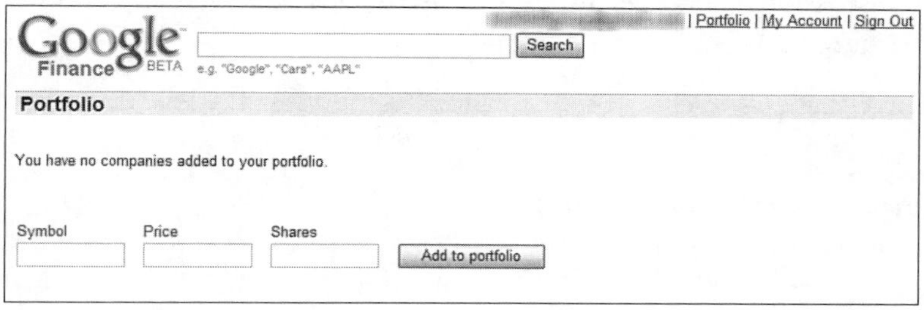

FIGURE 5.10
Adding new stocks to your Google Finance Portfolio.

Discussing Finances in Google Finance Groups

Savvy investors know that dry financial data can only tell you so much. Oftentimes it helps to get opinions and tips from other investors—to test the waters, so to speak, by talking to people who might have a little more information (or a few more opinions) about the company in question.

One of the best places to find like-minded investors is on the Google Finance Discussion Groups. This is a subset of the overall Google Groups discussion forums, tailor-made for financial discussions.

The Google Finance Discussion Groups differ from standard Google Groups in that the Google Finance discussions are moderated by Google staffers. The intent is to keep the junk off the boards; postings are monitored to find and delete spam, pornography, hateful or harassing content, and offers to buy or sell any security. It's kind of a sanitized version of the discussions you find at other financial information sites—sanitized for your protection, or so Google says.

tip You can also add a security to your portfolio by clicking the Add to Portfolio on any dedicated company/security page.

note Learn more about Google Groups in Chapter 28, "Using Google Groups."

Finding Google Finance Discussions

Google Finance discussions are organized by company. You access the discussions for a given company by going to the company's dedicated Google Finance page, scrolling down to the Discussions section, and clicking the More Discussions link. This displays a Discussions page, like the one shown in Figure 5.11.

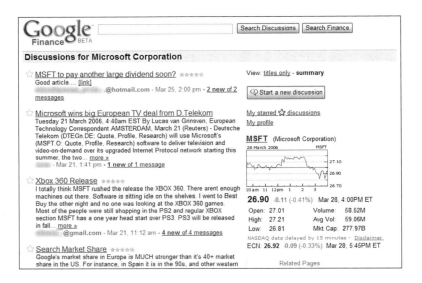

FIGURE 5.11

Viewing Google Finance discussions about a specific company.

Messages are listed in reverse chronological order, with the newest messages at the top of the left column. To view older messages, scroll to the bottom of the page and click the Older link.

Reading and Rating Messages

To read a complete message, all you have to do is click the message header. This displays a page like the one shown in Figure 5.12, where the message you clicked and all other messages in the same thread are displayed, in chronological order. For each message, you see the poster's Google Account ID, a link to the poster's profile, the date posted, a rating for this message, and then the message text.

The message rating is an interesting feature. Readers are encouraged to vote on the messages they read, assigning each message a rating on a scale of 0 to 5 stars. It's an attempt to highlight those messages that other users find the most useful.

Creating a Google Finance Profile

Before you can rate a message—or start a new discussion—you have to create a Google Finance profile. It isn't enough simply to have a Google Account; you have to enter a little information about yourself before Google deems you worthy to comment in a group.

FIGURE 5.12
Reading Google Finance messages.

To create your Google Finance profile, follow these steps:

1. Go to any company's Discussions page.

2. Click the My Profile link in the right column.

3. When the My Profile page appears, it should be relatively empty. Click the Edit link.

4. When the Edit My Profile page appears, as shown in Figure 5.13, enter your real name, the nickname

note If all you want to do is read messages and not post any messages of your own, you don't have to create a profile.

you want to use, your location, title, industry in which you work, personal website or blog (if you have one), favorite companies, stocks owned, investment style, and optional quote.

5. Click the Save button.

FIGURE 5.13

Creating your Google Finance profile.

Your completed profile is now displayed. You can edit your information at any time by repeating these steps.

Replying to Messages

To reply to a message, click the Reply link below the message text. This opens a Reply text box, as shown in Figure 5.14. Enter your reply into this box, and then click the Post button. Your reply will now be added to the thread in progress.

Starting a New Discussion

You're not limited to replying to existing messages, of course. You should feel free to start your own discussions, about topics that interest you.

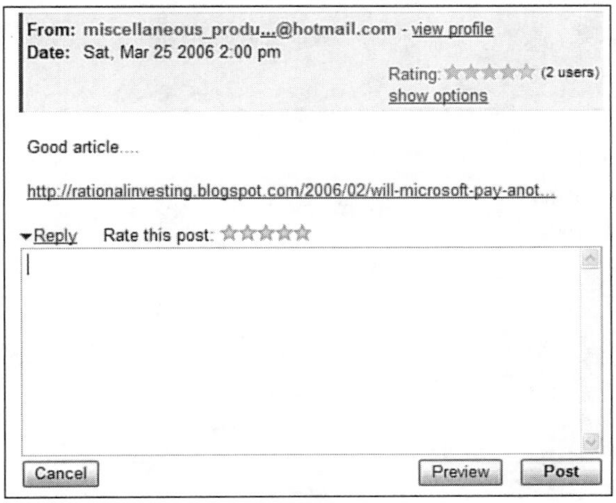

From: miscellaneous_produ...@hotmail.com - view profile
Date: Sat, Mar 25 2006 2:00 pm

Rating: ★★★★☆ (2 users)
show options

Good article....

http://rationalinvesting.blogspot.com/2006/02/will-microsoft-pay-anot...

▼Reply   Rate this post: ☆☆☆☆☆

Cancel   Preview   Post

FIGURE 5.14

Replying to a message.

To start a new discussion about a particular company, follow these steps:

1. Go to the company's main Discussions page.

2. Click the Start a New Discussion button.

3. The first time you post, you'll see the Finance Posting Application page. Assuming you agree with the terms, check the I've Read and Accepted... option, and then click the Next Step button. You'll now see your Google Finance profile; if you've not yet filled in the blanks, do so now, and then click the Next Step button.

4. When the Start a New Discussion page appears, as shown in Figure 5.15, enter a subject for the message, and then enter your message text. (You can preview your in-progress message by clicking the Preview button.)

5. If you want a copy of the message emailed to you, check the Send Me a Copy of This Message option.

6. When you're done composing your message, click the Post Message button.

Your message will now be reviewed by Google staff. If you pass muster, the message will be posted to the discussion group.

caution If your message is *not* approved, Google will notify you via email. If you don't receive an email, your message was approved and posted as normal.

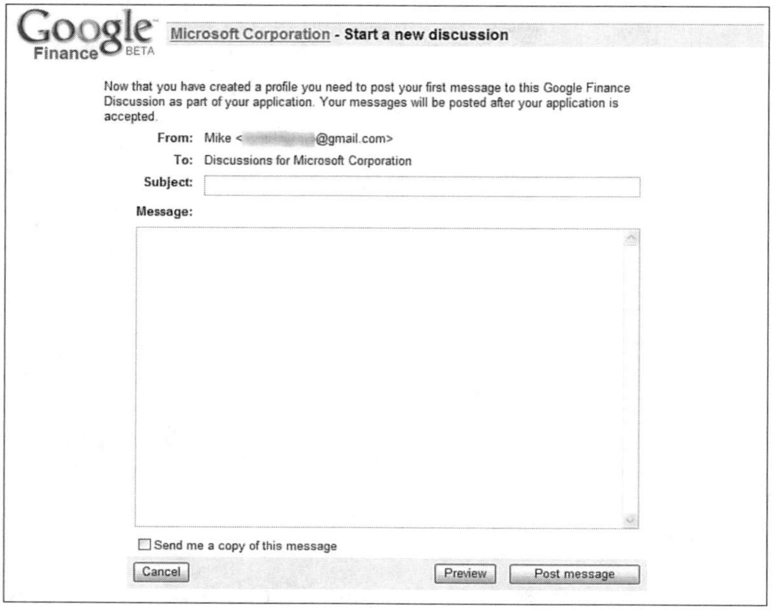

FIGURE 5.15

Posting a new message in the discussion group.

The Bottom Line

Although not quite as robust as some other online finance sites, Google Finance is a good one-stop-shop for basic company and stock information. The easy incorporation of Google Groups discussions and blog searches makes Google Finance even more useful; I also like the interactive stock charts.

Of course, for quick financial information, you can't beat Google's simple search box search. When you want stock quotes fast, just enter the company's ticker symbol into the ever-present Google search box. It's the fast way to get basic info!

6

Searching Blogs and Blog Postings

I f you've been on the Internet for any length of time, you're probably familiar with message boards, discussion groups, and Usenet newsgroups, all of which let users post and respond to messages in organized threads. You're probably also familiar with the concept of blogging, which is one of those new phenomena that's caught on so quickly that it already feels like it's been around forever. A blog— short for "web log"—is like a message board, but a little more owner-driven.

The typical blog is a personal website that is updated frequently with commentary, links to other sites, and anything else the author might be interested in. Many blogs also let visitors post their own comments in response to the owners postings, resulting in a community that is very similar to that of a message board. It's a 21st century version of self-publishing, enabled by the Internet.

If you want to start your own blog, Google offers its own blog-hosting service called Blogger; we'll discuss Blogger in more depth in Chapter 23, "Using Blogger." But if all you want to do is read blog postings, there are literally hundreds of thousands of blogs you can choose from, covering just about any topic you can think of. How do you find the blog that contains the information and opinions you're interested in?

Once again, Google comes to the rescue. When you want to find a particular blog or blog posting, you can use Google Blog Search. This is a specialized subset of the main Google search engine, fine-tuned to search the far-reaching blogosphere. Read on to learn more.

How Google Blog Search Works

Before Google Blog Search, it was a bit of a crap shoot trying to find information in the blogosphere. There is no single organized directory of blog sites, nor of the frequently updated content of all the blogs that exist today. The blogosphere is quite chaotic, and constantly changing; Google's traditional method of crawling the web for updated information, which normally takes a few weeks to update, was simply too slow to index blog content.

The solution to this problem came in the form of site feeds. A site feed is an automatically updated stream of a blog's contents, enabled by a special XML file format called RSS (Real-time Simple Syndication). When a blog has an RSS feed enabled, any updated content is automatically published as a special XML file that contains the RSS feed. The syndicated feed is then normally picked up by RSS feed reader programs and RSS aggregators for websites.

Google hit upon the idea of using these RSS feeds to seed its blog search index. By aggregating RSS feeds into its index, Google Blog Search is constantly (and almost immediately) updated with new blog content. The structured format of the RSS files also makes it relatively easy to accurately search for specific information and date ranges within the blog index.

While some users think that Google Blog Search only searches blogs hosted by Google's Blogger service, that isn't true. Google Blog Search searches every blog on the Internet that publishes a site feed, using either RSS or Atom formats. Google's blog index only holds posts created since the launch of Google Blog Search, however; for most blogs, that means posts made before June 2005 aren't available for searching.

note Atom is a feed format similar to RSS, with a few extra features.

How to List Your Blog with Google Blog Search

If you have your own blog, what do you need to do to make sure it's included in Google Blog Search results? The answer is, not much. You don't have to submit your blog to Google for indexing; all you have to do is make sure you've enabled a site feed for your blog. You can choose either an RSS or Atom feed; either one works. If you're not sure how to enable the site feed feature, contact your blog host for more information.

COMMENTARY

SURFING THE BLOGOSPHERE

When you take all the blogs on the Web together, you get something called the *blogosphere*. It's important to think of the blogosphere as separate from the Web, because of all the interlinking going on. Look at any blog, and you're likely to see a list of related blogs (sometimes titled "friends of..."). Bloggers like to link to other blogs that they like—as well as to news stories, photos, audio files—you name it.

In fact, a lot of blogs are nothing more than links to interesting blog entries—there isn't always a lot of original content there. The blogger finds something interesting, and then uses his own blog to draw attention to that other posting. In this way, bloggers are a lot like radio disc jockeys, "spinning" links and snippets the same as a DJ spins songs.

These bloggers not only sort through the blogosphere to find the most interesting articles, they also provide some background and organization to these postings, and in many cases add their own commentary. The best blogs have a definite point of view, no matter what content they're linking to.

The way to get the most efficient use of the blogosphere is to find one or two bloggers that you really like for a specific topic, and then use those blogs as a kind of guide to the rest of the blogosphere. Let the bloggers lead the way—and be prepared to spend some time jumping from link to link!

6

Searching for Blogs—And Blog Posts

Now that you know the background, how do you use Google Blog Search to search for information in the blogosphere? It's relatively easy; a simple search returns links to both entire blogs and individual blog postings.

Four Ways to Search

There are actually four different ways to use Google Blog Search.

First, you can go to the main Google Blog Search page (blogsearch.google.com), shown in Figure 6.1. Enter your query into the search box, and then click the Search Blogs button.

FIGURE 6.1

The main Google Blog Search page.

Alternatively, if you're a Blogger user and like the Blogger interface, you can use the Blogger Blog Search page (search.blogger.com), shown in Figure 6.2. This page works just like the Google Blog Search page; enter your query into the search box, then click the Search Blogs button.

Blogger users also have access to the Blogger Dashboard, shown in Figure 6.3, which you use to manage both your Blogger account and your blog settings. (As a Blogger user, you access the Dashboard at www.blogger.com.) Just scroll down to the Blog Search section, enter your query, and click the Search button.

Finally, when you visit any Blogger-hosted blog (a blog with a blogspot.com address), you can use the navigation bar at the top of the page to conduct a full Google Blog Search. As shown in Figure 6.4, enter your query into the search box and then click the Search All Blogs button.

However you do it, it's the same search, and will return the same results.

note The Search This Blog button limits your search to postings within the current blog only.

FIGURE 6.2
The Blogger Blog Search page.

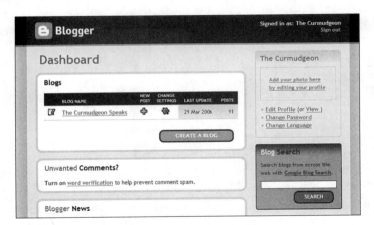

FIGURE 6.3
Searching via the Blogger Dashboard.

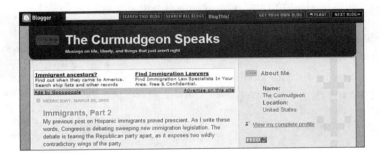

FIGURE 6.4
Searching via the navigation bar at the top of every Blogger blog.

Evaluating Blog Search Results

When you enter your blog search query, Google searches its index of RSS feeds and returns a page of blogs and blog postings that best match your query. As you can see in Figure 6.5, there are two main parts of this page.

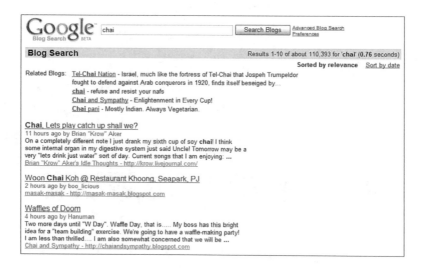

FIGURE 6.5

The results of a Google Blog Search.

At the top of the page is a short listing of blogs that have some relevance to your query. Click the blog name to view the entire blog.

Below that is a listing of individual blog posts. The title of the post is at the top of each listing; click the title to view the full posting. Below the title is a line that tells you when the posting was made, and who posted it. Then there's the first few sentences of the post, serving as a summary. And, finally, there's a link to the blog itself, listing both the blog's title and URL; click the link to view the entire blog.

To view additional postings that match your query, scroll down to the bottom of the page and click the Next link or the Page Number link.

> **tip** By default, blog postings are listed by relevance—the best matches are at the top of the list. If you'd rather view the results in chronological order, click the Sort by Date link at the top-right corner of the search results page.

Fine-Tuning Your Blog Search Query

Entering a Google Blog Search query is very similar to entering a standard Google web search query. Just enter one or more keywords into the search box, click the Search button, and you're on your way.

There are, however, some advanced search options you can apply to fine-tune your search results. Read on to learn more.

Using Advanced Search Operators

It's important to know that all the search operators you learned about in Chapter 2, "Searching the Web," can be used with Google Blog Search. Remember to enclose phrase searches in quotation marks, to use the + and - and **OR** operators, and to use advanced operators such as **link:** and **intitle:** as appropriate.

In addition, Google Blog Search has its own collection of blog-specific search operators that you can use. These operators are detailed in Table 6.1:

Table 6.1   Google Blog Search Operators

Operator	Description	Usage
inblogtitle:	Limits the search to words contained in the blog's title.	inblogtitle:*keyword*
inposttitle:	Limits the search to words contained in the titles of individual blog postings.	inposttitle:*keyword*
inpostauthor:	Limits the search to postings by a specific poster.	*keyword*:inpostauthor:*name*
blogurl:	Limits the search to a particular blog, as defined by the blog's web address (URL).	*keyword* blogurl:*www.blogurl.com*

Using the Advanced Search Page

If you don't like using search box operators, you can achieve the same results by using the Google Blog Search Advanced Search page. You get to this page by clicking the Advanced Search link on the main Google Blog Search page.

As you can see in Figure 6.6, the Advanced Search page contains a number of search restrictions, all accessible by filling in the appropriate blanks or selecting items from a pull-down list. Table 6.2 details the advanced search options available on this page:

6

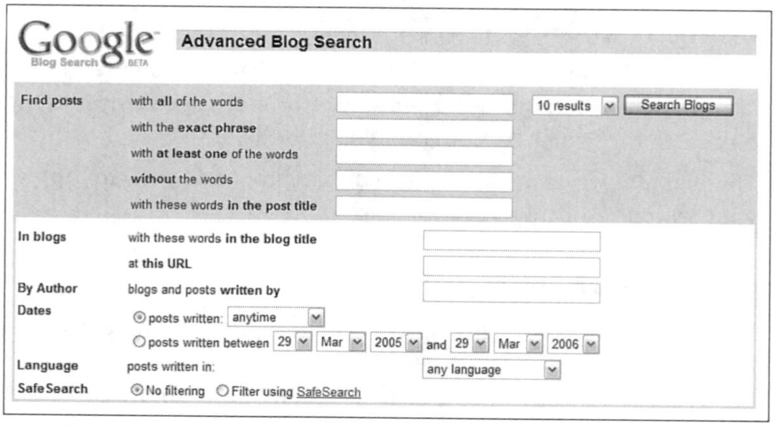

FIGURE 6.6

Google Blog Search's Advanced Search page.

Table 6.2	Google Blog Search Advanced Search Options	
Option	**Description**	**Same As This Operator**
Find posts with *all* of the words	Standard Google search, assuming the **AND** operator before each keyword.	N/A
Find posts with the *exact phrase*	Searches for exact phrases only.	" "
Find posts with *at least one* of the words	Searches for either one keyword or another.	**OR**
Find posts *without* the words	Excludes words from the search results.	-
Find posts with these words *in the post title*	Searches the titles of blog postings only.	**inposttitle:**
In blogs with these words *in the blog title*	Searches blog titles only.	**inblogtitle:**
In blogs at *this URL*	Searches posts within a specific blog.	**blogurl:**
By Author: blogs and posts *written by*	Searches posts made by a specific user.	**inpostauthor:**
Dates: posts written	Searches only those posts written in the last hour, last 6 hours, last 12 hours, last day, past week, past month, or anytime.	N/A
Dates: posts written between	Searches only those posts written within a specified date range.	N/A
Language: posts written in	Searches only those posts written in the specified language.	N/A
SafeSearch	Turns on or off Google's SafeSearch content filtering.	**safesearch:**

Advanced Searching from Blogger

If you use the Blogger Blog Search page instead of the Google Blog Search page, you have access to a different set of advanced search options. You can view a similar Advanced Search page (shown in Figure 6.7) by clicking the Advanced Search link, or view a more user-friendly subset by clicking the Use Search Options link. When you click this link, the main search page changes to include the following options, shown in Figure 6.8:

FIGURE 6.7

The Advanced Search page at Blogger Blog Search.

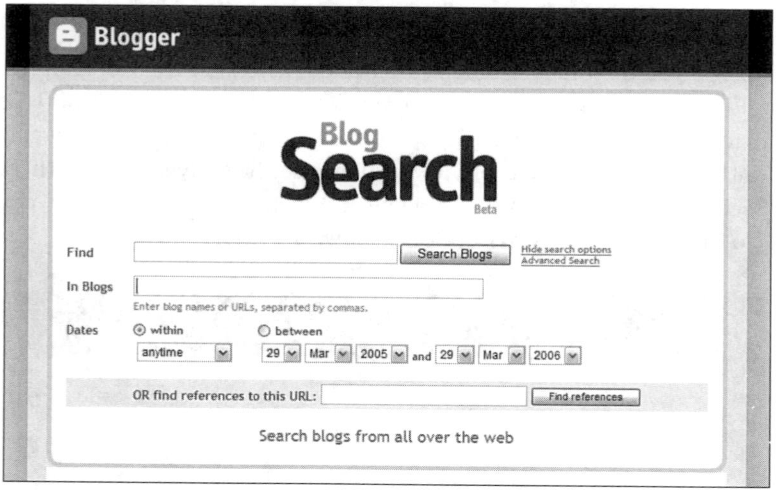

FIGURE 6.8

The expanded search options available at the main Blogger Blog Search page.

- In blogs (searches specific blogs only)
- Dates within (searches postings made within the last hour, 6 hours, 12 hours, day, week, or month)
- Dates between (searches postings made within a specified date range)
- Find references to this URL (searches postings that include a link to the specified web address)

Subscribing to Blog Search Results

Back at the beginning of this chapter I talked a little about how Google got its blog search results, by using RSS feeds. Well, Google uses this same technology to feed you updates to the postings you find on the search results page. That's right, Google syndicates its blog search results via RSS and Atom.

When you subscribe to an RSS or Atom search results feed, Google automatically

> **note** It should come as no big surprise that Google offers its own feed aggregator site called Google Reader. Learn more in the "Reading Blog Feeds with Google Reader" section, later in this chapter.

notifies you of any new postings that match your search query. The notification occurs in the feed reader or feed aggregator of your choice; as new search results are found, they show up as new postings within the feed.

To subscribe to a feed of search results, follow these steps:

1. Conduct your blog search as normal from the Google Blog Search main page.

2. When the search results appear, scroll to the bottom of the search results page, as shown in Figure 6.9, and then right-click either the 10 Results or 100 Results link for Atom or RSS. (The first link displays the 10 most recent search results in your feed reader; the second option displays the 100 most recent results.)

3. From the pop-up menu, select Copy Shortcut (or Copy Link Location in Firefox). This copies the URL for the selected feed.

4. Move to your feed reader program or feed aggregator website and paste this URL into the appropriate "new feed URL" box.

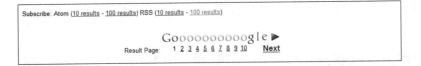

FIGURE 6.9

Right-click a link to copy the feed URL into your feed reader or aggregator.

Once the URL has been added to your list of feeds, any new postings that match your search query will now appear in your feed reader or aggregator. (Figure 6.10 shows a Google Blog Search feed in the Bloglines feed aggregator.) It's a great way to keep up-to-date on information pertaining to a search of interest!

caution   Always check to see which type of feeds your feed reader or aggregator supports. To be safe, use the RSS feed; more programs and websites support RSS than do Atom.

6

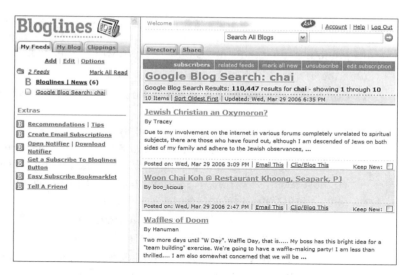

FIGURE 6.10

Viewing a Google Blog Search feed in Bloglines.

Reading Blog Feeds with Google Reader

When you want to read your blog feeds—from Google Blog Search or other sources—you need some sort of feed reading mechanism. That can be a feed reader software program, or a website that aggregates feeds from a variety of sources.

Google Reader is such a feed aggregator. Actually, it's more than that; Google Reader is a web-based reader that lets you read feeds from both blogs and from news sites. You can use Google Reader to read the latest blog postings *and* the latest news headlines. All you have to do is subscribe to the content on a site or blog, and then use Google Reader to read the latest postings or stories.

You access Google Reader at reader.google.com. Google Reader lets you read both blog feeds and news feeds. That means you can use Google Reader to display the latest news headlines from popular news sites, as well as catch the latest ponderings from your favorite bloggers. All you need to do is know which feed you want to subscribe to; Google Reader automatically displays the latest content, all in one place.

note To use Google Reader, you must have a Google Account—and be signed into that account.

As you can see in Figure 6.11, the most recent postings from the feeds you've subscribed to are displayed in the left list. To read a posting, just highlight it in this list; the fulltext of the posting is now displayed in the big right-hand window.

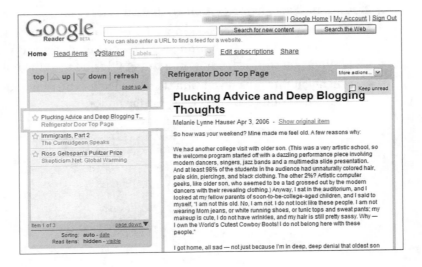

FIGURE 6.11

Reading blog and news feeds with Google Reader.

By default, postings you've already read are not displayed in the posting list. To view previously read posts, just click the Visible link below the posting list.

To read *all* the postings for a selected blog, highlight a posting for that blog and then click the blog's name; this switches the view to display the most recent postings for this blog only. You can return to your entire subscription list by clicking the Home link.

There are several ways to add a feed to Google Reader—which we'll examine next.

Search for Feeds

If you're not sure which feeds you want to subscribe to, you can use Google's search feature to search for feeds by topic

> **tip** If you'd rather read a posting on the original blog site itself, rather than in Google Reader, click the Show Original Item link next to the post title. The selected post on the original blog site will now open in a new browser window.

or content, and then subscribe to the feeds you find in the search results. Here's how to do it:

1. From the main Google Reader page, enter your query into the top-of-page search box.

2. Click the Search for New Content button.

3. When the search results page appears, as shown in Figure 6.12, read through the results. Each listing is for a particular news story or blog posting; you can click any story/posting title and read the full article.

4. When you find a blog you want to subscribe to, enter an optional label for the feed and then click the Subscribe button.

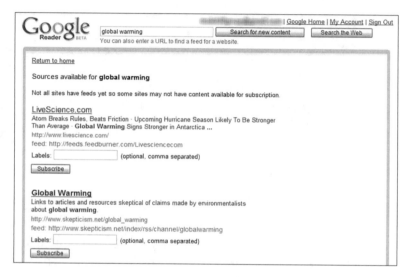

FIGURE 6.12

Searching for a feed to subscribe to.

Google Reader now redisplays the search results page, with the message "You have subscribed to..." at the top of the page. You can now continue to add more feeds, conduct a new search, or click the Return to Home link to return to the main Google Reader page.

Enter the Site's URL

If you know where a blog or website is (that is, if you know the site's address), you

note Google Reader accepts feeds in both RSS and Atom formats.

can search for that blog within Google Reader, and then make your subscription. Here's how it works:

1. From the main Google Reader page, enter the URL of the blog or news site into the top-of-page search box.

2. Click the Search for New Content button.

3. Google Reader now displays a page for the site you entered, as shown in Figure 6.13. This page lists the blog title and the most recent posts. (The currently highlighted post is also displayed; highlight a different post to read it, instead.)

4. To subscribe to the feed for this blog, click the Subscribe button.

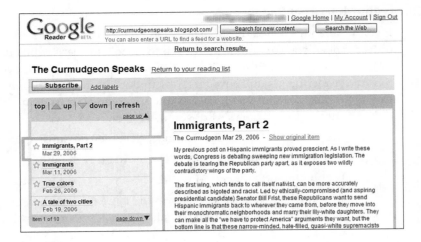

FIGURE 6.13
Reading a blog's contents—and subscribing to the blog feed.

Enter the Feed URL

If you know a feed URL (different from the blog or website URL), you can enter that URL directly into Google Reader to subscribe. Here's how to do it:

1. From the main Google Reader page, click the Edit Subscriptions link.

2. When the next page appears, click the Add a Feed button.

3. Enter the feed URL into the Feed URL box, as shown in Figure 6.14.

4. Click the Preview button.

5. Google Reader now displays a page for the site you entered. To subscribe to this feed, click the Subscribe button.

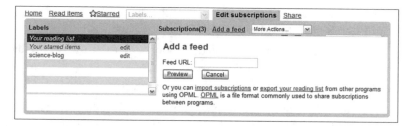

FIGURE 6.14

Subscribing by entering a feed URL.

Import Feeds from Other Readers

If you've already created a list of feed subscriptions in another feed aggregator or feed reader, you can import that list into Google Reader—which definitely beats re-entering your feeds by hand. This assumes, of course, that your previous feed reader/aggregator saved its subscription list in industry-standard OMDP format, and that you have that file stored on your computer's hard disk. All that assumed, here's what you need to do:

1. From the main Google Reader page, click the Edit Subscriptions link.
2. When the next page appears, click the Add a Feed button.
3. Click the Import Subscriptions link.
4. When the page refreshes, as shown in Figure 6.15, click the Browse button to find and select the OMDP file that holds your feed subscriptions.
5. Click the Upload button.

That does the trick. All the feeds in your old subscription file will now appear as subscriptions in Google reader.

Editing Your Subscriptions

Want to change your subscription list—to delete a feed, or change information about a feed? It's easy enough to do from Google Reader's Edit Subscriptions page. All you have to do is click the Edit Subscriptions link on the main Google Reader page, and you'll see the page shown in Figure 6.16. The bottom of the page (not shown in the figure) is a rehash of the main page; the top of the page is where you do your editing.

> **tip** Google Reader isn't the only feed aggregator site on the web. Some popular competing aggregators include Bloglines (www.bloglines.com) and NewsGator (www.newsgator.com). Alternatively, you can read your blog feeds in a freestanding feed reader software program, such as FeedDemon (*www.feeddemon.com*).

FIGURE 6.15

Importing a list of subscribed-to feeds.

FIGURE 6.16

Editing your Google Reader subscriptions.

To delete a feed, all you have to do is click the Edit link for a feed in the Subscriptions list, then click the Unsubscribe link (as shown in Figure 6.17). To change the labels you've assigned to a feed, click the Edit link for the feed in the subscriptions list, and then delete, edit, or add new labels in the Labels box.

FIGURE 6.17

Deleting a feed—or editing its labels.

Sharing Your Favorite Postings

One of the cool features of Google Reader is that you can highlight the particular feeds you like and then share those feeds with friends and colleagues via Gmail. Here's how it works.

1. Start by "starring" a favorite feed. You do this by clicking the dimmed-out star next to a posting in the posting list; when you click the star, it displays in full color.

2. After you've starred your favorite feeds, click the Share link at the top of the main Google Reader page.

3. When the next page appears, click the label for the list you want to share.

4. When the next page appears, as shown in Figure 16.18, click the Send Email button.

5. When the Gmail window shown in Figure 16.19 appears, enter the person's email address, edit the default text as you like, and then click the Send button.

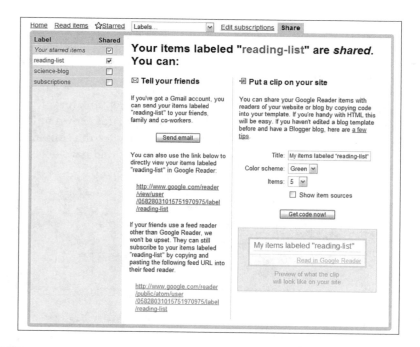

FIGURE 6.18

Sharing a feed via email.

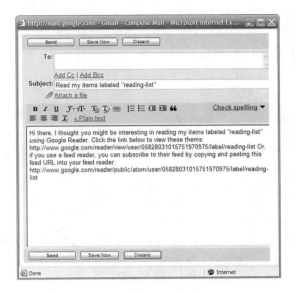

FIGURE 6.19

Getting ready to email a favorite feed to friends and colleagues.

Putting Your Favorite Feeds on Your Own Web Page

The other way you can share your favorite feeds is to put them on your own personal web page, in a feed box like the one shown in Figure 6.20. This requires a basic knowledge of HTML, of course—or at least access to your page's HTML code.

Here's what you need to do:

1. Start by "starring" a favorite feed. You do this by clicking the dimmed-out star next to a posting in the posting list; when you click the star, it displays in full color.

2. After you've starred your favorite feeds, click the Share link at the top of the main Google Reader page.

> **tip**
>
> You can also email individual blog postings to anyone you like. From the main Google Reader page, select the posting, pull down the More Actions list, and then select Gmail This. When the Gmail window appears, enter the recipient's email address, make any edits you'd like, and then click the Send button.

6

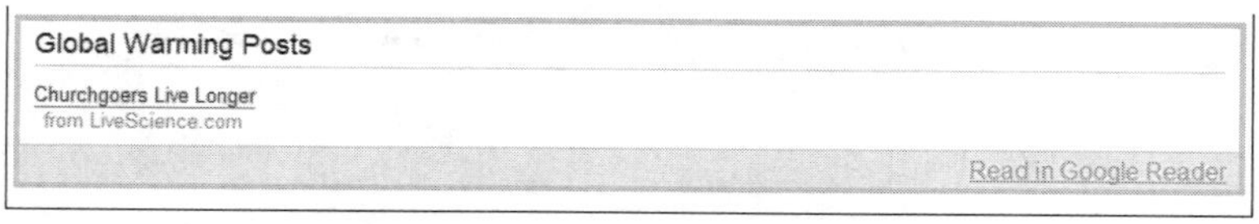

Global Warming Posts

Churchgoers Live Longer
from LiveScience.com

Read in Google Reader

FIGURE 6.20

A feed listing box on your personal web page.

3. When the next page appears, click the label for the list you want to share.

4. When the next page appears, move to the right column and enter a title for the list display, choose a color scheme, and select how many items you want to display.

5. If you want to display a reference back to the original blog, check the Show Item Sources option.

6. Click the Get Code Now! Button.

7. When the HTML code appears, copy it by selecting the entire listing and pressing Ctrl+C on your computer keyboard.

8. Open your HTML editor program, display the code for your personal web page, position the cursor where you want the listing box to appear, and then press Ctrl+V to paste the copied code into your web page code.

That's it. When you post your edited web page, the new listing box will be displayed, constantly updated with new posts from the blog you selected.

The Bottom Line

Blogs are here to stay, and they're becoming an increasingly important medium for the distribution of information and opinions. Google Blog Search came along at just the right time to help users like you and me find specific information in the increasingly large and chaotic blogosphere, which makes it one of the most valuable of Google's new search tools. The additional benefit of subscribing to a feed of your search results is just icing on the cake.

Searching for Scholarly Information

As great as Google is for the average Internet user, it can also be a librarian's worst nightmare. Many students and researchers are abandoning bricks and mortar libraries (as well as proprietary online research services) in favor of Google's free online searches. Almost any piece of information, it seems, can be found with a standard Google web search.

Or can it?

Google's web search engine indexes only that part of the Internet that is accessible to the general public. It doesn't access the tons of information stored in private research databases, or that exists in print journals and reference books found only in university and research libraries. While you *could* use Google to conduct research or write a scholarly paper, the amount of true scholarly information available to you would be limited—and difficult to separate from all the home-grown information out there. Google, it seems, is more for the hobbyist than for the serious student or professional researcher.

To their credit, the folks at Google recognized this deficiency and acted on it. The result is a relatively new service called Google Scholar. Google Scholar enables anyone—students, researchers, even the general public—to search a database of scholarly journals and articles, free of charge. Now students and researchers can conduct their research from the comfort of their dorm rooms and offices, without having to trudge down to the local library.

> **note** Scholars and researchers sometimes refer to Google Scholar as "Schoogle" (pronounced *skoogle*). Searching Google Scholar is known as "Schoogling."

How Google Scholar Works

Within a few short months of its launch, Google Scholar drew raves from its scholarly audience and established itself as a viable (and free) alternative to the expensive research databases offered by Elsevier, Thomson, and other scholarly publishers. While some librarians say that Google Scholar doesn't offer quite the quality and quantity of results of its more established rivals, others praise it for its easy access and simple operation.

As you can see in Figure 7.1, the Google Scholar search page closely resembles the traditional Google web search page. You access Google Scholar at scholar.google.com.

FIGURE 7.1
The Google Scholar main search page.

When you search Google Scholar, you receive a list of matching articles, journals, papers, theses, books, and the like, along with a brief summary of each item. Much of the information displayed on the search results page is available online free of charge. Some is available online only for subscribers to a particular service. Some is available online only for members of a particular library. And some is available in printed format only.

The information in the Google Scholar database is also available via a traditional Google web search, although it's often buried deep in the search results. The advantage of Google Scholar is that it focuses your search solely on the scholarly literature, and returns results in a format familiar to students and researchers. The search itself is also fine-tuned for the scholarly crowd; you can confine your search to specific disciplines, authors, and publications.

Put another way, Google Scholar is a way for students and researchers to find academically appropriate and peer-reviewed literature without having to wade through all the nonprofessional information that clutters the public Internet.

Identifying Scholarly Content

To identify content for inclusion in the Google Scholar database, Google uses an algorithm that guesses at what it thinks is scholarly content. As with Google's PageRank algorithm, the Google Scholar algorithm is a closely guarded secret.

What we do know is that the algorithm tries to identify credentialed authors and searches for citations for each article. These citations are extracted and analyzed; at least in part, Google examines the connections between other documents that cite the article in question. This citation analysis is also used to help rank documents within the Google Scholar results. (Google Scholar also takes into consideration the full text of each article, the article's author, and the publication in which the article appeared to make its rankings.)

Searching Beyond the Public Internet

Google Scholar not only searches the public web for scholarly information, it also strives to include articles, journals, and books from major scholarly publishers. If the full text of a document is not available for dissemination via the public web, Google still includes an abstract from the document; you can then choose whether or not to pay for access (if that option is available; some materials require a subscription to the host library for access).

note Another benefit to this citation analysis is a Cited By link next to each search result listing. When you click on this link, you see a list of all pages and documents that point to the current article.

7

Some of this nonpublic information is available by Google's partnering with major scholarly research services and libraries. For example, Google Scholar derives some of its content from the Open WorldCat database, which contains records of materials owned by libraries that participate in the Online Computer Library Center (OCLC) project. (You can learn more about OCLC and Open WorldCat at www.oclc.org.)

> **note** When dealing with scholarly literature, it's often the case that the same paper is hosted in more than one database. In these instances, Google identifies what it believes is the "best" version and provides links to other available versions.

Including Print-Only Content

In the case of some scholarly literature, the publication itself is not actually online; only the abstract and citations are available over the Internet. This is a benefit to including information sourced from various library databases—you can find out what documents a library has available, even if you can't download them from the Internet.

> **caution** As useful as Google Scholar is, it only searches a fraction of the published scholarly literature. For more comprehensive scholarly research, use the search function provided by your local research library to search the many field-specific databases that cover scholarly publications, such as ABI/Inform, ERIC, Medline, and Proquest.

COMMENTARY

FINDING "INVISIBLE" INFORMATION

One of the interesting things about Google Scholar is that much of the material included in its database is already available to the general public—if only the public went to libraries. That's because Google Scholar includes listings of articles and books that are only available in print format or via electronic research databases, and only made available to libraries. The information is out there; you just have to go to the library to find it. And since fewer and fewer people are going to libraries these days, the information becomes invisible to the PC-bound user.

That's one of the nice things about Google Scholar—it directs you use your local library. Yes, you use Google Scholar to determine the availability of information, but then you have to hit the library to read some of it. (Some information, of course, is readily available online.) This is, in my opinion, a good thing; more hands-on exposure to books and literature benefits us all.

Another benefit of Google Scholar is that it provides at least limited access to online information that is normally locked behind subscription barriers. Most search engines—including Google—simply can't search private, subscription-only databases. The information in these databases creates what some call the "deep web," or what others call the "invisible web." The information's there, all right, but you wouldn't know it (and couldn't access it) without a subscription to the proprietary database service.

In some instances, this formerly password-protected information is made available to Google Scholar users, thanks to arrangements made between Google and the subscription services. In other cases only an abstract of the information is available; to read the full text, you have to subscribe to the service or pay a one-time fee to access the article. (You may also have to frequent a library that has a subscription to the service.) In any case, Google Scholar makes you aware of this previously "invisible" information, which is also a good thing.

Understanding Google Scholar Search Results

When you conduct a Google Scholar search, the results returned are limited primarily to scholarly articles, journals, theses, books, and the like. (In fact, articles tend to make up the bulk of Google Search results.) Figure 7.2 shows a typical Google Scholar search results page.

Different Types of Results

The information you see about a particular search result depends on what type of document it is. Let's work through the possibilities.

If it's an article available online, the title will be clickable. When you click the title, you're taken either to the full text of the article or (if the article itself is available only via subscription) the article's abstract. If the article is available via purchase via the British Library, a BL Direct link is displayed; click this link for purchase information.

7

1. Citation—not available online
2. Book—not available online
3. Article—available online
4. Title—click to read full-text or abstract
5. Bibliographic information
6. Click for list of documents that cite this article
7. Click to locate libraries that carry this book
8. Click to search for information about this work online
9. Click to purchase full-text article via the British Library
10. Click to view other documents in this group of works

FIGURE 7.2

A typical Google Scholar search results page.

If it's an article *not* available online, the title will *not* be clickable, and the word [CITATION] will appear beside the title. In this instance, you may be able to find the information you want by displaying the article's citations.

If it's a book that's available in electronic form online, the word [BOOK] will appear beside the title and the title will be clickable. When you click the title, you'll be taken either to the full-text of the book or (if the book itself is available only via subscription) the book's abstract.

If it's a book that's *not* available online, the word [BOOK] will appear beside the title and the title will *not* be clickable. You'll also see a Library Search link; click this link to find a library that carries the hardcopy book.

caution Articles marked with [CITATION] are referred to online, but not yet available online. Unfortunately, a large amount of scholarly literature is still available offline only—although this is apt to change over time.

Listing Information

For each item listed on the search results page, you'll see the following information:

caution Not every source listed in Google Scholar is free. Many citations link directly to the websites of the articles' publishers, many of which charge a fee for access.

- Title of the book or article. If the full text or abstract is available online, the title will be a clickable link.

- Bibliographic information (in green), including author, publisher, and so on.

- Cited By link, which links to a list of other articles and documents that cite this particular article.

- View As HTML link, which lets you view a PDF-format article in normal web page format.

- Web Search link, which lets you search for information about this article in the main Google web index.

- Library Search link, available when a book is listed, which lets you view a list of real-world libraries that carry copies of the book.

- BL Direct link, available when an article is available for purchase via the British Library.

- Group Of link, visible when an article is one of several in a group of scholarly works. Click the link to view a list of the other articles.

How to Use Google Scholar Results

To best use Google Scholar results, you should first try clicking on the article title. If this option isn't available, or if you're taken to an abstract only, then you can use the Cited By and Web Search links to search for related articles and information. (You can also try to find the full-text article at your local library, of course.)

If you find a book that looks interesting, and if the book isn't available for online reading (most aren't), then it's time to head to the library. Click the Library Search link to find a list of libraries that carry the book, and then put on your jacket and make a visit.

tip If you're accessing Google Scholar from a university or research library, you may see a FindIt @ link next to selected search results. Click this link to locate an electronic version of the work via your library's online resources.

7

Searching Google Scholar

Now that you're somewhat familiar with the kind of scholarly information that Google Scholar finds, let's dive head-first into the research waters and learn how to find that information.

Conducting a Basic Search

You can perform most of your research directly from the Google Scholar main page. Just enter your query into the search box and click the Search button, same as you would a normal Google web search.

Using Advanced Search Operators

Scholarly research, however, is a little more exacting than typical web searching. More often than not you're searching for articles by a particular author, or for articles from a specific publication. To fine-tune your search in this manner, you can use most of the same search operators we discussed in Chapter 2, "Searching the Web"—in particular, +, -, " ", **OR**, and **intitle:**.

There's also one new operator specific to Google Scholar. This is the **author:** operator, which lets you search for articles written by a specific author. To use this operator, enclose the author's name in quotation marks and place it directly after the operator, as shown in Figure 7.3: **author:"m miller"**. If you're interested in finding *references* to works by that author (as opposed to the author's works themselves), skip the **author:** operator and simply enclose the author's name in quotation marks as an exact-phrase search.

FIGURE 7.3
Searching for articles written by a specific author.

The exact phrase operator is also useful when you're searching for a particular article or publication. Simply enclose the article/publication title in quotation marks, as shown in Figure 7.4: **"discovering peer to peer"**. No other operator is necessary.

tip Given the vagaries of format, you may need to search for the author by first initial, first initial followed by a period, and full first name. For example, to search for me, you could enter **author:"m miller"**, **author:"m. miller"**, or **author:"michael miller"**.

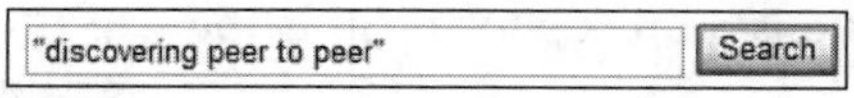

FIGURE 7.4

Searching for a specific article or publication.

Using the Advanced Scholar Search Page

Even more fine-tuning is available from the Google Scholar Advanced Search page. You access this page, shown in Figure 7.5, by clicking the Advanced Scholar Search link on the main Google Scholar page.

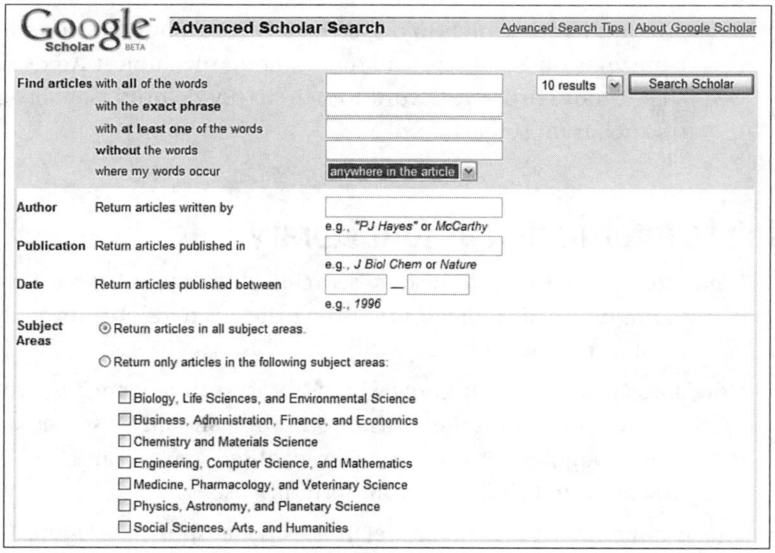

FIGURE 7.5

Using the Advanced Scholar Search page.

As you can see, the top part of this form offers pretty much the same type of fine-tuning available from the normal Google Advanced Search page (or by using advanced search operators). You have the option of searching for all the words (default), an exact phrase (" "), at least one of the words (**OR**), and without the words (-). The new option here is the last one, which lets you specify where in the article to search—in the title only, or anywhere in the article (default).

The other options on this page include the following:

- To find articles written by a specific author, use the Author option and enter the author's name.

- To find articles published in a specific publication, use the Publication option and enter the publication's name.

> **caution** Searches by publication are often incomplete. This is due to missing or incorrect information included with many citations, which often don't bother to mention where the article was actually published.

- To find articles published within a specified date range, use the Date option and enter the starting and ending year.

- To limit your search to a specific subject area (biology and life sciences, business and finance, and so on), go to the Subject Areas section and click those areas you want to search. (By default, Google Scholar searches all subject areas.)

Linking to Information at Your Library

I mentioned previously that some search results might have a FindIt @ link next to the title. This indicates that the article is available for reading from your local or university library.

How does Google Scholar know which library you're using? If you're logging on from a campus computer, this information should be sensed automatically. But if you're logging on from another location, you can manually inform Google Scholar which library you normally use.

This is done from the Scholar Preferences page, shown in Figure 7.6. You get to this page by clicking the Scholar Preferences link on the main Google Scholar page.

From the Scholar Preferences page, scroll down to the Library Links section, enter the name of your library, and click the Find Lbrary button. You'll now see a list of available libraries, like the one in Figure 7.7. You can select up to three libraries from this list, although you may be prompted to log on before accessing the associated FindIt @ links. Click the Save Preferences button when you're done.

> **tip** It's also a good idea to check the Open WorldCat option, so that you can search items listed in the Open WorldCat library database.

7

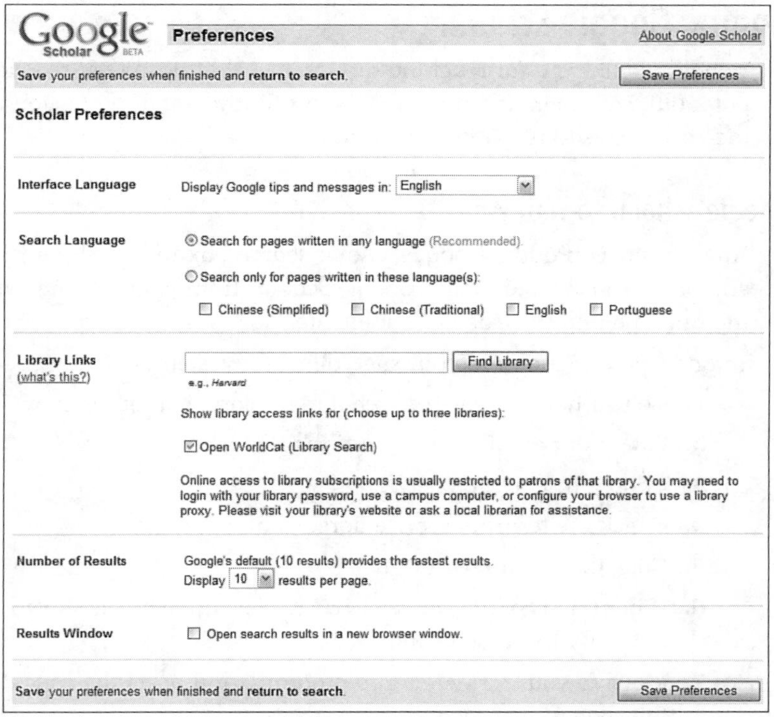

FIGURE 7.6

Configuring Library Link access (and other settings) from the Scholar Preferences page.

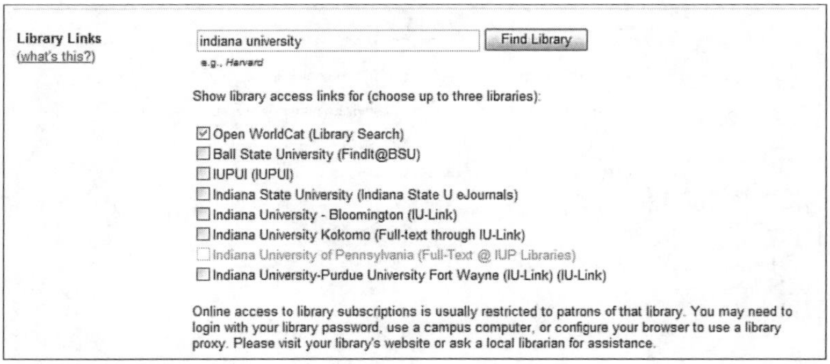

FIGURE 7.7

Select up to three libraries from the Library Links list.

Expanding Google Scholar

Google Scholar is a far-reaching service, one that hasn't yet reached its full potential. Let's look at a number of ways that research professionals can increase access to the Google Scholar database.

Add Google Scholar to Your Website

Any website can add a Google Scholar search box to its web pages. This enables site visitors to search Google Scholar from your website, without exiting and opening the Google Scholar site.

To add Google Scholar to your site, follow these steps:

1. Go to scholar.google.com/scholar/scholarsearch.html, shown in Figure 7.8.
2. Enter your email address into the first box.
3. Choose a search box style.
4. Check the terms of service agreement.
5. Click the Continue button.
6. When the resulting page of HTML code appears, as shown in Figure 7.9, copy the code listing.
7. Move to your HTML editing program, and paste the copied code into the code for your web page.

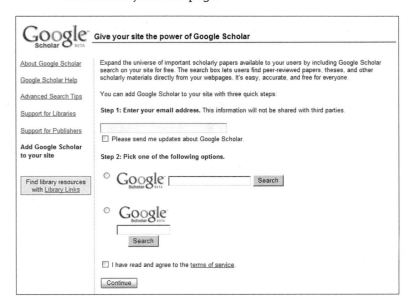

FIGURE 7.8

Getting ready to add Google Scholar to your web page.

FIGURE 7.9

Copy the HTML code into the code for your web page.

Google Scholar for Libraries

As you might have gathered from reading through this chapter, Google Scholar is particularly useful for school libraries. There are two ways that a library can participate in Google Scholar—by offering Google Scholar access to library users, and by making library materials available to the Google Scholar database.

To make Google Scholar available to a library's patrons, the library needs to contact their link resolver vendor. In some instances, Google Scholar is now an option on the vendor's configuration pages; in other instances, you may need to set up specific procedures. When you've joined the Library Links program, all on-campus users will see FindIt @ links to library materials within the standard Google Scholar search results.

To include your library's materials in the Google Scholar database (so that they appear when a user clicks the Library Search link next to a search result), the library has to join the OCLC Open WorldCat program. You can also contact Google directly for more information at scholar-library@google.com.

And here's something all libraries will appreciate. Both the Library Links and Library Search programs are completely free! No budget demands, here.

7

Google Scholar for Publishers

If you're a publisher of scholarly content and would like to see your works included in the Google Scholar database, you should contact Google at scholar-publisher@google.com. You can opt to provide full-text articles, abstracts, or even subscription-controlled content—it's your choice.

note If you opt not to provide full-text articles (or to provide subscription-only content), you still have to provide Google with a complete abstract they can display to their users.

The Bottom Line

Google Scholar is a real boon for students and research professionals. Even though much of the information found by Google Scholar isn't available online (or for free), it still opens the curtain to the world of the invisible web, and lets you discover content that you otherwise wouldn't have found via traditional web search engines. Yeah, you may still need to trundle down to the library, but at least you'll know exactly what you're looking for.

Searching for University, Technical, and Government Information

As you learned in Chapter 7, "Searching for Scholarly Information," Google Scholar offers a great resource for those searching for scholarly articles, papers, and the like. But Google Scholar isn't the only Google site of interest to students and researchers. There's a lot of good information to be found on the websites of major colleges and universities, which Google facilitates through the site-specific Google University Search.

Google University Search is just one of several "special searches" that Google offers to its users. Of similar construct are four technology-related searches (for Microsoft, Apple, Linux, and BSD Unix) and a single large U.S. Government Search, which searches governmental websites. All of these special searches work in the same fashion, automatically restricting searches to a range of sites most appropriate to the search.

Read on to learn more.

8

Using Google's University Search

Google makes it easy to search specific university sites using University Search. As you can see in Figure 8.1, University Search works by limiting your search to pages housed on a specific university website; you're searching a single university site, not the entire Web.

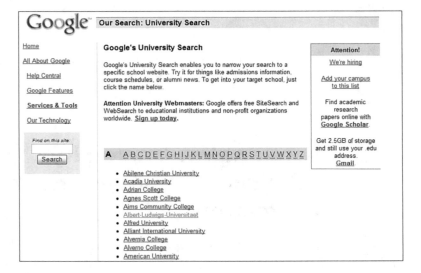

FIGURE 8.1
More than 600 universities are listed on Google's University Search.

As of this writing, Google lists site-specific searches for more than 600 institutions worldwide, from Abilene Christian University to York University. You can use University Search to search for course schedules, admissions information, and the like.

To use Google's University Search, follow these steps:

1. Navigate to the University Search page located at www.google.com/options/universities.html.

2. Scroll through the list of universities until you find the one you want to search, and then click that university's link.

3. When the next page appears, as shown in Figure 8.2, enter your search query.

4. Click the Search button; Google now returns a list of matching pages found on the selected university's website.

8

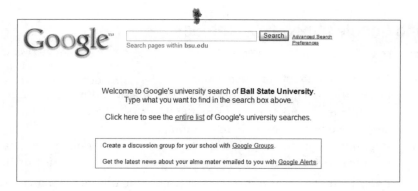

FIGURE 8.2

Conducting a university-specific search.

COMMENTARY

MAKING GOOGLE PART OF YOUR COLLEGE LIFE

Google would like to get in on the ground floor with college students. I guess the company figures if it hooks users when they're in college, they'll stay Google users all their lives.

To that end, Google offers a combination of services that it calls College Life. There's nothing new or unique about these services; College Life just puts them together in one place for interested students.

You access Google College Life at www.google.com/university/. The services offered here include Gmail, Google Talk, Google SMS (for text messaging on cell phones), Blogger, Google Desktop, Google Scholar, and Picasa.

In many ways, Google College Life is a lot like Google Pack, which we'll discuss in Chapter 35, "Using Google Pack." The big difference is that the Google College Life services are primarily online services, not software—and, as such, aren't bundled together for a single installation. (Since they're online, there's little installation to be done.) And, while all these services should be of use to the typical college student, there's nothing specifically college-centric about them. Still, if you're wanting to use this pseudo-suite of Google services, the College Life home page is as good a place as any to start.

Using Google's Special Technology Searches

note BSD (Berkeley Software Distribution) Unix is a specific version of the Unix operating system developed at the University of California at Berkeley.

As you've no doubt surmised, Google's University Search works by restricting the search to a specific domain, using the (hidden) **site:** operator. Well, there's nothing stopping Google from using a similar strategy to offer other site- and topic-specific searches—which leads us to our next batch of special searches.

Knowing that a large number of people use the Internet to search for computer- and technology-related information, Google has created several technology-related special searches. You can use these specialty searches to find technical support, software updates, downloadable software, and other computer-related information and services.

There are four of these technology-related searches, each focused on a specific computer platform. These searches include

- Google Microsoft Search (www.google.com/microsoft), shown in Figure 8.3, which searches the main www.microsoft.com domain and other Microsoft-related sites.

- Google Apple Macintosh Search (www.google.com/mac), shown in Figure 8.4, which searches the main www.apple.com domain and other Apple-related sites.

- Google Linux Search (www.google.com/linux), shown in Figure 8.5, which searches a variety of Linux-related sites.

- Google BSD Unix Search (www.google.com/bsd), shown in Figure 8.6, which searches a variety of sites that specialize in the BSD version of the Unix operating system.

FIGURE 8.3
Google Microsoft Search.

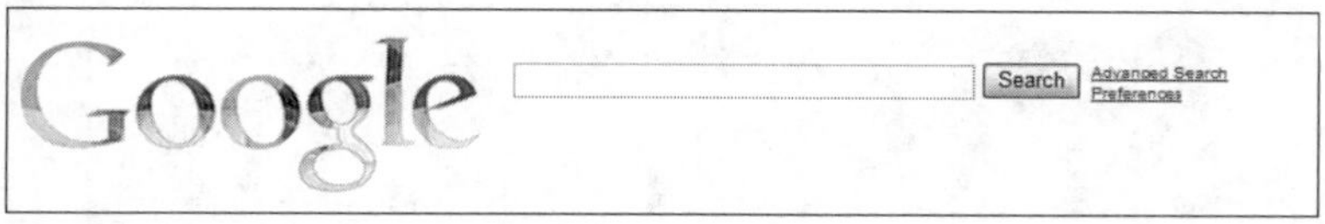

FIGURE 8.4
Google Apple Macintosh Search.

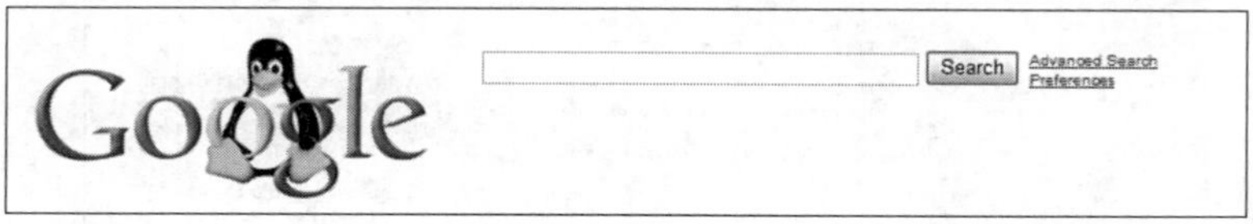

FIGURE 8.5
Google Linux Search.

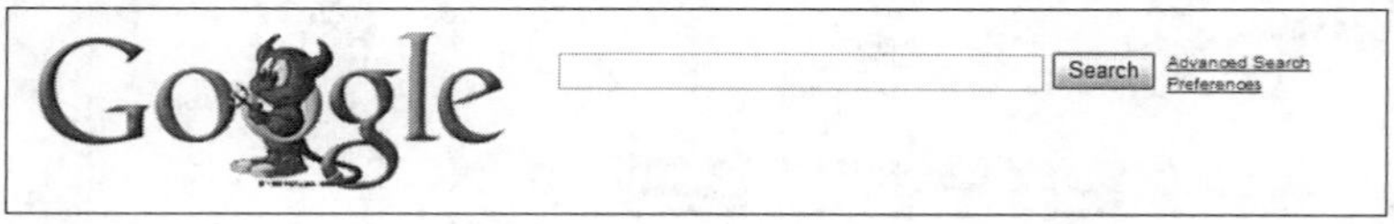

FIGURE 8.6
Google BSD Unix Search, for Unix users.

As an example, if you go to the Google Microsoft Search page and enter **windows media center** as your query, the first results, as you can see in Figure 8.7, come from Microsoft's own website. But other prominent results come from Paul Thurrott's SuperSite for Windows, Matt Goyer's Media Center Blog, The PodcastNetwork (for The Media Center Show podcast), the Wikipedia, ZDNet News, and so on. The results are tightly focused, culled from legitimate technical websites, and are happily free of personal website clutter.

You get similar results from each of the other specialty technology searches. When you're looking for technical or computer-related information, this is a great shortcut to the most useful results.

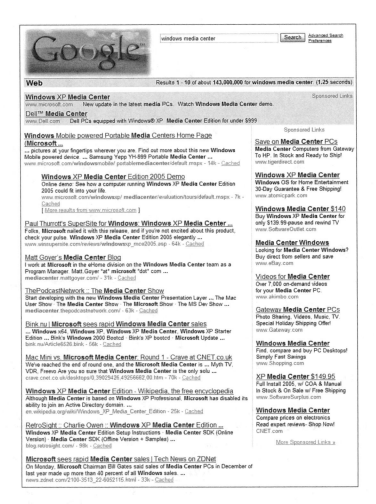

FIGURE 8.7

The results of a Google Microsoft Search.

Using Google U.S. Government Search

There's one other topic-related specialty search I'd like to mention. This is Google's U.S. Government Search, shown in Figure 8.8. As you might suspect, this search focuses its attention solely on U.S. government websites—which makes it the best place to search for official government forms, information, reports, and the like.

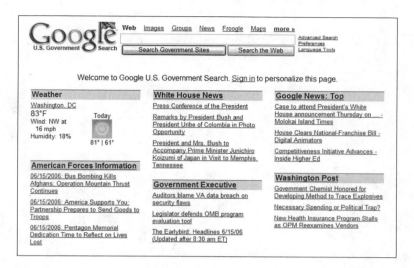

FIGURE 8.8
Searching government websites with Google's U.S. Government Search.

There are a few neat things about Google's U.S. Government Search (usgov. google.com). First, when you search from this page, Google directs your query to all the sites within the .gov domain, which includes sites for all major U.S. government agencies, Congress, and the White House. And, not to be too fed-eralist about it, U.S. Government Search also searches all the individual state government sites in the .us and .gov domains. Suffice to say, if it's at all government-related, U.S. Government Search can find it.

The second neat thing is that U.S. Government Search is more than just a simple search page. You also get the latest news headlines in a number of government-related categories (White House News, Government Executive, and Armed Forces Information), the top headlines from the Washington Post, and today's Washington, DC weather. It's a one-stop shop for everything inside the beltway—and the perfect home page for government insiders.

The Bottom Line

There's nothing about these specialty searches that you can't do or find using a standard Google web search and the appropriate advanced search opera-tors. However, since these searches do the filtering for you, they make it easier to find site- and topic-specific information. Most users aren't aware that these sites exist, so adding them to your search toolbox will put you one up on other users.

Searching for Words and Definitions

Want to look up the definition of a particular word, but don't want to bother pulling out the old hardcover dictionary? Not sure of a specific spelling? Then use Google as an online dictionary to look up any word you can think of. It's easy—and there are two ways to do it.

Using a "What Is" Search

The first approach to looking up definitions is to use a little-known Google feature, known as a "what is" search. All you have to do is enter the keywords **what is** in your query, followed by the word in question. (No question mark is necessary.) For example, to look up the definition of the word "defenestrate," enter **what is defenestrate**, as shown in Figure 9.1.

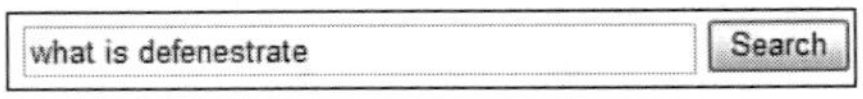

what is defenestrate	Search

FIGURE 9.1

Looking up definitions with a "what is" search.

When you use a "what is" search, Google returns a standard search results page (typically with several useful definition links in the list), as well as a single web definition at the top of the page. As you can see in Figure 9.2, this mini-section includes a short definition of the word and two useful links. The first link, disguised as the result title, is actually a link to other definitions of the word on the web. The second link, Definition in Context, displays an example of the word used in a sentence. (This in-context usage is supplied by the same site that supplies the main definition.)

FIGURE 9.2

The special results of a "what is" definition search.

There's something even more useful on the "what is" search results page, however. If you look in the statistics bar, you'll see the word you searched for displayed as a link. Click this link and Google displays the full dictionary definition of this word from the Answers.com website. As you can see in Figure 9.3, the Answers.com page includes a pronunciation of the word, as well as one or more definitions.

note Answers.com (www.answers.com) offers all sorts of information, including—but not limited to—dictionary definitions. Its definitions are sourced from *The American Heritage Dictionary*.

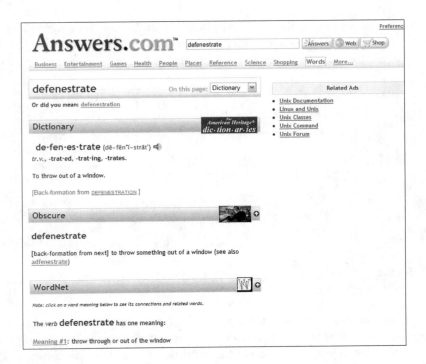

FIGURE 9.3

A typical dictionary definition from Answers.com.

Using the Google Glossary

Even more definitions are available when you use the Google Glossary feature. Google Glossary is what Google calls it, anyway; really, it's just another advanced search operator that produces some very specific results.

The operator in question is **define:**. Use this operator before the word you want defined, with no spaces between. So, for example, if you want to define the word "defenestrate," enter the query **define:defenestrate**, as shown in Figure 9.4.

FIGURE 9.4

*Searching for definitions with the **define:** operator.*

When your query includes the **define:** operator, Google displays a special defini-tions page, as shown in Figure 9.5. This page includes all the definitions for the word that Google found on the Web; click a link to view the full definition.

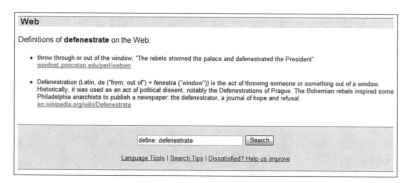

FIGURE 9.5

*Results of a search using the **define:** operator.*

Depending on the word you're searching for, Google might recognize one or more related words or phrases. If so, Google displays these related phrases as a series of links at the top of the definition results page, as shown in Figure 9.6, for a search based on the term "bluetooth." Click a link to initiate a search for that related word or phrase.

FIGURE 9.6

Sometimes Google recognizes related phrases to the one you're searching for.

And here's something else to know. If you want to define a phrase, use the **define:** operator but put the phrase in quotation marks. For example, to define the phrase "peer to peer", enter the query **define:"peer to peer"**, as shown in Figure 9.7.

> **tip** If you enter the keyword **define**—*not* the **define:** operator—with a space between it and the word you want defined, Google returns the same results as if you entered a "what is" query.

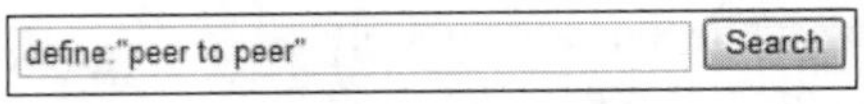

define:"peer to peer"	Search

FIGURE 9.7
Searching for the definition of a phrase.

COMMENTARY

RELYING ON THIRD-PARTY INFORMATION

Google is, without a doubt, a search site. It doesn't purport to be a content site, as some search portals have tried to evolve into. Google is all about searching for information, not about providing proprietary content.

While this purity of purpose is notable (and one of the defining features of the Google experience), it means that when you want standard reference information, Google has to direct you elsewhere. This is what happens when you search Google for word definitions; Google serves up the search results, but you have to click through to another site to read the actual definition.

This is in contrast to how some other sites handle the same process. For example, Yahoo! licenses dictionary information from Houghton Mifflin's *American Heritage Dictionary of the English Language* and feeds dictionary search results directly from its own Yahoo! Education site (education.yahoo.com/reference/dictionary/). You can search for a definition and view that definition without ever leaving the Yahoo! site. With Google, on the other hand, you only do your searching on the Google site; Google hands you off to any number of third-party sites to view definitions.

I'm not sure which approach is best. The all-in-one Yahoo! dictionary results are very convenient, but Google offers a wider variety of definitions from multiple websites. Google's approach is a bit of a trade-off that ensures a lack of editorial prejudice—even if it requires a little more clicking (and comparing) on your part.

Finding Similar Words with Google Sets

Our final word-related search feature is one that's still in development at Google Labs. I'm talking about Google Sets, which lets you enter two or more related words, and Google Sets displays other similar terms to complete the set.

You access Google Sets at labs.google.
com/sets/. As you can see in Figure 9.8, the
main Google Sets page is actually a form.
All you have to do is enter a few terms
from the set you want to complete, and then
click either the Large Set or Small Set button.

note Learn more about
Google Labs in Chap-
ter 42, "Exploring Google Labs."

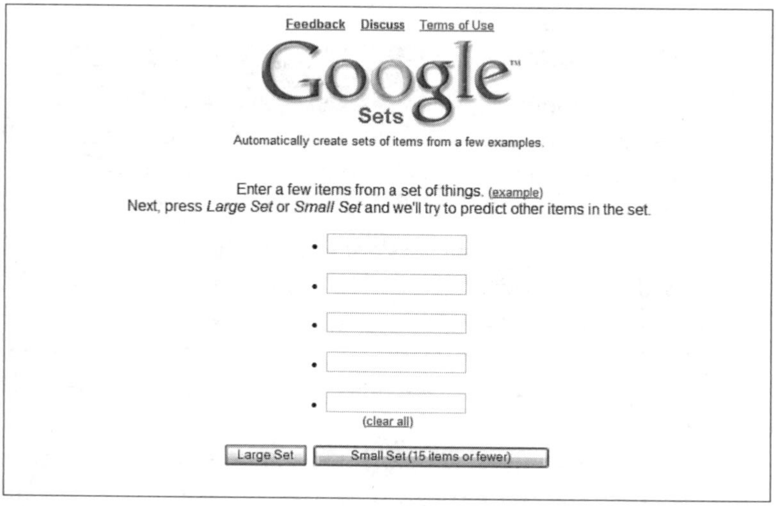

Feedback   Discuss   Terms of Use

Google™
Sets

Automatically create sets of items from a few examples.

Enter a few items from a set of things. (example)
Next, press *Large Set* or *Small Set* and we'll try to predict other items in the set.

(clear all)

Large Set   Small Set (15 items or fewer)

FIGURE 9.8

Searching for related words with Google Sets.

The resulting page, like the one shown in Figure 9.9, displays a longer list of
terms predicted from the short list you entered. You can expand this list by
clicking the Grow Set button beneath the list.

For example, if you enter the terms **round**, **square**, and **rectangle**, Google
Sets returns the terms **triangle**, **oval**, **circle**, **hexagon**, and so forth. If you
enter the terms **dog**, **cat**, and **bird**, Google Sets returns the terms **horse**, **rab-
bit**, **fish**, **snake**, and so forth.

How might you use Google Sets? One use is to help you "fill in the blanks"
when you're writing or creating lists. Another use might be to expand your
own set of query terms when you're using Google to search an unfamiliar
subject.

Google Sets is interesting, in any case—even if you can't find a direct application to your current task.

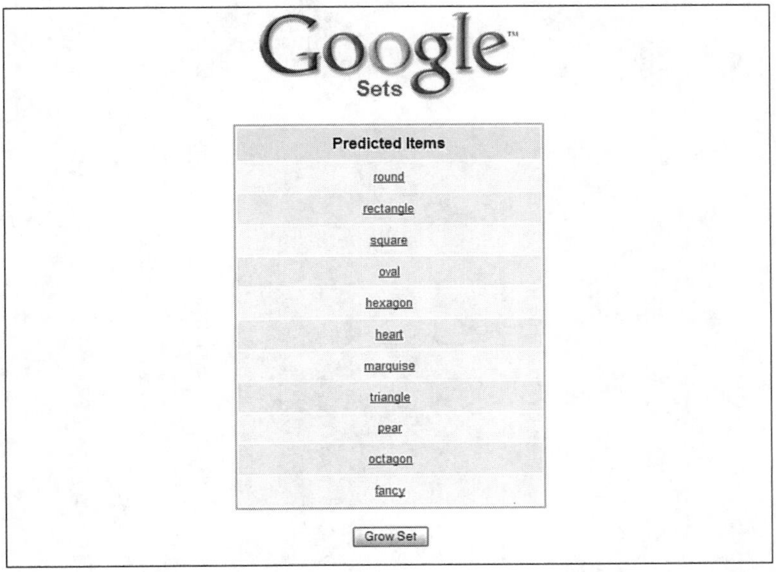

FIGURE 9.9
The results of a Google Sets search.

The Bottom Line

Google's definition-searching features, while relying on third-party websites for the actual content, are still a welcome and useful addition to the standard Google search interface. It's nice to know that you can search for just about anything you want—including definitions—from a single search box. In fact, that's one of the things that makes Google so useful; you don't have to use multiple sites to find multiple types of information.

Searching for Other Special Information

As you've read through the previous chapters, you've no doubt received a sense that there's a lot more hidden behind the standard Google search page than most users realize. Well, you're right—and there's more where that came from.

For example, did you know that you can use Google to search for tracking information from UPS, FedEx, and other shipping companies? Or find up-to-the-minute airport and flight status information? Or find out when a particular movie is showing at your local theater? Or display the latest weather forecast?

That's right, Google makes a lot of special information available from its main search page. All you have to do is know how to search for it!

Searching for Facts

When you're looking for hard facts, Google might be able to help. Yes, Google always returns a list of sites that match your specific query, but if you phrase your query correctly—and are searching for a fact that Google has preidentified—you can get the precise information you need at the top of the search results page.

What types of information are we talking about, here? Fact-based information, such as birthdates, birthplaces, population, and so on. All you have to do is enter a query that states the fact you want to know. For example:

- To find the population of San Francisco, enter **population san Francisco**.
- To find where Mark Twain was born, enter **birthplace mark twain**.
- To find when President Bill Clinton was born, enter **birthday bill clinton**.
- To find when Raymond Chandler died, enter **die raymond chandler**.
- To find who is the president of Germany, enter **president germany**.

The answers to these questions are displayed at the top of your search results page, as shown in Figure 10.1. You get the precise answer to your question, according to the referenced website. Click the associated link to learn more from this source.

Web	Results 1 - 10 of about 8,340,000 for william shakespeare die (0.28 seconds)

William Shakespeare — Date of Death: 23 April 1616
According to http://www.who2.com/williamshakespeare.html - More sources »

FIGURE 10.1

A typical top-of-page Google Q&A fact.

This capability to display "quick answers to straightforward questions" is called Google Q&A, and the information presented is typical reference information, the kind of stuff you might find in a desk reference or almanac. Google Q&A isn't always consistent about the sources of this info, nor about the specific facts that are displayed. For example, searching for **distance to mars** returns no quick fact; neither does **height empire state building** or **size football field**. So accept what you get, and recognize that Google is selective about the facts it knows.

caution If a fact isn't in the Google Q&A database, it won't be displayed on the search results page.

Searching for Weather Information

Did you know that Google can be used to find and display current weather conditions and forecasts? It's a pretty easy search; all you have to do is enter the keyword **weather**, followed by the location. You can enter the location as a city name, city plus state, or ZIP Code. For example, to view the weather forecast for Minneapolis, enter **weather minneapolis**, as shown in Figure 10.2.

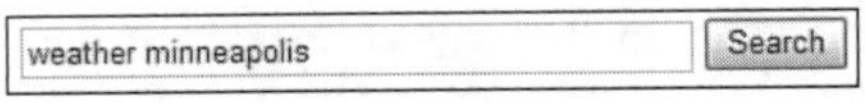

weather minneapolis	Search

FIGURE 10.2

Searching for the weather forecast for a specific city.

As you can see in Figure 10.3, Google displays current weather conditions and a four-day forecast at the top of the search results page. And, while this is a good summary report, you may want to click through to the more detailed forecasts offered in the standard search results listings below the four-day forecast.

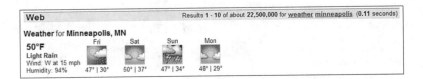

FIGURE 10.3

Google's weather search results.

Searching for Travel Information

Weather information is important to travelers, as is information about flight and airport delays. Fortunately, you can use the main Google search page to search for this information, just as you did with weather forecasts.

Viewing Airport Conditions

To search for weather conditions and delays at a particular airport, all you have to do is enter the airport's three-letter code, followed by the word **airport**. For example, to view conditions at the Minneapolis-St. Paul International Airport (with the code MSP), enter **msp airport**, as shown in

note Google's weather search results are provided by Weather Underground (www.wunderground.com).

Figure 10.4. This displays a link to conditions at the chosen airport, as provided by the FAA and shown in Figure 10.5. Click this link for detailed information, as shown in Figure 10.6.

tip To find the code for any airport anywhere in the world, go to www.world-airport-codes.com.

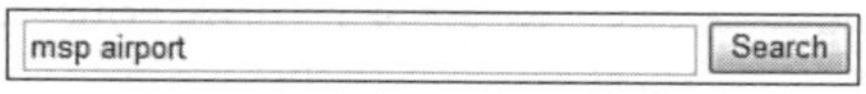

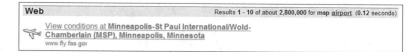

FIGURE 10.4

Searching for airport conditions.

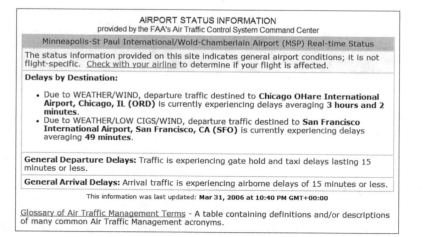

FIGURE 10.5

Click the link to view airport conditions.

FIGURE 10.6

Airport conditions, provided by the FAA.

Tracking Flight Status

Google also lets you track the status of any U.S. flight, and many international flights. All you have to do is enter the flight number into the Google search box. For example, to find out the status of United Airlines flight 116, enter **ua116**, as shown in Figure 10.7.

As you can see in Figure 10.8, Google now displays links to three sites that let you track the flight status—Travelocity, Expedia, and fboweb. Click one of these links to view real-time flight status. (Figure 10.9 shows the flight status as displayed by Travelocity.)

FIGURE 10.7

Searching for flight status.

FIGURE 10.8

Click a link to view the flight status.

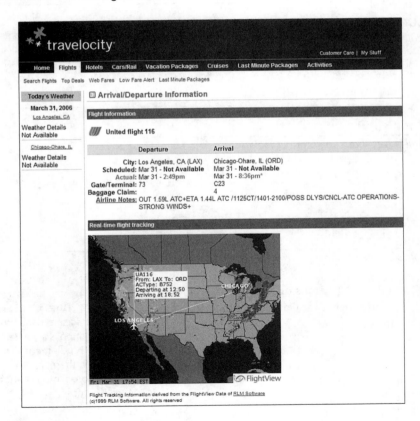

FIGURE 10.9

Flight status information via Travelocity.

Searching for Numbers

Airline flights aren't the only numbers you can look up with Google. Google lets you enter all sorts of numbers into its main search page, and then displays the relevant information at the top of the search results page.

For example, if you want to track a package that was sent via UPS, all you have to do is enter the UPS tracking number. If you want to see what product is attached to a specific UPC (universal product code), just enter the bar code number. If you have an area code and want to know which city it serves, enter the area code. (The results of these searches are shown in Figures 10.10, 10.11, and 10.12, respectively.)

FIGURE 10.10

Google's UPS tracking number lookup.

FIGURE 10.11

Google's UPC bar code product lookup.

FIGURE 10.12

Google's area code lookup.

Table 10.1 details all the different types of numbers that Google can look up for you:

note In most instances, all you have to enter is the number itself, with no associated operator. The only exception is if you're searching for an FCC equipment ID or patent number; in these instances, enter the keyword **fcc** or **patent** before the ID number.

Table 10.1   Google Number Lookups

Type of Number	Example
FedEx tracking numbers	123456789012
United States Postal Service tracking numbers	1234 1234 1234 1234 1234 12
UPS tracking numbers	1Z1234W123456789012
UPC bar codes	123456789012
Area codes	123
Vehicle ID numbers (VIN)	AAAAA123A1AA12345
FAA airplane registration numbers	a123bc
Patent numbers	patent 123456
FCC equipment IDs	fcc A1B-12345-DEF

Searching for Movies

Numbers aren't the only types of information available via a Google lookup.
You can also use the standard Google search box to look up movie reviews
and showtimes. All you have to do is enter the word **movies** followed by the
name of the movie. For example, to find out when *V for Vendetta* is showing in
your neighborhood, enter **movies v for vendetta**, as shown in Figure 10.13.

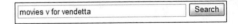

FIGURE 10.13

Searching for movie information.

Google now displays a movie information section at the top of the search
results page, as shown in Figure 10.14. This is where the fun starts.

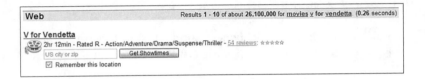

FIGURE 10.14

Google's gateway to movie reviews and showtimes.

To view a list of reviews for this movie, click the movie title. As you can see in Figure 10.15, this reviews page not only lists a plethora of reviews from professional movie critics (along with a brief summary of each review), you also have the option of showing only the positive reviews, or the negative ones, or even the neutral ones. You can even search within the reviews, if you like.

FIGURE 10.15

An extensive list of reviews for a specific movie.

Back to the search results page, to find out showtimes at a theater near you, enter your ZIP Code and click the Get Showtimes button. This displays a list of movie theaters near you, as shown in Figure 10.16, with today's showtimes for the movie listed. To view showtimes for another day, just click the day link at the top of the listings. You can even view any theater on a map (or get driving directions), by clicking the Map link next to a theater's name.

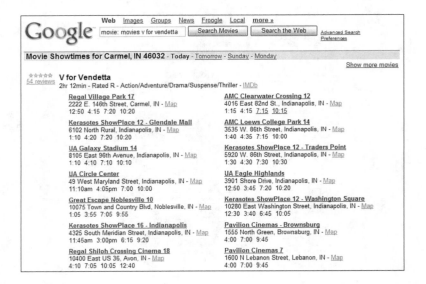

FIGURE 10.16

Today's showtimes for the movie in question.

And if you can't remember the name of a given movie, you can use Google to figure it out for you. Just enter the **movie:** operator, followed by whatever information you do know—an actor's name, the movie's director, a plot detail, or whatever. As you can see in Figure 10.17, Google returns a list of movies that match your search criteria, along with reviews for each movie listed. Click the movie title to view more reviews for that movie.

tip
To avoid entering your ZIP Code every time you search for a movie, check the Remember This Location option.

tip
If you want to find pictures of movie posters and other images from a movie, go to the Google Image Search page (images.google.com) and enter your **movie:** query from there.

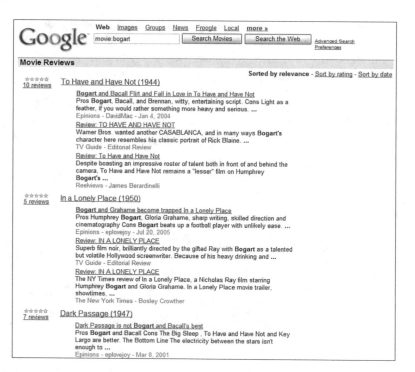

FIGURE 10.17

Searching for movies by actor.

Searching for Music

Google not only lets you search for movie information, it also is a great search engine for music—in particular, popular music artists. Google knows the names of tens of thousands of popular performers; all you have to do is enter the performer's name in the search box, and Google returns specific information about that performer.

For example, when you search for **norah jones**, Google displays a Norah Jones section at the top of the search results page, as shown in Figure 10.18. This section includes a brief listing of the artist's most recent (or most well-known) albums and songs.

FIGURE 10.18

The result of a music artist search.

Click the performer's name and you see a visual listing of the artist's albums, as shown in Figure 10.19. Click any album art or title and you see a listing of album tracks, a link to album reviews, and links to download tracks from the album from a variety of online music stores, as shown in Figure 10.20. Back on the main artist page, there are also links to websites devoted to the artist, news about the artist, photos of the artist, and mentions of the artists in Google Groups discussion forums.

FIGURE 10.19

The artist's albums; click for detailed info.

The amount of information available from this simple performer search is surprising, and sometimes a little overwhelming. Most users have no idea that this much quality information is available by merely Googling a performer's name!

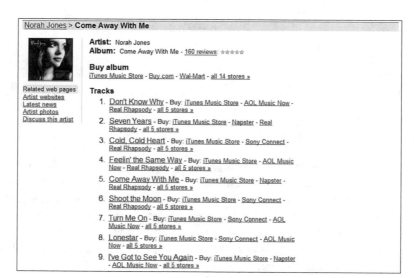

FIGURE 10.20
Detailed track and purchase information for the selected album.

The Bottom Line

There's a lot of hidden information available from the standard Google search box. If you don't know whether or not Google serves up the precise data you're looking for, take a chance; enter what you know into the search box and see what happens!

Additional Search Features

11 Customizing Google and the Google Home Page

12 Making Google Safe for Kids

13 Using Google in Other Languages

14 Using Google as a Calculator and Converter

15 Keeping Updated with Google Alerts

Customizing Google and the Google Home Page

The main Google search page is an exercise in simplicity, pretty much just a search box and a search button—none of the clutter you see at other search sites. That doesn't mean that you can't customize the way the page looks, however slightly. And it also doesn't mean that Google doesn't offer a portal-like page filled with custom content. (This latter page is simply at a different address than the main search page.)

Read on to learn more about applying your own personal preferences to the way Google looks and acts.

Setting Google Search Preferences

Most users aren't aware that they can personlize the way in which Google displays search results—and, to a small degree, the way the main search page looks. Well, you can, thanks to Google's Preferences page.

You get to the Preferences page by clicking the Preferences link on Google's home page. As you can see in Figure 11.1, there are a handful of items you can configure here; we'll discuss each separately in the following sections.

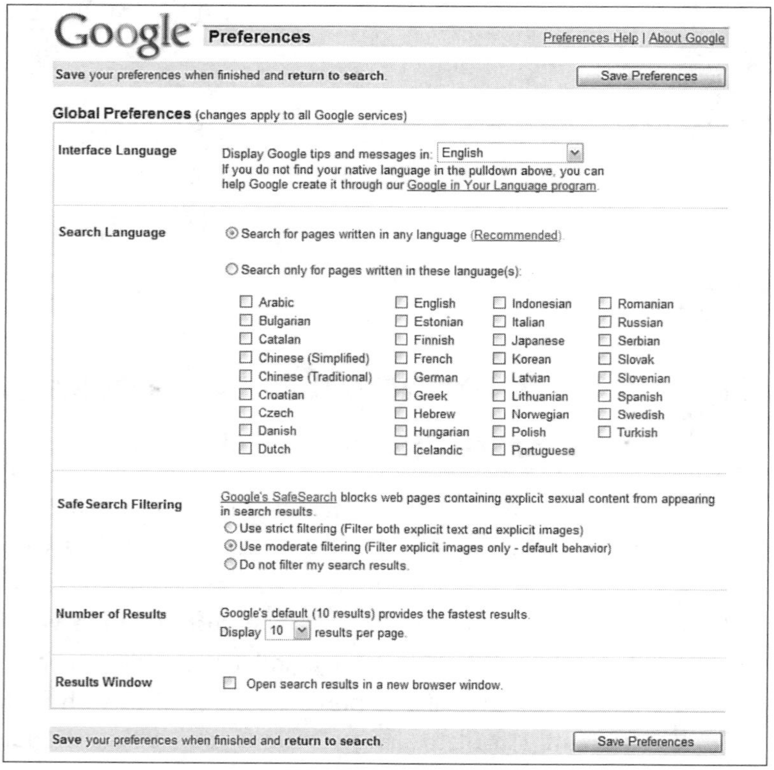

FIGURE 11.1
Customize the way Google looks and acts on the Preferences page.

When you're done configuring your preferences, clicking the Save Preferences button applies your choices to your current and all future Google searches across all Google services. That's all there is to it.

Display Google in a Different Language

By default, the Google interface displays with all the text in English. Google can, however, display its main page in dozens

caution Google tracks and applies your preferences via the use of browser cookies. If you have cookies disabled in your browser, your preferences won't be retained.

of local languages, from Afrikaans to Zulu. To select the interface language, just pull down the Interface Language list and make a selection.

> **note** Learn more about Google's interface language and search language features in Chapter 13, "Using Google in Other Languages."

Search in a Different Language

When you search Google, your query automatically searches for web pages created in any language. You may, however, want to restrict your searches to pages created in a specific language—especially if you only speak that one language.

To that end, you can instruct Google to restrict all your searches to pages created in a specific language. To do this, check the Search for Pages Written in These Languages option, and then click the language(s) you want your results restricted to. The choices range from Arabic to Turkish; English is somewhere in the middle there.

Search Safely

When your children are searching the Web, you probably don't want them exposed to adult content in Google's search results. Fortunately, Google offers a SafeSearch content filtering option that identifies and filters out any potentially offensive content from any Google search. You activate the SafeSearch filtering option from the Preferences page; you can choose from strict filtering (filters both words and images), moderate filtering (filters images only), and no filtering (Google's default configuration). Just check the option you want.

Display More Results Per Page

By default, Google displays 10 results per page for each search you make. This allows for a fairly fast display of results. If you want to see more results on your page, go to the Number of Results section of the Preferences page and change the setting to 20, 30, 50, or 100. As you might expect, choosing a larger number of results per page will slow down the display of results—and make it a little harder to chug through the results.

Open a New Results Window

By default, Google displays your search results in the same browser window you used to initiate your search. If you prefer to

> **note** Learn more about Google's SafeSearch content filtering in Chapter 12, "Making Google Safe for Kids."

have Google open a new browser window containing your search results, go to the Results Window section of the Preferences page and select the Open Search Results in a New Browser Window option. With this option selected, any time you click the Search Google button, a new browser window will open with the search results listed.

Creating Your Own Personalized Homepage

By now you're undoubtedly familiar and comfortable with the Spartan Google home page. But that's not the only way into the Google search engine; Google also offers a separate start page that you can use as a portal not just to Google, but to the entire World Wide Web.

This Google start page, called (rather unimaginatively, in my opinion) the Personalized Homepage, can be found at www.google.com/ig/. (Don't ask me what the "ig" in the address stands for; I have no idea.) You have to have a Google Account to create your Personalized Homepage; you can then log into your account from any computer to see your home page wherever you might happen to be.

When you first see your Personalized Homepage, it looks like the one in Figure 11.2. There's not a whole lot there yet, just the standard Google search box and options, a Top Stories section, sections for Quote of the Day and Word of the Day, and the weather forecast for someplace called Happy, Texas. (It's in Swisher County, near Highway 87, in case you're wondering.) But this is just a start; the whole point of creating a personal start page is to personalize the content—which we'll learn how to do next.

FIGURE 11.2

The default Personalized Homepage—not much content yet.

Personalizing Start Page Content

Personalizing Google's Personalized Homepage involves choosing which content you want to display, as well as how you want to display it. We'll start with the content-picking part, first.

To create your own personalized page, you start at the default Google Personalized Homepage and click the Personalize Your Google Homepage link. (Alternatively, after you've created your Personalized Homepage, you can click the Add Content link at the top-left corner of the page.) Google now displays a page full of content modules, as shown in Figure 11.3.

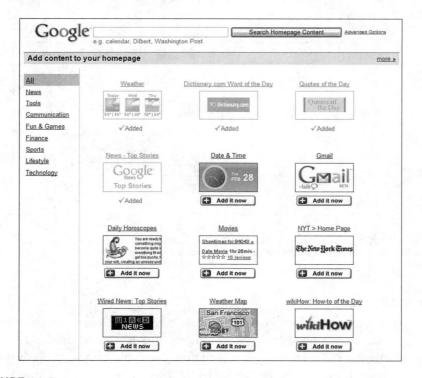

FIGURE 11.3
Available content modules for Google's Personalized Homepage.

The content modules you see are just a few of the many that are available. The content is organized by type (News, Tools, Communication, and so on); just click a content link at the left side of the page to see those modules of that particular type. And make sure you scroll down to the bottom of the page and click the More link to see all the modules that didn't fit on this first page.

Not surprisingly, Google also lets you search for content to include on the Personalized Homepage. Just enter your query into the search box at the top of this page, and then click the Search Homepage Content button; content that matches your query will now be displayed.

note Google's content modules are sometimes called *gadgets*.

To view what a full content module looks like (and see more details about the content), click the module title; this displays a content information page, like the one in Figure 11.4. To add a content module to your home page, click the Add It Now button, either on the main module listing or on the detailed content information page.

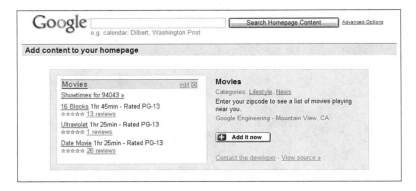

FIGURE 11.4
Viewing detailed information about a particular content module.

Adding RSS Feeds

You're not limited to adding the prepackaged content that Google offers to your Personalized Homepage. You can also use the Personalized Homepage to display RSS feeds from blogs and other feed-enabled websites. All you need to know is the URL of the RSS feed, and then follow these steps:

1. From the Google Personalized Homepage, click the Add Content link.

2. When the Add Content to Your Homepage page appears, click the Add by URL link.

note Some modules require additional information, such as your ZIP Code, to work properly. You can add this information from the Personalized Homepage itself by editing the module in question, as we'll discuss later in this chapter.

3. The page now expands to include an Add by URL box, as shown in Figure 11.5. Enter the URL for the RSS feed into this box, and then click the Add button.

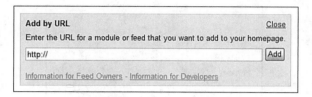

FIGURE 11.5

Use the Advanced Options box to add RSS feeds to your Personalized Homepage.

Customizing Individual Content Modules

Once you've added some content modules to your Personalized Homepage, you may want to customize the way they're displayed. Some modules let you specify the number of headlines that are displayed; others let you display information for a particular location.

You customize a module by clicking the Edit link next to the module title.

If a module lets you change the number of headlines displayed, you'll see a pull-down number list, like the one in Figure 11.6. Select the number of stories from the list, and then click the Save button.

FIGURE 11.6

Select how many headlines to display from the pull-down list.

If particular content requires localization, clicking the Edit link displays the necessary options for your selection. For example, Figure 11.7 shows the editing options for the Weather module; you can choose to display the temperature in Fahrenheit or Celsius, which country or region to display, and add cities that you want to view. Click the Add button and the selected cities will be added to the Weather module's display. (In this instance, you'll need to click the Close link when you're done adding cities to the module.)

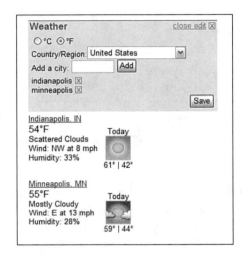

FIGURE 11.7
Adding cities to the Weather module.

Similarly, the Stock Market module lets you add any security to the list. As you can see in Figure 11.8, when you click the Edit link you enter a ticker symbol into the box, and then click the Add button. Again, you need to click the Close Edit link to end the editing session.

FIGURE 11.8
Adding stocks to the Stock Market module.

Rearranging Content Modules

With some personalized start pages, you have to access a separate "design" page to rearrange content on the page. Not so with Google's Personalized Homepage. Google's page has a set three-column design, and any content module can appear anywhere in any column.

To rearrange modules on the Personalized Homepage, all you have to do is use your mouse to drag a module to a different location. The layout of the page is "live" all the time; just position your cursor in the title bar for a module, click and hold the left mouse button, and then drag the module to where you want it to appear. It's that easy.

Deleting Content Modules

It's also easy to delete any content module you no longer want to appear on the Personalized Homepage. Just click the "X" in the modules title bar, and the module is deleted from the page. Simple.

Adding Even More Content

The question remains—just what content can you add to your Personalized Homepage? All of Google's official modules are displayed when you click the Add Content link; you can also view the modules at www.google.com/ig/ directory. There are several hundred available modules, with more being added daily.

You're not limited to Google's official modules, however. Google has published the API for its Personalized Homepage, which opens up the development of new modules to anyone with programming skills.

Google's directory of Personalized Homepage modules includes a lot of these homegrown content modules, but there's even more available elsewhere on the Web. One good source for "unofficial" content modules is Google Modules (www.googlemodules.com).

As you can see in Figure 11.9, Google Modules includes a ton of specialty modules from a variety of developers— everything from a PacMan module to a Travelocity flight search hack to a constantly updated list of President Bush's language-garbling "Bushisms." Adding one of these modules to your Personalized

tip If you're interested in developing your own Google Personalized Homepage modules, you'll need to use the Google Homepage API. Find out more at www.google.com/apis/homepage/.

Homepage is as easy as clicking the Add Module link next to each module description; when Google displays the confirmation page, click the Add to Google page to confirm the addition.

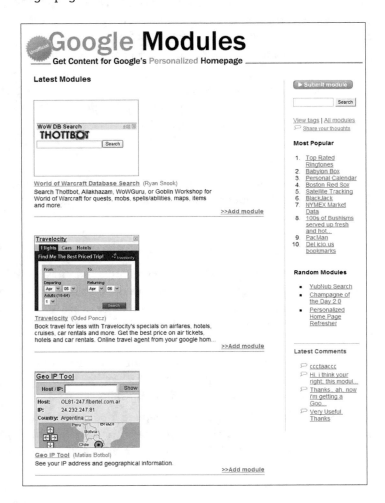

FIGURE 11.9

Find unofficial Google modules at the Google Modules website.

Other good sources of unofficial modules are GoogleWidgets.net (www. googlewidgets.net), Hot Modules (www.hotmodules.com), and widQ.com (www.widq.com).

Your Final Personalized Homepage

When you're done adding, editing, and deleting, you have a start page that's as personalized as you like. It's great to have all the content you're interested in assembled on a single page—and still have the handy Google search box at the top. Figure 11.10 shows what my Personalized Homepage looks like— what about yours?

FIGURE 11.10

A fully customized Personalized Homepage.

COMMENTARY

PERSONALIZED PORTAL VERSUS PURE SEARCH

For a half-dozen years, one of the most attractive things about Google was its bare-bones, totally uncluttered home page. Unlike other former search-only sites, such as Yahoo!, Google resisted the urge to turn its search engine into a web portal. Google's search-only page was clean and to the point, where Yahoo! and similar sites were crammed full of all manner of content.

To be honest, I hate the portalization of sites like Yahoo! and Excite. When I want to search, I want to search—and I don't want to be distracted by unwanted and mostly irrelevant content. That's one of the reasons why Google long ago became my search site of choice.

On one level, the adoption of a portal-like approach for Google's Personalized Homepage disturbs me. On another level, I really like it. Oh, to be conflicted!

I'm disturbed because Google is all about purity of search, and throwing all this other stuff into the mix dilutes that purity. On the other hand, Google does the personalized start page thing quite well; the results are at least as appealing as what you get with My Yahoo! (my.yahoo.com) or My Way (www.myway.com). And, to Google's credit, they've kept the personalized portal separate from the standard search page. When you want search and nothing but search, you still go to www.google.com. When you want the portal interface, you go to www.google.com/ig/.

As long as Google continues to keep pure search separate from the personalized portal, they'll please both types of users—searchers and browsers. Let's hope that the folks in Mountain View never abandon their core search audience, and that the Personalized Homepage is merely a supplement to what Google does best.

Making Google Your Home Page

Whether you use the standard Google home page or Google's Personalized Homepage, you can easily set this page as the home page for your web browser. This way Google will be the first thing you see when you start web browsing every day.

Instructions for all major web browsers are listed in Table 11.1:

Table 11.1	Instructions for Setting Google As Your Browser's Home Page
Web Browser	**Instructions**
Internet Explorer	1. Select Tools, Internet Options. 2. Select the General tab. 3. Enter either **www.google.com** or **www.google.com/ig/** into the Address box. 4. Click OK.
Mozilla Firefox	1. Select Tools, Options. 2. Select the General preferences. 3. Enter either **www.google.com** or **www.google.com/ig/** into the text box. 4. Click OK.
Opera	1. Select Tools, Preferences. 2. Select the General tab. 3. Pull down the Startup menu and select Start with Home Page. 4. Enter either **www.google.com** or **www.google.com/ig/** into the Home Page field. 5. Click OK.
Netscape	1. Select Edit, Preferences. 2. Select the Navigator category. 3. Enter either **www.google.com** or **www.google.com/ig/** into the Home Page text box. 4. Click OK.
Safari	1. Select the Preferences menu. 2. Select General preferences. 3. Enter either **www.google.com** or **www.google.com/ig/** into the Home Page field. 4. Close the Preferences window.

The Bottom Line

While there is a little bit of customization you can do to the "classic" Google home page, if you want a true personalized portal, you can turn to Google's Personalized Homepage. You retain the standard Google search box at the top of the page, but what goes below that is entirely up to you. Between Google's in-house developers and a small army of independent programmers, there are hundreds of content modules you can add to your own Personalized Homepage. The potential exists to create a start page that contains all the content you're interested in, a true gateway to those parts of the web that most interest you, if that's your thing. If not, the traditional Google home page is still there, ready for your next search—and nothing but the search.

12

Making Google Safe for Kids

L ike it or not, there's a lot of unsavory content on the Web. When you perform a Google search, some of these undesirable pages can end up in your search results—which is not a great thing if it's your kids who are doing the searching.

Fortunately, Google offers a content filter that you can apply to your Google searches. Google's SafeSearch filter screens the Google index for sites that contain adult information and then elminates those pages from your search results. Google uses proprietary technology to check keywords, phrases, URLs, and Google Directory categories against a list of objectionable words and topics. When you activate SafeSearch, you're blocked from viewing results that contain these undesirable words and topics.

Read on to learn more.

How SafeSearch Filtering Works

Given all of the complex algorithms and technologies Google applies to its standard searching, the SafeSearch content filter is surprisingly simple. SafeSearch is nothing more than a filter that looks for the appearance of certain "naughty" words,

caution SafeSearch settings are stored in a cookie on your hard disk. If you have cookies disabled in your browser, you can't use the SafeSearch filter across multiple search sessions.

such as "sex," "porn," and "girls." (The exact list is a Google secret, of course, but you can bet it includes all those words the publisher won't let me list here.) When a web page contains one or more of these objectionable words (in either the page text or the URL), the page is omitted from Google's search results.

Like I said, surprisingly simple.

There are two levels of SafeSearch filtering:

- **Moderate.** Blocks objectionable images from Google Image Search results only; it doesn't block any pages based on objectionable text. This is the default configuration.

- **Strict.** Blocks both objectionable words and images—and also includes a stricter image filter than the moderate filtering option.

It's important to note that the SafeSearch filter only applies to those results returned from a Google search. Google doesn't block access to any specific web page, it just omits objectionable pages from its search results. You can still enter the URL for an objectionable page into your web browser; Google won't keep you from going directly to that page.

It's also important to note that while SafeSearch does a good job of filtering out objectionable pages, it isn't perfect—and won't catch all obscene material. So it's possible (if not likely) that some objectionable links might creep into your search results, even with SafeSearch activated. To that end, SafeSearch is not a substitute for adult supervision when your kids are searching the Web.

Enabling the SafeSearch Filter

There are four ways to enable (or disable) the SafeSearch filter—from the Preferences page, by using the Advanced Search page, by using the **safesearch:** search operator, or by modifying the URL of any search results page. We'll look at each method in turn.

SafeSearch Filtering from the Preferences Page

To turn on or off SafeSearch filtering on a global basis (for all future searches), use the settings on Google's Preferences page. Follow these steps:

1. From Google's main search page, click the Preferences link.

2. When the Preferences page appears, scroll down to the SafeSearch Filtering section (shown in Figure 12.1).

3. Select one of the three options: Use Strict Filtering (affects both text and image searching), Use Moderate Filtering (affects image searching only), or Do Not Filter My Search Results (turns off SafeSearch filtering). Moderate Filtering is selected by default.

4. Click the Save Preferences button.

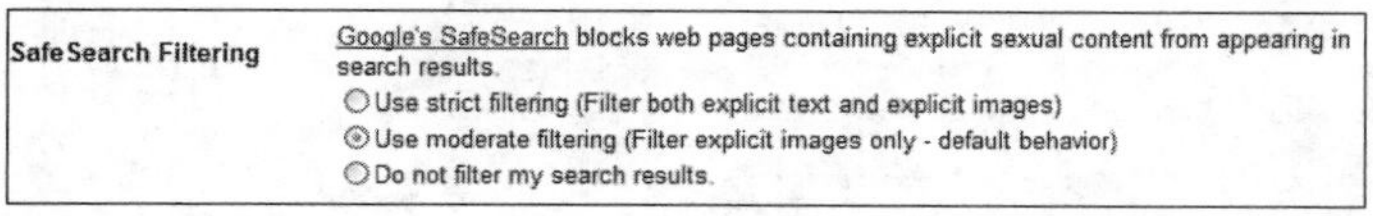

SafeSearch Filtering	Google's SafeSearch blocks web pages containing explicit sexual content from appearing in search results.
	○ Use strict filtering (Filter both explicit text and explicit images)
	⊙ Use moderate filtering (Filter explicit images only - default behavior)
	○ Do not filter my search results.

FIGURE 12.1

Enabling SafeSearch filtering on the Preferences page.

SafeSearch Filtering from the Advanced Search Page

Google's Advanced Search page also features a SafeSearch option, which is great for when you want to filter (or not filter) a specific search request only—without affecting your overall SafeSearch settings. To apply content filtering from the Advanced Search page, follow these steps:

1. From Google's main search page, click the Advanced Search link.

2. When the Advanced Search page appears (as shown in Figure 12.2), select the Filter Using SafeSearch option.

3. Enter the rest of your search query.

4. Click the Google Search button.

SafeSearch Filtering from the Standard Search Box

If you prefer to fine-tune your searches from the standard search box, using advanced search operators, you can

note The Advanced Search page enables strict filtering for both text and image searching. You can enable moderate filtering for image searching by using the Advanced Image Search page, discussed in Chapter 24, "Searching Google Images."

12

enable or disable SafeSearch filtering on a search-by-search basis by using the **safesearch:** operator. All you have to do is add the **safesearch:** operator at the beginning of your query. For example, if you're searching for **breast cancer** and want to filter out any adult sites that might pop up (due to the inclusion of the word "breast"), modify your query to **safesearch: breast cancer**, as shown in Figure 12.3.

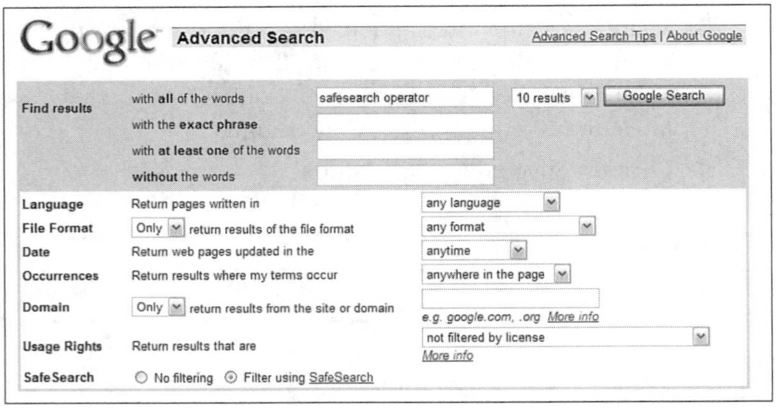

FIGURE 12.2
Enabling SafeSearch filtering on the Advanced Search page.

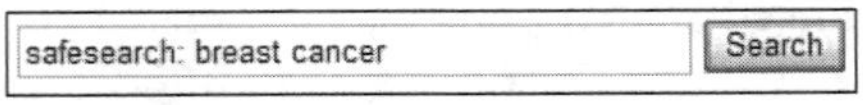

FIGURE 12.3
*SafeSearch filtering with the **safesearch:** operator.*

SafeSearch Filtering by Editing the Search Results URL

Back in Chapter 2, "Searching the Web," we discussed how you can modify search results by editing the URL of any search results page. Well, there's a URL parameter you can apply for SafeSearch filtering, which is great if you want to conduct a search contrary to your normal SafeSearch settings. It works like this:

- If you normally have SafeSearch turned on and you want to expand your search results to include potentially objectionable material, add `&safe=off` to the end of the search results page URL, and then rerun the search. (Figure 12.4 shows how this might look.)

■ If you normally have SafeSearch turned off and you want to remove objectionable material from the results, add &safe=on to the end of the search results page URL, and then rerun the search.

FIGURE 12.4
Expanding your search results by turning off the SafeSearch filter from the search results page URL.

When *Not* to Use SafeSearch

As nice as SafeSearch is, especially if you have kids, sometimes it can get in the way. That's because its relatively simple nature (looking for a list of objectionable words) casts a fairly wide net. For example, an innocent search for "breast," in regards to women's health, can get caught up in the filtering net if you have SafeSearch turned on.

For that reason, you probably want to disable SafeSearch filtering when you're searching health or medical subjects. You should also consider disabling SafeSearch if you're not satisfied with any normal search; it's sometimes hard to tell just what the content filter is filtering until you turn it off.

COMMENTARY

12

SAFESEARCH—HELP OR HINDRANCE?

Personally, I'm not a big fan of content filters—especially when those filters are somewhat unsophisticated. Unfortunately, Google's SafeSearch falls into this category.

The problem with an unsophisticated content filter is that it's fairly dumb. All SafeSearch does is look for a list of words, and does its blocking based on appearance in that list. Just because a site contains one of those words, however, doesn't automatically mean that the site itself is objectionable—the example of breast cancer sites, which contain the word "breast," being a good example.

These dumb filters also catch a lot of innocent sites in their net. CNET recently reported that PartsExpress.com found itself being blocked by Google's SafeSearch filter, because the letters s-e-x were contained in the site's URL. It wasn't a sex site, obviously, but that's the way these content filters work—by brute force.

Google's brute force approach to content filter is the way almost all content filters used to work—ten years ago. Most third-party content filtering programs today are more sophisticated in the way they look for potentially objectionable sites; they may start with a word filter list, but apply various algorithms to try to put those words in context on a site. The results are still less than perfect, and still block a number of legitimate sites, but at least it's progress.

If you have kids on your PC, Google's SafeSearch filter is a good way to help protect them from seeing things they shouldn't be seeing. But if you're searching on your own, you might find the results *too* limiting. If so, do the smart thing—and turn off the filter.

The Bottom Line

Google's SafeSearch content filter works by looking for sites that contain objectionable words and phrases, and then excludes those sites from the search results. You can apply the SafeSearch filter from Google's Preferences and Advanced Search pages by using the **safesearch:** operator and by modifying the search results page URL. Know, however, that SafeSearch won't catch all objectionable content, and may in fact block some sites that aren't objectionable at all. It's a good—but not perfect—tool.

12

Using Google in Other Languages

Google may have been born in sunny California, but it's become an international force on the Internet. Not only can you use Google to search for web pages from different countries, you can also use Google to translate those pages you find. Google's main search page can also be configured to display in different languages, plus there are dozens of country-specific Google sites.

In other words, Google wants to be your one-stop search shop, no matter where you live or what language you speak.

Searching for Language- and Country-Specific Pages

While many users may think of English as the default language of the Web, it isn't the only language—not by any means. As the World Wide Web becomes more worldwide, more and more pages are posted in a variety of native languages. In fact, more than 30% of all web pages are in a language other than English, and that number is growing daily.

When you want access to *all* the information that's out there, you can't limit your search to just English-language pages; doing so leaves a third of the Web unsearched. For that reason, savvy searchers know how to open their Google searches to foreign-language pages—or restrict them to pages written in a specific language.

> **note** Vilaweb reports that English remains the number-one language of the Web, used in 68.4% of all web pages. Japanese is number-two (5.8%), followed by German (5.7%), Chinese (3.8%), and French (2.9%).

Changing Your Default Language Search

By default, Google searches for pages written in any language. If you want to limit your search to pages written in a specific language, follow these steps:

1. From Google's main search page, click the Preferences link.
2. When the Preferences page appears, go to the Search Language section, as shown in Figure 13.1.
3. To search for pages in any language, check the Search for Pages Written in Any Language option. (This is the default Google search.)
4. To restrict your search to pages written in one or more specific languages, check the Search Only for Pages Written in These Language(s) option, and then check the specific languages.
5. Click the Save Preferences button.

FIGURE 13.1
Configuring Google's search language preferences.

Conducting a Language-Specific Search

Configuring your language preferences from the Preferences page affects all your

> **tip** To restrict your searches to English-language pages only, check the English option on the Preferences page.

searches, globally. When you want to conduct a one-off language-restricted search, you need to use the search option on Google's Language Tools page. Here's what to do:

1. From Google's main search page, click the Language Tools link.
2. When the Language Tools page appears, go to the Search Specific Languages or Countries section, as shown in Figure 13.2.
3. Pull down the Search Pages Written In list and select the specific language you want to search.
4. Enter your query into the Search For box.
5. Click the Google Search button.

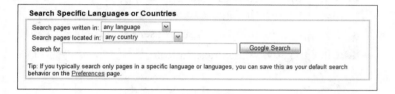

FIGURE 13.2

Limiting your search to pages written in a specific language, or located in a specific country.

Google now returns a list of pages that match your query, limited to those pages written in the language you selected.

Conducting a Country-Specific Search

Similarly, you can restrict your search to pages located in a specific country—no matter what language they're written in. Just follow these steps:

1. From Google's main search page, click the Language Tools link.
2. When the Language Tools page appears, go to the Search Specific Languages or Countries section.
3. Pull down the Search Pages Located In list and select the specific country you want to search.
4. Enter your query into the Search For box.
5. Click the Google Search button.

> **tip**
> You can also restrict your search to a specific language by using the Language option located on Google's Advanced Search page.

Displaying Google in Another Language

By default, Google displays all the text and buttons on its pages in English—unless you're accessing one of Google's international sites, of course. (We'll discuss these in the next section.) But, assuming you're accessing the standard English-language Google site, everything is in English.

You can, however, configure Google's English-language site to display in other languages. As of this writing Google can display its pages in more than 100 different languages, from Afrikaans to Zulu. Here's how to change your interface language:

1. From Google's main search page, click the Preferences link.

2. When the Preferences page appears, go to the Interface Language section, as shown in Figure 13.3.

3. Pull down the language list and select a language.

4. Click the Save Preferences button.

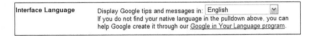

FIGURE 13.3

Configuring Google's interface language preferences.

After you've made your choice, all of Google's text and controls will display in the new language. (Figures 13.4, 13.5, and 13.6 show the Google interface in Arabic, Japanese, and Spanish, respectively.)

FIGURE 13.4

Google in Arabic.

FIGURE 13.5

Google in Japanese.

FIGURE 13.6

Google in Spanish.

And here's something fun. In addition to real languages, the Google interface is also available in a number of fake languages. My favorites? Klingon, Pig Latin (shown in Figure 13.7), Elmer Fudd ("I'm Feewing Wucky"), Hacker (shown in Figure 13.8), and Bork, Bork, Bork!—the pseudo-Swedish spoken by the Muppets' Swedish Chef.

FIGURE 13.7

Google in Pig Latin.

13

FIGURE 13.8

Google in Hacker language.

Using Country-Specific Google Sites

Displaying Google's main interface in another language is fine, but if you live in another country you probably have a country-specific version of Google that you can use, instead.

Google has dedicated sites for 138 different countries. For example, Figure 13.9 shows Google's South Korea site; Figure 13.10 shows the U.K. Google site; and Figure 13.11 shows the Israel Google site.

FIGURE 13.9

Google South Korea.

FIGURE 13.10

Google U.K.

FIGURE 13.11
Google Israel.

The advantage of using a country-specific Google site is you have the option, right on the home page, of restricting your search to pages located in that country. The URLs for each of Google's country-specific sites are listed in Appendix A, "Google's Site Directory," and can also be found on Google's Language Tools page.

Translating Text and Web Pages from One Language to Another

Now here's a Google feature that most users aren't aware of. Not only can you display Google in other languages and use Google to search for pages written in other languages, you can also use Google to translate those pages written in other languages. In fact, you can use Google's language tools to translate not only complete web pages, but also any phrases of text that you enter.

You can access Google's language tools by clicking the Language Tools link on Google's main page, or by going directly to www.google.com/language_tools. As you can see in Figure 13.12, the top part of the page is where you search for pages written in a specific language (or located in another country); below that are Google's translation tools. (And below that are links to each of Google's country-specific sites.)

> **tip**
>
> I use Google's translation tools when I receive emails from readers in countries that don't speak English. I simply cut the text of the message from the email, and then paste into the Translate Text box; when I click the Translate button, I can read the translated message. Without this translation feature, I'd have no idea what my foreign readers were writing to me about!

13

FIGURE 13.12
Google's Language Tools page.

Languages Translated

Google lets you translate text or web pages between the languages shown in Table 13.1:

Table 13.1 **Google's Translation Languages**	
From This Language	**To This Language**
English	Arabic
English	Chinese (Simplified)
English	French
English	German
English	Italian
English	Japanese

Table 13.1   Continued

From This Language	To This Language
English	Korean
English	Portuguese
English	Spanish
Arabic	English
Chinese (Simplified)	English
French	English
German	English
Italian	English
Japanese	English
Korean	English
Portuguese	English
Spanish	English
French	German
German	French

Translating Text Passages

Translating text passages is a fairly simple process. Just follow these steps:

1. On Google's Language Tools page, enter (or copy) the original text into the Translate Text box.

2. Pull down the From list and select the original and the translated language.

3. Click the Translate button.

Google now displays the Translate page, shown in Figure 13.13. The translated text is shown in the first text box; the text in its original language is shown in the second text box.

tip If you accidentally selected the wrong original language (it's not always easy to tell which language is which, especially if you don't speak them), just make a different selection from the From list on the Translate page. This retranslates the original text.

13

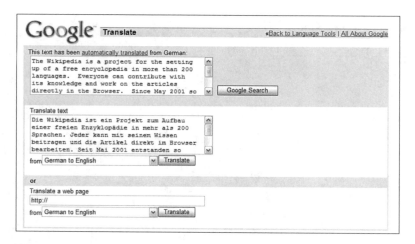

FIGURE 13.13

The results of Google's automatic text translation.

Translating Web Pages

You can also use Google's translation tools to translate complete web pages from one language to another. This is particularly useful if one of the pages in your search results is in a language other than English. Here's how to do it:

1. On Google's Language Tools page, enter (or copy) the URL from the web page into the Translate a Web Page box.

2. Pull down the From list and select the original and the translated language.

3. Click the Translate button.

Google now displays a translated version of the original page in your web browser. At the top of the translated page is a link to view the original page (in its original language); click this link to return to the native-language page. (Figures 13.14 and 13.15 show the CNN Japan page in its original Japanese and in the Google-translated English version, respectively.)

caution Google can only translate the text on a web page; it can't translate the graphics, which will appear in their original language.

13

FIGURE 13.14

The original Japanese-language page…

FIGURE 13.15

…and Google's English-language translated version.

13

Translating from Google's Search Results

When you're searching the Web, you can use Google's web page translation feature without first having to go to the original foreign-language page. When you encounter a foreign-language page in Google's normal search results, you see a Translate This Page link, as shown in Figure 13.16. Click this link and Google will automatically display the translated version of the page.

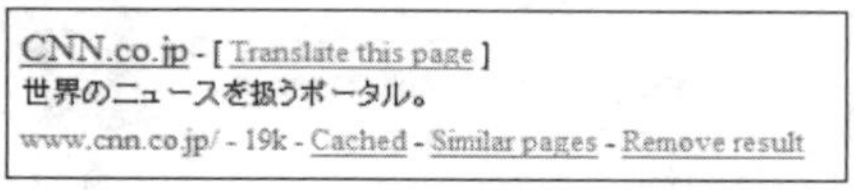

<u>CNN.co.jp</u> - [<u>Translate this page</u>]
世界のニュースを扱うポータル。
www.cnn.co.jp/ - 19k - <u>Cached</u> - <u>Similar pages</u> - <u>Remove result</u>

FIGURE 13.16
Click the Translate This Page link to automatically translate a foreign-language page in Google's search results.

Translating Web Pages from the Google Toolbar

If you have the Google Toolbar installed in your web browser, you have one more way to translate web pages. Just click the down-arrow on the Translate button (shown in Figure 13.17) and then select Translate Page Into English; Google's translation tool does the rest.

FIGURE 13.17
Using the Translate feature on the Google Toolbar.

Translating Words from the Google Toolbar

Here's another translation tool you can apply from the Google Toolbar. The WordTranslator function, when enabled, allows you to translate any English word into your chosen foreign language, just by hovering your cursor over the word on a web page. As you can see in Figure 13.18, the chosen-language definitions for the selected word appear in a tooltip-like pop-up.

> **note** Learn more about the Google Toolbar in Chapter 31, "Using the Google Toolbar."

FIGURE 13.18

Translating words on the fly with Google Toolbar's WordTranslator.

To use the WordTranslator feature, you have to first choose the destination language, and then activate the tool. You choose the language by selecting Settings, Options, clicking the Translator Settings button, and then choosing a language from the pull-down list. You activate WordTranslator by clicking the down arrow next to the Translate button and checking the Enable WordTranslator option.

COMMENTARY:

MACHINE TRANSLATION

Google's automatic translation function, like all translation tools you find on the Web, is accomplished via the use of technology. It's basically a word-by-word translation that doesn't always "get" the structure and rules of a language. This means that a lot of sentences and syntax get garbled; even single-word translations are sometimes off a little, due to a lack of context sensitivity.

As I said, all automatic translation services—sometimes called *machine translation*—suffer from the same problems. While the technology behind these machine translators is constantly improving, it's still not as good as what a professional human translator or dual-language speaker can accomplish. This is yet another case of technology not being quite as accurate as good old human beings; machine translation is constantly a step behind.

In addition, Google's translation tool isn't quite as far-reaching as some of the other similar tools you find on the Web. As of this writing, for example, Google doesn't do Russian to English translations, or English to Norwegian. For that you have to turn to some alternative sites, such as FreeTranslation.com (www.freetranslation.com), WorldLingo (www.worldlingo.com/en/products_services/worldlingo_translator. html), or my personal favorite, Alta Vista's Babel Fish (babelfish.altavista.com). All of these tools offer more translation options than Google—even if the quality of the translations are not noticeably more accurate.

13

The Bottom Line

Google makes it easy for you to use their search services, no matter what language you speak or what country you're in. You can even search for non-English web pages, and then automatically translate those pages into English. Just click the Language Tools link on Google's home page, and a whole new world is waiting for you to use.

13

Using Google As a Calculator and Converter

When you can't be troubled to reach over and pick up the handheld calculator sitting on your desk, you can use Google as a high-tech web-based calculator—the world's most overly complex calculator, to be sure, but a calculator nonetheless.

But I jest. It's actually quite convenient to enter an equation into the Google search box and get an answer right in your web browser. I'm not sure exactly why Google added this functionality to their site, but I know it's getting a bit of use—from me personally, if from no one else.

Performing Basic Calculations from the Google Search Box

To use Google as a calculator, all you have to do is enter your equation or formula into the search box, and then click the Google Search button. The result of the calculation is displayed on the search results page, as shown in Figure 14.1. It's that simple.

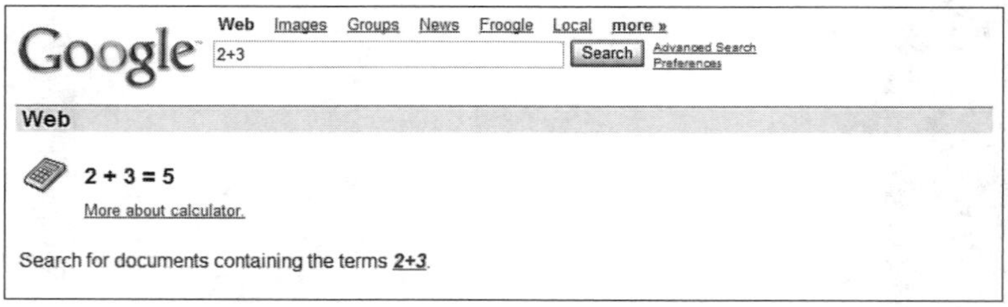

FIGURE 14.1

Using Google to add two numbers together.

You can use a number of algebraic operators to construct your calculations. Table 14.1 details the operators that Google recognizes.

Table 14.1	Google's Basic Calculator Functions		
Function	**Operator**	**Example**	**Result**
Addition	+ *or* plus *or* and	2 + 1	3
Subtraction	- *or* minus	2 - 1	1
Multiplication	X *or* × *or* times	2 × 1	2
Division	/ *or* over *or* divided by	2 / 1	2

Note that several functions have multiple operators you can use. For example, for addition you can use either +, **plus**, or **and**. That means you can add the numbers 2 and 3 in three different ways:

- **2 + 3**
- **2 plus 3**
- **2 and three**

And you don't have to enter spaces between the operator and the numbers (unless you're spelling them out). So **2 + 3** is just as good a query as **2+3**. Google's smart enough to figure out what you're doing.

Here's another example. Let's say you want to divide 72 by 8. Just enter **72 / 8** into the search box (as shown in Figure 14.2), and then click the Search button. (You could also enter **72 over 8** or **72 divided by 8**.)

tip

If you really wanted to search for documents that contain the equation you entered, rather than calculate the results of the equation, click the Search for Documents Containing the Term link on the search results page.

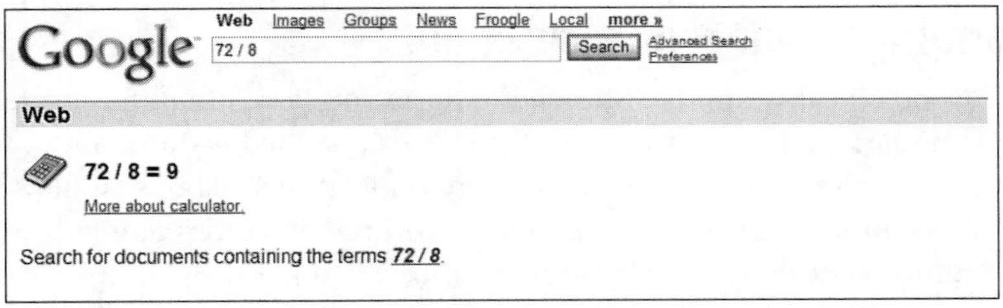

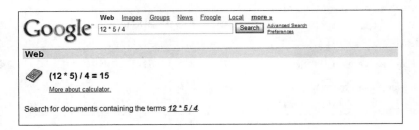

FIGURE 14.2
Dividing two numbers.

Google also lets you string multiple operations together. For example, if you want to calculate 12 times 5 divided by 4, enter **12 * 5 / 4**, as shown in Figure 14.3. The calculations work from left to right, multiplying and dividing first, and then adding and subtracting. So, using another example, 2 + 3 * 3 equals 11, not 18.

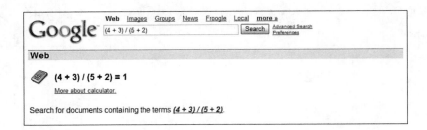

FIGURE 14.3
Stringing together multiple operations

You can also create nesting equations by using appropriately placed parentheses. So, to divide the sum of 4 plus 3 by the sum of 5 plus 2, you'd enter **(4 + 3) / (5 + 2)**, as shown in Figure 14.4. You can get as complex or as creative as you want; Google can handle it.

FIGURE 14.4
Entering a nesting equation.

14

Performing Advanced Calculations

Google's calculator isn't limited to basic addition and multiplication. It can also handle more advanced calculations (detailed in Table 14.2), trigonometric functions (Table 14.3), inverse trigonometric functions (Table 14.4), hyperbolic functions (Table 14.5), and logarithmic functions (Table 14.6). If you know what these functions are, I assume you know the proper way to use them. If you don't, then get yourself a good math book or don't bother with them.

Table 14.2   Google's Advanced Mathematic Functions

Function	Operator	Example	Result
Percent (X percent of Y)	% of	20% of 10	2
Square root	Sqrt	sqrt(16)	4
Root	nth root of	5th root of 32	2
Exponents (raise to a power)	^ *or* ** *or* to the power of	4^2	16
Factorial	!	10!	3,628,800
Modulo (finds the remainder after division)	% or mod	14%3	2
Choose (determines the number of ways of choosing a set of Y elements from a set of X elements)	Choose	9 choose 3	84

Table 14.3   Google's Trigonometric Functions

Function	Operator	Example	Result
Sine	Sin	sin(100)	-0.506365641
Tangent	tan *or* tangent	tan(100)	-0.587213915
Secant	sec or secant	sec(100)	1.15966382
Cosine	cos or cosine	cos(100)	0.862318872
Cotangent	cotangent	contangent(100)	-1.70295692
Cosecant	csc or cosecant	csc(100)	-1.97485753

Table 14.4   Google's Inverse Trigonometric Functions

Function	Operator	Example	Result
Inverse sine	Arcsin	arcsin(1)	1.57079633
Inverse tangent	Arctan	arctan(1)	0.785398163
Inverse secant	Arcsec	arcsec(1)	0
Inverse cosine	Arccos	arccos(1)	0
Inverse cotangent	arccotangent	arccotangent(1)	0.785398163
Inverse cosecant	Arccsc	arccsc(1)	1.57079633

Table 14.5   Google's Hyperbolic Functions

Function	Operator	Example	Result
Hyperbolic sine	Sinh	sinh(1)	1.17520119
Hyperbolic cosine	Cosh	cosh(1)	1.54308063
Hyperbolic tangent	Tanh	tanh(1)	0.761594156

Table 14.6   Google's Logarithmic Functions

Function	Operator	Example	Result
Logarithm base 10	Log	log(100)	2
Logarithm base 2	Lg	lg(100)	6.64385619
Logarithm base e	Ln	ln(100)	4.60517019

Looking Up the Values of Constants

In addition to performing calculations, Google also knows a variety of mathematical and scientific constants, such as pi, Avogadro's Number, and Planck's Constant. It also knows the radius of the Earth, the mass of the sun, the speed of light, the gravitational constant, and a lot more.

Let's check this out. Not sure what the value of pi is? Enter **pi** and Google returns 3.14159265, as shown in Figure 14.5. How about the speed of light? Enter **speed of light**, and Google returns 299,792,458 m/s, as shown in Figure 14.6. What about the radius of the Earth? Enter **radius of earth**, and Google returns 6378.1 kilometers, as shown in Figure 14.7.

14

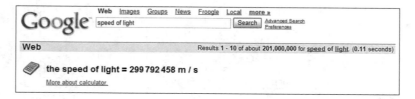

FIGURE 14.5

The value of pi.

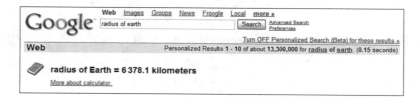

FIGURE 14.6

The speed of light.

Now let's get fancy. Try dividing the radius of the Earth by pi. Enter **(radius of earth) / pi**; Google's answer is 2030.21229 kilometers, as shown in Figure 14.8. Or how about multiplying the radius of the Earth by the speed of light and then dividing the answer by Avogadro's Number? I'm not sure why you'd want to do this, but the query looks like this: **(radius of earth) * (speed of light) / (avogadro's number)**. (The answer, shown in Figure 14.9, is $3.17512652 \times 10^{-09}$ m²/s.)

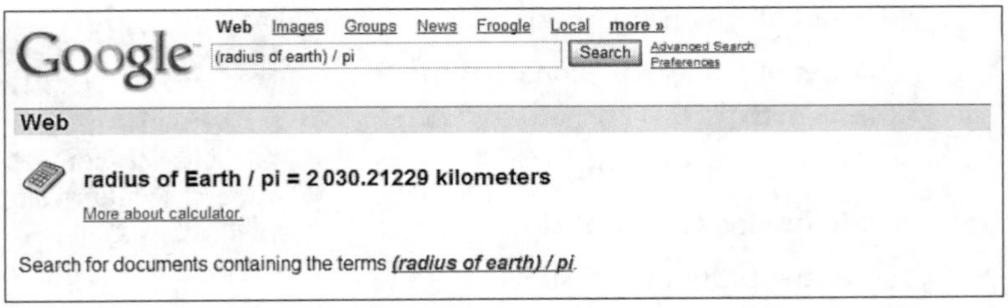

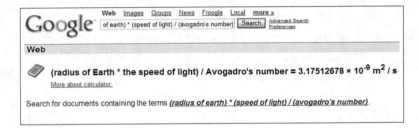

FIGURE 14.8
The radius of the Earth divided by pi.

FIGURE 14.9
The radius of the Earth times the speed of light divided by Avogadro's Number.

And what constants does Google know? Here's a short list, with shorthand entries in parentheses:

- Atomic mass units (amu)
- Astronomical Unit (au)
- Avogadro's Number
- Boltzmann Constant (k)
- Electric Constant (epsilon_0)
- Electron mass (m_e)
- Electron volt (eV)
- Elementary charge
- Euler's Constant
- Faraday Constant
- Fine-structure Constant
- Gravitational Constant (G)
- Magnetic flux quantum

14

- Mass of moon (m_moon)
- Mass of *planet* (m_*planet*, as in **m_earth**)
- Mass of sun (m_sun)
- Molar Gas Constant (R)
- Permeability of free space
- Pi
- Planck's Constant (h)
- Proton mass (m_p)
- Radius of moon (r_moon)
- Radius of *planet* (r_*planet*, as is **r_mars**)
- Radius of sun (r_sun)
- Rydberg Constant
- Speed of light (c)
- Speed of sound
- Stefan-Boltzmann Constant

caution When dealing with mathematical constants, Google's calculator sometimes interprets uppercase letters different from lowercase letters.

For example, if you wanted to find the speed of light, you could enter **speed of light**, or you could just enter a capital **C**. Google knows the value both ways.

Converting Units of Measure

Another surprise is that Google's calculator also handles conversions. It knows miles and meters, furlongs and light years, seconds and fortnights, and even angstroms and Smoots—and can convert from one unit of measurement to another.

The key to using the Google calculator as a converter is to express your query using the proper syntax. In essence, you want to start with the first measure, followed by the word "in," followed by the second unit of measure. A general query looks like this: *x* **firstunits in secondunits**.

Let's look at some examples.

Don't know how many feet equal a meter? Then enter the query **1 meter in feet**, as shown in Figure 14.10. Not sure how many teaspoons are in a cup? Enter **1 cup in teaspoons**, as shown in Figure 14.11. Want to convert 100 U.S. dollars into Euros? Then enter **100 usd in euros**, as shown in Figure 14.12. Or how about converting 72 degrees Fahrenheit to Celsius? Then enter **72**

degrees Fahrenheit in Celsius, as shown in Figure 14.13. Or maybe you want to find out your weight in kilos, or your age in seconds? Enter the queries **180 pounds in kg** or **45 years in seconds**, as shown in Figures 14.14 and 14.15.

note Google's currency conversion rates are provided by Citibank N.A., and may not always be the most current rates.

FIGURE 14.10
Converting meters to feet.

FIGURE 14.11
Converting cups into teaspoons.

FIGURE 14.12
Converting U.S. dollars into Euros.

14

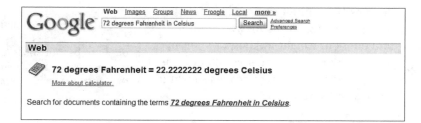

FIGURE 14.13

Converting degrees Fahrenheit to degrees Celsius.

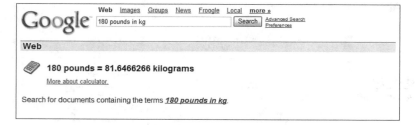

FIGURE 14.14

Converting pounds into kilograms.

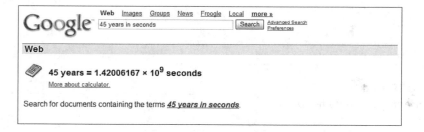

FIGURE 14.15

Converting years into seconds.

That's right, all the formulas necessary for these types of conversions are hard-wired into the Google search engine. Just state your query as clearly as possible and Google will do the rest.

What units of measure does Google know? Table 14.7 provides just *some* of what you can find when you search Google.

14

Table 14.7 Google's Units of Measure

Type of Measurement	Units
Currency	U.S. dollars (USD), Australian dollars (AUD), Canadian dollars, British pounds (GBP, pounds), Euros
Mass	Grams (g), kilograms (kg), pounds (lbs), grains, carats, stones, tons, tones
Distance (length)	Meters (m), kilometers (km), miles, feet (ft), Angstroms, cubits, furlongs, nautical miles, Smoots, light years
Volume	Gallons, liters (l), pints, quarts, teaspoons, tablespoons, cups
Area	Square miles, square kilometers, square feet, square yards, acres, hectares
Time	Days, hours, minutes, seconds (s), months, years, centuries, sidereal years, fortnights
Electricity	Volts, amps, ohms, henrys
Power	Watts, kilowatts, horsepower (hp)
Energy	British thermal units (BTU), joules, ergs, foot-pounds, calories, kilocalories (Calories)
Temperature	Degrees Fahrenheit, degrees Celsius
Speed	Miles per hour (mph), kilometers per hour (kph), kilometers per second, knots
Data	Bites, bytes, kilobytes (kb), megabytes (mb), gigabytes (gb), terabytes (tb)
Quantity	Dozen, baker's dozen, gross, great gross, score, googol
Numbering systems	Decimal, hexadecimal (hex), octal, binary, roman numerals

Some more examples. Let's say you want to convert the year 2006 into Roman numerals; enter **2006 in roman**, as shown in Figure 14.16. Maybe you want to convert the decimal numeral 47 into hexadecimal; enter **47 in hex**, as shown in Figure 14.17. How about converting 70 miles per hour into kilometers per hour; enter **70 mph in kph**, as shown in Figure 14.18. Or maybe you want to convert 100 land miles into nautical miles; enter **100 miles in nautical miles**, as shown in Figure 14.19.

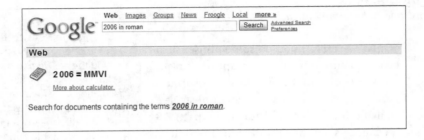

FIGURE 14.16

Converting years into Roman numerals.

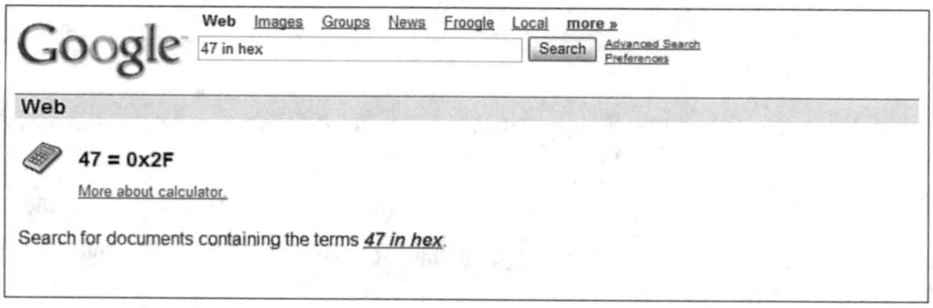

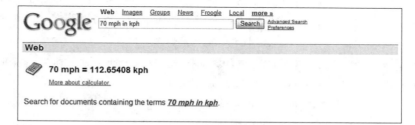

FIGURE 14.17

Converting numbers into hexadecimal.

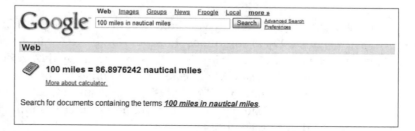

FIGURE 14.18

Converting miles per hour into kilometers per hour.

FIGURE 14.19

Converting miles into nautical miles.

Google even lets you do some nonsensical conversions. You can query **speed of light in knots** or **1 foot in smoots**. You can also use these conversions to create nonsense calculations, such as **(radius of earth) / 3 teaspoons**, as shown in Figure 14.20. It doesn't make any sense, but Google can do it.

> **tip** Google's calculator has been hardwired to include the answers to some fairly complex—and fairly fanciful—calculations. My favorite is to enter the query **what is the answer to life the universe and everything.** Google's answer (42) should delight long-time fans of Douglas Adams's *The Hitchhiker's Guide to the Galaxy*.

14

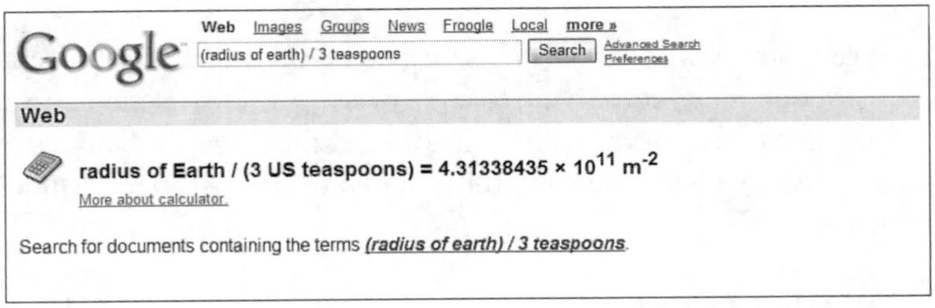

FIGURE 14.20

Google lets you divide the radius of the Earth by 3 teaspoons—but why would you want to?

COMMENTARY:

FUN WITH NUMBERS

If Google wasn't amazing enough, the addition of the calculator feature ups the ante several degrees. The calculator—combined with the database of constants, values, and conversions—is, in my opinion, one of the most eminently useful features on the entire Google site.

But let's not go too overboard. By sticking to its search box–oriented interface, Google has created what is essentially a command-line calculator. While it's fairly loaded with functionality, it shares the same drawbacks as any command-line calculator—notably, forcing the user to memorize a list of mathematical functions.

Compare this to the way a typical keyboard calculator works. You don't have to remember that to enter **arcsin** when you want to find the inverse sine, nor do you have to create a tortured expression like **21^2** when you want to square a number. On a keyboard calculator, each advanced function is assigned to its own key; when you want to use the function, you just have to press the associated key.

So Google's command-line calculator has its limitations, which is the kind of compromise Google is forced to make when it stands steadfastly by its simple, search box entry system. While I have nothing against simplicity, in the case of calculators, online or otherwise, it might be more helpful for Google to offer an alternative graphical keyboard interface, like the one found on the X-Number site. Google wouldn't have to abandon the simple search box interface; the graphical calculator could be a separate page, a link away.

14

> I admire Google's focus on its well-recognized simple approach, but enough is enough. Trying to cram every possible function into a single search box is maybe a little obsessive-compulsive. Perhaps it's time to investigate alternative interfaces for various nonsearch functions.

An Easier Way to Calculate

While most of Google's calculator functions are fairly easy to remember, you may not want to bother with all the proper operators and syntax. If that's the case, check out Soople's Calculator page (www.soople.com/soople_intcal-chome.php). Soople is a third-party site that provides an alternative interface to many of Google's harder-to-use functions, and the Calculator page, shown in Figure 14.21, breaks out several Google calculator functions into their own discrete visual search boxes.

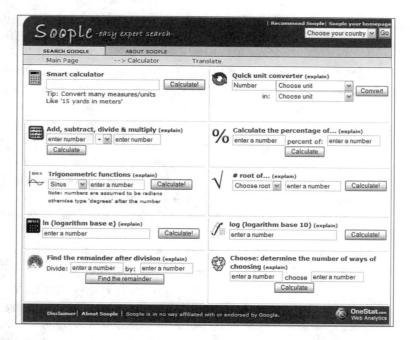

FIGURE 14.21
Soople's Calculator page.

Soople offers the following discrete calculators, all of which feed into the official Google calculator:

- Smart Calculator (same as the standard Google search box)
- Quick Unit Converter (conversions)
- Add, Subtract, Divide, & Multiply (simple mathematic calculations)
- Calculate the Percentage Of (percents)
- Trigonometric Functions (trig operators)
- # Root Of (roots—square and otherwise)
- ln (logarithm base e)
- log (logarithm base 10)
- Find the Remainder After a Division (modulo)
- Choose (set choosing)

And that's not the only third-party Google calculator interface around. X-Number has developed a keyboard interface for the Google calculator, which you can find at www.xnumber.com/google_calc.htm. As you can see in Figure 14.22, you can use your mouse to click the number/function keys onscreen, or just enter numbers with your computer keyboard's number keys. Your input is fed to Google, and the results output on a standard Google calculator results page. Cool!

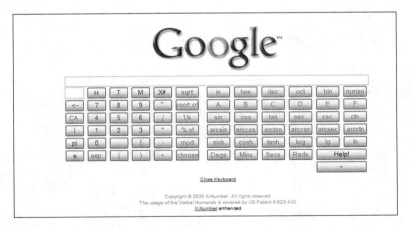

FIGURE 14.22

X-Number's keyboard interface for the Google calculator.

14

The Bottom Line

Google's calculator is one of the most useful "hidden" functions on the entire Google site. Most users don't know that they can use Google to perform virtually all of their mathematic calculations and conversions, but they can—and it's surprisingly easy to use. Just enter your equation, using common mathematical operators, and Google will return the solution to your calculation. It's a lot quicker (and a little easier) than starting up the Windows Calculator—because you're already at the Google site!

Keeping Updated with Google Alerts

If you do a lot of Googling, you may get tired of entering the same searches over and over, trying to find the latest search results. Wouldn't it be great if Google could email you when new web pages appear that match your search criteria? Or if there are recent news articles that match your interests?

That's where Google Alerts come in. A Google Alert is an email that Google sends you when it finds new items of interest. All you have to do is sign up for an alert, and then wait for your email inbox to fill up.

Different Kinds of Alerts

Google offers four different types of alerts you can choose to receive. Each type of alert is based on a specific type of Google search:

■ **News alerts** search Google News for new headlines that match your query.

■ **Web alerts** search Google's web index for new web pages that match your query.

■ **News & Web alerts** search both Google News and Google's web index for new items that match your query.

■ **Groups alerts** search Google Groups for new messages that match your query.

You can opt to receive news alerts once a day, once a week, or as it happens. For most users, the once a day option (shown in Figure 15.1) is best; this way you can see what new web or Google Groups information appeared in the last 24 hours.

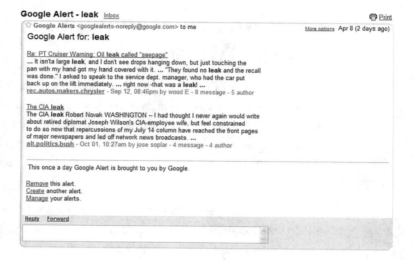

FIGURE 15.1

A once-a-day Groups alert.

However, if you're wanting the latest headlines via a News alert, you should opt for the as-it-happens option. As you can see in Figure 15.2, this type of News alert includes the latest headline (at the bottom of the message), with previous headlines collapsed above it. Click a headline to expand it and read the story synopsis, or click the Expand All link at the top of the message to expand all the headlines.

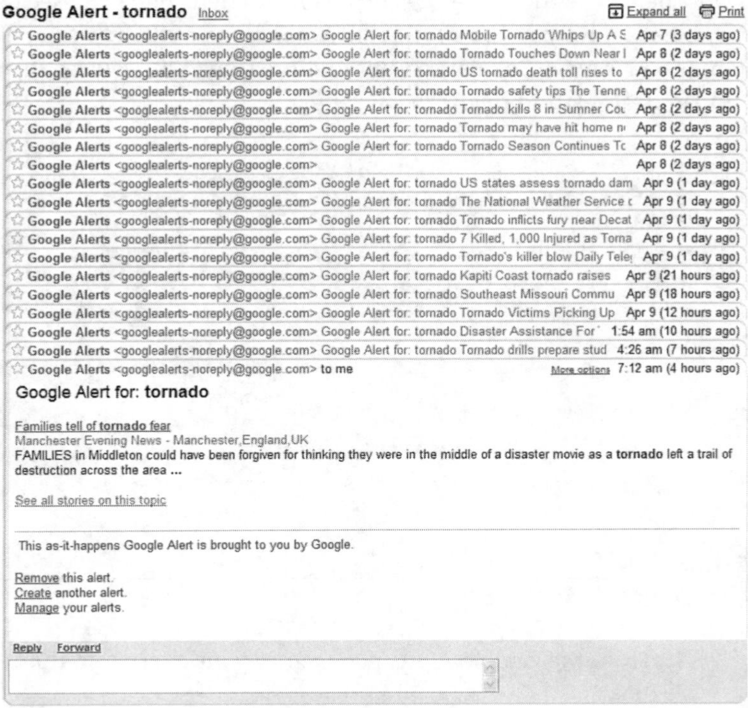

FIGURE 15.2
An as-it-happens News alert.

In all instances, Google Alerts won't notify you of *all* items that match your query—otherwise you'd be getting literally hundreds of email messages a day. Instead, Google Alerts only search the most relevant results, based on Google's PageRank Algorithm. So if you sign up for News alerts, you'll be notified only of those new stories that make it into the top 10 results for your query; if you sign up for Web alerts, you'll be notified only of those new pages that make it into the top 20 results for your query; if you sign up for Groups alerts, you'll be notified only of those new messages that make it into the top 50 results for your query.

Signing Up for Alerts

Signing up for a Google Alert is as easy as entering a search query, and then activating the alert service. You do all of this from the Google Alerts home page (www.google.com/alerts/).

Now here's the tricky thing. Which Google Alerts page you see depends on whether or not you have a Google Account, and whether or not you're signed in. If you have a Google Account and are signed in, you see the page shown in Figure 15.3, and follow these steps:

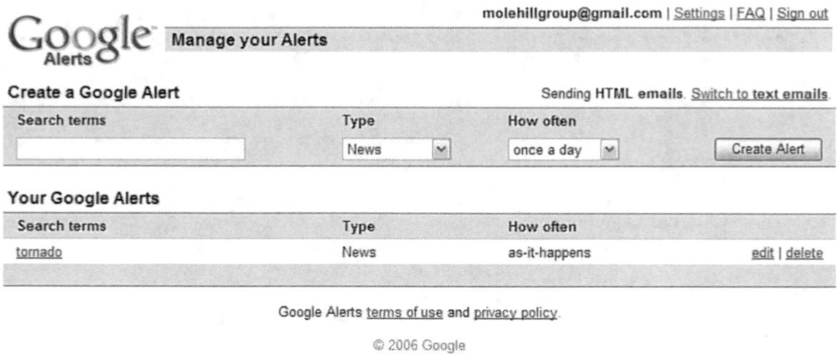

FIGURE 15.3

Creating a new Google Alert.

1. From the Google Alerts page, enter your query into the Search Terms box.

2. Pull down the type list and select which type of alert you want to receive—News, Web, News & Web, or Groups.

3. Pull down the How Often list and select how often you want to receive alerts—Once a Day, Once a Week, or As-It-Happens.

4. Click the Create Alert button.

If you don't have a Google Account or aren't signed in, you first see the page shown in Figure 15.4. The procedure for using this page is similar to the one just discussed, except that you also have to specify which email address you want to use to receive your Google Alerts. If you use this method of creating an alert, you'll receive a notification message in your email inbox, like the one shown in Figure 15.5; click the Verify This Google Alert Request link to verify your alert.

note If you have a Google Account and a Gmail account, your Google Alerts are automatically sent to your Gmail inbox. If you don't have a Gmail account, you'll need to specify which email address you want your alerts sent to.

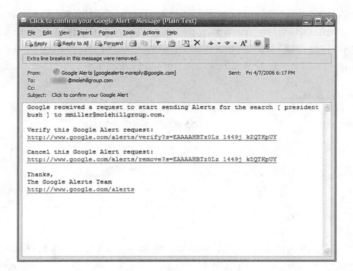

FIGURE 15.4
Creating a new Google Alert—without a Google Account.

FIGURE 15.5
Verifying your new Google Alert.

Customizing and Editing Your Alerts

To manage your existing alerts, you must be signed in with your Google
Account. Then, when you access the Google Alerts page, you see a list of your
Google Alerts, like the one shown in Figure 15.6.

FIGURE 15.6

Getting ready to edit your Google Alerts.

To edit the parameters of an alert, click the Edit link next to that alert. This expands the alert, as shown in Figure 15.7. You can now edit your search query, change the type of alert, or change the frequency of the alert. Click the Save button when you're done making changes.

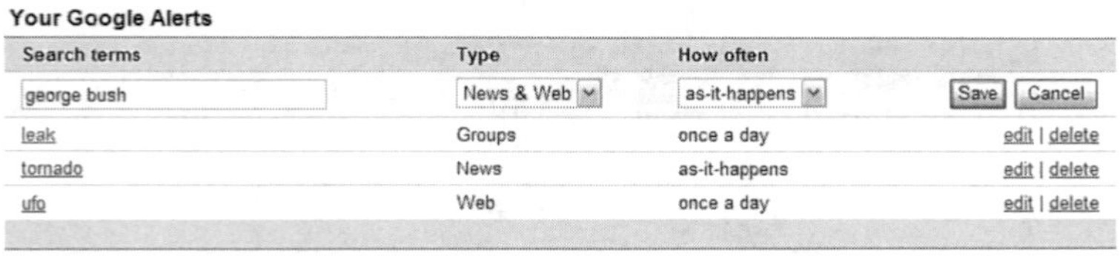

FIGURE 15.7

Editing the parameters of a Google Alert.

By default, your Google Alerts come to you with fancy HTML formatting. If you'd rather receive plain-text email messages, click the Switch to Text Emails link at the top of the Google Alerts page. (You can always switch back by clicking the resulting Switch to HTML Emails link.)

Deleting Google Alerts

There are two ways to stop receiving a Google Alert you've created:

- Click the Delete link next to the alert on the Google Alerts page.

> **tip** To view the current results of the search you saved as an alert, go to the Google Alerts page and click the name of the alert. This will run the specified search, and display a normal search results page.

▪ Click the cancellation link at the bottom of any Google Alert email you receive.

The Bottom Line

Google Alerts are a great way to receive notification of new information as it becomes available. It doesn't matter whether you're searching for new web pages, news stories, or group postings, Google Alerts will keep you completely up-to-date—from the comfort of your email inbox.

Shopping and Product Searches

16 Searching for Bargains with Froogle and Google Catalogs

17 Buying and Selling—Online and Locally—with Google Base

Searching for Bargains with Froogle and Google Catalogs

The most important development in the history of online shopping is the creation of the price comparison site. This is a site that uses a shopping bot to automatically search a large number of online retailers for current prices on available products. This product and pricing information is used to create a large database that you, the consumer, can access at will. When you search a price comparison site, you're looking up the most recent pricing information in its database. In essence, you let the price comparison site do your shopping for you; all you have to do is evaluate the results.

As you might expect, searching for bargains is right up Google's alley; it plays right into Google's strength with search technologies. So I now introduce you to Froogle, Google's shopping search engine. Read on to learn more—and find some great bargains.

Froogle: It's Different from Other Price Comparison Sites

note In case you didn't figure it out on your own, Froogle's name is a Googlized version of the word *frugal*.

Before we get into how Froogle works, it might prove beneficial to first understand how the other price comparison sites on the Web work. That's because Froogle works differently from all those competing sites.

How Most Price Comparison Sites Work

If you've ever used BizRate (www.bizrate.com), NexTag (www.nextag.com), Shopping.com (www.shopping.com), and similar price comparison sites, you might be under the impression that these sites scour the Web for prices from a wide variety of online retailers. That's a false impression; instead, these sites build their price/product databases from product links submitted and paid for by participating retailers. That's right, most price comparison sites charge retailers to be included in their listings. The more retailers a site signs up, the more products there are for you to search through.

To be fair, these price comparison sites do appear to honestly present the lowest prices—from participating merchants, that is. The prices presented are legitimate, no matter who's paying what. The only thing is, it's possible that lower prices might exist at a retailer who doesn't sign on to a site's program.

How Froogle Works

Froogle isn't like all the other price comparison sites. Unique among these sites, Froogle is completely objective; Froogle doesn't take money for its listings, instead sending its spider software to independently scour the Web for merchants and products.

That's right, Froogle is a pure search engine, just like its Google parent. Froogle searches all the online retailers it can find, and doesn't accept any paid listings. That makes Froogle's price comparisons more legitimate than those at other sites. (And, in the name of full disclosure, it should be noted that merchants can also submit their product listings to Froogle—they just don't have to pay for this privilege.)

Not only are Froogle's results untainted by product placement, it also typically returns more results for any given item you're shopping for. That's again because of the way Froogle scours the Web for product listings; it's not limited to results submitted by participating retailers. If it's for sale on the Web, chances are Froogle knows about it.

Searching for the Lowest Prices

Froogle's main page (froogle.google.com), shown in Figure 16.1, bears more than a passing resemblance to Google's main page. You use Froogle as you would Google, by searching for products you want to buy. (Unlike other price comparison sites, Froogle offers no product category browsing capability; it's a search-only interface.)

> **note** Retailers don't actually pay price comparison sites on a per-listing basis; instead, they pay when customers click their product listings. This is called a *pay-per-click (PPC)* model, and the individual fee is referred to as a *cost per click (CPC)*. CPCs run anywhere from a nickel to more than a buck, depending on the site and the product category.

FIGURE 16.1
The results of a Froogle search.

Basic Searching

Because Froogle is an offshoot of Google, it's no surprise that it works so well as a product search engine. In most cases, all you have to do is enter a product description, name, or model number into the search box at the top of the home page, and then click the Search Froogle button.

Understanding Froogle's Search Results

Froogle displays all matching products on a search results page, such as the one shown in Figure 16.2. By default, the results are displayed in list view; if you click the Show Grid View link, you'll see the products displayed in a visual grid, as shown in Figure 16.3, which shows more items in the same amount of space (but with fewer immediate options for each listing).

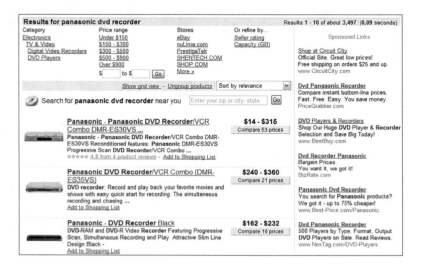

FIGURE 16.2

The results of a Froogle search.

Also by default, Froogle organizes its results based on relevance, which is measured by customer demand. You can also use the pull-down list at the top of the results listing to sort products by price (low to high or high to low), product rating, or merchant rating.

Above the product listings is a section of search refinements you can use to narrow down the search results. These refinements differ by type of product, but typically include filters that let you restrict your search by category, price range, features, and so on. Click a link to redisplay the results as appropriately filtered.

When you find a product you're interested in, you can do a few things:

caution Watch out for the advertisements on Froogle's search results page. These are the listings in the Sponsored Links section on the right side of the page; they're not really search results, but rather listings paid for by Froogle's advertisers.

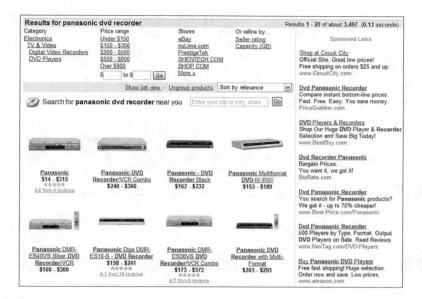

FIGURE 16.3

Froogle's product results page displayed in grid view.

- ■ To display a detailed product page for that product, click either the product's name or the Compare Prices button. A typical product page includes a third-party description of the product, a rating for that product (from zero to five stars), a link to a review of that product, and a list of merchants that offer that product for sale—along with their current selling prices. (More on those price listings in a minute.)

- ■ To read reviews of that product, click the Product Reviews link below the item description. (More on product reviews later in this chapter.)

- ■ To add this item to your Froogle shopping list, click the Add to Shopping List link. (More on Froogle's shopping list later in this chapter, too.)

Getting the Most from the Product Detail Page

When you get to the product detail page, like the one shown in Figure 16.4, you'll want to pay particular attention to the price listings. By default, these listings are sorted by seller rating, with the highest-rated merchants first.

FIGURE 16.4

A Froogle product detail page.

However, there are two potential problems with this type of ranking. First, the seller rating doesn't always correspond to the lowest price. Second, not all sellers have been ranked, which more often than not leaves a huge number of unranked retailers jumbled at the bottom of the page.

Fortunately, there are other, more useful, ways you can sort the results:

- To sort by online retailer (alphabetically), click the Seller Name link above the merchant column.

- To sort by price (lowest to highest), click the Price link above the price column.

Understandably, most shoppers will choose to sort by price. Note, however, that the lowest price may sometimes be a used or reconditioned unit, or sometimes even an accessory for the item you're shopping for. In other words, sorting by price is sometimes less useful than the other methods of ranking results.

Advanced Searching

If you find that Froogle is returning too many (or too few) search results, you can use the Advanced Search page to fine-tune your query. The Advanced Froogle Search page, shown in Figure 16.5, is similar to the Google Advanced Search page; you get there by clicking the Advanced Froogle Search link on Froogle's main page.

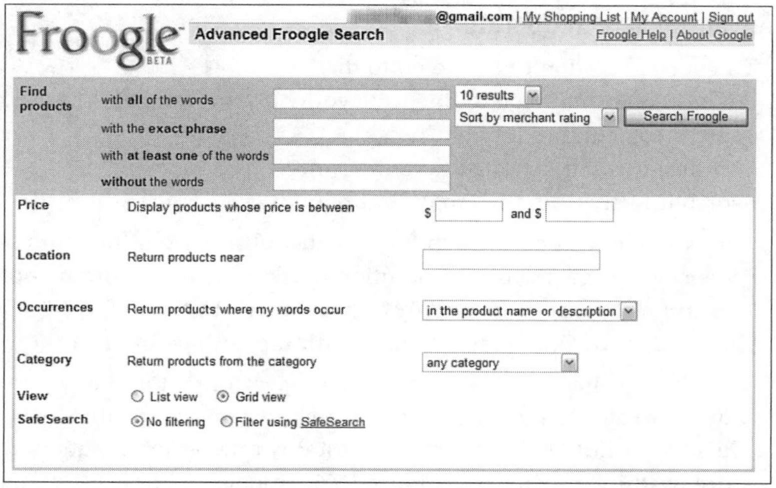

FIGURE 16.5
Advanced Froogle searching.

The Advanced Froogle Search page offers a number of different search parameters, as detailed in Table 16.1:

Table 16.1   Advanced Froogle Search Options

Option	Description	Comparable Search Operator
Results (pull-down list)	Selects how many listings are displayed on the search results page	N/A
Find products with *all* of the words	Google's default search mode	N/A
Find products with the *exact phrase*	Searches for the exact phrase entered	" "
Find products with *at least one* of the words	Searches for either one word or another	OR
Find products *without* the words	Excludes products that contain the specified word(s)	-
Price	Displays products priced within the specified range	...
Occurrences	Searches for products where the keywords occur in the product name, description, or both	N/A
Category	Searches for products within a specified product category	N/A
View	Displays results in either list or grid view	N/A
SafeSearch	Turns on or off SafeSearch content filtering	safesearch:

Using Advanced Search Operators

Of course, you don't have to go to the Advanced Search page to fine-tune your search. You can use any of Google's advanced search operators to refine your search directly from the Froogle search box.

note Learn more about Google's search operators in Chapter 2, "Searching the Web."

For example, you can search for an exact phrase from the main search box by enclosing the phrase in quotation marks, like this: **"nikon coolpix 2100"**. You can also exclude a word from your search by using the "-" sign in front of the word, or do an either/or search with the **OR** operator.

There's also one Froogle-specific search operator you might want to use. The **store:** operator lets you limit your search to a specified online store. For example, to see what DVD players that Best Buy sells, enter the query **dvd player store:bestbuy**, as shown in Figure 16.6. Froogle will now list all matching products offered for sale by the specified merchant.

dvd player store:bestbuy	Search

FIGURE 16.6

Restricting your search to a single online store.

Getting Ready to Buy

When you find an item you want at the price you want, it's time to visit that merchant's site and continue the shopping process. This is as easy as clicking the merchant's name on the product detail page; this should take you directly to that item's listing on the merchant's site.

By the way, if you want to see what other items a merchant has for sale, click the All Items from Seller link on the product detail page. This takes you to a listing of that merchant's available products, as shown in Figure 16.7. You can filter this list by price or brand, if you like.

caution Froogle's prices aren't always totally current. Since Froogle spiders the Web for information, the price data it collects can be several days to several weeks old. Don't be surprised to click a merchant link and find a different price listed, or discover that the item is no longer available.

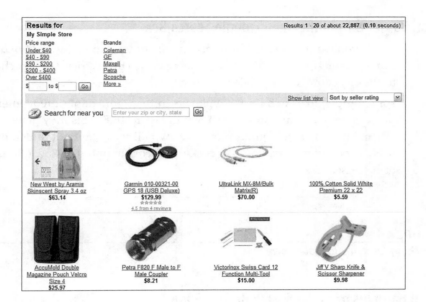

FIGURE 16.7

All items for sale by a particular seller.

Shopping for Local Bargains

By default, Froogle searches the entire Web for the products you're shopping for. But sometimes you don't want to buy from a merchant clear across the country (or the globe); sometimes a big item is best purchased from a traditional retailer close by, or you can get faster shipping from someone local.

When you want to find merchants near you that are selling the merchandise you're looking for, you can use the Google Maps service. We'll talk more about Google Maps in Chapter 18, "Using Google Maps"; for now, all you need to know is that Google Maps includes a vast database of local merchants. When Google Maps is combined with Froogle, you get a database of merchandise available locally.

There are several ways to use Froogle's Google Maps connection, as we'll now discuss.

Local Bargains from the Main Froogle Search Box

When you want to search for items for sale in your area, just add **near** *location* or **near** *zipcode* to the end of your query. This restricts the search results to the city, state, or ZIP Code you specify.

For example, to search for DVD players in the Minneapolis area, enter **dvd players near minneapolis**, as shown in Figure 16.8. This may generate a list of local results, although it's more likely you'll see a "did not match any products" page. From here, you can click the Local Shopping or Local Results link, as discussed next.

dvd players near minneapolis   Search

FIGURE 16.8

Searching for items for sale where you live

Local Bargains from the Search Results Page

At the top of every search results page there's a Search for *Item* Near You section, like the one in Figure 16.9. Sometimes you'll also see a Local Results link at the top of a search results page, with a Google Maps icon (like the one in Figure 16.10). Enter the appropriate information (or click the link) and Froogle displays a list of local merchants that have the item in question for sale, as shown in Figure 16.11.

Search for **panasonic dvd recorder** near you   Enter your zip or city, state   Go

FIGURE 16.9

Display local Google results by entering your ZIP Code.

See 1800 local results for **dvd players** near **minneapolis**

FIGURE 16.10

Click the Local Results link to view items for sale locally.

This list of local merchants also includes a Google Map of the area, with the merchants pinpointed on the map. Click a pin on the map to display information about that product and merchant, as shown in Figure 16.12.

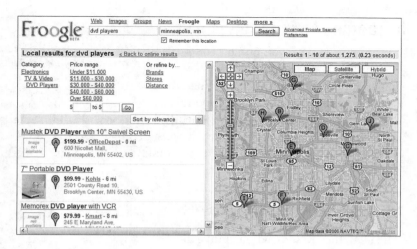

FIGURE 16.11
A list of local merchants with the specified item for sale.

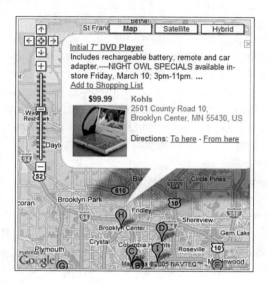

FIGURE 16.12
Click a pin on the map to view product/merchant details.

Using Froogle's Merchant Reviews

What do you do if you find a good price for an item on Froogle, but have never heard of the merchant before? When the quality of the merchant is as important as the price of the product, turn to Froogle's merchant reviews. It's a good way to steer your business toward reliable retailers, and avoid those that underserve their customers.

Froogle's merchant reviews, alas, aren't provided by Froogle—or by Froogle's users. Instead, they're sourced much like all of Froogle's and Google's content, by spidering the Web. Froogle's spider searches out merchant reviews at other product comparison sites (such as PriceGrabber.com, ResellerRatings.com, and Shopping.com), and then lists and collates them for your shopping convenience. The original reviews, in most instances, are provided by customers of that retailer.

The first place you see the merchant reviews is, after you search for a product, on the resulting product details page. As you can see in Figure 16.13, the initial results are ranked according to seller rating, on a scale of zero to five stars. The Seller Rating column displays the retailer's rating, as well as how many user reviews that merchant has received.

When you click the seller's rating link, you're taken to that retailer's rating/reviews page. As you can see in Figure 16.14, this page displays the seller's overall star rating, along with the most relevant reviews of that seller. (Relevance, in this instance, relates to reviews of similar products to that you searched for.)

If the sheer number of reviews is overwhelming, you can click the appropriate links to

- Show positive reviews only
- Show neutral reviews only
- Show negative reviews only
- Sort reviews by date (instead of relevance)

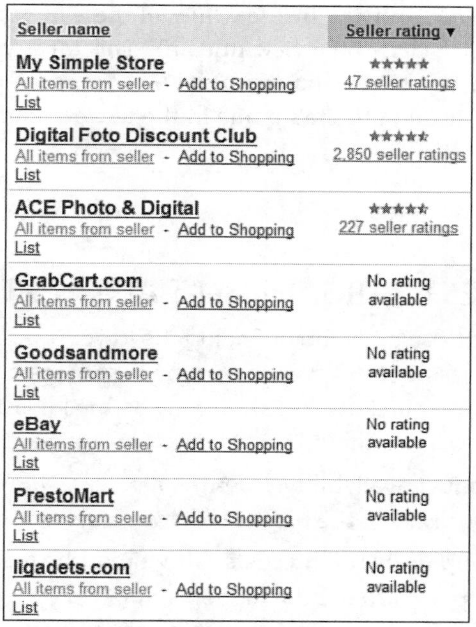

FIGURE 16.13
Froogle's seller ratings, on the product details page.

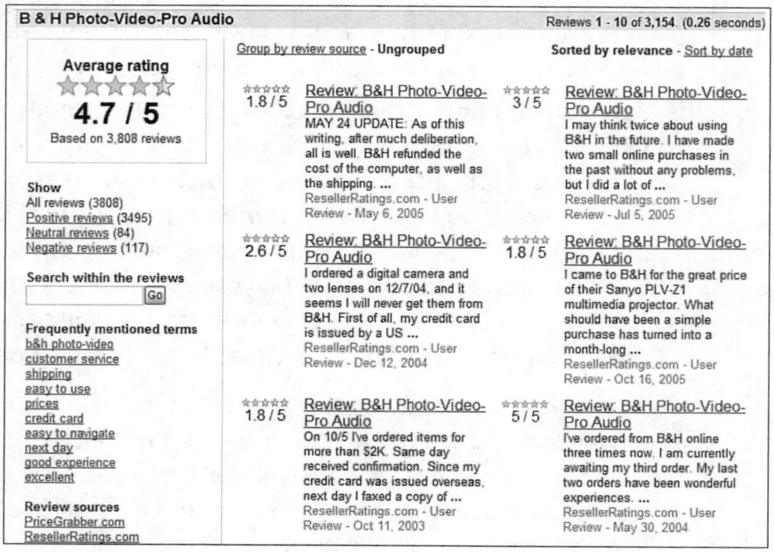

FIGURE 16.14
A seller's rating/reviews page.

Froogle displays only the first few lines of these merchant reviews. To read a full review, just click the review title link. This takes you to the original review on its original website. (You can also go to the main page of the reviewing website by clicking the site's name in the Review Sources section of the left column.)

COMMENTARY:

THE BEST BARGAIN ISN'T ALWAYS THE LOWEST PRICE

Froogle does a great job of finding the lowest prices online, but the lowest price doesn't always mean the best bargain. While it's tempting to base your purchase decision solely on the lowest price, there are other factors you should consider before you make your purchase:

- **Product availability.** Does the merchant with the lowest price actually have the product in stock and ready to ship?

- **Shipping/handling costs.** Oftentimes the merchant with the lowest price also has the highest shipping costs. Look for merchants that offer free or low-cost shipping, and then compare the *total* price—the product price plus the shipping costs.

- **Product condition.** Froogle's product listings display not only new, in-the-box products, but sometimes also list used or refurbished items. Don't fall for a super-low price on a refurbished product when what you really want is a brand-new one.

- **Merchant reputation.** Not all online retailers are created equal. Some are actually bait-and-switch artists, or offer poor service, or take forever to ship, or otherwise promise to disappoint. This is where you want to take advantage of Froogle's merchant ratings and compare different retailers by reading the reviews and ratings from previous customers. When you find a low price from a merchant you've never heard of before, take the time to read the customer reviews—and skip those merchants that rate poorly.

You read a lot of stories about consumers getting cheated or scammed or just being disappointed when dealing with one or another online retailer. On the Internet, just as in the real world, *caveat emptor* is the motto *du jour*. The smarter you shop, the safer and more satisfied you'll be. That means not automatically buying from the retailer from the lowest price—and doing your homework before you click that "purchase now" button.

Creating Your Own Froogle Shopping List

Here's a great bonus feature of particular value around the holidays. You can use Froogle to create a "wish list" of products you'd like to receive (or buy yourself) at particular merchants. This Froogle Shopping List feature is stored online at Froogle, so you can access it from any computer—which means you can share it with friends and family.

Adding an Item to Your Shopping List

To add an item to your Froogle Shopping list, you start by conducting a normal product search from the Froogle main page. When the search results page appears, you have two options.

First, you can click the Add to Shopping list link below a product's description, as shown in Figure 16.15. This adds the product to your shopping list, and displays the My Shopping List page.

FIGURE 16.15

Click the Add to Shopping List link next to a product on the search results page.

Second, you can continue through from the search results page to the product detail page. From there, you can click the Add to Shopping List link below any merchant's description, as shown in Figure 16.16; this also adds the product to your shopping list, and also displays the My Shopping List page.

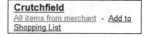

FIGURE 16.16

Click the Add to Shopping List link next to a merchant on the product details page.

Viewing and Managing Your Shopping List

To view the contents of your shopping list, all you have to do is click the My Shopping List link at the of any Froogle page. This displays all the items you've added to your list, as shown in Figure 16.17.

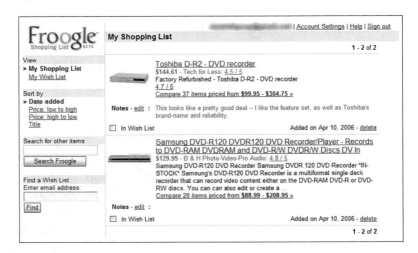

FIGURE 16.17

The contents of your shopping list on the My Shopping List page.

You can add your own personal notes to any item on your list by clicking the Edit button next to the product listing. This opens an editing text box like the one in Figure 16.18. Type your notes into the box, and then click the Save button.

FIGURE 16.18

Adding a note to a shopping list product listing.

To delete an item from your list, just click the Delete link below the product listing.

Creating a Wish List

If you want your shopping list to serve as a wish list for generous gift givers, Froogle can accommodate your wishes. A Froogle Wish List is separate from a Froogle Shopping List, although they both start at the same place. That is, you can designate items from your shopping list to add to your wish list, simply by clicking the In Wish List option next to any shopping list product listing.

You display your wish list by clicking the My Wish List link in the left column of the My Shopping List page. As you can see in Figure 16.19, this page looks similar to the My Shopping List page. (But containing your wish list items, of course.) The big difference is the link at the top of the page that displays the URL for this page. You can copy this URL and send it to your friends and family; this way, they can see what you want for your birthday or the holidays, and plan their purchases accordingly.

FIGURE 16.19
The contents of your Froogle My Wish List page.

Shopping Online with Google Catalogs

Froogle isn't the only online shopping aid that Google offers. Also available is Google Catalogs, a service that makes catalogs from a variety of major merchants, such as L.L. Bean and Crate and Barrel, available for your online browsing.

You access Google Catalogs at catalogs.google.com. As you can see in Figure 16.20, you can search for a specific catalog (using the standard Google-like search box) or browse through all catalogs in a particular product category (by clicking through the category links). There's even an Advanced Catalog Search so you can fine-tune your search parameters; it works pretty much like the Advanced Froogle Search page.

FIGURE 16.20

Searching for product catalogs with Google Catalogs.

Searching for Specific Catalogs

Searching for catalogs brings up the expected search results page, shown in Figure 16.21. The only thing really different about this page is that you get to see a thumbnail picture of each catalog in the search results. Click the thumbnail picture or the catalog title to view the contents of that catalog.

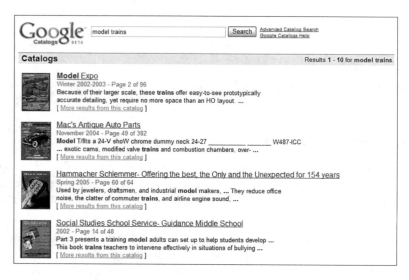

FIGURE 16.21

The results of a Google Catalog search.

Browsing by Product Category

Browsing by product category brings up a category page like the one shown in Figure 16.22. Again, you can view the contents of a catalog by clicking the catalog's thumbnail picture. You can also go directly to the catalog merchant's website, or click a link in the left column to view a smaller list of catalogs within selected product subcategories.

FIGURE 16.22
Browsing catalogs by product category.

Viewing Catalogs Online

However you find a catalog, Google Catalogs lets you view the contents of that catalog online—which is the coolest thing about this entire subsite. Every catalog listed in the Google Catalogs directory has been converted into graphics files, and is ready for your detailed viewing within your web browser.

You can display a catalog one page at a time (as shown in Figure 16.23), two pages per page (Figure 16.24), four pages up

tip The enlarged view is useful for reading all that fine print you find on a typical catalog page.

(Figure 16.25), or in an enlarged view (Figure 16.26). Just select the view from the buttons above the page graphic; flip through the pages using the right and left arrows below the page graphic.

FIGURE 16.23

A catalog in full-page view.

FIGURE 16.24
A catalog in two-page view.

FIGURE 16.25
A catalog in four-page view.

FIGURE 16.26

A catalog in enlarged view.

It's important to note that unlike most Google services, Google Catalogs relies completely on submissions by third parties—in this case, the catalog suppliers. So if you find any incorrect information, don't blame Google; all the content is supplied by the catalog merchant.

The Bottom Line

It should be no surprise that Google offers top-flight product and shopping search services; as you've previously learned, the company's core search technologies can be applied to all sorts of specialized searches.

In the case of Froogle, there's a lot to like—and a few things not to like. The big plus is Froogle's complete impartiality, as it doesn't take any paid listings (as do competing price comparison sites). The major minus is that Froogle's austerity also keeps it from offering honest-to-goodness head-to-head product comparisons, as you can find on Shopping.com and similar sites.

For these reasons, I use Froogle when I know what I'm looking for but don't know where to buy it. If I'm still in the stage of deciding what specific product I want, then Shopping.com is my site of choice; there's a lot more product information there than you'll find on Froogle.

16

Buying and Selling—Online and Locally—with Google Base

Google Base is a new Google service that's not entirely easy to describe. Some have described it as a site for online classified ads, like the increasingly popular Craigslist. Others have described it as an online marketplace, kind of like eBay without the auctions. Still others view Google Base as a giant database of products and information—and it's this description that's probably the most accurate.

Google describes Google Base as "a place where you can easily submit all types of online and offline content that we'll host and make searchable online." That sounds a lot like a big database to me. You can use Google Base to post items that you want to sell; other users can search the Google Base database to find items they want to buy. When a match is made, you and the other user arrange payment and shipping, outside of the Google system. (That's why some say Google Base is a lot like eBay, because eBay is also a "middleman" to individual transactions between users.)

Understanding Google Base

Okay, so it's probably best to think of Google Base (base.google.com) as a giant database of products and services. As Google says, the goal of Google Base is to "collect and organize information and to expose it to the world." Of course, most of the "information" that Google talks about is actually physical products, for sale by owner; the amount of free information offered in Google Base is a small subset of the total listings.

The reason that Google talks about collecting information is because that's exactly what they collect—information about physical products for sale, as well as other offline and online content. Google deals in the information about the items for sale, not in the items themselves.

The nice thing about Google Base is that it's a totally free service for both buyers and sellers. Items you post for sale on Google Base are available to users of the Google Base site; depending on their relevance (that is, their popularity vis a vis links from other websites), they may also appear on Google proper, Froogle, or Google Maps.

What kinds of items can you post on Google Base? Obviously, you can post information about physical items you're selling, from clothing to cars and just about anything in-between. You can also post nonphysical items for sale, such as poems, short stories, informational guides, cooking recipes, electronic books, digital artwork, and the like. You can even post items or information for free distribution; Google Base doesn't have to be just for selling.

And you can choose how—or, more precisely, *where*—you sell or distribute your items. If you want to use Google Base as a classified advertising service to sell items for local pickup or delivery, you can. If you want to offer items online for shipment anywhere in the country (or the world), you can. It's your choice.

After you've posted an item, it's available for searching by other Google Base users. It's possible that your item will also show up on Google proper (or on Froogle or Google Maps), but don't hold your breath; it has to build up relevance the old-fashioned way, via lots of links from other sites, before Google adds it to its normal search index.

> **note** When you post an item on Google Base, you describe it by assigning multiple keywords in the form of *labels* and *attributes*. Think of a label as the major product category (automobile, clothing, short story, and so on) and attributes as subcategories or descriptors (Ford, Taurus, 4-door, black, and so on). Potential buyers use these attributes to fine-tune their searches.

What's *Not* Permitted on Google Base

Google doesn't let you post just anything on Google Base; there are certain types of information and items that are prohibited. Most of this is common sense, but here's a short list of what you can't promote on Google Base:

- Affiliate sites or products sold through an affiliate marketing relationship
- Body parts or human remains
- Bulk marketing products, such as email lists and bulk email software
- Cable and satellite descramblers and black boxes
- Child pornography
- Copyright unlocking devices and mod chips
- Counterfeit and unauthorized goods
- Dialers
- Discounted currencies or currency exchanges
- Drug test circumvention aids
- Duplicate posted content or mirrored sites or products
- Fake government IDs and documents
- Fireworks
- Goods or services that are illegal in your country
- Illegal drugs and drug paraphernalia
- Illegal knives and weapons
- Information on how to create explosive devices
- Items and websites that promote violence or advocate violence against a protected group
- Manuals, how-to-guides, or other information that enable illegal access to software, servers, or websites—in other words, hacking and cracking materials
- Multilevel marketing or pyramid schemes
- Nonconsensual adult material
- Online casinos, sports books, or bingo games
- Prescription drugs (without valid SquareTrade certification, which is available to legitimate pharmacies in the U.S. and Canada)
- Prostitution services

17

- Rare, scarce, or valuable metals
- Toxic, explosive, flammable, or radioactive materials and substances
- Unauthorized copies of copyrighted media and software
- Unsubstantiated health cures or remedies

You also can't post on behalf of Google (unless you actually work for Google, that is), or otherwise pass yourself off as a Google employee. Google also prohibits "keyword stuffing," where you include excessive, repetitive, or irrelevant keywords in your listing.

Finding Items on Google Base

As you can see in Figure 17.1, Google Base looks a little like the main Google search page, with the addition of a handful of clickable product categories at the bottom of the page. You can find items either through searching (no surprise), or by clicking through the product categories.

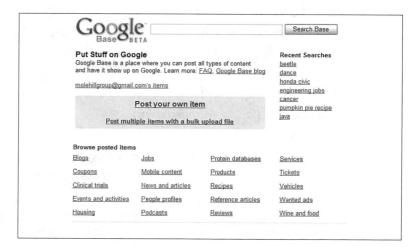

FIGURE 17.1
The Google Base main page.

Searching for Items

Searching for items on Google Base is just like searching for items on Google proper, with the addition of search refinements based on those user-assigned attributes we discussed previously.

To conduct a product search, all you have to do is enter your query into the top-of-page search box, and then click the Search Base button. Google Base now displays an initial search results page, as shown in Figure 17.2. Unfortunately, the results on this page are probably too broad to use, as it lists all the items posted in a specific category.

> **tip** You can use any of Google's advanced search operators to refine your Google Base search.

FIGURE 17.2

General results from a Google Base search.

What you want to do now is refine your search by clicking on one of the attributes listed above the search results. For example, when you search for **dvd player**, you see the following list of attributes: Products, Reviews, Vehicles, Car Catalogs, Housing, and Jobs. (There's also a Show More link, which lists additional—although less-common—attributes.) Click one of these attribute links and you see a more relevant list of results.

For example, if you're searching for a DVD player to buy, you would click the **Products** attribute link at the top of the initial search results page. This displays a page of DVD player products, like the one in Figure 17.3. If you see what you want on this page, great. If not, you may need to refine your search even more by clicking another attribute link at the top of this search results page—Location, Payment, Condition, Brand, Manufacturer, UPC, and so on. Keep refining your search by selecting more and more relevant attributes, until you find the exact items you want.

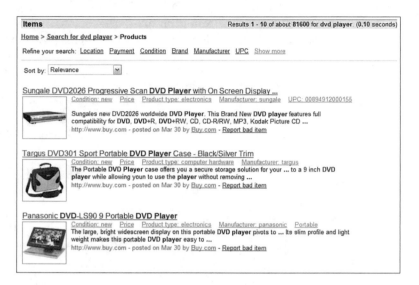

FIGURE 17.3

Search results refined by clicking on an attribute link.

For most shoppers, the location is an important attribute—chances are you're looking for something nearby, presumably within easy driving distance. When you click the **Location** attribute, Google Base displays a Location option at the top of the page, as shown in Figure 17.4. Pull down the first list to select how far away you want to search; enter your city or ZIP Code into the second box to fix your location. Check the Remember This Location option to make this your default location for future searches; click the Go button when you're ready to refine your search.

FIGURE 17.4

Limiting your search to a specific location.

Google Base now displays items for sale near you. As you can see in Figure 17.5, each listing includes the item name, a short description, the location of the item (typically the address), and a variety of links. Each of these links is a further attribute; clicking one of these attribute links doesn't display more information about the selected item, but rather redisplays the search results list with the results filtered yet again by the newly selected attribute. (I must warn you, all these attribute links can get a tad confusing; it's not necessarily the way I'd personally choose to refine my product search.)

FIGURE 17.5

A typical Google Base product listing.

When you want to find out more about a particular item listing, *don't* click one of those attribute links! Instead, click the title of the listing; this takes you directly to the product page, often hosted off-Google at a third-party site. If you then choose to purchase the item, you arrange payment and shipping directly with the seller. Your interaction with Google Base is now over.

While many items listed on Google Base are actually hosted on another site, there are also many items hosted by Google Base itself. For example, Figure 17.6 shows a Google Base–hosted apartment listing page. To contact the seller, scroll down the Contact section and click the Contact the Poster link.

Browsing for Items

In addition to the standard product search, Google Base lets you browse through some of the most popular product categories. Note, however, that browsing is seldom an efficient method of finding stuff.

You start your browsing by clicking a product category on the main Google Base page. Let's say you're searching for local housing, so you click the **Housing** link. This displays a search results page with all available housing listings in the entire Google Base database—not very useful.

note Many of Google Base's product listings are hosted by ShopLocal.com, a site used by big retailers to post local listings. You can tell where the listing originates by viewing the green URL at the end of each product listing.

What is useful is the list of attributes at the top of the page or, in the case of the Housing category, the top-of-page refinement controls shown in Figure 17.7. If you're looking for housing, you can specify any or all of the following attributes:

- Location
- Listing type (for rent, for sale, room for rent)
- Bathrooms (number)
- Price
- Bedrooms (number)
- Property type (apartment, bungalow, condominium unit, and so on)

FIGURE 17.6

An apartment rental page hosted by Google Base.

Other categories have similar refinement controls and attributes; make your selection to narrow down the available choices.

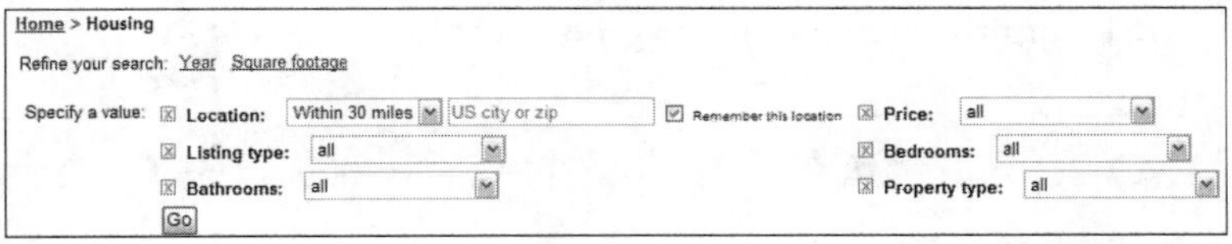

FIGURE 17.7

Refining your browsing for housing.

Buying Items with Google Payments

Remember when I said that all purchase transactions are solely between the buyer and the seller, that Google Base isn't directly involved? Well, that's only partially true.

As I write these words, Google is evaluating a system that would let buyers purchase products directly from a Google Base listing page, using their Google Accounts. Of course, for this to work, Google would have to institute some sort of electronic payment service, similar to eBay's PayPal service; not surprisingly, Google has already done this, in the form of what Google dubs Google Payments.

The Google Payments program lets any seller accept payment via credit card; Google Payments handles the entire credit card transaction, so that the process is transparent to the buyer. When a seller accepts payment via Google Payments, you'll see a Buy button on the seller's product listing page, like the one in Figure 17.8. You'll also see the "I accept payment through Google" line in the Payment section of the page.

When you click the Buy button, you'll see a Review Order Details page, like the one shown in Figure 17.9. Fill out all the information on this page, including your credit card number and billing address, and then click the Agree and Continue button.

Google now displays the Confirm Purchase page shown in Figure 17.10. Click the Place Your Order Now button on this page and your payment is entered and the transaction concluded. Google displays a thank you screen and sends you a confirmation email. It's pretty painless.

FIGURE 17.8

This seller accepts payment via Google Payments.

Remember, though, that sellers are not required to accept Google Payments. So don't expect every item listed on Google Base to include the Buy button or Google Payment option.

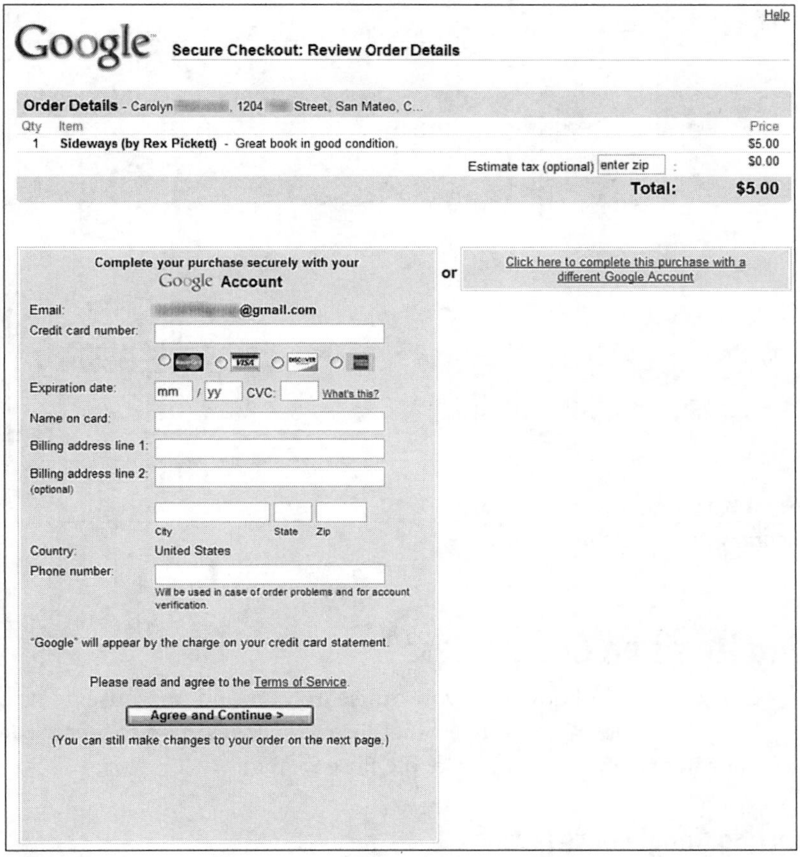

FIGURE 17.9
Entering billing and credit card information.

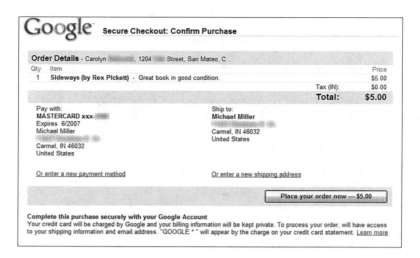

FIGURE 17.10
Completing your Google Base purchase.

Selling Items on Google Base

Okay, now you know how you can search for and purchase items on Google Base. But what if you have something to sell? Read on to learn how to post your items for sale on the Google Base system.

Submitting Google Base Listings

Creating a listing with Google Base is a relatively easy process. All you have to do is follow these steps:

1. From the main Google Base page, click the Post Your Own Item link.

2. The next page, shown in Figure 17.11, prompts you to select an item type. This should be the main product category for your listing. You can probably find a category that fits by pulling down the Choose an Existing Item Type list; if not, enter a new category into the Create Your Own Item Type box. Click the Next button to continue.

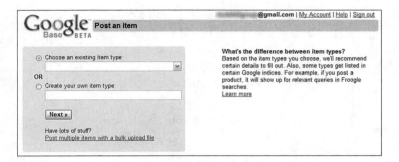

FIGURE 17.11

Selecting an item type.

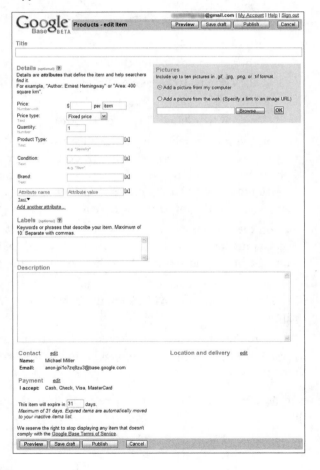

FIGURE 17.12

Entering product details.

3. The next page, shown in Figure 17.12, is where you enter all the details about what you're selling. While the specific details will vary by item type, here's what you're likely to encounter:

tip   You'll need to click the Edit link in the Location and Delivery section to specify your shipping costs for this item.

- Title (the heading of your item listing)
- Price
- Price type (fixed price, minimum price, or negotiable)
- Quantity
- Product type
- Condition
- Brand
- Other attributes (below the Brand box)
- Labels (up to 10 keywords that describe your item, separated by commas)
- Description (detailed text description)

4. Still on the same page, move to the Pictures section (top right) and add up to 10 photos of your item. You can add a picture hosted on another website by entering the photo's complete URL, or you can click the Browse button to upload pictures stored on your PC. Click OK after you've entered the information for each photo.

5. Still on the same page, scroll down to the bottom of the page and check your Contact, Payment, and Location and Delivery information. Click the appropriate Edit link to change any of this info.

6. Still on the same page, enter the length of time you want this listing to last into the This Item Will Expire in *XX* Days field. Your listings can run a maximum of 31 days.

7. When you're done entering information, click the Preview button to preview your listing, or the Publish button to finalize and post your listing.

The resulting listing, like the one in Figure 17.13, is now live. Good luck with the selling!

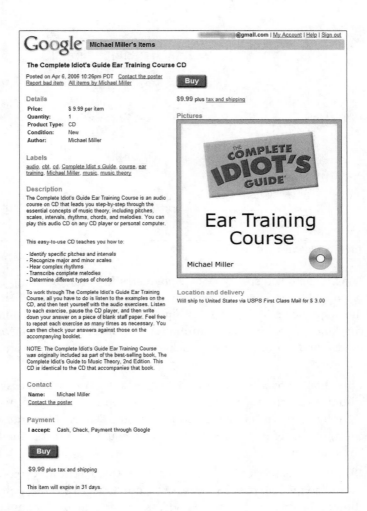

FIGURE 17.13

A live Google Base listing.

Accepting Google Payments

If you want to accept payment via Google Payments (which lets you accept credit card payments), you'll need to specify this separately when you're creating the product listing. When you click the Edit button in the Payment section, you'll see the section expand to display the options shown in Figure 17.14. Check the Accept Payment Through Google option and then complete the rest of your item listing.

17

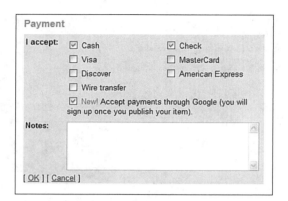

FIGURE 17.14

Selecting the Google Payments option.

The first time you specify Google Payments for an item listing, you'll be prompted to sign up to accept payments through Google. When you see the page shown in Figure 17.15, enter your name, address, phone number, checking/savings account information (for direct deposit of payment funds), and so on. When you click the Next button, your account is activated.

Why should you sign up for Google Payments? Well, it's an easy way for individuals to accept payment via credit card—which is the preferred form of payment by most buyers. Google handles all the details of the transaction; in effect, the buyer pays Google, and then Google deposits the funds in your bank account.

Of course, this service isn't free. (What is?) Google charges you 2.5% of the transaction value, plus 25 cents per transaction. This is less than PayPal charges for similar services on eBay; it's a fair deal, and should be factored into your cost of doing business.

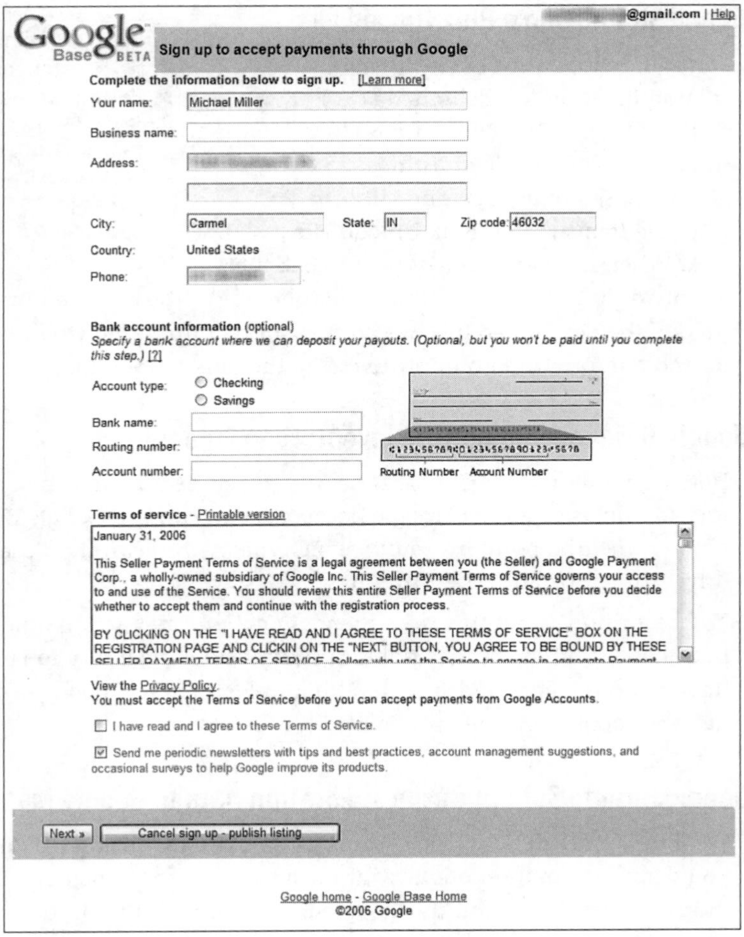

FIGURE 17.15
Entering information to establish your Google Payments account.

Uploading Bulk Items

The process previously described is the way to list individual items for sale. But if you have a lot of items to post, you're better off using Google Base's bulk upload function. You can prepare your list of items offline, and then upload them all in a single file.

Creating and Submitting a Bulk Upload File

For bulk uploading, Google accepts information in either tab-delimited (TSV) or XML (RSS 1.0, RSS 2.0, or Atom 0.2) formats. To upload a file of listings, go to the Google Base home page and click the Post Multiple Items with a Bulk Upload File link. When the next page appears, click the Specify a Bulk Upload File link, and then follow the onscreen instructions to upload the designated file. See base.google.com/base/howtobulkupload.html for more information on how to create the bulk upload file.

> **tip** If you want more exposure for your Google Base posting, consider using Google's AdWords program. Learn more in Chapter 37, "Making Money with Google AdSense and AdWords."

Using Google Base to Submit Store Inventory to Froogle

Here's another use for Google Base—it lets retailers submit their store inventory for inclusion in the Froogle database. You can use Google Base to submit both online and retail inventory, which means you can then use Froogle to drive traffic to your local location.

The best thing about this is it's the identical process used to upload bulk postings to Google Base. That's right, to submit store inventory to Froogle all you have to do is create and submit a bulk upload file to Google Base. Learn more at www.google.com/sellonfroogle/.

Using Google Base to Submit Business Location Data to Google Maps

We'll talk more about Google Maps in Chapter 18, "Using Google Maps." If you want information about your local business to be included in the Google Maps database, you can use Google Base to submit that information.

Again, the process to upload business location data is the same for submitting any bulk upload file to Google Base. You'll need to create a file with your business location information (in tab-delimited or XML format), and then upload that file from the Google Base main page. Get explicit instructions at base.google.com/base/business_feed_instructions.html.

> **note** This process is specifically for businesses with 10 or more unique locations. If you have fewer locations, you can submit them using the Google Local Business Center, as explained in Chapter 18.

COMMENTARY:

GOOGLE VERSUS EBAY?

Here's a question for you. If Google Base lets individuals advertise items to other individuals online, and if Google Base offers an online payment service that lets individuals accept credit card payments, then how is Google Base different from eBay?

While the folks at Google insist that Google Base isn't meant to compete with eBay, it's quite clear that it will—to one degree or another. Google Base is, quite simply, an online marketplace that brings together buyers and sellers and facilitates their transactions. That's exactly what eBay does.

Of course, there are differences. Google Base doesn't offer an online auction function, which eBay does. (Although Google Base does offer a "negotiated price" option, where you can haggle with an interested buyer.) Google Base is also a bit more than a simple product marketplace, in that it offers craigslist-style classified ads. And, at this point in time, Google Base is much, much smaller than eBay—although that could change as the months go by.

Then there are the costs. eBay charges a fee to list an item for sale, and another fee when the item is sold. Google Base charges neither. eBay also charges when you include more than one photo of your item, which Google Base doesn't. There's even a difference in the sites' online payment services; eBay's PayPal charges 2.9% of the final transaction price plus 35 cents per transaction, where Google Payments charges just 2.5% of the final transaction price plus 25 cents per transaction. If this price differential holds, a seller could save $8 or so on a $100 transaction. That's not peanuts, folks.

But maybe the folks at Google are sincere about not viewing Google Base as direct competition to eBay. Obviously, Google is okay with generating less revenue per transaction than eBay does. No, it's likely that Google views Google Base as yet another vehicle for generating advertising revenue. And, as you recall from my commentary in Chapter 1, "Inside Google," Google is very much an advertising-based business, in spite of its superficial focus on search technology. The more listings that appear on Google Base, the more opportunities Google has to sell ad space. It may be that simple.

17

In addition, Google may be able to use its Google Payments system to generate immediate revenue from the ads it serves. Imagine a user clicking an ad, and then being offered the immediate opportunity to purchase the advertised product—facilitated by Google Payments, of course. It's a win-win for Google.

All that said, consumers' perception matters. And if online buyers and sellers perceive that Google Base is an attractive alternative to eBay, Google will find itself competing head-to-head with the world's current largest online marketplace. Is that a battle Google can win? I don't know; to date, both Google and eBay have been companies you don't bet against. How they fare in a direct battle is impossible to call.

The Bottom Line

Google Base is a new online marketplace that lets users offer all manner of goods and services for sale or free distribution over the Internet. These products can be purely for local delivery or pickup, or for shipment across the country or around the world. Interested buyers can search the Google Base database for items they want, and then make their purchases using credit cards, thanks to the new Google Payments online payment service.

Yes, it sounds like a mash-up of eBay, craigslist, and Google's existing search technology—which is what it is. The success or failure of Google Base will depend on how many sellers the service attracts (to create a critical mass of items for sale), as well as how many potential buyers are drawn to the site.

Is Google Base for you? The answer is a qualified "maybe." Since Google doesn't charge any fees to list an item for sale (you only pay if the item sells and the buyer pays via Google Payments), there's no harm for sellers to give Google Base a spin. And as a buyer, there's also no harm in shopping; if you find something to buy, great, if not, no big deal.

So that's Google Base. Check it out and see what *you* think.

Maps and Directions

18 Using Google Maps

19 Using Google Map Mashups

20 Using Google Earth

Using Google Maps

Not sure how to get to a particular location? In the old, pre-Internet days you had to try to find addresses on your AAA roadmap, or humble yourself by stopping and asking directions at the local gas station. Thanks to the Internet, however, you can now use Google Maps to generate online maps and driving directions.

You'll never stop for directions again.

Introducing Google Maps

Of all the cool Google features, I find Google Maps the absolute coolest. Not only does Google Maps compete head-to-head with other online mapping sites, such as MapQuest and Yahoo! Maps, but it offers a raft of unique and, dare I say, *fun* features. It'll help you get to where you want to go, and show you a lot of neat and useful information on the way there.

Google Maps (maps.google.com) offers a ton of useful mapping services, all packed into an easy-to-use interface. Yes, you can generate maps for any given address or location, but you can also click and drag the maps to view adjacent sections, overlay the map info on satellite images of the given area, display nearby businesses as a series of pushpins on the map, and have Google Local plot driving directions to and from this location to any other location.

And all this map and direction stuff is done from the familiar Google search box. Unlike other map sites, there are no forms to fill out; just enter what you want to see into the search box, and let Google Maps do the rest.

COMMENTARY:

FROM MAPS TO LOCAL AND BACK AGAIN

Here's something interesting. The Google Maps you know and love wasn't always called Google Maps. Oh, that was its original name, but for about six months in 2005–2006, Google changed the name to Google Local. It doesn't matter that Google Local was previously the name of another Google service that housed a database of local merchants; Google rolled the two services together and gave the whole thing the name Google Local.

Why was this? In October 2005, the Taiwanese government protested against its listing in Google Maps. Google Maps had displayed the label "Taiwan, Province of China," which offended the Taiwanese, who view themselves as a sovereign nation. The People's Republic of China, however, views Taiwan as a renegade province. By labeling Taiwan as a province of China on its maps (which, by the way, is the same way the United Nations refers to Taiwan), Google inadvertently created an international incident.

Google's solution was uniquely creative. It accelerated the merger of the technologies behind Google Maps and Google Local, renamed the whole thing Google Local, and changed the label for Taiwan to remove the "Province of China" text. Google could claim to Taiwan that it had bowed to their concerns (by changing the map), while at the same time saying to China that it didn't actually change the map, it launched a completely new service. Like I said, a creative solution.

The problem with this solution, of course, is that Google's users continued to refer to the service as Google Maps. It didn't matter that the Google Local logo was at the top of the page, it was "Google Maps" as far as most users were concerned. So, in May 2006, Google relented and rechristened the site Google Maps—the name it should have kept all along.

Searching for Maps

As the name implies, Google Maps is all about the maps. To display a map of a given location, all you have to do is enter information about that location into the top-of-page search box, shown in Figure 18.1. When you click the Search button, a map of that location is displayed on the page.

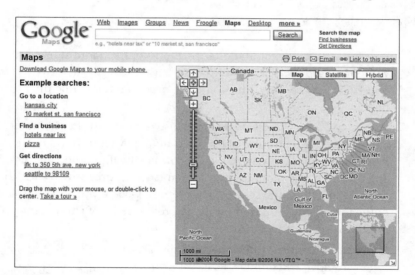

FIGURE 18.1
The Google Maps home page.

Searching by Address

The most obvious way to display a map of a given location is to enter the location's street address or general location. There are a number of ways you can enter an address or a location, as detailed in Table 18.1:

Table 18.1   Google Maps Address Formats

Address Format	Example
city, state	indianapolis, in
zip	46204
address, city, state	101 e washington street, indianapolis, in
address, city, zip	101 e washington street, indianapolis, 46204
street intersection, city, state	e washington and n Pennsylvania, indianapolis, in (can use the & sign instead of the word "and")
street intersection, zip	e washington and n Pennsylvania, indianapolis, 46204 (can use the & sign instead of the word "and")
latitude, longitude	39.767, -86.156
airport code	LAX
subway station, country (in UK and Japan only)	paddington, uk

Remember to put a comma after each part of the address. In most instances, you don't need to spell out words like "east," "street," or "drive"; common abbreviations are okay, and you don't need to put a period after the abbreviation.

For many major cities, Google Maps also accepts just the city name. For example, entering **miami** gives you a map of Miami, Florida; entering **san francisco** displays a map of the California city. If, on the other hand, you enter a city name that's fairly common (such as **greentown**—which appears in Indiana, Ohio, and several other states), Google will either display a map of the largest city with that name, or provide a list of cities or matching businesses for you to choose from.

If you want to enter latitude and longitude, you have two options. First, You can enter latitude and longitude as decimal degrees, using the - sign to express west longitude or south latitude. Second, you can use N, S, E, and W designations. What you *can't* do is express latitude and longitude using degrees-minutes-seconds (such as 28 24' 23.4"); Google doesn't recognize the ' and " syntax.

If Google doesn't recognize an address you entered (such as when an address could

> **caution** You can't enter just a state name or abbreviation. While Google recognizes most cities, it doesn't recognize states or countries.

> **tip** You can use any of Google's advanced search operators (discussed in Chapter 2, "Searching the Web") to fine-tune your Google Maps searches.

either be on an "east" or a "west" street, or the same address for a "drive" and a "lane"), Google will display a list of possible addresses, as shown in Figure 18.2. Assuming you can identify the correct address from this list, click the link to display the map of that location.

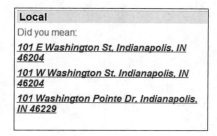

Local

Did you mean:

101 E Washington St, Indianapolis, IN 46204

101 W Washington St, Indianapolis, IN 46204

101 Washington Pointe Dr, Indianapolis, IN 46229

FIGURE 18.2

Google Maps sometimes asks for an address clarification.

Searching by Landmark

Sometimes you don't need to know the exact address to generate a Google map. Google has hard-coded many landmarks and institutions into its map database, so that you only have to enter the name of the landmark or location into the search box.

For example, entering **golden gate bridge** generates the map shown in Figure 18.3; entering **fenway park** generates the map shown in Figure 18.4.

FIGURE 18.3

Golden Gate Bridge on a Google map.

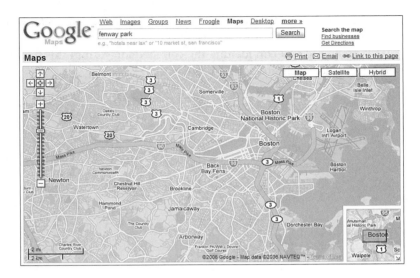

FIGURE 18.4

Fenway Park on a Google map.

Displaying Google Maps by Entering a URL

As you learned back in Chapter 2, any time you enter a Google search, the resulting page is identified by a unique URL. This URL contains the keywords in the query, as well as parameters that define how the results are displayed.

Google uses this same approach to generate its map URLs. If you know the parameters that Google uses to create certain types of maps, you can create your own map URLs, and enter these URLs directly into the address box of your web browser.

Now, this might seem like a lot of work for something that Google does automatically, but manually entering a map URL has certain benefits. The chief benefit is that you can use this technique to generate maps from your own custom data. Let's say, for example, that you have a spreadsheet of your co-workers' names and addresses. If you want to generate maps of your colleagues' locations, you can use the URL manipulation technique to create the map URLs, thus bypassing the standard data entry process.

The key to doing this, of course, is understanding the components of Google's map

caution What landmarks are and are not in the Google Maps database is somewhat arbitrary. It's always worth trying, but don't be disappointed if what you're looking for isn't so easily found.

URL. While these URLs might look complex at first glance, they're actually fairly straightforward.

Let's look at a typical map URL:

```
maps.google.com/maps?q=minneapolis,mn&hl=en
```

Dissecting this URL, we see that the first part of the address (maps.google .com/maps) gets us to the Google map server. The next bit (?q=) specifies the start of the query. Next comes the location entered (minneapolis,mn), in this example in the form of *city,state*. Finally, the whole thing ends with a &hl=en parameter, which tells Google to display the map in English.

The real trick here is inserting the location after the ?q= and before the &hl=en parameters. You want to enter the location exactly as you would in the Google Maps search box, with the stipulation that you replace every space in the location with a + sign. So, for example, if you wanted to display a map of New York City, you'd enter **new+york,ny**; if you wanted a map of Apple Valley, Minnesota, you'd enter **apple+valley,mn**.

The same thing goes with full street addresses. Enter the address as you would normally, but with + signs in place of any and all spaces in the address. Take, for example, the following address: 101 E Washington Street, Indianapolis, 46204. When you convert this into URL format, the full address looks like this:

```
maps.google.com/maps?q=101+e+washington+street,+indianapolis,+46204
```

You can also use additional parameters to further dictate what type of map is displayed:

- **&t=*x*.** Defines the imagery type. Replace *x* with **k** to display a satellite map, or **h** to display a hybrid map.

- **&ll=*x,y*.** Displays a map centered on a specific latitude (x) and longitude (y).

- **&spn=*x,y*.** Defines the size of the map area, in degrees latitude (x) and longitude (y).

- **&z=*x*.** Also defines the map area in terms of level of zoom. Replace *x* with a number between 3 (maximum zoom in) to 12 (maximum zoom out).

Like I said, it looks complicated, but it's really quite simple.

Displaying Street Maps from a Google Web Search

Here's another tip. You don't have to go to the Google Maps page to display a Google map. When you enter a street address, city, and state (or ZIP Code)

18

into the standard Google web search box, the OneBox listing search results page will be a Show Map listing like the one in Figure 18.5. This listing includes a link to the location's map on Google Maps, Yahoo! Maps, and MapQuest. Click the desired link to display the associated map full-size.

FIGURE 18.5

Map results from the standard Google search page.

Navigating a Google Map

Once you have a Google map displayed onscreen, there are many, many different ways to navigate around, into, and out of the map—both with your mouse and with your computer keyboard. Table 18.2 describes the ways:

Table 18.2   Google Map Navigation

Navigation	With Mouse	With Keyboard
Pan left (west)	Click the left arrow button	Press the left-arrow key—or pan wider with the Home key
Pan right (east)	Click the right arrow button	Press the right-arrow key—or pan wider with the End key
Pan up (north)	Click the top arrow button	Press the up-arrow key—or pan wider with the Page Up key
Pan down (south)	Click the bottom arrow button	Press the down-arrow key—or pan wider with the Page Down key
Zoom out (wider area)	Click the - button *or* drag the zoom slider down	Press the - key
Zoom in (smaller area)	Click the + button *or* drag the zoom slider up	Press the + key

You can drag the map in any direction by positioning the cursor anywhere on the map, clicking and holding the mouse button, and then dragging the map around. You can also reposition the map by dragging the little blue rectangle in the inset map (located in the lower-right corner of the main map) to a new location. And you can simply center the map on a new location by positioning the cursor over that location and then double-clicking the mouse.

The closer you zoom in, the more detail displayed on the map. You won't see specific road information until you're fairly zoomed in; even then, major roads are displayed

tip

To re-display the last map you viewed, click the Return to Last Result button in the middle of the arrow buttons on the map.

first, and then minor roads displayed on more extreme zoom levels. For example, Figures 18.6, 18.7, and 18.8 show different levels of zoom over Branson, Missouri; note the emergence of detailed road info at the closer zoom levels.

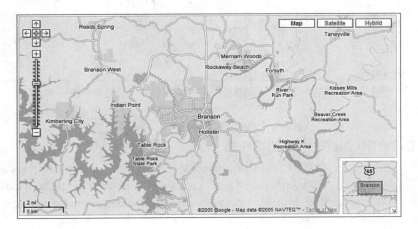

FIGURE 18.6

Branson, Missouri—not so close up.

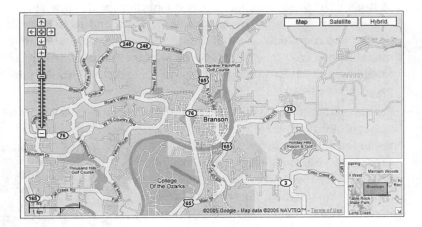

FIGURE 18.7

Branson, viewed a little closer—note the major highway labeling.

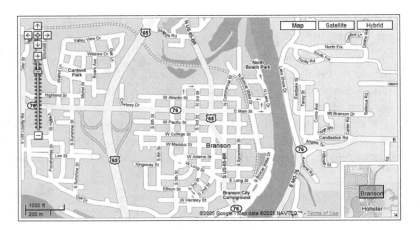

FIGURE 18.8

Branson at a more extreme zoom—even the smallest streets are labeled.

Displaying Satellite Images

By default, Google Maps displays a standard map of any location you enter. But that's not the only way you can view a location. Google Maps also incorporates satellite images, which lets you get a bird's eye view on the actual location. It's like having access to your very own spy satellite!

The View from Above

To display the satellite image of a location, click the Satellite button at the top of the map. You can use the standard navigation and zoom controls to pan around and zoom into or out of the satellite image. Depending on the level of magnification, you may be able to see rooftops and trees. (Figure 18.9 shows a satellite map of Shea Stadium—if it were game day, you could almost see the people in the seats!)

If you zoom in too far, you may reach the limits of the satellite imagery. That is, not all locations have super high-resolution satellite photos. When you zoom in too far, you'll see a screen like the one in Figure 18.10, with the repeated message "We are sorry, but we don't have imagery at this zoom level for this region." If you see this message, zoom out a little to see what you can see.

> **note** Google Maps sources its map from NAVTEQ and TeleAtlas. It sources its satellite images from DigitalGlobe and EarthSat. Note that the satellite images are apt to be less current than the map data.

FIGURE 18.9

A satellite map of Shea Stadium.

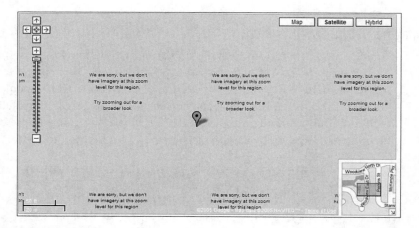

FIGURE 18.10

Oops—you zoomed in too far!

And here's something kind of creepy. Some satellite images have been digi-tally altered, supposedly for "national security" reasons. For example, Figure 18.11 shows 1 Observatory Circle in Washington, DC, the official residence of the Vice President. As you can see, the entire area has been pixilated on the map to keep anyone (terrorists included, I suppose) from seeing what's going on there. (Interestingly, a similar view of the White House is completely unpixelated, which makes one wonder what it is about the VP's place that makes it more top secret than the President's house...)

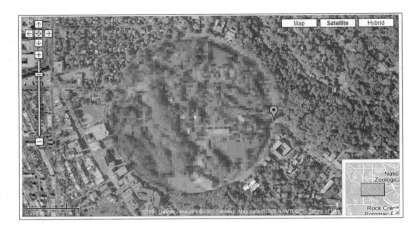

FIGURE 18.11

A digitally altered satellite image of the Vice President's residence.

Displaying Hybrid Satellite Maps

Satellite maps are fun (try looking up the map for your own house!), but not always as useful as a standard map, especially when you're going to be driving somewhere. What you might want to try, instead, is what Google calls a "hybrid" map. What this is, as you can see in Figure 18.12, is a satellite image with map info overlaid on top of it. It's actually a nice compromise of visual identification and useful data; just click the Hybrid button to see for yourself.

FIGURE 18.12

A hybrid map that overlays street names on a satellite image.

Sharing Maps

Once you've created a map of a given location, it would be great if you could save the map for use in the future—rather than re-entering the location and manipulating the navigation and zoom controls. Fortunately, there are several ways to save and share the maps you create. Read on to learn more.

Linking to a Specific Map

The key to saving or sharing any map you've created is that Google assigns every possible map its own unique URL. When you know the URL, you can share it with others—or save it to your computer desktop.

Here's how it works:

1. Create a map for the desired location.

2. Click the Link to This Page link.

3. Google now displays a long URL in the Address box of your web browser. Highlight this URL, right-click your mouse, and select Copy from the pop-up menu.

4. To paste this link into an email message or text document, position your cursor in the message, right-click your mouse, and select Paste from the pop-up menu.

Alternatively, you can save the map as a shortcut on your desktop. To do this, create the map, click the Link to This Page button, and then drag the URL from your browser's Address box onto your desktop.

Emailing a Map

There's an even easier way to email a map to friends and family—or to yourself, so you'll have a link to the map as a message in your inbox. Just follow these steps:

1. Create a map for the desired location.

2. Click the Email link.

3. This opens a new email message in your default email program. As you can see in Figure 18.13, the link to the map is displayed in the text of the message; enter the recipient's email address, and then click the Send button.

tip If you're running Google Desktop, Google offers a Maps gadget for the sidebar. Learn more in Chapter 32, "Using Google Desktop."

18

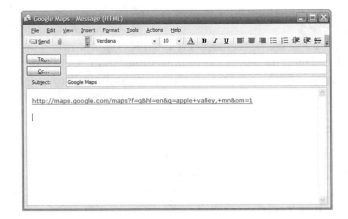

FIGURE 18.13

Emailing a link to a map you created.

Printing a Map

Of course, you can also just print a hard copy of the map. This is as easy as clicking the Print link above the map you've created; nothing more is necessary.

Displaying Driving Directions

Google Maps does more than just display maps; it can also generate driving directions from one location to another. It's a simple matter of entering two locations, and letting Google get you from point A to point B.

Generating Turn-by-Turn Directions

To generate driving directions, follow these steps:

1. From the Google Maps main page, click the Get Directions link in the top-right corner of the page.
2. The top of the page now changes to include two search boxes, as shown in Figure 18.14. Enter your starting location into the left Start Address box, and your ending location into the right End Address box.
3. Click the Search button.

FIGURE 18.14

Entering Start and End addresses.

Google also lets you generate driving directions directly from the Google Maps search box. Just enter your first location, followed by the word **to**, followed by the second location. For example to drive from San Francisco International Airport to the Transamerica Building in downtown San Francisco, enter **SFO to 505 sansome st, san Francisco, ca**, as shown in Figure 18.15.

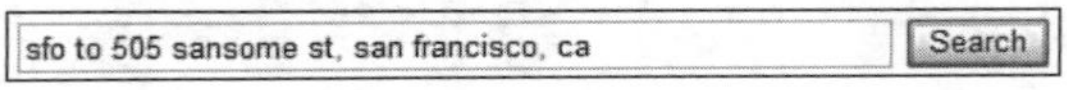

> sfo to 505 sansome st, san francisco, ca   Search

FIGURE 18.15

Generating driving directions from the search box.

You can also generate driving directions to or from any location you've previously mapped. When the location is pinpointed on the map, you see an info box like the one in Figure 18.16. To generate driving directions to or from this location, click either the To Here or From Here links. The info box now changes to include a Start Address or End Address box, as shown in Figure 18.17; enter the second address, and then click the Get Directions button.

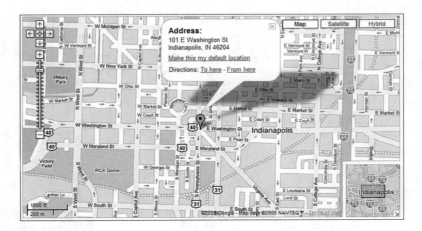

FIGURE 18.16

Generating driving directions from a previously mapped location.

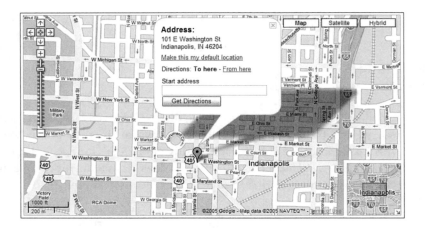

FIGURE 18.17
Entering the second address from the previously mapped location.

Following Directions

However you enter the two locations, Google now generates a page of driving instructions, as shown in Figure 18.18. The step-by-step directions are listed on the left side of the page; an overview map is displayed on the right.

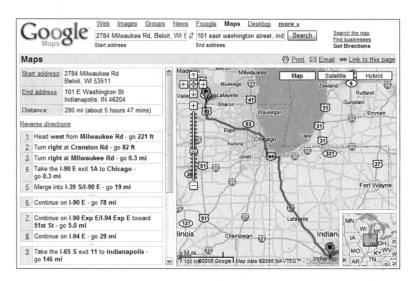

FIGURE 18.18
Driving directions and a map of your route.

It seems pretty straight ahead so far, but there's a neat little feature hidden on this page. When you click any of the numbered steps on the left, a magnified map pops up on top of the overview map, detailing that particular step, as shown in Figure 18.19. This is a great way to see those detailed directions that are easy to misunderstand.

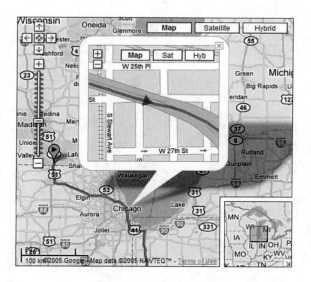

FIGURE 18.19

A pop-up map that zooms into a particular piece of your route.

In addition, you have the option of displaying a standard map (as shown in Figure 18.20), a satellite image of your route (as shown in Figure 18.21), or a hybrid map with your route overlaid on a satellite image (as shown in Figure 18.22). I prefer the hybrid map, but use whichever type of map that works best for you.

Getting Back Home Again

When you're driving from point A to point B, at some time you probably want to drive back to point A again. With Google Maps you don't have to re-enter your start and end locations again (in reverse order, of course); instead, you can simply click the Reverse Directions link. This displays a new route from your original end location back to your original start location. It's a snap.

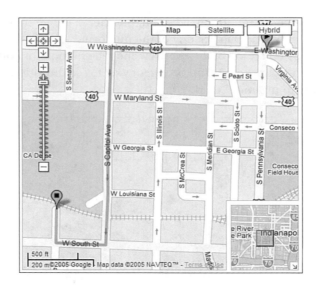

FIGURE 18.20
Your route displayed as a standard map.

FIGURE 18.21
Your route displayed as a satellite image.

FIGURE 18.22
Your route displayed as a hybrid map/satellite image.

Printing Your Directions

One last thing. Google Maps' driving directions are great, but they won't do you any good if they're displayed on your home PC screen while you're on the road. To take a copy of your directions with you, just click the Print link. This makes a hard copy printout of the directions page, map and all.

COMMENTARY:

BAD DIRECTIONS

I've learned from experience that Google's driving directions aren't always perfect. Sometimes they provide a longer or more circuitous route than you might prefer; sometimes they include roads that are under construction or closed; and sometimes they're just plain wrong. As an example, Google recently directed my girlfriend to turn the wrong way into a one-way street—not an ideal route!

Google recognizes this, and provides the following caution in the Google Maps help system:

Google Maps may occasionally display incorrect locations or directions. You may also find that the icon for a location you've mapped on a satellite image is off by a house or two. Please be assured that we're continually working to improve the accuracy of this service.

Like that really helps when you've just turned into a road that isn't there. While it's good to know they admit they have occasional problems, I'd rather not have to deal with bad directions from the start.

If you're served up bad directions or a faulty map, you can let Google know about it by going to maps.google.com/support/bin/request.py. This page leads to a series of web forms that let you input your complaints and criticisms—including specific errors you encounter. Use it, but be polite.

I've also found that Google Maps sometimes offers different routes than served up by MapQuest, Yahoo! Maps, and other competing map sites. I'm not sure why this is; perhaps the different services use different algorithms to determine the shortest or most direct route. In any case, I recommend inputting your coordinates into several map sites when you're planning a longer trip; you might find a better route than the one Google Maps provides.

Then there's the matter of what Google Maps *doesn't* do. In particular, Google Maps doesn't let you create multiple-stop driving directions. That is, you can only create directions for getting from point A to point B. If your trip involves going from point A to point B with a stop at point C, you're out of luck.

To be fair, most online map sites are like Google Maps in this regard; they only provide point-to-point driving directions. One exception to this is the Rand McNally travel site (www.randmcnally.com). While this site's standard driving directions are point-to-point, like Google's, if you go to the Road Trip Planner page, you can create a trip with multiple stops. So if you want to drive from Las Vegas to Los Angeles to San Francisco to Portland, Rand McNally will generate driving directions for each leg of the trip. With Google Maps, you'd have to treat each leg as a separate set of directions; I give the edge to Rand McNally (a little-known site, to be sure) in this instance.

Setting Your Default Location

Whether you're using Google Maps to display maps or driving directions, chances are you'll be dealing with one location more than others—typically your home or office, as the "start" location. Instead of entering this address every time you log onto the Google Maps site, you can set this location as Google Maps' default location. This default location is automatically entered as the default map and as the start address for driving directions.

To enter an address as your default location, start by entering the address into the search box, and then click the Search button. When the map appears, click the Make This My Default Location link in the pinpoint info box. That's all there is to it.

To remove a default location you've set, start by logging on fresh to the Google Maps site. Your default location now appears as the main screen map, and there's a Starting At… section on the left side of the page, as shown in Figure 18.23. Click the Clear link next to the Starting At… entry, and the default location will be removed.

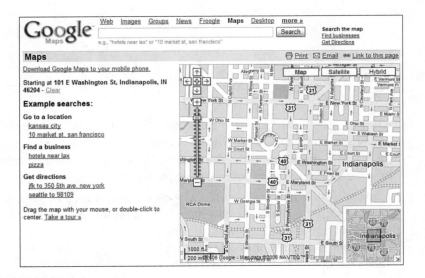

FIGURE 18.23

Google Maps programmed with a default starting location.

Finding Nearby Businesses

Before Google Maps became Google Maps, there was a separate Google Local service that included a large database of local retailers for your searching pleasure. Well, that Google Local service is now part of Google Maps, which means you can search any mapped location for nearby businesses.

Thanks to the database of local retailers, you can use Google Maps to search within any area or neighborhood, or near any address. You use the **near** operator to search for local merchants, in the following formats:

- *service near zip*, as in **pizza 46032** or **pizza near 46032**, as shown in Figure 18.24.
- *service near city, state*, as in **pizza carmel, in** or **pizza near carmel, in**, as shown in Figure 18.25.

| pizza 46032 | Search |

FIGURE 18.24

Searching for pizza in a specific ZIP Code.

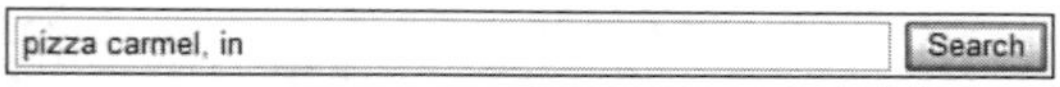

| pizza carmel, in | Search |

FIGURE 18.25

Searching for pizza in a given city.

If you already have a location called on a map, you don't even have to enter the location into the search box. Just enter the type of service you want (**pizza**, for example) into the Google Maps search box, and the current map location will be searched for matching businesses.

When you click the Search button, Google displays a map of the specified location with matching businesses pinpointed on the map and listed on the left side of the page, as shown in Figure 18.26. Matching categories are also listed above the business list; click a category link to expand or narrow your search, accordingly.

> **tip** You can skip the **near** operator if you like, and simply enter *service zip* or *service city, state*.

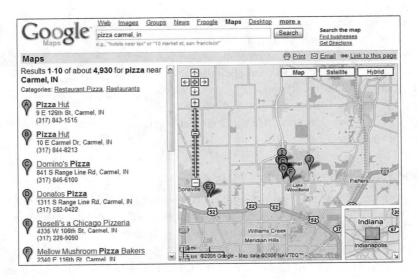

FIGURE 18.26

The results of a Google Maps business search.

When you click a business name or pinpoint, an information box appears, as shown in Figure 18.27. Most info boxes have two tabs. The Address tab lists the business name, address, phone number, website URL, and so on. The Details tab lists additional information, including links to online reviews and mentions, if any exist. Click the appropriate links to display more information.

FIGURE 18.27

Displaying more information about a given business.

Note that Google Maps only lists 10 businesses per page. To display the next page
of results, you have to scroll down the left
side of the page and then click the Next
link. The map will change (zoom in or out)
to display this next batch of businesses;
Google Maps typically lists the closest businesses first, and then expands its
results, geographically.

> **tip** You can also use the Local Business Center to correct or delete existing business information.

Adding Your Business to Google Maps

Google Maps gathers the bulk of its local retailer information from various
Yellow Pages directories. Since these directories are not always accurate or up-
to-date, it's possible that some businesses (newer ones, especially) might not be
included.

If you run a local business that for some reason doesn't show up in the Google
Maps results, you can contact Google to add your business info to the database. You do this from the Local Business Center (www.google.com/local/add/),
shown in Figure 18.28. Follow the onscreen instructions to submit your business info.

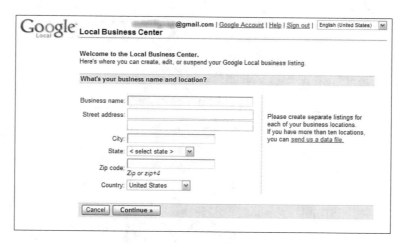

FIGURE 18.28

Adding information on your business to Google Maps.

Using Google Maps on Your Cell Phone

The maps and directions in Google Maps aren't limited to use on your desktop or notebook PC; you can also take them with you on your cell phone. We'll talk more about all of Google's mobile services in Chapter 30, "Using Google Mobile Services," but let's take a quick look now at Google's mobile mapping services.

Sending Map Info to Your Cell Phone

First, you can send any page of business information in Google Maps to any U.S. cellular phone number that includes a text messaging service. It's part of Google's Send to Phone feature, and it's really easy to use.

Whenever you pinpoint a business on a Google map, you'll see an info box for that business, as shown in Figure 18.29. Within this info box is a Send to Phone link. When you click this link, Google displays a Send to Phone info box, like the one in Figure 18.30. This info box displays the information that you'll be sending; enter your phone number into the To: box, and then pull down the Carrier list and select your cell phone carrier. When you click the Send button, this information will be messaged to your cell phone.

FIGURE 18.29

Click the Send to Phone link to send business info to a cell phone.

FIGURE 18.30

Enter your cell phone number and carrier to send the info.

Querying Google Maps via Text Message

Here's a cool—and free—feature most users don't know about. You can use your cell phone to send a text message to Google containing a standard map-based query, and Google will message you back with the necessary information or driving directions.

All you have to do is send a message to **46645** (**GOOGL** on most phones). The message should contain your normal "what's where" query (such as **pizza carmel in**), or start and end addresses, if you want directions. If you entered a "what's where" search, Google sends you back a text message containing a list of matching businesses. If you entered two locations, Google sends you back a text message containing step-by-step driving directions. It's pretty neat, and it's completely free—save for any text message charges from your phone carrier, of course.

Using Google Maps for Mobile

Google also offers a version of Google Maps for use on your cellular phone. The download to your phone is free; you'll have to pay your normal phone service charges, of course.

There are two ways to use Google Maps for Mobile—as a phone-based application, or via a web page specially designed for mobile phone use.

You can download the Google Maps for Mobile application at www.google.com/gmm/; the application displays a menu of options like the one shown in Figure 18.31. To use the web-based application, use your phone's web browser to go to mobile.google.com/local, shown in Figure 18.32.

Both the application and the website let you enter specific or general locations, and then display movable/zoomable maps (like the one in Figure 18.33), satellite images, or driving directions.

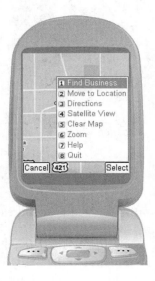

FIGURE 18.31

Using the Google Maps for Mobile application on a typical cell phone.

FIGURE 18.32

Using the Google Maps for Mobile phone-friendly website.

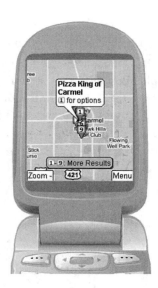

FIGURE 18.33

Displaying a map with Google Maps for Mobile.

The Bottom Line

Google Maps is a worthy competitor to more established map sites such as MapQuest and Yahoo! Maps. What sets Google Maps apart is its interactive zoomable and movable maps, and its capability to display satellite imagery and hybrid maps in addition to traditional maps. You also get a great search function you can use to find local businesses, as well as some nifty functions you can access from your mobile phone. I used to use MapQuest, but I've switched all my map-based activities to Google Maps; it's that much better.

Google Maps also lets anybody (anybody with programming expertise, that is) access their map database to create a Google map "mashup"—that is, a specialized application that adds new data to a standard Google map. There are tons of neat Google map mashups on the Web, which we'll examine in Chapter 19, "Using Google Map Mashups"; we'll also discuss how to make your own mashups in Chapter 41, "Creating Google Map Mashups." It's a cool technology, and one of the neatest things about Google Maps; read ahead to learn more.

Using Google Map Mashups

One of the coolest things about Google Maps is that Google has made the map API public. This means that anyone can create his or her own custom Google map, overlaid with his or her own personal data, and post it on his or her own website. This overlaying of third-party data points on a Google map is called a Google map *mashup*, and there are literally thousands of them on the Web today.

We'll learn more about making your own mashups in Chapter 41, "Creating Google Map Mashups." But you don't have to be a programmer to enjoy the wide variety of information and entertainment available from other people's mashups. Read on to discover just a small part of the public mashups available for your viewing pleasure.

Finding Google Map Mashups

Where, pray tell, does one find all these Google map mashups? One can search Google with the query **google map mashup**, of course, or one can just go to Google Maps Mania (googlemapsmania.blogspot.com). As you can see in Figure 19.1, this is a blog that lists the best and the latest map mashups. It's an "unofficial" blog, but it's the de facto directory to the world of Google map mashups.

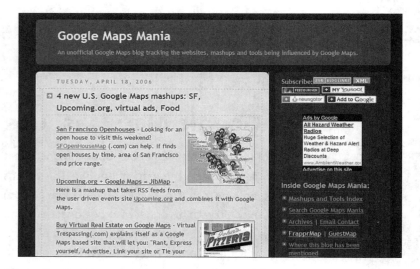

FIGURE 19.1

Discover the latest map mashups at the Google Maps Mania blog.

Another good source of map mashups is CommunityWalk (www. communitywalk.com). As you'll learn in Chapter 41, this is a site that lets you create your own mashups, based on simple web-form entry. The upshot is that the CommunityWalk site, shown in Figure 19.2, also is host to a ton of user-created mashups. It's worth a look.

Then there's the easy route to finding the best mashups—just finish reading this chapter. I'll list some of the most useful and interesting (not always the same thing) mashups I've found on the Web, organized by type. Remember, though, that since these mashups are all created by parties other than Google, their continued availability may vary.

FIGURE 19.2
Find user-created mashups at the CommunityWalk site.

News and Weather Mashups

We'll start our tour by looking at mashups that map news stories and weather-related information. Here's a short list of some of the best news-related mashups:

- **Associated Press News Mashup** (www.81nassau.com/apnews/)—A mashup that maps current AP news stories across the U.S., as shown in Figure 19.3

- **Maplandia News Centre BBC World News Map** (www.maplandia.com/news/)—Mapping news stories globally

- **Local News by ZIP Code** (www.mibazaar.com/localnews/)—Enter your ZIP Code and find a list of local news stories

Now let's look at a few of the weather-related map mashups:

- **WeatherBonk** (www.weatherbonk.com)—Live weather conditions, forecasts, webcams, and such, as shown in Figure 19.4, compiled primarily from local weather stations

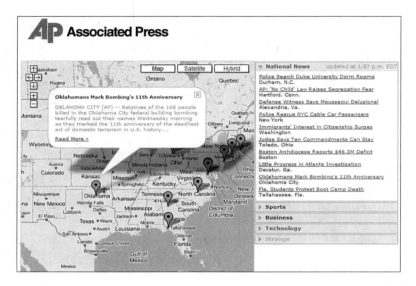

FIGURE 19.3
The Associated Press news mashup.

- **Google Weather Maps** (maps.gokulsoundar.com)—Local weather maps mapped to a Google map mashup

- **Personal Weather Stations** (www.wunderground.com/stationmaps/gmap.asp)—A map of personal weather stations registered with the Weather Underground website

- **Storm Report Map** (www.stormreportmap.com)—Tracks the progress of hurricanes and major thunderstorms, using data from the National Weather Service Storm Prediction Center

- **Floodwater Mapper** (flood.firetree.net)—Displays floodwater conditions around the globe

FIGURE 19.4
WeatherBonk weather conditions in Chicago.

Local Information and Services

Need to find a doctor in your area? Or a public library? Or the lowest gas prices? Here are some mashups you might find useful...

- **JibMap** (www.jibmap.com)—The Upcoming.org local event finder mashed with a Google maps interface, as shown in Figure 19.5

- **EVMapper** (www.mapbureau.com/evmapper/)—Another map-based event finder, this one using the EVDB event database

- **Healthia Doctor Search** (www.healthia.com/doctor/doctorsearch. php)—Search for doctors in your area, by specialty

- **Libraries411.com** (www.libraries411.com)—Fnd the nearest public library

- **My WikiMap Cheap Gas Prices** (www.mywikimap.com)—With gas prices going through the roof, use this mashup, shown in Figure 19.6, to find the lowest prices in your area

> **note** EVDB stands for Events and Venues Database. Learn more about this third-party database technology at www.evdb.com.

■ **HotelMapper** (www.720510.com/gmap/other/final/)—Find hotel rooms in a given area on the map

■ **Judy's Book Maps** (maps.judysbook.com)—Find and map local businesses, courtesy of the Judy's Book website

■ **BroadwayZone** (www.broadwayzone.com)—Broadway plays and shows, mapped

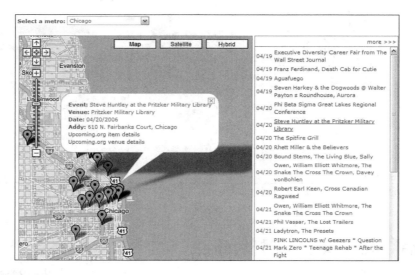

FIGURE 19.5

Local Chicago events mapped on Upcoming.org

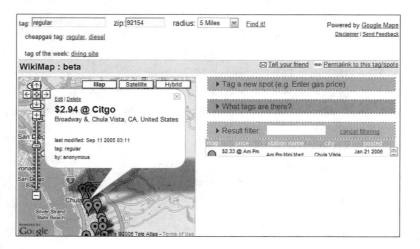

FIGURE 19.6

Checking gas prices in the San Diego area with My WikiMap.

Housing

To my mind, one of the most practical uses of Google map mashups is to find and display available housing on a map-based interface. When you're in the market for a new home or apartment—or want to find out the going price of houses in a given location—check out these useful mashups:

- **Trulia** (www.trulia.com)—Search for real estate across the U.S.
- **HousingMaps** (www.housingmaps.com)—Homes for sale or rent, by city and price range, using data from Craigslist, as shown in Figure 19.7
- **Real Estate Advisor** (www.realestateadvisor.com)—Homes for sale across the U.S.
- **RealEstateAuctions.com** (www.2realestateauctions.com)—Maps top eBay real estate auctions
- **Apartment Ratings** (www.apartmentratings.com)—Maps a database of apartment ratings and reviews
- **Zillow.com** (www.zillow.com)—Find the value of any home in the U.S. via a map-based interface
- **HomePriceMaps.com** (www.homepricemaps.com)—Maps current home prices across the U.S.
- **WikiBroker Real Estate Maps** (www.wikibroker.com)—Maps the dollar values of sold houses by city, state, neighborhood, street, or address; currently live for California, Florida, Georgia, Nevada, and Texas only
- **Homes Sold** (homesold.fidelitylabs.com)—Displays which homes have sold in a specific neighborhood; currently in beta testing for Connecticut, Massachusetts, and Rhode Island, with intentions to expand across the country

19

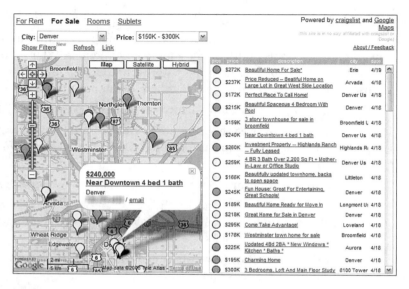

FIGURE 19.7

Browsing homes for sale in Denver via HousingMaps.

Food, Dining, and Entertainment

Can't find a good restaurant? Need a quick beer? Let these Google map mashups help.

- **Chompster** (www.chompster.com)—Restaurant locations across the country

- **toEat.com** (www.toeat.com)—A great listing of U.S. restaurants, as shown in Figure 19.8

- **U.S. Fast Food Locations** (www.hardtoremember.org/fastfood/)—As the name implies, fast food across the U.S.

- **Menumap** (menumap.monkeythumb.net/map)—Restaurant and menus for New York, Boston, Chicago, and San Francisco

- **Chicago Hot Dog Stands** (www.asta.chicago.il.us/chicagohotdogs/)—The best places to get a good dog on the street in the Windy City

- **Kosher Food and Kosher Restaurant Maps** (www.pilotyid.com/kosher-map.php)—Find kosher food anywhere in the U.S.

- **Beermapping.com** (www.beermapping.com/us-brewery-map/)—Maps breweries and brew pubs across the U.S.

- **NYC Beer and Music Map** (www.crooked-beat.com/maps/venuemap. aspx)—The best places to drink and hear music in New York City
- **Local Lush** (www.locallush.com)—Maps bars and clubs by city
- **ClubFly** (www.clubfly.com)—A gay and lesbian bar and club finder

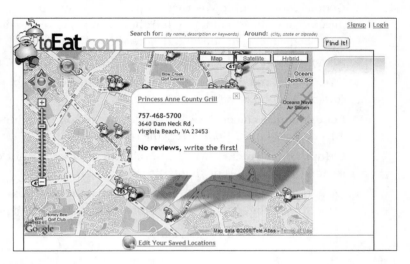

FIGURE 19.8

Mapping Virginia Beach restaurants with toEat.com.

Transportation

When you want to get from point A to point B, there's nothing more useful than a Google map—unless it's a Google map mashup, augmented with other essential information. Here are just a few of these Google transportation mashups:

- **onNYTurf** (www.onnyturf.com/subwaymap.php)—Map mashups of the New York City subway system
- **NYC Transit Maps** (www.transit-maps.com)—Calculate the quickest route between any two points in New York City
- **Chicago Transit Authority** (www.tastypopsicle.com/maps/cta.asp)— Map mashups of the CTA
- **NextBus** (www.nextbus.com/predictor/)—Find out how long it's likely to be until the next bus arrives in the San Francisco bay area

19

- **BART Map/Schedule** (www.acme.com/bart/)—Transit maps and schedules for the San Francisco bay area

- **The T** (www.bostonsubway.info)—Massachusetts Bay Transportation Authority subway stations and maps

- **Google-Yahoo Traffic-Weather Maps** (traffic.poly9.com)—A terrific mashup of traffic conditions (via Yahoo! Traffic), local weather maps, and Google maps, as shown in Figure 19.9

- **Alkemis Local** (local.alkemis.com)—Live traffic cams around the U.S.

- **NYC Trafficland** (www.trafficland.com/nyc/findacamera.php)—Ttraffic cameras around New York City

- **Roadsideamerica.com** (www.roadsideamerica.com/map.html)—Map offbeat tourist attractions across the country

- **GMaps Flight Tracker** (www.gmapsflighttracker.com)—Track the in-air location of major airline flights, as shown in Figure 19.10

- **FAA Flight Delay Information** (www.usaflightinsurance.com/gmap.htm)—Find out the current status of major airline flights

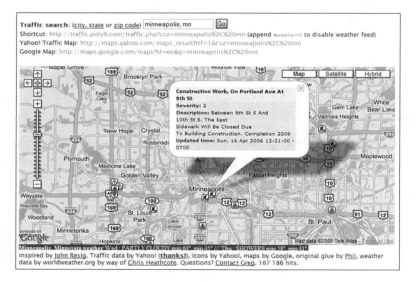

FIGURE 19.9

Viewing Minneapolis traffic conditions via Google-Yahoo Traffic-Weather Maps.

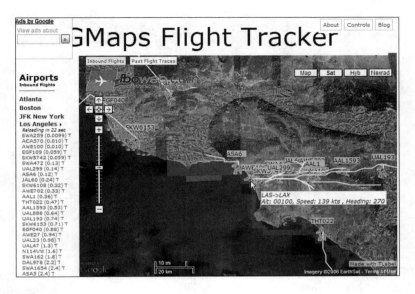

FIGURE 19.10
Tracking incoming Los Angeles flights with GMaps Flight Tracker.

WiFi and Cellular

When you're traveling, it's nice to be able to find free WiFi service, and to know if and where your cell phone is going to work. If you're a connected traveler, here are a few high-tech mashups you might find useful.

- **Cell Phone Reception and Tower Search** (www.cellreception.com)— Find out where the nearest cell phone tower is, and what kind of reception you should expect

- **gWiFi.net** (www.gwifi.net)—A map mashup of free WiFi hotspots across the country, as shown in Figure 19.11

- **Sharemywifi.com** (www.sharemywifi.com)—Find out which of your neighbors have unencrypted WiFi networks that you can leech off of

- **findu.com** (www.tech-software.net/findu.php)—If you're into old-school wireless technology, you'll love this ham radio call sign finder

19

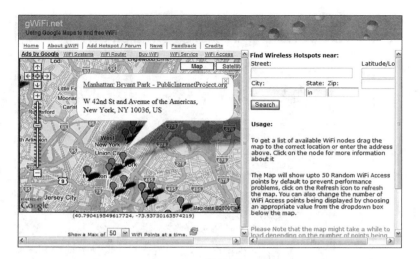

FIGURE 19.11

Free WiFi hotspots in New York, courtesy of gWiFi.net.

Demographic Information

The U.S. government collects tons of useful and interesting information every 10 years as part of the census process. It's no surprise that several enterprising individuals have managed to map some of that data for public consumption, courtesy of Google map mashups.

- **gCensus** (www.gcensus.com)—Displays basic census data for any zoomed-in area of the map, including population, housing units, land area, and water area

- **World Wide Webfoot** (maps.webfoot.com)—Displays a variety of maps derived from Census Bureau information, including race and population density, age distribution, housing units, household composition, total population density, population percentage by gender, average household size, and so on, as shown in Figure 19.12

- **CityRanks** (www.cityranks.com)—Displays population density for major U.S. cities

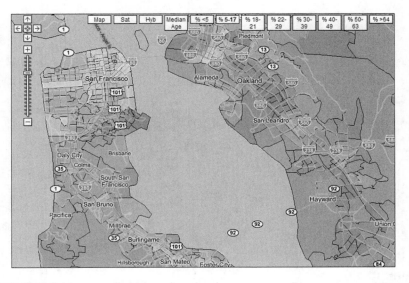

FIGURE 19.12
Age distribution in the San Francisco area, courtesy of World Wide Webfoot.

Colleges and Universities

Where are the best universities in the U.S? Find out from these map mashups:

- **Top Business Schools Map** (www.mibazaar.com/education/business_school.html)—Based on *U.S. News & World Report* rankings, as shown in Figure 19.13

- **Top Engineering Schools Map** (www.mibazaar.com/education/engineering_school.html)—Similar ranking of the nation's top engineering schools

- **Top Medical Schools Map** (www.mibazaar.com/education/medical_school.html)—The best medical schools in the U.S.

19

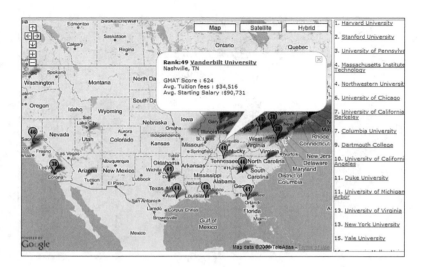

FIGURE 19.13

The best business schools in the U.S. in a Google map mashup.

Photo Maps

Photo map mashups let you post your pictures online, and have them browsable by map location. These sites, all very similar in features, are a great way to share photos with other photo lovers—and illustrate the most scenic sights across the globe.

- **JoeMap** (www.joemap.com)
- **Panorama Explorer** (www.panoramaexplorer.com), shown in Figure 19.14
- **Panoramio** (www.panoramio.com)
- **Pixagogo** (maps.pixagogo.com/maps/start.aspx)
- **smugMaps** (maps.smugmug.com)

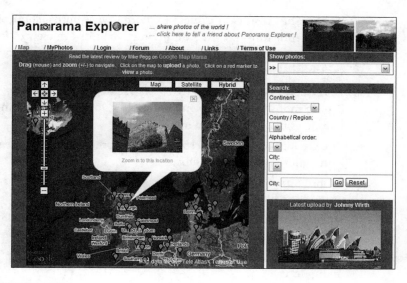

FIGURE 19.14
A scenic castle in Scotland, as posted to Panorama Explorer.

Sports and Training

Sports are big online, as well as in the world of Google map mashups. Whether you're a spectator or a participant, you'll find these mashups particularly fun.

- **NFL Stadiums** (www.axlf.com/maps/)—As the name implies, a mashup showing maps of major league football stadiums and their surrounding areas, complete with nearby restaurants and merchants

- **MapGameDay.com** (www.mapgameday.com)—Interactive maps of college campuses and football stadiums; includes ticket locations, parking, tailgate parties, and so on

- **Gmaps Pedometer** (www.gmap-pedometer.com)—Maps the distance between locations, as shown in Figure 19.15

- **WalkJogRun** (www.walkjogrun.net)—A running route planner with distance/speed calculator

- **GymPost** (www.gympost.com/gymsearch/map.php)—A map database of local gyms, athletic clubs, Pilates studios, fitness centers, and such

- **World Golf Map** (www.golfworldmap.com)—Maps of golf courses around the world

19

- **BunkerShot.com Golf Course Explorer** (www.bunkershot.com/b/map_menu.cfm)—Provides an interactive birds-eye view of famous golf courses, including Augusta National, Pebble Beach, and Pinehurst, as shown in Figure 19.16

- **1001 Secret Fishing Holes** (www.1001seafoods.com/fishing/fishing-maps.php)—As the name implies, tons of local fishing holes mapped on a Google map mashup

- **The Oz Report Flight Parks** (www.ozreport.com/flightparks.php)—Hang gliding parks and clubs

- **Global Surfari** (www.globalsurfari.com)—Surf forecasts for surfers around the globe

- **HockeyCat Rink Guide** (www.hockeycat.com/rinkmapguide.html)—A huge database of indoor hockey rinks

- **ScubaMAP** (www.scubamap.net/map/)—The best locations for scuba diving in the U.S.

- **Wannadive.net** (www.wannadive.net/spot/list.html)—Mappable dive sites around the world

- **SkiBonk** (www.skibonk.com)—Ski resorts, weather conditions, and such

- **Find a Local Racetrack** (www.localtracks.net/find_a_local_race_track)—And find a place to place your bets

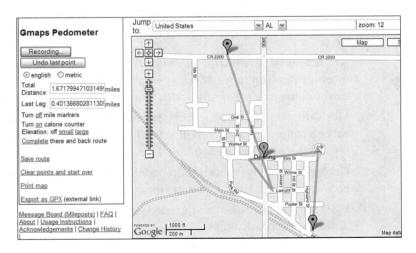

FIGURE 19.15

Mapping a running route in Alabama (1.67 miles!) with Gmaps Pedometer.

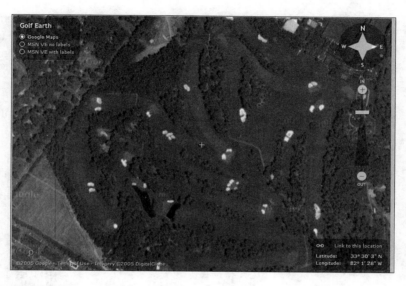

FIGURE 19.16
A satellite view of the Augusta National golf course, courtesy of the BunkerShot.com Golf Course Explorer.

Games

There are two types of map mashup game sites—those that support specific real-world and online games, and those that use Google maps as the basis for new online games. In the first category, here are two sites that help you find other gamers to play with:

- **PokerMashup** (www.pokermashup.com)—Find a real-world poker game anywhere in the U.S.

- **Xbox Live Gamer Map** (www.xboxusersgroup.com/forums/vbgamermap.php?do=showmain)—Maps Xbox Live players online

Now we come to the category of mashup games. These are games that utilize Google map mashups as part of the game:

- **Find the Landmark** (landmark.mapsgame.com)—Locate specified landmarks on a Google map of the world, as shown in Figure 19.17

- **Google Map Attack** (www.googlemapattack.com)—Similar to Find the Landmark; you follow a series of hints to find a location anywhere in the world

- **Road Sign Math** (www.roadsignmath.com)—A do-it-yourself game of identifying road signs that have mathematical significance (such as a 2 and a 3 over a 5, or a 4 over a 16, and so on)

- **Scavengeroogle** (www.bloglander.com/scavengeroogle/)—A maps-based online scavenger hunt

- **Tripods** (www.thomasscott.net/tripods/)—Battle invading tripod markers on a Google map of Manhattan

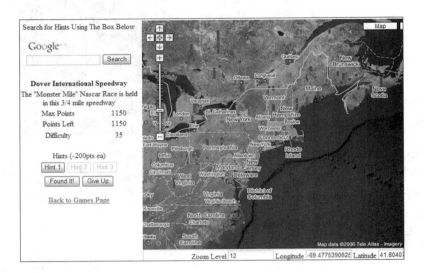

FIGURE 19.17

Searching for the Dover International Speedway as part of the Google Map Attack game.

Celebrity Sightings

If you've ever had a close encounter with a big-name celebrity, you can map it on one of these celebrity-sighting sites:

- **Spotted.at** (www.spotted.at)—Maps celebrity sightings and encounters

- **Gawker Stalker** (www.gawker.com/stalker/)—Maps celebrity sightings in and around New York City, as shown in Figure 19.18, courtesy of the infamous Gawker website

FIGURE 19.18
Stalking celebrities online at the Gawker Stalker site.

COMMENTARY:

DOWN WITH GAWKER

The Gawker Stalker website might sound familiar to you, especially if you follow celebrity comings and goings. The site has become famous for its ability to accurately track celebrities in the Manhattan area, which annoys the heck out of celebrities trying to maintain some degree of anonymity. By mapping where celebrities have been sighted, Gawker Stalker and similar sites also make it easier for the general public (and the occasional obsessed fan) to stalk their favorite celebs.

This fact was not lost on famous movie star George Clooney, who took personal offense at his whereabouts being made public via Gawker Stalker. Clooney decided to strike back, and encouraged his friends and colleagues to flood the Gawker Stalker site with false sightings, thus inducing false information overload and burying the real sightings among the bogus.

Here's the email that Clooney sent out to various show-business publicists:

19

"There is a simple way to render these guys useless. Flood their Web site with bogus sightings. Get your clients to get 10 friends to text in fake sightings of any number of stars. A couple hundred conflicting sightings and this Web site is worthless. No need to try to create new laws to restrict free speech. Just make them useless. That's the fun of it. And then sit back and enjoy the ride. Thanks, George."

Being recognized in public and fawned over by fans is part and parcel of being a successful movie star; if they don't want the fame, they shouldn't take the money. That said, it's easy to sympathize with people who just want a little privacy, and find that privacy being encroached upon by web-fueled celebrity stalkers. Does that make sites like Gawker Stalker a bad thing? I don't know—but I do know that I wouldn't want *my* every move tracked on a publicly posted Google map!

Other Fun—And Informative—Mashups

Many Google map mashups don't fall under any common category. Some of these miscellaneous mashups are entertaining, some are informational—but they're all quite interesting.

- **PackageMapper.com** (www.packagemapper.com)—One of the most useful mashups I've found; it maps FedEx, USPS, and DHL packages en route to their destinations, as shown in Figure 19.19

- **GeoBirds** (www.geobirds.com/yourlocal?option=com_staticxt&staticfile= local.html)—For serious bird watchers, maps bird sightings around the country

- **U.S. Presidential History** (www.mibazaar.com/ushistory/)—Marks the birthplaces of all U.S. presidents

- **BeenMapped.com** (www.beenmapped.com)—Lets you create your own location bookmarks to help you remember places you've visited

- **Platial** (www.platial.com)—Billed as "the people's atlas," lets you create customized maps where you can tell stories and show where events happened

- **Where I Had My First Kiss** (www.whereihadmyfirstkiss.com)—as the name says, a map of places users had their first kiss

- **HotorNot + Google Maps** (hotmaps.frozenbear.com)—Uses Google maps to find people from the HotorNot personals site by location, as shown in Figure 19.20

- **Highest Elevation Points** (www.geology.com/state-high-points.shtml)— Maps the highest points in all 50 states

- **Area 51 Satellite and Aerial Photos** (gmaps.tommangan.us/groom_lake.html)—Find out what's really going on at that top-secret government site

- **Spacecraft Tracking** (gmaps.tommangan.us/spacecraft_tracking.html)—From the same guy who did the Area 51 mashup, this one goes into outer space to track the orbits of the Hubble space telescope and the International Space Station

- **The Big One** (www.ducklet.com/earthquake/)—Uses map mashups to create a simulation of the great San Francisco earthquake and fire

- **What Time Is It?** (www.gchart.com)—Click anywhere on this map to find the current time for any location in the world

- **MapSexOffenders.com** (www.mapsexoffenders.com)—Zoom in to find the location of registered sex offenders across the U.S.

- **Following the Dollars** (www.cs.indiana.edu/%7Emarkane/i590/contributors.html)—Maps political campaign contributions by area

- **FutureCrisis Avian Flu Outbreak Map** (www.futurecrisis.com/places/view.php)—Find out where the latest bird flu cases have broken out

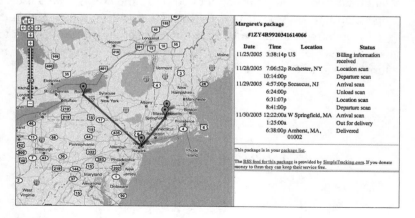

FIGURE 19.19

Tracking packages via PackageMapper.com.

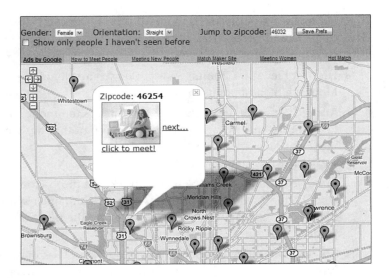

FIGURE 19.20

Looking for dates in Indianapolis with HotorNot + Google Maps.

The Bottom Line

You can spend hours browsing through all the different Google map mashups on the Web. There's some really cool and innovative mashups out there—and some that are actually useful. The ability to display virtually any type of content on a Google map puts a lot of power in the hands of web users and developers, and makes Google maps even more useful than they are on the Google Local site. I recommend you check out some of these mashups just to see what's possible, and then, if you're interested in creating your own mashups, jump ahead to Chapter 41 and get coding.

19

Using Google Earth

I f you like the maps you get with Google Maps, you're going to love Google Earth. Google Earth is a software program that lets you create, view, and save high-resolution, three-dimensional fly-bys of any location on the planet. This might sound like a high-end, expensive piece of software, and you'd be half-right; Google Earth (the basic version, anyway), is available free of charge for all users.

Read on to learn more.

Which Version Is for You?

Google offers three different versions of Google Earth, all downloadable from earth.google.com:

 Google Earth (free version), the version for most users that lets you perform a variety of general mapping functions. This version is a free download.

▓ Google Earth Plus, which can be purchased for $20. This version includes all the features of the basic version, and adds support for GPS devices (Magellan and Garmin units only), the ability to import spreadsheet data, a variety of drawing tools for annotation purposes, and high-resolution printing.

▓ Google Earth Pro, designed for professional and commercial use. This version, which costs $400, includes all the features of Google Earth Plus, augmented with multiple terabytes of detailed aerial and satellite images from cities around the world, the ability to import custom data and blueprints, and use a variety of add-on modules. The add-on modules (which cost $200 apiece) include a Movie Making Module (for creating WMV-format movies of zooms and tours), a Premium Printing Module, a GIS Data Importing Module, a CDT Traffic Counts Module, and an NRB Shopping Center Data Module.

Which version should you use? For most individuals, the free version is more than adequate. If you want to interface Google Earth with a GPS unit, spend the twenty bucks for Google Earth Plus. And if you intend to use Google Earth for professional use (commercial real estate, construction and engineering, insurance, intelligence and homeland security, and so on), investigate the much more robust Google Earth Pro.

For the purposes of this chapter, we'll focus on the free version of Google Earth.

Introducing Google Earth

When you first launch Google Earth, you see a large view of the planet Earth, as well as surrounding navigation and display controls, as shown in Figure 20.1. You can hide or display certain parts of the interface by checking them on or off in the View and Tools menu.

20

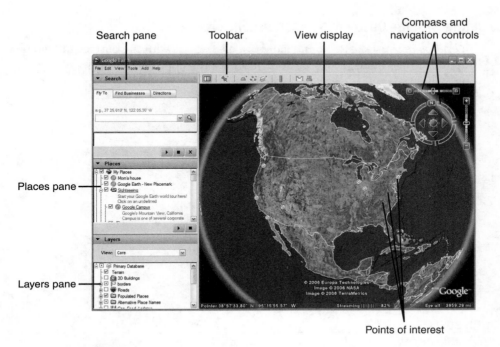

FIGURE 20.1
The Google Earth interface.

Navigating Google Earth

You start your journey through Google Earth from the 3D view of the globe.
You can zoom in on any location on the planet, and navigate from place to
place around the planet. All it takes is a mastery of Google Earth's navigation
controls.

Of course, since you're doing three-dimensional navigation, complete with
panning, tilting, and rotating, the navigation is a bit more complicated than
what you have with a flat web-based Google map. With Google Earth, you
can navigate around the 3D globe by using the navigation controls at the top-
right corner of the screen; by using your mouse; or by using select keyboard
commands. We'll look at each method in turn.

20

Navigating with the Onscreen Navigation Controls

Perhaps the easiest way to navigate Google Earth is with the onscreen navigation controls, shown in Figure 20.2. Just click the appropriate control with your mouse, and you can do the following:

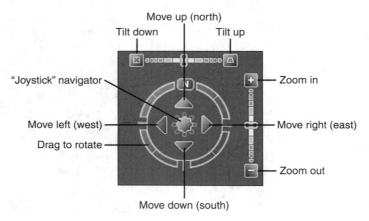

FIGURE 20.2

Google Earth navigation controls.

- Click the Zoom In and Zoom Out buttons (along with the corresponding slider control) to zoom into or out of the map. Clicking Zoom In displays a closer, more detailed view; clicking Zoom Out displays a further away, less detailed view.
- Click and drag anywhere on the rotation ring to rotate the view. You can rotate the view either clockwise or counterclockwise.
- Click the arrow buttons to move the 3D view up, down, right, or left.
- Click and hold the center control button to use your mouse like a 360-degree joystick. With the center control button held down, moving your mouse in any direction moves the map in the same direction.
- Click the Tilt Up and Tilt Down buttons (or move the corresponding slider control) to tilt the view accordingly.

Navigating with the Mouse

If you're handy with your mouse, you can use it alone (without the onscreen navigation controls) to zoom around Google Earth. In fact, Google Earth offers three different types of mouse-only navigation—Trackball, GForce, and Click-and-Zoom. We'll look at each in turn.

Trackball Navigation Mode

The default mouse navigation mode is the Trackball mode. Here's what you can do:

- To zoom in to a specific point, double-click on that point in the viewing pane.
- To generally zoom in, use your mouse's scroll wheel (if it has one) to scroll toward you. You can zoom in smaller increments by holding down the Alt key on your keyboard while scrolling.
- You can also generally zoom in by clicking and holding the *right* mouse button, and then moving your mouse up (away from you).
- To generally zoom out, use your mouse's scroll wheel to scroll away from you. You can also click and hold the right mouse button, and then move your mouse down (toward you).
- To zoom continuously in or out, hold down the right mouse button, briefly move the mouse up (to zoom in) or down (to zoom out), and then quickly release the mouse button. To stop the zoom, click once in the viewer.
- To move the map in any direction, click and hold the left mouse button, and then drag your mouse in the desired direction.
- To "drift" continuously in any direction, hold the left mouse button down, briefly move the mouse in the desired direction, and then quickly release the mouse button. To stop the drift, click once in the viewer.
- To tilt the view, hold down the Shift key on your keyboard and then move the mouse's scroll wheel up or down. Alternatively, if your mouse has a depressible scroll wheel or middle button, depress the scroll wheel or middle button and then move the scroll wheel up or down.
- To rotate the view, hold down the Ctrl key on your keyboard and then move the mouse either left or right. Alternatively, if your mouse has a depressible scroll wheel or middle button, depress the scroll wheel or middle button and then move the mouse either left or right.

If you use another mouse navigation mode, you can return to the Trackball mode by pressing Ctrl+T.

GForce Navigation Mode

The second mouse navigation mode makes your mouse behave as if it were a joystick. You enter GForce mode by pressing Ctrl+G.

When you're in GForce mode, the navigation cursor changes to an airplane shape. In addition, the effects of any mouse movement become more noticeable the closer you are to the terrain.

To pan left or right, simply left-click the mouse and move the mouse left or right. To tilt the view, left-click the mouse and move it toward or away from you.

To accelerate any movement, right-click and move the mouse forward; to decelerate, right-click and move the mouse back. To stop the current motion, press the spacebar on your keyboard.

Click-and-Zoom Navigation Mode

The final mouse navigation mode is the most limited. To activate Click-and-Zoom mode, select Tools, Options to open the Options dialog box; then select the Navigation tab and check the Click-and-Zoom option.

In Click-and-Zoom mode, you left-click to zoom in and right-click to zoom out. Press the spacebar to stop the zoom.

That's it; there's no other mouse movement possible in this mode.

Navigating with the Keyboard

You can also navigate through any Google Earth view by using your computer keyboard. Table 20.1 details the keyboard navigation commands:

> **tip** You can make more refined movements (that is, move more slowly), by holding down the Alt key in combination with most of these keyboard commands.

Table 20.1   Google Earth Keyboard Navigation Commands

Navigation	Keyboard Command
Move left	Left arrow
Move right	Right arrow
Move up	Up arrow
Move down	Down arrow

Table 20.1   Continued

Navigation	Keyboard Command
Zoom in	Ctrl+Up arrow *or* +
Zoom out	Ctrl+Down arrow *or* -
Tilt up	Shift+Up arrow *or* PgUp
Tilt down	Shift+Down arrow *or* PgDn
Rotate clockwise	Shift+Right arrow
Rotate counter-clockwise	Shift+Left arrow
Stop current motion	Spacebar
Reset tilt	u
Reset view to "north-up"	n
Reset both tilt and compass view	r

Taking a Quick Tour of Google Earth

Now that you know how to get around in Google Earth, let's take a quick tour.

Anytime you start Google Earth, the view defaults to the extended zoom of the planet Earth, focused on the continent of North America. This is a great place to start because you can get just about anyplace you want from here.

Let's start by panning east (to the right) until we focus on Europe. Click the right-arrow button to spin the Earth around until Africa appears, and then click the up-arrow button until Europe is centered onscreen, as shown in Figure 20.3.

The only problem with this view is that Europe is tilted in relation to due north; when we panned to the right from North America, we didn't actually spin the globe on its north-south axis. We can fix this problem by clicking the Rotate Right button, or (even better) by clicking the Reset North button. The resulting view is shown in Figure 20.4.

Next, we want to zoom into the map. Click the Zoom In button (or use the zoom slider control) until France fills up the screen, as shown in Figure 20.5. Now use a combination of zooming and panning until you see the city of Paris, as shown in Figure 20.6.

20

FIGURE 20.3

The Google Earth globe panned east and north, to focus on Europe.

FIGURE 20.4

The globe rotated so that due north is straight up.

FIGURE 20.5
Zooming in on France.

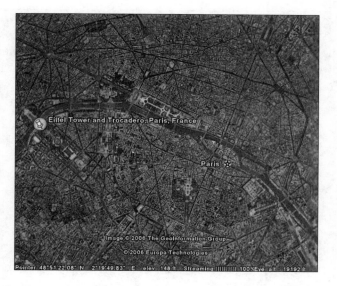

FIGURE 20.6
Zooming in on Paris.

By now you've noticed the big pushpin (called a *placemark*) that's labeled Eiffel
Tower and Trocadero, Paris, France. In Google Earth, you use placemarks to mark
specific places (no surprise); you zoom into a given location by double-clicking

the placemark, either on the map or in the Places pane. Do that now, for the Eiffel Tower placemark, and you'll zoom into the view shown in Figure 20.7.

FIGURE 20.7

Zooming in to the Eiffel Tower placemark.

Now for some fun. Start by zooming in a little closer, and then click the Tilt Down button a few times. What you get now is a bird's eye view of the bridge and the city beyond, as shown in Figure 20.8.

FIGURE 20.8

A birds-eye view of Paris.

Next, rotate around and zoom in a little more until you're looking down the bridge. As you can see in Figure 20.9, you can make out individual cars on the bridge—pretty neat!

FIGURE 20.9

An even closer view, looking down the bridge.

And, to demonstrate how easy it is to navigate directly to placemarked locations, go to the Places pane and double-click the Google Campus placemark. After a dizzying spin-and-turn around the globe, you'll see the Googleplex appear, as shown in Figure 20.10. Feel free to zoom in and see exactly what Google's world headquarters looks like—up close and personal!

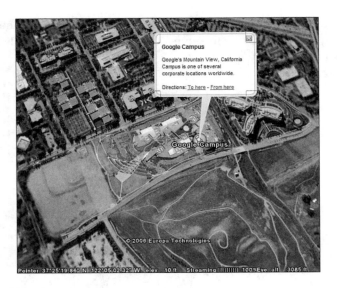

FIGURE 20.10

A Google Earth view of Google's worldwide headquarters.

Making Google Earth More Three-Dimensional

Google Earth offers two options to make its three-dimensional views look even more realistic—by displaying 3D buildings and terrain.

Let's look at the 3D buildings option first. Start by going to the Places pane and then double-clicking the Chicago River placemark. Zoom in and tilt the map a little, until you see the view shown in Figure 20.11. Now check the 3D Buildings option in the Layers pane, and Google Earth will add the blocky 3D buildings shown in Figure 20.12—a much more realistic perspective of what the actual city looks like.

The 3D terrain option is a good one when you're viewing an area of hilly terrain. You turn this on by checking the Terrain option in the Layers pane. You can see this option at work by going to the Colorado River View placemark. The view without the 3D terrain function enabled is shown in Figure 20.13; Figure 20.14 shows the much more realistic look with the 3D terrain.

note Google Earth has 3D buildings in many major cities—but not all. Turn on this feature when zooming into a city to see what's available.

FIGURE 20.11
A non-3D view of the Chicago River area.

FIGURE 20.12
The same view of the Chicago River, with 3D buildings added.

20

FIGURE 20.13
A non-3D view of the Colorado River area.

FIGURE 20.14
The same view of the Colorado River, with 3D terrain.

By the way, you exaggerate these height effects by selecting Tools, Options, and when the Options dialog box appears, select the View tab and enter a higher number for Elevation Exaggeration. Figure 20.15 shows the Mount Saint Helens placemark at the standard elevation; Figure 20.16 shows an exaggeration effect of 3.0 (the maximum amount). Cool!

FIGURE 20.15

Mount Saint Helens at normal elevation.

FIGURE 20.16

Mount Saint Helens at an exaggerated elevation.

Configuring View Options

That last bit of our tour draws our attention to the various view options available in Google Earth. There are a lot of options, more than we can cover here, but we'll try to address some of the most popular and useful ones.

Setting View Preferences

Most of Google Earth's view options are set from within the Options dialog box, shown in Figure 20.17. You open this dialog box by selecting Tools, Options.

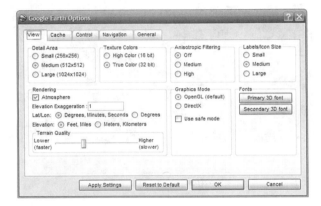

FIGURE 20.17

The Options dialog box.

Within the Options dialog box, you want to select the View tab. From here you can adjust the settings detailed in Table 20.2:

Table 20.2	Google Earth View Settings
Setting	**Description**
Detail Area	Determines how much area within the viewer has high-resolution focus, calculated in pixels. Medium is the default setting; you should select Large only if your PC's graphics card has at least 32MB memory.
Texture Colors	Sets the color depth of the display; True Color (32 bit) displays a more realistic view.
Anistropic Filtering	This is a texture mapping technology that produces a smoother looking image, especially around the horizon (when viewing a tilted angle). You should turn this on only if your graphics card has at least 32MB memory.
Labels/Icon Size	Determines the default size for labels and icons in the viewer.

Table 20.2   Continued

Setting	Description
Rendering	Checking Atmosphere shows the atmosphere around the globe when viewed at full horizon or from space.
Elevation Exaggeration	Choosing a higher number exaggerates the height of tall objects (terrain and buildings) in the viewer.
Lat/Lon	Displays latitude and longitude in either degrees, minutes, and seconds or just degrees.
Elevation	Displays elevations in either feet and miles or meters and kilometers.
Terrain Quality	Adjust to display more or fewer terrain details.
Graphics Mode	Google Earth is a graphics-intensive application. If your PC has a high-powered graphics card, it can run in the better-looking Direct X mode. If, however, your PC has a less powerful graphics card (as do most notebook PCs), then you can run Google Earth in the less-demanding OpenGL mode. (Safe mode is used only when you're experiencing display problems.)
Fonts	Determines which fonts are used to display labels in the viewer.

Using Full-Screen Mode

By default, the Google Earth viewer appears in a window within the Google Earth window. To display the viewer full-screen, press the F11 key (or select View, Full Screen). To return to the standard mode, press F11 again.

Displaying a Latitude/Longitude Grid

To overlay a latitude/longitude grid on any Google Earth view, press Ctrl+L (or select View, Lat/Lon Grid). This grid tilts along with the overall view tilt; Figure 20.18 shows what this grid looks like.

Displaying the Overview Map

There's one more view setting that can help you navigate Google Earth. This is the Overview map, which you switch on by pressing Ctrl+M (or by selecting View, Overview Map). As you can see in Figure 20.19, this is a similar map overview as you see in Google Maps.

The Overview map shows you where you are in the viewer in relation to the rest of the world. You can double-click anywhere in the Overview map to navigate to that location.

20

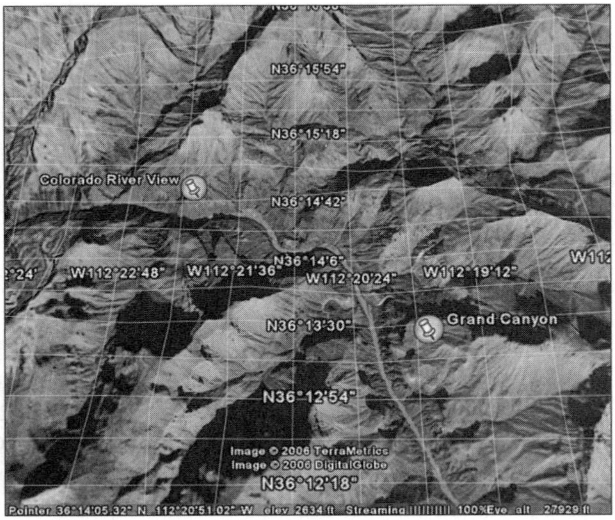

FIGURE 20.18

Google Earth with a latitude/longitude grid overlaid on the standard view.

FIGURE 20.19

The Overview map displayed in the Google Earth viewer.

20

Saving and Printing a View

You can save any image displayed in the Google Earth viewer by selecting File, Save Image. You can also print the current image in the viewer by selecting File, Print. Note, however, that the free version of Google Earth prints images only at screen resolution; the $20 Google Earth Plus prints images at a much higher resolution, about 2400 pixels, according to Google.

Searching for Locations to View

You know how to zoom and pan around the Google Earth globe—but this isn't always the easiest way to zoom into a specific location. Fortunately, Google Earth lets you search for places just as you do in Google Maps, and then zoom directly into the desired location.

To search for a location, make sure the Fly To tab is selected in the Search pane and then enter the location into the search box. When you click the Search button, Google Earth zooms into the location you entered, as shown in Figure 20.20.

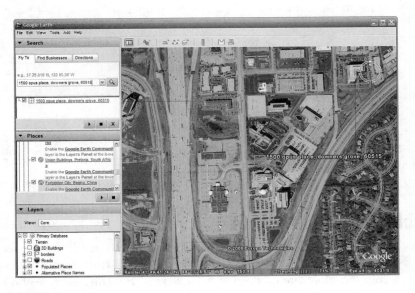

FIGURE 20.20

Searching for a location—and zooming into it.

As with Google Maps, Google Earth lets you search using a variety of entry formats. Table 20.3 details the different ways to search for a location:

note Street-level searching is limited to locations in the U.S., U.K., and Canada only.

Table 20.3 Google Earth Search Formats	
Format	Example
country	France
city country	paris france
city, state	minneapolis, mn
zip	60515
number street, city, state	1500 opus place, downers grove, il
number street, city, zip	1500 opus place, downers grove, 60515
cross street, city, state	42nd and broadway, new york, ny
latitude, longitude (in decimal)	37.7, -122.2
latitude, longitude (in DMS format)	37 25'19.07"N, 122 05'06.24"W

By the way, Google Earth also lets you search for businesses and landmarks by using the Find Business tab in the Search pane, shown in Figure 20.21. You can search within the current view, or within any city, state, or country you enter. Items that match your query are pinpointed in the view pane.

FIGURE 20.21

Searching for businesses with Google Earth.

Displaying Driving Directions

You can also use Google Earth to map driving directions, just as you can with Google Maps. The big difference in using Google Earth for this purpose is that your directions are mapped in a 3D view, so you can bet more of a birds-eye view of where you'll be driving.

Getting Directions

The easiest way to generate driving directions is to click the Directions tab in the Search pane, and then enter your Start and End addresses. When you click the Search button, your route is mapped onscreen, with each turn place-marked on the map, as shown in Figure 20.22. You can zoom into, rotate, pan, and tilt the map as you like, as well as zoom into any specific direction by double-clicking that placemark. As you can see in Figure 20.23, zooming into a placemark like this gives you a very good idea of what you'll encounter when you make your trip.

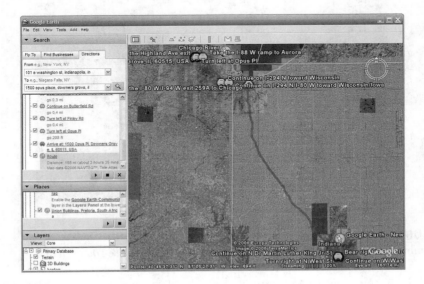

FIGURE 20.22
Using Google Earth to generate driving directions.

Touring Your Route

And here's an even neater feature. Once you have your route displayed onscreen, you can use Google Earth's tour feature to "fly" the complete route in the viewer. Just select the Route item at the end of the directions listing, click the Play Tour button, and get ready for a wild ride!

Printing and Saving Directions

To print step-by-step directions for your route, all you have to do is click the Click Here for a Printable View link in the directions listing. This will open a

20

Google Maps web page on the bottom half of your screen, with the directions displayed in that window. From this window, click the Print link to print the directions.

FIGURE 20.23

Zooming into a specific turn-by-turn instruction—it's almost like you're there!

To save your route for future use, select File, Save As. Enter a new filename for your trip, and then click the Save button.

Displaying and Using Layers

One of the things that makes Google Earth so useful is its capability to overlay other data on top of its maps. This data is added in the form of *layers*; available layers can be enabled via the Layers pane.

You've already seen several different types of layers in use. When you enabled the 3D buildings and terrain features, you added these layers to the underlying map. Disable the feature, and the layer is taken away.

There are many other kinds of layers you can add to most Google Earth maps. Table 20.4 details some of what's available:

> **tip** In the Layers pane, layers are organized in folders. Double-click a folder to see and activate specific layers within the major layer category.

Table 20.4   Google Earth Layers

Layer	Description
3D buildings	Displays three-dimensional buildings in major metropolitan areas
Airports/transportation	Displays airports, heliports, and airport maps
Alternative place names	Displays locations in different languages—English, French, Italian, German, Spanish, Dutch, and Portuguese
Banks/ATMs	Displays nearby bank and ATM locations
Bars/clubs	Displays the locations of nearby nightclubs and bars
Borders	Displays border information, including countries, states, counties, coastlines, and the like
Census	Overlays various census data, where available
Churches/cemeteries	Displays the location of nearby churches and cemeteries
City boundaries	Displays city limit borders
Coffee shops	Displays the location of nearby coffee shops
Community showcase	The best of user-created layers
Crime stats	Displays local crime statistics, where available
DG coverage	Displays cloud cover information
Dining	Displays the locations of nearby restaurants
Earthquakes	Displays the location of recent earthquakes
Fire/hospitals	Displays the locations of nearby fire stations and hospitals
Gas stations	Displays the locations of nearby gas stations
Geographic features	Displays bodies of water, mountains, and other features
Golf	Displays the locations of nearby golf courses
Google Earth community	Displays placemarks created by Google Earth users
Grocery stores	Displays the locations of nearby grocery stores
Lodging	Displays the locations of nearby hotels and motels
Major retail	Displays the locations of nearby major retailers
Movie/DVD rentals	Displays the locations of nearby movie rental stores

20

Table 20.4   Continued

Layer	Description
National Geographic Magazine	Displays a variety of special layers created by the editors of *National Geographic* magazine
Parks/recreation areas	Displays nearby parks and recreation areas
Pharmacy	Displays the locations of nearby pharmacies
Populated places	Displays cities, towns, villages, capitals, and so on
Postal code boundaries	Displays boundaries of U.S. postal codes
Railroads	Displays railroad tracks
Roads	Displays the names/numbers of major highways, county roads, and streets
School districts	Displays boundaries for elementary, secondary, and unified school districts
Schools	Displays the locations for nearby schools
Shopping malls	Displays the locations for nearby shopping malls
Sports venues	Displays nearby sports stadiums, ballparks, and the like
Terrain	Displays 3D elevation for the viewing region; this layer is limited to natural geographic features, like mountains and canyons, and is not available for cities and buildings
Transit	Displays local and commuter rail lines
U.S. Congressional districts	Displays boundaries for U.S. Congressional districts
Volcanoes	Displays known volcanoes
Water	Displays bodies of water

For example, Figure 20.24 shows a view of La Jolla, California with the Roads layer enabled; Figure 20.25 shows the same area with the Lodging layer enabled. At a longer view, Figure 20.26 shows the San Diego area with the Postal Codes layer enabled. You get the point.

caution Not all layers contain information for all locales. For example, you won't find 3D building data for the middle of the Nevada desert.

FIGURE 20.24
Roads in La Jolla.

FIGURE 20.25
Restaurants in La Jolla.

20

FIGURE 20.26

Postal code areas in San Diego.

Displaying Points of Interest

Many of the layers available in Google Earth contain what are known as points of interest (POI). These are specific locations overlaid on a map, such as ATMs, restaurants, gas stations, and the like.

When you click a POI, Google Earth displays an information box for that item, like the one shown in Figure 20.27. Within this info box you can generate driving directions to or from that point, or click the Search Google link to display web-based information about that location.

Right-click a POI and you get a pop-up menu that lets you copy or save this location (as well as generate driving directions). Saving the POI puts it in your My Places folder in the Places pane, so you can return to it at any future time. Alternatively, you can copy the POI and then paste it into a specific subfolder in the My Places folder.

20

FIGURE 20.27
Viewing information about a point of interest.

Creating Custom Placemarks

About that My Places folder. This is a folder where you can store any item for future use. You can store pre-existing POIs, as we just discussed, or store custom placemarks that you create yourself.

To mark any place on any Google Earth map as a placemark, follow these steps:

1. Zoom into the location you want to placemark.

2. Click the Add a Placemark button on the Toolbar (or select Add, Placemark).

3. A new, blank placemark is now placed on the map, as shown in Figure 20.28. If the placemark is not in the correct location, use your mouse to drag it around the map as necessary.

4. Also appearing at this time is a New Placemark dialog box, like the one shown in Figure 20.29. Enter a new name for the placemark, along with any descriptive text you'd like, and then click the OK button.

FIGURE 20.28

Adding a new placemark to a map.

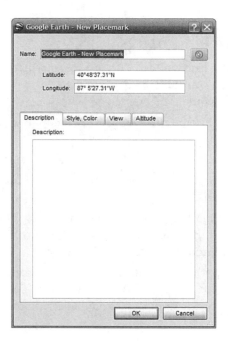

FIGURE 20.29

Entering information about the new placemark.

As you can see in Figure 20.30, the placemark is now set on the map, with the name you provided. The placemark is also stored in the My Places folder (or other folder you selected).

FIGURE 20.30
The new placemark, properly named and placed.

Measuring Distance Along a Path

Ever wonder precisely how far it is from one point to another? Wonder no more, because Google Earth lets you measure distances along a line or path.

It's quite easy, really. Just follow these steps:

1. Zoom into a location to create the desired view.

2. Press the U key on your keyboard to make sure you're viewing the map from a top-down view.

3. Select Tools, Ruler.

4. This displays the Ruler dialog box, shown in Figure 20.31. To measure a straight line, select the Line tab; to measure a more complex route, select the Path tab. (From here on, I'll assume you're measuring a Path.)

> **tip**
> You can further customize a placemark by checking the Advanced option in the New Placemark dialog box. This expands the dialog box so you can choose a different icon, icon color, or icon size, as well as set more precise coordinates for the placemark.

FIGURE 20.31

Getting ready to measure distance on a map.

5. Return to the viewer pane and click the mouse at the starting point of the route you want to measure.

6. Move the mouse to the first turn in your route, and click the mouse again. This draws one line segment, with a red dot at the start point and a green one at the end of this segment.

7. Move the mouse to the next turn in your route, and click the mouse again. This draws another line along this segment of your route.

8. Repeat step 7 until you've reached the final end point of your route, as shown in Figure 20.32.

FIGURE 20.32

The path of your route, drawn on the map.

The length of your route is now displayed in the Ruler dialog box. Close the dialog box when you're done measuring.

> **tip** To change the units of measure (miles, by default), use the pull-down list to select a new unit.

Using Google Earth with GPS Devices

If you upgrade to Google Earth Plus and you have a Global Positioning System (GPS) device, you can connect the GPS unit to your computer and import your way-point and track data into Google Earth.

> **note** At this point in time, Google Earth supports imports from Garmin and Magellan GPS devices only.

Waypoints are imported as placemarks; routes and trackpoints are imported as paths.

Importing your data is as simple as following these instructions:

1. Connect the GPS device to your computer.
2. Turn on the GPS device.
3. From within Google Earth, select Tools, GPS.
4. When the GPS dialog box appears, select your device's manufacturer, the types of data you want to import, and other preferences.
5. Click the OK button.

That's it. Your imported data appears in the Places pane, labeled by your device (Garmin GPS Device or Magellan GPS Device, depending).

The Bottom Line

Google Earth is an incredibly feature-rich application. Even if you're just a casual user, you can have lots of fun zooming into specific locations, doing route fly-bys, and the like. The program's 3D capabilities take basic mapping to a new level—and provide added functionality.

Bottom line? I like Google Earth a lot. I don't use it for all my mapping needs (Google Maps is just fine for most things, to be honest), but when I want an added bit of realism, it's the way to go. It's certainly worth your time and money (it's free, remember) to give it a look.

> **tip** Google Earth also lets you add your own overlays to the built-in maps, in the form of custom layers. If you're using Google Earth Plus or Pro, you can also import spreadsheet data to create points of interest. There's not enough space in this chapter to go into these custom functions; consult the program's help file for detailed instructions.

20

Communications Services

21 Sending and Receiving Email with Gmail

22 Instant Messaging with Google Talk and Gmail Chat

23 Using Blogger

Sending and Receiving Email with Gmail

Everybody has an email account—at least one. You probably have a home email account from your Internet service provider (perhaps with additional addresses for your spouse and kids), as well as a work email account. Chances are you also have a web-based email account from MSN Hotmail or Yahoo! Mail, as either a backup or just to have it.

So why, then, would you want yet another email account? And from Google, of all places?

That's right, Google has its own web-based email service, called Gmail, that competes with MSN Hotmail and Yahoo! Mail. What makes Gmail unique, though, is the massive amount of storage it offers, as well as its insistence on a non-folder, pure search approach to organization.

Given all the other email offerings available today, is Gmail right for you? That's a good question, and one you'll have to read on to figure out.

What Makes Gmail Unique

At first blush, Gmail (mail.google.com) looks a lot like MSN Hotmail and Yahoo! Mail. It's free, it lets you send and receive email from any web browser, and the interface even looks similar to its competitors.

But Gmail offers a few unique features that sets it apart from the web-based email crowd. In particular:

- Gmail gives you more than 2.7 gigabytes of storage. In comparison, the free version of MSN Hotmail only offers 250MB storage, while the free version of Yahoo! Mail offers just 1GB.

- Gmail is completely free. Unlike MSN Hotmail and Yahoo! Mail, which try to push subscription services with additional features, Gmail offers all its features to all its users, free of charge.

- Gmail doesn't use folders. That's right, with Gmail you can't organize your mail into folders, as you can with the other services. Instead, Gmail pushes the search paradigm as the way to find the messages you want—not a surprise, given Google's search-centric business model.

- Gmail groups your emails into message threads (it calls them "conversations") that let you follow the back and forth of a continuing email message exchange.

Probably the most notable points here are the storage capacity and the search-instead-of-folders organizational approach. The huge storage capacity means that you really don't need to delete old emails, and that you can use Gmail as kind of an online backup service for your key data files. (Just email your files to yourself, and they're stored on Google's servers.) The search-based paradigm, however, takes a little more getting used to, especially if you're a highly organized type; this may be one instance where Google's reliance on search technology might not be totally practical for the application at hand.

COMMENTARY:

EMAIL WITHOUT FOLDERS?

The whole bit about "searching not sorting" deserves special consideration. If you're like me, you're used to storing different types of email messages in different folders within your email program. You might have a folder for messages from family members, another for messages from work colleagues, and still others for specific projects or events. If you want to look back through the messages from that person or relating to that project/event, all you have to do is open the folder. It's the way we tend to organize things, as witnessed by the huge sales of physical file folders at your local office supply store.

Google, however, has thrown that paradigm out the window. You simply can't create folders in Gmail; your messages are all dumped into the same massive inbox (or, in the case of older messages, archived in the All Mail box). If you want to see all the messages from your Aunt Peg or if you want to read all messages related to a given project, you have to search for them.

(Nitpickers will take this opportunity to remind me that individual messages can be labeled, and that you can assign the same label to all related messages, and that this is kind of sort of like filing your messages. But labeling is only like filing if you happen to throw all your labeled papers into one massive file folder. You still have to search for messages that bear a given label; therefore, the search-not-sort paradigm holds.)

Of course, Google is the king of search, so it should come as no surprise that they try to push the search paradigm in every service they offer. And, in some instances and for some users, that's fine. But not all users think that way, especially when you're looking at an email inbox that over time might hold tens of thousands of individual messages. Do you really want to search through that inbox every time you want to view all messages on a given topic? Wouldn't it be easier to sort the messages by topic beforehand, using the tried and true folder approach?

I have to give Google credit for sticking with their core search paradigm in everything they offer, even if it doesn't always make sense. (It is, after all, how they distinguish themselves from their folder-happy competition at Microsoft.) But, in the case of Gmail, don't count me as a complete fan. I like the massive storage capability, I like the interface, I even like the "conversation" grouping. But I don't like not being able to create and use folders to organize my messages. Would it have killed the Google powers-that-be to let their Gmail customers use folders in addition to search? I simply don't see where *not* offering a feature (such as folders) gives Gmail a competitive advantage. A best-of-both-worlds approach would have offered the traditional folder paradigm, as well as Gmail's enhanced search functionality.

Are you listening, Google?

21

Signing Up (It's Free!)

Here's one more thing that's unique about Gmail. You can't just go to the Gmail website and sign up. In fact, at this point in time Gmail is a bit of a closed club, for some unfathomable reason; the general public can't use it. Instead, you have to be invited by another Gmail user.

tip   You can invite another user directly from your Gmail inbox page. Just scroll down to the Invite a Friend section, enter the friend's current email address, and click the Send Invite button. (Currently, Google lets you invite up to 15 friends.)

So, if you know someone else who uses Gmail, you can ask them to send you an invitation. When you respond to the invitation, you create your Gmail account.

There's one other way to get a Gmail account, however. If you have a cellular phone with text messaging capability, you sign up using your mobile phone. All you have to do is go to mail.google.com (shown in Figure 21.1) and click the Sign Up for Gmail Using Your Mobile Phone link. When prompted, enter your cell phone number, and Google will send you a text message with the invitation code you need to create your account.

A little complicated, yes, but worth the trouble.

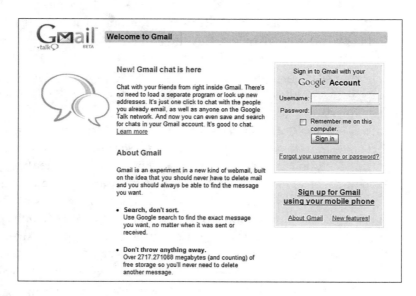

FIGURE 21.1

The Welcome to Gmail page, for new users.

21

Getting to Know the Gmail Interface

Once you sign up for your Gmail account, you get assigned your email address (in the form of *name*@gmail.com) and you get access to the Gmail inbox page, shown in Figure 21.2.

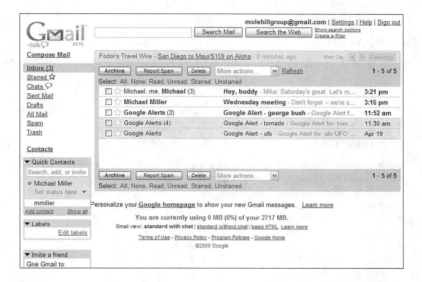

FIGURE 21.2
The Gmail inbox.

The default view of the Gmail page is the inbox, which contains all your received messages. You can switch to other views by clicking the appropriate links at the left side or the bottom of the page. For example, to view all your sent mail, simply click the Sent Mail link on the left; to view only unread messages, click the Unread link at the bottom.

Each message is listed with the message's sender, the subject of the message, a short snippet from the message itself, and the date or time the message was sent. (The snippet is typically the first line of the message text.) Unread messages are listed in bold; once a message has been read, it's displayed in normal, nonbold text.

To perform an action on a message or group of messages, put a check mark by the message(s), and then click one of the buttons at the bottom of the page. Alternatively, you can pull down the More Actions list and select another action to perform.

21

Sending and Receiving Email

Obviously, the Gmail interface is fairly easy to understand. (If Google does nothing else, they create simple, easy-to-understand interfaces.) Now let's get down to brass tacks, and learn how to use Gmail for basic message sending and receiving.

Reading Messages

To read a message, all you have to do is click the message title in the inbox. This displays the full text of the message on a new page, as shown in Figure 21.3.

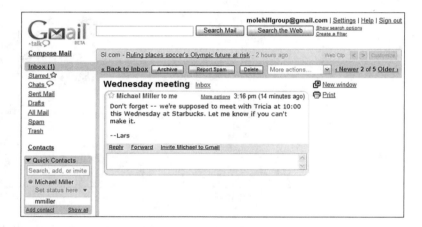

FIGURE 21.3

Reading an email message in Gmail.

If you want to display this message in a new window, click the New Window link. To print the message, click the Print link. To return to the inbox, click the Inbox link.

Viewing Conversations

One of the unique things about Gmail is that all related email messages are grouped together in what Google calls *conversations*. A conversation might be an initial message and all the replies (and replies to replies) to that message; a conversation might also be all the daily emails from a single source with a common subject, such as messages you receive from subscribed-to mailing lists.

21

A conversation is noted in the inbox list by a number in parentheses after the sender name(s), as shown in Figure 21.4. If a conversation has replies from more than one person, more than one name is listed.

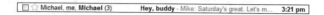

FIGURE 21.4

A conversation consisting of three messages.

To view all the messages in a conversation, simply click the message title. As you can see in Figure 21.5, all the messages in the conversation are stacked on top of each other, with the text of the newest message fully displayed. To expand any single message within the conversation, simply click that message's subject. To expand *all* the messages in a conversation, as shown in Figure 21.6, click the Expand All link.

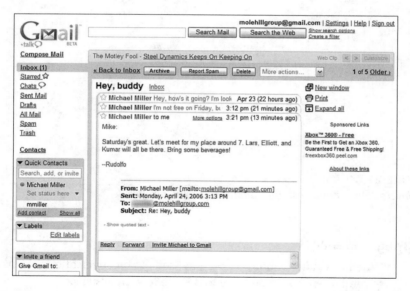

FIGURE 21.5

Viewing all the messages in a conversation.

FIGURE 21.6
A conversation expanded so that all messages are displayed.

Replying to Messages

Whether you're reading a single message or a conversation, it's easy enough to send a reply. All you have to do is follow these steps:

1. In the original message, click the Reply link. This expands the message to include a reply box, like the one shown in Figure 21.7.

2. The text of the original message is already quoted in the reply; add your new text above the original text.

3. The original sender's address is automatically added to the To: line, so click the Send button when to send the message on its way.

FIGURE 21.7

Replying to an email message.

Forwarding Messages

Sometimes you might want to forward a message to a third party, instead of simply replying to the original sender. You do this by following these steps:

1. In the original message, click the Forward link. This expands the message to include a forward box, like the one shown in Figure 21.8.

2. Add the recipient's email address to the To: box.

3. Enter your cover message into the main message box.

4. Click the Send button to send the message on its way.

21

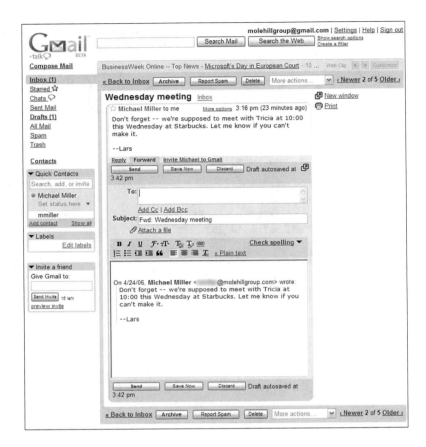

FIGURE 21.8

Forwarding an email message to a third party.

Composing and Sending New Messages

Creating a new message from scratch isn't a whole lot harder than replying to a preexisting message. All you have to do is follow these steps:

1. Click the Compose Mail link at the top of any Gmail page.

2. When the Compose Mail page appears, as shown in Figure 21.9, enter the recipient's email address into the To: box. Separate multiple recipients with commas.

tip You can cc (carbon copy) and bcc (blind carbon copy) additional recipients byvf clicking the Add Cc and Add Bcc links; this expands the message to include Cc or Bcc boxes, into which you enter the recipients' addresses. (A bcc sends the message to the intended recipients, but hides their addresses from the main recipients; a cc displays the recipients' addresses.)

3. Enter a subject for the message into the Subject box.

4. Enter the text of your message into the large text box. Use the formatting controls (bold, italic, font, and so forth) to enhance your message as desired.

5. When you're done composing your message, click the Send button.

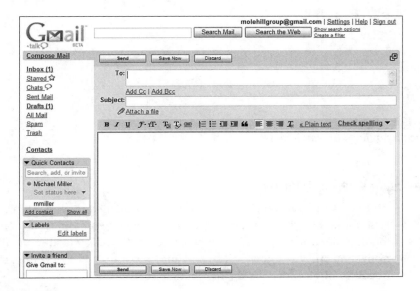

FIGURE 21.9

Composing a new email message.

Attaching Files

One of the key features of Gmail is its capability to store large amounts of data. You can use this feature to email files to yourself for backup purposes; of course, you can also email files to other users, as you wish.

To attach a file to a Gmail message, follow these steps:

1. Compose a new message as discussed previously.

2. From the new message page, click the Attach a File link.

tip

Gmail provides spell checking for all your outgoing messages. Just click the Check Spelling link, and then accept or reject suggested spelling changes throughout your document.

21

3. When the Choose File dialog box appears, navigate to and select the file you want to attach, and then click the Open button.

The file you selected now appears under the Subject box on the new message page, as shown in Figure 21.10. To attach another file to this same message, click the Attach Another File link; otherwise, continue composing and sending your message as normal.

FIGURE 21.10

Attaching a file to an email message.

Opening or Viewing Attached Files

What do you do if someone sends you a file attached to an email message? First, make sure that you're expecting the attachment, and that it's not a virus tagging along for the ride. If you're confident that it's a legitimate attachment from someone you know and trust, you can opt to either view the attachment (ideal for photos) or save the attachment to your hard drive.

When you receive a message with an attachment, you see a little paper clip icon next to the message subject/snippet, as shown in Figure 21.11. To view or save an attachment, follow these steps:

1. Click the message to open it.

2. If the attachment is an image file, the photo will display in the opened message, as shown in Figure 21.12. To view other types of files, or to view a photo in a separate window, click the View link.

3. To save the file to your hard disk, click the Download link. When the File Download dialog box appears, click the Save button, select a location for the file, and then click the second Save button.

caution While you can send Word documents, Excel spreadsheets, MP3 music files, JPG picture files, and the like, Gmail won't let you send any executable program files. (These are files that have an EXE extension.) You can't even send EXE files when they're compressed into ZIP files. Gmail blocks the transmittal of all EXE files, in an attempt to prevent potential computer viruses.

21

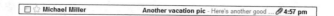

FIGURE 21.11

A message with a file attached.

FIGURE 21.12

Attached photos display automatically when you open a message.

Deleting Messages

There are two ways to delete messages in Gmail:

■ From the inbox page, check the message and then click the Delete button.

■ From any open message, click the Delete button.

Either of these two approaches moves the selected message to the Trash bin. Messages stay in the Trash bin for 30 days; after that, they're permanently deleted.

Searching Your Inbox

As noted previously, Gmail organization is based on Google's popular search paradigm. That is, to find a specific message in your crowded inbox, you have to search for it.

> **tip** You can view the messages in the Trash bin by clicking the Trash link. You can then undelete any message by checking it and then clicking the Move to Inbox button.

21

Basic Search

For most users, Gmail's basic search feature will quickly and easily find the messages you're looking for. All you have to do is follow these steps:

1. Enter one or more keywords into the search box at the top of any Gmail page.

2. Click the Search Mail button.

> **caution** Unlike Google's web search, Gmail search doesn't offer automatic stemming—which means it doesn't recognize matches to partial strings, plurals, misspellings, and the like. If you search for **dog**, Gmail won't recognize **dogs**, **dogged**, or **doggy**.

Gmail now returns a search results page, like the one shown in Figure 21.13. This page lists messages in which the queried keywords appear anywhere in the message—in the subject line, in the message text, or in the sender or recipient lists. Click a message to read it.

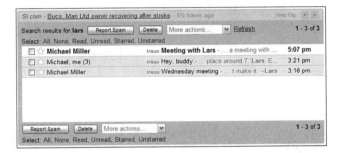

FIGURE 21.13

Viewing the results of a Gmail search.

Searching with Search Options

The more messages in your inbox, the more you'll need to fine-tune your mail searches. Fortunately, Gmail makes this easy with a simple checkbox interface. When you click the Show Search Options link (beside the search box), the top of the Gmail page expands, as shown in Figure 21.14. From here, you can search according to the parameters listed in Table 21.1:

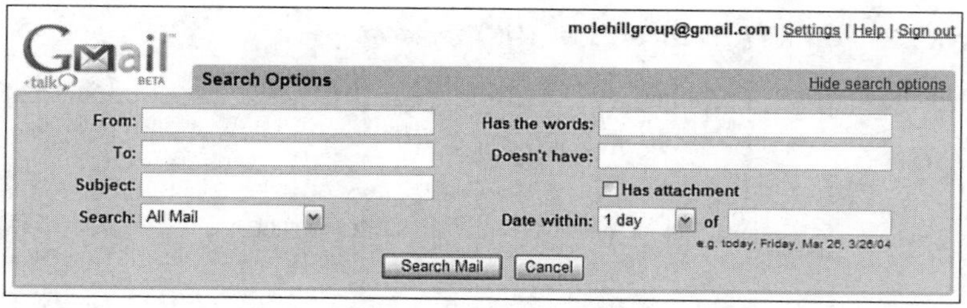

FIGURE 21.14
Fine-tuning your search with Gmail Search Options.

Table 21.1	Gmail Search Options
Search Option	**Description**
From:	Searches within the sender (From:) field only
To:	Searches within the recipient (To:) field only
Subject	Searches within the message subject line only
Search	Pull down to search within All Mail (including archived messages), Inbox, Starred, Chats, Sent Mail, Drafts, Spam, Trash, All Spam & Trash, Read Mail, or Unread Mail
Has the words	Searches for messages that contain all the words listed
Doesn't have	Searches for messages that don't contain the words listed
Has attachment	Limits searches to messages with files attached
Date within	Narrows searches to a specific timeframe (1 day, 3 days, 1 week, 2 weeks, 1 month, 2 months, 6 months, 1 year) of the specified date

Just enter your keywords into the box(es) next to the criteria you want, and then click the Search Mail button.

Searching with Advanced Operators

If you prefer to do your searching from the search box only, Gmail offers a slew of advanced search operators you can employ. These operators work just like the regular search operators we discussed in Chapter 2, "Searching the Web," except they're specialized for the task of email searching.

Table 21.2 details the available Gmail search operators.

21

Table 21.2   Gmail Advanced Search Operators

Search Operator	Description	Example
from:	Searches for messages from a specific sender	from:sherry *or* from:sherry@example.net
to:	Searches for messages sent to a specific recipient	from:mike *or* from:mike@gmail.com
subject:	Searches for words contained in the message subject line	subject:meeting
OR	Searches for messages containing one or another word (OR must be in all caps)	sherry OR mike
-	Excludes messages that contain a specific word	-meeting
label:	Searches for messages by label	label:friends
has:attachment	Searches only for messages with files attached	has:attachment
filename:	Searches for attachment by name or filetype	filename:sherry.jpg *or* filename:pdf
" "	Searches for an exact phrase	"friday meeting"
( )	Used to group words in a query	from:(sherry OR mike) *or* subject:(dinner movie)
in:*location*	Searches for messages in specific areas of your account: anywhere, inbox, trash, spam	in:anywhere
is:*state*	Searches for messages that are read, unread, or starred	is:unread
cc:	Searches for recipients in the cc: field	cc:melinda
bcc:	Searches for recipients in the bcc: field	bcc:oliver
after:*year/month/day*	Searches for messages sent after a given date	after:2006/06/15
before:*year/month/day*	Searches for messages sent before a given date	before:2006/09/01

Obviously, you can combine any or all of these operators. For example, to search within a certain date range, combine the **after:** and **before:** operators, like this: **after:2006/06/15 before:2006/09/01**. To search for unread messages from a certain person, enter this query: **from:gary is:unread**. And so on.

note When you use the **in:anywhere** operator, it searches for messages anywhere in your account *except* in Spam or Trash.

Other Ways of Organizing Your Email Messages

If searching doesn't get the complete job done for you, Gmail offers a few other ways to organize your messages—short of offering folders, of course. Still, any little bit helps.

Starring Important Messages

If you find a message that you think is more important than other messages, you can "star" that messages. In effect, Gmail "starring" is the same as the "flagging" feature you find in competing email services and programs.

To star a message, just click the empty star next to the message in your inbox. Once clicked, the star appears in solid colors (a nice shade of gold with a blue border). Figure 21.15 shows both a starred and an unstarred message.

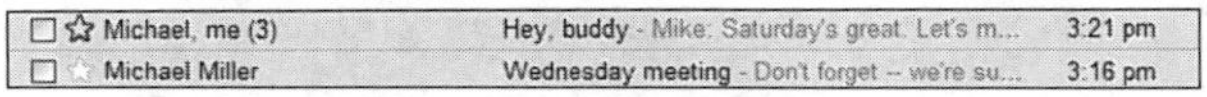

FIGURE 21.15

A starred message (above an unstarred message).

The advantage of starring messages is that Gmail lets you display only starred messages, if you like. Just click the Starred link to the left of the message window, and just the starred messages will be listed.

Applying Labels

Another way to organize your Gmail messages is to assign each message with a *label*, which is akin to attaching metadata to a photo or music file. In Google, this system is supposed to be equivalent to (and superior to) foldering, although I'm not so sure. Still, as I said before, every little bit helps.

You can assign one or more labels to every message in your inbox. Once labeled, you can then recall all messages that share a given label—which is kind of sort of like opening a folder.

To assign a label to a message, follow these steps:

1. In the inbox, check those messages you want to share the same label.
2. Pull down the More Actions list and select New Label. (Or, if you've already created a label, select this label from the pull-down list.)
3. If prompted (via a separate dialog box), enter the label you want to apply to the selected message(s).

21

To apply another label to the same message(s), just repeat this procedure. Once labeled, the label appears before the message's subject line, as shown in Figure 21.16.

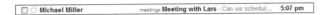

FIGURE 21.16

A labeled message.

Each of your labels also appears in the Labels box, at the bottom left of the inbox window, as shown in Figure 21.17. To view all messages with the same label, just click the label name in the Labels box; Gmail now displays all the messages labeled as such. (You can also use the **label:** operator in the search box to search for messages with a specific label.)

FIGURE 21.17

The Labels box.

Archiving Old Messages

If you're a busy little emailer, chances are your inbox will get very large very quickly. This is particularly so with Gmail, as you can't offload messages from the inbox into folders.

When your inbox becomes too cluttered with messages, Gmail lets you archive older messages. When you archive a message, it moves out of the inbox into a larger store called All Mail. Since all your Gmail searches search the All Mail messages, one strategy is to archive all messages after you've read them, thus freeing up the inbox for only your most recent messages.

> **tip** To edit or delete a label, click the Edit Labels link in the Labels box, and then click either the Rename or Remove Label link.

> **tip** Given Gmail's 2.7GB+ storage capacity, Google recommends archiving old messages rather than deleting them—just in case you ever need them. It's kind of a pack rat approach to email management, but that's what happens when storage is virtually unlimited and search tools are fairly effective.

To archive one or more messages, follow these steps:

1. From the Gmail inbox, check those messages you want to archive.

2. Click the Archive button.

> **tip**
> You can return archived messages to the inbox by clicking the All Mail link, checking the message(s) you want to move, and then clicking the Move to Inbox button.

That's it; the messages you marked are now removed from the inbox, but remain accessible from the All Mail link or whenever you perform a Gmail search.

Filtering Incoming Mail

Here's another way to organize your messages—specifically, to manage what happens to them when they arrive in your inbox. Gmail lets you create up to 20 filters that identify certain types of incoming messages and then handle them in a specified manner.

For example, you might want to create a filter that applies a label to all messages with certain words in the subject line. Or maybe star all messages that come from a particular person. Or forward all messages from one sender to another recipient. Or just automatically delete all messages from a particular sender, or on a particular subject.

Gmail lets you choose from five different actions for your filters:

- Skip the inbox (automatically archive the message)
- Star it
- Apply the label (choose from a list, or create a new label)
- Forward it to (a specified email address)
- Delete it

Here's how you create a filter:

1. From the Gmail inbox, click the Create a Filter link (beside the search box).

2. The Create a Filter section shown in Figure 21.18 now appears at the top of the inbox page. Enter the search criteria to identify which messages you want the filter applied to, and then click the Next Step button.

21

FIGURE 21.18
Specifying which messages the new filter will apply to.

3. When the next page appears, as shown in Figure 21.19, select the action you want the filter to initiate.

4. Click the Create Filter button.

FIGURE 21.19
Specifying the action you want the filter to apply.

All future messages that match your search criteria (as well as matching messages already in your inbox) will now have the specified action performed on them.

Dealing with Spam and Viruses

Google, like any responsible email provider, offers several features designed to reduce the amount of unwanted spam

tip To view all your current filters (and edit or delete selected filters), click the Settings link at the top of the Gmail inbox page, and then select the Filters tab.

messages you receive in your inbox, as well as reduce the risk of computer virus infection. These features are applied automatically, but it's nice to know how they work.

Blocking Spam Messages

Google applies a variety of internal spam filters to identify spam as it enters the Gmail system, and thus block it from appearing in users' inboxes. In most cases, you never see the spam; Google blocks it before it ever gets to you.

Sometimes spam makes it past Google's main filter but then is caught on the receiving end. When this happens, the spam message appears in the Spam section of your inbox. You can view purported spam messages by clicking the Spam link.

If Google happens to route a legitimate message to your Spam list (it happens sometimes), just check the message and click the Not Spam button. This will move the message out of the Spam list back into your general inbox.

If you inadvertently receive a spam message in your Gmail inbox, you can help train Google's spam filters by reporting it. You do this by checking the message in your inbox, and then clicking the Report Spam button. This action both removes the spam message from your inbox and sends information about the message back to Google.

Scanning Your Attachments for Viruses

Gmail also takes steps to protect you from email-borne computer viruses. These viruses typically come as file attachments, even more typically as EXE files attached to email messages.

To that end, Gmail automatically blocks the sending and receiving of all EXE files. It's a fairly draconian approach; there's no way around the system to send a legitimate EXE file, so don't bother trying.

Google also scans all the attached files you send and receive via Gmail, no matter what the file extension. If a virus is found in an attachment, Gmail tries to clean the file (remove the virus); if the virus can't be removed, you won't be able to download or send the file.

Working with Contacts

Every email program or service offers some sort of address book, a list of your most-frequent contacts. Gmail is no exception; its Contacts list lets you store

21

contact information (including but not limited to email addresses) for thou-sands of people. Even better, every time you send a message to a new email address, Gmail automatically adds that address to your Contacts list.

Adding a New Contact

As I just said, Google automatically adds any email address to which you send a message to your Contacts list. You can also manually add contacts to your list by following these steps:

1. Click the Contacts link on the left side of any Gmail page.
2. When the Contacts page appears, as shown in Figure 21.20, click the Create Contact link.
3. When the Add Contact page appears, as shown in Figure 21.21, enter the person's name and email address into the appropriate blanks.
4. Enter any additional information about this person into the Notes box.
5. Click the Save button to create the contact.

FIGURE 21.20

Gmail's Contacts page.

You can add even more information about a contact by clicking the Add More Contact Info link on the Add Contact page. This expands the page to include sections for phone number, address, and other information, as shown in Figure 21.22. You can even add your own custom fields and sections by click-ing the Add Another Field and Add Section links, respectively.

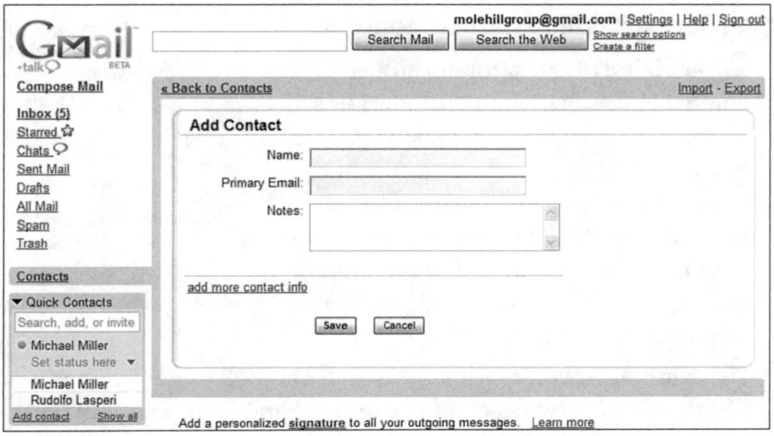

FIGURE 21.21
Adding a new contact.

FIGURE 21.22
Adding additional contact info.

Importing Contacts from Another Program

If you already have a lot of contacts entered in another email program or service, such as Microsoft Outlook or MSN Hotmail (and you probably do), you can import those contacts into your Gmail Contacts list. All you have to do is export your contacts from the other program or service into a CSV-format file, and then import that file into Gmail.

tip You can also add a sender's email address to your Contacts list whenever you receive a new email message. All you have to do is open the message, click the More Options link, and then click Add Sender to Contacts List.

For example, if you're using Microsoft Outlook as your primary email program, you start by selecting File, Import and Export (within Outlook), and then use Outlook's Import and Export Wizard to export your contacts into a Comma Separated Values (CSV) file.

Once the CSV file is created, you follow these steps to import the contacts into Gmail:

1. From the Gmail inbox, click the Contacts link.
2. When the Contacts page appears, click the Import link.
3. When the Import Contacts dialog box appears, as shown in Figure 21.23, click the Browse button to locate the file you want to import.
4. Once you've selected the file, click the Import Contacts button.
5. Once the contacts have been imported, click the Close link to close the dialog box.

Your contacts should now appear in Gmail's Contacts list.

Displaying Contacts

When you click the Contacts link on Gmail's inbox page, you display the Contacts list. There are three tabs within this list:

- Frequently Mailed, which displays only those contacts to whom you send the most messages
- All Contacts, which displays all your contacts, even those you never send email to
- Groups, which displays groups of contacts that you create

note We'll talk more about groups in the "Using Contact Groups" section, later in this chapter.

Click a tab to view the contacts within that tab.

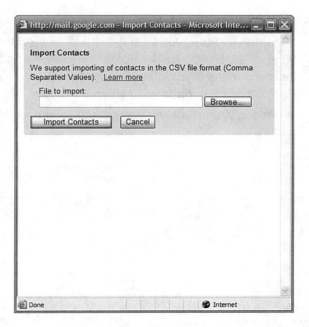

FIGURE 21.23
Importing contacts into Gmail.

Searching for Contacts

If you have a ton of contacts in your Contacts list, you may need to search for the ones you want to use. To search for a particular contact, go to the Contacts list, enter the name of that contact into the search box, and then click the Search Contacts button. You can search by a person's first name, last name, or both; you can also search by domain or email address.

Using Contact Groups

Most email programs let you create mailing lists that contain multiple email addresses, which makes it easier to send bulk mailings to groups of people. Gmail also offers a mailing list–like feature, which it calls contact groups. When you want to send a message to all members of a group, you only have to select the group name—not every contact individually.

To create a contact group, follow these steps:

1. From the Gmail inbox page, click the Contacts link.

2. When the Contacts page appears, as shown in Figure 21.24, click the Groups tab.

21

3. Click the Create Group link.

4. When the Create Group page appears, as shown in Figure 21.25, enter a name for this group into the Group Name box.

5. Enter the contacts you want included in this group into the Add Contacts box; use commas to separate names.

6. When you're done adding names to the group, click the Create Group button.

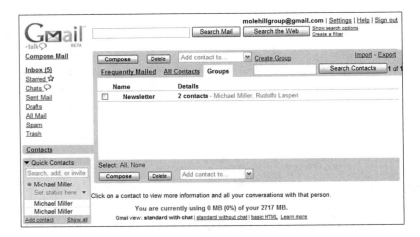

FIGURE 21.24

The Groups tab on Gmail's Contacts page.

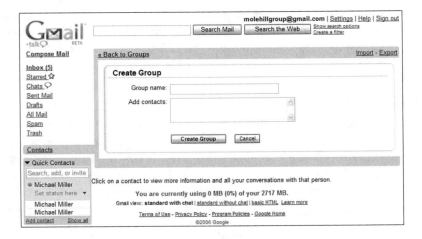

FIGURE 21.25

Creating a new contact group.

Sending a Message to a Contact or Contact Group

The whole point of creating contacts and contacts groups is to make it easier to send email messages—without having to remember all those email addresses every time. To that end, there are two ways to send messages to people or groups in your contacts list.

tip You can also add contacts to a group from either the Frequently Mailed or All Contacts tab. Just check the contacts you want to add, and then pull down the Add Contact To... list and select the name of the contact group.

First, you can send messages directly from the Contacts page. Select one of the three tabs, check the name of the person or group you want to email, and then click the Compose button. This creates a new blank message, with that person or group's email address(es) already added to the To: line.

Alternatively, you can click a contact's name in the Quick Contacts box, located on the left side of the Gmail page. As you can see in Figure 21.26, the Quick Contacts box lists those contacts with whom you've recently communicated, and also lets you search for people in your contacts list. When you click a contact name, a separate window opens with a new blank message displayed.

FIGURE 21.26

Gmail's Quick Contacts box.

Using Gmail with Other Email Programs and Accounts

Here's another neat thing about Gmail. Google lets you send your Gmail messages to any POP email program, or forward your messages to another email account. Both of these options let you read your Gmail messages in Microsoft Outlook or Outlook Express, as you like.

21

Reading Gmail in Another Email Program

You don't have to access Gmail from your web browser. Google lets you retrieve your Gmail messages through any POP email program, such as Microsoft Outlook, Outlook Express, Eudora, or Mozilla Thunderbird.

To do this, you have to enable POP email for your Gmail account. Follow these steps:

tip Because programs like Outlook allow you to put email into folders, this is one way around the lack of support for foldering in Gmail. However, keep in mind that any messages moved from your Gmail account into a folder in a separate email client won't be accessible if you access Gmail via the Web.

1. From the Gmail inbox, click the Settings link at the top of the page.

2. When the Settings page appears, select the Forwarding and POP tab, shown in Figure 21.27.

FIGURE 21.27

Setting up POP downloading and Gmail forwarding.

3. In the bottom half of this page, check the Enable POP for All Email option.

4. Pull down the When Messages Are Accessed with POP list and select either Keep Gmail's Copy in the Inbox (so that all messages are still accessable from Gmail over the Web), Archive Gmail's Copy (so that all messages are also sent to Gmail's All Mail list), or Delete Gmail's copy (so that messages do not appear on the Gmail website).

5. Click the Save Changes button

6. Open your POP email program and create a new account for your Gmail messages. When prompted, enter **pop.gmail.com** as the incoming mail server, and **smtp.gmail.com** as the outgoing (or SMTP) mail server.

From now on, you should be able to retrieve your Gmail messages from your existing POP email program.

Forwarding Gmail to Another Account

You can also forward your Gmail messages to another of your email accounts. This is different from reading your messages in another program, in that copies of your messages are sent to your other email address. You then retrieve these copies of your Gmail messages whenever you check the mail in your other account.

To set up Gmail forwarding, follow these steps:

1. From the Gmail inbox, click the Settings link at the top of the page.
2. When the Settings page appears, select the Forwarding and POP tab.
3. In the top half of this page, check the Forward a Copy of Incoming Mail To option.
4. Enter the address of your other email account into the email address box.
5. From the pull-down list, select how you want to handle the original Gmail messages—Keep Gmail's Copy in the Inbox, Archive Gmail's Copy, or Delete Gmail's copy.
6. Click the Save Changes button.

Either of these options, by the way, are great for when you're on vacation. You can forward your Gmail to whichever account you read when you're away from home—or simply use your other email program to read your Gmail messages at your leisure.

Putting Gmail into Vacation Mode

Speaking of vacation, Gmail also has a dedicated vacation mode. When you activate vacation mode, anyone who sends you a message automatically gets a response that you're on vacation.

Here's how to activate Gmail's vacation mode:

1. From the Gmail inbox, click the Settings link at the top of the page.
2. When the Settings page appears, select the General tab and scroll down to the Vacation section, shown in Figure 21.28.
3. Check the Vacation Responder On option.
4. Enter a subject for the messages you want the responder to automatically send out, something along the lines of "I'm on vacation."
5. Enter the text of your vacation message.

21

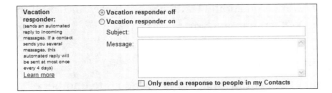

FIGURE 21.28

Gmail's vacation settings.

6. If you want only your contacts to receive this vacation message, check the Only Send a Response to People in My Contacts option.

7. Click the Save Changes button.

That's it. With the vacation responder activated, anyone who sends you a message automatically receives your vacation message in reply. When you return from vacation, return to the Settings page and check the Vacation Responder Off option.

Viewing RSS Feeds in Gmail

If you've worked with Gmail at all, you've probably noticed the little headlines and links that appear at the top of the inbox list, like the one in Figure 21.29. Google calls these things Web Clips, and you use them to view news headlines and blog postings via RSS or Atom feeds. It's a great way to keep up on the newest postings in your favorite blogs.

FIGURE 21.29

A Web Clip at the top of the Gmail inbox list.

Unless you specify, Google just plants a random feed at the top of your inbox. To specify which feeds you display as Web Clips, follow these steps:

1. From the Gmail inbox, click the Settings link at the top of the page.

2. When the Settings page appears, select the Web Clips tab, shown in Figure 21.30.

3. By default, Gmail cycles through headlines and clips from all the sites and blogs listed on the Web

> **tip** To scroll through additional Web Clips, click the left and right arrows next to the current clip.

Clips tab. To remove any site/blog from this assortment, click the appropriate Remove link.

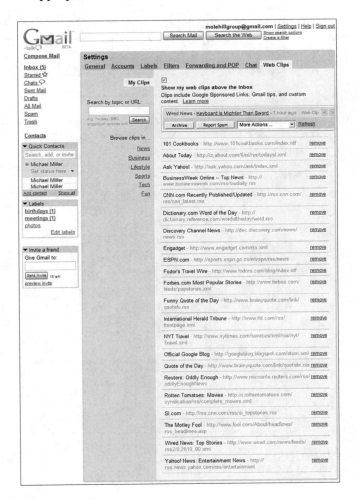

FIGURE 21.30
Selecting which Web Clips to display at the top of your inbox list.

4. To add a new blog or feed to the Web Clips assortment, enter the URL or the name of the feed into the search box, and then click the Search button. When the Search Results page appears, as shown in Figure 21.31, click the Add button next to the feed you want to add.

If you prefer *not* to view Web Clips at the top of your inbox list, simply uncheck the Show My Web Clips Above the Inbox option.

21

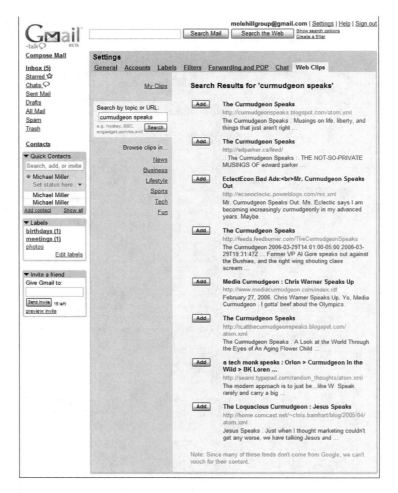

FIGURE 21.31

Searching for feeds to display as Web Clips.

Adding a Signature to Your Messages

If you want to add a personalized signature to the bottom of all your email messages, you don't have to manually enter that signature every time you send a message. Instead, you can configure Gmail to automatically add the signature. Just follow these steps:

1. From the Gmail inbox, click the Settings link at the top of the page.
2. When the Settings page appears, select the General tab, shown in Figure 21.32.

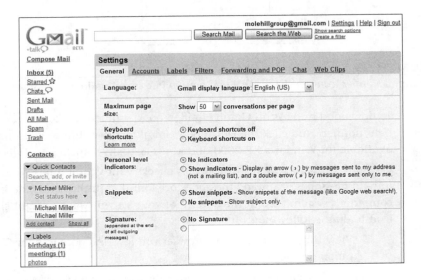

FIGURE 21.32
Configuring Gmail's signature settings.

3. Scroll down to the Signature section and check the second option (the one below No Signature).
4. Enter your signature into the large text box.
5. Click the Save Changes button.

If you prefer not to include a signature, check the No Signature option.

Getting Notified of New Gmail Messages

As convenient as Gmail is, it can be even more convenient if you're automatically notified when you receive new messages in your inbox. There are two ways to do this—via the Gmail Notifier program, or via the Google Toolbar.

Using the Gmail Notifier

Gmail Notifier is a utility that displays an icon in your system tray when you have new Gmail messages, like the one in Figure 21.33. It can even display the subjects, senders, and snippets from those messages, all without you having to go to the Gmail site.

FIGURE 21.33

The Gmail Notifier icon (on the far left) and pop-up info about an inbox message.

To download and install Gmail Notifier, go to mail.google.com/mail/ help/notifier/ and click the Download Gmail Notifier button. Versions are available for Windows XP/2000 and Mac OS 10.3.9+ (including Tiger).

Once the Gmail Notifier is installed, it checks your Gmail inbox for any unread messages. If unread messages are found, it displays an icon in your computer's system tray, at the bottom of your screen. You can right-click this icon to do the following:

- View Inbox (opens a new browser window and goes to your Gmail inbox on the Web)
- Check Mail Now (rechecks your inbox for new messages)
- Tell Me Again (displays info about unread inbox messages in a pop-up window above the system tray)
- Options (configures the utility)
- About (displays version number and other info)

Using the Google Toolbar

Alternatively, if you have the Google Toolbar installed, you can view unread messages by clicking the down arrow next to the Gmail button, as shown in Figure 21.34. To open a new browser window and go directly to your Gmail inbox on the Web, just click the main Gmail button.

FIGURE 21.34

Viewing new Gmail messages from the Google Toolbar.

The Bottom Line

While I don't particularly like the lack of folders, I grudgingly admit that Google has created a pretty good web-based email service with Gmail. I particularly like the huge storage capability, which just encourages my pack-rattish tendencies. It's a worthy competitor for the more established MSN Hotmail and Yahoo! Mail services.

And there's more. Gmail also offers a live chat function, which we'll discuss in Chapter 22, "Instant Messaging with Google Talk and Gmail Chat." Turn the page to learn more.

note Learn more about the Google Toolbar in Chapter 31, "Using the Google Toolbar."

tip If you have an Internet-enabled cell phone or other mobile device, there's one more way to check your Gmail messages. All you have to do is point your phone's web browser to m.gmail.com, and follow the onscreen instructions from there.

21

Instant Messaging with Google Talk and Gmail Chat

America Online has its AOL Instant Messenger (AIM) service. Microsoft has its MSN Messenger service. Yahoo! has Yahoo! Messenger. It should come as no surprise, then, that Google is now offering an instant messaging service called Google Talk.

What is surprising is that you can access Google Talk from the standalone Google Talk client (similar to what's offered with both AIM and MSN Messenger) or from the Gmail web page. That's right, you can instant message your friends from Google's web-based email service. Cool.

Instant Messaging with Google Talk

Google Talk is the name of both Google's instant messaging network and its IM client. You can download the Google Talk client and learn more about the Google Talk network at talk.google.com.

As with competing IM systems, Google Talk lets you send and receive both text-based instant messages and voice-over-IP Internet phone calls. To use Google Talk as a text-based IM client, all you need is your computer and an Internet connection; to use Google Talk for Internet phone calls, you'll also need a microphone and a speaker for your PC.

> **note** To use Google Talk or Google Chat, you must have a Gmail username and password. Learn more about signing up for Gmail in Chapter 21, "Sending and Receiving Email with Gmail."

Finding Someone to Talk To

Once you have Google Talk installed, you need to find someone to talk to. Here's where there's a bit of a speed bump. You see, Google Talk only lets you instant message with other Google Talk subscribers. If your friends are all using AIM or MSN Messenger, you can't talk to them with Google Talk. None of these IM networks are interchangeable; none of them interface with each other.

Sorry.

You can, however, talk to any other Google Talk user, or any other person who's using Google's Gmail service. And you can invite new users to sign up for Gmail and Google Talk. All you have to do is click the +Add button at the bottom of the Google Talk window; when the Invite Your Friends to Google Talk dialog box appears, enter your friend's email address and click the Next button.

If your friend already has a Gmail account, he'll get an invite to download the Google Talk client. If not, you'll be prompted to send a Gmail invitation in addition to the Google Talk invite.

As to chatting with other Gmail or Google Talk users, all your Gmail contacts are pre-loaded into Google Talk, the most frequently emailed contacts first. Contacts who already have Google Talk have a colored ball next to their names; a gray ball means they're offline, a red ball means they're busy, an orange ball means they're idle (away from the keyboard), and a green ball means they're online and available to chat.

Initiating a Text-Based Chat

Google Talk, like most IM clients, starts automatically every time you turn on your computer. You're prompted to sign in, using your Gmail ID, and then you see the

> **note** Unlike some other IM services, you can't currently use Google Talk to send photos or other files to the person you're chatting with.

Google Talk window. As you can see in Figure 22.1, all your friends are listed in the bottom half of the window. Friends who are available to IM have a green ball next to their names.

FIGURE 22.1

The main Google Talk window.

To start a chat with one of your friends, just click on that person's name. This opens a new chat window, like the one in Figure 22.2. Enter a message in the bottom text box, and then press Enter. Your ongoing discussion is displayed in the main window.

FIGURE 22.2

Chatting in Google Talk.

Blocking Other Users

Every now and then you run into some jerk online that you really don't want to talk to again. Fortunately, Google Talk lets you block incoming messages from selected users. You can do this in one of two ways:

> **tip** To send a private email to the person you're chatting with, click the Email button.

- If the person is in your Friends list, right-click the name and select Block.
- If you're currently chatting with the person, click the Options button (in the chat window) and select Block.

To unblock a previously blocked user, click the Settings link (in the main Google Talk window) to open the Settings dialog box, select Blocked, select the person to unblock, and then click the Unblock button.

Saving Your Chat History

By default, Google Talk saves copies of all your chats. Some users like this ability to revisit a chat history, just in case something important got discussed that you'd like to refer to again.

Each complete chat session is saved as a message in your Gmail account. When you click the Chat link on the Gmail inbox page, you see a list of all your chats, as shown in Figure 22.3. Click a chat to read the history, or delete the chats you don't really want to keep.

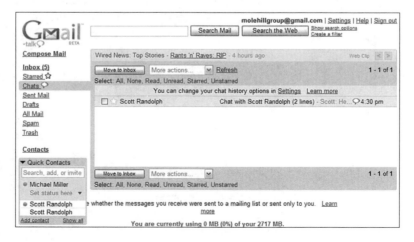

FIGURE 22.3

Revisiting chat histories in Gmail.

At any point in any IM session, you can go "off the record" and halt the history recording. All you have to do is click the Options button (in the top-left corner of the chat window) and select Go Off the Record. To resume recording the chat history, click the Options button and select Stop Chatting Off the Record. (By the way, once you go off the record with a given user, all your subsequent chats—for this and other users—will be off the record until you choose to go on the record again.)

tip

If you prefer not to save a history of your chats, click the Settings link in the main Google Talk window; when the Settings dialog box appears, select Chat and then check the Don't Save Chat History in My Gmail Account option.

Changing Your Status—And Signing Out

To change your online status, click the Available list under your name in the Google Talk window. You can choose to sign out completely, display your status as busy (with a standard message or a custom message), or display your status as available (again, with a standard message or a custom message). To sign out completely, select Sign Out.

Initiating a Voice-Based Chat

Google Talk also lets you conduct voice-based chat sessions with your fellow users. These Internet phone sessions are possible only if both computers are equipped with a microphone and speaker (or, alternatively, a telephone headset).

There are two ways to initiate a voice phone call:

- Click the phone icon next to a name on your Friends list.
- During an ongoing text-based chat, click the Call button in the chat window.

If your computer is not equipped with a microphone and speaker, you won't see the Call button.

Customizing Google Talk

There are many ways to personalize the way Google Talk looks and acts. These settings are all accessed via the Settings dialog box, shown in Figure 22.4. You open this dialog box by clicking the Settings link in the main Google Talk window.

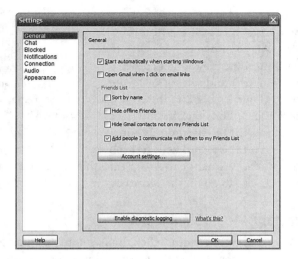

FIGURE 22.4

Configuring general Google Talk settings.

Some of the more important settings include

- To keep Google Talk from automatically launching whenever you turn on your computer, select General and then uncheck the Start Automatically When Starting Windows option.

- To not save chat history, select Chat and then check the Don't Save Chat History in My Gmail Account option.

- To change how you're notified when someone wants to chat with you, select Notifications and check the appropriate options.

- To change the look of Google Talk, select Appearance and make a new selection from the Chat Theme list (Figure 22.5 shows one of the alternate chat themes).

FIGURE 22.5

Choosing a new chat theme.

Chatting via Gmail with Gmail Chat

One of the most unique features of Google Talk is that you don't need the Google Talk client to instant message other users. You can, if you choose, do all your chatting from within Gmail, using your normal web browser.

Initiating a Chat

There are a few different ways to start a chat from within Gmail. You can

- Click the person's name in your Quick Contacts list.
- Hover over the person's name in your Quick Contacts list to display detailed information, and then click the Chat button.
- Click the Contacts link to display your Contacts list; you can then hover over the person's name and click the Chat button.

Once you've done one of these actions, a message window appears in the lower-right corner of your web browser, as shown in Figure 22.6. If you prefer to view the chat in a separate window, like the one in Figure 22.7, click Pop-out. In either case, you enter your messages in the bottom text box, and then press Enter; the full chat is shown in the space above.

FIGURE 22.6

Chatting from within the Gmail browser window.

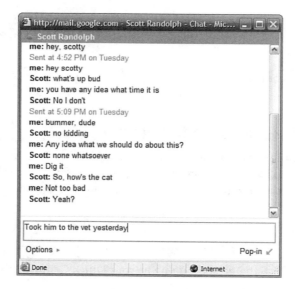

FIGURE 22.7

Viewing Gmail chat in a separate pop-out window.

And, of course, you can go off the record or block a user the same way you do with the Google Talk client, just by clicking the Options menu.

Changing Your Status—And Ending Your Chat Session

When it's time to end a chat session, you can sign out of Google Talk by pulling down the Set Status Here menu in the Contacts section of the Gmail inbox page. Here are your options:

22

- Sign out of chat
- Busy
- Busy with custom message
- Available
- Available with custom message

Select Sign Out of Chat to sign out, or just click Busy if you're only going to be temporarily unavailable.

COMMENTARY:

THE TROUBLE WITH GOOGLE TALK

To quote the movie *Soylent Green*, the problem with Google Talk is *people*. There simply aren't enough of them.

You see, Google is a latecomer to the instant messaging game, and really doesn't offer anything new or unique for users. In fact, Google Talk doesn't have quite as many features as AIM or MSN Messenger; you can't send files via Google Talk, for instance, which you can with the other systems. In other words, there is no compelling new technology- or feature-related reason to switch from another IM system to Google Talk.

That is readily apparent when you consider how few people are using Google Talk. No hard numbers are available, but you can easily see for yourself; how many of *your* friends are online with Google Talk, versus those who are currently using AIM, MSN Messenger, or Yahoo! Messenger? Instant messaging, at the end of the day, is all about your friends. You have to have someone to talk to; if none of your friends are using Google Talk, you're talking to yourself.

Until Google Talk attracts more users, however, it remains one of Google's little-known and lesser-used features. That might change, however, when Google connects with AOL's instant messaging network, which Google says is in the works. (It's part of Google's strategic alliance with—and $1 billion investment in—America Online.) Look for Google Talk/AIM interoperability within the next year or so.

22

Using Google Talk with Other IM Networks

note Learn more about the Jabber open instant messaging protocol at www.jabber.org.

As I noted previously, Google Talk doesn't connect with other instant messaging networks; with Google Talk, you're pretty much limited to IM'ing with other Google Talk users.

Unless, that is, you know the trick.

You see, Google has always had the goal of connecting Google Talk to the other large IM networks. To that end, Google Talk is built on the Jabber protocol, which allows for interoperability between compatible IM services. Unfortunately, the list of compatible IM services today is short and not very extremely useable.

There, is, however, a hack that lets you use the Google Talk client to connect to the AIM, ICQ, MSN Messenger, and Yahoo! Messenger networks. What you have to do is connect Google Talk to a Jabber server, and from there use a specialized transport to connect to your IM network of choice.

Here's how to make it work:

1. Download and install the Psi Jabber client from psi-im.org.
2. Launch the Psi client, as shown in Figure 22.8.

FIGURE 22.8

The Psi Jabber client.

3. Click the Psi button in the lower-left corner and select Account Setup.

4. When the Jabber Accounts dialog box appears, click the Add button.

5. In the Name: field, type **Google Talk**, and then make sure the Register New Account option is *not* checked.

6. Click the Add button.

7. When the Account Properties dialog box appears, select the Account tab (shown in Figure 22.9).

note To connect to another IM network in this manner, you must be a subscriber to that network. You'll be prompted to enter your username and password for any IM service you try to connect to.

FIGURE 22.9
Configuring Psi to connect to Google Talk.

8. Enter your full Gmail email address in the Jabber ID field.

9. Select the Connection tab, shown in Figure 22.10.

10. Check all the options on this tab, and then enter **talk.google.com** into the Host field.

11. Click the Save button.

12. Back in the main Psi window, click the Psi button and select Service Discovery, Google Talk.

FIGURE 22.10

Configuring Google Talk options in Psi.

13. When the Service Discovery dialog box appears, enter the address of any public Jabber server into the Address box and then press Enter. (You can find a list of public Jabber servers on the www.jabber.org site; you may have to try more than one server to find one that offers the IM transport you want.)

14. As shown in Figure 22.11, you should now see a list of available IM transports (among other things). Click the transport for the IM network you want to connect to.

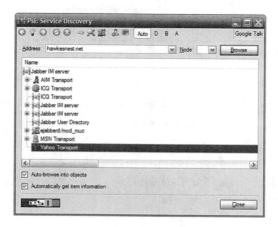

FIGURE 22.11

Viewing available IM transports.

15. Wait a few seconds for Psi to gather the appropriate data for the selected transport, and then right-click on the transport and select the Register option.

16. When the Registration dialog box appears, as shown in Figure 22.12, enter your username and password for that IM network and then click the Register button.

FIGURE 22.12

Registering for the selected IM network.

17. Psi will now connect to the selected IM network and retrieve your contacts.

18. Once your contacts have been retrieved, exit Psi.

The next time you launch Google Talk, all your contacts from the selected IM service should be listed in your Google Talk Friends list. When you click any of that IM network's contacts from within Google Talk, you automatically connect to that network and can IM to your heart's content.

This is, admittedly, a bit of a hassle—and it doesn't always work perfectly. Still, if you're technically competent, you might want to give it try—and see if you can use Google Talk to connect to AIM, Yahoo! Messenger, or another large IM network.

The Bottom Line

Google Talk works pretty much like AIM and MSN Messenger, although it isn't quite as feature-rich as those more-established IM clients. It also isn't near as popular; perhaps the biggest drawback to Google Talk is that too few people are using it.

note As Psi adds your IM contacts, you'll probably receive a series of system messages asking you to okay the addition of each contact. Click the Add/Auth button to authorize each contact.

22

Bottom line, you want to use the IM system that all your friends are using, and for now that probably means AOL Instant Messenger or MSN Messenger—at least until Google Talk offers official connection to the AIM network.

Using Blogger

If you want to create your own personal blog, you have two ways to go. You can use blogging software to create a blog on your own website, using your own web hosting service. Alternatively, you can create a blog at one of the many blog hosting communities.

A blog hosting community is a site that offers easy-to-use tools to build and maintain your blog, and then does all the hosting for you—typically for free. Creating your own blog on one of these sites is as simple as clicking a few buttons and filling out a few forms. And once your blog is created, you can update it as frequently as you like, again by clicking a link or two.

Perhaps the most popular blog hosting community on the Web today is Blogger, which Google just happens to own. Now, you might think that Blogger has very little to do with Google's core competency in search technology, and you'd be right. But Blogger does offer Google lots of opportunities to sell advertising space, and as we've discussed throughout this book, that's how Google makes its money.

So, since Blogger is an important part of the Google empire, it gets covered in this book. It also helps that Blogger is very good at what it does, perhaps the best (and definitely the biggest) of all the blog hosting communities on the Web today. If you want to launch your own personal blog, you could do worse than use Blogger.

How Blogs Are Organized

Before we delve into the ins and outs of Blogger, let's take a minute to look at how blogs work, in general. As we first discussed in Chapter 6, "Searching Blogs and Blog Postings," a blog is kind of like a personal diary made public on the Web, a kind of message forum that any user can create. After you launch your blog, you populate it as frequently as you want with your various and sundry musings, in the form of individual blog posts. Other users can respond to your postings, and you can respond to their responses. In this way, a blog is an organic thing.

And, while blogs reside on the Web and are viewed via web browsers, they're organized much differently than normal websites. Instead of the standard home page plus subsidiary page structure, a blog typically has just a single page of entries. This main page contains the most recent posts, and might require a bit of scrolling to get to the bottom. There's no introductory page; this main page serves as both introduction and primary content.

Older posts are typically stored in the blog archives. You'll normally find a link to the archives somewhere on the main page; there might be one huge archive, or individual archives organized by month.

The blog posts themselves are arranged in reverse chronological order. That means that the most recent post is always at the top of the page, with older posts below that. Comments to a post are typically in normal chronological order; you may have to click a link to see a separate page of comments.

Beyond this basic structure, that's all the organization you're likely to find in most blogs. That's because, for many bloggers, blog entries are a stream of consciousness thing. Bloggers blog when they find something interesting to write about, which makes the typical blog a little like a public diary. Don't look for a logical flow or organization; that's not what blogs are about. Instead, post your thoughts and opinions as they occur. It's the way the blogosphere works.

COMMENTARY:

WHY BLOG?

Blogging takes time—even when you utilize an easy-to-use tool like Blogger. Not only do you have to create the blog, you then have to keep it updated on a fairly frequent basis. For some bloggers, this means daily posts; for others, several posts a day. Knowing this, how do so many bloggers find time for all these postings—and why?

For what it's worth, there isn't a single answer to that question.

You see, some people view their blogs as a kind of personal-yet-public scrapbook—an online diary to record their thoughts for posterity. Even if no one else ever looks at it, it's still valuable to the author as Arepository of thoughts and information he or she can turn to at any later date.

But that isn't always the case. While some blogs are completely free-form, many other blogs have some sort of focus. For example, Tech Blog (talkingtechs.blogspot.com) is a blog all about technology-related topics; High Fiber Content (highfibercontent.blogspot.com) is a blog about quilting. Other bloggers write about music or videogames or travel or cooking or whatever they're interested in. Their blogs include their thoughts on the topic at hand, as well as links to interesting news articles and websites.

Other people blog for a cause. Liberal blogs link to left-leaning stories and pages; conservative blogs contain commentary and links that reinforce their right-leaning viewpoints. There are blogs for every point on the political spectrum, and some you've never thought of.

In a way, the most serious bloggers are like columnists in the traditional media. They write with a passion, point-of-view, and personal sensibility that makes their blogs extremely interesting to read. Even bloggers who don't inject personal comments still offer a viewpoint based on what they choose to include and link to in their blogs. It's an interesting world out there in the blogosphere, and it's revolutionizing journalism (and journals) for the new online reality.

Getting to Know Blogger

Blogger (www.blogger.com) was a freestanding site with more than a million users long before Google acquired it in 2003. Since then, it's only gotten bigger—and better. In fact, Blogger is one of the crown jewels of the Google empire; its user base is now well over 3 million, or about 10% of all blogs on the Web. (And Google says the number of Blogger blogs is doubling every six months!)

If you're new to Blogger, the home page you see looks like the one in Figure 23.1. From here you can search through Blogger's millions of blogs and blog postings or opt to create your own blog (it's free).

FIGURE 23.1

Blogger's home page for new users.

Once you've registered with Blogger, you go directly to the Blogger Dashboard, shown in Figure 23.2. From here you can manage all your blogs, create new blog posts, manage your Blogger account and profile, search other Blogger blogs, and access Blogger's help system.

FIGURE 23.2

The Blogger Dashboard.

Creating a Blog

Before you can create a blog, you have to create a Blogger account. This account is separate from your Google account, so you'll have to go through the process even if you use Gmail, Google Talk, or other Google services.

Creating a Blogger account is a piece of cake. In fact, Blogger combines the process of creating your account and creating your first blog. It's a simple three-step process.

Start on the new user home page, and click Create Your Blog Now. This opens the Create an Account page, shown in Figure 23.3, where you enter your desired user name, password, display name (separate from your user name, if you like), and email address.

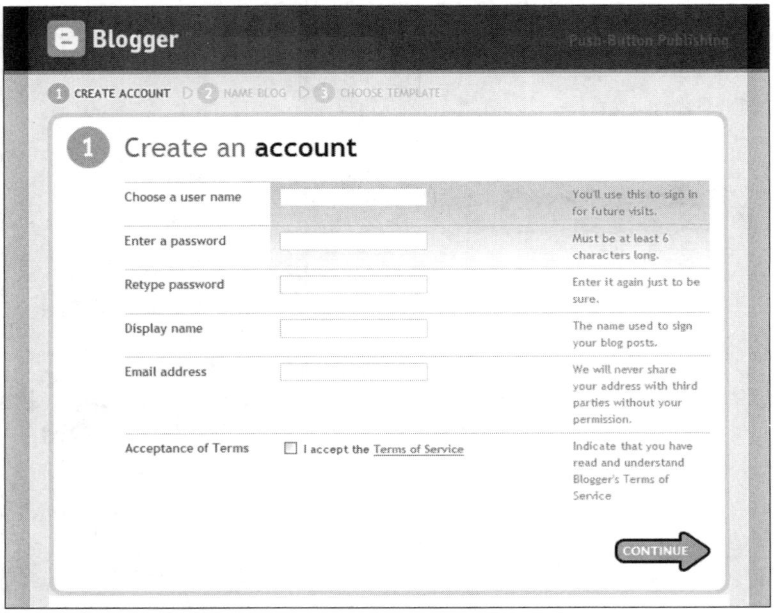

FIGURE 23.3

Creating your Blogger account.

When you click Continue, you see the Name Your Blog page, shown in Figure 23.4. Enter a title for your blog, a corresponding blog address (the part of the URL that goes before Blogger's blogspot.com domain), and click Continue.

Next, you get to choose a template for your blog. As you can see in Figure 23.5, a template is a pre-designed combination of page layout, colors, and fonts. Try to choose a template that's easily readable, especially for the types of postings you think you'll be doing. (You can preview any template at full size by clicking the Preview Template link under the template's thumbnail picture.) After you make your choice, click the Continue button.

note By default, Blogger serves as host for your blog, and assigns you a URL in the blogspot.com domain. If you'd rather host your blog on another website, read the "Changing Where Your Blog is Hosted" section, later in this chapter.

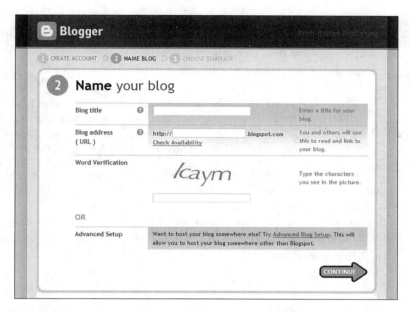

FIGURE 23.4
Naming your blog.

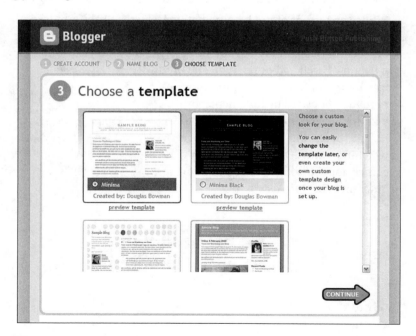

FIGURE 23.5
Choosing a template for your blog.

Blogger now creates your blog and displays a confirmation page. If now is a good time to write your first blog post, click the Start Posting link. Otherwise, you can create posts at any later time.

note Chances are you'll be happy with one of the default templates that Blogger offers. If not, you can change templates at any time, or use Blogger's various editing tools to customize the look and feel of your blog. Learn more in the "Changing Where Your Blog is Hosted" section, later in this chapter.

Viewing Your Blog

You can view your blog by entering the URL that was previously assigned, or by going to the Dashboard (www.blogger. com), clicking the blog name, and then clicking the View Blog tab. As you can see in Figure 23.6, a typical blog includes a Blogger search bar at the top of the page, with the title of the blog just below that. Blog posts take up the balance of the page, with assorted personal information in a narrow column to the right or left of the postings.

Each blog post is accompanied by a date and time stamp (sometimes above the post, sometimes below), as well as links to any reader comments or other blogs that have linked to this post. Click the Comments link to read any comments; click the Links to This Post link to see the links.

While the format of the blog posts themselves is fairly standard, the elements in the narrow column are highly customizable. Most blogs include an About Me section (which may or may not include a photo), a listing of recent posts, a listing of archived posts (typically organized by month), and any other information you choose to include here. For example, I've customized my blog to include books I'm reading, DVDs I'm watching, and CDs I'm listening to. You can customize your blog in a similar—or different—fashion, as you like.

note Specific blog elements and the placement thereof differ from blog to blog and from template to template. Your blog will probably look different from the one shown here.

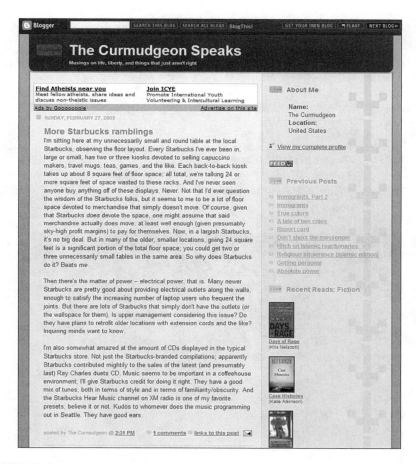

FIGURE 23.6

The author's blog—The Curmudgeon Speaks.

Posting New Blog Entries

Once you've launched your blog, it's time to write your first blog post. When you're ready to post, the place to start is the Blogger Dashboard. All you have to do is follow these steps:

1. From the Blogger Dashboard, click the New Post icon for this particular blog (as shown in Figure 23.7).

FIGURE 23.7
Click the New Post icon to create a new blog post.

> **2.** When the Posting page appears, as shown in Figure 23.8, enter a title for this post.

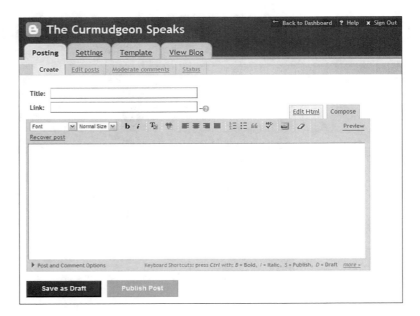

FIGURE 23.8
Creating a new blog post.

> **3.** If this post refers to another page on the Web, enter the URL for that page into the Link box.
>
> **4.** Enter the text for your post into the large text box. If you like, you can format the text (bold, italic, colors, etc.) using the formatting toolbar above this text box.
>
> **5.** If you want to apply more sophisticated formatting (and you know how to code in HTML), click the Edit HTML tab and enter your own HTML codes.

6. To check the spelling in your post, click the Check Spelling button and follow the onscreen instructions.

7. To view a preview of your post, click the Preview link.

8. To save a draft of your post for editing and posting at a future time, click the Save As Draft button.

9. When you're done writing and formatting, click the Publish Post button.

Blogger now publishes your post, and then displays the screen shown in Figure 23.9. Click the View Blog button to view your blog, with the new post at the top of the page.

FIGURE 23.9
Your post has been posted!

Blogging from the Google Toolbar

Thanks to Blogger being part of the Google family, there's another way to create blog posts. Assuming you have the Google Toolbar installed, you can reference any web page you visit in a new Blogger post. Here's how it works.

1. Navigate to a web page that you want to blog about.

2. From the Google Toolbar, shown in Figure 23.10, click Send To, Blogger.

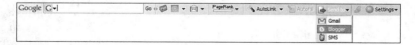

FIGURE 23.10
Sending the current web page to your Blogger blog.

3. When the Blog This! window appears, as shown in Figure 23.11, the name of the page appears in the main text window as a link. (It also appears as the title of this new post.) You can add more text, if you like, or change the title of the post.

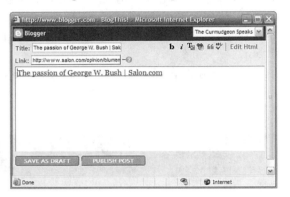

FIGURE 23.11
Creating the new post, based on a recently visited web page.

4. When you're done creating the new post, click the Publish Post button.

Any posts you create in this manner are published to your blog exactly the same as posts created from within the Blogger site. It's a quick and easy way to make note of interesting items you find on the Web!

Editing Your Posts

No one's perfect. Every now and then you'll post something to your blog and then discover an egregious spelling error, or a bad link, or maybe just something you wished you'd never written in the first place. Have no fear, gentle blogger; Blogger lets you edit any post you like.

To edit a Blogger post, follow these steps:

1. From the Blogger Dashboard, click the link for your blog.

2. When the list of recent posts appears, as shown in Figure 23.12, click the Edit button next to the post you want to edit.

3. When the Edit Post window appears, as shown in Figure 23.13, edit your post accordingly.

4. When done editing, click the Publish Post button.

note If you're managing more than one blog, you'll need to pull down the blog list at the top-right corner of the Blog This! window and select which blog you want to post this to.

FIGURE 23.12
Click the Edit button to edit any recent post.

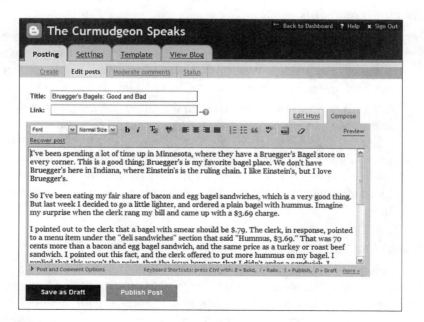

FIGURE 23.13
Editing a post.

Managing Comments—And Fighting Spam

By default, anyone can post comments to your blog postings. These comments appear below each posting, when you click the Comments link.

Limiting Comments

If you'd rather not have everyone and their brother comment on your blog, you can limit comments to either registered Blogger users or members of your blog. You do this by following these steps:

1. From the Blogger Dashboard, click the Change Settings icon next to your blog name.
2. When the Settings page appears, click the Comments tab, as shown in Figure 23.14.
3. Pull down the Who Can Comment? list and select either Anyone (the default setting), Only Registered Users, or Only Members of This Blog.
4. Click the Save Settings button.

Moderating Comments

The Comments tab of the Settings screen also lets you configure several other ways comments are displayed on your blog. One of the key settings concerns comment moderation. When you choose to moderate comments, you must approve any comments to your blog before they can be posted.

You turn on moderation by checking the Enable Comment Moderation? option on the Comments tab of the Settings page. This displays a new Moderate Comments tab on the Posting screen, which is where all user comments appear after they've been written. (You'll also be notified via email of all new comments.) On this page you can choose to publish or reject any listed comment; click the Publish button and the comment is posted to your blog.

Fighting Comment Spam

Another problem with blog comments is that, without any moderation, they can be used for spam purposes. That's right, unscrupulous spammers use spam robots to seed blog postings with unwanted spam messages. It's all done automatically; don't be surprised if you wake up one morning and find a ton of comments to your blog that have nothing at all to do with your original postings.

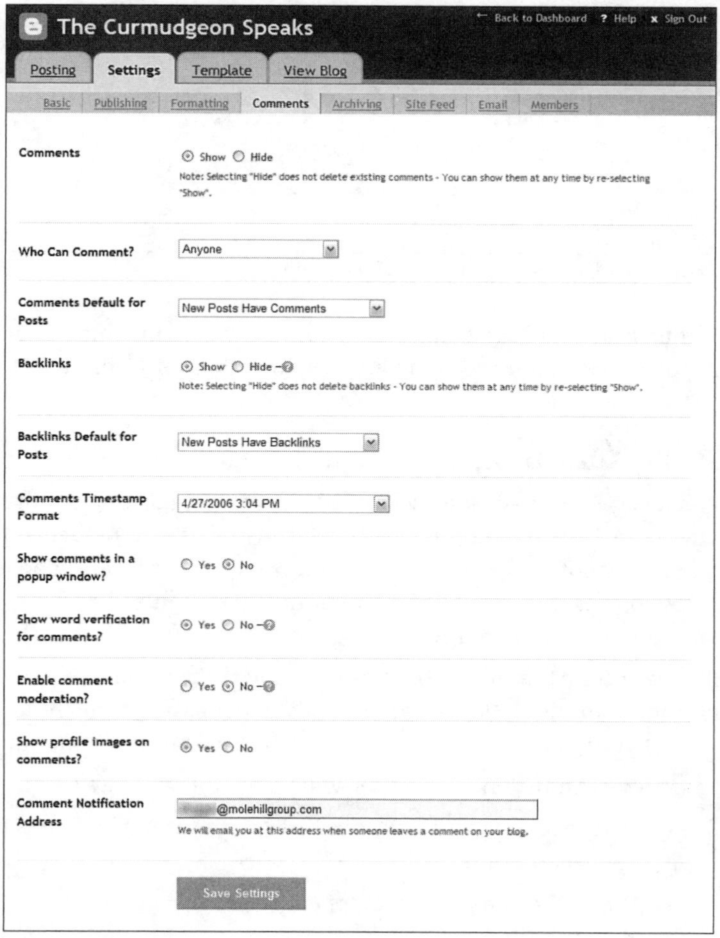

FIGURE 23.14

Configuring comments for your blog.

There's an easy way to defeat these spam robots. All you have to do is require some sort of human input for a comment to be posted. Blogger does this by adding a word verification section, like the one shown in Figure 23.15, to the comments posting page. Readers have to enter the word verification code before the comment can be posted; since robots can't read graphic images like this, they can't enter the word verification code, and no spam is left.

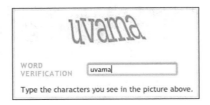

FIGURE 23.15

Word verification codes, like this one, stop blog spam.

You turn on word verification by going to the Comments tab on the Settings page and checking the Show Word Verification for Comments? option.

Syndicating Your Blog

Previously in this book we've talked a lot about RSS and Atom syndication. These are feeds that can be viewed with various feed readers and feed aggregators, so that interested users can view your most recent blog postings. When a new post is published, it is automatically recognized and displayed for anyone subscribing to your feed.

Blogger uses Atom for its blog syndication. When you activate Atom syndication for your blog, Blogger automatically generates a machine-readable version of your blog that can be read by most feed readers and aggregators.

To activate Atom syndication for your blog, follow these steps:

1. From the Blogger Dashboard, click the Change Settings icon next to your blog name.

2. When the Settings page appears, click the Site Feed tab, as shown in Figure 23.16.

3. Pull down the Publish Site Feed list and select Yes.

4. Pull down the Descriptions list and select either Full (to publish the full content of each post) or Short (to publish only the first paragraph or so of each post).

5. Click the Save Settings button.

note As you learned in Chapter 6, Google has its own Google Reader feed aggregator site, located at reader.google.com.

tip If you'd rather use RSS syndication instead of Atom, use the Feedburner service (www.feedburner.com).

FIGURE 23.16
Configuring Atom syndication.

Take notice of the URL for your site feed. It's typically your blog URL with
/atom.xml attached, like this: *myblog*.blogspot.com/atom.xml. To place a link
to this feed in your blog, add the following code to the sidebar section of your
HTML template:

```
<a href="<$BlogSiteFeedUrl$>" title="Atom feed">Site Feed</a>
```

Making Money from Your Blog

Here's something cool—and potentially profitable—about Blogger. Google lets
you insert context-sensitive text advertisements into your blog, which (in theory) could generate a bit of income for you.
Every time a visitor clicks on one of the ad
links, you earn a small commission. Just
how much of a commission you earn,
however, is not disclosed by Google—which
is a bit of an odd way to attract partici-
pants to their program, if you ask me.

note Learn more about
editing your tem-
plate's HTML in the "Changing
Where Your Blog is Hosted" section, later in this chapter.

These Blogger ads are served by Google's AdSense division. This is one of the key revenue-generating parts of the Google empire. It's to Google's benefit for you to add ads to your blog; the fact that you participate in the revenues is the carrot to get you to sign up.

To add AdSense ads to your blog, follow these steps:

1. From the Blogger Dashboard, click the Change Settings icon next to your blog name.

2. When the Settings page appears, select the Template tab and click the AdSense link.

3. When the AdSense page appears, as shown in Figure 23.17, pull down the Select Ad Format list and select an ad format. You can choose from various sizes and shapes of ads; the ad you select is previewed on the page below the pull-down list.

4. Pull down the Select Colors list and select a color scheme for your ad.

5. Click the Save button.

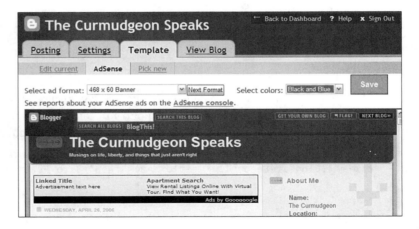

FIGURE 23.17

Adding AdSense ads to your blog.

After you've activated AdSense for your blog, you can view your ad activity in the AdSense console (www.google.com/adsense/). As you can see in Figure 23.18, the console tracks your click-through activity; you can also select the AdSense Setup and My Account tabs to manage the details of your account and ads.

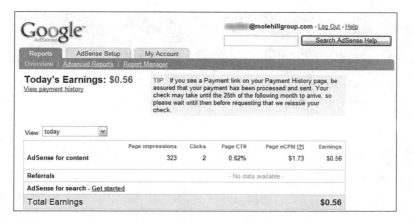

FIGURE 23.18

Managing your ads from the AdSense console.

Changing Where Your Blog Is Hosted

By default, your Blogger blog is hosted on the Blogger website, and has an address with the blogspot.com domain. You're not limited to using Blogger as a host, however; if you wish, you can host your blog on a different website, and give it a unique domain name.

To host your blog on another site, you first have to have another site, provided by a web hosting service. You also need to have FTP access to that site, since Blogger uses FTP to upload all blog postings.

Once your website is set up, you can then configure Blogger to use that site to host your blog. Here's what you need to do:

1. From the Blogger Dashboard, click the Change Settings icon next to your blog name.

2. When the Settings page appears, click the Publishing tab.

3. Click the FTP link. (Or, if your website host offers secure FTP, click the SFTP link.)

4. When the next page appears, as shown in Figure 23.19, enter the following settings:

> **note** Learn more about Google's AdSense program in Chapter 37, "Making Money with Google AdSense and AdWords."

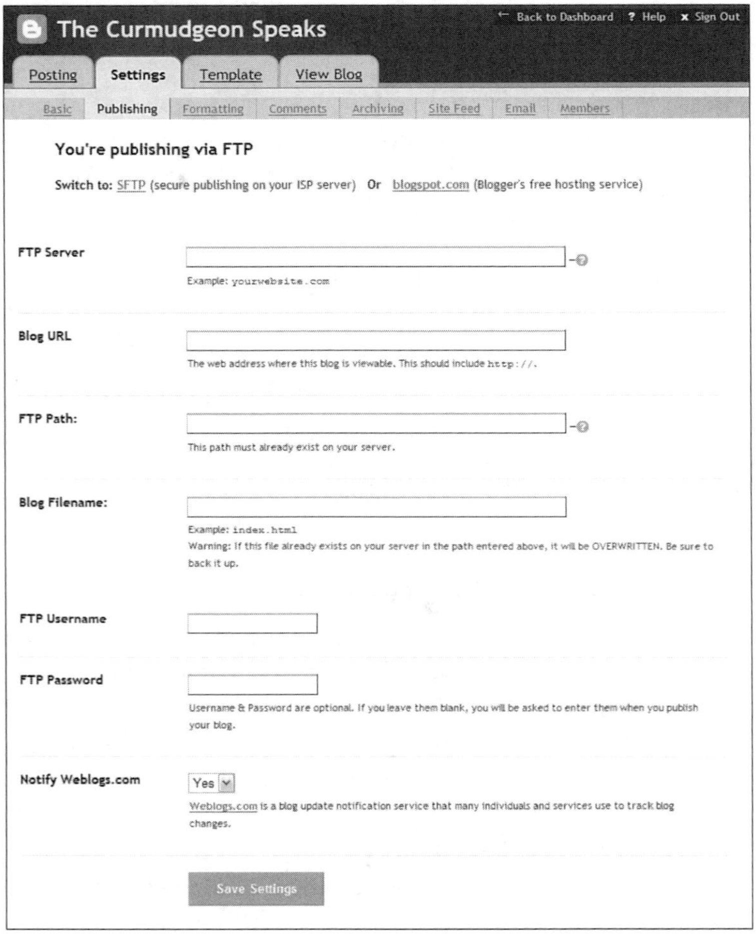

FIGURE 23.19

Setting up your blog to be published on another website.

- FTP server
- Blog URL (the URL you'll be using for your blog)
- FTP path
- Blog filename (the name of the file that will serve as the home page of the blog)
- FTP username
- FTP password
- Notify Weblogs.com (a web notification service)

5. Click the Save Settings button.

6. Click the Republish button.

Your blog will now appear on the website you selected. The blog will be physically hosted on the other server, and will appear with the website address you specified.

Changing Templates

The blog templates that Blogger offers are nice, but there aren't a lot of them. This means that it's likely that your blog will have the same look and feel as dozens—if not hundreds—of other blogs. If that bothers you, then you need to delve into the world of blog customization. Read on to learn more.

Choosing a Different Template

First things first. If you no longer like the template you originally chose for your blog, you can change it. Blogger offers more than 30 different blog templates, and there's no harm in switching from one to another to suit your mood. Here's how to do it:

1. From the Blogger Dashboard, click the Change Settings icon next to your blog name.

2. When the Settings page appears, select the Template tab and click Pick New.

3. All of Blogger's templates are now displayed, as you can see in Figure 23.20. (This is actually a larger selection of templates than was visible when you first created your blog.) Click the Use This Template button next to the template you'd like to use.

4. Click the Republish button.

Using Third-Party Templates

If you don't like the templates that Blogger provides, you can use a template created by someone else. There are lots of third-party sites on the web that offer Blogger templates; the most popular of these sites include

caution When you choose a new template, any editing you've done to your previous template will be lost. You probably want to copy the code for your old template to a text file, and then use that code to edit your template as necessary.

- Blog Templates (www.ehsany.com)
- Blogger Templates (blogger-templates.blogspot.com), shown in Figure 23.21
- BlogSkins (www.blogskins.com)
- diaphaneity.com (www.diaphaneity.com/layouts/)
- Eris' Template Generator (www.erisfree.com/d2/apart.php)
- Free Blogger Templates (blog-templates.ravasthi.name)
- Noipo.org Blogger Templates (blogtemplates.noipo.org)

FIGURE 23.20

Choosing a new template for your blog.

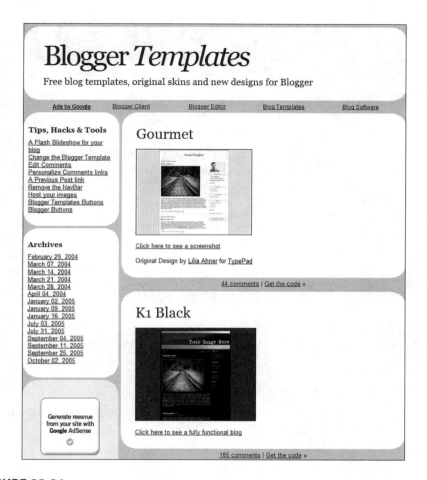

FIGURE 23.21

Third-party templates from the Blogger Templates site.

To use one of these third-party templates, follow these steps:

1. Select all the code for the new template and copy it to your computer's clipboard. (Press Ctrl+C to copy.)

2. From the Blogger Dashboard, click the Change Settings icon next to your blog name.

3. When the Settings page appears, select the Template tab and click Edit Current, as shown in Figure 23.22.

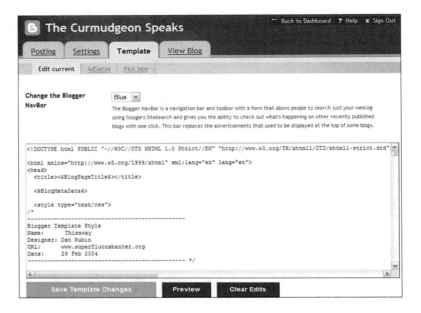

FIGURE 23.22

Use the Edit Current page to edit your template code—or paste the code for a third-party template.

4. Delete all the code from the main text box.

5. Position your cursor in the empty text box and click Ctrl+V to paste the new template code.

6. Click the Save Template Changes button.

7. Click the Republish button.

Modifying Blogger Templates with HTML and Blogger Tags

Let's take another look at the Edit Current page on the Template tab. That big text box in the middle of the page is filled with lines of code that looks a little like HTML. Well, that's because the code *is* HTML—or most of it is, anyway. Your blog is constructed from HTML code, with a few special Blogger tags thrown in for good measure.

If you know your way around HTML, you can use the Edit Current page to customize your Blogger template. Changing colors or fonts, deleting unwanted elements, even adding new elements is as simple as editing the appropriate codes.

Understanding Essential Codes

I won't go into all the intricacies of HTML here; I'll assume that if you're editing code, you know what you're doing. What I will do is point out some of the more important codes, as well as talk about those Blogger-specific tags.

First, know that Blogger uses Cascading Style Sheets (CSS), so that most of the font and color information is set at the very top of the code. Look for the code that starts with the following line:

```
<style type="text/css">
```

Everything in-between this tag and the closing `</style>` tag defines all the elements used in the template's style sheet. When you make changes to the definitions within this section, it affects the look of the entire style sheet.

The main content of your blog is prefaced by the following tag:

```
<div id="main-content">
```

After this tag you'll find code that inserts your blog posts, comments, and similar content. You probably want to leave this part of the template as-is.

The sidebar, however, is where you'll do the most customization. You can add a ton of content here, using both Blogger tags (for Blogger-generated content) and your own HTML. This section of the template starts with the following line of code:

```
<div id="sidebar">
```

Understanding Blogger Tags

Most of the content in your template is generated by Blogger tags. When you use a Blogger tag, a single tag is used to insert all manner of dynamic content. For example, the single `<$BlogItemBody$>` tag displays the entire content of a post. You don't have to enter the content into the code; this tag inserts it, dynamically.

It's important, then, to get to know the various Blogger tags. These tags fall into two general groups; *item-level* tags, which insert content from Blogger's database, and *page-level* tags, which define when and where the content from item level tags will

caution Unlike normal HTML code, Blogger tags are case-sensitive. You must use the proper in-tag capitalization for the code to work.

appear on the page. You can tell an item-level tag from the dollar signs surrounding the tag name. For example, `<$BlogItemUrl$>` is an item-level tag that inserts the URL for a given post; `<BlogItemURL>` is a page-level tag that defines where the URL will appear.

There are quite a few of these Blogger tags, which are detailed (by type) in Tables 23.1 through 23.7.

Table 23.1   General Tags

Tag	Type	Description
`<Blogger>` and `</Blogger>`	Page-level	Container tags that surround all your blog content
`<$BlogEncoding$>`	Item-level	Inserts the encoding section from your template's Formatting tab
`<$BlogMetaData$>`	Item-level	Inserts all blog metadata via a single tag
`<$BlogPageTitle$>`	Item-level	Inserts "smart" titles for your blog ("Blog Name" for the index page, "Blog Name: Date Info" for archive pages, and "Blog Name: Post Title" for individual post pages)
`<$BlogTitle$>`	Item-level	Inserts the title of the blog
`<$BlogDescription$>`	Item-level	Inserts the description for the blog
`<BlogDateHeader>`	Page-level	Defines the placement of the date headers for each post
`<$BlogDateHeaderDate$>`	Item-level	Inserts date headers for each post; typically used in conjunction with the `<BlogDateHeader>` tag, like this: `<BlogDateHeader><$BlogDateHeaderDate$></BlogDateHeader>`

Table 23.2   Posting Tags

Tag	Type	Description
`<BlogItemTitle>`	Page-level	Defines the placement of a post's title
`<BlogItemURL>`	Page-level	Defines the placement of post's URL
`<$BlogItemURL$>`	Item-level	Inserts the URL for a post
`<$BlogItemBody$>`	Item-level	Inserts the content of a post
`<$BlogItemAuthor$>`	Item-level	Inserts the first and last name of a post's author
`<$BlogItemAuthorNickname$>`	Item-level	Inserts the display name of a post's author
`<$BlogItemAuthorEmail$>`	Item-level	Inserts the email address of a post's author

Table 23.2   Continued

Tag	Type	Description
`<$BlogItemAuthorURL$>`	Item-level	Inserts the home page URL of a post's author
`<$BlogItemDateTime$>`	Item-level	Inserts the date and/or time of a post
`<$BlogItemNumber$>`	Item-level	Inserts the ID number of a post
`<$BlogItemArchiveFileName$>`	Item-level	Inserts the archive filename of a post
`<$BlogItemPermalinkURL$>`	Item-level	Inserts the permalink of a post
`<$BlogItemControl$>`	Item-level	Inserts the quick edit link of a post
`<BlogDateFooter>`	Page-level	Defines the placement of a post's output date footer
`<BloggerPreviousItems>`	Page-level	Defines where previous items will appear
`<$BlogPreviousItemTitle$>`	Item-level	Inserts the 10 posts previous to the current post

Table 23.3   Comment Tags

Tag	Type	Description
`<BlogItemCommentsEnabled>` and `</BlogItemCommentsEnabled>`	Page-level	Turns on the display of comments
`<BlogItemComments>` and `</BlogItemComments>`	Page-level	Defines where comments will appear
`<$BlogItemCommentCount$>`	Item-level	Inserts the comment count
`<$BlogItemCommentFormOnClick$>`	Item-level	Inserts a link to the blog comment form
`<$BlogCommentNumber$>`	Item-level	Inserts the comment number
`<$BlogCommentBody$>`	Item-level	Inserts the comment text
`<$BlogCommentPermalinkURL$>`	Item-level	Inserts the URL for the comment's permalink
`<$BlogCommentAuthor$>`	Item-level	Inserts the name of the comment's author
`<$BlogCommentDateTime$>`	Item-level	Inserts the date/time the comment was created
`<$BlogCommentDeleteIcon$>`	Item-level	Inserts a delete button for each comment
`<$BlogItemCreate$>`	Item-level	Inserts a link that lets users add new comments
`<$BlogItemCommentCreate$>`	Item-level	Inserts a link that lets users add new comments

23

Table 23.4   Profile Tags

Tag	Type	Description
`<$BlogOwnerNickname$>`	Item-level	Inserts the blog owner's display name
`<$BlogOwnerFirstName$>`	Item-level	Inserts the blog owner's first name
`<$BlogOwnerLastName$>`	Item-level	Inserts the blog owner's last name
`<$BlogOwnerFullName$>`	Item-level	Inserts the blog owner's first and last name
`<$BlogOwnerEmail$>`	Item-level	Inserts the blog owner's email address
`<$BlogOwnerLocation$>`	Item-level	Inserts the blog owner's location
`<$BlogOwnerAboutMe$>`	Item-level	Inserts the blog owner's complete profile
`<$BlogOwnerProfileUrl$>`	Item-level	Inserts a link to the blog owner's profile

Table 23.5   Archive Tags

Tag	Type	Description
`<BloggerArchives>`	Page-level	Defines the placement of the archive post list
`<$BlogArchiveURL$>`	Item-level	Inserts the URLs for the archive post list
`<BlogArchiveName$>`	Item-level	Inserts the names for the archive post list

Table 23.6   Site Feed Tags

Tag	Type	Description
`<BlogSiteFeed>`	Page-level	Defines the placement of RSS feed information
`<$BlogSiteFeedUrl$>`	Item-level	Inserts the URL for your site feed; typically used in conjunction with the `<BlogSiteFeed>` tag, like this: `<BlogSiteFeed><$BlogSiteFeedUrl$></BlogSiteFeed>`
`<$BlogSiteFeedLink$>`	Item-level	Outputs the URL for your site feed inside a `<link>` tag

Table 23.7   Conditional Tags

Tag	Type	Description
`<MainPage>` and `</MainPage>`	Page-level	Contents between the on and off tags will only appear when visitor is viewing the main page of your blog

Table 23.7	Continued	
Tag	Type	Description
`<ArchivePage>` and `</ArchivePage>`	Page-level	Contents between the on and off tags will only appear when a visitor is viewing the archive page of your blog
`<ItemPage>` and `</ItemPage>`	Page-level	Contents between the on and off tags will only ppear when a visitor is viewing an item page in your blog
`<MainOrArchivePage>` and `</MainOrArchivePage>`	Page-level	Contents between the on and off tags will only appear when a visitor is viewing the main or archive pages of your blog

In some cases, all you have to do is insert the appropriate tag. For example, to insert your username and profile, insert the following tags into the sidebar section of the template code:

```
<$BlogOwnerNickname$>
<$BlogOwnerAboutMe$>
```

Using some of the other tags, however, can be a bit tricky. I recommend you study the existing template code to see how these tags are used, and then consult the Blogger help system for more detailed instructions.

Using Other HTML Tags

When you're customizing your blog template, you may want to include a variety of personal information about yourself, typically in the template's sidebar. All you have to do is go to the sidebar section of code (which starts with the `<div id="sidebar">` tag) and insert the appropriate HTML.

For example, to insert a photo in the sidebar, use the following code:

```
<img src="imageurl" width="100">
```

Replace *imageurl* with the full URL and filename of the graphic you want to insert. The `width` attribute sizes the picture to a 100-pixel width, which should be a good size to fit within the sidebar; experiment with different widths, if you like.

Some bloggers, myself included, like to include a list of books they're reading or CDs they're listening to, like the one shown in Figure 23.23. You can manually insert a reading or listening list in your sidebar, along with pictures and links to each item on Amazon.com, by using the following code:

FIGURE 23.23

A CD listening list added to the blog sidebar.

```
<h2 class="sidebar-title">Recent Reads</h2>
<font size=1>

<a href="http://www.amazon.com/exec/obidos/ASIN/amazonASIN">
<IMG
SRC="http://images.amazon.com/images/P/amazonASIN.01.THUMBZZZ.jpg"
align=top>
Book/CD title
</a>

<a href="http://www.amazon.com/exec/obidos/ASIN/amazonASIN">
<IMG
SRC="http://images.amazon.com/images/P/amazonASIN.01.THUMBZZZ.jpg"
align=top>
Book/CD title
</a>

<a href="http://www.amazon.com/exec/obidos/ASIN/amazonASIN">
<IMG
SRC="http://images.amazon.com/images/P/amazonASIN.01.THUMBZZZ.jpg"
align=top>
```

```
Book/CD title
</a>

</font>
```

In this code, replace *amazonASIN* within both the link and the image URLs with the actual Amazon ASIN number. (You can find this number on any Amazon product page.) Replace *Book/CD title* with the title of the book or CD. You can include as many items as you like in your list by adding more lines of code.

And, as discussed previously, you can add a link to your blog's Atom feed by inserting the following lines of code:

```
<a href="<$BlogSiteFeedUrl$>" title="Atom feed">Atom Feed</a>
```

In this instance, you're using the `<$BlogSiteFeedUrl$>` Blogger tag to dynamically insert the URL for your blog's Atom feed.

As you can see, there's a lot you can do to customize your blog template—more than I can describe in this single chapter. If you're technically inclined, I recommend you check out the help system on the Blogger site, which offers a wealth of more advanced information. And don't be afraid to experiment—as long as you create a backup copy of your existing blog template first!

How Popular Is Your Blog?

One last thing. If you're hosting a blog, eventually you're going to get curious about how many people are reading it. Unfortunately, Blogger doesn't offer any built-in statistics or visitor counters. You can, however, utilize third-party hit counters and tools to track your blog's traffic. Some of the most popular of these tools include:

- Bravenet Counter and Site Stats (www.bravenet.com/webtools/counter/)
- FreeStats (www.freestats.com)
- Site Meter (www.sitemeter.com)
- StatCounter (www.statcounter.com)

The Bottom Line

If you want to blog, Blogger makes it easy. Creating your own blog takes less than five minutes, and it's just as quick and easy to

tip Want to learn more about Blogger? Get the latest Blogger news—and discover lots of insider tips and tricks—at the official Blogger Buzz blog (buzz.blogger.com).

create new blog posts. And, if you want a truly personalized blog, Blogger lets you get your hands dirty and tinker with the underlying HTML to your heart's content—or, if you're less technically inclined, to simply choose another pre-designed blog template. In any case, blogs are all the rage these days, and Blogger is the most popular blog host for a reason. What have you got to lose? (It is free, after all.)

23

PART

VII

Multimedia

24 Searching Google Images

25 Downloading Video Entertainment from Google Video

Searching Google Images

A mong Google's many specialized searches, perhaps the most popular is Google Image Search, also known as Google Images. This is a subset of Google's basic web search that lets you search for photos, drawings, logos, and other graphics files on the Web. It's perhaps the best way I know to find pictures online.

The fact that Google can find pictures that match your search criteria is something short of amazing. After all, pictures aren't like web pages; pictures don't have any text that Google can parse and index. Instead, Google analyzes the file extension, image caption, text on the host web page adjacent to the image, and other factors to try and determine what the image is a picture of. It's to Google's credit that most of the time it gets it right.

Searching for Images

There are two ways to access Google Image Search, shown in Figure 24.1. You can click the Images link on any Google search page, or you can go directly to images.google.com.

FIGURE 24.1

The home page for Google Image Search.

Basic Searching

For most users, searching Google Image Search is as easy as entering your query into the search box and clicking the Search Images button. Nothing to it.

You can, of course, use any of Google's advanced search operators within your query. Of particular use is the **filetype:** operator, which you can use to limit your search to JPG or GIF image files.

Advanced Searching

If you want to fine-tune your image search, the best way to do it is to use the Advanced Search page. When you click the Advanced Image Search link on the main Image Search page, you see the form shown in Figure 24.2. From here you can fine-tune your search in a number of ways:

- **Find results.** Narrow your search by searching for all the words, the exact phrase, any of the words, or for pictures not related to the words

- **Size.** Search only for images that are small, medium, or large in size

- **Filetypes.** Search only for JPG, GIF, or PNG-format files

- **Coloration.** Search only for black and white, grayscale, or full-color images

> **note** Learn more about advanced search operators in Chapter 2, "Searching the Web."

■ **Domain.** Search only for images within a specified domain or website

■ **SafeSearch.** Apply moderate, strict, or no filtering to the image search results

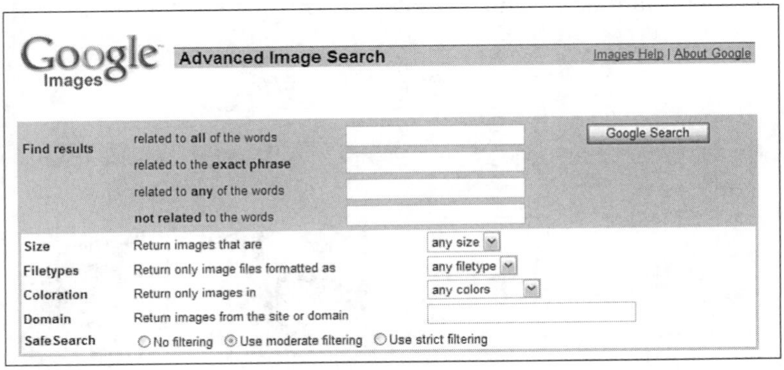

FIGURE 24.2

Fine-tuning your search from the Advanced Image Search page.

The Advanced Image Search page is great if you're looking for images of a particular file type—for example, if you're looking only for JPG images. It's also good if you're looking for a larger or higher-resolution picture for print purposes (both of which are likely to be of a larger file size), or a smaller or lower-resolution picture for web use (both of which are likely to be of a smaller file size).

This begs the question, of course, of how small is small. Or how large is large, for that matter. The answers to these questions are detailed in Table 24.1.

Table 24.1	Google Image Search Size Parameters
Size	**Approximate Dimensions (in pixels)**
Small	150×150 or smaller
Medium	Larger than 150×150 Smaller than 500×500
Large	500×500 or larger

Viewing Image Search Results

When you click the Search Images button, Google returns the first page of results. As you can see in Figure 24.3, the matching images are displayed in a grid of thumbnail pictures, ranked in terms of relevance.

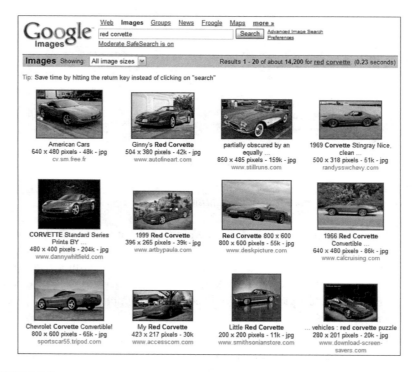

FIGURE 24.3

The results of a Google image search.

For each thumbnailed image, Google lists an image caption, the size of the image (in both pixels and kilobytes), the filetype, and the host website. To view any image, all you have to do is click the thumbnail.

When you click a thumbnail image, the original page is displayed in a frame at the bottom of the next page, as shown in Figure 24.4. At the top of the page is the Google Images frame, which includes the image thumbnail, information about the image, and a few important links:

tip If you'd rather limit the results to images of a particular size (small, medium, or large), pull down the Showing: list at the top of the page and make the appropriate selection.

FIGURE 24.4
Viewing an image found with Google Image Search.

- To view the host page without the Google frame, click the Remove Frame link
- To view the picture full-size, click the See Full-Size Image link
- To return to your search results, click the Image Results link

Saving and Printing Images

Any image you find on the Web can be saved to youy hard disk or printed on your printer. (Unless the page designer has implemented some form of copy protection for the image, that is.) Saving and printing images is a function of your web browser, but here's how to do it in Internet Explorer.

To save an image to your hard disk, right-click the picture and select Save Picture As. When the Save Picture dialog box appears, select a location for the picture, and then click the Save button.

caution Commercial use of copyrighted images is prohibited—so be careful how you use the pictures you find with Google Image Search.

To print a picture (without printing the surrounding web page), right-click the image and select Print Picture. When the Print dialog box appears, click the Print button.

note Learn more about SafeSearch content filtering in Chapter 12, "Making Google Safe for Kids."

Filtering Out Dirty Pictures

One of the bad things about searching the Web for pictures is that, depending on your query, you're likely to stumble across a few adult-oriented pictures in your search results. Assuming that you don't want (or don't want your kids) to see these dirty pictures, Google enables its moderate SafeSearch content filter by default when you use Google Image Search. (Moderate SafeSearch filtering blocks the display of questionable images only, not text.)

If you'd prefer to view your search results unfiltered, you have two options:

- From any search results page, click the Moderate SafeSearch Is On link. This takes you to the Preferences page, shown in Figure 24.5; check the Do Not Filter My Search Results option, and then click the Save Preferences button.

- From the main Google Image Search page, click the Preferences link. When the Preferences page appears, check the Do Not Filter My Search Results option, and then click the Save Preferences button.

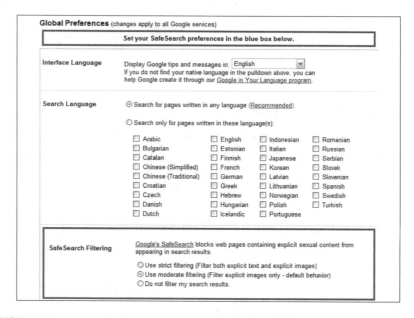

FIGURE 24.5

Turning off SafeSearch filtering on the Preferences page.

Removing Your Images from Image Search

If you're an artist or photographer, you might find that your copyrighted images are appearing in Google Image Search. This might be okay with you, or it might not. If you'd prefer that your images not be displayed in Google Image Search, you can request Google remove them.

To remove a copyrighted image from Google Image Search, you have to add a special text file to the root directory of your website. This file should be labeled robots.txt, and needs to include specific information about the images you want to protect.

If you want to remove a specific image file from the Google search index, add the following lines to the robots.txt file:

```
User-agent: Googlebot-Image
Disallow: /subdirctory/file.jpg
```

Naturally, replace *subdirectory* with the name of the subdirectory where the image file is located, and replace *file.jpg* with the name and extension of the file you want to protect.

Alternately, you can instruct Google to remove all images on your site from the Google search index. In this instance, you want to add the following lines to the robots.txt file:

```
User-agent: Googlebot-Image<
Disallow: /
```

When the GoogleBot spider crawls your site, it automatically reads the content of the robots.txt file for instructions. If your site includes a robots.txt file, the spider will follow the instructions you specify, and not add the image file(s) you noted.

COMMENTARY:

FAIR USE

On February 17, 2006, a Los Angeles federal judge ruled that Google Image Search violated the copyrights held by an adult website, by displaying thumbnail versions of copyrighted photos.

The Perfect 10 website (www.perfect10.com) had sued Google over use of the photos in Google's search results. The site claimed—and the judge agreed—that the free availability of the photos on Google Image

Search, even in thumbnail form, could harm Perfect 10's ability to sell small versions of its photos as downloads to cell phones.

The judge ruled that Google's creation and display of the Perfect 10 thumbnail images "likely do not fall within the fair use exemption." Fair use, for those of you unschooled in copyright law, is the legal standard that allows for limited use of copyrighted works for specific purposes, such as news reporting, criticism, or comment.

Google, obviously, disagreed. The company pointed out that it doesn't display full-sized versions of the photos in question; when a user clicks a thumbnail image, he leaves Google and is taken to the Perfect 10 website. For these purposes, Google argued that display of thumbnail images is fair use.

While I'm all for artist's rights, it seems to me that the display of thumbnail images for navigational purposes doesn't do anyone any harm. If Google were displaying the full-sized images without permission, that would be another thing. But displaying thumbnails is what makes Google Image Search particularly useful, and I'd wager that having Perfect 10's photos listed in Google's search results drives a lot of traffic to the (paid) Perfect 10 site. By forcing Google to remove thumbnails of their images, Perfect 10 is likely to see a decrease in traffic—which is a "cut off your nose to spite your face" sort of scenario.

Google is appealing this ruling, and hope they win on appeal. If other websites force Google to remove their thumbnail images from its search results, it will negatively affect the usability of Google Image Search. The fewer images you can see, the less useful Image Search will be.

The Bottom Line

I like Google Image Search. It's easy to use, and it normally returns quite accurate results. I use it often, and particularly like the ability to filter results by image size. It is, in my mind, the best image search engine available today.

Downloading Video Entertainment from Google Video

Google Video is a new way to watch your favorite television programs, films, and videos over the Internet. You can browse or search through thousands of free and paid programs, ranging from short video clips to full-length television shows and movies, all commercial-free.

Many independent videos can be downloaded and viewed free of charge. Other videos can be purchased outright for unlimited viewing, or rented for viewing during a specified time period. You can watch videos directly in your web browser or you can download videos for future playback using the Google Video Player. Videos available from Google Video Store can be played back on any personal computer, and selected videos are available for download to Apple's Video iPod and Sony's Playstation Portable devices.

Play around with Google Video a bit and you'll discover that watching videos on your own timetable is kind of cool. Read on to learn more.

Searching for and Downloading Videos

As you can see in Figure 25.1, Google Video (video.google.com) looks and feels a bit different from Google's main search site. Yes, there's a search box at the top of the page, but there are also a ton of video thumbnails pre-displayed. Google's featured videos are displayed at the top of the main page, with lists of "popular" and "random" videos below that.

FIGURE 25.1

Google Video—your home for video entertainment on the Internet.

Maybe you'll find what you want listed on the home page; maybe not. For most of us, however, finding a video entails either browsing or searching the entire Google Video library.

Browsing by Category

Unlike just about all of Google (except for the Google Directory), Google Video doesn't rely exclusively on searching to find what you want. That's right, Google

> **note** The Featured category on the Google Video home page doesn't actually list individual videos. Instead, it lists categories or groupings of videos by Google's video partners. Click a thumbnail to view the videos offered.

Video offers category browsing, which for many users is a preferred way of finding videos in a particular category.

To browse through Google's video categories, click one of the category links at the top of the main Google Video page. Google Video organizes its offerings into seven major categories (Top 100, Comedy, Music Videos, Movies, Sports, Animation, and TV Shows), plus a number of additional categories (under the More link). Click one of these categories and you see all the videos in that category, ranked by date (newest first).

Changing the Thumbnail Display

By default, Google videos within a category are displayed in a thumbnail grid, as shown in Figure 25.2. If you prefer, you can display these videos in list format instead (as shown in Figure 25.3) by clicking the List link. (The list format displays a bit more information about each video.)

FIGURE 25.2

Viewing videos in the default grid view.

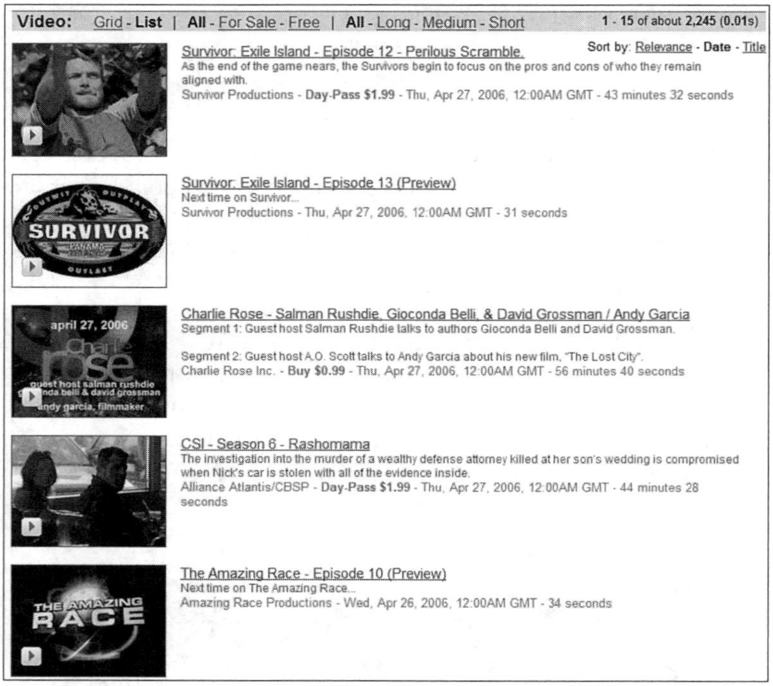

FIGURE 25.3

Viewing videos in list view.

Also by default, Google videos are listed in reverse chronological order, with the newest videos first. If you like, you can choose to display the videos by relevance or title, by clicking the appropriate links in the Sort By section of the page.

You can also opt to display only certain subsets of videos. At the top of the page you can choose to display only those videos For Sale or those available for Free. (By default, all videos are displayed.) In addition, you can choose to display only videos of a given length—Long, Medium, or Short. (Again, the default is to display videos of all sizes.)

note Google Video does not, at this time, offer SafeSearch content filtering. However, since Google Video doesn't distribute videos that include pornography or obscenity, your family is probably safe from accidentally viewing objectionable content.

Basic Video Searching

As the number of videos in the Google Video library increases, browsing by category will become increasingly unwieldy. If you have a particular video in mind, the better approach is to search for it.

Searching for videos is just like searching for anything on Google. Enter one or more keywords into the search box, and then click the Search Video button. All videos that match your query are displayed in a grid on the subsequent search results page.

note How does Google know the video content to return appropriate search results? Simple; it searches the text descriptions provided by the videos' producers as well as the text of the videos' closed captioning.

Searching by Title

If you want a more refined search, however, you're a bit out of luck. That's because Google Video does not as yet offer an advanced search page or the use of advanced search operators.

There is one exception, however. Google Video does let you use the **title:** operator in your video searches. Use this operator to search for videos by title. Just enter the **title:** operator (with no space following) followed by the title of the video.

For example, to search for episodes of *Law and Order*, enter **title:law and order**, as shown in Figure 25.4.

FIGURE 25.4
Searching for videos by title.

Viewing the Top 100 Videos

One of the neat things about Google Video is that you can easily discover what "hot" videos your fellow users are viewing. When you click the Top 100 link at the top of any Google Video page, you'll see a list of the 100 most popular videos, in order, as shown in Figure 25.5. Click a thumbnail to view the entire video.

25

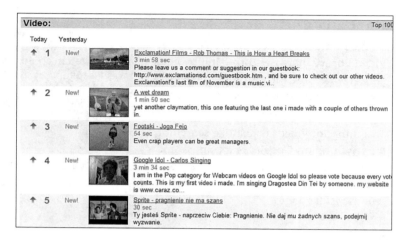

FIGURE 25.5
Viewing Google's Top 100 videos.

Viewing Google Picks Videos

Even more cool videos are available in the Google Picks section of the Google Video. Google Picks are videos that have been selected by your fellow users as being the coolest of the cool—not necessarily the most popular (ala the Top 100), but rather the hippest and most interesting. Click the Google Picks link (under the More link) to view today's coolest videos.

Viewing Past Picks (and More) at the Google Video Blog

Old Google Picks videos don't fade away, they simply migrate to the official Google Video Blog (www.googlevideo.blogspot.com). As you can see in Figure 25.6, the Google Video Blog highlights user-produced videos, submitted via the Google Video Upload program.

There are also several unofficial blogs devoted to Google Video. These include:

- Best Google Videos (bestgooglevideos.blogspot.com)
- Google Idol (www.googleidol.com)
- Google Video of the Day (gvod.blogspot.com)
- Google Video Latest (googlevideos.blogspot.com)
- In Search of Google Videos (www.videofinds.com)

note Learn more about Google Video Upload in the "Distributing Your Own Videos via the Google Video Upload Program" section, later in this chapter.

FIGURE 25.6

The official Google Video Blog.

COMMENTARY:

VIDEO COMPETITION

The market for downloadable videos is growing by leaps and bounds. Viewers like the opportunity to download copies of their favorite TV shows to watch at their leisure; there's also much voyeuristic enjoyment that comes from viewing homemade videos from users around the world.

Unfortunately for Google, Google Video doesn't have this market all to itself. For example, YouTube (www.youtube.com) has emerged as the premiere source for homegrown videos, and Apple's iTunes Video Store (www.apple.com/itunes/videos/) is striking numerous deals for exclusive paid video content. Other big players in this space are MSN Video (video.msn.com) and Yahoo! Video (video.yahoo.com).

At this point in time, Google Video does not have a demonstrable edge on the competition. In fact, it's a poor second in both viral videos (to

YouTube) and downloadable TV shows (to iTunes). And this game is all about content; viewers will go where the content is.

For Google Video to be a dominant player in the downloadable video market, they have to become more aggressive in striking deals with major video producers. The company's typical "if we search it, they will come" attitude won't cut it in an environment where Universal, CBS/Viacom, Time Warner, and the other biggies are trying to get the best bang for their bucks.

It remains to be seen whether Google Video will be a player in this space, or whether Apple will take the same sort of dominant share it did in the downloadable music market. At present, Apple's in the lead.

Viewing Videos

Once you find a video, you want to watch it. Google Video offers several different viewing options, depending on the type of video. Some videos can be viewed free of charge while others can be purchased or rented—and all videos can be previewed, right from the category or search results page.

Previewing Videos

On all video search results pages, the video thumbnails are accompanied by a Play button, like the one shown in Figure 25.7. When you click the Play button, a short preview of the video begins playback, right there on the search results page.

FIGURE 25.7

Click the Play button to view a preview of the video.

Understanding Google Video Viewing Options

There are three types of playback options available on Google Video, each at a different price point. These options include:

- **Free.** You can download the video at no charge. (Figure 25.8 shows a news clip available for free download.)

- **Purchase.** You can pay a set price to download the video. Once you've downloaded it, it's yours to view as often as you want. (Figure 25.9 shows a music video with the Buy option.)

- **Day Pass.** You can *rent* the video for viewing within a 24-hour period. You pay a set fee and can watch the video an unlimited number of times within 24 hours. After the 24-hour period is up, the video can no longer be viewed—unless you rent it again, of course. (Figure 25.10 shows an episode of *Survivor* available for Day Pass rental.)

FIGURE 25.8

This video is available free of charge.

FIGURE 25.9

This video must be purchased.

Survivor - Episode 5 - For Cod's Sake
Survivor Productions
Day-Pass $1.99 - 43 min 32 sec - Mar 2, 2006

FIGURE 25.10

This video can be viewed via a 24-hour Day Pass.

Some videos come with two viewing options. For example, the movie in Figure 25.11 is available for purchase for $19.99, or available for Day Pass rental for $2.99. You can choose whichever option you want.

Rat Pack
Image Entertainment
Buy $19.99 - Day-Pass $2.99 - 1 hr 44 min 48
sec - Oct 18, 2005

FIGURE 25.11

This video can be either purchased or rented for 24 hours.

Playing Streaming Videos on the Google Video Web Page

To view a video, you start by clicking the video's thumbnail on the category or search results page. This displays the video playback page, like the one shown in Figure 25.12.

Most free videos let you view them directly from this page via the built-in video viewer. Use the transport controls under the video window to play, pause, fast forward, and rewind the video.

note Viewing streaming video requires that you have Macromedia Flash Player 7.0+ installed on your computer. If you don't have a Flash Player plug-in installed, you can download it from www.macromedia.com.

25

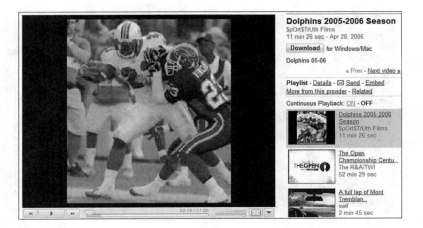

FIGURE 25.12

A typical video playback page.

By default, streaming videos appear within the video window. You can view these videos in a full-screen window by clicking the full-screen button at the bottom right of the video window. To return to the original video window, repeat the procedure.

Downloading Videos

If you prefer to download the video to your hard drive for future viewing, click the Download button on the video playback page. This automatically downloads the video file to your hard disk; once downloaded, you can watch the video at your convenience.

If the video is available for purchase or Day Pass rental, you'll see buttons for Buy High Quality or Day-Pass High Quality. For example, Figure 25.13 shows a video that has both purchase and Day Pass options; click the appropriate button to make your purchase and download the video. (When a video is available for purchase or rental, the large video viewing window shows a preview of the video only.)

caution Downloading isn't an option for all videos. Some video producers restrict viewing to online streaming only in an effort to combat piracy.

25

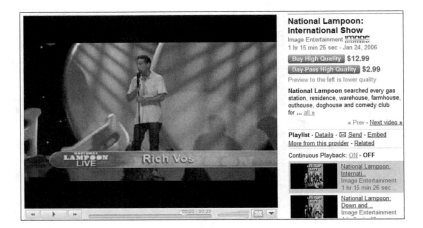

FIGURE 25.13
A video with both purchase and Day Pass options.

Watching Videos You've Downloaded

Any movie you download—for free or purchased—can be viewed in any video player program. The default playback program is Google's very own Google Video Player, which is automatically installed when you download your first video.

Using the Google Video Player for Playback

The first time you download a video from Google Video, you also download and install the Google Video Player. The Google Video Player, shown in Figure 25.14, is a video player program you can use to view all your downloaded videos—not just those you download from Google Video.

Google Video Player looks a lot like the video viewer window on the Google Video video playback page. You have the same transport controls (play, pause, fast forward, and rewind) as well as a full-screen button to display the window full-screen. There's a also a thumbnail button; when you click this button, Google Video Player displays all the chapters of the video as a series of onscreen thumbnails, as shown in Figure 25.15.

FIGURE 25.14

The Google Video Player.

FIGURE 25.15

Viewing chapter thumbnails in Google Video Player.

When you click the Google Video button at the lower-right corner of the Google Video Player window, you have several options available to you. You can select from various playback window sizes (Half Size, Original Size, Double Size, and Full Screen), as well as view information about the current video (Video Properties), go to this video on the Google Video website, or just go to the Google Video home page.

There's also a "search videos" box in the Google Video Player window. You can use this search box to perform a Google Video search—assuming you're online at the time, of course.

When you download a video from Google Video, the Google Video Player starts automatically. If you want to play back a video you've previously downloaded, just open Google Video Player manually, select File, Open, and select the file you want to view.

note Your computer has to be connected to the Internet when you're watching a purchased or Day Pass video you've downloaded. This is because Google Video Player has to communicate with Google to verify the purchase information and decrypt the encrypted files.

Playing Downloaded Videos on Another Video Player

Most videos you purchase (and many you download for free) are copy protected. You can only play these copy-protected videos from within Google Video Player.

If you download a non-copy protected video, however, you can view that video in any video player that plays AVI-format files. Just open the file from within your video player program as you would any other video file.

How do you know if a downloaded video is copy protected? It's simple. If, when downloading the program, it was available for both Windows and Macintosh, it's not copy protected. If it was only available for Windows downloads, it is copy protected.

Playing Purchased Videos on Another Computer

You can, however, view any video you purchase on another computer. Assuming, that is, you have Google Video Player installed on that computer.

What you have to do is re-download the video from Google Video to your other computer. You'll need to sign in with your original Google account ID, and then click the Purchased Videos link at the top of the Google Video page. This will display a list of all the videos you've purchased. Click the video you want to download to your second computer, and then click Download. This will automatically download the video to this computer, without charging you again for the purchase.

Downloading Videos to Portable Devices

Some (but not all) videos on Google Video are available for download to either the Apple Video iPod or Sony PSP portable devices. Read on to learn more.

Downloading to an Apple Video iPod

If a video is available for iPod download, you'll see this option on the video's video playback page. Next to the Download button is a pull-down list; look for videos that have a Video iPod option on this list, like the one in Figure 25.16.

FIGURE 25.16

A video available for download to the Apple Video iPod.

25

To download a video to your Video iPod, follow these steps:

1. From the video's video playback page, pull down the Download list and select Video iPod.

2. Click the Download button and save the video to your computer's hard drive.

3. Connect your iPod to your computer.

4. Open the iTunes application.

5. From within iTunes, select File, Add File to Library.

6. When the Add to Library dialog box appears, browse for and select the video you just downloaded, and then click Open.

7. Select Edit, Preferences.

8. When the iTunes dialog box appears, select the iPod tab, click Videos, Automatically Update All Videos, and then click OK.

iTunes now copies the video to your iPod. To play the video on your iPod, select Videos, Movies.

Downloading to a Sony Playstation Portable

If a video is available for PSP download, you'll see the Sony PSP option in the pull-down list next to the Download button on the videos' video playback page, as shown in Figure 25.17. To download a video to your PSP, follow these steps:

FIGURE 25.17

A video available for download to the Sony PSP.

1. From the video's video playback page, pull down the Download list and select Sony PSP.

2. Click the Download button and save the video to your computer's hard drive.

3. Use My Computer or a similar utility to rename the downloaded file to MAQ*****.MP4, where the asterisks are digits from 0–9.

4. Copy the renamed file to the \MP_ROOT\101ANV01 folder on your PSP memory stick.

Distributing Your Own Videos via the Google Video Upload Program

Ever dream of becoming a big-time movie director? Well, all big-time movie directors have to start somewhere—and Google Video is as good a place as any.

Google offers the Google Video Upload program to all aspiring filmmakers out there. The program lets you upload your own videos and home movies to the Google Video site, where they can be viewed and downloaded by anyone on the Web.

> **tip** If you're a professional video producer with more than 1,000 hours of video you want to upload, you can take advantage of Google Video's Premium Program. Learn more at services.google.com/inquiry/video/.

Understanding Upload File Guidelines

To upload a video file to Google Video, it must meet the following format and content requirements:

- The video must be in either AVI, ASF, QuickTime (MOV), Windows Media (WMV), Real Audio (RA or RAM), or MPEG file formats.
- For videos originating from a low-quality source (VHS videotape, web-cams, camera phones, and the like), upload the file at the original quality level.
- For videos originating from a DV camcorder or other high-quality source, encode the video at full-frame size and a high bitrate (good results are obtained with interlaced MPEG2 video encoded at greater than 5Mbps and either 720 × 480 or 720 × 576 resolution).
- You can't upload pornographic or adult content.

Uploading Videos

To upload videos to Google Video, all you have to do is follow these steps:

1. From any Google Video page, click the Upload and Share Your Videos link.
2. When the next page appears, as shown in Figure 25.18, click the Browse button and select the file you want to upload.
3. Enter a Title and Description for the video, select a Genre and Language, and check the box to agree to Google's terms and conditions.
4. Click the Upload Video button.

Charging for Your Video

If you want to charge users for downloading your video, you can do this. You can assign either purchase or Day Pass status to your video, at whatever price you want.

To do this, go to the Google Video home page and click the Uploaded Videos link. All the videos you've uploaded are listed here on the Video Status page, as shown in Figure 25.19.

25

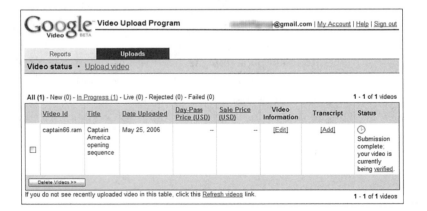

FIGURE 25.18

Uploading a video with the Google Video Uploader.

FIGURE 25.19

Viewing the status of all the videos you've uploaded.

Click the Edit link in the Video Information column for the video you want to add. This displays the Add/Edit Video Information page. From here, click the Advanced Options link. This expands the page to include the section shown in Figure 25.20. From here you can select the following payment options:

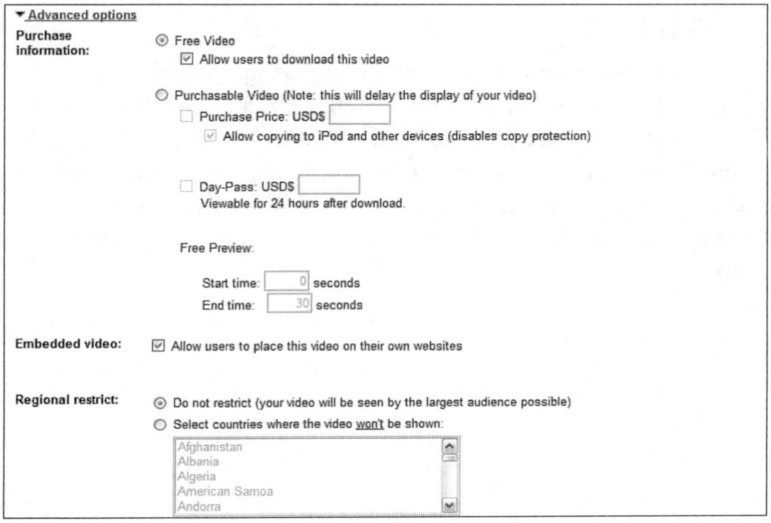

FIGURE 25.20

Specifying purchase options for your video.

- Free video (with an option to download; if you don't select this option, the video can be streamed online only)

- Purchasable video (with the purchase price you specify, and the option to download to an Apple iPod or other portable device)

- Day-Pass (with the price you specify, for use within a 24-hour period)

- Free preview (specifies how long a preview you want to display—with the exact start and stop times for the preview)

- Embedded video (allows purchasers to embed this video in their websites, or not)

- Regional restrict (blocks downloads to users of specific countries)

Make your changes, and then click the Save Video Information button. Purchases will be applied to your Google Payments account.

> **note** Learn more about Google Payments in Chapter 17, "Buying and Selling—Online and Locally—with Google Base."

The Bottom Line

As the demand for online video grows, Google Video promises to be a really big deal. As a viewer, you can search for video programming to watch online or download to view at your own convenience. There's a lot of material available, from homegrown efforts to commercial television programs, music videos, and movies. It's a great way to catch up on your favorite TV shows (at a few bucks a download), or just see what your fellow Google Video users are up to.

25

Other Google Services

26 Using Google Answers

27 Using Google Book Search

28 Using Google Groups

29 Using Google News

30 Using Google Mobile Services

Using Google Answers

I f you can't find what you're looking for on Google (and, despite Google's advanced search technology, this sometimes happens), you can always have an expert do the searching for you. Google Answers is a service that lets you pay for answers to your questions; the answers are provided by more than 500 professional researchers. When you ask a question, the Google Answers researchers search the public web and a variety of private databases for the information you request. It's a great way to conduct personalized research—without actually doing the research yourself.

Understanding Google Answers

Google Answers is an interesting service. Spend a little time here and you'll see that a vibrant little community has been created, utterly devoted to the task of helping and informing other users. In fact, most of the answers provided by Google Answer researchers are augmented by (unpaid) comments from other users who want to pitch in with what they know. It's kind of neat, actually.

What Kinds of Questions Can You Ask?

In essence, Google Answers lets you ask any question that has a concrete answer. You can ask numerical questions or word questions; historical questions or philosophical questions; easy questions and hard questions.

What you can't—or rather, shouldn't—ask are open-ended questions that don't have firm answers. Ask a question like "What color is prettiest, red or blue?", and you're likely not to get any answers. If the answer to a question exists and can be looked up, no matter how hard it might be to find, you're much more likely to get an acceptable response.

You also shouldn't try to ask questions that relate to illegal activities, request private information about individuals, refer to adult content, or are meant to advertise or sell products or services. Also, Google discourages students from using Google Answers to answer homework or exam questions; if you're a student, you shouldn't be paying someone else to do your work for you!

Finally, Google would like you to know that Google Answers "is not a substitute for professional advice or services." While it's okay to ask legal, medical, or business-related questions, you shouldn't overly rely on the answers you receive; you're better off paying a lawyer, doctor, or accountant for true professional advice.

Who Answers Your Questions?

The questions you ask via Google Answers are answered by a volunteer team of more than 500 researchers. By volunteer, I mean that they're not paid a salary by Google; they earn their money from the fees users pay to get their questions answered.

Google's researchers, by the way, are not always (if ever) experts in their field. What they are are expert researchers. A researcher is someone who can find specific information, which is exactly what Google's researchers do. You ask a question, and they research it; the result of their research is, ideally, the answer you were searching for.

Google says that the company has a stringent process for screening researchers. Each applicant must submit an essay, as well as answer a series of test questions. To maintain the quality level, Google periodically boots researchers whose ratings fall below acceptable levels. (This is why it's

note In addition to the price you set for your question, Google tacks on a non-refundable $0.50 listing fee for every question you submit.

important for you to rate the answers you receive.)

In addition to these paid researchers, any Google Answers user can post comments to any question. Users don't get paid for these comments, and their comments aren't always on-base. Still, additional informa- tion and opinions can sometimes be help-

> **note** The researcher who answers your ques- tion keeps 75% of the fee you paid; Google keeps the other 25%. (Researchers keep 100% of all tips you leave at the end of the process.)

ful, as long as you realize that these aren't responses from the paid Google researchers.

How Much Should You Pay for Answers?

Using the Google Answers service comes at a price. You can set your price as low as $2.00, or as high as $200.

Obviously, the more you pay, the more likely you are to get a rapid and detailed answer. And it's certainly appropriate to pay more for more-detailed and hard-to-answer questions. The longer a researcher has to work to find the answer, the more he or she should be paid.

You're only charged, however, when your question is actually answered. If Google's researchers draw a blank, you don't have to pay.

In addition, when you rate the answer you receive, you can also opt to tip the researcher; just enter an amount between $1 to $100 in the tip box next to the rating. This is a good way to reward particularly good work on the part of an individual researcher.

Asking Questions—and Viewing Answers

As you can see in Figure 26.1, the main Google Answers page (answers. google.com) is where you ask your questions—and get your answers. You can even browse or search through previously answered questions, which is a good way to start your research. (There's no point reinventing the wheel, after all.)

Viewing Previously-Answered Questions

While asking your own questions is the bread-and-butter of Google Answers, you can also view the answers to questions that other users have asked. All previously answered questions are organized by category; you can browse through the categories or search for available answers using the Search Google Answers box.

26

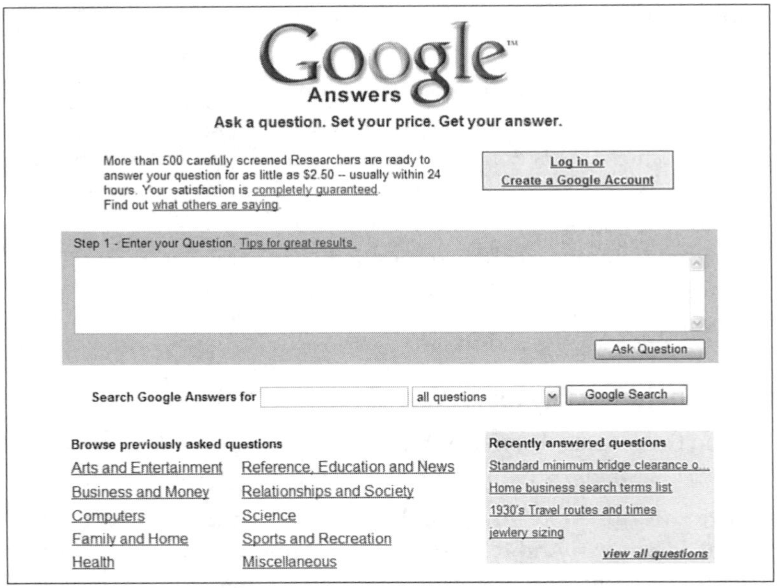

FIGURE 26.1

Google Answers—where you pay for professional research.

Browsing for previously answered questions is as easy as clicking through the categories listed at the bottom of the Google Answers home page. When you click a category link, you see a list of questions asked in that category, as well as additional subcategories of questions, as shown in Figure 26.2.

You can also search the Google Answers database for particular questions. Just enter your query into the Search Google Answers box, select whether you want to view all questions, answered questions only, or unanswered questions only, and then click the Google Search button. You'll now see a list of questions similar to that shown in Figure 26.2.

On the search results page, questions that have been successfully answered are noted by the word Answered in the Status column. Questions that are still waiting to be answered have an *X* Days Left status; questions that were not answered within 30 days are listed as Expired. The price that the original questioner paid for the answer is listed in the Price column; as a latecomer to the discussion, you can view the answer for free.

To view a question and its answer, start by clicking the question title. This displays the View Question page, like the one shown in Figure 26.3. The original question is listed at the top of this page, followed by the accepted answer.

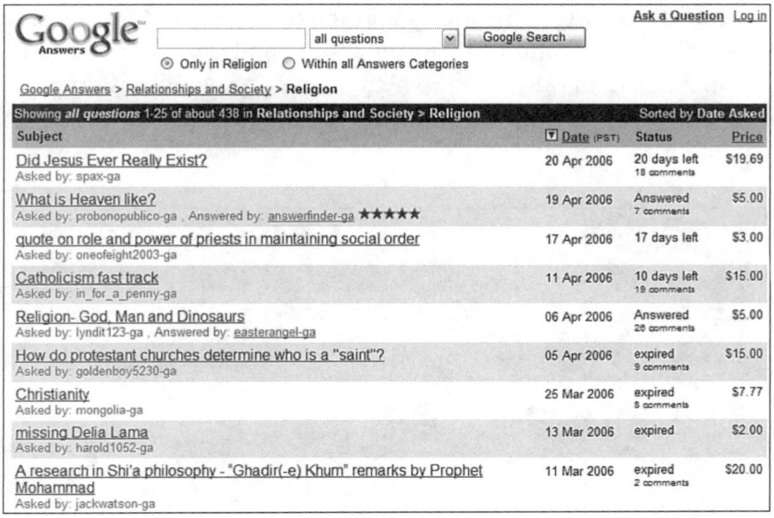

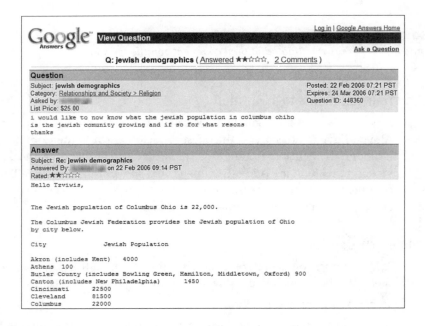

FIGURE 26.2
Viewing previously asked questions.

FIGURE 26.3
A question and resulting answer.

26

Below the answer is the rating that the original questioner gave to the answer, along with any comments the questioner had (see Figure 26.4). Below that are comments from other users, which often add valuable information to the original answer. (Take these comments with a grain of salt, however; they're not paid for!)

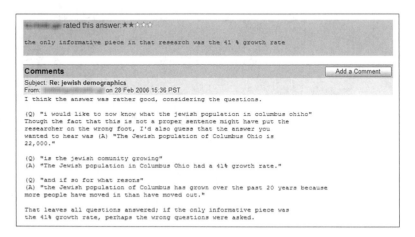

FIGURE 26.4

Comments on the answer, and additional comments on the question.

Adding Your Comments to a Question

Any registered user of Google Answers can comment on any question asked. All you have to do is access the question, scroll down to the Comments section, and then click the Add a Comment button. This expands the Comments section to include the Add a Comment box, shown in Figure 26.5. Enter your comments and then click the Post Comment button; your comments will now be added to the end of that question's Comments section.

Asking a New Question

Asking a question is pretty much as simple as asking the question, and then specifying how much you'll pay for the answer.

To ask a new question, follow these steps:

   1. On the main Google Answers page, enter your query into the Enter Your Question box, and then click the Ask Question button.

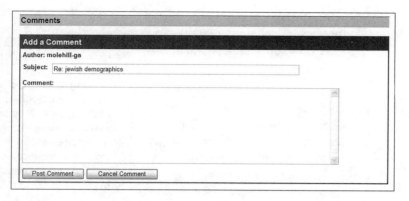

FIGURE 26.5

Adding your own comments to a question.

2. When the Ask a Question page appears, as shown in Figure 26.6, expand on your initial question, if you like. (The more details you provide, the more accurate the answers are likely to be.)

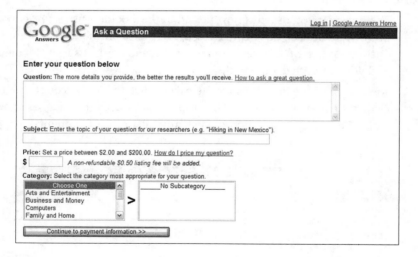

FIGURE 26.6

Entering your question.

3. Enter a subject for your query.

4. Set the price that you'll pay for the answer. The minimum you can pay is $2.00; the maximum, $200. (Google Answers automatically adds a $0.50 listing fee to your bill.)

5. Select the category and subcategory that best matches your question.

6. Click the Continue to Payment Information button.

7. If you're new to Google Answers, you're now prompted to create a Google Answers account. This is separate from your normal Google account; enter the appropriate information, and then click the Create My Google Answers Account button.

> **note** Once a researcher starts work on your question, it is "locked" to ensure that only one researcher at a time is working on it. Questions are locked for four hours, unless the question price is $100 or more (in which case the question is locked for eight hours). During this period, no other researcher can answer the question, nor can other users make comments.

8. You're now prompted for your credit card number and other payment information. Enter the necessary information and then click the Pay Listing Fee and Post Question button.

Getting the Answer

The question you asked is now posted to the Google Answers researcher community, and a Google Answers researcher takes on the task of obtaining answers. When an answer is found, the researcher posts it to Google Answers, and you're notified via email.

To view all of the questions you've asked, click the My Account link on the Google Answers main page. This displays your account page, as shown in Figure 26.7. Click a question to view any answers or comments.

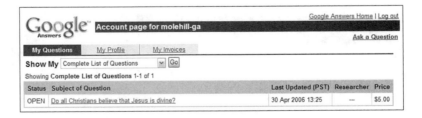

FIGURE 26.7

Viewing all questions you've asked.

COMMENTARY:

ASKING BETTER QUESTIONS—FOR BETTER ANSWERS

Since you're paying for it, it makes sense to phrase your question in a way that generates the best possible response. Here are some tips you should keep in mind:

- Don't ask open-ended questions—that is, questions that don't have a hard-and-fast answer. Researchers aren't philosophers.

- If you already know part of the answer, include it as part of the question. There's no point paying a researcher to tell you something you already know.

- If you think you know where some or all of an answer may be found, mention it in your question. It never hurts to give the researcher a little head start.

- If your question is overly complex, break it up into multiple questions. Researchers are less willing to answer questions that have a multiple-part answer; it's like you're asking them to answer multiple questions but only want to pay them once.

- Be very clear about the answer you want. For example, instead of asking for "recent" results, specify an exact time frame. Don't leave the interpretation up to chance.

Finally, don't underestimate the power of the dollar. It's possible to post a price for a question that's just too low to justify the time commitment required for an answer. It's not a hard and fast rule, but in general the more you pay, the better the answers you'll receive.

Clarifying Your Question—And Your Answers

Once you've submitted a question, you may find that you're not getting any answers. If this is the case, you may want to clarify your question, in the hopes of better attracting willing researchers. To do this, go to your account page, open the question you want to clarify, and then click the Clarify Question button. This lets you enter additional information about the question. (You can't, however, edit the question itself.)

Sometimes it will be the researcher who needs a question clarified. If this is the case, the researcher will issue a Request for Question Clarification, which you'll receive via email. Return to the question page and click the Clarify Question page to answer the researcher's queries.

Finally, you may not always like the answers you receive to your questions. If you get a particularly muddy answer from a researcher, you can ask the researcher for clarification. To request such a clarification, open the question in question and click the Clarify Answer button. Enter your additional questions, and then click Post Clarification to let the researcher know what you need.

Ratings, Refunds, and Reposts

After you get a response to your question, you should provide feedback to the researcher (and to other users) by rating the answer. Researcher ratings not only provide guidance to other potential questioners, they also help Google track the overall performance of each researcher.

To rate an answer, go to the question page and click the Rate Answer button. You can rate an answer from 1 to 5 stars, with 5 being the best rating. You can also provide comments about the answer, to help clarify your numerical rating.

If you feel an answer is totally unsatisfactory, you can reject it and request a refund. You can also, if you like, repost the question, to give another researcher a crack at it. You perform both of these actions from the answered question page. (You'll need to provide explanations for both the refund and repost request.)

The Bottom Line

Google Answers is a great alternative to the standard Google web search—particularly if you have trouble finding the desired information on your own. The team of Google Answer researchers, along with the Google Answers user community, do a good job of answering most questions; these folks are expert researchers, which means they can find just about any information that can be found.

When a particular piece of information is important to you—important enough to pay for it—turn to Google Answers. The results are, more often than not, worth the cost.

Using Google Book Search

There's a lot of great information out there on the Web. But it pales to the amount of information available in printed books. If there were a way to create a repository of all the world's book content, it would put the Internet to shame.

For better or for worse, Google is working to create that legendary global book repository. Imagine, if you will, every book ever published, available for searching online, from your web browser. That's what Google is trying to accomplish with Google Book Search, in conjunction with the Google Books Library Project. If Google is successful (and there's no guarantee of that, of course; the project is rather daunting), the collected wisdom of the ages will be just a mouse click away.

The Story Behind Google Book Search

Google's ultimate goal with Google Book Search is to let you search the full text of any book ever published, and then provide the option of reading that book online (for selected books), purchasing the book (from selected book-sellers), or finding out where you can borrow a copy of the book (from participating libraries). To achieve this goal, of course, Google must have the full text of all these books in its database—which is a formidable challenge.

Google is now in the process of adding the contents of as many books as possible to its Google Books database. This book content is coming primarily from two sources—publishers and libraries.

Google Books Partner Program

Publishers can submit their books for inclusion in the Google Books database via the Google Books Partner Program. This program is being pushed as a way for publishers to promote their books online, via exposure to Google's vast user base.

When a publisher signs up for a Google Books account, the company sends Google a list of their books they want included in Google Book Search. Ideally, the publisher also sends Google a printed copy of each book or the text of each book in PDF format. (The publisher can also just have Google add them to the Google Books database when they're scanned at a library—which we'll get into in a moment.)

Just because Google has the full text of the book in its database, however, doesn't mean that users can read the entire book online, for free. To protect the publishers' copyrighted content, Google only lets readers view a handful of pages online; in addition, all copy, save, and print functions are disabled, so freeloading readers can't download or print books for free. The only reason that Google archives the full text of the book is so readers can search the entire book, and then read short snippets of matching text.

In other words, Google Book Search is not intended as a way for readers to read entire books online. Instead, you use Google Book Search to discover what books contain the information you're looking for; you can then opt to purchase the book or borrow it from a library.

27

Google Books Library Project

The other way that Google is obtaining content for its Google Books database is from participating libraries, as part of the Google Books Library Project. To date, Google has agreements with four academic libraries (Stanford, Harvard, Oxford, and the University of Michigan) and with the New York Public Library to scan the books in their collections, and to make those books available for searching online. The result is like having all the books from these libraries available in your web browser, with Google Book Search serving as a kind of online card catalog to all that book content.

> **note** If a publisher or copyright holder doesn't want its books included in Google Book Search, they can ask Google not to scan selected library texts. For more information on excluding titles from the database, see books.google.com/partner/exclusion-signup.

Of course, the library doesn't own the content of all the books in its collection. While Google may be able to scan a library's books, it can't legally distribute those books (or provide access to those books electronically) unless the books' publishers have given Google permission to do so. Unless, that is, a given book is old enough so that its copyright has expired.

So the library collections available through Google Book Search contain searchable indexes of all available texts, and full-text versions of works in the public domain. It's not quite the same as having the full content of a library available for reading online, but it's getting close.

Searching—And Viewing—Book Content

The Google Books database is accessible in two different ways—from the regular Google web search page, or from the dedicated Google Book Search page.

Searching from the Standard Web Search Page

You don't have to go to the Google Book Search page to search for book content. Google Books results can appear as the result of a standard Google web search—assuming the book(s) in question have something to do with the query at hand. In this instance, matching books appear at the top of the search results page, as shown in Figure 27.1.

27

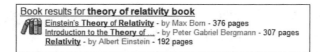

FIGURE 27.1

Google Books results from a standard web search.

Searching from Google Book Search

The other way to conduct a book search is from the Google Book Search page (books.google.com), shown in Figure 27.2. This page functions like Google's standard web search page; enter your query into the search box, and then click the Search Books button.

FIGURE 27.2

Searching for books with Google Book Search.

There's one option on the Google Book Search page you need to be aware of. You have the option of searching all books (the default setting), or only those books for which the full text is available (full view books). Select which option you want underneath the search box.

Conducting an Advanced Book Search

Google Book Search also offers an Advanced Book Search page, accessible when you click the Advanced Book Search link. As you can see in Figure 27.3, this page offers many of the advanced search options you find on Google's regular Advanced Search page, as well as a few book-specific search options.

All these search options are detailed in Table 27.1.

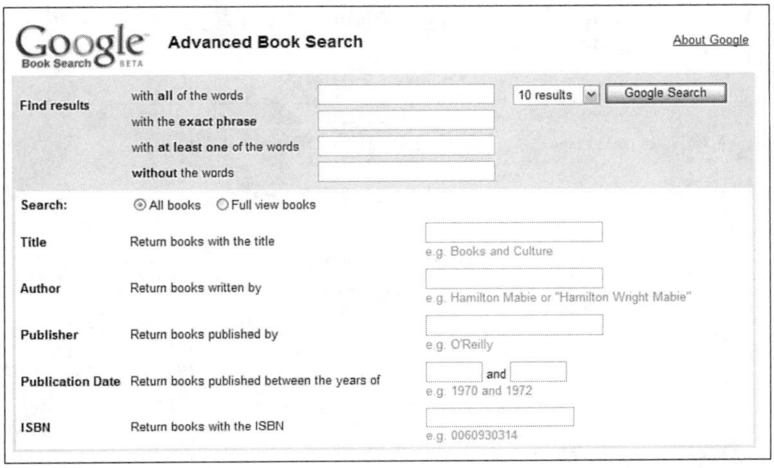

FIGURE 27.3
Google's Advanced Book Search page.

Table 27.1   Advanced Book Search Options

Option	Description
Find messages with *all* of the words	Default search mode
Find messages with the *exact phrase*	Searches for messages that contain the exact phrase entered
Find messages with *at least one* of the words	Searches for messages that contain either one word or another
Find messages *without* the words	Excludes messages that contain the specified word(s)
Search	All books in the database, or only those "full view" books that have the full text available for viewing
Title	Search for words in the book's title
Author	Search for books written by a specific author
Publisher	Search for books published by a specific publisher
Publication date	Search for books published between two given years
ISBN	Search for a book with a specific ISBN number

Viewing Book Content

After you enter your search query, Google returns a list of matching books, like the one shown in Figure 27.4. Books in this list can have four different viewing options, depending on the book's copyright status and publisher/author wishes:

FIGURE 27.4
Search results from a Google Book Search.

- **Full view.** The full text of these books is available for reading online. (Figure 27.5 shows a typical full view book.)

- **Limited preview.** These books have only a limited number of pages available for reading online, as kind of a preview to the rest of the book. The full text of the book is not available for reading online. (Figure 27.6 shows a typical preview page.)

- **Snippet view.** Similar to limited preview books, these books only offer a few small snippets of text for preview. These snippets show a few instances of the search term in content; the full text of the book is not available for reading online. (Figure 27.7 shows some snippets from a typical book.)

- **No preview available.** For these books, no previews or snippets are available. Obviously, the full text of the books is also not available for reading online. (Figure 27.8 shows the information for a typical no-preview book.)

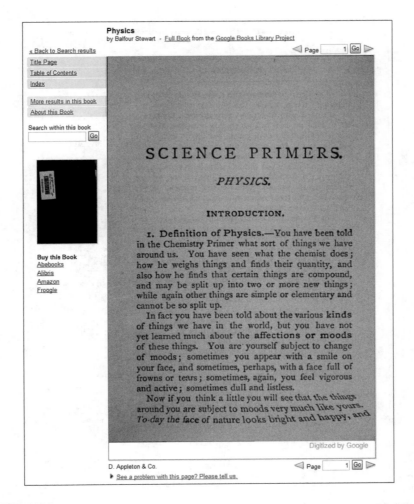

Physics
by Balfour Stewart - Full Book from the Google Books Library Project

« Back to Search results

Title Page
Table of Contents
Index

More results in this book
About this Book

Search within this book

Buy this Book
Abebooks
Alibris
Amazon
Froogle

Page 1 Go

SCIENCE PRIMERS.

PHYSICS.

INTRODUCTION.

1. **Definition of Physics.**—You have been told in the Chemistry Primer what sort of things we have around us. You have seen what the chemist does; how he weighs things and finds their quantity, and also how he finds that certain things are compound, and may be split up into two or more new things; while again other things are simple or elementary and cannot be so split up.

In fact you have been told about the various kinds of things we have in the world, but you have not yet learned much about the **affections or moods** of these things. You are yourself subject to change of moods; sometimes you appear with a smile on your face, and sometimes, perhaps, with a face full of frowns or tears; sometimes, again, you feel vigorous and active; sometimes dull and listless.

Now if you think a little you will see that the things around you are subject to moods very much like yours. To-day the face of nature looks bright and happy, and

Digitized by Google

D. Appleton & Co.

Page 1 Go

▶ See a problem with this page? Please tell us.

FIGURE 27.5

A full view book.

27

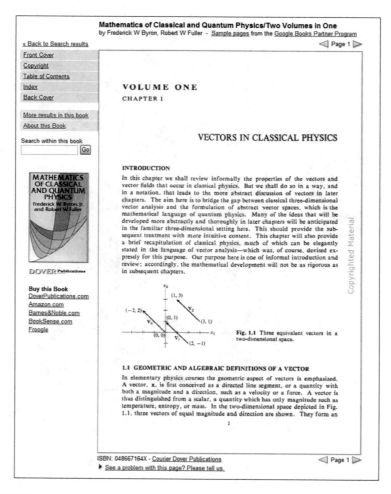

FIGURE 27.6

A book with a limited preview.

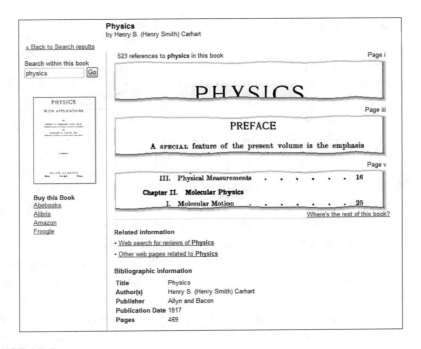

FIGURE 27.7

Book snippets.

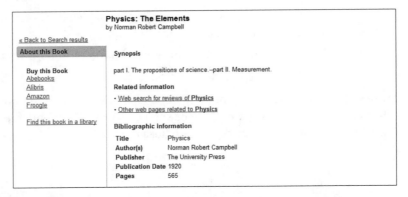

FIGURE 27.8

A book with no preview available.

Getting More Information

Once you've accessed a book page (full view or otherwise), you have several options for obtaining more information. Depending on the book, you can

note The Find It In a Library function utilizes the OCLC Worldcat database. Learn more about the Online Computer Library Center (OCLC) at www.oclc.org.

- Read the book online (for full view books). Click the right and left arrow buttons to turn the pages, or click the links at the left to go to specific sections of the book. (You can also enter a page number below the page window to go directly to a specific page in the book.)

- Search within the book. Use the search box at the left side of the page to search for instances of words and phrases within the book.

- Read bibliographic information about the book (author, publisher, publication date, and so on), located below the book page display.

- Read more about this book (synopsis, et al.) by clicking the About This Book link.

- Read online reviews of the book. (Click the links below the book page display.)

- Learn more about the book's publisher by clicking the publisher name below the book page display.

- Buy the book from selected bookstores; click the bookstore link to go directly to a purchase page.

- Find this book in a nearby library by clicking the Find It In a Library link and entering your ZIP Code.

Know, however, that not all of these options are available for all books. Many books simply let you see a preview or snippet, some brief bibliographical information, and a link or two to purchase the book online.

COMMENTARY:

GOOGLE VERSUS THE PUBLISHING COMMUNITY

As the Google Books Library Project goes about its business of scanning in hundreds of thousands of library books, it's important to note that Google is scanning those books without first seeking the approval of those books' authors or publishers. That has caused a great deal of friction between Google and the publishing community—and at least one major lawsuit.

The so-called "publishing community" is separate from the library community, and it's the libraries that Google is working most closely with. Publishers and libraries have significantly different mindsets, which is at the core of this conflict.

You see, publishers (and authors), whatever their artistic intent, are ultimately in the business to make money, which they do by selling books. Libraries, on the other hand, exist to disseminate information, most often for free. It's this age-old conflict between generating revenues and distributing information that Google has deliberately walked right into the middle of.

When it comes to allowing their books to be available via Google Book Search, publishers are of decidedly mixed minds. Some publishers view it as a promotional opportunity and another potential outlet for book sales; other publishers view it as interfering with their own internal sales plans. That's why you see some publishers cooperating with Google on this project, but many more publishers shying away. These less-enthusiastic publishers want to protect their copyrights and restrict access to the books they publish; they're more likely to partner with an online bookseller like Amazon.com than with a site that, in their view, gives content away for free.

Authors face a similar dilemma. Should they embrace Google Book Search as a way for readers to find out about their less-visible works, or should they be afraid of Google lessening the value of their content by giving it (or some of it) away for free?

Opposing Google's effort is the Authors Guild. The Guild, along with individual authors Herbert Mitgang, Betty Miles, and Daniel Hoffman, have sued Google over the Book Search program, alleging that Google is engaging in massive copyright infringement at the expense of the rights of individual writers.

Authors Guild president Nick Taylor had this to say about the situation:

"This is a plain and brazen violation of copyright law. It's not up to Google or anyone other than the authors, the rightful owners of these copyrights, to decide whether and how their works will be copied."

The problem, as many authors see it, is that Google is scanning all library books by default, and then requiring disinterested authors and publishers to opt out of the program. A better approach would be to

27

ask permission before scanning, instead of assuming that permission and then allowing proactive opt-outs. As currently constructed, the program can inadvertently include content that authors (or publishers) do not want distributed online.

That said, many authors think that Google Book Search can increase the visibility of the books they've written. For example, here's what author Paul Andrews says about the program:

"As a longtime dues-paying member of the Authors Guild, I'm party to a lawsuit against Google over its new book-search service called Google Book Search. As an author of two books, though, I'm not sure I want to be suing Google. Every writer wants his or her work to be read. But to be read, a work needs to be found. Digital search is fast becoming the *de facto* way to be found, [and] Google Book Search aims to do for books what Google has done for the Web."

Author Cory Doctorow puts it more distinctly:

"Thank you, thank you, thank you Google, for providing a way to put books back into the daily round of average people."

As an author, I can see both sides of the conflict. On one hand, I really don't want Google or any other entity giving away copies of my books (electronic or otherwise) for free, without paying me any royalties. On the other hand, if only snippets of my books are available for online browsing, what's the harm? In fact, if viewing a page or so online encourages a potential reader to actually purchase a printed copy of one of my books, I benefit from the exercise.

The spanner in the works, however, is whether readers of nonfiction works can find the information they want from a Google search result snippet, and therefore not have to purchase the printed book. It's possible, for example, that someone searching for information about Google Book Search might be able to read this very page online, and therefore not have to purchase the entire book. In this instance, Google Book Search becomes a deterrent to book sales, which isn't a good thing. (At least it's not a good thing for authors and publishers; for readers, it might be a different story.)

My gut tells me that as long as Google Book Search only shows short snippets of book content, it actually works to promote the sale of printed books, especially those books that don't receive a lot of promotion or appear on the best-seller lists. If the program evolves to providing the full text of works online, without the approval of or compensation to the legal copyright holder, then the program is more akin to intellectual property theft than it is to providing useful information for web searchers. As pundits are fond of saying, only time will tell the ultimate impact of the Google Books program.

The Bottom Line

The Google Books project is an interesting and ambitious endeavor. While the prospect of having all the world's printed books available online is deceptively attractive, it's also somewhat impractical. Google can't, after all, make available copyrighted material without the permission of the book's copyright holders. This means that most of books in print today won't be available for reading online, at least not for free.

As such, the value of having book content searchable but not readable is debatable. You can try Google Book Search for yourself to see what you think, but be prepared; a lot of the information you find will be tantalizingly out of reach.

Using Google Groups

Not all the information on the Internet resides on the World Wide Web. For many years, Usenet, an assemblage of topic-specific discussion groups, was one of the most dominant parts of the Internet. Though less influential than it once was, Usenet still exists—and, when it comes to searching for information, the messages exchanged in Usenet newsgroups often contain information relevant to the search queries you might have.

The problem with Usenet is that it's difficult to perform a "live" search among all the current newsgroups. Not only are there tens of thousands of groups to search through, you're also faced with the problem of currency. Because individual postings stay available in a newsgroup for only a limited period of time, messages "scroll off" particularly active newsgroups within a matter of days.

Fortunately for all of us, Google maintains a comprehensive archive of Usenet newsgroup messages, past and present. And Google's done Usenet one better, enabling the average user to create his or her own topic-specific discussion groups as part of its Google Groups service.

For all these reasons, Google Groups is a particularly important part of the Google empire. Read on to learn more.

The History of Usenet and Google Groups

Most users today might not realize it, but Usenet is the largest and oldest existing online community in the world. Predating the World Wide Web—but still using the Internet's underlying infrastructure—Usenet is a collection of more than 30,000 online discussion groups, organized by topic. Usenet ties into Google via Google Groups, which functions as a newsreader for Usenet newsgroups, an archive of historical newsgroup postings, and a host to thousands of user-created (non-Usenet) discussion groups.

How Newsgroups Work

Before we get into Google Groups, let's spend a little time discussing Usenet. Usenet is a network that piggybacks on the larger Internet, and in fact was one of the first components of the Internet, predating the web and the so-called public Internet. The Usenet network is designed to host and convey messages from users organized around topic categories called *newsgroups*.

In essence, a Usenet newsgroup is an electronic gathering place for people with similar interests. Within a newsgroup, users post messages (called *articles*) about a variety of topics; other users read these articles and, when so disposed, respond. The result is a kind of ongoing, freeform discussion in which dozens—or hundreds—of interested users can participate.

Usenet newsgroup messages are stored on a network of Usenet servers. These servers communicate with one another via the Internet. Users access the messages using a dedicated Usenet newsreader program (such as Agent, downloadable from www.forteinc.com), or an email program that also reads newsgroups (such as Outlook Express), or the Google Groups website.

note Unlike some web-based discussion forums or blogs, most Usenet newsgroups are unmoderated, meaning that no one's watching the message content to ensure that subject discussions stay on track. The result is a kind of only slightly organized chaos, typically with a lot of off-topic messages and thinly concealed advertisements mixed in with the on-topic and useful messages.

Understanding Newsgroup Hierarchies

Trying to find one newsgroup out of the 30,000 or so available is like trying to find the proverbial needle in a virtual haystack.

Fortunately, Usenet organizes its newsgroups in an extremely logical fashion, using a series of hierarchies.

A newsgroup name looks a little like a website address, with single words or phrases separated by periods. Newsgroup names are more logical, however, in that each break in the name signifies a level of greater granularity. The left-most part of the name places the newsgroup in one of several major domains, with each subsequent component denoting a subset of the major domain. (It's kind of like moving through the folders and subfolders on your hard disk.)

So as you read a newsgroup name, your focus moves from left to right, until you zero in on a very specific topic. For example, the rec.arts.cinema group tells you that the newsgroup is in the *recreational* section of Usenet, and that it discusses the *art* of the *cinema*.

There are dozens of different top-level domains. The most important of these are detailed in Table 28.1.

Table 28.1   Major Usenet Top-Level Domains

Domain	Coverage
alt.	Alternative topics not covered elsewhere on Usenet.
biz.	Business-related products and services.
comp.	Computer-related topics.
humanities.	Literature, fine arts, and other humanities.
k12.	Education-related issues for grades kindergarten through 12.
misc.	A broad variety of topics that don't easily fit into one of the other domains.
news.	Newsgroup-related issues.
rec.	Recreation and popular entertainment.
soc.	Societal and cultural issues.
sci.	Science-related issues, for both professionals and laymen.
talk.	All manner of issues, open for public debate.

There are also many regional and company-specific Usenet domains. For example, the japan. domain contains Japanese-oriented newsgroups, and the microsoft. domain includes newsgroups about Microsoft products. Some of the larger regional domains include their own hierarchies that resemble the over-all Usenet hierarchy in complexity.

28

Google Groups: Archiving Usenet Articles

Usenet is a kind of living beast, with new articles being posted daily and old articles fading away into the ether. Except that you really don't want those old articles fading away, as they contain (among the expected chaff, of course) some very important discussions and information that simply don't exist anywhere else on the Internet.

For that reason, there have long been attempts to archive historical Usenet postings. The most successful of these archives was DejaNews (later called Deja.com), which Google purchased in 2001. Google subsequently turned DejaNews into Google Groups, which continues to function as both an archive of historical Usenet articles and a web-based newsreader for current Usenet newsgroups. You can use Google Groups to search the newsgroup archives or to browse the current messages in any Usenet newsgroup.

Today, Google Groups is more than just Usenet. Yes, Google Groups continues to serve as a Usenet newsreader and as a comprehensive Usenet archive, but it's also home to thousands of user-created discussion groups that have nothing to do with Usenet. When you search Google Groups, you're searching both Usenet postings and postings made within these user-created groups; as far as Google Groups is concerned, one type of group is just as good as the other.

Searching the Newsgroups

In the past, you had to use a newsreader program to browse through Usenet newsgroups and read individual newsgroup articles. This was fine for the time, and marginally acceptable if you were only interested in following a handful of newsgroups, but just didn't cut it if you were power searching for specific information across multiple newsgroups. For that, you need a more powerful tool, a true Usenet search engine— which is where Google Groups comes in.

Searching for Groups

You access Google Groups, shown in Figure 28.1, by clicking the Groups link on Google's home page or by going directly to groups.google.com. From here you can search for specific groups, browse through available groups, or search across all groups for specific information.

note Don't be put off by Google Groups' "beta" designation; it's been in so-called beta testing since its 2001 launch! Calling something a beta version is just Google's way of rolling out new services. After five years online, it's safe to say that Google Groups has been thoroughly tested, and is more than ready for prime time.

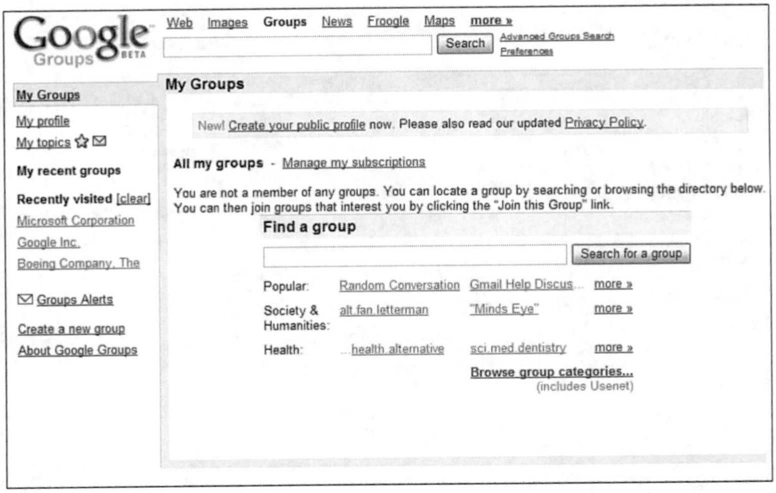

FIGURE 28.1

The Google Groups home page.

When you want to read the current articles in a specific group, you start by searching for that group. To conduct a group search, enter your query into the Find a Group box (in the middle of the page), and then click the Search for a Group button.

The search results page, shown in Figure 28.2, lists several different items. At the top of the page is a series of filters that you can click to list only those matching groups within a specific topic, language, activity level, or size (number of members). Below that is a list of the groups themselves, listed in order of activity (high to low).

For each group, Google lists the group name, a link to matching messages within the group, the category and language of the group, the group's activity level and number of users, and whether or not it's a Usenet newsgroup. (If the word "Usenet" doesn't appear, it's a user-created Google Group.)

Browsing Through the Groups

You can also browse for groups by category. Just scroll down to the bottom of the Google Groups page and click the Browse Group Categories link. This displays the Group Directory, shown in Figure 28.3. Click through a major category and through the various subcategories until you find the specific group you want.

FIGURE 28.2

Searching for a specific group.

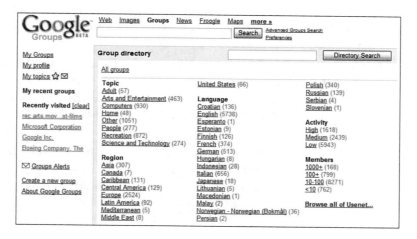

FIGURE 28.3

Browsing through the Group Directory.

28

Searching Across All Groups

If, instead of reading the messages in a specific group, you want to search for messages about a given topic across all groups, you can do that. Searching the Google Groups archive is as simple as entering a query into the search box at the top of the Google Groups page, and then clicking the Search button.

tip   To browse through Usenet newsgroups by hierarchy, click the Browse All of Usenet link on the Group Directory page.

This displays a list of individual messages that match your search criteria, like the one in Figure 28.4. Click a message header to read that message, or click the group name below that message to go to the hosting group.

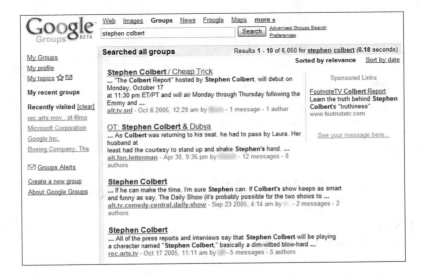

FIGURE 28.4

Searching for messages across all groups.

Using Advanced Search Operators

When you're searching for messages across groups, you can use any of three Groups-specific advanced search operators to fine-tune your search. Just enter the operator into the search box; Table 28.2 details these three operators.

Table 28.2	Google Groups Advanced Search Operators	
Operator	**Description**	**Example**
author:	Searches for posts by a specific author	author:molehill
group:	Limits your search to a specific group	group:alt.movies
insubject:	Limits your search to the subject lines of messages only	insubject:abba

28

Performing an Advanced Search

Google Groups also offers an Advanced Groups Search page, shown in Figure 28.5, which lets you fine-tune your search from a simple web form. You access this page by clicking the Advanced Groups Search link on the Google Groups page.

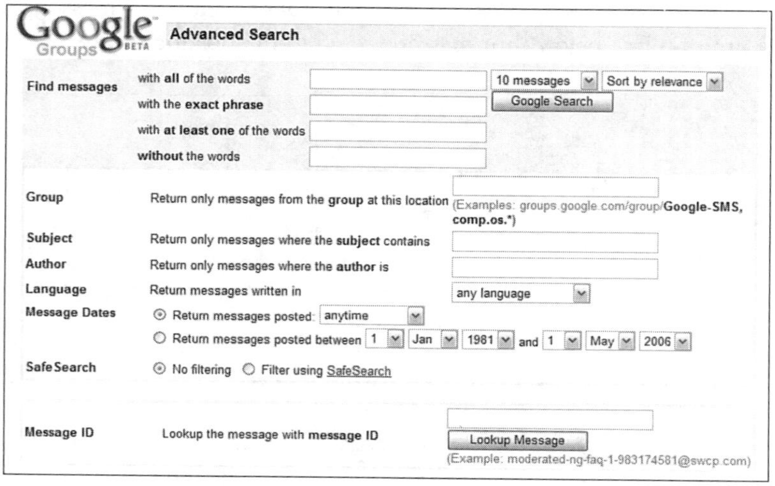

FIGURE 28.5

The Advanced Groups Search page.

Table 28.3 details the search options available on the Advanced Groups Search page.

Table 28.3   Advanced Groups Search Options

Option	Description
Results	Selects how many listings are displayed on the search results page
Sort by	Sorts messages by relevance or date
Find messages with *all* of the words	Default search mode
Find messages with the *exact phrase*	Searches for messages that contain the exact phrase entered
Find messages with *at least one* of the words	Searches for messages that contain either one word or another
Find messages *without* the words	Excludes messages that contain the specified word(s)
Group	Searches for messages within the selected group
Subject	Searches only within the subject line of messages
Author	Searches for messages from the specified user

Table 28.3	Continued
Option	Description
Language	Restricts search to messages written in the specified language
Message Date	Restricts search to messages created between the specified dates
SafeSearch	Activates the SafeSearch content filter for this search
Message ID	Searches for a specific message number

Make your choices, and then click the Google Search button to initiate the search.

Participating in Google Groups

Once you find a group you like, you have a couple of options. You can opt to visit the group and read messages on an infrequent basis, or you can subscribe to the group so that you're notified when new messages are posted.

Visiting Groups and Reading Messages

To view any Google group, all you have to do is search for or browse to the group, and then click the group name. This displays the group page, shown in Figure 28.6.

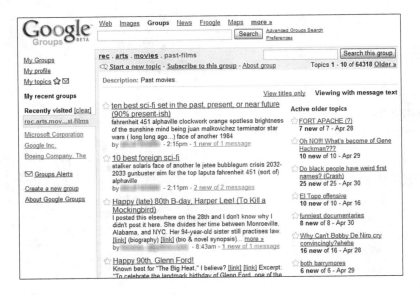

FIGURE 28.6
The home page for a Google Group.

On this page you see a list of the most recent topics (in Usenet parlance, "threads"), with a snippet of the most recent message in each thread. A list of older topics is displayed in the right column; you can also, if you like, search the messages within this group, by using the second search box on the page (next to the Search This Group button).

To read all the messages on a given topic (in a given thread, that is), click the title of the thread. This displays the message page, like the one in Figure 28.7. Messages are listed in chronological order (the first message at the top and the last at the bottom).

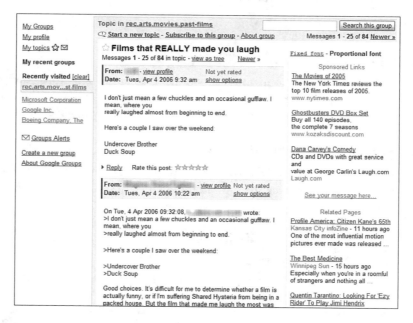

FIGURE 28.7

Reading all the messages in a thread.

Subscribing to a Group

If you want to keep up-to-date on all the new messages in a group, you may want to *subscribe* to the group. When you subscribe to a group, you're automatically notified of new messages posted to the

tip To find other articles from specific users, go to any message page and click the poster's name (in the From: field). This displays a summary of articles posted to various groups by the author of the current article.

28

group via email; you don't have to visit the group page to manually read messages.

To subscribe to a group, just go to the main group page and then click the Subscribe to This Group link at the top of the page. When the Join page appears, as shown in Figure 28.8, select how you want to be notified of new messages:

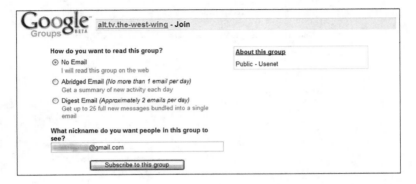

FIGURE 28.8

Subscribing to a group.

- **No email.** You don't receive any notification of new messages; you have to go to the Google Groups site to read the group's messages.

- **Abridged email.** You get one email a day that contains a summary of all the new messages.

- **Digest email.** You get one or more emails a day containing the full text of up to 25 messages. If a group has more than 25 messages in a day, you'll receive additional digest emails containing the excess messages.

Once you've made your selection, enter the nickname you want to use, and then click the Subscribe to This Group button.

Posting to a Group

Once you're on a group page, you have the option of simply reading messages, replying to messages, or posting a message on a new topic.

tip To unsubscribe from a group, go to that group's page, click the Unsubscribe or Change Membership link, and then click the Unsubscribe button on the Change My Membership page.

28

To reply to a message, start by opening the message thread. At the bottom of each message in the thread is a Reply link; click this link and the page expands to show a Reply box, like the one shown in Figure 28.9. Enter your reply into the box, and then click the Post button. Your reply will be added to the end of the current thread.

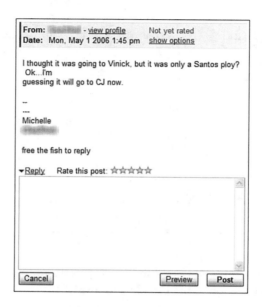

FIGURE 28.9

Replying to a message.

Creating a New Message Thread

You're not limited to replying to existing message topics. You can also start a new message thread (what Google calls a topic), with a new message.

To do this, go to the main group page and click the Start a New Topic link at the top of the page. This displays the Start a New Topic page, shown in Figure 28.10. Enter a name for the new topic into the Subject box, and then enter the text of your message into the Message box. When you click the Post Message button, your new message appears as the first in a new topic/thread on the main group page.

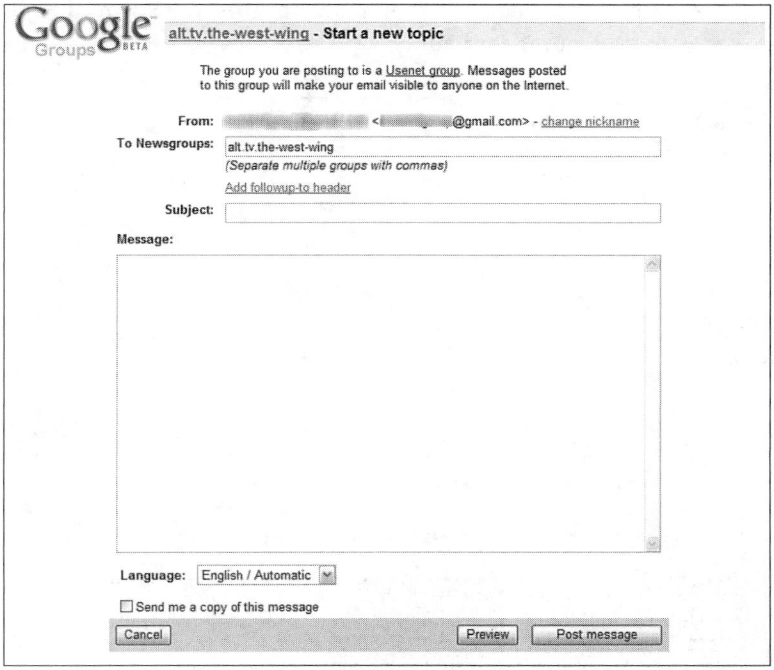

FIGURE 28.10
Creating a new post on a new topic.

Creating Your Own Google Group

With the tens of thousands of groups (Usenet and otherwise) present on Google Groups, it's still possible that there's no group available for a given topic in which you're interested. If this is the case, you can always start your own Google Group, on just about any topic you desire.

Setting Up the Group

To start a new Google Group, follow these steps:

1. From the main Google Groups page, click the Create a New Group link (in the left column).

tip
To cross-post to more than one group, enter additional group names into the Subject box, separated by commas.

note
User-created groups are not Usenet newsgroups, and are available only to users of the Google Groups website. In this sense they're similar to the user groups hosted by Yahoo! Groups (groups.yahoo.com), but without all of Yahoo's bells and whistles; for example, Google doesn't let its groups host photos and other files.

28

2. When the Create a Group page appears, as shown in Figure 28.11, enter a name for your group.

FIGURE 28.11

Creating a new Google Group.

3. Enter an email address for your group. (This is typically the group name, followed by @googlegroups.com.)

4. Enter a brief description of your group.

5. If the group is likely to contain adult content or language, check the option This Group May Contain Content Which Is Only Suitable for Adults.

6. Select the desired access level for the group: Public (anyone can join, but only members can read messages), Announcement-Only (anyone can join, but only moderators can post messages), Restricted (only the people you invite can join). For what it's worth, most groups have Public access.

7. Click the Create My Group button.

Inviting Members to Your Group

Once you've created your group, it's time to find some members. You do this by inviting people to join your group, like this:

1. After you've click the Create My Group button, the Add Members page appears, as shown in Figure 28.12.

FIGURE 28.12

Inviting new members to your group.

2. Enter the email addresses of those people you wish to invite to your group. Enter one email address per line.

3. To automatically add each of these users to your group, select the Add option. To send each user an invitation instead, check the Invite option.

28

4. Select which type of subscription will appear as the default—No Email, Email, Abridged Email, or Digest Email.

5. Enter a welcome message to send to each of the people you signified.

6. Click the Done button.

You can also invite new members at any later date. Just go to your group page, click the Invite link (at the top of the page), and follow the onscreen directions from there.

Managing Your Group

Once you've created your group, you can manage it on a day-to-day basis. Just go to your group page and click the Manage link at the top of the page. This displays the Manage page, shown in Figure 28.13. From here you can change any of the group's settings, browse the group membership, invite new members, and so on.

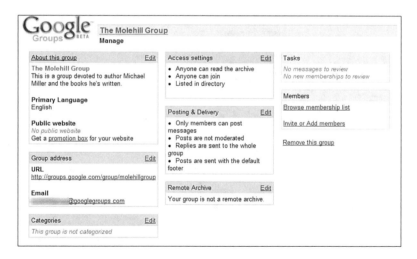

FIGURE 28.13

Managing your Google Group.

COMMENTARY:

NETIQUETTE

When you're posting on an online discussion group or blog, you need to follow a set of unstated rules, or you risk offending other users—and possibly setting off a so-called "flame war" of diatribes and personal attacks. Acceptable online behavior is sometimes called *netiquette*, and adheres to some of the following advice.

- Don't write in all capital letters—it looks like you're SHOUTING!
- Be specific when creating a message header; this helps readers determine which messages to read and which to avoid.
- Don't post off-topic messages. Users come to a group or blog to discuss a specific topic; off-topic postings just add unnecessarily to the clutter and noise level.
- Don't make your messages longer than they need to be. Brevity is a prized trait when communicating online.
- Don't post a message in more than one section in an online forum, or in more than one newsgroup. This is called *cross-posting*—it wastes valuable bandwidth, and is strongly frowned upon.
- Be polite. Don't use offensive language, and don't be unnecessarily insulting. Many passive-aggressive users adopt a much different persona when they're typing out semi-anonymous messages in cyberspace; it's better to write as if you were talking face-to-face, and treat others as you would like to be treated yourself.
- Don't advertise or spam. It isn't seemly, and it's sure to inspire a rash of vitriolic replies.

These netiquette rules apply equally to discussion groups (Google, Usenet, or other) and blogs. Good netiquette is universal; bad netiquette is always something to be avoided.

28

The Bottom Line

Continuing access to the Usenet newsgroup archive would be reason enough to celebrate Google Groups. The fact that Google Groups also lets you create your own discussion groups is just icing on the proverbial cake. (Notice that it's always the cake that's proverbial, and not the icing?) In any case, if you have a topic that especially interests you, Google Groups is the place to find others who share your interest. I particularly like the ability to receive message summaries and digests via email, so I don't have to visit the actual site if I don't particularly want to—after I've subscribed to all my favorite groups, of course!

Using Google News

S ure, Google's main gig is the super search engine we all know and love (and its main source of revenue is selling ads on all those search results pages), but Google has also become one of the primary online resources for newshounds worldwide. Not that you have to search the Google index for old news stories (although you can, if you want to); no, Google does all the hard work for you with its Google News service.

Google News is a news-gathering service that identifies, assembles, and displays the latest news headlines from more than 4,500 different news organizations. Google doesn't write any of its own news stories; it has no reporters or editors on staff. Instead, it uses its search technology to search major news sites on the Web and collate the most relevant, most up-to-date news headlines on a single web page. (Google News headlines are updated every 15 minutes.) You can then click any headline to read the full news story on its originating news site.

Of course, you can also use Google's search technology to search older news articles (up to 30 days past), which lets Google News function as kind of a news archive on the Web. This feature, along with its headline-gathering home page, makes Google News a one-stop shop for anyone interested in news and information online.

Viewing the Latest Headlines and Stories

You get to Google News directly at news.google.com, or by clicking the News link on any Google page. As you can see in Figure 29.1, Google News organizes its stories by category and lists a number of related stories under each lead headline. More headlines are displayed when you click the All Related link under each story, as shown in Figure 29.2.

FIGURE 29.1

The default Google News page.

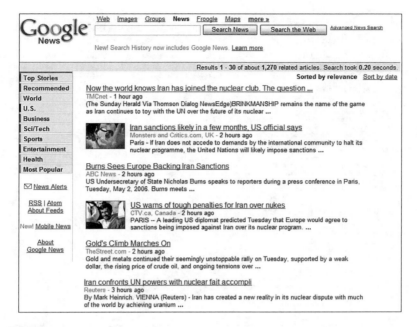

FIGURE 29.2

A list of related stories.

By the way, if you don't like the default headline+photos view, you can click the Text Version link to view an all-text version of the Google News page. As you can see in Figure 29.3, this version of Google News looks more like a standard Google search results page.

Google News organizes its stories into nine sections that roughly correlate with the topic-oriented sections you find in a major daily newspaper. You can view all the headlines in each section by clicking the section link in the left navigation box. The sections include

- Top Stories
- World
- U.S.
- Business
- Sci/Tech
- Sports
- Entertainment
- Health
- Most Popular

FIGURE 29.3

Google News in all-text view.

To read any story, just click the headline link. This takes you from Google to the story on its originating website, with the selected story displayed.

Viewing International News

Not surprisingly, Google News isn't just for American users. Google offers 34 country-specific versions of Google News, each version customized with news of interest to that country. For example, Figure 29.4 shows the U.K. version of Google News; Figure 29.5 shows the Mexican version.

To switch to a different country's news site, you can pull down the country list at the top of the Google News page, or click on a country link at the bottom of the page.

FIGURE 29.4

Google News for the United Kingdom.

FIGURE 29.5

Google News for Mexico.

Personalizing Google News

The default Google News page is good, but you can also create a version of Google News customized for your own personal tastes and interests. That is, you can personalize Google News to display only those types of stories that you want to see.

To personalize Google News, click the Personalize This Page link. This displays a Personalize This Page box, as shown in Figure 29.6.

FIGURE 29.6

Personalizing Google News.

From here, you can rearrange any of the standard modules by simply dragging and dropping them into new positions. To change the number of stories displayed within each module, or to delete a module from the page, click the link within any section module.

You can also click the Add a Standard Section link to add a module from any of the U.S. or international versions of Google News. Or, if you like, you can create your own custom news modules by clicking the Add a Custom Section link. This displays the Add a Custom Section box, shown in Figure 29.7.

Custom modules are essentially custom Google news searches; enter your query into the Keywords box, select how many stories you want to display in the module, and then click the Add Section button.

> **tip**
>
> To add a label or change the language for your custom section, click the Advanced link.

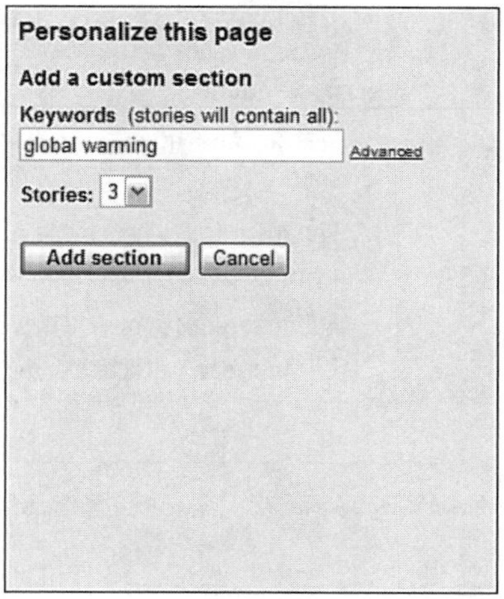

FIGURE 29.7

Creating a custom news module.

Once you have your personalized page configured the way you like it, you can display this page by clicking the Personalized News link at the top of the Google News page.

Searching for News Articles

While reading Google News' current headlines is nice, if you're searching for specific stories or older stories, you need to use Google's Advanced News Search. You access this advanced search from the Google News page by clicking the Advanced News Search link.

As you can see in Figure 29.8, you can use the Advanced News Search to search by a variety of parameters, as detailed in Table 29.1.

Table 29.1   Advanced News Search Options

Option	Description
Sort by	Specifies in what order results are displayed—by relevance or by date
Find results with *all* of the words	Default search mode
Find results with the *exact phrase*	Searches for the exact phrase entered
Find results with *at least one* of the words	Searches for either one word or another
Find results *without* the words	Excludes pages that contain the specified word(s)
News source	Searches for articles from a specified newspaper or news site

Table 29.1	Continued
Option	Description
Location	Searches for articles from news sources located in a specific country or state
Occurrences	Returns articles where the keywords occur in the article's headline, body, URL, or anywhere in the article
Date	Returns articles published between two specific dates, or within the last hour, day, week, or month

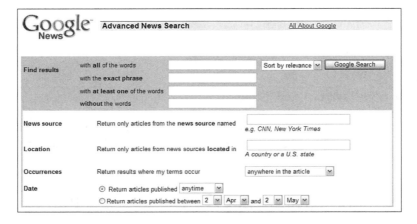

FIGURE 29.8
The Advanced News Search page.

Reading Google News Feeds

I've discussed blog feeds and news feeds several times in this book, so there's no need to go into what a feed is at this point. Suffice to say, you can sign up for RSS or Atom feeds from any Google News section or custom search, and then read the latest headlines for that section or search as a feed in your favorite feed reader or aggregator.

tip Once you create a query for a specific topic, you can bookmark the search results page in your web browser. Every time you access this bookmark, you'll display an updated search results page containing the latest news stories on the specified topic. You can even put a shortcut to this bookmark on your desktop and double-click it when you want up-to-date news on the topic at hand.

Google lets you sign up for three types of news feeds:

note Learn more about feeds and the Google Reader feed aggregator in Chapter 6, "Searching Blogs and Blog Postings."

- News section feeds, which contain headlines from a given Google News section. Click any section link to go to that section page, and then use the RSS or Atom link in the left column.

- News search results feeds, which contain headlines that match any news search you initiate. Conduct your search, and then use the RSS or Atom link in the left column of the search results page.

- Customized news feeds, which contain all the headlines from your personalized version of Google News. Click the Personalized News link at the top of the main Google News page, and then use the RSS or Atom link in the left column of the personalized page.

Signing Up for News Alerts

Back in Chapter 15, "Keeping Updated with Google Alerts," you learned all about Google Alerts. As you recall you can use Google Alerts to notify you via email when news articles appear online that match the topics you specify. This way you can monitor breaking news stories, keep tabs on industries or competitors, or just stay up-to-date on specific types of events.

To sign up for a Google News Alert, follow these steps:

1. From the Google News page, click the News Alerts link.

2. When the Google Alerts page appears, as shown in Figure 29.9, enter your query into the Search Terms box.

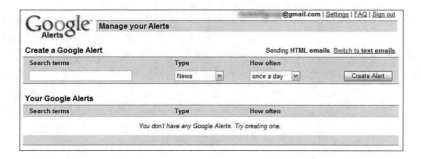

FIGURE 29.9

Setting up a Google News Alert.

3. Pull down the type list and select News.

4. Pull down the How Often list and select how often you want to receive alerts—Once a Day, Once a Week, or As-It-Happens.

5. Click the Create Alert button.

You'll now receive email messages, on the schedule you specified, containing the latest news headlines on that specific subject.

tip As-It-Happens is the best option for receiving alerts about breaking news stories.

note Learn more about all of Google's mobile services in Chapter 30, "Using Google Mobile Services."

Getting News on the Go

There's one more way to get the latest Google News headlines, and it doesn't involve your computer. That's right, you can receive Google News headlines on your cellular phone or other mobile device. It's a great way to keep up-to-date when you're on the go.

You access Google Mobile News by going to www.google.com on your mobile phone and clicking News. You can then browse the top headlines by section, or search for news stories as you would on the Google News web page. Learn more by clicking the Mobile News link on the main Google News page.

COMMENTARY:

NEWS ON THE WEB

As much as I like Google News, it's not the only site I use to get my daily news fix. There are tons of great news sites on the Web, including those run by major broadcast news organizations, newspapers, and magazines. There are even sites that offer databases of archived news articles—great for researching older issues and topics. Let's look at some of the best of these sites.

■ **Broadcast news online.** ABCNews (abcnews.go.com), BBC News (news.bbc.co.uk), CBSNews (www.cbsnews.com), CNN (www.cnn. com), FOXNews (www.foxnews.com), and MSNBC (www. msnbc.com)

■ **Magazines online.** *Business Week* (www.businessweek.com), *Entertainment Weekly* (www.ew.com), *National Review* (www. nationalreview.com), *Newsweek* (www.newsweek.com), *People* (www.people.com), *Time* (www.time.com), *U.S. News and World Report* (www.usnews.com)

■ **Newspapers online.** *Boston Globe* (www.boston.com/news/ globe/), *Chicago Tribune* (www.chicagotribune.com), *Denver Post* (www.denverpost.com), *Detroit Free Press* (www.freep.com), *Los Angeles Times* (www.latiems.com), *Miami Herald* (www.herald. com), *Minneapolis Star Tribune* (www.startribune.com), *New York Times* (www.nytimes.com), *San Francisco Chronicle* (www.sfgate. com), *USATODAY* (ww.usatoday.com), *Wall Street Journal* (www. wsj.com), and the *Washington Post* (www.washingtonpost.com)

By the way, if you're looking for more local newspaper sites, you should definitely check out the Newseum (www.newseum.org/todaysfrontpages/flash/). This site presents the front pages of daily newspapers from around the country and around the world. Click on any location to view today's image of that city's newspaper; click further to read the paper online.

The Bottom Line

I find Google News one of the best sources of news available online. By assembling stories from literally hundreds of different newspapers, magazines, and websites, it provides a depth of coverage that simply isn't possible from single-source sites like CNN.com. Granted, Google News focuses on the top stories only, but where else can you go to read coverage from the *New York Times*, the *Melbourne Herald Sun*, and the *Arabic News*—all on the same page?

Using Google Mobile Services

oogle is a great tool for anyone with a personal computer and a connection to the Internet. But it's also quite useful if you have a cell phone or other mobile device (such as a PDA). That's because Google offers a variety of mobile services, under the umbrella of Google Mobile.

That's right, you can access many of Google's most popular features from your mobile phone. You can use Google Mobile to search the Web, find local restaurants and businesses, download maps and directions, view the latest news headlines, and even send and receive email messages. All you need, in most instances, is a web-enabled mobile phone, and you're ready to go.

Searching Google on Your Web-Enabled Mobile Phone

Most of Google's mobile search services require the use of a web-enabled mobile phone—that is, a mobile phone with a built-in web browser and access to the Internet. (If you have a non-web phone that offers text messaging, you can use the Google SMS service for some of these functions; read on to the "Searching Google via Text Messaging" section, later in this chapter.)

note Learn more about all of Google's mobile services at www.google.com/mobile/.

tip If your mobile phone doesn't want to open the www.google.com page, try using www.google.com/xhtml instead.

Using Google Web Search

Google's known for its web search engine, so Google Web Search is the first Google Mobile function we'll talk about. You access the main Google Mobile search page by pointing your cell phone browser to www.google.com.

Google's web interface will look a little different from phone to phone, but in general should resemble the screen shown in Figure 30.1. To conduct a web search, follow these steps:

FIGURE 30.1

Google's web search for mobile phones.

1. Check the Web option.
2. Use your phone's keypad to enter a query into the search box.
3. Highlight and click the Google Search button.

Search results should now appear on your phone's screen, as shown in Figure 30.2. Ten results are displayed on each screen; scroll down the screen to view additional results.

FIGURE 30.2
The results of a mobile web search.

Conducting Specialized Web Searches

Google Mobile's Web Search lets you conduct a variety of specialized searches, direct from the main search box. These specialized searches include the following:

- Weather conditions and forecasts—enter the word **weather** followed by **city, state** or **zipcode**
- Local business listings—enter the business name followed by **city state** or **zipcode**
- Stock quotes—enter the stock symbol
- Sports scores and schedules—enter the school or team name
- Movie showtimes—enter the name of the movie or (for all showtimes) the word **movies** or **showtimes**, followed by **city state** or **zipcode**
- Definitions—enter the word **define** followed by the word you want defined

Using Google Mobile Web Search

The unfortunate thing about Google Mobile's default web search is that it searches the entire web—and not all web pages are optimized for display on mobile devices. If you want to limit your search to sites designed for display on small mobile screens, use Google's Mobile Web Search. This search is activated when you check the Mobile Web option on the main Google Mobile screen.

note Learn more about Google's web-based image search in Chapter 24, "Searching Google Images."

Using Google Image Search

Google also lets you conduct image searches from your mobile phone. This is a good way to find wallpapers and screensavers for your mobile phone.

To access Google's mobile Image Search, check the Images option on the main Google Mobile screen. Each search results page displays three images, which you can scroll through on your phone display. (Figure 30.3 shows what a typical image looks like displayed on your mobile phone.)

FIGURE 30.3

An Image Search result on Google Mobile.

Using Google Local Search

When you check the Local Listings option on the main Google Mobile screen, you can now search for local businesses. Enter the type of business you're searching for, click the Google Search button, and your screen now changes to that shown in Figure 30.4. From here, enter the location into the second search box (**city,state** or **zipcode**), click the Google Search button, and your phone displays matching businesses on a small map, as shown in Figure 30.5.

FIGURE 30.4
Searching for local businesses on Google Mobile.

FIGURE 30.5
Local businesses displayed on your cell phone.

From here, you can do a few neat things. To call a specific business, just highlight its phone number and click Enter. To display more information about a given business, click the business name. And to display driving directions to or from this location, click the business name and then click the Driving Directions link.

Searching Google via Text Messaging

If your phone doesn't have a web browser built-in, you can still access some of Google's search features via text messaging using the Google SMS service. Essentially, you send a text message to

tip You can also access Google Mobile's Local Search directly by entering **mobile.google.com/local** into your phone's web browser.

Google containing your query; Google sends you a message in reply that contains the search results.

Here's how it works:

1. Type a text message into your phone that contains the keywords in your query.

2. Send the text message to the number **46645** (that's **GOOGL**, if you do letters instead of numbers).

3. Wait for Google to send you a text message containing the search results.

What kinds of queries can you ask via text messaging? You can search for businesses (**business zipcode**), movie show times (**movie zipcode**), weather forecasts (**weather zipcode**), stock quotes (**symbol**), driving directions (**city state to city state**), and so forth. Essentially, you can send any standard Google query via text messaging, and get the text-based results in a return message.

Downloading Google Maps and Directions on Your Mobile Phone

As we discussed in Chapter 18, "Using Google Maps," you can have Google maps and directions sent to your mobile phone. The mobile version of Google Maps is actually a Java application that you download to your mobile phone. Once downloaded, you can view full-screen interactive maps of any location (like the one in Figure 30.6), find and map local businesses and locations, display satellite images, and show detailed map-based driving directions.

FIGURE 30.6

An interactive Google Map displayed on your cell phone.

To download the Google Maps application, point your phone's web browser to www.google.com/gmm.

note Learn more about Google News in Chapter 29, "Using Google News."

Viewing Google News on Your Mobile Phone

Just because you're on the road doesn't mean you have to be out of touch. Google Mobile lets you view all the latest news headlines on your mobile phone, as shown in Figure 30.7. Just go to the main Google Mobile screen, and then scroll down and click News. You can browse through the headlines, and then click any headline to read the full story.

FIGURE 30.7
Reading the latest news on Google Mobile.

Sending and Receiving Gmail on Your Mobile Phone

If you have a Gmail account, you can send and receive email messages from your mobile phone. You access Gmail Mobile by pointing your phone's web browser to m.gmail.com.

As you can see in Figure 30.8, all the messages in your Gmail inbox appear on your phone's display. Click a message or conversation to read the contents, or click the Compose Mail link to create a new message. The great thing about using Gmail

note Learn more about Gmail in Chapter 21, "Sending and Receiving Email with Gmail."

Mobile is that it's completely in synch with your regular Gmail inbox; when you read a message on your cell phone, it's marked as read when you next access Gmail from your computer.

note Learn more about Froogle in Chapter 16, "Searching for Bargains with Froogle and Google Catalogs."

FIGURE 30.8

Viewing inbox messages with Gmail Mobile.

Searching Froogle on Your Mobile Phone

Google also lets you search for products from your cell phone with the Froogle Mobile service. Just point your phone's web browser to wml.froogle.com and enter what you're looking for into the search box. Your phone now displays a list of matching products, just like the regular Froogle website does.

Personalizing Your Google Mobile Home Page

Finally, you can personalize the Google Mobile page you see on your phone when you go to www.google.com. If you like, you can design your page to show a local weather report, favorite stock quotes or sports scores, interesting news headlines, you name it. (Figure 30.9 shows a typical personalized mobile home page.)

In essence, your phone displays a small-sized version of the personalized home page you create for viewing on your computer. When you go to the Google Mobile page on your phone, click the Personalized Home link. Your phone will now display the content of your personalized home page.

FIGURE 30.9
A personalized Google Mobile home page.

The Bottom Line

I have to admit, I've never quite got the hang of using my cell phone for sending text messages and web browsing. (It's an age thing, I think.) That said, if you are a savvy phone user (and have a web-enabled cell phone), you can access some of Google's most useful features from your phone's keypad. When it comes to Google Mobile, you *can* take it with you!

> **note** Learn how to create a personalized Google home page in Chapter 11, "Customizing Google and the Google Personalized Home Page."

Google Software Tools

31 Using the Google Toolbar

32 Using Google Desktop

33 Using Google Calendar

34 Using Picasa

35 Using Google Pack

Using the Google Toolbar

Believe it or not, I seldom use Google's website—even though I search with Google a dozen or more times a day. That's because you don't have to go to the Google site to use Google search. If you have the Google Toolbar installed in your web browser, you can conduct all your searches from the Toolbar's search box, so there's no need to open the Google web page.

Even better, the Google Toolbar provides a wealth of direct shortcuts to some of Google's most popular functions and services. If you're a big Google user, installing the Google Toolbar is a must; it will save you a ton of time.

Getting to Know the Google Toolbar

If you use Google a lot (and use a recent version of Internet Explorer), you'll like the Google Toolbar. Everything you normally do on the Google site is right there on the Toolbar, just a click away. It's easy to use and—even better—it doesn't take up much screen real estate.

To install the Google Toolbar, go to toolbar.google.com and click the Download Google Toolbar button. Follow the onscreen instructions to download the software and complete the installation.

Once installed, the Google Toolbar appears just below the other toolbars in your web browser. You can customize the Toolbar to display a variety of different buttons; Figure 31.1 shows the default configuration.

tip If you use Mozilla Firefox instead of Internet Explorer as your web browser, Google offers a version of its Google Toolbar just for Firefox users. It's quite similar to the IE Toolbar, but with a few Firefox-specific features (such as a "subscribe to feed" option).

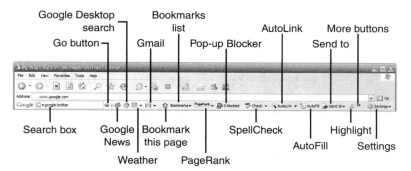

FIGURE 31.1
The Google Toolbar in its default configuration.

We'll look at these and other available features next.

Using Google Toolbar's Default Buttons

The Google Toolbar, in its default configuration, displays a variety of buttons you can click for direct access to various Google features. And, as you'll learn later in this chapter, you can add even more buttons to the Toolbar than what you see by default.

Let's take a quick look at each of the available buttons for the Google Toolbar.

Enhanced Search Box

Probably the most important part of the Google Toolbar is the search box. This is the thing that I constantly use; just enter

note This chapter describes version 4 of the Internet Explorer version of the Google Toolbar. If you're using a previous version, upgrade today to get the latest features.

your query into the search box, click the Go button, and you'll conduct a Google web search without having to first go to the Google website.

And, if that's all the Google Toolbar offered, that would be plenty. But what at first glance appears to be a standard search box is in fact an *enhanced* search box, offering more features that what you get on the Google site itself.

You can see how the enhanced search box work just by entering a new query. As you type your query, the Toolbar displays a list of useful suggestions, like the one shown in Figure 31.2. This list is based on popular searches from other users, spelling corrections, and your own search history and bookmarks. If your query is displayed on this list, just select it and press Enter.

FIGURE 31.2

Enter a keyword and see a list of suggested queries.

You can also use the Toolbar to perform more than just standard web searches. Click the G button (with the down arrow) in the search box and you'll see a drop-down menu full of other Google searches you can perform, as shown in Figure 31.3. Select a search from this list, finish entering your query, and when you click Go your search will be directed as noted.

FIGURE 31.3

Click the G button to see other available searches.

Google News

This one's easy. Click the Google News button and you go directly to the Google News site.

tip You can make the Toolbar's search box wider or narrower by dragging the separator to the right of the Go button.

Google Desktop

If you have Google Desktop installed on your PC, clicking the Google Desktop button opens the Google Desktop program (in your web browser) so you can conduct a search of your computer's hard disk.

note Learn more about Google Desktop in Chapter 32, "Using Google Desktop."

Weather

Once configured, clicking this button displays the search results for weather in your area. Hovering over this button displays the current weather conditions; clicking the down-arrow button displays a four-day forecast, as shown in Figure 31.4.

FIGURE 31.4

Displaying weather forecasts from the Google Toolbar.

You configure the Toolbar's weather settings by following these steps:

1. Click the Settings button and select Options.
2. When the Toolbar Options dialog box appears, select the Buttons tab.
3. In the Custom Buttons list, select the Weather button.
4. Click the Edit button.
5. When the Edit Button dialog box appears, as shown in Figure 31.5, enter your ZIP Code and click OK.
6. Click OK to close the Toolbar Options dialog box.

FIGURE 31.5
Configuring the Google Toolbar's Weather button.

31

Gmail

The Gmail button is your direct link to Google's Gmail service. Hover your cursor over the Gmail button and a pop-up will tell you if you have new messages in your inbox. Click the down-arrow next to the button and you see a list of inbox messages. Click the button itself and you're taken directly to the Gmail inbox page.

Bookmarks

Not that you really need them, but the Google Toolbar lets you create a set of bookmarks separate from those normally stored in your web browser. The advantage to these Google bookmarks is that they can follow you from computer to computer; when you log onto your Google account, your stored bookmarks are displayed in whichever browser you're using at the time.

To bookmark the current page, all you have to do is click the Bookmark button. (That's the one with the blue star.) To view all your bookmarks, click the Bookmarks button (that's plural—the one with the down arrow.)

tip You can sign into your Google or Gmail account directly from the Google Toolbar. All you have to do is click the Settings button and select Sign In. When you're signed in, the Settings button displays green; when you're not signed in, it's gray.

PageRank

This section of the toolbar displays Google's ranking of the currently displayed page. The greener the bar, the higher the ranking.

If you click the PageRank button, several informational options are displayed. You can view a cached snapshot of the current page; view a list of similar pages; or display a list of pages that link to the current page ("backward links"). Click an option to display the info.

Pop-up Blocker

The Google Toolbar includes its own pop-up blocker, the better to block those pesky pop-up windows. The "*x* blocked" number on the button tells you how many pop-ups it has blocked, in total.

To allow pop-ups on any given page, just click this button; the button text changes to "Popups Okay." Click the button again to turn the pop-up block back on.

SpellCheck

This isn't one of the most useful buttons, in my opinion—but then, I'm a pretty good speller. What the SpellCheck button does is find any spelling mistakes you've made when typing data into a web form. That in itself isn't that useful, but it also works as a spell checker for any web-based email service, such as Gmail. Click the SpellCheck button to go through the words you've typed one at a time; click the down arrow and select AutoFix to have the spell checker automatically correct any misspelled words, without your input.

AutoLink

When AutoLink is activated, Google automatically evaluates each page you load for addresses, locations, and the like. When it finds these items on a web page, the AutoLink button changes to a Look for Map button; click the down arrow next to the button to display a list of found addresses and locations. Click an address or location and a new browser window will open, a Google Map of that location displayed.

AutoLink can also link package tracking numbers to delivery status, VIN numbers to vehicle history, and ISBN numbers to Amazon.com book listings. It's kind of cool; give it a try and see what it finds!

> **note** When AutoLink finds different kinds of items, the button text changes accordingly. For example, when it finds an ISBN number on a page, the button text changes to "Show Book Info."

AutoFill

When you activate this feature, clicking the AutoFill button will automatically complete web forms with the personal information you've previously entered. Given the increasing number of forms on all manner of websites, it's a great time saver.

Before you can use AutoFill, of course, you have to enter the data you want to use to fill in all those forms. Here's what you do:

1. Click the Settings button and select Options.

2. When the Toolbar Options dialog box appears, select the Features tab.

3. Click the AutoFill Settings button.

4. When the AutoFill Settings dialog box appears, as shown in Figure 31.6, enter the appropriate information.

5. To enter your credit card data (necessary if you want to use AutoFill for online shopping), click the Add/Edit Credit Card button. When the Credit Card Information dialog box appears, enter your credit card data, and then click the Set Password button. Enter a password, click OK, and then click OK to close the Credit Card Information dialog box.

6. Click OK to close the AutoFill Settings dialog box, and then click OK again to close the Toolbar Options dialog box.

You enter data with AutoFill simply by clicking the AutoFill button whenever a web form is displayed. If you use AutoFill to automatically enter credit card information, you'll be prompted to supply a password before the credit numbers are entered.

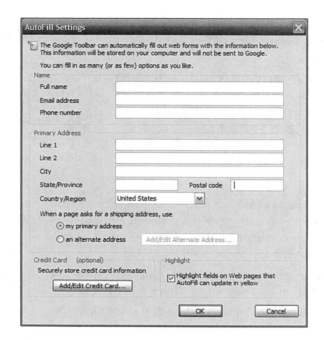

FIGURE 31.6

Entering your AutoFill information.

Send To

When you click the Send To button, you're presented with three options, as shown in Figure 31.7:

FIGURE 31.7

Sharing a page or selected text with the Send To button.

- **Gmail.** Sends the page or selected text to another user via email
- **Blogger.** Uses the page or selected text to create a new Blogger blog entry
- **SMS.** Sends the text of the current page or selected text to a cell phone number via text messaging

If no text on the page is selected, the entire page is sent to the selected service. If you first select a block of text, only that text is sent.

Highlight

When you click the Highlight button, Google automatically highlights (in yellow) the words you searched for on the current web page. (Figure 31.8 shows a web page with the keyword **spenser** highlighted throughout.)

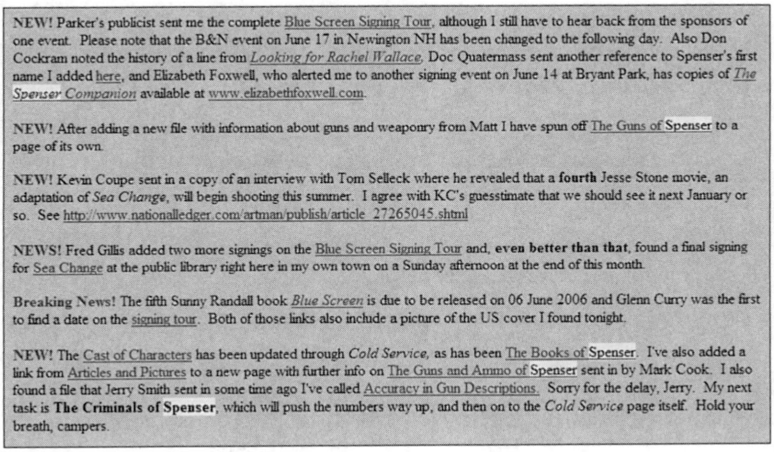

NEW! Parker's publicist sent me the complete Blue Screen Signing Tour, although I still have to hear back from the sponsors of one event. Please note that the B&N event on June 17 in Newington NH has been changed to the following day. Also Don Cockram noted the history of a line from *Looking for Rachel Wallace*. Doc Quatermass sent another reference to Spenser's first name I added here, and Elizabeth Foxwell, who alerted me to another signing event on June 14 at Bryant Park, has copies of *The Spenser Companion* available at www.elizabethfoxwell.com.

NEW! After adding a new file with information about guns and weaponry from Matt I have spun off The Guns of Spenser to a page of its own.

NEW! Kevin Coupe sent in a copy of an interview with Tom Selleck where he revealed that a **fourth** Jesse Stone movie, an adaptation of *Sea Change*, will begin shooting this summer. I agree with KC's guesstimate that we should see it next January or so. See http://www.nationalledger.com/artman/publish/article_27265045.shtml

NEWS! Fred Gillis added two more signings on the Blue Screen Signing Tour and, **even better than that**, found a final signing for Sea Change at the public library right here in my own town on a Sunday afternoon at the end of this month.

Breaking News! The fifth Sunny Randall book *Blue Screen* is due to be released on 06 June 2006 and Glenn Curry was the first to find a date on the signing tour. Both of those links also include a picture of the US cover I found tonight.

NEW! The Cast of Characters has been updated through *Cold Service*, as has been The Books of Spenser. I've also added a link from Articles and Pictures to a new page with further info on The Guns and Ammo of Spenser sent in by Mark Cook. I also found a file that Jerry Smith sent in some time ago I've called Accuracy in Gun Descriptions. Sorry for the delay, Jerry. My next task is **The Criminals of Spenser**, which will push the numbers way up, and then on to the *Cold Service* page itself. Hold your breath, campers.

FIGURE 31.8

*The keyword **spenser** highlighted on a web page.*

Word Find

To the right of the Highlight button are a series of "word find" buttons. These are buttons representing the words you just searched for; click a word find button to jump to the next occurrence of that word on the current page.

Customizing the Google Toolbar

So far, we've discussed just those buttons that are displayed by default when you

> **tip**
> When the Google Toolbar is installed, a stealth feature is applied to your browser's address box. The browse by name feature lets you enter a site name, instead of its URL, into the address box; Google will then take you to that site automatically, without you having to enter the site's full address.

install the Google Toolbar in your web browser. But there are a lot more buttons available—once you know how to add them.

tip If you have more buttons activated that can fit horizontally on the Toolbar, a "more buttons" button appears at the far right of the Toolbar, just to the left of the static Settings button. Click this button to display a list of the remaining buttons you have installed.

Adding and Removing Buttons

You add and remove buttons to and from the Google Toolbar from the Toolbar Options dialog box, shown in Figure 31.9. You display this dialog box by clicking the Settings button on the Toolbar, and then selecting Options.

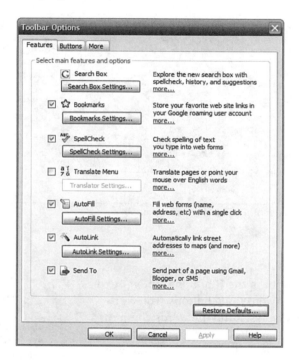

FIGURE 31.9

Adding new buttons from the Toolbar Options dialog box.

New buttons are available on all three tabs (Features, Buttons, and More); the More tab is also used to configure selected buttons.

To add a button to the Toolbar, just check the box next to the button; to remove a button, uncheck that button's box.

Using the Optional Toolbar Buttons

What other buttons can you add to the Google Toolbar? Table 31.1 provides a list:

Table 31.1   Optional Google Toolbar Buttons

Button	Description
Translate	Use to translate the current page into another language (or, if you enable WordTranslator, hover your cursor over a word on the page to see it translated into Spanish)
Search Site	Click to search within the current website
Google Images	Displays the Google Images search page
Google Local	Displays the Google Maps page
I'm Feeling Lucky	Automatically takes you to the first page listed in the search results for the current query
Google Groups	Displays the Google Groups page
Froogle	Displays the Froogle page
Google Earth	Opens the Google Earth application
Button Gallery	Displays a list of additional buttons
Up	Navigates up one level in the current website
Next	Displays the next page listed in the current search results
Previous	Displays the previous page listed in the current search results
Voting	Use to "vote" on the page to determine its overall PageRank

Adding Custom Buttons to the Toolbar

Google and third-party developers have created a slew of custom buttons you can add to the Google Toolbar. You can see a list of available buttons when you click the Button Gallery button, or go directly to www.google.com/tools/toolbar/buttons/gallery. As you can see in Figure 31.10, there are a lot of buttons available!

> **note** You can even create your own custom Google Toolbar buttons—providing you know how to program with the Google API, that is. Learn more in Chapter 40, "Creating Custom Search Applications."

FIGURE 31.10

The Google Toolbar buttons gallery.

Other Ways to Search Google from Your Web Browser

The Google Toolbar is just one way to search Google from within your web browser. There are also a few other tools you can employ—all of which let you search directly, without having to go to the Google website.

Making Google Your Default Search Engine in Internet Explorer

Did you know that you can enter a query in your Internet Explorer address bar, click the Go button, and get a list of search results? By default, your queries are sent to Microsoft's MSN Search (no surprise), but you can easily change this to send your searches to Google, instead.

To make Google your default search engine in Internet Explorer, follow these steps:

1. Click the Search button in the Internet Explorer toolbar.

2. When the search pane opens, click the Customize button.

3. When the Customize Search Settings dialog box appears, as shown in Figure 31.11, check the Use Search Assistant option.

4. In the Choose a Search Provider for Address Bar Searches list, select Google.

5. Click the Okay button.

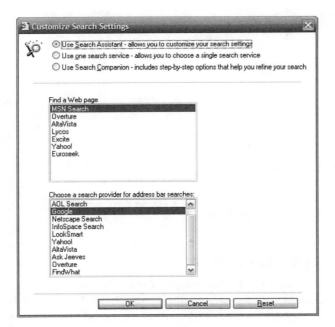

FIGURE 31.11

Customizing Internet Explorer's search settings.

Once configured, all in-browser searches will default to the Google site. IE will also display a Google search pane, like the one shown in Figure 31.12, when you click the Search button in the Internet Explorer toolbar.

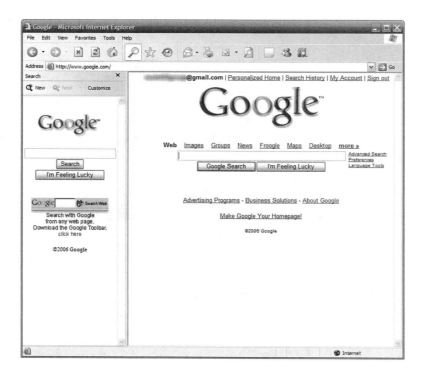

FIGURE 31.12

The Google search pane in Internet Explorer.

Installing Google Browser Buttons

You can also add special Google browser buttons to your web browser's Links or personal toolbar, as shown in Figure 31.13. You can add these buttons to either the Internet Explorer or Netscape browsers (versions 4.0 or later).

FIGURE 31.13

Google browser buttons added to the IE Links toolbar.

There are two buttons you can add:

- **Google Search.** Initiates a Google search when you highlight any word on a web page and then click this button

- **Google.com.** Takes you to the Google home page

To install these Google browser buttons in your web browser, go to www.google.com/options.buttons.html and click the Get Your Google Buttons Here link. Follow the onscreen instructions to complete the installation.

The Bottom Line

I love the Google Toolbar. I use it several times every day—if not every hour. In fact, I seldom go to the Google home page; instead, I do all my searching from the Toolbar. I also like the Send To button when creating blog entries, and the Weather button for viewing current weather conditions. All in all, I recommend that all Google users add the Google Toolbar to their browsers; it is, perhaps, the fastest way to do your Google searching.

31

Using Google Desktop

You use the Google website to search the Web, but there's a lot of information you need to find on your own computer, as well. So why can't you use Google to search your hard disk?

Well, you can, thanks to the Google Desktop software program. Google Desktop installs on your PC and automatically indexes all your data files, email messages, and the like. When you conduct a Google Desktop search, the program searches this index and returns a list of matching files and messages. It's just as easy as using the Google website, and it lets you find all those "lost" documents that are buried somewhere on your hard disk.

As an added bonus, Google Desktop includes a sidebar that sits on your computer desktop and provides access to different content modules. Assuming you have the available desktop real estate, the Google Desktop sidebar lets you view your Gmail inbox, the latest news, local weather conditions, your instant messaging contacts, and lots, lots more, all stacked together on the edge of your computer screen.

I'm not sure what's best about Google Desktop, the local searching or the sidebar content. They're both really cool and very useful, so read on to learn more.

Welcome to the Google Desktop

At first glance, the Google Desktop is a sidebar that sits to the right of your computer desktop, as shown in Figure 32.1. The content of the sidebar is totally customizable; as we'll learn later in this chapter, you can add a variety of different "gadgets" to the sidebar, each with a different and unique function.

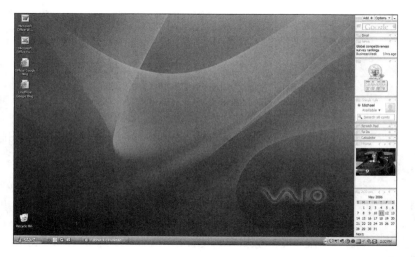

FIGURE 32.1

Google Desktop installed on your computer desktop—it's all in the sidebar on the right side of the screen.

The sidebar, however, is just the icing on the cake. The key ingredient in the Google Desktop is a PC-centric version of the Google search engine. Once installed, you use Google Desktop to search your hard disk (or your entire network) for files and email messages that match a specific query. You do your searching from your web browser, which displays a special Google Desktop page; it works pretty much like a standard Google web search, except that it's not searching the Web—it's searching the contents of your computer's hard disk.

With all this functionality, you might expect Google Desktop to cost an arm and a leg. Well, you can hold onto your limbs, because Google Desktop is freeware. You can downloaded it completely free of charge from desktop.google.com.

note Google Desktop is only available for computers running Windows XP or Windows 2000 with Service Pack 3+ installed. The program is not currently available for Apple Macintosh computers.

When you first download Google Desktop, a few things happen. First, the default sidebar is built and displayed on your desktop; you'll be able to configure this to your liking later. Second, the Google Desktop search engine starts up and begins to index the contents of your PC. Depending on the size of your hard disk and how much of it is used, this could take anywhere from a few minutes to a few hours. Although you can use Google Desktop while this index is being created, you probably don't want to conduct any searches until all your disk's contents have been indexed.

What types of items does Google Desktop index? Not every type of file, obviously; for example, it doesn't index executable program files. Here's the complete list of what's indexed:

- Email (including messages from Microsoft Outlook, Outlook Express, Gmail, Mozilla Thunderbird, and Netscape Mail)
- Chats (from Google Talk, AOL Instant Messenger, and MSN Messenger)
- Web history (.HTM and .HTML files from Internet Explorer, Mozilla Firefox, and Netscape browsers)
- Microsoft Word documents (.DOC files)
- Microsoft Excel spreadsheets (.XLS and .XLW files)
- Microsoft PowerPoint presentations (.PPT files)
- Adobe Acrobat documents (.PDF files)
- Media files (image files, audio files, and video files)
- Text files (.TXT format)
- Other files from Microsoft Outlook and similar programs (contacts, calendar appointments, tasks, notes, and journal entries)
- Compressed files (.ZIP files—including the full content of each compressed file)

32

Searching Your Hard Disk

Google Desktop is really two applications under a single guise. The sidebar, which we'll discuss later in this chapter, is really quite separate from the desktop search engine. In fact, you can't quickly do a desktop search from the sidebar; to search the contents of your PC, you have to launch the Google Desktop program separately.

Conducting a Basic Search

When you click the Google Desktop icon on your desktop (or select Start, All Programs, Google Desktop, Google Desktop), a new web browser is opened. As you can see in Figure 32.2, the browser is loaded with a page that looks almost identical to the main Google web page. The main differences are that you're not connected to the Internet, the search function is set to Desktop, and there are a few new options at the bottom of the page. (We'll get to them in a minute.)

FIGURE 32.2

The Google Desktop search page.

Searching your hard disk is as easy as entering a query into the search box, and then clicking the Search Desktop button. (If you click the Search the Web button instead, Google Desktop connects to the main Google website and initiates a traditional web search.)

Viewing Your Results

The results of your search are now displayed, as shown in Figure 32.3. This search results page looks a bit different from a standard web search results page, for two reasons.

FIGURE 32.3
The results of a Google Desktop search.

First, the results are, by default, sorted by date instead of relevance, with the most recent results listed first. (You can switch to a relevance list by clicking the Sort by Relevance link at the top of the page.)

Second, the results page contains several different types of results. Google Desktop searches for—and finds—the following types of items:

- Emails
- Files (of various types)
- Web pages you've viewed
- Chat transcripts
- Other (Outlook tasks, appointments, and the like)

The type of item found is easily discerned by the icon next to each search result. For example, email messages are displayed with an envelope icon; files are displayed with the appropriate filetype icon; web

tip
Some types of items (such as JPG files, MP3 files, and recently visited web pages) also have a thumbnail of that item displayed to the right of the item listing. Click the thumbnail to view the item (or, if it's a web page, a cached version of the page).

pages are displayed with an icon representing the web page's logo or a generic web page icon.

For each item listing, Google Desktop displays the item or filename, a brief description of or excerpt from the item, and the location of the file on your hard disk. You can open the file by clicking the filename, or open the folder that holds the file by clicking the Open Folder link. Click the Cached link to view a cached version of the folder comments; click the Date link to view all items created on the same date. (This last option is good for finding related email messages.)

Filtering Your Results

By default, Google Desktop displays all items in the same list. You can filter the list, however, to display only a single type of item, by clicking the Emails, Files, Web History, Chats, or Other links at the top of the page. (Figure 32.4 shows a search filtered to display only files; note the filetype icons to the left, and the thumbnails for photo and music files to the right.)

FIGURE 32.4

Desktop search results filtered to display only computer files.

Depending on the type of item displayed, you may have additional filtering options. For example, if you display just emails, you can filter the results to include only those messages to or from specific users, as shown in Figure 32.5. If you display just files, you can filter the results to include only specific file types, as shown in Figure 32.6. If you display "other" items, you can filter the results to include only contacts, calendar appointments, tasks, and the like, as shown in Figure 32.7.

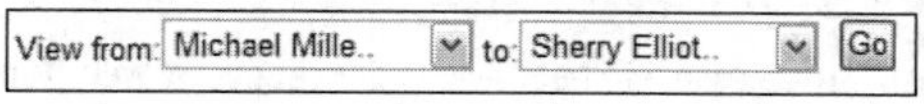

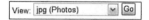

FIGURE 32.5

Filtering email results.

FIGURE 32.6

Filtering file results.

View: **All 8 other** - <u>2 contacts</u> - <u>5 calendar</u> - 1 task ⌄ Go

FIGURE 32.7

Filtering "other" results.

Conducting an Advanced Desktop Search

Of course, it's often easier to refine your query than it is to filter your results. To that end, Google Desktop offers a Search Options page, accessible from the Advanced Search link on the main page. As you can see in Figure 32.8, this page offers various filters you can apply to your query—although the filters available vary by type of item you're searching for. Table 32.1 details the available options.

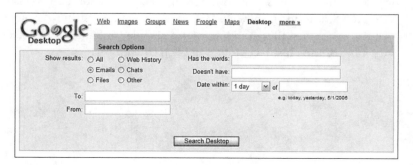

FIGURE 32.8

Fine-tuning your search from the Search Options page.

Table 32.1 Google Desktop Search Options

Type of Search	Available Options
All	*Has the words, doesn't have*, and *date within* (search within a date range)
Emails	*To:* and *From:* (restricts search to emails sent to or from specific users)
Files	*File type* and *In the location* (restricts search to specific file types or files stored within a specific folder)
Web History	*In the site* (restricts search to pages viewed on a specific website)
Chats	No specific options available
Other	*Other types* (restricts search to contacts, appointments, tasks, notes, and journal entries)

Viewing Items in Timeline View

Searching by keyword is the way most people will find things on their hard drives, but sometimes it's not the best way to approach the problem. There are times when you remember *when* you sent or received a message or created a file, not necessarily *what* the message or file was about.

For these times, Google Desktop offers the Timeline view. This view lets you view everything created or modified on a particular day.

You access Timeline view by clicking the Browse Timeline link on the main Google Desktop page. As you can see in Figure 32.9, Timeline view lists all your desktop items by date, in reverse chronological order (newest first), starting with today. You can view items from another date by clicking that date on the calendar on the right side of the page; you can also filter items to display only emails, files, web history, or chats.

Viewing the Contents of Your Index

Want to see exactly what (and how much) Google Desktop has indexed? Then click the Index Status link on the main Google Desktop page. This displays the Desktop Status page, shown in Figure 32.10, which lists how many emails, chats, web pages, files, and total items Google Desktop has indexed, as well as the time of the most recent item in each category.

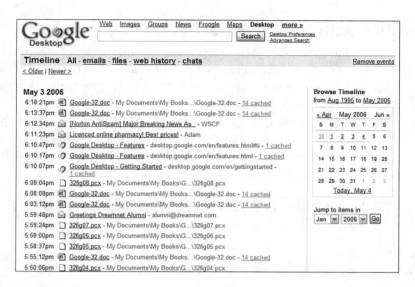

FIGURE 32.9

Viewing items by date in the Timeline view.

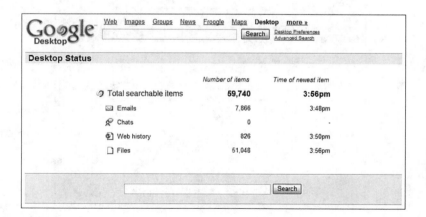

FIGURE 32.10

Viewing how many items Google Desktop has indexed, on the Desktop Status page.

Searching within Microsoft Outlook

When you install Google Desktop, it also installs a special search bar in Microsoft Outlook (assuming you're using Outlook, of course). This lets you search Outlook's emails directly from the Outlook program—no need to start up Google Desktop separately.

As you can see in Figure 32.11, the Google Desktop toolbar installs at the far right of the normal Outlook toolbar. Enter your query and click the Search button to search all your Outlook mailboxes; matching emails are listed in a separate search results window, as shown in Figure 32.12.

FIGURE 32.11
The Google Desktop toolbar in Microsoft Outlook.

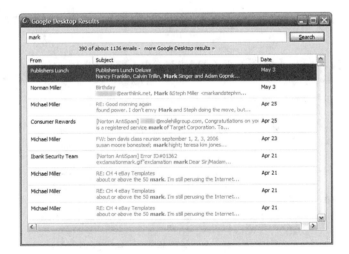

FIGURE 32.12
Results from searching your Outlook email messages.

Searching Other Computers on Your Network

Google Desktop isn't limited to searching your PC's hard disk. You can also use it to search other computers on your wireless or Ethernet network.

To use Google Desktop across multiple computers on a network, you must have a Google account (just one) and you must have copies of Google Desktop installed on all computers you want to include in the search. The reason you need a Google account is that each computer's index is transmitted via the Internet to Google's servers; when you search "across computers" you're actually searching the index for your network, as stored on Google's servers.

tip

Since the index informa-tion for all your PCs is stored on Google's servers, you can use this feature to view your desktop PC's files and messages from your laptop PC when you're on the road—or vice versa. Just make sure that Google Desktop is running on both PCs, and that they're both connected to the Internet.

To set up Google Desktop to search across multiple computers, follow these steps:

1. Open Google Desktop and click the Desktop Preferences link. (Alternatively, you can right-click the Google Desktop icon in the Windows system tray, and select Preferences from the pop-up menu.)

2. When the Preferences page appears, click Gmail and Search Across Computers.

3. When the next page appears, as shown in Figure 32.13, check the Index and Search My Documents and Viewed Web Pages Across All My Computers option.

4. Enter a name for this computer.

5. Check which items from this PC you want to be able to search from other PCs: documents and web history, documents only, web history only, or nothing. (The "nothing" option lets this computer search other computers, but doesn't let them search this PC.)

6. Click the Save Preferences button.

You'll need to repeat these steps for each computer you want to include in the Google Desktop search. You'll also need to log onto the same Google account on each PC; this is how Google keeps track of the computers to include in the search index.

32

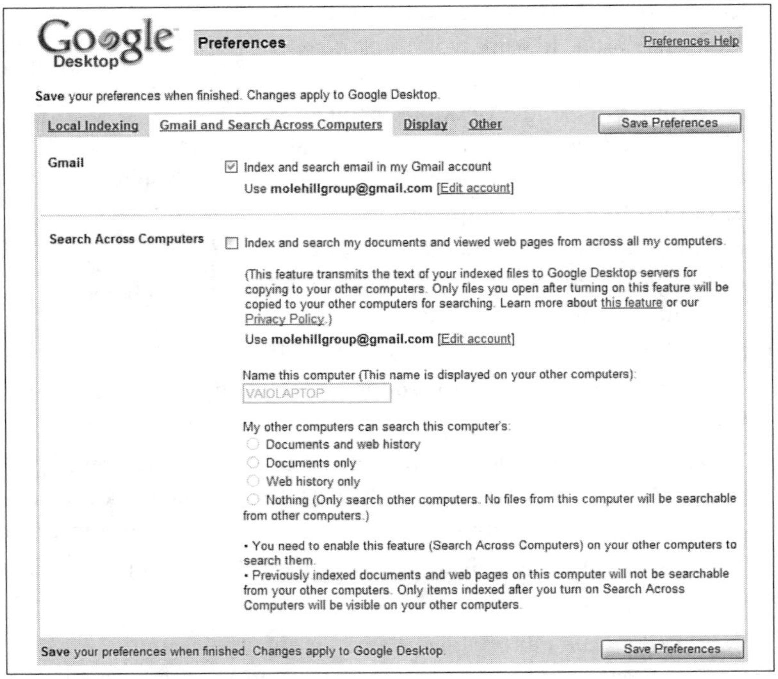

FIGURE 32.13
Configuring Google Desktop to search across multiple computers.

Searching the Web from Google Desktop

The Google Desktop program not only lets you search your desktop, it also lets you conduct normal Google web searches—assuming your computer is connected to the Internet, that is. (You don't have to be connected to the Internet to search your own computer, of course.) There are several ways you can do this; we'll look at each, in turn.

Searching from the Google Desktop Window

If you have the Google Desktop window open, searching the Web is a snap. Just enter your query as normal, and then click the Search the Web button (instead of the Search Desktop button). Google Desktop now connects to the Google website and displays the expected page of search results.

Searching from the Sidebar

The Google Desktop sidebar includes a standard search box, as shown in Figure 32.14. This search box is for searching the Web, *not* for searching your desktop—although it can be used for searching your desktop, too.

FIGURE 32.14

The Google Desktop sidebar search box.

To search the Web from the sidebar, just enter your query and press the Enter key on your keyboard. By default, your search is sent to the Google website and displayed in a new browser window.

To use the sidebar search box to search your desktop, instead, enter your query but then wait for the menu of options to appear, as shown in Figure 32.15. From this menu, select Search More, Search Desktop, and *then* press Enter. Your desktop search results will now appear in a new browser window.

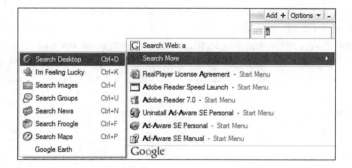

FIGURE 32.15

Accessing other search options—including desktop search—from the sidebar search box.

Searching from the Quick Search Box

There's another way to search the Web from Google Desktop, and it's maybe the coolest one. When Google Desktop is running, a special Quick Search Box feature is

> **tip**
>
> Alternatively, you can select another option from the Search More menu to send your query to Google Images, Google Groups, Froogle, and the like.

also activated. This isn't something that sits on your desktop; you don't even see it unless you call it up.

You display the Quick Search Box by pressing the Ctrl key *twice*. As you can see in Figure 32.16, the Quick Search Box appears on top of whatever program you're currently using. Enter your query into the box and press the Enter key, and your query is sent to the Google website; results are returned in a new browser window.

tip Google Desktop also lets you display a search deskbar in the Windows taskbar, a floating search deskbar anywhere on your desktop, or a permanent Quick Search Box on your desktop background. Just select Desktop Preferences, click display, and then check the display option you want.

FIGURE 32.16

Press Ctrl twice to display the Quick Search Box.

32

Like the sidebar search box, the Quick Search Box can also be used to search the files and messages on your computer's hard disk. Just enter your query and wait for the menu of options to appear, as shown in Figure 32.17. From this menu, select Search More, Search Desktop, and *then* press Enter. Your desktop search results will now appear in a new browser window.

FIGURE 32.17

Other search options available from the Quick Search Box.

Using the Google Desktop Sidebar

As I noted in the introduction to this chapter, Google Desktop is more than just a desktop search. It's also about putting more information on your desktop, via the Google Desktop sidebar.

As you can see in Figure 32.18, the sidebar resides on the far right of your computer desktop (by default, anyway—you can change this) and includes a variety of different content modules, which Google calls *gadgets*. You can choose from hundreds of different gadgets to display all sorts of information.

FIGURE 32.18
The Google Desktop sidebar.

Different Ways to Display the Sidebar

The sidebar is activated by default when you first install the Google Desktop program. You can turn it off by selecting Options, Close. (That's clicking the

Options button at the top of the sidebar, and then selecting Close.) To redisplay it, right-click the Google Desktop icon in the Windows system tray and select Sidebar from the pop-up menu.

By default, the sidebar appears on the right side of your desktop. You can move it to the left side of the desktop by selecting Options, Dock Sidebar, Left. To change the width of the sidebar, just drag the left (or right) side of the sidebar until the sidebar is the desired size.

If you don't want the sidebar taking up all that screen real estate, consider using the auto-hide feature. When this option is selected, the sidebar is hidden until you move the cursor to the far right side of the screen. When you do this, the sidebar pulls out for your use. To activate auto-hide, select Options, Auto-Hide.

Working with Sidebar Gadgets

The fun thing about using the Google Desktop sidebar is selecting which gadgets you want displayed. There are tons of different gadgets available, as we'll discuss in the next section; you can insert as many as you have room for.

To add a new gadget to the sidebar, click the Add button. This displays the Add/Remove Gadgets dialog box, as shown in Figure 32.19. From here you can view gadgets in a number of different categories (By Google, New, Finance, Technology, Communication, and so on); click the Add button next to a gadget to add it to your sidebar.

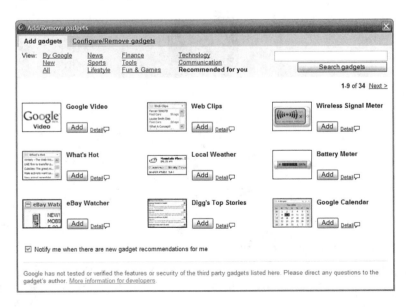

FIGURE 32.19

Selecting new gadgets for the sidebar.

To remove any gadget from the sidebar, click the down arrow in that gadget's title bar, and then select Remove. (You can always restore the Gadget by clicking the Add button at the top of the sidebar, if you like.)

In the sidebar, any gadget can be displayed at any height, or collapsed to just its title bar. Making a gadget taller or shorter is a simple matter of dragging the top border up or down with your mouse. Collapsing the gadget entirely is done by clicking the gadget's down arrow, and then selecting Collapse.

You can rearrange the gadgets in your sidebar in any order. It's a dynamic process; just grab the gadget's title bar with your mouse and drag it into a new position. The other gadgets rearrange themselves to make room for the moved gadget.

Most gadgets have an expanded view, which you display by clicking the left arrow in the gadget's title bar. This expands the gadget to the left, where (in most cases), more options are available than in the standard gadget. (Using the expanded view is also a necessity when you have the gadget collapsed.) For example, Figure 32.20 shows the expanded view of the Photos gadget— with an additional expansion for the selected photo.

Click the Options button to customize a specific gadget

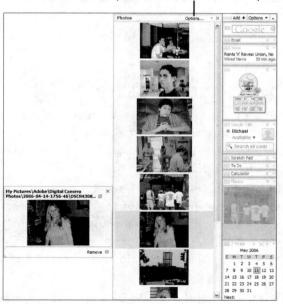

FIGURE 32.20

The Photos gadget in expanded view.

Individual gadgets can also be undocked from the sidebar. When you click the down arrow in the gadget title bar and then select Undock from Sidebar, the gadget is moved from the sidebar to its own window on the desktop. (Figure 32.21 shows the undocked version of the Weather gadget.) To redock a gadget, click the gadget's down arrow and select Dock to Sidebar.

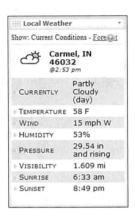

FIGURE 32.21

An undocked gadget.

32

COMMENTARY:

GADGETS AND WIDGETS

The concept of putting content modules on your desktop didn't start with Google Desktop. The most recent implementation of this concept is Apple's Dashboard, which lets you add a variety of "widgets" to the Mac desktop. It's proven very popular.

On the Windows side, the widget concept was adopted by Konfabulator, which was recently purchased by Yahoo! and renamed (not surprisingly) Yahoo! Widgets. Like the Apple Dashboard, Yahoo! Widgets can be placed anywhere on your computer desktop; each widget is a separate mini-application that floats above the desktop, ready for your use.

Into this fray comes the Google Desktop sidebar. Unlike the Apple Dashboard and Yahoo! Widgets, Google's gadgets are by default docked onto a sidebar that sits to the right side of the desktop. Each gadget can be undocked, however, to float on the desktop like a Dashboard or Yahoo! widget.

This whole area gets a lot more complicated in 2007 when Microsoft releases Windows Vista, the latest implementation of the Windows operating system. Windows Vista will include the Windows Sidebar, which looks and feels a lot like the Google Desktop sidebar. The Windows Sidebar, of course, is built into the operating system; like the Google Desktop sidebar, it sits on the side of the screen and is filled with individual gadgets.

All of these widgets and gadgets are designed with the same goal in mind—to put more content, information, and functions at your fingertips. It's handier to have these content modules floating on the desktop or docked on a sidebar than it is to dig through layers of menus to open up each application individually. For that reason, I'm a big fan of both the Google Desktop toolbar and of Yahoo! Widgets; I imagine I'll learn to love the Windows Sidebar, too, when Windows Vista ships.

The Bottom Line

I liked Google Desktop even before it added the sidebar. The ability to quickly and easily search your hard disk for files and emails is something that should be built into the operating system, but Windows' built-in search function has been notoriously slow and quirky; Google Desktop does it a lot better. (Sorry, Microsoft.) Add the sidebar and all that marvelous gadget content, and you have a winning application—one that's both useful and fun.

Trust me on this one; once you install Google Desktop, you'll use the desktop search a lot and you'll be constantly trying out new sidebar gadgets. The desktop search is an invaluable tool, and the sidebar is just plain addictive. It's something you'd pay for—except you don't have to, because it's free.

Using Google Calendar

The next Google application we'll discuss isn't a software program per se, but rather a web-based application accessible from any computer over the Internet, using any web browser. In the case of Google Calendar, that's a good thing, as you can keep track of your schedule and appointments wherever you're at, even if you're away from home or the office. All you have to do is log onto the Google Calendar website from any web browser, and all your appointments and schedules are displayed.

Read on to learn more.

All About Google Calendar

Google Calendar (calendar.google.com), shown in Figure 33.1, looks like every other web-based calendar you've ever seen. (And like most software-based calendars, too.) You enter your appointments (which Google calls "events") directly into the calendar, which you can display in either daily, weekly, or monthly views. You can also, if you like, view your weekly agenda on a single page.

FIGURE 33.1

Google Calendar—not just another calendar application.

Nothing unusual about any of that. So, compared to all the other calendar applications out there, what's unique about Google Calendar?

First, Google Calendar is a web-based calendar. This means that your calendar information is stored on Google's servers, not on your own computer. The advantage of this is that you can access your calendar from any computer anywhere in the world. Just log onto the Google Calendar page, and your calendar and all events are there.

Second, since Google Calendar is web-based, you can use it to create not only a private calendar for yourself, but also public calendars for your company or organization. Create a public calendar and all employees or attendees can access it via the Web. In addition, special event invitation features make it easy to invite others to an event—public or private.

Third, Google allows you create several different—and different types of—calendars. You can create one calendar for home, another for work, and yet another for your son's soccer team. Then you can view all your calendars from the same Google Calendar page.

Fourth, since Google Calendar is part of the Google empire, it integrates smoothly with Gmail. Google Calendar can scan your email messages for dates and times and, with a few clicks of your mouse, create events based on the content of your Gmail messages.

Finally, Google Calendar tries to be as universal as possible. That means relatively seamless integration with the information you've previously created with any other calendar programs you may be using, such as Yahoo! Calendar or the Microsoft Outlook calendar.

Bottom line, Google wants to make it both beneficial and easy to move from your current calendar program to Google Calendar. Give it a try and see what you think.

> **note** While Google Calendar imports events and appointments from Microsoft Outlook, it doesn't (as yet) offer dynamic synchronization with Outlook. That means you can't make a change in Google Calendar and have it reflected in Outlook, or vice versa. Google is purportedly working to add this feature at a later date.

COMMENTARY:

TARGETED ADS

For Google, Google Calendar offers yet another opportunity to sell profitable advertising space. Although, to be fair, Google Calendar is not yet littered with these pesky little things. But rest assured, that's why Google created Google Calendar—as yet another vehicle to deliver highly targeted ads.

Think through all the detailed information Google Calendar is collecting about you and your activities, and then imagine how that information can be used from an advertising perspective. For example, if you create an event to go to a movie on Saturday night, Google can theoretically parse that information and then sell targeted ad space to movie studios or theater chains—or maybe even restaurants in the nearby neighborhood. The more information you enter, the more targeted Google's ads can be.

It sounds cynical, I know, but why else would Google offer such a service with no supporting direct revenue stream? The rewards for such an investment come from future advertising—in this case, very targeted, and thus very profitable, advertising.

Don't like the idea of Google keeping all this personal information on their company servers? Then don't use Google Calendar, or any other web-based calendar application, for that matter. The benefits of a web-based calendar are purchased at the cost of personal privacy; even though Google says your private information will stay private, they can still use that information to send event-specific ads in your direction. If

33

the privacy issue bothers you, switch to a software-based calendar, instead—and forgo the ability to share events and calendars with your friends and colleagues. That's the trade-off you have to consider.

Setting Up Your Google Calendar

Google Calendar is designed to be easy to use. To that end, Google succeeds.

Setting Up a Basic Calendar

Setting up your first calendar is comically easy. In fact, there's nothing to set up. When you first sign into the Google Calendar page, your calendar is already there, waiting for your input. There's nothing to create, nothing to configure. Can you get any easier than that?

Setting Up Multiple Calendars

One of the key features of Google Calendar is the ability to create and manage multiple calendars. For example, you might want to create one calendar with work events and another with social events.

To create a second (or third or fourth) calendar, follow these steps:

1. From the main Google Calendar page, click the + button next to My Calendars in the Calendars box.
2. When the Create New Calendar page appears, as shown in Figure 33.2, give the calendar a name and description, and then enter other appropriate information.
3. Click the Create Calendar button.

As you can see in Figure 33.3, all of the calendars you create are listed in the Calendars box on the left side of the Google Calendars page, under My Calendars. To switch to another calendar, just click its link in this box; you can also view events from multiple calendars on the same page by checking each calendar you wish to view.

Setting Up Other Types of Calendars

Google Calendar lets you create four different types of calendars:

- **Personal calendars**, like your default calendar.
- **Public calendars**, which others can access via the Web. (See the "Creating a Public Calendar" section, later in this chapter, for more information.)

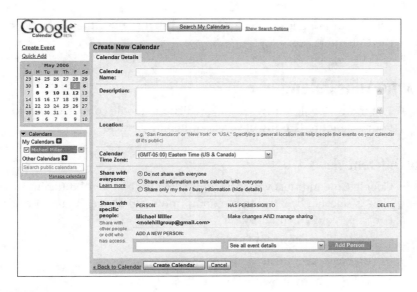

FIGURE 33.2
Creating a new calendar.

FIGURE 33.3
Viewing all your calendars.

- **Friend's calendars**, which you import from their Google Calendar web pages. To import a friends' calendar, click the + button next to Other Calendars in the Calendar box, select Friend's Calendars, enter the URL for your friend's calendar page, and then click the Add button.

- **Holiday calendars**, which add national holidays to a basic calendar. To create a holiday calendar, click the + button next to Other Calendars in the Calendar box, select Holiday Calendars, and then click the Add Calendar button next to the specific calendar you want to add.

All of your nonpersonal calendars are listed in the Other Calendars section of the Calendars box.

Viewing Your Calendar

The main Google Calendar page (calendar.google.com) is where you view all your calendars—in any of several different views.

Using Different Views

Google Calendar lets you view your calendar in several different ways. Each view is selected by clicking the appropriate tab above the main calendar. You can view your calendar by

- Day, as shown in Figure 33.4
- Week, as shown in Figure 33.5
- Month, as shown in Figure 33.6
- Next 4 days, as shown in Figure 33.7
- Agenda, as shown in Figure 33.8

FIGURE 33.4

Google Calendar Day view.

FIGURE 33.5

Google Calendar Week view.

FIGURE 33.6

Google Calendar Month view.

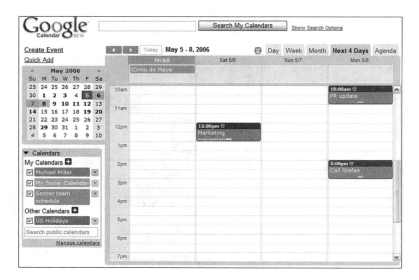

FIGURE 33.7

Google Calendar Next 4 Days view.

FIGURE 33.8

Google Calendar Agenda view.

For each view, you can move backwards and forwards in time by clicking the left and right arrow buttons at the top right of the calendar. To center the calendar on the current day, click the Today button.

> **tip**
> The Agenda view is different from the other views in that it lists all scheduled events on your calendar, in chronological order.

You can also create customized calendar views for any number of days. For this, you use the mini-calendar on the left side of the Google Calendar page. Just click and drag your mouse across the mini-calendar from the first to the last day you wish to view; the main calendar will change to reflect the number of days you select.

Viewing Multiple Calendars

The main calendar on the Google Calendar page can display any single calendar individually, or multiple calendars simultaneously. It all depends on which—and how many—calendars you check in the Calendars box.

Every calendar that is checked is displayed in the main calendar. To display only a single calendar, check that calendar and uncheck all the others. To view the events from more than one calendar, check those calendars; all the events will be displayed on the main calendar, color-coded appropriately.

Viewing Your Calendar from Other Calendar Applications

Google Calendar can export its event information in either XML or iCal formats. (iCal is used on the Macintosh; XML is used by most web-based calendar applications.) This lets you read your Google Calendar data in other calendar applications.

The key is to distribute your calendar's private address to another calendar application. To do this, follow these steps:

1. In the Calendars box, click the down arrow next to the calendar you want to share, and then select Calendar Settings.

2. When the Details page appears, as shown in Figure 33.9, scroll down to the Private Address section.

> **note**
> Sharing your calendar's private address lets others read your calendar information, but not add to or change that information.

3. Click either the XML or iCal buttons in the Private Address section. (Use

33

iCal to share your calendar with the Apple iCal program; use XML for most other programs.)

4. A pop-up window containing your calendar's address now appears, as shown in Figure 33.10; copy this address into the other calendar application.

caution You use the private address to view your calendar within another calendar application that you are personally using. To share your calendar publicly with other users, use the calendar's *public* address.

FIGURE 33.9

Accessing details for the selected calendar.

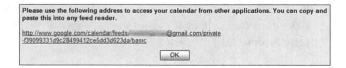

FIGURE 33.10

Copy your calendar's private address into the other calendar application.

Working with Events

All the items scheduled on your calendar are called *events*. An event can include all sorts of information—some of which is augmented by information provided by the Google website.

Adding an Event to Your Calendar

Google provides several different ways to add events to your calendar. Let's look at each, in turn.

First, you can simply click the hour or the day on your calendar that you'd like to create a new event; if you add an event to a daily calendar, click and drag your cursor over the entire timeframe of the event. This opens a new event balloon, like the one shown in Figure 33.11. Enter the name of the event into the balloon, and select which calendar you want to add the event to.

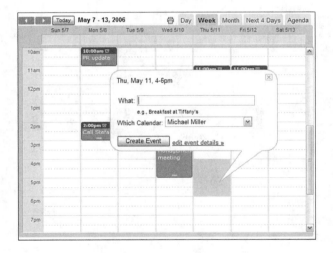

FIGURE 33.11

Adding information to a new event balloon.

If you use this approach on a monthly calendar, unfortunately, you can't easily determine the length of the event. To fine-tune these and other details of the event, click the Edit Event Details link in the event balloon. This opens the page shown in Figure 33.12, where you can enter the following information:

- What (name of the event)
- When (start and end times—or days)

- Repeats (use for repeating events)
- Where (the event's location)
- Calendar (which of your calendars the event should be added to)
- Description (a brief overview of the event)
- Reminder (how much in advance you want to be reminded of the event, if at all)
- Show Me As (either available or busy, for anyone viewing a public calendar)
- Privacy (determines whether the event is private, public, or your default setting)
- Guests (enter the email addresses of any guests you want included; you'll be prompted to email them with notice of the event, if you like)
- Guests Can (either invite others to your event, see the guest list, or neither)

FIGURE 33.12

Entering more detailed event information.

You can also add an event by clicking the Create Event link in the upper-left corner of the Google Calendar page. This also opens the page shown in Figure 33.12; enter the appropriate information, and then click the Save button.

Adding an Event via Quick Add

Perhaps the easiest way to add an event, however, is with Google Calendar's Quick Add feature. When you click the Quick Add link (or type the letter Q), the Quick Add entry box appears, as shown in Figure 33.13. Enter the name and time of the event, and then press Enter. This method is quite intelligent; if you enter **Lunch with George at noon Monday at the Macaroni Grill**, Quick Add translates the text and enters the appropriate event at the specified date and time.

FIGURE 33.13

Using Quick Add to add an event.

Adding an Event from Gmail

Here's a neat feature that arises from the integration of Google Calendar and Gmail. When you're reading a Gmail message that contains information pertaining to a possible event, just pull down the More Action menu and select Create Event. This opens a New Event window, as shown in Figure 33.14; enter the appropriate information, click Save Changes, and the event will be added to your Google Calendar.

33

Importing Events from Other Applications

If you're already using another calendar application, you can import the events from that application to Google Calendar. Importing events in this fashion is a lot easier than re-entering all those events by hand!

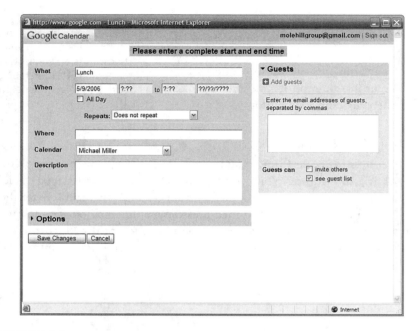

FIGURE 33.14

Adding an event from a Gmail message.

For example, if you're using Microsoft Outlook, you can import calendar events by following these steps:

1. From within Microsoft Outlook, select File, Import and Export.

2. When the Import and Export Wizard appears, select Export to a File and then click Next.

3. Select Comma Separated Values (Windows) and click Next.

4. Select the calendar you want to export, and then click Next.

5. Select a location for the exported file, and then click Next.

6. When the final window appears, click Finish.

7. From within Google Calendar, click the Settings link.

8. When the Calendar Settings page appears, click the Import Calendar tab.

9. Click the Browse button and select the .CSV file you just created.

10. Pull down the Choose Calendar list and select which calendar you wish to import these events into.

11. Click the Import button.

You would follow similar steps to import events from other calendar applications. Just remember to export your other calendar data as a .CSV (comma separated values) file, and then import that file into Google Calendar.

> **tip** To receive event notifications on your mobile phone, go to the Settings page, select the Notifications tab, and then enter your cell phone number, carrier, and other necessary information.

Inviting Others to an Event

When you first created an event, you had the option of adding guests to this event's information. If you did so, you were prompted to send email invitations to those guests.

After you've created an event on your calendar, you can invite more guests at any time. Just follow these steps:

1. Open the selected event to display the event page.

2. Enter the email addresses of your guests into the Add Guests box. Separate multiple addresses with commas.

3. Click the Save button.

4. Google Calendar now displays the message, "Would you like to notify guests of your changes?" To send email invitations to your new guests, click the Send button.

Google now sends invitations to all the guests you added. As you can see in Figure 33.15, each invitation includes links for the guest's response—Yes, No, or Maybe. When the guest clicks one of these links, he is taken to a Submit Response web page. His response is then automatically entered into the event in your Google Calendar, as shown in the Guests section of the event page (see Figure 33.16).

> **tip** You can also add a Google Calendar event button to your personal website; any visitor clicking on this button adds the event to their own Google Calendar. For instructions on how to add an event button via HTML, read the Google Calendar Event Publisher Guide (www.google.com/googlecalendar/event_publisher_guide.html).

33

FIGURE 33.15

An email invitation to a Google Calendar event.

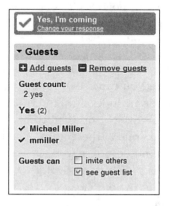

FIGURE 33.16

Guests attending a specific event.

Creating a Public Calendar

So far, we've dealt with private calendars—those calendars that you, and only you, view on your own PC. As discussed previously, Google Calendar also lets you create *public* calendars that anyone can access via the Web. These public calendars are great for sharing information and schedules about public events and organizations. For example, you could create a public calendar to track games and events for your school's basketball team, or for your company or organization. Just create the public calendar and share its address with all interested parties.

To create a public calendar, follow these steps:

1. In the Calendar box on the Google Calendar page, click the + button next to My Calendars.
2. When the Create New Calendar page appears, enter the name, description, and other information as normal.
3. Scroll down to the Share with Everyone section of this page, and then check the Share All Information on This Calendar with Everyone option.
4. Click the Create Calendar button.

Next, you want to share this calendar with all interested parties. To do this, you have to create and then share the calendar's web address. Follow these steps:

1. In the Calendars box, click the down arrow next to this calendar and select Calendar Settings.
2. When the Details page appears, go to the Calendar Address section and click the XML button.
3. When the Calendar Address box appears, copy the URL generated. (But don't distribute it yet; this isn't the final address for your calendar.)
4. Go to www.google.com/googlecalendar/event_publisher_guide.html and paste the URL you just copied into the box at the bottom of the page.
5. Click the Create URL button.
6. Google now generates a usable URL for your calendar. Copy this URL into another application, or into an email message that you send to other members of your organization or team.

33

Searching Your Calendar—And Public Calenders

As could be expected, Google integrates some interesting search features into the Google Calendar application. Not only can you search for events in your own calendars, you can also search all public calendars for interesting events.

Searching Your Private Calendars

If you have a lot of events stored in multiple calendars, finding a particular event might be problematic. To that end, you can utilize Google's search feature. Just enter some information about the event (a person's name, a place, or whatever) into the top-of-page search box, and then click the Search My Calendars button. Google now displays a list of matching events, as shown in Figure 33.17; click an event to view more details.

FIGURE 33.17

Results from a Google Calendar event search.

Searching Public Calendars

Google Calendar also lets you search all public calendars for events. You do this from the Search Public Calendars box in the Calendar box on the left side of the main Google Calendars page. Events that match your search are displayed on a new page. Click the link under each event to view details of that event; click the Add Calendar button to add this complete calendar to your own Google Calendar page.

The Bottom Line

There are many benefits to using a web-based calendar, chief of which is the ability to share event information publicly. If this matters to you—or if you simply like the ability to check your calendar from any available PC—then Google Calendar is worth a spin. It's free to use, if you don't mind posting your private information across the Internet on Google's company servers.

34

Using Picasa

O
f all of Google's software products, I like Picasa the best. Why do I like Picasa so much? Because it does just about everything that a program like Adobe Photoshop Elements or Paint Shop Pro does, but with a much smaller footprint (very small file size—very quick to download) and for free. Whether you need to fix bad digital pictures or just organize all the photos on your hard drive, Picasa will do it with ease.

Installing and Configuring the Program

As I just mentioned, Picasa is a free program you can download from picasa.google.com. The program is actually quite small, so the download isn't time-consuming at all. Just click the download link, and you'll be ready to go in no time.

The first time you launch the program, Picasa scans your computer for picture files. As you can see in Figure 34.1, you can have Picasa scan your entire hard disk, or only those files in your My Documents, My Pictures, and Desktop folders. Obviously, it takes less time to scan these selected folders than it does to scan your entire hard disk; if you're well organized, select this second option. (If not... well, you might as well have Picasa search everywhere for files you might have haphazardly stored.)

> **note** This chapter is based on Picasa 2. If you're using an older version of the program, you should upgrade to the new version at your earliest convenience.

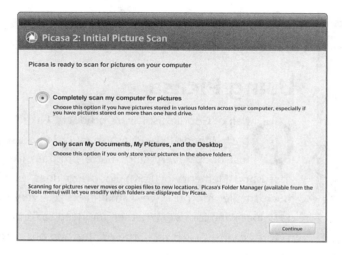

FIGURE 34.1

Picasa scans your hard disk for all available picture files.

The picture files that Picasa finds are used to create an index within the Picasa program. This picture index is used to organize your photos into visual albums; most users will find it's easier to locate pictures from within Picasa's albums than it is by using the My Pictures folder in Windows.

The balance of this chapter is devoted to showing you how to use Picasa to organize and edit your photos. Since Picasa has so many features one could write an entire book about it (is my editor reading this?),

> **note** Picasa 2 is only available for computers running Windows XP or Windows 2000. Picasa 2 does not run on older versions of Windows, nor on Apple Macintosh computers.

page count constraints force me to limit coverage to those common tasks that the typical user is likely to perform.

Getting to Know the Picasa Desktop

By default, Picasa shows all photos in its picture library, as shown in Figure 34.2. The individual folders in your library are displayed in the left folders pane; the photos within the selected folder are displayed in the main window. You can also use the scroll bars to scroll up and down through all the photos in Picasa's index.

FIGURE 34.2

Picasa's picture library.

When you select a photo, it's surrounded by a blue border and displayed as a thumbnail in the Picture Tray at the bottom left of the screen. You can select more than one picture at a time; the thumbnails are then resized to fit them all within the Picture Tray.

Also along the bottom of the screen are various function buttons. These buttons are described in Table 34.1.

Table 34.1	Picasa's Function Buttons
Button	**Description**
Hold	Holds selected pictures in the Picture Tray
Clear	Clears all pictures from the Picture Tray
Label	Adds a label to pictures in the Picture Tray
Star	"Stars" selected photos for future use
Rotate counter-clockwise	Rotates the picture 90 degrees to the left
Rotate clockwise	Rotates the picture 90 degrees to the right
Print	Prints the selected pictures
Email	Emails pictures (using either your default email program, Gmail, or Hello's Picasa Mail)
Collage	Creates a collage of the selected photos (like the one in Figure 34.3)
Hello	Connects to Google's Hello photo-sharing service
Blog This!	Sends the selected photo to your Blogger blog (as a new photo posting)
Order Prints	Orders prints of selected photos from an online photo print service
Export	Saves a copy of any photo that you've edited

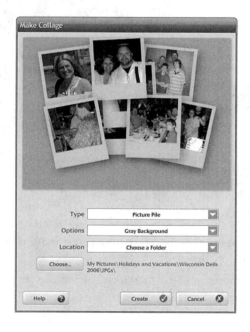

FIGURE 34.3

A photo collage, created with Picasa.

Just above all the function buttons, at the bottom right of the main display, is a zoom slider control. You use this slider to adjust the size of the photos that appear in the main display.

At the top of the Picasa window are four buttons and a search box. The buttons let you import new photos; display the pictures in the selected folder as a slideshow; display your photos in an innovative timeline view (shown in Figure 34.4); or burn selected photos to a "gift" CD. The search box lets you search your hard disk for photos that match specific criteria.

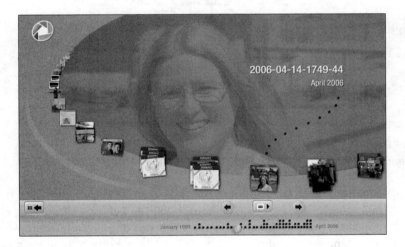

FIGURE 34.4
Picasa's timeline view.

Organizing Your Photos

One of the neat things about Picasa is how easy it is to reorganize your photos. You can easily move photos from one folder to another or rename your photos, all from Picasa's library view.

Moving Photos

Picasa displays all your photos in their original folders, with the folders listed in the folder pane. To move a picture from one folder to another, simply drag it from the library window to a new folder in the folder pane. To move *all* the pictures in the folder to another folder, just drag and drop that folder in the folder pane.

Renaming Photos

It's equally easy to rename a photo. Just select the picture you want to rename, and then select File, Rename. When the Rename Files dialog box appears (as shown in Figure 34.5), enter a new name for the file and click the Rename button. (Alternatively, you can check the options to automatically include the picture's date and/or image resolution in the filename.)

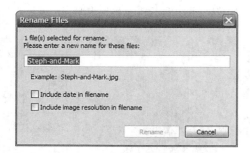

FIGURE 34.5
Renaming picture files.

To rename a group of photos, select all the photos you want to rename, and then select File, Rename. This time when the Rename Files dialog box appears, enter the common name you want all photos to share. When you click Rename, the photos will be renamed accordingly, with each individual photo having a "-1," "-2," and so on appended to the common name.

Fixing Common Photo Problems

If you're like me, not every photo you take is a "keeper." Some of my photos are too dark, some are too light, some have a bad color balance, some aren't composed properly, some are shots of people with really bad red eye...you get the picture. (No pun intended.) The nice thing about taking photos digitally (as opposed to shooting on film) is that fixing bad pictures is a simple matter of moving the appropriate digital bits and bytes around—which is something that Picasa does with aplomb.

When you want to fix a picture, you start by double-clicking it in the photo library.

> **tip** You return to Picasa's photo library by clicking the Back to Library button.

This displays a large version of the photo in the main window, along with a new control pane on the left side of the window, as shown in Figure 34.6. The control pane has three different tabs; each tab contains a variety of controls you can use to edit and manipulate the selected picture.

FIGURE 34.6
Editing a picture.

Read on to learn how to perform some of the more common fixes.

Fixing a Dark (or Light) Picture

If you shoot a lot of photos indoors, chances are you'll run across a few shots that are underlit—that is, the photos appear too dark. Conversely, shooting outdoors in bright sunlight can result in some photos being too light, or washed out. Fortunately, Picasa can fix both these problems.

Whether your picture is too dark or too light, there are several different methods you can use to fix the problem. The easiest method, and the first to try, is to select the Basic Fixes tab (shown in Figure 34.7) and click the Auto Contrast button. Nine times out of ten, this will do the trick.

34

FIGURE 34.7

Picasa's Basic Fixes tab.

If using Auto Contrast doesn't fix the problem, try adjusting the Fill Light slider (also on the Basic Fixes tab). Moving the slider to the right lightens the picture as if you shot it with additional fill light; moving the slider to the left removes the fill light and darkens the picture.

Additional adjustments can be made from the Tuning tab, shown in Figure 34.8. From here you can (once again) adjust the Fill Light, as well as Highlights (lightens or darkens only the brightest areas of the picture) and Shadows (lightens or darkens only the darkest areas of the picture).

Fixing an Off-Color Picture

Another problem with shooting indoors is that you don't always get the right colors. Shooting under fluorescent lights can turn everything a little green, while shooting under too low a light can give everything a warmish orange cast.

To fix tint problems (the entire picture looking the wrong color), go to the Basic Fixes tab and click the Auto Color button. If this doesn't do the trick, go to the Tuning tab and adjust the Color Temperature control. Moving this slider to the left creates a "cooler" picture (more blue), while moving it to the right creates a "warmer" picture (more red).

> **tip**
> You can undo any change you make by clicking the Undo button in the Control Panel. Reapply the change by clicking the Redo button.

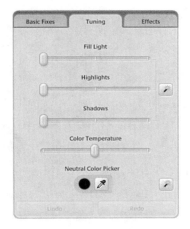

FIGURE 34.8

Picasa's Tuning tab.

You might also consider using the Neutral Color Picker on the Basic Fixes tab. Click the eyedropper button and then click the cursor on an area in your picture that should be neutral white or black. This will adjust all the other colors to match.

If you need more control over the picture's tint, go to the Effects tab (shown in Figure 34.9) and click Tint; this displays the Tint control. Click your cursor within the Pick Color box to display the screen shown in Figure 34.10. Move the cursor around the color box until you find the proper tint, and then click the cursor to confirm.

FIGURE 34.9

Picasa's Effects tab.

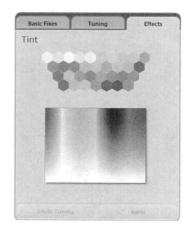

FIGURE 34.10

Adjusting the tint of a picture.

Finally, if a picture has too much (or too little color), you need to adjust the photo's color saturation. You do this from the Effects tab. Click the Saturation control, and then adjust the Amount slider to the left (to remove color from the picture) or the right (to increase the amount of color).

Fixing Red Eye

When you shoot indoors with a flash, you sometimes get what is called the "red eye" effect. (You know this one; it's when your subject looks like the red-eyed spawn of a devil.) Fortunately, Picasa makes removing red eye a snap. Here's what you do:

1. Select the Basic Fixes tab.

2. Click the Redeye button.

3. When the Redeye Fixes control appears, as shown in Figure 34.11, click and drag your mouse over the first eye you want to fix. Picasa automatically removes the red from the selected eye.

4. Repeat Step 3 for the other eye you want to fix.

5. Click the Apply button to confirm the fix.

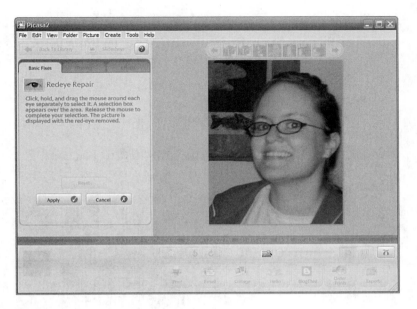

FIGURE 34.11

Fixing red eye.

Cropping a Picture

Sometimes, for whatever reason, you don't properly compose a picture. Maybe your subject isn't centered; maybe your subject is too far away. Whatever the case, you can crop the photo to put the subject front and center in the picture, using Picasa's Crop control.

To crop a picture, follow these steps:

1. Select the Basic Fixes tab.

2. Click the Crop button.

3. When the Crop Picture control appears, as shown in Figure 34.12, select what size you want the resulting picture to be: 4 × 6, 5 × 7, 8 ×10, or a custom size (Manual). This fixes the dimensions of the crop area.

34

4. Click your mouse at the top-left area where you want to crop.

5. Hold down the mouse button and drag the cursor down and to the right until you have selected the area you want to remain in the final picture.

6. Release the mouse button.

7. Click the Apply button to confirm the crop.

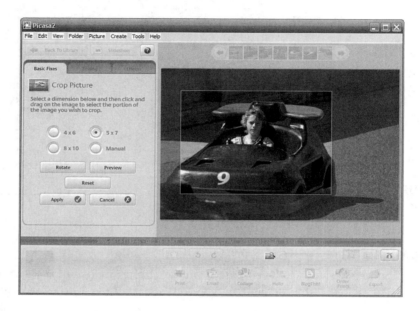

FIGURE 34.12

Cropping a photo.

Applying Special Effects

Picasa's Effects tab not only lets you adjust tint and color saturation, it also lets you apply a bevy of special effects to your photos. Table 34.2 details the available special effects.

34

Table 34.2   Picasa's Special Effects

Special Effect	Description
Sharpen	Sharpens the edges of the photo
Sepia	Converts the photo to sepia tone, like old-time photos
B&W	Removes all color from the photo
Warmify	Boosts the warm tones in the photo (good for skin tones)
Film Grain	Adds a film-like grain to the photo
Tint	Lets you adjust the photo's tint
Saturation	Lets you adjust the color saturation of the photo
Soft Focus	Adds a soft focus effect to the edges of the photo, while keeping the center of the photo in sharp focus (as shown in Figure 34.13)
Glow	Adds a gauzy glow to the photo
Filtered B&W	Creates the effect of a black and white photo taken with a color filter
Focal B&W	Similar to the soft focus effect, removes color from the edges of the photo while keeping the center of the photo in full color
Graduated Tint	Applies a gradated filter to the photo (useful for shooting skies and landscapes)

FIGURE 34.13

A portrait with a soft focus effect.

Saving Your Changes

Once you've completed editing and adding special effects to your photos, it's time to save your changes. Picasa always retains your original photo in its original state, just in case you want to return to it for different editing in the future; your edited photo is exported (saved) under a new filename.

Saving an Edited File

To save an edited photo, follow these steps:

1. Click the Export button.
2. When the Export to Folder dialog box appears, as shown in Figure 34.14, check the Use Original Size option.
3. Click the OK button.

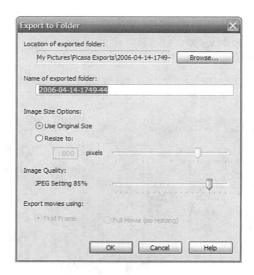

FIGURE 34.14
Exporting an edited photo.

Picasa now saves your edited picture in the My Pictures/Picasa Exports folder on your hard disk. Note that Picasa only saves files in the JPG format.

Resizing a Photo for the Web

Here's something else you can do from the Export to Folder dialog box—resize your photos to use on a web page.

If you have a high megapixel camera and you're shooting at the highest quality setting, you're creating some very large photos, too large to fit comfortably on a web page. You don't want photos any wider than 800 pixels on a web page—and probably a lot smaller than that. For this reason, you should resize your photos to make them small enough for web use.

Picasa lets you resize any photo when you export it. All you have to do is check the Resize To option in the Export to Folder dialog box, and then adjust the slider to a new width (in pixels). You can also enter a custom width in the corresponding box. It's that easy.

> **tip**
>
> Picasa can also export a folder full of pictures as a photo web page, which you can then upload to your website. Select Folder, Export As Web Page to begin the process.

Printing and Sharing Your Photos

There are many ways to share your digital photo. You can make photo prints (either on your own printer or using a photo printing service), email the photos, or burn them onto a picture CD. Picasa lets you do all these tasks, quite easily.

Printing Photos on Your Personal Printer

To print one or more photos on your own photo printer, follow these steps:

1. From the photo library, select the photo(s) you want to print.

2. Click the Print button.

3. When the Print dialog box appears, as shown in Figure 34.15, select the print size or layout you want. You can select from twelve wallet-sized prints, four 3.5 × 5 prints, two 4 × 6 prints, two 5 × 7 prints, one 8 × 10 print, or a full-page print.

4. Select whether you want the photo resized to fit the print area, or cropped to fit the print area.

5. Select how many copies you want to print.

6. Click the Print button.

Printing Photos via an Online Print Service

If you don't have a photo printer, or would rather have more professional prints, Picasa lets you send your photos to an online photo printing service. Your photos are sent over the Internet to the print service; your prints are then mailed to you when completed.

To send one or more photos to a print service, select the photo(s) in the photo library and then click the Order Prints button. When the Picasa Prints and Products dialog box appears (as shown in Figure 34.16), click the button for the service you want to use, and then follow the specific onscreen instructions from there.

FIGURE 34.15

Printing a photo.

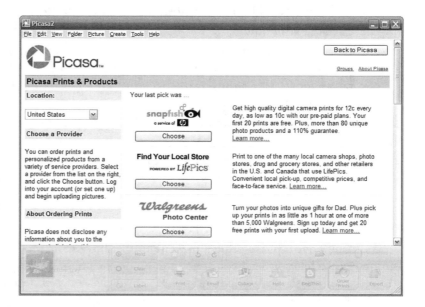

FIGURE 34.16

Choosing an online photo print service.

Sharing Your Photos with Picasa Web Albums

If you want to share your photos with all your family and friends, what better way to do it than via the Web? That's where Picasa Web Albums comes in. This is a new Google service that lets you upload your pictures to a special photo-sharing website; you then send invitations to whomever you want to view your photos. And, like all things Google, it's all free.

You upload your photos from within the latest version of Picasa. Select the pictures you want to share, then click the Web Album button. Once uploaded, go to the Picasa Web Albums site (picasaweb.google.com) and click the Share button; follow the onscreen instructions to send email invitations to whomever you want. The email contains a link back to your Picasa photo album.

Viewing photos on the Picasa Web Albums site is a piece of cake. Visitors can view one picture at a time, or sit back and enjoy a web-based slideshow.

Signing up for Picasa Web Albums is totally free, for both you and your visitors. You get 250MB of free storage space, which can hold at least 1,000 normal-sized digital photos. If you need more storage space, you can pay $25 per year and get an additional 6GB of storage. Check it out!

Sharing Your Photos with Hello

Picasa isn't Google's only photo-related application. Hello is a kind of photo-oriented instant messaging program that lets you send photos to your friends in real-time. When you and a friend are connected at the same time, it's a matter of a few mouse clicks to send a photo.

You can learn more about Hello at www.hello.com, or by clicking the Hello button in Picasa. The first time you use Hello, you'll be prompted to create a username and process; signing up is free. You'll also have to download and install the Hello application, which is relatively quick and easy.

Once online, you add users to your friends list the same way you do with any instant messaging program. When a friend is online, he shows up in his own tab in the Hello window. You can then use the Send Pictures button to share photos with your friend; he can do the same on his end. The result, as shown in Figure 34.17, is an online chat composed primarily of pictures.

I'll be honest; I really don't see the purpose of Hello. It's a big hassle, since both you and your friends have to be online at the same time to share photos. And if you're already using an instant messaging program that lets you send files to other users, such as AIM or MSN Messenger, why bother with yet another program to do the same thing? You may disagree and really like Hello, but I find it a superfluous application. Still, it's well integrated with Picasa, if you want to use it.

34

FIGURE 34.17

Viewing a photo sent via Hello.

Emailing Photos

Even simpler than doing the whole instant messaging thing, Picasa lets you quickly and easily email photos to your friends and family. Just follow these steps:

1. In Picasa's photo library, select the photo(s) you want to send.

2. Click the Email button.

3. When the Select Email dialog box appears, select which email service you want to use to send your photo(s).

4. If you selected Gmail, you'll see the Gmail dialog box shown in Figure 34.18. (If you selected another option, you'll see that application's send email screen.) Enter the name of the recipient into the To: box, and then click the Send button.

If you like, you can have Picasa automatically resize photos you send via email to make for faster uploading/downloading. All you have to do is Select Tools, Options to display the Options dialog box, and then select the E-Mail tab, shown in Figure 34.19. In the Output Options section, use the slider to select an output size (anything less than 800 pixels wide is safe), and then check the *xx* Pixels, As Above option for the When Sending Single Pictures selection.

34

FIGURE 34.18
Sending a photo via Email.

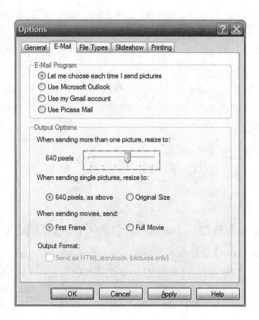

FIGURE 34.19
Configuring Picasa to automatically resize photos sent via email.

Burning Photos to a Picture CD or DVD

Another way to share your photos with others is to burn and distribute a CD or DVD containing those photos. Picasa makes this a relatively painless process, all things considered. Just follow these steps:

1. In Picasa's photo library, select the photos you want to burn to CD or DVD.

2. Click the Gift CD button (above the library window). The bottom of the window now changes as shown in Figure 34.20.

3. If you want to include an automatic slideshow for your photos, check the Include Slideshow option.

4. To include the pictures at less than their original size, pull down the Picture Size list and select a new size.

5. Enter a name for the disc into the CD Name box.

6. If you want to include a copy of the Picasa program on the disc, check the Include Picasa option.

7. Insert a blank CD or DVD into your PC's CD/DVD drive, and then click the Burn Disc button.

FIGURE 34.20

Getting ready to burn a picture CD.

COMMENTARY:

OTHER PHOTO-EDITING PROGRAMS

Picasa isn't the only photo-editing program out there, of course. It is, however, one of the few free applications; most photo-editing software costs at least $100, in some cases much, much more. And, from my experience, Picasa does at least as good a job as most of the lower-end photo-editing programs; only Adobe Photoshop offers superior photo-editing features.

34

That said, let's take a quick look at some of the competing photo-editing programs:

- **IrfanView (www.irfanview.com).** Like Picasa, a free application—although it isn't quite as full featured as Picasa, in my opinion.
- **Adobe Photoshop Elements (www.adobe.com).** A lower-priced, less fully featured subset of the venerable Photoshop CS program, designed with the amateur photographer in mind. Elements has always been one of my favorite programs, but it doesn't really offer much more than what you get with Picasa—and it costs $90.
- **Corel Paint Shop Pro (www.corel.com).** This program is a little more fully featured than Photoshop Elements, but not quite as advanced as Photoshop CS. It's priced in the same range as Elements ($99).
- **Microsoft Digital Image Suite (www.microsoft.com).** Microsoft's somewhat undistinguished entry into the photo-editing market, similar to Paint Shop Pro in functionality and price ($99).
- **Adobe Photoshop CS (www.adobe.com).** Photoshop is the standard for professional photographers and image editors. It does just about anything you can dream of—but it has a very steep learning curve, as well as a very steep price ($649).

Bottom line, if you're a casual or amateur photographer who wants something inexpensive and easy to use, I'd recommend Picasa over any of the competing products (Photoshop Elements, Paint Shop Pro, et al). If, on the other hand, you're a professional photographer or designer, you probably need everything Photoshop CS offers—and can afford the price.

The Bottom Line

As I said at the beginning of this chapter, I really like Picasa. Practically anything I can do in Photoshop Elements, I can also do in Picasa—in many cases, faster and easier. And, unlike Elements and other $100+ programs, Picasa is free. It's a great little program that all amateur photographers should be using; it makes it easy to fix those occasional bad photos that we all take.

Using Google Pack

I f you like the Google applications we've discussed in this section and throughout the rest of this book, you'll probably like Google Pack, too. Google Pack is, in Google's words, "a free collection of essential software."

In essence, Google Pack lets you download the best of Google's software applications, as well as a handful of useful third-party applications, in one fell swoop. A few clicks of your mouse lets you download the entire Google Pack, and installation of the individual programs is pretty much a one-step process. It's a convenient way to get a lot of useful programs in one simple package.

What's in Google Pack?

Just what applications are included in Google Pack? Google includes a core group of programs, as well as four optional programs you can download if you choose. At present, the core programs in Google Pack include

- Google Earth (discussed in Chapter 20, "Using Google Earth")

note At present, Google Pack is only available for Windows PCs. It isn't available for Apple Macintoshes.

- Google Toolbar (discussed in Chapter 31, "Using the Google Toolbar")

- Google Desktop (discussed in Chapter 32, "Using Google Desktop")

- Picasa (discussed in Chapter 34, "Using Picasa")

- Google Pack Screensaver (photo screensaver, exclusive to Google Pack)

- Mozilla Firefox with Google Toolbar (an alternative to the Internet Explorer web browser, with Google Toolbar preinstalled)

- Norton Antivirus 2005 Special Edition (antivirus software)

- Ad-Aware SE Personal (anti-spyware program)

- Adobe Reader 7 (PDF reader)

Google also offers four optional programs that can be downloaded as part of Google Pack:

- Google Talk (discussed in Chapter 22, "Instant Messaging with Google Talk and Gmail Chat")

- Google Video Player (discussed in Chapter 25, "Downloading Video Entertainment from Google Video")

- RealPlayer (media player)

- GalleryPlayer HD Images (high-quality artwork and photos)

All the programs in Google Pack are free—although some of the non-Google programs are limited versions of programs that have more fully featured paid versions. (You don't have to upgrade to the paid versions, however; you can use all the programs in Google Pack immediately after downloading.)

Installing Google Pack—And Keeping It Up-to-Date

Google Pack can be downloaded for free from the Google website. Downloading is managed by the Google Updater; this useful utility is also used to update the software in Google Pack, or to uninstall any program you don't want to keep. Once installed, you'll see a Google Updater icon in your Windows system tray; this icon displays notifications when there are updates available for any Google Pack program.

35

To download and install Google Pack, go to pack.google.com and click the Download Google Pack button. If you don't want to install all the Google Pack programs, wait for the next page to appear and click the Add or Remove Software link; this takes you to a page where you can select which programs you want to install. Otherwise, follow the onscreen instructions to start the Google Updater program and install all the Google Pack programs.

> **tip** You can install Google Pack even if you already have some of the included programs installed. Google Updater checks to see if you have the latest version of any installed program; if you do, it doesn't reinstall the program unnecessarily.

As you can see in Figure 35.1, Google Updater begins the download process automatically, after checking your PC for any previously installed programs. After Google Pack is installed, you may be requested to restart your computer for the installation to take effect.

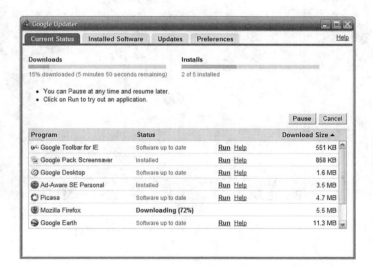

FIGURE 35.1

Installing Google Pack applications with Google Updater.

The nice thing about Google Pack is that not only do you not have to install each program separately, you also don't have to configure each program individually. The normal configuration process for each

> **tip** To uninstall any Google Pack program, open Google Updater, select the Installed Software tab, and then click the Uninstall link next to the program you want to uninstall.

35

program is handled by the Google Updater program, with all your personal information added automatically.

Using the Google Pack Screensaver

The one new Google program exclusive to Google Pack is the Google Pack Screensaver. This program displays selected digital photos as your Windows screensaver.

By default, the Google Pack Screensaver displays pictures in your My Pictures folder in a photo collage, like the one shown in Figure 35.2. You can also choose to display pictures sequentially, with either a wipe or fade effect; you can also select other folders or subfolders to include in the display.

FIGURE 35.2
The Google Pack Screensaver in action.

To reconfigure the screensaver in this fashion, follow these steps:

1. Right-click on an open area of the Windows desktop and select Properties from the pop-up menu.

2. When the Display Properties dialog box appears, select the Screen Saver tab.

3. Pull down the Screen Saver list and make sure Google Pack Screensaver is selected.

4. Click the Settings button.

5. When the Google Pack Screensaver dialog box appears, select the Visual Settings tab, shown in Figure 35.3. Pull down the Visual Effect list to select a new effect; adjust the slider to set how long each picture is displayed.

6. To select which pictures are displayed, select the Picture Folder Settings tab, shown in Figure 35.4. Check which folders and subfolders you want to display, or click the Add button to add more folders or subfolders.

7. When you're done adjusting the settings, click the OK button.

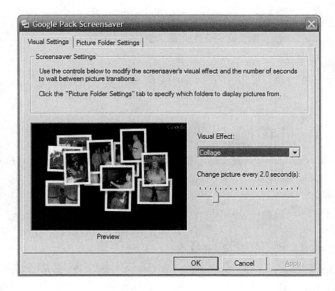

FIGURE 35.3
Configuring the screensaver's visual settings.

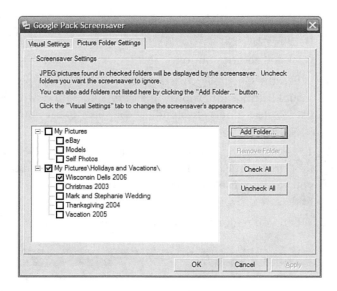

FIGURE 35.4

Determining which photos to display in the Google Pack Screensaver.

Using the Third-Party Software in Google Pack

I've covered the other Google programs included in Google Pack elsewhere in this book; turn to those chapters to learn more about Google Earth, Google Desktop, Google Toolbar, Picasa, and the like. Let's now turn our attention to the non-Google programs included in Google Pack—all of them free.

Surfing the Web with Mozilla Firefox

Chances are you use Microsoft's Internet Explorer as your web browser. That's fine, but IE isn't the only browser available.

Google Pack includes a copy of Mozilla Firefox, a top-notch web browser that many people are using as an alternative to Internet Explorer. As you can see in Figure 35.5, Firefox offers tabbed browsing, where multiple websites can be displayed on different tabs within the browser—instead of in separate browser windows. This version of Firefox also comes with the Google Toolbar preinstalled. (Find out more at www.mozilla.com/firefox/.)

35

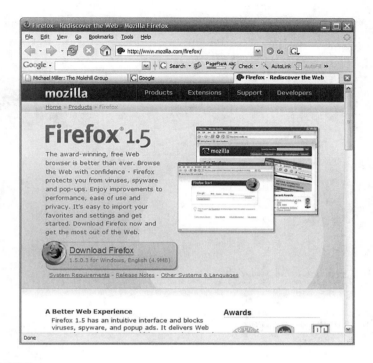

FIGURE 35.5
The Mozilla Firefox web browser.

Fighting Viruses with Norton Antivirus 2005 Special Edition

Norton AntiVirus is, as the name implies, a program that protects your computer against computer viruses, worms, and the like. It not only scans and cleans the files on your computer's hard disk, it also scans incoming and outgoing email attachments, blocks viruses in instant messages, and automatically downloads new virus definitions on a regular basis.

The version of Norton AntiVirus in Google Pack is the only program that isn't completely free. While it comes with a six-month free trial, you'll have to pay for a subscription to keep it up-to-date after that point.

Fighting Spyware with Ad-Aware SE Personal

Antivirus programs stop computer viruses; to stop spyware, you need an antispyware program—such as Ad-Aware SE Personal. This program protects against all manner of spyware, including adware, browser hijakckers, and the like. The version of Ad-Aware that comes with Google Pack, shown in Figure 35.6, is completely free. (Find out more about Ad-Aware at www.lavasoftusa. com.)

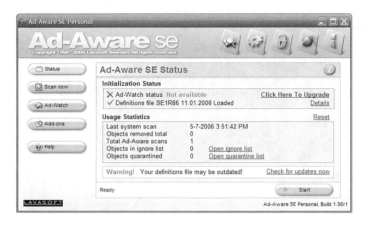

FIGURE 35.6

The Ad-Aware antispyware program.

Viewing PDF Files with Adobe Reader

Adobe Reader is the program you use to view PDF files. You probably already have a version of Adobe Reader installed on your PC; the version that comes with Google Pack is the latest version available. (Find out more at www.adobe.com.)

Playing Music and Videos with RealPlayer

When you want to play digital music, CDs, downloaded videos, and the like, you need a media player program. Playing media is what RealPlayer does, as you can see in Figure 35.7; you can also use the program to transfer songs to your iPod or other portable audio player device. (RealPlayer is an optional component of Google Pack; find out more at www.real.com.)

Viewing GalleryPlayer HD Images

The final item in Google Pack isn't really a program, it's a collection of high-resolution images, like the ones shown in Figure 35.8. These images are provided by GalleryPlayer, a company that packages fine-art photos and images for purchase; the images included with Google Pack are free, however. (GalleryPlayer HD Images is an optional component of Google Pack; find out more at www.galleryplayer.com.)

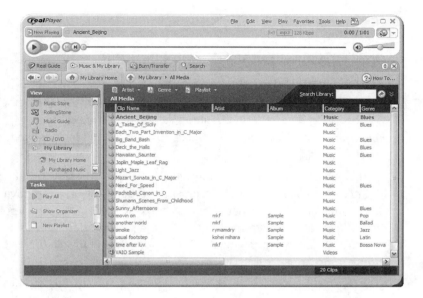

FIGURE 35.7
The RealPlayer music and video player program.

FIGURE 35.8
A selection of GalleryPlayer images.

COMMENTARY:

WHY GOOGLE PACK?

Why in the world does Google Pack exist?

Well, for users, it's a convenient way to download and install Google's various programs. It's also possible that you might need a web browser, a media player, and the like, so having them included in the pack is an added bonus.

To be fair, however, you probably already have Internet Explorer and Windows Media Player installed on your PC, so installing alternative programs might not be necessary. Calling Google Pack "essential software" might be overstating the case. These programs are only essential if you have a computer with absolutely nothing else installed; let's call these applications "desirable" rather than "essential," okay?

For Google, Google Pack is an opportunity to compete directly with Microsoft in both the browser and desktop application markets. Google doesn't (as yet) offer its own web browser or media player, so bundling Firefox and Real Player fills some very real gaps in the big G's product lineup—and provide an added incentive to download and install Google's own applications.

That said, I do have trouble seeing both the appeal of Google Pack to consumers and the value of Google Pack to Google. It's nice and all, but it's not compelling—in my opinion, anyway.

The Bottom Line

What some users will find appealing about Google Pack is that it includes some of the most useful and popular utility programs available today, bundled together with a common installer program. Consumers don't have to fret about choosing one program over another; Google Pack simplifies both the choices and the installation so it's pretty much a one-step process. And, best of all, all the programs in Google Pack are free—if you need these programs, downloading them via Google Pack is definitely the way to go.

PART

X

Google for Businesses

36 Submitting Your Site—and Increasing Your Ranking

37 Making Money with Google AdSense and AdWords

38 Using Google within Your Organization

Submitting Your Site—And Increasing Your Ranking

I f you have your own personal website or manage a commercial website, making sure your site appears in Google's search results is a very important issue. Not only do you want to ensure that your site appears when someone searches Google for the appropriate subject, but you also want your site to rank as high as possible in those results. Appearing as the 99,999th result in a list of 100,000 isn't a good thing.

While submitting your site to Google is a relatively easy process, increasing your site's ranking is a more involved process—so much so that an entire industry has risen around the topic of search engine optimization. So if you want to improve your Google search ranking, roll up your sleeves and get ready for a little hard work!

How to Submit Your Site to the Google Index—The Easy Way

While you could wait for the GoogleBot crawler to find your site on the Web, a more proactive approach is to manually submit your site for inclusion in the Google web index. It's an easy process—in fact, the easiest thing we'll discuss in this chapter.

All you have to do is go to www.google.com/addurl/, shown in Figure 36.1. Enter the URL for your home page into the appropriate box (including the http://), add any comments you might have, and then click the Add URL button. That's it; Google will now add your site to the GoogleBot crawl list, and your site will appear in appropriate search results.

FIGURE 36.1

Submitting your site to the Google index.

Note that you only have to add the top level URL for your site; you don't have to add URLs for any subsidiary pages. (For example, if your home page is http://www.homepage.com/index.html, enter only http://www.homepage.com.) GoogleBot will crawl the rest of your site once it finds the main URL.

How to Remove Your Site from the Google Index

tip To disallow other specific crawlers and spiders, see the (long) list at www.robotstxt.org/wc/active/html/.

If, for some reason, you want to remove your website from the Google index, the process is slightly more involved. What you need to do is place a special text file in the root directory of your website's server. This file should be named robots.txt, and should include the following text:

```
User-agent: Googlebot
Disallow: /
```

This code tells the GoogleBot crawler not to crawl your site. If you want to remove your site from *all* search engines (by preventing all robots from crawling the site), include the following text instead:

```
User-agent: *
Disallow: /
```

If you only want to remove certain pages on your site from the Google index, insert the following text into the robots.txt file, replacing *page.html* with the filename of the specific page:

```
User-agent: Googlebot
Disallow: /page.html
```

Finally, you can use the robots.txt file to exclude all pages within a specific directory. To do this, insert the following text, replacing *directory* with the name of the directory:

```
User-agent: Googlebot
Disallow: /directory
```

How to Submit a Complete Sitemap

Google has a new program that enables you to submit the URLs for your entire website, manage the status of your pages, and receive reports about the visibility of your pages on Google. It's called the Google Sitemaps program, and it's worth considering if you manage a large website.

Google Sitemaps serves two general purposes. First, it helps to keep Google informed of all the new and updated pages on your site—in other words, to improve the freshness of the Google index. Second, the program should help to increase the coverage of all your web pages in the Google index. The first goal benefits Google; the second benefits you; and both goals should benefit

36

Google's search users. Participation in Google Sitemaps is free.

Note that the Google Sitemaps program supplements, rather than replaces, the usual methods of adding pages to the Google index. If you don't participate in Google Sitemaps, your pages may still be discovered by the GoogleBot crawler, and you may still manually submit your site for inclusion in the Google index.

> **note** Google also has a separate Mobile Sitemaps program to add pages to its Mobile Web Index. Learn more information at www. google.com/webmasters/ sitemaps/docs/en/mobile.html.

Basic Site Submittal

There are two ways you can submit your site for inclusion in the Google Sitemaps program. We'll discuss the easy way first.

> **note** To participate in the Google Sitemaps program, you first need to sign into your Google account.

If you don't want to bother with submitting a detailed sitemap of your website, you can simply provide Google with the URL of your site. You do this from the My Sites page (www.google.com/webmasters/sitemaps/).

Once you submit your site, you have to verify that you're the site owner. You can do this either by adding a specified <META> tag to the HTML of your site's index page, or by creating and uploading a new HTML page as directed by Google. You do this verification from your new My Sites page (shown in Figure 36.2); click the Verify link and follow the instructions on the following page.

FIGURE 36.2
The Google Sitemaps My Sites page.

When you submit your site in this basic fashion, Google lets you view a variety of statistics about your site in the Google index. It doesn't, however, guarantee that all the pages in your site will appear in the Google index. For that, you need to submit a *sitemap* of your site; read on to learn more.

Submitting a Complete Sitemap

To take full advantage of the Google Sitemaps program, you need to submit a complete sitemap of your website. A sitemap is simply a listing of all the pages in your site, URL by URL, with basic information about the contents of each page.

Submitting a sitemap is the preferred way to submit your site, as Google's crawler will never know about all the pages on your site—especially if some of those pages are generated dynamically or changed frequently. By explicitly telling Google about all the pages on your site, in a format that Google understands, you enhance the chances of those pages being included in Google search results.

> **note** Even when you submit a complete sitemap, Google doesn't guarantee that it will crawl or index all the URLs on your website. However, since Google uses the data in your sitemap to learn more about your site's structure, it should improve the crawler schedule for your site, and ultimately improve the inclusion of your site's page in Google's search results.

Google can accept your sitemap file in a variety of formats (including a plain text file with one URL per line), but the best way to do it is to create an XML file. The file should include the URLs for all the pages in your site, along with optional information about when the page was last changed and the frequency of changes. You should automatically notify Google when your sitemap changes, so Google can work with the latest version.

Creating and Submitting Your Sitemap

To create your sitemap, you can use the Google Sitemap Generator tool or avail yourself of the increasing number of third-party sitemap generator tools. I'll discuss these third-party tools in a moment; to download the Google Sitemap Generator, follow the instructions at www.google.com/webmasters/sitemaps/docs/en/sitemap-generator.html.

Once you've created your sitemap, you upload it to your Google Sitemaps account by following these steps:

1. Upload your sitemap file to the highest-level directory (typically the root directory) on your web server.

2. Go to your My Sites page and click the Sitemaps tab.

3. Click the Add a Sitemap link.

4. When prompted, select which type of sitemap you're adding—a general web sitemap, or a mobile sitemap (for mobile web pages).

> **tip** Google Sitemaps also accepts RSS and Atom site feeds for your site. This is the way to go if your site includes a blog, message board, news headlines, or other dynamically generated content.

5. The Add Sitemap page now expands, as shown in Figure 36.3. Check that you've created the sitemap in a supported format and uploaded your sitemap to your website's highest-level directory.

6. Enter the URL for the sitemap file.

7. Click the Add Web Sitemap button.

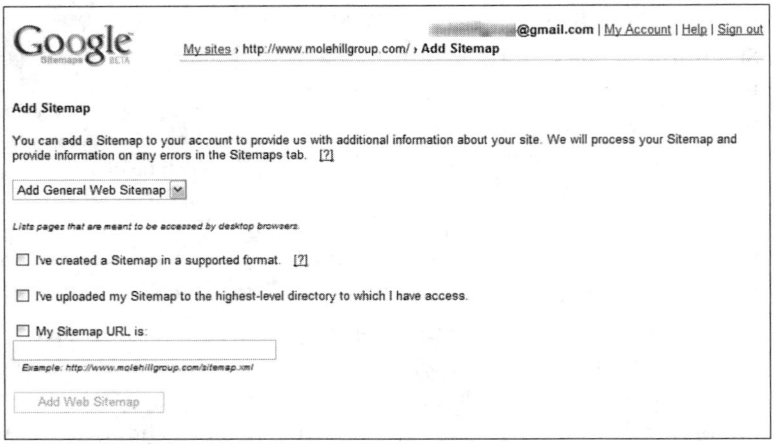

FIGURE 36.3
Adding a sitemap for your website.

Using Sitemap Generator Tools

The Google Sitemap Generator is, admittedly, a bit wonky. For most users, an easier way to generate a sitemap is to use one of the many third-party sitemap generator tools, which are quite a bit more user friendly than the tool that Google provides.

For most of these tools, generating a sitemap is as simple as pressing a button. Once the sitemap file is generated, you can then upload it to the root directory of your website and submit it to Google Sitemaps.

Some of these tools are web-based, some are software programs, and most are free. The most popular of these tools include the following:

- G-Mapper (www.dbnetsolutions.co.uk/gmapper/)

- GSiteCrawler (www. johannesmueller.com/gs/)

- Gsitemap (www.vigos.com/ products/gsitemap/)

tip Learn more about Google Sitemaps at the Inside Google Sitemaps blog (sitemaps.blogspot.com).

■ IntelliMapper (www.intelli-mapper.com)

■ Site Magellan (www.sitemagellan.com)

■ SitemapsPal (www.sitemapspal.com)

Viewing Sitemap Diagnostics and Statistics

Google Sitemaps provides quite a bit of statistical analysis and some useful diagnostics for your site. You get to this data by clicking the Manage Site link on your My Sites page; this displays the Summary diagnostic page, shown in Figure 36.4.

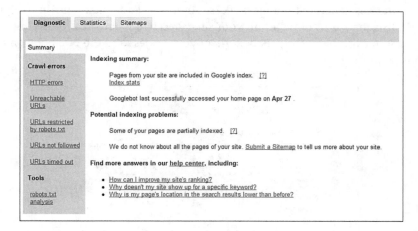

FIGURE 36.4
Viewing summary diagnostics for your site.

There are three tabs on this page, with additional pages for each tab. Table 36.1 details what you'll find here.

Table 36.1   Google Sitemaps Diagnostics and Statistics

Tab	Contents
Diagnostics	Summary (indexing summary and problems)
	Crawl errors
	HTTP errors
	Unreachable URLs
	URLs restricted by **robots.txt**
	URLs not followed
	URLs timed out
	Tools
	robots.txt analysis

Table 36.1	Continued
Tab	**Contents**
Statistics	Query stats (top search queries and search query clicks)
	Crawl stats (page status and PageRank data)
	Page analysis (content type, encodings, and common words on your site and in external links to your site)
	Index stats (links to standard Google site linkage and cache info)
Sitemaps	Management of sitemaps for one or more sites

For example, the Query Stats page, shown in Figure 36.5, lists the top search queries that visitors used to find your site, as well as which of those search queries generated the most clicks. The Crawl Stats page, shown in Figure 36.6, lists the status of pages on your site (successfully crawled, URLs timed out, and so forth), the average PageRank of your pages, and the one page on your site with the highest page rank.

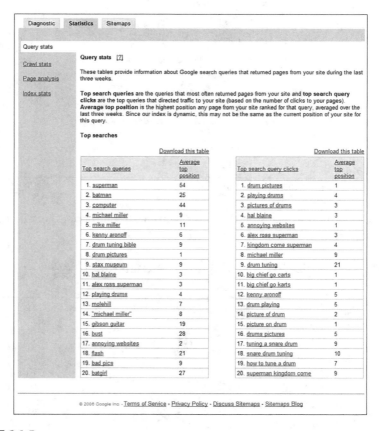

FIGURE 36.5
Google Sitemaps' Query Stats page.

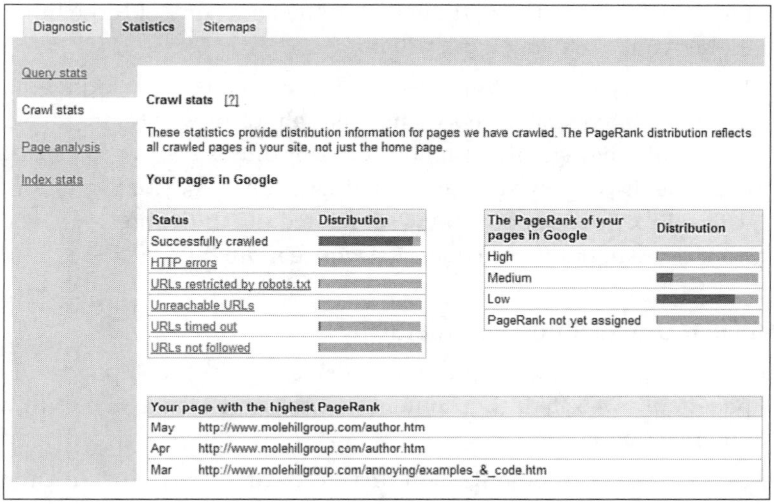

36

FIGURE 36.6
Google Sitemaps' Crawl Stats page.

How to Optimize Your Site's Ranking

Making sure your web pages are included in the Google search index is one thing; working to ensure a high PageRank within those results is something else. The process of tweaking your website to achieve higher search results on Google and other search sites is called *search engine optimization (SEO)*, and it's a major consideration for all big-time webmasters.

To increase your site's ranking in Google's search results, you have to increase your site's PageRank. There are a number of ways to do this, almost all of which involve manipulating the content and HTML code of your site. Read on to learn some of the most effective techniques.

Increase the Number of Links to Your Site

Probably the biggest impact you can have on your site's PageRank is to increase the number of sites that link to the pages on your site. As you learned back in Chapter 1, "Inside Google," the PageRank rating is based on a complex and proprietary algorithm, which is heavily weighted in favor of links to your site. The more sites

> **tip**
> For more search engine optimization tricks, check out the SEO Chat website (www.seochat.com).

that link to your site—and the higher the PageRank of those links sited—the higher your site's PageRank will be.

To increase your PageRank, then, you want to get more higher-quality sites to link back to your site. And it's not enough for those sites to have a high PageRank; they should also have content that is relative to your site. For example, if you have a site about NASCAR racing, you'll get more oomph with a link from another NASCAR-related site than you would with a link from a site about Barbie dolls. Relevance matters.

Create a Clear Organization and Hierarchy

The GoogleBot crawler can find more content on a web page and more web pages on a website if that content and those pages are in a clear hierarchical organization.

Let's look at page organization first. You want to think of each web page as a mini-outline. The most important information should be in major headings, with lesser information in subheadings beneath the major headings. One way to do this is via standard HTML heading tags, like this:

```
<h1>Most important information
    <h2>Less important information
        <h3>Least important information
```

This approach is also appropriate for your entire site layout. Your home page should contain the most important information, with subsidiary pages branching out from that containing less important information—and even more subpages branching out from those. The most important info should be visible when a site is first accessed via the home page; additional info should be no more than a click or two away.

This hierarchical organization is easily seen when you create a sitemap for your users. (This is distinct from the sitemap you create for and submit to Google Sitemaps.) A visible sitemap, looking for all the world like a big outline, not only makes it easier for visitors to find information on your site, it also gives the GoogleBot crawler some very meaty information to process.

Include Appropriate Keywords

Just as important as a page's layout is the page's content. You want to make sure that each and every page on your site contains the keywords that users might use to search for your pages. If your site is all about drums, make sure your pages include words like **drums**, **percussion**, **sticks**, **heads**, **drumset**,

cymbals, snare, and the like. Try to think through how *you* would search for this information, and work those keywords into your content.

Put the Most Important Information First

Think about hierarchy and think about keywords, and then think about how these two concepts work together. That's right, you want to place the most important keywords higher up on your page. The GoogleBot will only crawl so far, and you don't want it to give up before key information is found. In addition, PageRank is partially determined by content; the more important the content looks to be on a page (as determined by placement on the page), the higher the PageRank will be.

Make the Most Important Information Look Important

Google also looks to highlighted text to determine what's important on a page. It follows, then, that you should make an effort to format keywords on your page as bold or italic.

Use Text Instead of Images

Here's something you might not think about. At present, Google parses only text content; it can't figure out what a picture or graphic is about, unless you describe it in the text. So if you use graphic buttons or banners (instead of plain text) to convey important information, Google simply won't see it. You need to put every piece of important information somewhere in the text of the page—even if it's duplicated in a banner or graphic.

If you do use images on your site, make sure you use the <ALT> tag for each image, and assign meaningful keywords to the image via this tag. GoogleBot will read the <ALT> tag text; it can't figure out what an image is without it.

Link via Text

Following on the previous tip, make sure that you link from one page to another on your site via text links—not via graphics or fancy JavaScript menus. Google will find and use the text links to crawl other pages on your site; if the links are non-text, GoogleBot might not be able to find the rest of your site.

caution Similarly, don't hide important information in Flash animations, JavaScript applets, video files, and the like. Remember, Google can only find text on your page—all those nontext elements are invisible to the GoogleBot.

Incorporate <META> Tags

When calculating PageRank, Google not only considers the visible content on a page; it also evaluates the content of key HTML tags—in particular, your site's <META> tags. You want to make sure that you use <META> tags in your page's code, and assign important keywords to each of those tags.

note There are many more <META> attributes than the ones listed here (such as **CHANNEL, DATE**, and so on), but neither Google nor most other search engines read them. It's safe to stick to the attributes in Table 36.2, and ignore other possible <META> attributes.

The <META> tag, which (along with the <TITLE> tag) is placed in the head of your HTML document, can be used to supply all sorts of information about your document. You can insert multiple <META> tags into the head of your document, and each tag can contain a number of different attributes. The most common attributes are listed in Table 36.2:

Table 36.2   <META> Tag Attributes

Attribute	Description
DESCRIPTION	Provides a brief description of the page's content
KEYWORDS	Lists all important keywords that might be used to search this page
ROBOTS	The NOINDEX parameter is used if you *don't* want this page included in the Google index

You use separate <META> tags to define different attributes, using the following format:

```
<META name="attribute" content="items">
```

Replace *attribute* with the name of the particular attribute, and *items* with the keywords or description of that attribute.

For example, to include a description of your web page, you'd enter this line of code:

```
<META name="DESCRIPTION" content="All about stamp collecting">
```

To add keywords that GoogleBot can index, enter this line of code:

```
<META name="KEYWORDS" content="stamps, stamp collecting, collectable
stamps, stamp history, stamp prices">
```

Note that you separate each keyword by a comma, and that a "keyword" can actually be a multiple-word phrase. You can include up to 10 keywords with this attribute.

Finally, if you don't want Google to include this page in its search index, enter the following line of code:

```
<META name="ROBOTS" content="NOINDEX">
```

note If you want your page indexed by Google, you shouldn't include **ROBOTS <META>** code in your document.

You can include all three of these <META> attributes in the head of your HTML document, each in separate lines of code, one after another, like this:

```
<META name="DESCRIPTION" content="All about stamp collecting">
<META name="KEYWORDS" content="stamps, stamp collecting, collectable
stamps, stamp history, stamp prices">
<META name="ROBOTS" content="NOINDEX">
```

Make Good Use of the <TITLE> Tag

The <TITLE> tag is just as important as the <META> tag—which is why you shouldn't fall into the trap of assigning only your site name to the tag. Instead, the <TITLE> tag should contain two to three important keywords, and then followed by the site name. Google places major importance on the <TITLE> tag when determining a site's content; you want to make sure that your site's most important content is listed within this tag.

For example, if your stamp collecting site is called The Stamp Shop, you might use the following <TITLE> tag:

```
<TITLE>The Stamp Shop - Collecting, Prices, and History</TITLE>
```

Use Heading Tags Instead of CSS

This is a tough one. Most cutting-edge web designers have switched from standard heading tags (<H1>, <H2>, and so on) to Cascading Style Sheet (CSS) <DIV> and <SPAN> codes. That's unfortunate, as Google looks for the old-fashioned heading tags to determine the content (and thus the PageRank) of your site. If you want to optimize your ranking in the Google index, you'll switch back to the <H1> and <H2> tags for your page headings—and make sure you use the content of those tags wisely.

Update Your Code Frequently

GoogleBot crawls the Web with some frequency, looking for pages that have changed or updated content. If your site hasn't changed in awhile, this can affect your PageRank. So you'll want to make sure you change your content on a regular basis; in particular, changing the content of your heading tags can have a big impact on how "fresh" Google thinks your site is.

Use RSS Feeds for Dynamic Content

Contrary to the previous advice, Google actually has a problem tracking some frequently updated content—in particular, the type of dynamic content generated by blogs, news sites, and the like. Put simply, GoogleBot doesn't crawl dynamic pages as well as it does static pages. (It has to do with how long it takes some dynamic pages to load; spiders only allocate a certain amount of time per page before they move on to the next site to index.)

There are two solutions to this problem. One is to use a content management system (CMS) that loads fast enough to appease the GoogleBot crawler. The second solution is to publish your dynamic content as an RSS feed. This second solution is probably the best one, as Google does a really good job digesting RSS feeds to populate its search index. When in doubt, make sure that you generate an RSS feed for all your dynamic content.

Use an OPML File

Including an OPML file on your site can also help increase your PageRank. That's because an OPML file contains in-depth hierarchical information about the way the data on your pages is organized; Google can make good use of this information in a way that benefits your site's ranking.

For Google to use your OPML file, it should describe content that exists on a page that can be reached from your site's main page. In addition, the OPML file must be a reasonably close representation of the actual page. Finally, you must provide a link from the page to the OPML file, so the GoogleBot crawler can find it.

How *Not* to Optimize Your Site's Ranking

Now that you know the things you can do to increase your site's ranking, let's take a quick look at the things you *shouldn't* do— that is, things that can actually *decrease* your site's PageRank.

> **note** OPML stands for Outline Processor Markup Language, and is an XML-based format that enables the exchange of outline-structured information between applications. Learn more about OPML at www.opml.org.

Site Design Problems to Avoid

Some web designers work against their own best interest by embracing methods that actually decrease a site's ranking in the Google index. Here are some of the most common problems you should try to avoid:

- Don't use **&id=** as a parameter in your URLs. (Google doesn't include in its index pages with this parameter—which is typically used to specify session IDs or individual page or article numbers.)

- Don't use dynamic URLs. (Google can only index static URLs, not those that are dynamically generated.)

- Don't create hidden or invisible text or links on your page. (This is when you disguise keywords or links by making them the same or similar color as the page background, using a tiny font size, or hiding them within the HTML code itself. Google pretty much ignores hidden text, although this practice can sometimes actually decrease your page's ranking.)

- Don't include irrelevant words on a page or in a page's meta tags. (Google looks for targeted keywords; a keyword that is too dissimilar to other content on a page makes Google think that your page might be a "doorway" page.)

- Don't create a "doorway" page that contains little or no original content. (A doorway page is one that is optimized for a number of terms that aren't connected to a site's primary content; Google doesn't like doorway pages.)

- Don't overuse keywords in your content or meta code. (This is known as "keyword stuffing," and Google views this as a kind of search-related spam; too high a keyword density and Google will categorize your page as a doorway page, which is not good.)

- Don't duplicate content on multiple pages within your site, or via the use of multiple domains or subdomains. (Google utilizes a type of duplicate content filter that will filter out duplicate sites from its search results; it's always possible that your main site will be filtered out, while the duplicate content remains!)

> **tip**
> To determine if your page's keyword density is too high, use the GoRank keyword density analyzer tool (www.gorank.com).

> **tip**
> To scan for duplicate copies of your page on the Web, use the CopyScape tool (www.copyscape.com).

- Don't use cloaking or sneaky redirects. (See the next section to learn more about these practices.)

- Don't link to a site that's been dropped or banned from the Google index. (Just search Google for the site in question; if it doesn't appear in the results, you don't want to link to it.)

> **tip** To simulate what GoogleBot and other spiders see when they visit your website, check out the Search Engine Crawler Simulator (www.seobench.com/search-engine-crawler-simulator/). If you don't see a lot of text when you enter your page's URL, neither will GoogleBot.

- Don't have more code than you do actual text. (That means avoiding too many code-heavy effects, such as nested tables or JavaScript effects; if your important text is buried under hundreds of lines of code, you'll be at a disadvantage compared to a well-optimized site.)

- Don't include so much content (particularly large images) that your pages take too long to load. (GoogleBot doesn't like long load times, remember; along the same lines, hosting your pages on a very slow server could also drive off the GoogleBot.)

- Don't create messy code. (Neatness counts; messy HTML can confuse GoogleBot and cause it to miss important content.)

Deliberate Practices to Avoid

The previous section talked about things you might accidentally do that can adversely affect your PageRank rating. There are also some practices that sneaky web designers deliberately do to increase their page rank; Google takes issue with these practices, and can ban you from their index if you're caught.

To that end, here are some of the more nefarious outlawed optimization practices:

- **Google bombing.** Sometimes called *Google washing* or *link bombing*, this is an attempt to increase your PageRank by having a large number of sites link to a page by using identical anchor text. For example, you might register several domains and have all them link to a single site using the same anchor text for

> **note** Any attempt to influence search engine rank via misleading methods is referred to as *search engine spamming* or *spamdexing*. The practice of creating a website solely for the purpose of achieving a high PageRank is called *Googleating* (pronounced "Google-ating," not "Google-eating").

the links. Searching for the term used in the link anchor text will return the linked-to site high in the search results. (Google bombing often occurs in blogs, where a site owner will "bomb" multiple blog postings with replies linking to the owner's site.)

> **note** Doorway pages are also known as gateway pages, landing pages, bridge pages, portal pages, zebra pages, jump pages, and entry pages.

- **Keyword stuffing.** This is when you insert hidden, random text on a page to increase the keyword density, and thus increase the apparent relevancy of a page. For example, if your page is about trains, you might insert several lines of invisible text at the bottom of the page repeating the keyword **train**, over and over. In the past, some search engines simply counted how often a keyword appeared on a page to determine relevance; today, Google employs algorithms to detect keyword stuffing. (A related technique is *meta tag stuffing*, where keywords are stuffed into HTML meta tags.)

- **Doorway pages.** This is a web page that is low in actual content, instead stuffed with repeating keywords and phrases designed to increase the page's search rank. Doorway pages typically require visitors to click a "click here to enter" link to enter the main website; in other instances, visitors to a doorway page are quickly redirected to another page.

- **Link farms.** This is a group of web pages that all link to one another. The purpose of a link farm is to increase the number of links to a given site; since PageRank is at least partially driven by the number of linked-to pages, using a link farm can make it appear as though a large number of sites are linking to a given site.

- **Mirror websites.** This is the hosting of multiple websites, all with the same content, but using different URLs. The goal is to increase the likelihood that any one (or more) of the mirror sites will appear on Google's search results pages.

- **Cloaking.** This is an attempt to mislead Google by serving up a different page to the GoogleBot crawler than will be seen by human visitors. This is sometimes used for *code swapping*, where one page is optimized to get a high ranking, and then swapped out for another page with different content.

■ **Scraper sites.** This is a site that "scrapes" results pages from Google and other search engines to create phony content for a website. A scraper site is typically full of clickable ads.

Using Search Engine Optimizers

Optimizing a website to achieve the most favorable Google ranking can be a very time-consuming process, especially if you're not technically inclined. For that reason, many website owners choose to enlist the aid of a search engine optimizer—a software tool, web-based service, or company that optimizes your web pages for you.

SEO Software

For many users, search engine optimization can be accomplished via a software-based tool that analyzes your web pages, makes appropriate suggestions or changes, and then submits your pages to Google and other major search engines. There are many different types of SEO programs available, for all levels of websites—from personal pages to commercial sites. Pricing typically runs $150 or more.

Some of the most popular of these programs include

■ Internet Business Promoter (www.axandra-web-site-promotion-software-tool.com/top-10-ranking.htm)

■ OptLink (www.optilinksoftware.com)

■ Search Engine Optimizer (www.se-optimizer.com)

■ SEO Toolkit (trellian.vendercom.com/seotoolkit/)

■ Web CEO (www.webceo.com)

■ WebPosition Gold (www.web-position-gold-pro-software.com)

SEO Services

If you run a large website, you may want to engage the services of a firm that provides custom search engine optimization. Pricing is dependent on the services rendered and the size of your site; some firms charge by the number of clicks generated.

Some SEO services you might want to check out include:

■ High Rankings (www.highrankings.com)

■ Priority Submit (www.prioritysubmit.com)

- SEO Logic (www.seologic.com)

- SiteLab (www.sitelab.com/organic_seo_optimization.html)

- Submit Express (www.submitexpress.com)

- Submitawebsite.com (www.submitawebsite.com)

- Submit-It (www.submit-it.com)

- SubmitToday.com (www.submittoday.com)

- TopRank (www.toprankresults.com)

COMMENTARY:

TOO GOOD TO BE TRUE

Beware search engine optimizers that promise you specific results, or that claim a "special relationship" with Google. There is no way to guarantee a number-one ranking in Google's search results; all anyone can do is follow the good design practices detailed in this chapter.

Search engine optimization, unfortunately, is an area that attracts a number of scam artists. And, given that the topic of search results and optimization is confusing even to experienced web designers, it's easy to be taken in by false claims and unrealistic promises.

A legitimate search engine optimizer only promises to do what can be done—that is, optimize your site to attempt to achieve a higher page rank. Legitimate firms will not and can not promise specific results, nor will they try to sell you position or placement.

How can you tell a legitimate SEO from a fraudulent one? There are some warning signs to look out for; in particular, beware any SEO that

- Guarantees ranking

- Doesn't distinguish between actual search results and sponsored ads that appear on search result pages

- Gets traffic from fake search engines or spyware

- Puts links to their other clients on doorway pages

- Offers to sell keywords in the address bar

- Owns shadow domains (these are registered domains that funnel users to another site by using deceptive redirects)

36

- Is not itself listed in the Google index, or has had domains removed from the Google index
- Operates with multiple aliases or falsified WHOIS info

No legitimate SEO will attempt to falsify results, generate phony results or traffic, or use deceptive spamdexing methods. When it comes to improving your Google search ranking, there is no magic formula; if a firm's promises sound too good to be true, they probably are.

The Bottom Line

Google makes it easy to get listed in their web index, but getting listed is just the start. Making sure that your listing appears high in Google's search results requires a lot of hard work, a bit of technical savvy, and—oh, yeah—useful and relevant content. In fact, too many webmasters get hung up on arcane search engine optimization techniques, when they should be focusing on creating sites that more visitors actually want to visit. If you spend your time creating a compelling and well-designed website, a high Google ranking will, more often than not, naturally follow.

Making Money with Google AdSense and AdWords

A s you recall from Chapter 1, "Inside Google," Google only looks to be a search technology company. While it does develop and distribute all manner of search-based services, Google makes its money—and lots of it—by selling advertising.

Google sells ads on its own search results pages, as well as throughout its entire network of sites (Gmail, Froogle, you name it). It also sells ads on other sites, both big and small. As I said, that's where the money comes from.

Now you can share in some of Google's advertising profits. Google's AdSense program lets you add Google advertising to your own website, and take a cut of all moneys generated. You can then spend your profits by buying ads on Google's site, via the AdWords program—and let those ads drive traffic to your site, where you can sell more merchandise or generate more clicks or whatever it is that you do.

Read on to learn how you can make your website more profitable with Google AdSense—and how to advertise your site on Google.

Adding Advertising to Your Website with Google AdSense

Any website, no matter how small, can generate revenue. On the Web, one of the primary ways of generating revenue is from advertising; you place an ad on your site, and whenever a visitor clicks through the ad to the advertiser's website, you collect a small fee.

The problem with this scenario, of course, is that you're not in the advertising business; you have no sales force to sell advertising on your site, nor do you have the technology required to place the ads, track click-throughs, and then collect funds due from advertisers. You might be able to generate a bit of revenue, if only you could get the ads placed and managed.

This is where Google AdSense comes in. The AdSense program places content-targeted ads on your site, sells those ads to appropriate advertisers, monitors visitor click-throughs, tracks how much money is owed you, and then pays you what you've earned. Granted, a typical personal website or blog isn't going to generate a lot of click-throughs on its ads, but even a few click-throughs a week will generate a bit of spare cash that you didn't have otherwise. All you have to do is sign up for the program, insert a few lines of code into your web page's underlying HTML code, and then sit back and let Google do the rest of the work.

Google AdSense is actually two programs in one. Google AdSense for Content is that part of the program that places targeted ads on your web pages; Google AdSense for Search lets you add Google search to your website, and thus generate even more traffic and advertising revenue.

Understanding Google AdSense for Content

The main part of the AdSense program is dubbed Google AdSense for Content. This is the part of the program that puts ads on your web pages, and then generates revenue whenever visitors click on the ad links.

AdSense ads aren't just random advertisements; Google utilizes the same technology it uses to analyze web pages for its search index to determine the content of a page and place a content-appropriate ad on that page. For example, if your web page is about teeth, Google might place an ad for dentists; if your web page is about books, it might place an ad for book clubs. And so on and so forth.

37

The nice thing about ads that actually relate to your page's content is that they're more appealing to your site's visitors. One can assume that if you have a page about teeth, your visitors are interested in all things teeth-related, and thus are likely to respond positively to ads selling teeth-related merchandise and services. At the very least, the ads Google places should be more relevant to your toothsome visitors than, say, ads for motor oil or Viagra. And the more relevant the ad, the higher the click-through rate will be—which means more profits, for both Google and you.

note Google calls this "contextual targeting," and it works—more often than not. Google's content parser can only determine which words are used on your page, not how those words are used. So if you have a page that's critical of the dentistry profession, it will still generate ads for dentists and dental hygienists.

37

Even better, AdSense ad selection is automatic; you don't have to do a thing. Google automatically crawls your page to determine its content, and places ads appropriately. Your involvement is to activate the AdSense service, insert the appropriate HTML code (just once), and then sit back and let Google do everything else. You don't even have to notify Google if you change your site's content; AdSense automatically monitors your site for changes, and places new ads accordingly.

Understanding Google AdSense for Search

Then there's AdSense for Search, to which you get access when you sign up for AdSense for Content. The Search component lets you add a Google search box to your website. This is a good thing, as it keeps users on your site longer; they don't have to leave your site to conduct a web search.

Keeping visitors on your site longer increases the chances of them clicking through any ad placed on your site. In addition, you now collect a small percentage of the ad revenue when a visitor clicks through an ad on the search results page. It's only pennies (or fractions of a penny) per click, but it can add up fast.

You can actually put two different Google search boxes on your web pages. You can utilize the standard Google web search box, of course, or you can create a box that lets visitors search within your own website. Either option is free; you can choose either or both.

As to how you get the ads onto your site, it's a simple matter of feeding some key information to Google, having Google generate the appropriate HTML code, and then you pasting that code into the code for your web page. Once the code is inserted, the AdSense ads automatically appear. And every time a visitor clicks one of the ads on your site, you receive a percentage of the fee that the advertiser paid to Google. It's that simple.

How to Profit from AdSense

If you're like me, one of the first questions you have about AdSense concerns the money—just how much money can you make from the AdSense program? There's no easy answer to that question, unfortunately.

First, you have to know that Google simply doesn't disclose how much money you can make; it doesn't tell you how much it charges its advertisers, nor what percentage of the take you receive. That's right, when you sign up for the AdSense program, you're doing so with absolutely no idea what your earnings will be. It doesn't really sound like a fully informed contractual agreement to me, but that's the way it is.

That said, we do know in general how the AdSense program works. The ads you display on your pages can be placed on either a cost-per-click (CPC) or cost-per-thousand-impressions (CPM) basis. That is, the advertiser pays either when someone clicks an ad, or when someone simply views the ad. You have no choice on whether you get CPC or CPM ads on your site.

Whenever an advertiser pays Google (for either a click or an impression), you receive a cut of that payment, in the form of a commission. How much of a commission you make depends on how much the advertiser is paying Google for that particular ad. The payment varies by advertiser and by quality of content; competition for the most popular content and keywords causes advertisers to bid up the price accordingly.

What does that mean in terms of dollars? It all depends; I've heard of payments running anywhere from 2 cents to $15 per click. You get a percentage of that. (And what percentage that is, Google doesn't disclose.)

So the amount you earn is dependent on the price that advertisers are paying, the amount of targeted traffic your site receives, and the number of visitors that view or click the ads on your site. To that last point, there are things you can do to improve your ads' visibility and click-through rate; I'll impart some tips in the "Ten Tips for Improving Your AdSense Earnings" section, later in this chapter.

note AdSense for Search ads are sold exclusively on a cost-per-click basis.

Joining the AdSense Program

Signing up for the Google AdSense program is easy enough to do. You start at the main AdSense page (www.google.com/adsense/), and then click the Click Here to Apply button. On the next page, shown in Figure 37.1, you get to fill out an application form. On this form, you need to supply the following information/make the following choices:

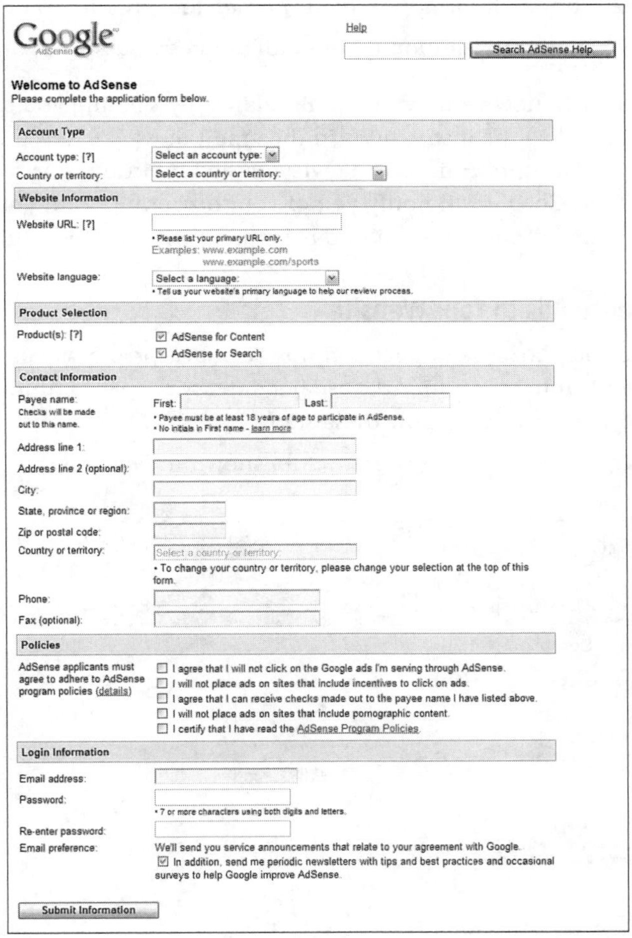

FIGURE 37.1

Applying to the Google AdSense program.

- Account type (individual or business)
- Country or territory (U.S. or otherwise)
- Website URL (Google needs this to generate the HTML ad code; enter the top-level URL of your site only)
- Website language (English or otherwise)
- Products (AdSense for Content and/or AdSense for Search)
- Contact information (your name, address, and so on)
- Login information (your email address, password, and so forth)

Google will now verify your email address by sending you a confirmation email. Follow the instructions in the email message, and then Google will review your application. The review period typically runs two to three days, and then Google will notify you of your acceptance and you'll be ready to log into your AdSense account and get started with the rest of the process.

Adding AdSense Ads to Your Website

Once your AdSense application has been accepted, you can log into your account from the main AdSense page (www.google.com/adsense/). To add an ad to your website, follow these steps:

1. Select the AdSense Setup tab, shown in Figure 37.2.

FIGURE 37.2

Getting ready to set up an AdSense ad.

2. Click the AdSense for Content link.

3. When the AdSense for Content page appears, as shown in Figure 37.3, select whether you want to display an ad unit (a block advertisement) or a link unit (a list of linked topics). If you choose to display an ad unit, you also need to pull down the list and select the type of ads you want—text only, image only, or text and image (default). Click the Continue button to continue.

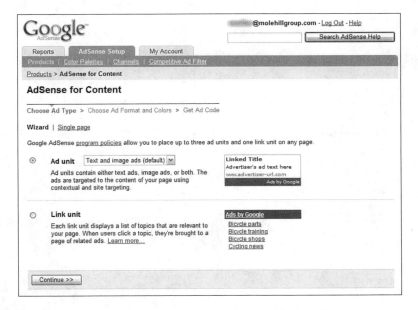

FIGURE 37.3
Choosing the type of ad to display—an ad unit or link unit.

4. When the next page appears, as shown in Figure 37.4, select the ad format and color scheme you want. Available ad formats include three sizes of horizontal ads, three sizes of vertical ads, and five sizes of square ads. Click the Continue button to continue.

5. The final page, shown in Figure 37.5, displays the code that Google generated for your ad. Copy the code from this page and then paste it into the HTML code for your web page.

note The Choose Ad Format and Colors page also includes a number of other options for your ads. You can specify a custom channel for your ads (you can create different channels for different pages on your site), tell Google if the ad will be appearing on a framed page, and select what type of content to display if no ads are available for your page.

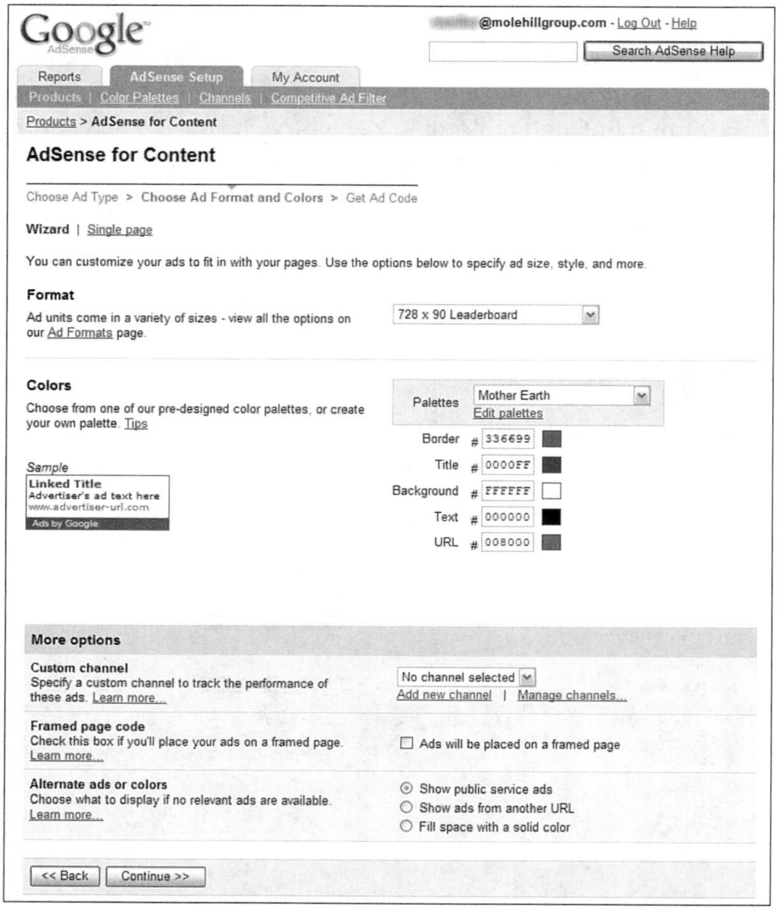

37

FIGURE 37.4

Choosing the ad format and color scheme.

If you want to include the same type of ad (format and color) on every page of your site, you'll need to copy the final code into each page's HTML. If you want to generate different types of ads on different pages, you'll need to repeat this entire process for each different ad type on your site.

tip

Google makes it even easier to add AdSense ads to your Blogger blog. Go to the Blogger Dashboard, click the Change Settings icon, select the Template tab, and then click the AdSense link. From here all you need to do is select the ad format and color you want, and Blogger does the rest—no code-pasting required on your part.

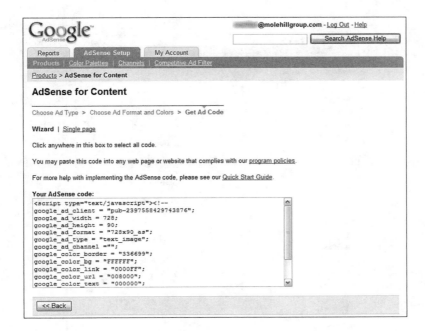

FIGURE 37.5
The final ad code—copy it into your web page's HTML.

Note that Google generates different ads for the unique content on each page of your site. You only need to create new ad code if the format of the ad (size, type, color, and so on) changes from page to page.

Adding a Google Search Box to Your Site

If you want to add a Google search box to your pages, follow these steps from the main AdSense page:

1. Select the AdSense Setup tab.

2. Click the AdSense for Search link.

3. Click the Get Started Now! button.

4. When the AdSense for Search page appears, as shown in Figure 37.6, select whether you want to include Google Web Search only or Web Search plus Site Search; if you select the latter option, you'll need to enter up to three URLs for your site.

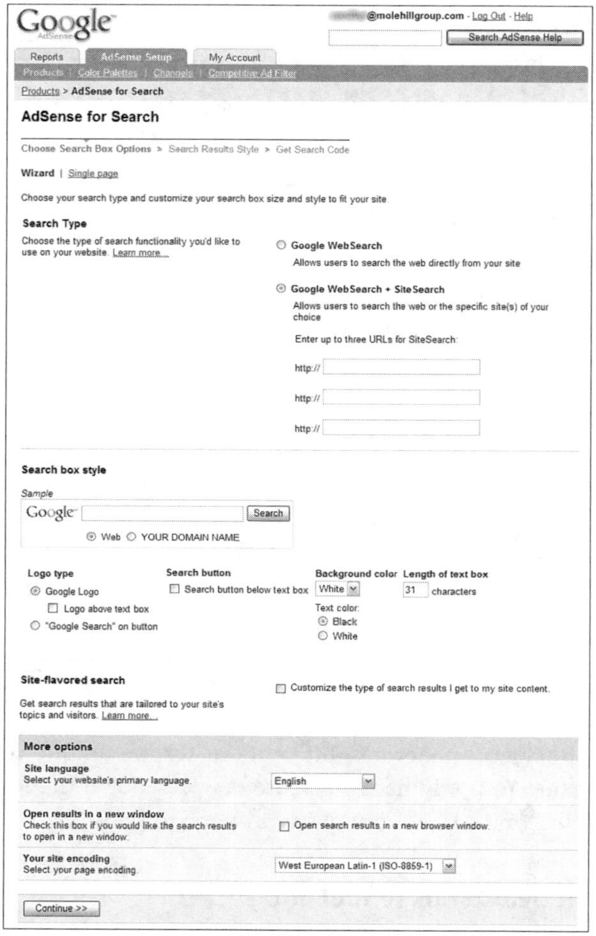

FIGURE 37.6
Adding Google search to your site.

5. In the Search Box Style section, select the logo type you want (separate Google logo or the words "Google Search" on the Search button), whether you want the Search button below the search box (it's to the side by default), the background color of the search box, and the length of the search box.

6. In the Site-Flavored Search section, check the Customize the Type of Search Results option if you want search results tailored to the contents of your site.

7. In the More Options section, select your site's language, whether you want search results opened in a new browser window, and the page encoding for your site.

8. Click the Continue button to continue.

9. When the next page appears, as shown in Figure 37.7, enter a URL for the logo you want to include on the search results page, as well as a destination URL for when the logo is clicked.

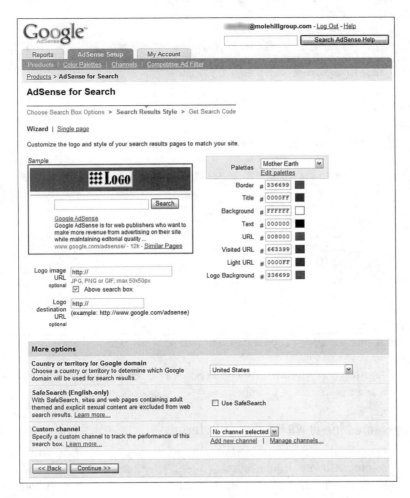

FIGURE 37.7

Configuring your Google search options.

10. Select a color scheme for the search results page, as well as any other options at the bottom of the page.

11. Click the Continue button to continue.

12. The final page, shown in Figure 37.8, displays the code that Google generated for the search box. Copy the code from this page and then paste it into the HTML code for your web page.

FIGURE 37.8

The final search box code—copy it into your web page's HTML.

Again, you'll need to copy this code into each page on your site where you want a search box to appear.

Making More Money with AdSense Referrals

Google offers yet another way to make money by referring your site's visitors to other Google products and services. For example, you can earn $2 every time a visitor installs Google Pack from a button you put on your web page, or $1 if a visitor installs Picasa. At present Google lets you refer the following items to your site's visitors:

- Google AdSense
- Google AdWords
- Google Pack
- Mozilla Firefox
- Picasa

You can add one referral button (and one button only) to each of your web pages. Just follow these steps:

1. Select the AdSense Setup tab.
2. Click the Referrals link.
3. When the Referrals page appears, as shown in Figure 37.9, check the product you want to refer, then click the Continue button.

FIGURE 37.9
Selecting a product to refer.

4. When the next page appears, select the type of referral button you want to use, and then click the Continue button (see Figure 37.10).

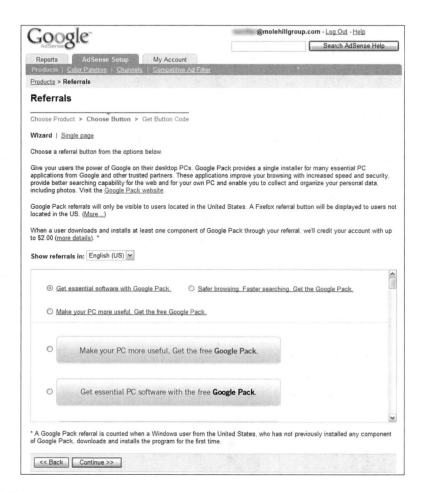

FIGURE 37.10

Choosing the type of referral button to display.

5. The final page, shown in Figure 37.11, displays the code that Google generated for the referral button. Copy the code from this page and then paste it into the HTML code for your web page.

FIGURE 37.11
The final referral button code—copy it into your web page's HTML.

Monitoring Your AdSense Performance

Once you have AdSense ads active on your website, you can monitor the performance of those ads—how many clicks you're generating, and how much that means in terms of earnings. Just go to the AdSense site and click the Reports tab. The default report, shown in Figure 37.12, details your page impressions, clicks, click through rate (CTR), the effective cost per 1,000 impressions (eCPM), and total earnings; you can show this information for today, yesterday, the last seven days, this month, last month, and all time.

Additional custom reports can also be generated from this page. For example, you can view performance by day (as shown in Figure 37.13), top queries by day (for AdSense for Content), and other similar reports.

FIGURE 37.12
Viewing your AdSense performance.

Ten Tips for Improving Your AdSense Earnings

Just putting an AdSense ad on your website doesn't guarantee that you'll make a lot of money from it. The key to generating significant earnings is to get a lot of visitors to view or click-through the ads; that means both increasing your site traffic and the visibility and appeal of the ads themselves.

To that end, here are ten things you can do to improve the earnings potential of your AdSense ads:

Tip #1: Give your ads prominent position. If you hide your AdSense ads, no one will see them—and if no one sees them (or clicks them), you won't generate any earnings. Place your ads in a prominent position, and your earnings will increase. The best position is one that a visitor can see without scrolling, which means near the top of your page, either centered above your main content or in the top left corner. It's also important to place your ads near important content; you want visitors to see the ads when they view must-read content. (A good position is directly below the end of an article or other editorial content.) Also good is placement near navigational elements, such as menus and back/up buttons.

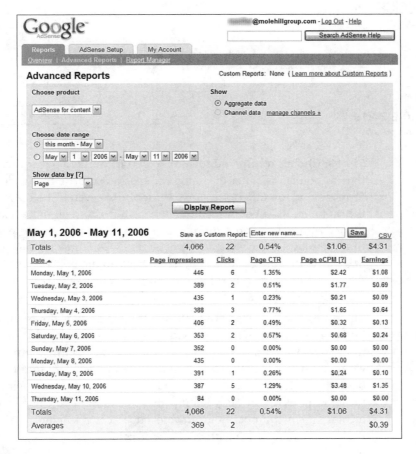

FIGURE 37.13

An earnings-by-day report.

> **Tip #2: Display text and image ads.** When you create your AdSense ad, you have a choice of a text ad (shown in Figure 37.14) or image ad (shown in Figure 37.15). You should choose the option to display both types of ads. That's because some advertisers choose the text format only and others choose the image format only; when you opt to display both types of ads, you have a wider pool of potential advertisers who can display their ads on your page.

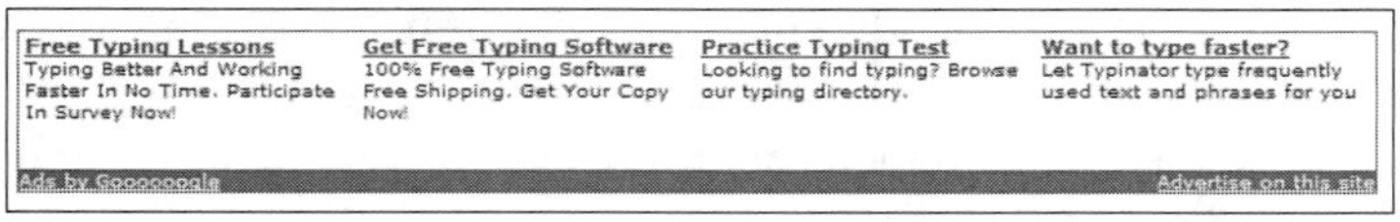

FIGURE 37.14

A text ad.

FIGURE 37.15

An image ad.

Tip #3: Choose a large ad format. When it comes to advertising effectiveness, bigger is better. It should come as no surprise that wider ad formats tend to outperform narrower formats—even if the narrower ad is also taller. It's all about readability; visitors can read more text at a glance with a wider ad than they can with a taller one. Google says that the most effective formats are the 336 × 280 large rectangle, the 300 × 250 medium rectangle, and (contrary to the previous advice) the 160 ×600 wide skyscraper; I've also had good luck with the 728 × 90 leaderboard and 468 × 60 banner.

Tip #4: Format your ads to look like they're part of the regular page. Here's a test: What type of ad performs best—one that stands out from your regular page template or one that blends in? Contrary to what you might initially think, it's the ad that blends in that performs best; visitors tend to view such an ad as part of the page content, rather than as an ad. So when it comes to choosing ad colors, go with a color scheme that is similar to your page's color scheme. Avoid colors that contrast too much with your page's colors.

Tip #5: Surround your ad with images. You can draw more attention to your AdSense ad if you surround it with images—attractive images that your visitors would want to look at, anyway. This probably means putting an image above or below (or both above and below) the AdSense module. It's even better if the images have something to do with the ad content. For example, if you have a page about notebook PCs, and you're fairly sure that AdSense will serve up an ad related to notebook PCs, then surround that ad with pictures of notebook PCs.

This approach not only draws attention to the ad, it actually makes the ad appear to be more integrated into your page's content.

Tip #6: Put multiple ads on your page. If you have a large web page (one with a lot of scrolling content), you have room to put more than one ad on the page. Google lets you put up to three ad units on each page, in addition to one link unit and one referral button. The more ads you include, the more earnings you can generate.

caution Just because you can put multiple ads on your page doesn't mean you should. If you make your page too ad-heavy, you'll turn off visitors who might think your site is nothing but ads—and not enough content.

37

Tip #7: Add link units to your pages. You're not limited to placing just ads on your page. AdSense also lets you place *link units*, like the one in Figure 37.16, anywhere on your page. A link unit is a list of topics relevant to your site's content; when a visitor clicks one of these links, he's shown a page of ads related to that topic. You'll earn more money when the visitor clicks one of these topic-related ads.

FIGURE 37.16

An AdSense link unit.

Tip #8: Add AdSense for Search to your pages. You're missing out on potential earnings if you don't add AdSense for search to your site. There's certainly no harm to be done by including a Google web search or site search box to your site; if and when visitors use the search box, you'll earn money. It's as simple as that.

Tip #9: Configure AdSense to display alternative ads. There's no guarantee that Google will always have advertisers interested in purchasing space on your site. For those times when ads aren't ready to serve, let AdSense display alternative ads instead. It's better to have *something* filling that ad space, rather than have open space on your page; plus, running a public service ad is a good thing to do.

Tip #10: Improve your site's content—and increase your traffic. Here's the most valuable tip of all. The better and more timely your site's content, the more visitors you'll attract. And the more visitors, the more click-throughs your ads will receive. To increase your ad revenue, improve your site; it's as simple as that.

COMMENTARY:

CONTENT-SENSITIVE ADVERTISING

The neat thing about both AdSense and AdWords is that they use Google's search technology to serve content-focused ads. And an ad that is somehow related to the content of your site will be more interesting to your visitors than an ad about a random product or service.

Google uses a rather complex algorithm to determine the content of a page before it serves an appropriate ad. It's not just simple keyword matching; Google's algorithm analyzes keywords on your page, word frequency, font size, and the overall link structure to figure out, as well as it can, what a page is about. Then it finds an ad that closely matches that content, and feeds that ad to the page.

For example, my personal website (www.molehillgroup.com) is all about the books I've written. On a recent day Google served up ads for "Top Book Club Selections" and "Books for Dummies"; the individual page for my book *Absolute Beginner's Guide to eBay* had ads titled "BidSlammer Snipes eBay," "eBay Sniping Since 1998," and "Bidz.com Auctions."

That doesn't mean that Google always gets it right. A recent post on my blog deriding the dental profession was accompanied by an ad for dental hygienist insurance and another for a dental school. Close, but no cigar.

That said, enhancing ad selection by matching ads to page content is a good thing—for both advertisers and consumers. As an advertiser, this technology helps to identify more likely buyers; for consumers, at least you're seeing an ad that has something to do with the page you're reading. It's much better than the kind of random mass-market advertising we're used to in most media, and it's a good application of Google's core search technology.

Advertising on Google with Google AdWords

Where do all those AdSense ads come from? The ads that Google places on your web pages come from another Google program called Google AdWords.

AdWords is where Google sells all the ads it places, both on users' sites and on its own search results pages.

If you want to place an ad (excuse me, a "sponsored link") on selected Google search results pages, you need to sign up for the AdWords program. You purchase your space by selected keyword; when you buy a keyword, your advertisement will appear on results pages for searches involving that keyword. (Figure 37.17 shows a typical AdWords ad.)

> Books by Michael Miller
> How-to books by popular author
> Computers, music, eBay, and more!
> www.molehillgroup.com

FIGURE 37.17

A typical Google AdWords ad.

That's right, Google AdSense makes use of Google's "contextual advertising" technology to place your ad alongside the most relevant content. That means your ad not only appears on matching Google search results pages, but also on third-party websites that feature similar content. This ensures that your advertising reaches qualified consumers who are interested in what you're offering; you're not blanketing the market blind, you're targeting specific consumers.

Where Google AdWords Advertises

Google claims that its AdWords program reaches more than 80% of all Internet users. That's due to the huge reach of the Google site itself, as well as the company's partners in the Google Network.

The Google Network includes all of Google's sites (Froogle, Gmail, and the rest), the hundreds of thousands of small and medium-sized sites that participate in the Google AdSense program, and a number of major websites. These third-party sites include the following:

- About.com
- AOL
- Ask.com
- AT&T WorldNet
- Business.com
- CompuServe
- EarthLink
- Food.com

- HGTV.com
- How Stuff Works
- InfoSpace
- Lycos
- Netscape Netcenter
- The New York Times
- Reed Business
- Shopping.com

Determining Your Costs—And Choosing a Payment Option

Advertising with Google AdWords isn't like a traditional advertising buy; there are no contracts and deadlines and such. You pay a one-time $5.00 activation fee, and then are charged either on a cost-per-click (CPC) or cost-per-thousand-impressions (CPM) basis. (You can choose either payment method.) You control your costs by specifying how much you're willing to pay (per click or per impression) and by setting a daily spending budget. Google will never exceed the costs you specify.

How much does AdWords cost? It's your choice. If you go with the cost-per-click method, you can choose a maximum CPC click price from $0.01 to $100. If you go with the CPM method, there is a minimum cost of $0.25 per 1,000 impressions. Your daily budget can be as low as a penny, up to whatever you're willing to pay.

If you go the CPC route, Google uses AdWords Discounter technology to match the price you pay with the price offered by competing advertisers for a given keyword. The AdWords Discounter automatically monitors your competition and lowers your CPC to one cent above what they're willing to pay.

You can opt to prepay your advertising costs, or to pay after your ads start running. With this last option, Google charges you after 30 days of when you reach your initial credit limit of $50, whichever comes first. Even small advertisers can participate, as Google accepts payment via credit card, debit card, direct debit, or bank transfer.

Creating an AdWords Ad

It's surprisingly easy to create and activate an AdWords ad. You need to determine which keywords you want to buy upfront, of course, but from there it's a simple matter of filling in the appropriate web forms.

Here's how it works:

1. From the Google AdWords home page (adwords.google.com), shown in Figure 37.18, click the Click to Begin button.

2. When the next page appears, as shown in Figure 37.19, choose either the Starter Edition or Standard Edition option. (If this is your first time listing, I recommend going the Starter Edition route—which is what I'll discuss throughout the rest of these numbered steps.)

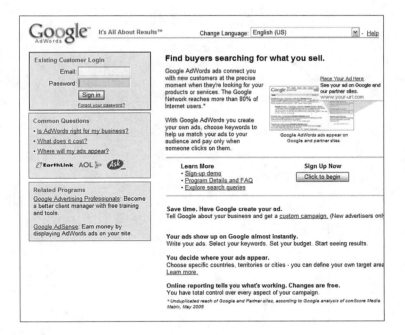

FIGURE 37.18
The home page for Google AdWords.

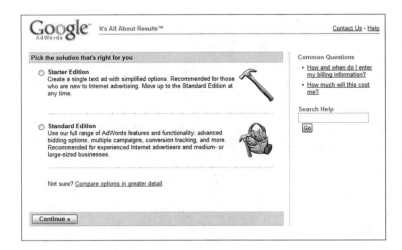

FIGURE 37.19
Choosing either the Starter Edition or Standard Edition solutions.

3. When the next page appears, as shown in Figure 37.20, enter your location and language.

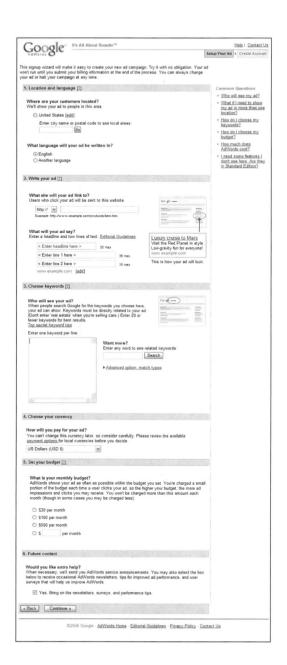

FIGURE 37.20

Entering information about your ad.

4. Scroll to the Write Your Ad section and enter the following information: the URL of the website you want the add to link to, your ad's title (25 characters max), and two lines of text (35 characters max each).

5. Scroll to the Choose Keywords section and enter up to 20 keywords that you want your ad linked to. (Enter one keyword or phrase per line; a "keyword" can actually be a multiple-word phrase.)

6. Scroll to the Choose Your Currency section and enter the currency you'll be paying in.

7. Scroll to the Set Your Budget section and select your monthly AdWords budget—$30, $100, $500, or a custom amount.

8. When you're done entering information on this page, click the Continue button.

9. Google now prompts you to sign in to your Google account, or to create a new AdWords-specific account. Follow the onscreen instructions to proceed.

10. Google will now email you with instructions on how to set up billing information for your account. Follow tthe instructions in this email to activate your account and launch your ads.

If you chose a Standard Edition campaign, you have a few more options to consider. In contrast to the Starter Edition, the Standard Edition lets you

- Create multiple ads (instead of the Starter Edition's single ad)
- Choose from a variety of pricing options, including keyword-specific bidding, content bidding, ad position preference, and so on
- Control how much you're willing to pay per day, as well as the maximum you're willing to pay when someone clicks your ad (the cost-per-click)
- Target specific websites for ad placement
- Utilize a variety of advanced planning and reporting tools, including conversion tracking, the AdWords traffic estimator, and a variety of sophisticated statistics and reports

As I said earlier, the Starter Edition is probably the best way to get started. Once you get a few ad campaigns undert your belt, then you can graduate to the advanced options available with the Standard Edition.

Monitoring Your Ads' Performance

Once your ad campaign is started, you can monitor performance from the main AdWords page. Once you sign intot this page, select the My Ad Campaign tab, as shown in Figure 37.21. You can view the performance of each keyword you selected, in terms of impressions, clicks, and total cost to-date.

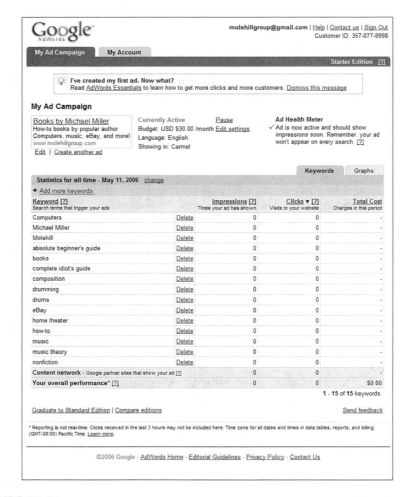

FIGURE 37.21

Viewing the performance of your ad campaign.

This page also lets you change the parameters of your campaign. You can add more keywords (by clicking the Add More Keywords link) or delete existing keywords (by clicking the Delete link next to an individual keyword). You can also upgrade to the Standard Edition option at any time by clicking the Graduate to Standard Edition link.

The Bottom Line

If you run a website, there is no reason not to sign up for the Google AdSense program. Instead of being a drain on your finances, AdSense lets any website generate some amount of revenue. Even if it's just a few dollars per month, it might be enough to let your site pay for itself.

And if you want to drive more traffic to your site (to help generate more AdSense earnings), you can tap into the power of Google search via the AdWords program. AdWords lets any website—no matter how small—advertise on Google's search results pages. It's a sure-fire way to get your site noticed by Google's millions of users.

Use AdSense to generate revenue for your site, and AdWords to generate traffic. The first doesn't cost you anything, and the second very well could pay for itself in terms of increased traffic and ad revenues. If you're serious about your website, these are two programs you must participate in.

37

Using Google Within Your Organization

Google isn't just for searching the Web. Information technology (IT) professionals should be pleased to discover that Google distributes several products designed for finding information across corporate networks. Plus, Google makes versions of its Google Toolbar and Google Desktop applications specifically for use in corporate environments.

So if you're looking for a way to incorporate first-class search capabilities across your enterprise network, Google has something for you.

Searching the Corporate Network with the Google Toolbar for Enterprise

We'll start by taking a quick look at Google Toolbar for Enterprise. This is pretty much the same Google Toolbar available for standalone PCs, but with several additional features designed specifically for network administration and use.

The enterprise-specific features include

- A Windows-based Installer package that lets administrators install and configure the Toolbar for employees across a corporate network

> **note** Learn more about the Google Toolbar in Chapter 31, "Using the Google Toolbar."

- Standards-based administration lets administrators manage all user preferences using Microsoft Group Policy settings
- Integration with the Google Search Appliance and Google Mini lets users search across a corporate network
- Ability to create customized search buttons to let users directly search specific sites (including the company's public website or subscription research sites)
- Whitelist so administrators can designate which sites allow pop-up windows

Like the regular Google Toolbar, the Google Toolbar for Enterprise can be downloaded for free. See www.google.com/tools/toolbar/T4/enterprise/ for more information.

Searching the Corporate Network with Google Desktop for Enterprise

Google's other desktop search application, Google Desktop, is also available in a corporate version. Google Desktop for Enterprise offers similar features to the standard Google Desktop program, supplemented with the following enterprise-specific features:

- A Windows-based Installer package that lets administrators install and configure the program for employees across a corporate network
- Standards-based administration lets administrators manage all user preferences using Microsoft Group Policy settings
- Integration with the Google Search Appliance and Google Mini lets users search across a corporate network
- Ability to find email messages from Microsoft Outlook Express, Netscape Mail, Mozilla Mail, Mozilla Thunderbird, Gmail, and IBM Lotus Notes

> **note** Learn more about Google Desktop in Chapter 32, "Using Google Desktop."

- Support for shared workstation environments, so users can have secure searches across just the files they have access to on shared workstations

- Ability to encrypt all user data and search index files using Encrypted File System (EFS)

Like the consumer version of Google Desktop, Google Desktop for Enterprise can be downloaded for free. See desktop.google.com/enterprise/ for more information.

Searching Small Business Data with the Google Mini

When you want to activate Google search capability across your entire organization, Google has a one-stop solution for you. The Google Mini is an integrated hardware and software solution that plugs into your corporate network and lets any network user search all the content you have available.

As you can see in Figure 38.1, the Google Mini is based on a plug-and-play hardware unit that connects via Ethernet to your corporate network. Installation and setup should take less than an hour; just plug it in, point it at the content on your network, and you're ready to go.

FIGURE 38.1
The Google Mini.

Employees access the Google Mini—and your corporate information—via either a customized search box on your website, the Google Toolbar for Enterprise, or Google Desktop for Enterprise. It can search across multiple file servers, and recognizes more than 220 different file formats, including all the popular corporate file formats—.DOC, .XLS, .PPT, .PDF, and the like.

The nice thing about using the Google Mini is that it lets employees search your corporate information using the familiar Google search interface. If they're used to using Google on the Web (which they probably are), they'll have no problem finding corporate information on a Mini-enabled network.

You can also use the Mini to power search across your company's public website; it can serve search results with different interfaces for different departments or websites.

The Google Mini comes in multiple versions. The most affordable version costs $1,995 and searches up to 50,000 documents. Additional versions search 100,000, 200,000, or 300,000 documents for $2,995, $5,995, and $8,995, respectively. You can learn more—and purchase the Mini online—at www.google.com/enterprise/mini/.

Adding Enterprise-wide Search with the Google Search Appliance

The Google Mini can handle searches for up to 300,000 documents. If your corporate storehouse is bigger than that, it's time to turn to the Google Search Appliance.

The basic Google Search Appliance, shown in Figure 38.2, can search up to 500,000 corporate documents; larger versions can search literally tens of millions of documents. Like the Google Mini, the Google Search Appliance is an integrated hardware and software solution; install the hardware, and then let the built-in software crawl your network's content (including all connected servers, databases, and content management systems) to create a master index of documents. The master index is then searchable by any employee, using either the Google Toolbar for Enterprise or Google Desktop for Enterprise; security features ensure that users can access only that information they have permission to view.

FIGURE 38.2

The Google Search Appliance (GB-1001).

The base version of the GB-1001 Google Search Appliance costs $30,000 and can search up to 500,000 documents; an upgraded version that can search 1,000,000 documents costs $50,000. Google also offers the larger GB-5005, which can search up to 5 million documents, and the GB-8008, which can search tens of millions of documents. Prices on the larger models are available by quote only. Learn more at www.google.com/enterprise/gsa/.

note What kinds of companies use Google Earth Enterprise? The list includes architecture and engineering firms, commercial real estate developers, real estate brokers, insurance companies, government agencies, and other firms that deal with massive amounts of geocentric information.

Creating Geo Data with Google Earth Enterprise

note Learn more about Google Earth in Chapter 20, "Using Google Earth."

38

If your company deals in geographic data, consider investing in Google Earth Enterprise. This corporate application lets you combine enterprise data with ASP-delivered Google Earth data—including satellite imagery and GIS data. You can then publish this data throughout your organization or to the public.

Google Earth Enterprise is comprised of three distinct elements:

- Google Earth Fusion, which integrates your corporate data, including raster images, GIS, terrain, and point data
- Google Earth Server, which streams this data to the Google Earth Enterprise Client
- Google Earth Enterprise Client, which you use to view and print your geo data

Google offers two versions of Google Earth Enterprise—Google Earth Enterprise Pro (a full enterprise solution) and Google Earth Enterprise LT (a smaller-scale version with local hosting of customized Google Earth basemaps). Learn more (and arrange for a sales call) at earth.google.com/earth_enterprise.html.

Creating 3D Models with Google SketchUp

If your company is using Google Earth for Enterprise (or, for that matter, the personal version of Google Earth), you may be interested in one of Google's more recent software acquisitions. Google SketchUp is a 3D modeling program that lets designers and artchitects create 3D models of buildings, vehicles, and the like, and then place them within a Google Earth map. You can use Google SketchUp to plan home additions, housing developments, building projects, and the like. (Figure 38.3 shows a housing development rendered in 3D with SketchUp.)

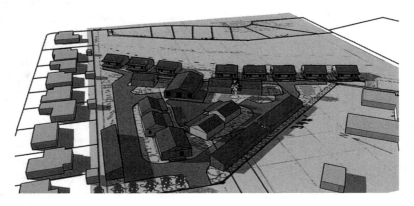

FIGURE 38.3

A Google SketchUp model of a housing development.

Google offers two versions of Google SketchUp. The basic version is free for personal use; SketchUp Pro is a more powerful tool for design professionals and costs $495. Both versions include thousands of pre-drawn components, let you create full 3D models with real-time shadow casting, and let you apply color and texture directly to your models. The Pro version lets you print and export raster images at higher-than-screen resolution, create animations and walkthroughs, and utilize all the expected 3D file formats (DWG, DXF, 3DS, OBJ, XSI, VRML, and FBX). Learn more at sketchup.google.com.

The Bottom Line

Google is reaching out to the enterprise with a variety of products that expand on its basic search tools and applications. Whether you want to implement Google search across your corporate network or utilize Google Earth to model your latest building designs, Google has a product for you. The nice thing about these professional applications is that they all look and act just like their consumer counterparts, which makes for a shorter learning curve and more productive employees. But then, would you expect less from Google, the reigning king of simplicity?

Google for Developers

39 Adding Google to Your Website

40 Creating Custom Search Applications

41 Creating Google Map Mashups

Adding Google to Your Website

Wouldn't it be great to have a Google search box on your own website—so that your visitors can either search the Web from your site, or use Google search technology to search your site itself? Back in Chapter 37, "Making Money with Google AdSense and AdWords," you learned how to add a Google search box via the AdSense for Search program. But you don't have to sign up for the AdSense program to add Google search to your site; Google offers several other ways to add a Google search box—and they're all free.

Adding Google Free WebSearch

Lots of webmasters add Google search boxes to their sites, because Google makes it easy to do so. Google's main program is called Google Free, and it comes in several different flavors—basic web search, web search with SafeSearch filtering, and web search with site search added.

The first of these options is Google Free WebSearch. It's easy to add; all you have to do is insert the following HTML code into your web page's code, where you want the search box to appear.

Here's the code:

```
<!— Search Google —>
<center>
<FORM method=GET action="http://www.google.com/search">
<input type=hidden name=ie value=UTF-8>
<input type=hidden name=oe value=UTF-8>
<TABLE bgcolor="#FFFFFF"><tr><td>
<A HREF="http://www.google.com/">
<IMG SRC="http://www.google.com/logos/Logo_40wht.gif"
border="0" ALT="Google" align="absmiddle"></A>
<INPUT TYPE=text name=q size=25 maxlength=255 value="">
<INPUT type=submit name=btnG VALUE="Google Search">
</td></tr></TABLE>
</FORM>
</center>
<!— Search Google —>
```

The result is a standard Google search box, like the one shown in Figure 39.1.

FIGURE 39.1
Adding a Google search box to your web page.

Adding Google Free SafeSearch

If you want your visitors to be protected against unwanted adult content when they search Google from your site, you can add a Google search box with the SafeSearch content filter enabled. To add a Google Free SafeSearch box to your site, use the following HTML code:

```
<!— Google SafeSearch  —>
<center>
<FORM method=GET action="http://www.google.com/search">
<input type=hidden name=ie value=UTF-8>
<input type=hidden name=oe value=UTF-8>
```

```
<TABLE bgcolor="#FFFFFF"><tr><td>
<A HREF="http://www.google.com/search?safe=vss">
<IMG SRC="http://www.google.com/logos/Google_Safe.gif"
 border="0" ALT="Google" width="115" height="45" align="absmid-
dle"></A>
<INPUT TYPE=text name=q size=25 maxlength=255 value="">
<INPUT type=hidden name=safe value=strict>
<INPUT type=submit name=sa value="Google Search">
</td></tr></TABLE>
</FORM>
</center>
<!— Google SafeSearch —>
```

This adds the search box shown in Figure 39.2 to your page, where you inserted the code. (Notice the "SafeSearch" logo is added to the Google logo.)

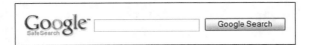

FIGURE 39.2
Adding a Google search box with SafeSearch to your web page.

Adding Google Free WebSearch with SiteSearch

Google also lets you search your own website using Google's search technology. This option is dubbed Google Free WebSearch with SiteSearch; just insert the following HTML code:

```
<!— SiteSearch Google —>
<FORM method=GET action="http://www.google.com/search">
<input type=hidden name=ie value=UTF-8>
<input type=hidden name=oe value=UTF-8>
<TABLE bgcolor="#FFFFFF"><tr><td>
<A HREF="http://www.google.com/">
<IMG SRC="http://www.google.com/logos/Logo_40wht.gif"
border="0" ALT="Google"></A>
</td>
<td>
<INPUT TYPE=text name=q size=31 maxlength=255 value="">
<INPUT type=submit name=btnG VALUE="Google Search">
```

```
<font size=-1>
<input type=hidden name=domains value="YOURDOMAIN"><br><input
type=radio name=sitesearch value=""> WWW <input type=radio
name=sitesearch value="YOURDOMAIN" checked> YOURDOMAIN <br>
</font>
</td></tr></TABLE>
</FORM>
<!— SiteSearch Google —>
```

For this option, you need to replace all instances of *YOURDOMAIN* with your own domain name (either with or without the leading www). As you can see in Figure 39.3, this inserts a search box with the option of searching the web ("WWW") or your own website.

FIGURE 39.3

Adding a Google search box with both web and site search to your web page.

Adding Customizable Google Free WebSearch

Here's another cool option for adding search to your site. With customizable Google Free WebSearch, you not only add a web search or web/site search box to your page, you also get to customize how the search results page will look. You can change the background color of the page, the color of the text, even add your own logo (as shown in Figure 39.4). And it's all a matter of filling in some simple web forms.

Just follow these steps:

1. Go to www.google.com/services/free.html and click the Customize Google for Your Site button.

2. When the next page appears, as shown in Figure 39.5, select whether you want WebSearch or WebSearch plus SiteSearch. If you choose WebSearch plus SiteSearch, enter the domain name of your site. Then click the Continue button.

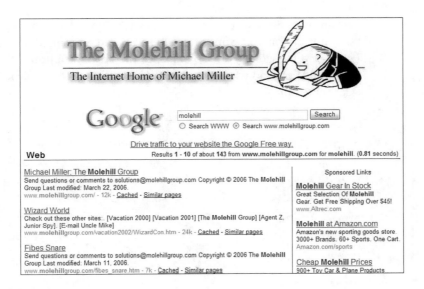

FIGURE 39.4

A Google search results page customized with a site's logo.

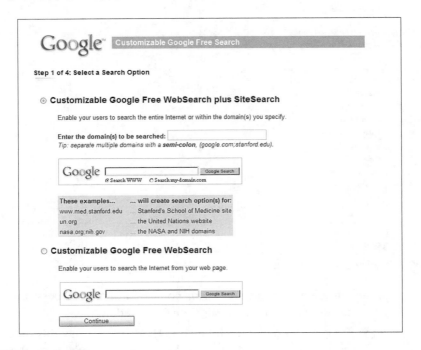

FIGURE 39.5

Choosing which type of custom search you want.

3. When the next page appears, as shown in Figure 39.6, enter any and all information you want—the URL, size, and alignment of your logo, page and text colors, and so on. Click the Preview button to see how this will look, and when you're satisfied with the results, click the Continue button.

FIGURE 39.6

Customizing Google Free WebSearch.

4. On the next page, enter your name, email address password, and other information, and then click the Continue button.

5. Google now generates a batch of HTML code. Copy this code, and then paste it into the code for your web page where you want the search box to appear.

Adding Site-Flavored Google Search

Finally, Google has a new way to add search to your website, in the form of Site-Flavored Google Search. This customizes the search results based on your site's content. All you have to do is fill out a profile of your site, and then Google generates the appropriate HTML code. When visitors search from your site using this new search box, they'll have the option to fine-tune the results based on the content profile you created.

To add Site-Flavored Google Search to your web page, follow these steps:

1. Go to www.google.com/services/siteflavored.html and click the Start Here to Customize Google for Your Site link.

2. When the next page appears, as shown in Figure 39.7, you can enter your website URL and click the Get Profile button to have Google automatically try to divine a profile for your site. (This doesn't always work, however.)

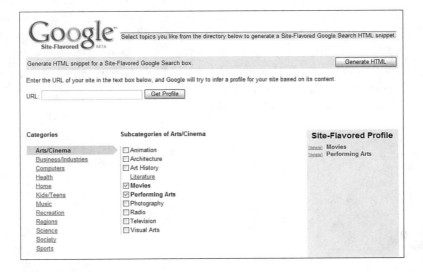

FIGURE 39.7
Creating a site-flavored Google search.

3. Instead, you may need to click through the categories listed (and one or more of the resulting subcategories) to create your profile.

4. When you're done creating your profile, click the Generate HTML button.

5. Google now generates a batch of HTML code. Copy this code, and then paste it into the code for your web page where you want the search box to appear.

When you insert this code, it creates a custom search box like the one shown in Figure 39.8. When a visitor uses this box to conduct a search, it generates a list of results "flavored" by the content selected in your site profile. The most relevant sites, based on the content profile, are listed at the top of the search results.

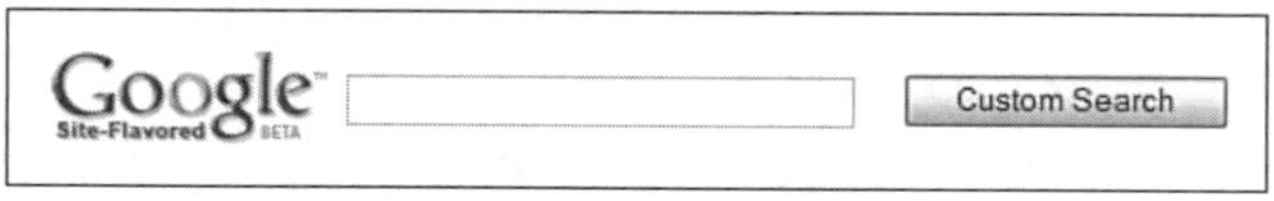

FIGURE 39.8
The Site-Flavored Google Search box.

The Bottom Line

I like the ability to add various types of Google searches to my website. Of all these methods, my favorite is the customized WebSearch plus SiteSearch; being able to add my logo to the search results page helps remind visitors of which site they were visiting when they conducted their search.

Remember, you can incorporate any of these Google searches into your own personal web pages. And they're all free; all you have to do is copy the code into your page's underlying HTML.

Creating Custom Search Applications

You can use Google to search the Web. You can use Google to search for data stored on your own computer. You can use Google to search for data stored on a corporate network. But did you know you can use Google within custom-developed software applications?

That's right. If you're a software developer, you can incorporate Google search into the programs you write. That's because Google makes its Application Programming Interface (API) available for public use. Developers can use the Google API when they're writing their own program code, and thus tie their programs into the Google search index.

And that's not all. Google publishes APIs for several of its other services, so that you can develop your own Google Desktop sidebar gadgets, or publish your own custom Google maps, or display your own custom interface to create Google Calendar events on your website.

Google's support of third-party developers is a very good thing, and it makes Google's services that much more usable. Read on to learn more.

Developing Your Own Google-Based Applications

If you're a software developer or web designer, here's a URL you need to know: code.google.com. This is the address of Google Code, the home base for all of Google's developer services.

note   API stands for Application Program Interface, a set of library-based routines that extend a programming language's functionality. SDK stands for Software Development Kit, a set of tools and utilities that enable programmers to create applications to run on a particular platform or work with an API. KML stands for Keyhole Markup Language, which is a programming language used for developing and storing geographic data.

As you can see in Figure 40.1, the Google Code home page links to all the APIs and programming tools that Google makes available for its various services. And just what tools are available? Table 40.1 provides the details.

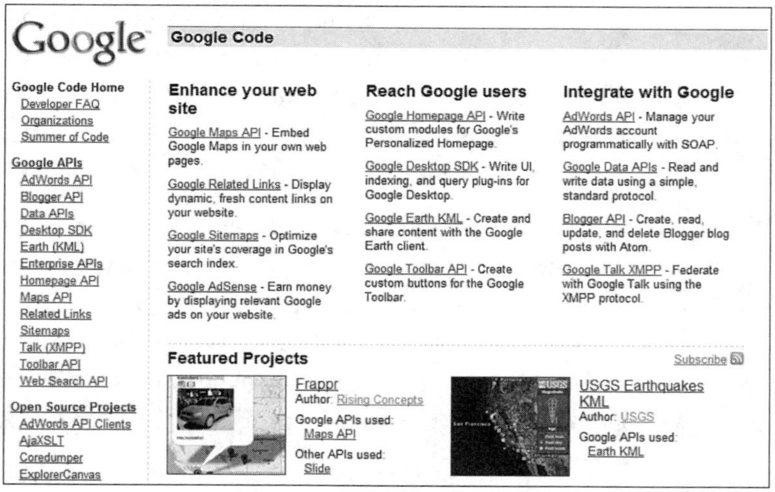

FIGURE 40.1
Google Code—the home page for third-party Google developers.

Table 40.1   Google Developer Tools

Tool	URL	Description
AdWords API	www.google.com/apis/adwords	Develop applications that interact directly with the AdWords server to manage large AdWords accounts and campaigns
Blogger Atom API	code.blogspot.com/archives/atom-docs.html	Retrieve, create, edit, and delete Blogger blog posts
Google Calendar Data API	code.google.com/apis/gdata/calendar.html	View and update Google Calendar events from third-party applications and web pages
Google Data APIs	code.google.com/apis/gdata/index.html	Read and write data on the Web using XML-based syndication tools
Google Desktop SDK	desktop.google.com/developer.html	Integrate Google Desktop into third-party applications, add new file formats for Google Desktop to index, and create new Sidebar gadgets
Google Earth KML	earth.google.com/kml/kml_intro.html	Model and store points, lines, images, and other geographic features in Google Earth
Google Gadgets API	www.google.com/apis/homepage	Create gadgets for the Google personalized home page
Google Maps API	www.google.com/apis/maps	Embed Google Maps in your own web pages
Google Search Appliance APIs	code.google.com/gsa_apis/xml_reference.html	Develop custom connectors to feed source data into the Google Search Appliance
Google Toolbar API	www.google.com/tools/toolbar/buttons/apis	Create custom buttons for the Google Toolbar
Google Webs API	www.google.com/apis	Query the Google search index from third-party applications

If you're developing any application that involves web search or other services that Google offers, you should make Google Code your starting point. From here you can download all the APIs, tools, and documentation you need to incorporate Google technology into the applications you develop.

Programming with the Google Webs API

Of all the APIs and development tools that Google makes available, the most popular

> **note** The hottest type of Google application development today involves the creation of Google map mashups using the Google Maps API. Learn more in Chapter 41, "Creating Google Map Mashups."

40

is the Google Webs API. This API lets you incorporate Google web search into the web pages and applications you develop, so your users can search all or part of the Web directly from the application.

The Google Webs API is a web service that uses SOAP and WSDL standards. You can use the Google Webs API to develop applications in whatever programming environment you prefer—Java (Apache SOAP and Apache Axis), Perl (SOAP::Lite), Ruby (SOAP4R), or C# in Microsoft Visual Studio .NET. The programs you develop use SOAP to connect remotely to the Google Webs API service, and thus return search results from the Google web index.

> **note** SOAP stands for Simple Object Access Protocol, and is an XML-based mechanism for exchanging information between different operating environments. WSDL stands for Web Services Description Language, and is used to describe how to interface with XML-based services.

Types of Google-Based Applications

By using the Google Webs API, you can add all sorts of functionality to your applications. You can enable your program to automatically issue search requests to Google's web index (or have users search manually), and then receive results as structured data in whatever format you specify. You can have your applications access historical data in the Google cache. You can even use the Google Webs API as a spell checker. (As you recall, Google has built-in spell-checking features.) Bottom line, the Google Webs APIs support the exact same search syntax as does the standard Google web search, so anything you can do from the Google website, you can do from within your applications.

What types of applications can you write using the Google Webs API? Here are a few ideas from the folks at Google:

- **Market research.** A program that regularly monitors the Web to display new information about a given subject

- **Data analysis.** A program that lets users analyze real-time information retrieved from the web, such as stock market quotes, news headlines, and the like

- **Trend analysis.** A program that retrieves and analyzes the amount of information available on a subject over time

- **Search interface.** A program that lets the user search for information using a non-HTML interface

■ **Spell checking.** A program that incorporates Google's spell-checking function

That's just the tip of the iceberg, of course. Recognizing just how much information Google puts at your fingertips, how you incorporate that information into your applications (using the Google Webs API) is up to you.

note At present, the Google Webs API can only be used to query the main Google web page index. It cannot be used to query Google Image Search, Google Groups, or the Google Directory.

Using the Google Webs API

To develop with the Google Webs API, you go through the following process:

1. Go to the Google Web APIs page (www.google.com/apis) and download the developer's kit. (The developer's kit includes all the documentation and example code you need to start programming with the Google Webs API.)

2. Click the link to create a Google Account (or sign into an existing account) and create a license key. The license key is then emailed to you.

3. Write your program code, incorporating hooks into the Google Webs API. Your code must also include your license key with each query you submit to the Google Webs API service.

The Google Webs API developer's kit includes a WSDL file describing the Google Web APIs service, a custom Java client library, documentation on how to use the service with Microsoft .NET or Perl, and example SOAP messages. This kit is downloadable for free, and Google doesn't charge any fees to obtain a license key and use the Google Webs API for noncommercial use. Your license key entitles your application to make 1,000 automated Google search queries per day. If you're developing an application for commercial resale, you must first obtain written consent from Google.

tip Get help and advice from other developers and the occasional Google employee at the google.public. web-apis Google Group (groups. google.com/group/google. public.web-apis). Some other good sources of information about using the Google Webs API are the books *Mining Google Web Services: Building Applications with the Google API*, by John Paul Mueller (Sybex, 2004), and *Google Hacks*, by Tara Calishain and Rael Dornfest (O'Reilly, 2005).

40

COMMENTARY:

WEB 2.0

By making its APIs public, Google is facilitating a ton of third-party development. All of this development essentially customizes existing Google information and services for specific purposes—by filtering search results, hiding Google access behind a different interface, or overlaying proprietary information on top of a Google map. In essence, an application built using a Google API isn't a freestanding application; it's a cooperative venture with Google, merging Google's public data with the application's interface or operation.

These Google-enabled applications are as good an example as any of what some people are calling Web 2.0. What is Web 2.0? Here's how tech pundit (and fellow publisher) Tim O'Reilly defined it:

"Web 2.0 is the network as platform, spanning all connected devices; Web 2.0 applications are those that make the most of the intrinsic advantages of that platform: delivering software as a continually-updated service that gets better the more people use it, consuming and remixing data from multiple sources, including individual users, while providing their own data and services in a form that allows remixing by others, creating network effects through an 'architecture of participation,' and going beyond the page metaphor of Web 1.0 to deliver rich user experiences."

That's a lot of technospeak, but I think Tim's onto something. In essence, Web 2.0 is a more collaborative web, where applications are virtual (not solely housed on a single computer or website); where data is freely shared between applications, users, and websites; and where operating systems are irrelevant and the Web itself becomes the platform.

In this aspect, Google-based applications and mashups demonstrate a first step toward Web 2.0. The applications built around the Google APIs aren't solely housed on a single computer or website; they require access to and coordination with Google's servers and databases. The data served by one of these applications isn't solely the developer's data; it's either mostly or partly Google's data, as shaped for the developer's needs. And these applications aren't Windows- or Mac-based apps; they're OS-independent, truly using the Web (or, more accurately, the Google API) as the platform.

When you encounter a Google map mashup or a custom Google search application, you're experiencing a little bit of the Web 2.0 future. In this Web 2.0 world, application developers depend on Google (and other companies that offer open access to their APIs and data) to complete their programs; users get as much value from Google's data as they do from the application itself. It's a cooperative effort, one in which the end user benefits tremendously.

The Bottom Line

Obviously, this chapter isn't the place to go into the intricacies of writing Perl code to hook into the Google Webs API service. Suffice to say that if you're an application developer, Google makes it fairly easy to add Google search and other services into your code. In fact, you can use the Google Webs API to shape specific queries and the results they generate, to the point that your users don't even have to know that you're tapping into Google's huge web index. It's a great way to add increased functionality to your applications, and it's all available to you for free.

40

Creating Google Map Mashups

In the previous chapter we discussed how developers can incorporate Google search into their applications using the Google Webs API. Search isn't the only Google feature you can incorporate, however; Google also lets you use the company's massive Google Maps database to add custom maps to your applications and web pages.

When you create a custom Google map, you're creating what is called a map *mashup*. That's because you're mashing together a Google map with your own personal data. That data might simply be a set of coordinates so that you map a specific location, or it might be a collection of locations that you want to display on a map.

The nice thing about creating custom Google maps is that you don't have to use a fancy programming language like Perl or C#. To create a custom Google map, all you need is a basic knowledge of HTML and JavaScript; it's not that hard, as you'll soon learn.

Creating Mashups—The Easy Way

There are two ways to create a Google map mashup based on your own custom data—the hard way and the easy way. The hard way involves writing your own HTML code and tying into the Google Maps API. The easy way involves entering the appropriate data into a web-based form. We'll look at the easy way, first.

If all you want to do is create a Google map of a specific location, to display on your website, using a Google map-builder website is the way to go. There are a number of these sites on the Web, including

■ CommunityWalk (www.communitywalk.com), shown in Figure 41.1

■ Google Map Maker (donkeymagic.co.uk/googlemap/)

■ Map Builder (www.mapbuilder.net)

■ myGmaps (www.mygmaps.com)

■ Strike Up Your Google Maps (www.martwebstudio.net/strike.up.your. gmaps/index.php)

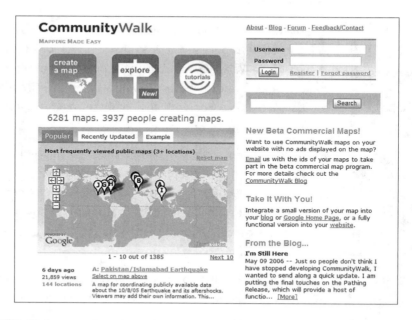

FIGURE 41.1

The CommunityWalk map building site.

These sites all work pretty much the same way. Enter your coordinates into the form, provide any additional information that may be necessary, and then click a button. The site then generates the HTML code required to create the map; copy and paste this code into your web page's HTML, and the map will now appear on your web page. It's that simple.

> **note** Discover a wealth of third-party map mashups in Chapter 19, "Using Google Map Mashups."

Programming with the Google Maps API

A better way to get precisely the map you want is to use the Google Maps API. This API lets you embed custom Google Maps in your own web pages. You need to know a little HTML and JavaScript, but it's not that hard to create a basic map.

To create more advanced map mashups, you just add more sophisticated code. For example, the Google maps API lets you add custom markers, info windows, and overlays to your maps. Each element is added via a distinct line of code, which then uses the Google Maps API to retrieve the appropriate map from Google. Like all of Google's other development tools, the Google Maps API is free for your noncommercial use.

Using the Google Maps API

To use the Google Maps API, you have to obtain a license key. This key can be used only on the web domain you specify—so if you plan on using a practice board or another website for development, you'll want to get a key for that site in addition to your main site.

You obtain your Google Maps API key at www.google.com/apis/maps. This is also where you download the API's documentation, access online help files, and link to the official Google Maps API Blog. (You can also access the blog directly at googlemapsapi.blogspot.com.)

To obtain a license key, you'll need to have a Google Account, and then enter the domain of your website. Google will then email you the key, which you'll include in all your Google Maps code.

Creating a Basic Map

To create a static map focused on a specific location, you need to create three blocks of JavaScript code. One block goes in the <HEAD> section of your document, the next augments the <BODY> tag, and the final block goes into the body of your document where you want the map to appear.

Let's start with the opening code. Insert the following lines of code between the **<HEAD>** and **</HEAD>** lines of your document:

```
<script
src="http://maps.google.com/maps?file=api&amp;v=2&amp;key=APIKEY"
type="text/javascript">
</script>
<script type="text/javascript">
//<![CDATA[

function load() {
if (GBrowserIsCompatible()) {
var map = new GMap2(document.getElementById("map"));
map.setCenter(new GLatLng(LATITUDE, LONGITUDE), ZOOM);
}
}

//]]>
</script>
```

In this code, replace *APIKEY* with the license key Google supplied to you. I stated this in the previous section, but it bears repeating: The key is specific to the web domain you specified when you applied for the key; if you use this code on another website, you'll need to edit the code to use a separate license key for that site.

You'll also need to replace *LATITUDE* and *LONGITUDE* with the precise latitude and longitude coordinates of the location you want to map. You can obtain these coordinates by generating a map on the Google Maps site, clicking the Link to This Page link, and then copying the coordinates from the resulting URL. (Latitude and longitude are listed in the URL following the **&ll** parameter.) For example, I generated a map for St. Catherine College in St. Paul, Minnesota; the latitude and longitude coordinates for this location are **44.928835, -93.185177**.

In addition, you want to replace *ZOOM* with a number from 0 to 17. The smaller the number the wider the view; to zoom into street level, try a zoom of 13 or larger.

Next, you need to edit the **<BODY>** tag to include the following parameters:

```
<BODY onload="load()" onunload="GUnload()">
```

41

Finally, insert the following line of code into the body of your document, where you want the map to display:

```
<div id="map" style="width: 500px; height: 300px"></div>
```

You can play around with this last line of code a bit. For example, you can make the map larger or smaller by using different width and height parameters, or center the map on the page by surrounding it with <CENTER> and </CENTER> tags. It's your choice in terms of formatting.

The resulting map, with a zoom level of 13, is shown in Figure 41.2. The same map, with the zoom level set to 15, is shown in Figure 41.3.

FIGURE 41.2

A map created with a zoom level of 13.

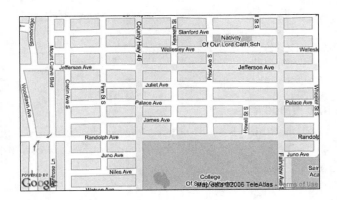

FIGURE 41.3

The same map with a zoom level of 15.

41

Adding Map Controls

You may have noticed that the map you created is just a map—it doesn't include any controls that let users zoom around or into or out of the default location. That's fine if you want a static map (of your company's headquarters, let's say), but if you want to make the map interactive, you have to add the appropriate map controls. You do this by adding the following lines of code between the **var map** and **map.setCenter** lines in the <HEAD> of your document:

```
map.addControl(new GSmallMapControl());
map.addControl(new GMapTypeControl());
```

The resulting map, shown in Figure 41.4, now includes the expected right, left, up, down, and zoom in/zoom out controls—as well as the Map/Satellite/Hybrid display controls.

FIGURE 41.4

Your map with map controls added.

Adding an Info Window

Another neat thing is to display an info window centered on the location you selected. The info window, like the one in Figure 41.5, can display whatever text you specify.

FIGURE 41.5

The map with an info window added for the default location.

To create an info window, enter the following lines of code directly after the **map.setCenter** line in the <HEAD> of your document:

```
map.openInfoWindow(map.getCenter(),
document.createTextNode("YOURTEXT"));
```

Naturally, you replace *YOURTEXT* with the text you want to appear in the info window.

Creating an Animated Map

Here's an example of a neat effect you can add to your map. By inputting two locations into the code, you can make your map pan from one location to another. This is a good effect to add when you're showing how to get from one location to another.

All you have to do is insert the following lines of code after the **map.setCenter** line in the <HEAD> of your document:

```
window.setTimeout(function() {
  map.panTo(new GLatLng(LATITUDE2, LONGITUDE2));
}, 1000);
```

Naturally, replace *LATITUDE2* and *LONGITUDE2* with the coordinates for the second location on the map. Increase the **1000** parameter if you want to slow down the speed of the pan.

Adding a Marker to Your Map

What's a map mashup without an icon to mark a specific location? Here's a quick way to add a single marker to your map, like the one in Figure 41.6. All you have to do is insert the following lines of code after the **map.setCenter** line in the <**HEAD**> of your document:

```
var point = new GLatLng(LATITUDE,LONGITUDE)
map.addOverlay(new GMarker(point));
```

FIGURE 41.6

The map with a location marker added.

Replace *LATITUDE* and *LONGITUDE* with the precise latitude and longitude of the marker's location, of course.

Adding Multiple Markers from Your Own Database

A first-class map mashup plots multiple markers on a map, based on a database of individual locations. Each location in the database has to be expressed as a latitude/longitude coordinate, of course; the database of coordinates can then be easily plotted as an overlay on the base Google map.

Let's start with the database of locations. You need to create an XML file named **data.xml**. The contents of the file should be in the following format:

```
<markers>
  <marker lat="LATITUDE1" lng="LONGITUDE1" />
  <marker lat="LATITUDE2" lng="LONGITUDE2" />
  <marker lat="LATITUDE3" lng="LONGITUDE3" />
  <marker lat="LATITUDE4" lng="LONGITUDE4" />
</markers>
```

Add as many **<marker>** lines as you like, each with its own coordinates.

You then call this file into your Google Maps code, using the **GDownloadUrl** command. You do this by adding the following lines of code after the **map.setCenter** line in the **<HEAD>** of your document:

```
GDownloadUrl("data.xml", function(data, responseCode) {
  var xml = GXml.parse(data);
  var markers = xml.documentElement.getElementsByTagName("marker");
  for (var i = 0; i < markers.length; i++) {
    var point = new
GLatLng(parseFloat(markers[i].getAttribute("lat")),

parseFloat(markers[i].getAttribute("lng")));
    map.addOverlay(new GMarker(point));
```

This adds a new overlay to your map, with each point from the **data.xml** file translated into its own marker on the map, like the one shown in Figure 41.7. Cool!

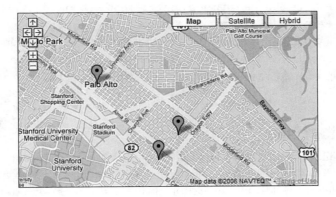

FIGURE 41.7
A map with multiple markers created from a database of locations.

And Even More...

This gives you a pretty good idea of how to add a simple Google map to your web page. To create more sophisticated mashups, you need to get more familiar with the Google Maps API and the use of overlays. That's more detail than we have space for here, but you can find all the documentation you need on the Google Maps API site. It's not that hard, especially if you know your way around a little JavaScript. And the results are worth it!

COMMENTARY:

MAKING MONEY FROM MAP MASHUPS

Google Maps mashups are becoming so popular that they're inspiring dollar signs in the eyes of crafty entrepreneurs. Anything this popular has to be profitable, doesn't it?

Maybe, maybe not. While there are a few high-profile mashup sites that have attracted significant venture capital backing, many investors have cold feet about the entire concept. In their eyes, most map mashups don't have a lot of profit potential, because they don't offer unique value to their users.

In this situation, both the words *unique* and *value* are important. If users can find the same information elsewhere, a mashup isn't unique. And if the information imparted isn't useful, there's no value to the user.

A successful map mashup must utilize the Google Maps API to add extra functionality to existing data. It's more than just presenting existing data as a series of map points; it's about giving users an experience unavailable previously. Find proprietary data that gains value when presented on a Google map, and you might just have a winner.

The Bottom Line

Unlike some other types of Google application development, adding a Google map to your web page is relatively easy—provided you're somewhat comfortable with HTML and JavaScript, of course. If you are, and can figure out latitude and longitude coordinates, adding a map to your page involves just a few lines of code. It's a great way to customize your web page—or, if you're more ambitious, create sophisticated Google Map mashups.

41

Into the Future

42 Exploring Google Labs

43 Beyond Search: What's Next for Google

Exploring Google Labs

A fter reading about all the various products and services currently offered by Google, you'd think the folks back at the Googleplex might be ready to sit back, relax a bit, and take a break. But you'd be wrong, because Google has even more search projects in the works, in an incubator they call Google Labs.

Google Labs (labs.google.com) is where Google's search experts concoct all manner of cutting-edge search projects. It's like a mad scientist's playground—and it's where the *next* Google features are often found.

Projects That Started in the Labs

Google Labs is, for all intents and purposes, a research and development (R&D) lab. The intent is to create new products and services that can be launched publicly within the Google universe. Granted, some of these projects are more theoretical than others and eventually fall by the wayside. But many Google Labs projects have graduated into full-blown products and services that are now presented alongside Google's more established offerings.

Which Google services first saw life in Google Labs? Here's a short list:

- **Google Desktop.** Search data on your computer's hard disk
- **Google Glossary.** Look up definitions for specific words
- **Google Groups 2.** Create and join topic-specific discussion groups
- **Google Maps.** View maps and driving directions
- **Google News Alerts.** Receive email alerts when new news stories appear online
- **Google Personal Homepage.** Create your own custom start page
- **Google Personalized Search.** Get search results more relevant to you
- **Google Scholar.** Search scholarly journals and articles
- **Google Search by Location.** Restrict your search to a specific geographic area
- **Google SMS.** Search Google via your mobile phone
- **Google Video.** Search and download TV programs and videos
- **Google Web Alerts.** Be notified of new web pages that match your search criteria

What's Cooking in Google Labs Today

At any given point in time, Google Labs has a dozen or so new projects percolating on the virtual test bench. Some of these projects will graduate into normal distribution; others will be incorporated into other products; and there will always be a few that just don't cut it and eventually wither away. With that in mind, let's take a quick look at what's currently being tested in Google labs.

Google Trends

Google Trends (www.google.com/trends) builds on the top searches compiled in the Google Zeitgeist to form a huge database of user information. Using a variety of data mining and analysis techniques, Google Trends lets you sort through search query data to determine the popularity of a given topic over time.

note The researchers at Google Labs are always working on new projects, so the projects available when you're reading this book may be different from the projects listed here.

42

For example, Figure 42.1 shows a trend analysis of the search query **Angelina Jolie**. As you can see, Angelina's popularity continues to trend upwards over time, with some obvious peaks coinciding with various news stories. At the bottom of the page is a list of the top cities that searched for this topic; it appears that the folks in Irvine, California, really like Ms. Jolie.

> **tip**
>
> The Google Zeitgeist (www.google.com/press/zeitgeist.html) presents the top search queries entered by Google users on a weekly, monthly, and yearly basis. For example, the top five searches in 2005 were, in order, **Janet Jackson, Hurricane Katrina, tsunami, xbox 360,** and **Brad Pitt.**

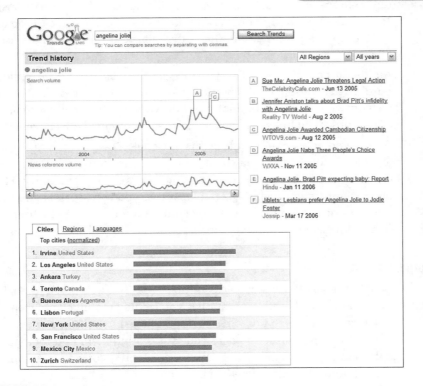

FIGURE 42.1

A Google Trends of Angelina Jolie.

When it officially launched Google Trends, the company pointed out that the service could be quite useful for its Google AdSense advertisers. Advertisers can use the Google Trends service to examine product trends over time—as well as trends in different regions. It's just one more clue that points to Google's core business being advertising, rather than technology.

Google Co-op

Google Co-op (www.google.com/coop) is
an experiment in user participation.
Google is pushing Google Co-op as a way
for Google users to improve Google search
by letting users label web pages and create
specialized links related to their own unique expertise.

note If you're a developer,
you can use the
Google Subscribed Links API to
add your services directly into
Google search.

For example, if you're an expert at a particular hobby, like digital photography, you can help categorize the digital photography pages you visit by giving them specific labels—Reviews, Sample Photos, Price Comparisons,
Troubleshooting, and so on. When other users search Google Co-op for digital
photography topics, they can then filter their results based on the user-created
labels.

Another aspect of Google Co-op is the *subscribed link*. This is, essentially, a
hard-wired sponsored link for related services that will appear at the top of
relevant search results. I'm not sure how valuable this really is to users; most
of the subscribed links I've seen so far are just glorified advertisements.

To that end, most of the contributors to Google Co-op (so far, at least) appear
to be large companies with content to sell. For example, the Destination
Guides category is heavily populated by Fodors, Frommer's Lonely Planet, and
other commercial travel guide publishers, as you can see in Figure 42.2. Now,
their contributions may be valuable, but it's a far cry from the user-populated
co-op that Google promised.

Google Notebook

Google Notebook (www.google.com/notebook) is a web-based (or, alternatively, a browser-based) tool that lets you create an online "notebook" to
organize all your web-based research on a given topic. You clip text, images,
and links from interesting pages you visit, storing them in a topic-specific
notebook page, like the one in Figure 42.3. It's a great way to organize typically chaotic web-based research activities.

The browser-based part of Google Notebook, by the way, comes in the form of
a Google Notebook button that installs on an Internet Explorer toolbar. Click
the button to display a list of Notebook-related actions, including saving a
link to the current web page in a given Notebook.

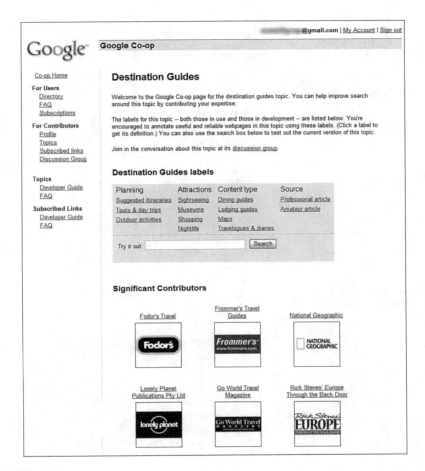

FIGURE 42.2
The Destination Guides category of Google Co-op.

Google Reader

As discussed previously in this book, Google Reader (www.google.com/reader) is a web-based RSS/Atom feed aggregator. Use Google Reader, shown in Figure 42.4, to automatically display the latest articles and headlines from blogs and websites that offer RSS and Atom feeds.

> **note** Learn more about Google Reader in Chapter 6, "Searching Blogs and Blog Postings."

42

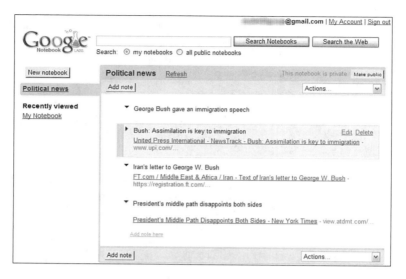

FIGURE 42.3

Organizing notes and web links in a Google Notebook.

FIGURE 42.4

The Google Reader feed aggregator.

Google Related Links

Google Links (www.google.com/relatedlinks) is a way to put related links on your own web page. Insert the proper HTML code, and Google places a box of topic links on your page. As you can see in Figure 42.5, these links are organized by Searches, News, and Web Pages; when site visitors click these links, they see a page of related Google news or search results.

> **note** Learn more about Google Sets in Chapter 9, "Searching for Words and Definitions."

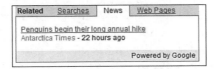

FIGURE 42.5

Add Google Related links to your web pages.

Google Sets

We also discussed Google Sets (labs.google.com/sets) earlier in this book. The concept here is to enter a few words that make up a type of list, and then let Google try to predict other items in the list. Figure 42.6 shows Google Sets at work.

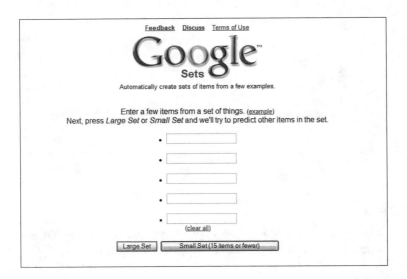

FIGURE 42.6

Filling in the blanks with Google Sets.

42

Google Page Creator

Here's a neat new tool that's definitely ready for prime time. When you want to create your own personal web page, you can turn to one of the many free web hosting communities (such as Yahoo! Geocities) or you can pay an expensive web hosting service. However, now you can use the recently launched Google Page Creator, a web-based tool that helps you create your own web pages—and then hosts those pages on Google's very own web page hosting community.

As you can see in Figure 42.7, Google Page Creator (pages.google.com) lets you create your web pages in a WYSIWYG environment. Just enter your page title, text, and pictures, and then click the Change Look and Change Layout links to customize the look and feel of your page. When you're done, click the Publish button and your website is published with its own unique URL, in the form of *yourname*.googlepages.com. Both the page creation and hosting are completely free.

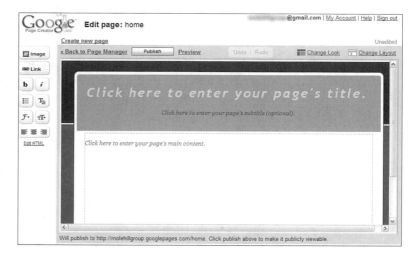

FIGURE 42.7

Creating your own web page with Google Page Creator.

Google Mars

If you like Google Maps and have an eye for the stars, you'll love Google Mars. As you can see in Figure 42.8, Google Mars (www.google.com/mars) is essentially Google Maps for the red planet, using detailed Martian maps, as supplied by NASA.

42

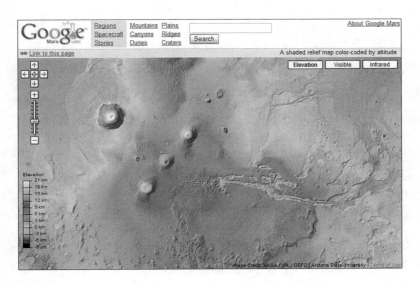

FIGURE 42.8
Navigate the Martian terrain with Google Mars.

Google Ride Finder

Google Ride Finder (labs.google.com/ridefinder) is a Google Maps mashup that lets you view the locations of taxis, shuttles, and limousines. Google Rider Finder contains real-time information for 15 major cities—Atlanta, Baltimore, Chicago, Dallas, Houston, Los Angeles, New York, Phoenix, Portland, San Francisco, San Jose, Seattle, St. Louis, Tucson, and Washington, DC. (Figure 42.9 shows the location of taxis in Chicago.)

Google Transit

Google Transit (www.google.com/transit) is another Google Maps mashup that lets you plan trips using public transportation. At present, it's only enabled for the Portland, Oregon area.

Froogle for Mobile

Froogle for Mobile (labs.google.com/frooglewml.html) lets you do comparison shopping in the real world. Just whip out your mobile phone when you're in a store, and query Froogle for Mobile to see if the current price is a good one.

42

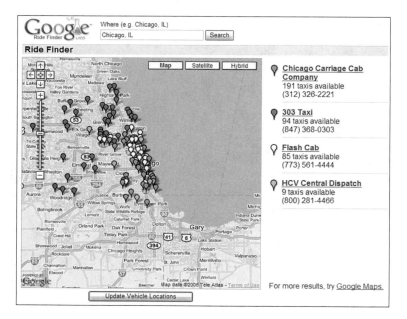

FIGURE 42.9
Google Ride Finder for Chicago.

Google Suggest

Google Suggest (www.google.com/webhp?complete=1&hl=en) is a technology that offers keyword suggestions as you enter a Google search query. At present, Google Suggest is included as part of the new Google Toolbar and Google Desktop search.

Google Dashboard Widgets for Mac

If you like the gadgets in Google Desktop but currently use a Macintosh computer, you're in luck. Google Dashboard Widgets for Mac (www.google.com/macwidgets/) translates several popular Google Desktop sidebar gadgets into widgets for the Apple Dashboard.

Google Extensions for Firefox

If you're using Mozilla Firefox instead of Internet Explorer as your web browser, Google Extensions for Firefox

note Google also offers Google Suggest in Japanese (www.google.co.jp/webhp?complete=1&hl=ja).

(www.google.com/tools/firefox) lets you add a variety of browser extensions to provide new functionality.

Google Web Accelerator

Google Web Accelerator (webaccelerator.google.com) is a technology that speeds up your web browsing by preloading popular web pages. It's free, and works on both dial-up and broadband connections.

Google Spreadsheeets

The latest, greatest application from Google Labs is Google Spreadsheets (spreadsheets.google.com), a web-based spreadsheet application that mimics some of the key features of freestanding spreadsheets, such as Microsoft Excel. As you can see in Figure 42.10, the basic interface looks pretty much like every other spreadsheet you've ever seen. You can enter numbers, words, formulas, functions, you name it, into any cell, and then format each cell as you like. (Functions are available by clicking the More link at the top right of the spreadsheet.) And, as with Excel, you can have multiple sheets in each spreadsheet. Sheets are selected from the tabs at the bottom of the main page.

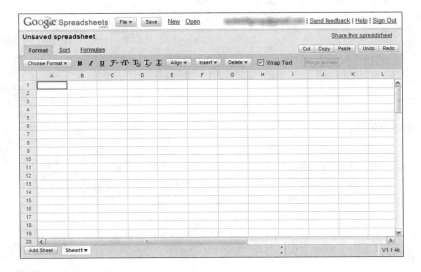

FIGURE 42.10

Google Spreadsheets—a full-function web-based spreadsheet application.

What's unique about Google Spreadsheets is that it's all web-based. The application and all your spreadsheets reside on Google's server, not on your computer. One nice thing about this is that your spreadsheets can be accessed wherever you are, from any PC; you'll never discover that the spreadsheet you need is located on your office PC when you're at home or away. The other nice thing is that, by being web-based, you can share your spreadsheets with others. That makes workgroup collaboration possible, which is something you don't have with Excel and other spreadsheet programs.

note To learn more about how to use Google Spreadsheets, check out my latest e-Book, *Using Google Spreadsheets*. You can purchase and download it at www.quepublishing.com/title/0768668336.

The other thing that's unique about Google Spreadsheets is that it's free. That's free, as in it costs zero dollars, unlike the increasingly more expensive Microsoft Excel. Being free makes it easy to take for a test drive, and even easier to add to your bag of applications. Many early users who've tried Google Spreadsheets have said that they're likely to switch from Excel; it can do almost everything Excel can do, from a numbers standpoint (there aren't any charts and graphs as yet), and it's perfect for corporate and small business environments. Give it a try!

Other Upcoming Google Projects

The projects in Google Labs aren't the only new Google projects being readied for market. Let's take a quick look at a few of the more promising future Google sites and services—so promising that they'll probably be "live" by the time you read this book!

tip Until Google Music launches, you can amuse yourself with Google Music Search (www.google.com/musicsearch?q). This is a direct link into the music search feature we first discussed in Chapter 10, "Searching for Other Special Information."

Google Health

Google Health (www.google.com/health) is designed as a one-stop portal for all health and medical-related issues. Look here for links to health-related news stories as well as content from various medical databases.

Google Music

Google Music (www.google.com/music) is rumored to be a repository for downloadable digital music files, and a potential competitor for Apple's iTunes Music Store. Whether Google Music will offer free downloads, paid downloads, or subscription services is not yet known.

note If you want to see an example of something that's not on Google's future release schedule, check out Google Romance (www.google.com/romance)—a remarkably well-thought-out April Fools' Day joke that fooled lots of folks on the Web.

Google Write

This may or may not be the final name for what is set to be a companion to Google Spreadsheets. Google Write will be a web-based word processor application, based on Writely, a recent Google acquisition. Expect Google Write to offer many of the same features of Microsoft Word, but in a web-based environment with document sharing and collaboration. And, like Google Spreadsheets, this one should be free—which will give Google a good start towards a Microsoft Office suite competitor.

Orkut

Orkut (www.orkut.com) is unlike some other sites in the Google network, in that Google acquired it ready-made, instead of building it from the ground up. Orkut is a social networking site, similar to MySpace, that lets you socialize with all your online friends, as well as find new friends, based on your own interests. (Figure 42.11 shows what an Orkut user profile looks like.)

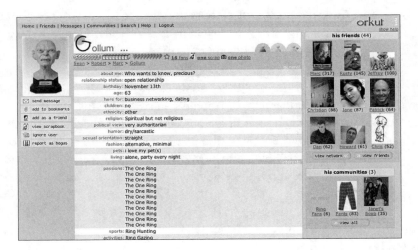

FIGURE 42.11

A typical (?) Orkut user profile.

COMMENTARY:

THE MOVING TARGET

Writing a book about Google is kind of like shooting at a moving target. That's because Google is constantly adding new features, services, and products—and updating all its existing ones.

Since I started writing this book, I've had to add no fewer than three new chapters to deal with newly launched Google features, and do midstream updates of a half-dozen other chapters. When I started writing, Google had yet to launch Google Calendar, Google Finance, Google Video, Google Notebook, or Google Co-op; Google Maps was still called Google Local; and Gmail didn't have half as many functions as it now does.

All these changes not only keep me on my toes as a writer, it also makes it difficult for the average user to keep up with all the new stuff that Google is doing. Let's face it; the average Google user doesn't use much more than the basic search page, so it's easy to miss some of the cool new features that get added on a regular basis.

To that end, I recommend two useful and informative Google-related blogs. The first is the Official Google Blog (googleblog.blogspot.com); as the name implies, this is Google's official blog, which is where all new products and services are officially introduced on launch. The other blog is the Unofficial Google Weblog (google.weblogsinc.com), which is a gossipy blog that always seems to have the inside scoop on what Google is about to be doing. I find both invaluable for keeping up on what Google is up to.

The Bottom Line

Google's newest products and services are often tested first in Google Labs, which functions as Google's R&D arm. Many Google Labs projects have graduated into real-world use; others are still in testing for Google to determine if they have appeal to a wide variety of users.

To find out what's cooking in Google Labs, go to labs.google.com. I know you'll find something interesting there!

Beyond Search: What's Next for Google

As big as the company is, Google just keeps getting bigger. In calendar year 2005, Google's revenues jumped an astounding 50%, to $6 billion—and its profits tripled to $1.6 billion.

How big can Google get? And what does it have to do to keep growing like this? The future of Google is the subject of much speculation on the part of market and financial analysts; there are clues, however, to Google's future direction—if you know where to look.

Google vs. Microsoft: Developing Competition

When a technology company gets as big as Google is, it attracts a lot of attention. A lot of this attention comes from competitors, of course, and the biggest competitor out there is Microsoft. In a war with the giant from Redmond, can Google win?

43

The short answer is, of course. But one questions whether Google and Microsoft are truly competing in the same space. Some analysts think so, as do many at Microsoft; for their part, however, Google seems to be less concerned.

"We try not to focus on what they (Microsoft) are doing," Google co-founder Larry Page said at a recent analyst's meeting. Google concentrates on innovation rather than competition, Page went on to say; Google is too busy creating new products and services to pay much attention on what Microsoft is doing.

Besides, just because Google is successful at one thing doesn't mean that Microsoft is suddenly less successful. Even though they're both broadly classified as technology companies, Google and Microsoft don't always compete head-to-head. As Google CEO Eric Schmidt noted, "There is room for more than one winner. Each of the strategies can coexist independent of the others."

That said, Google is increasingly veering into Microsoft's areas of core competency, and vice versa. For example, Microsoft is building an advanced search technology into its new Windows Vista operating system, which could be seen as directly competing with Google's own Google Desktop search—as well as its web search. Microsoft is also developing web-based advertising technologies and services to try to lure away some of Google's ad revenues.

On the other side of the table, many have viewed Google's development of web-based services as creating an alternative platform to Microsoft's Windows operating system. In this view, the "Google OS" becomes the main computing platform, not Windows. And, quite obviously, Google Spreadsheets and Google Write are direct competitors to Microsoft's Excel and Word applications. These are a real threat to Microsoft.

So there is definite competition between the two firms, especially when it comes to attracting key employees. In 2005, Google signed about eight new hires per day—many of them lured away from Microsoft. Some of these hires become contentious, such as Google's hiring of former Microsoft executive Kai-Fu Lee to head the company's Chinese operations. Microsoft took offense, and sued to keep Lee from jumping to Google; a judge ruled that Lee could make the move, providing he didn't work on some directly competitive products until his non-compete agreement expired.

Is Google competing with Microsoft? They're certainly competing for employees, which makes one think that the marketplace competition is real. As to whether Google is encroaching on Microsoft's turf or vice versa, that's an interesting question—the answer to which probably depends on whose side you're on.

Google vs. Yahoo!: Even More Competition

Microsoft isn't Google's only competitor. From the beginning, Google's chief competitor in the search field has been Yahoo! Not only was Yahoo! a more established search site, it also was the first search engine to expand into a full-featured portal with topic-focused vertical sites—something that Google is just now in the process of doing.

Of course, Google has already bested Yahoo! in terms of search index size and number of users. It's easy to see why, in retrospect; Google's incessant focus on search (and only search), along with the company's dedication to a clean interface and simple search experience, tapped into what the market wanted. People didn't want their search cluttered with all sorts of subsidiary nonsense; Yahoo! may have offered more non-search services, but Google did search better.

Today, Yahoo! remains a strong competitor in the search market, having improved its search effectiveness in recent years. Most endusers today don't realize that Yahoo! actually started as a directory, and only added a true search index with the acquisition of the Inktomi, Overture, AltaVista, and Fast search engines in 2003-2004. Yahoo! search still isn't as big or as targeted as Google search, but it's not half-bad—and Yahoo! still has millions of loyal users.

Even more important, Yahoo! is becoming a strong competitor to Google in its core Internet advertising business. In May, 2006, Yahoo! signed with eBay to become the exclusive third-party provider of graphic ads on eBay's auction site. Yahoo! also agreed to use eBay's PayPal payment system throughout its network of sites, and to co-develop "click-to-call" advertising technology. (With click-to-call, consumers can click an ad to place a phone call to an advertiser, using Internet phone technology supplied by eBay's Skype subsidiary.)

With both Microsoft and Yahoo! coming after Google's advertising cash cow, competition is heating up.

What Does Google Want to Be When It Grows Up?

Competition with Microsoft or Yahoo! aside, one does have to wonder just what kind of company Google intends to be five or ten years from now. It's obvious that Google is no longer the simple search technology company it was when Larry Page and Sergei Brin created their first search application in their Stanford University dorm room. As I've pointed out throughout this book, Google might look like a search company, but it generates virtually all of its revenues from selling advertising space—which makes Google a media company, similar to traditional newspaper and magazine publishers, but using 21st-century technology to deliver its ads and surrounding content. But will Google remain dependent on ad sales in the future—or is something else in store for the folks at the Googleplex?

It's tempting to look at everything Google is doing—from personalized searching to video downloads to wireless Internet service (see the sidebar later in this chapter)—and conclude that the company is simply working to refine its ad delivery technology. In essence, Google is working to (1) provide more settings to deliver its ads and (2) deliver ads that are more relevant to consumers. The former goal is met whenever Google rolls out a new product or service, each of which provides more ad space and more ad viewers. The second goal is met as Google refines its search technology and applies that to serving up content-relevant advertisements. The more of you that use Google's products and services, the more ads it can sell; the more it knows about you, the more relevant (and thus more profitable) those ads will be.

For example, look at Google Book Search. On the surface, it appears to be a highly useful service for consumers, if not slightly altruistic in its goal to provide access to a vast literary history. But it's really just another way to serve up those "sponsored links" that appear on all of Google's search results pages; each new user that queries Google Book Search is one more target for Google's advertising.

Consider, also, Google Desktop. Yes, Google makes it easier to find data stored on your personal computer, but by finding that data, Google also learns a lot about you. And the more Google knows about you (via the email messages you receive and the files you store), the more targeted it can make the ads that it serves to you. Personalized services equal personalized ads—and personalized ads just happen to be more effective, and thus more profitable for Google.

So it's important for Google to continue to develop its search and personalization technologies—not necessarily to improve users' search experience, but rather to attract more users and better target the ads that the company sells. It's also important, of course, for Google to continue to offer an effective and attractive search experience; if Microsoft or Yahoo! were to somehow eat into Google's share of online search, it would reduce Google's advertising base, and thus affect the company's ad-driven revenue stream. Being the best at what it does ensures a steady stream of advertising consumers, after all.

But is there growth left in the Internet-based ad market? The answer to that question is a definite yes. U.S. companies still spend more ad dollars on the traditional Yellow Pages than they do on online advertising; the Internet ad market accounts for less than 5% of overall ad spending. So there's plenty of growth left in Google's core business—not even counting the ad dollars to be had outside the U.S.

And the Internet may be only part of Google's future. Is it possible for Google to apply its technologies to other media besides the Internet? Google's Larry Page seemed to think so when he said "We're excited about taking the properties of search-based advertising... and applying that to the video space." Imagine Google serving up context-sensitive ads during your favorite television programs. Don't laugh; Google recently announced that it was entering the market for web-based video advertising, serving up "click-to-play" ads to its network of websites. It's only a short step from video ads on the web to similar ads on network TV.

So what kind of company will Google be when it grows up? My guess is that it will be much like it is today, except more so. More products and more services, not all of them directly search related, all of them offering more opportunities to deliver highly targeted advertising. More Google in more channels, more services in more media, more ads served by the Google advertising juggernaut. And better ads, because Google will know more about its users over time. The more of your life you hand over to the Googleplex, the more Google will know what you like, what you don't like, what you do, what you don't do, what you buy, and what you don't buy. Google will serve up increasingly relevant advertising, advertising targeted not only on your historical reading and viewing and buying patterns, but also on what you're currently doing. Activity-relevant advertising cross-indexed with past buying patterns should make for ads you might actually pay attention to—and certainly ads for which Google can charge companies top dollar.

You see, it's not all about the search, it's about the dollar. And Google knows that the best way to get advertisers' dollars is to attract more and more consumers with better and better products and services. The more that Google does for you, the more eyeballs it attracts to its ads—and the more eyeballs, the more advertising revenue. You get the picture.

43

COMMENTARY:

GOOGLE—WIRELESS SERVICE PROVIDER?

Whether you think of Google as a search technology company or an advertising company, here's a development that might have you scratching your head: Google is becoming a provider of wireless Internet service. In fact, Google is pursuing this direction in a number of different ways.

First, Google is partnering with EarthLink to offer city-wide WiFi service to the cities of San Francisco and Mountain View, California. It's an expensive proposition for Google; the infrastructure involved in the San Francisco rollout will cost upwards of $15 million.

How will Google make money on this type of project? It depends. San Francisco residents will have the option of paying $20/month for an ultra-fast 1 Mbps connection or of receiving free 300Kbps service. Users of the free service will be subjected to local advertisements on the web pages they view; Google, of course, makes money from selling the ad space.

So city-wide wireless Internet service is just another way to expand Google's advertising reach, in this case via the use of highly-profitable targeted local ads. As Google CEO Eric Schmidt recently noted, local advertising is an "increasingly meaningful contributor to revenue, and much more is coming." How is that coming? At least partly from Google's serving up free WiFi in selected cities.

The second way that Google is getting into wireless Internet service is by bidding on the Federal Communications Commission's auction for the 90MHz radio spectrum. Google is bidding against Time Warner and various cellular providers, which seems a bit odd at first. But several observers have speculated that Google is looking at the wireless spectrum as an alternative way to reach its users.

AT&T, Verizon, and other phone companies that provide DSL Internet service have been making noise about charging content owners and distributors, such as Google, additional fees to carry high-bandwidth content over their networks. Any Internet content owner not paying this toll would find their content relegated to second-class status.

By building its own access network in the wireless spectrum, Google could deliver its service directly to endusers. This would let Google neatly sidestep any access delays and avoid paying additional access charges. It's all about reaching the consumer directly—all the better to serve up those ads.

The Bottom Line

Google is a remarkable company, and a remarkable success story. It's more than just search, although it still offers the best search services on the Internet; the company is using its roots in search technology to expand the products and services it offers to its growing base of loyal and satisfied users. In fact, it's difficult to predict just what new products and services Google will offer in the months and years to come. The only surefire prediction is that Google will continue to excel at what it does, and to continue to expand its connection to its users' personal and professional lives.

Will Google still be king of search five years from now? One can't predict the future, but betting against Google is something that only fools do. The company is filled to the brim with smart and ambitious people, and they're the kind of people who almost always succeed at what they do.

Appendixes

A Google's Site Directory

B Google's Country Specific Sites

C Google's Advanced Search Operators

Google's Site Directory

Google Site	URL
Blogger	www.blogger.com
Blogger Blog Search	search.blogger.com
Froogle	froogle.google.com
Froogle for Mobile	labs.google.com/frooglewml.html
Gmail	mail.google.com
Google Accounts	www.google.com/accounts
Google Add Your URL	www.google.com/addurl
Google AdSense	www.google.com/adsense
Google AdWords	adwords.google.com
Google Alerts	www.google.com/alerts
Google Answers	answers.google.com
Google Apple Macintosh Search	www.google.com/mac
Google Base	base.google.com
Google Blog Search	blogsearch.google.com
Google Book Search	books.google.com
Google BSD Unix Search	www.google.com/bsd
Google Business Solutions	www.google.com/services

A

Google Site	URL
Google Calendar	calendar.google.com
Google Catalogs	catalogs.google.com
Google Code	code.google.com
Google College Life	www.google.com/university
Google Co-op	www.google.com/coop
Google Dashboard Widgets for Mac	www.google.com/macwidgets
Google Desktop	desktop.google.com
Google Directory	directory.google.com
Google Earth	earth.google.com
Google Enterprise Solutions	www.google.com/enterprise
Google Extensions for Firefox	www.google.com/tools/firefox
Google Finance	finance.google.com
Google Groups	groups.google.com
Google Health	www.google.com/health
Google Image Search	images.google.com
Google Labs	labs.google.com
Google Language Tools	www.google.com/language_tools
Google Links	www.google.com/relatedlinks
Google Linux Search	www.google.com/linux
Google Maps	maps.google.com
Google Mars	www.google.com/mars
Google Microsoft Search	www.google.com/microsoft
Google Mobile	www.google.com/mobile
Google More Products	www.google.com/options
Google Music	www.google.com/music
Google News	news.google.com
Google Notebook	www.google.com/notebook
Google Pack	pack.google.com
Google Page Creator	pages.google.com
Google Personalized Homepage	www.google.com/ig
Google Reader	reader.google.com

Google Site	URL
Google Ride Finder	labs.google.com/ridefinder
Google Scholar	scholar.google.com
Google Sets	labs.google.com/sets
Google Sitemaps	www.google.com/webmasters/sitemaps
Google SketchUp	sketchup.google.com
Google Software Downloads	www.google.com/downloads
Google Spreadsheets	spreadsheets.google.com
Google Talk	talk.google.com
Google Toolbar	toolbar.google.com
Google Transit	www.google.com/transit
Google Trends	www.google.com/trends
Google U.S. Government Search	usgov.google.com
Google University Search	www.google.com/options/universities.html
Google Video	video.google.com
Google Video Blog	www.googlevideo.blogspot.com
Google Web Accelerator	webaccelerator.google.com
Google Web Search	www.google.com
Google Webs API	www.google.com/apis
Google Zeitgeist	www.google.com/press/zeitgeist.html
Hello	www.hello.com
Official Google Blog	googleblog.blogspot.com
Orkut	www.orkut.com
Picasa	picasa.google.com

A

Google's Country-Specific Sites

Country	URL
Afghanistan	www.google.com.af
American Samoa	www.google.as
Anguilla	www.google.off.ai
Antigua and Barbuda	www.google.com.ag
Argentina	www.google.com.ar
Armenia	www.google.am
Australia	www.google.com.au
Austria	www.google.at
Azerbaijan	www.google.az
Bahamas	www.google.bs
Bahrain	www.google.com.bh
Bangladesh	www.google.com.bd
Belgium	www.google.be
Belize	www.google.com.bz
Bolivia	www.google.com.bo
Bosnia and Herzegovina	www.google.ba

Country	URL
Botswana	www.google.co.bw
Brazil	www.google.com.br
British Virgin Islands	www.google.vg
Bulgaria	www.google.bg
Burundi	www.google.bi
Canada	www.google.ca
Chile	www.google.cl
Colombia	www.google.com.co
Cook Islands	www.google.co.ck
Costa Rica	www.google.co.cr
Cote D'Ivoire	www.google.ci
Croatia/Hrvatska	www.google.hr
Cuba	www.google.com.cu
Democratic Republic of the Congo	www.google.cd
Denmark	www.google.dk
Djibouti	www.google.dj
Dominica	www.google.dm
Dominican Republic	www.google.com.do
East Timor	www.google.tp
Ecuador	www.google.com.ec
Egypt	www.google.com.eg
El Salvador	www.google.com.sv
Ethiopia	www.google.com.et
Fiji	www.google.com.fj
Finland	www.google.fi
France	www.google.fr
Gambia	www.google.gm
Germany	www.google.de
Gibraltar	www.google.com.gi
Greece	www.google.gr

B

Country	URL
Greenland	www.google.gl
Guatemala	www.google.com.gt
Guernsey	www.google.gg
Haiti	www.google.ht
Honduras	www.google.hn
Hong Kong	www.google.com.hk
Hungary	www.google.co.hu
Iceland	www.google.is
India	www.google.co.in
Indonesia	www.google.co.id
Ireland	www.google.ie
Isle of Man	www.google.co.im
Israel	www.google.co.il
Italy	www.google.it
Jamaica	www.google.com.jm
Japan	www.google.co.jp
Jersey	www.google.co.je
Jordan	www.google.jo
Kazakhstan	www.google.kz
Kenya	www.google.co.ke
Kyrgyzstan	www.google.kg
Latvia	www.google.lv
Lesotho	www.google.co.ls
Libyan Arab Jamahiriya	www.google.com.ly
Liechtenstein	www.google.li
Lithuania	www.google.lt
Luxemburg	www.google.lu
Malawi	www.google.mw
Malaysia	www.google.com.my
Malta	www.google.com.mt

B

Country	URL
Mauritius	www.google.mu
Mexico	www.google.com.mx
Micronesia	www.google.fm
Mongolia	www.google.mn
Montserrat	www.google.ms
Namibia	www.google.com.na
Nauru	www.google.nr
Nepal	www.google.com.np
Netherlands	www.google.nl
New Zealand	www.google.co.nz
Nicaragua	www.google.com.ni
Niue	www.google.nu
Norfolk Island	www.google.com.nf
Norway	www.google.no
Oman	www.google.com.om
Pakistan	www.google.com.pk
Panama	www.google.com.pa
Paraguay	www.google.com.py
Peru	www.google.com.pe
Philippines	www.google.com.ph
Pitcairn Islands	www.google.pn
Poland	www.google.pl
Portugal	www.google.pt
Puerto Rico	www.google.com.pr
Republic of Congo	www.google.cg
Republic of Korea	www.google.co.kr
Romania	www.google.ro
Russia	www.google.ru
Rwanda	www.google.rw
Saint Helena	www.google.sh
Saint Vincent and the Grenadines	www.google.com.vc
San Marino	www.google.sm

B

Country	URL
Saudi Arabia	www.google.sa
Senegal	www.google.sn
Seychelles	www.google.sc
Singapore	www.google.com.sg
Slovak Republic	www.google.sk
Solomon Islands	www.google.com.sb
South Africa	www.google.co.za
Spain	www.google.es
Sri Lanka	www.google.lk
Sweden	www.google.se
Switzerland	www.google.ch
Taiwan	www.google.com.tw
Tajikistan	www.google.com.tj
Thailand	www.google.co.th
Tonga	www.google.to
Trinidad and Tobago	www.google.tt
Turkey	www.google.com.tr
Turkmenistan	www.google.tm
Uganda	www.google.co.ug
Ukraine	www.google.com.ua
United Arab Emirates	www.google.ae
United Kingdom	www.google.co.uk
Uruguay	www.google.com.uy
Uzbekistan	www.google.uz
Vanuatu	www.google.vu
Venezuela	www.google.co.ve
Vietnam	www.google.com.vn
Virgin Islands	www.google.co.vi
Western Samoa	www.google.ws
Zambia	www.google.co.zm

B

Google's Advanced Search Operators

Operator	Description[1]
..	Searches within a range of numbers in the form *number..number*
-	Excludes pages that contain the specified word from the search results
""	Searches for the complete phrase in the form *word1 word2*
( )	Used to group keywords in a query
*	Whole-word wildcard; searches for missing words in a phrase ("") search
~	Searches for synonyms of the specified keyword
+	Includes the specified "stop" word in the query
after:	GMAIL—Restricts search to emails sent after a specified date
allinanchor:	Restricts search to the anchor text (link text) of web pages; used with multiple keywords
allintext:	Restricts search to the body text of web pages; used with multiple keywords

Operator	Description[1]
allintitle:	Restricts search to the titles of web pages; used with multiple keywords
allinurl:	Restricts search to the URLs of web pages; used with multiple keywords
author:	GOOGLE GROUPS and GOOGLE SCHOLAR—Searches for messages or articles by a particular author
bcc:	GMAIL and GOOGLE DESKTOP—Restricts search to the Bcc: lines of email messages
before:	GMAIL—Restricts search to emails sent before a specified date
blogurl:	GOOGLE BLOG SEARCH—Restricts search to the specified blog
book	Initiates a Google full-text book search
bphonebook:	Displays business phone book listings
cache:	Displays the cached version of the specified URL page as stored in the Google database
cc:	GMAIL and GOOGLE DESKTOP—Restricts search to the Cc: lines of email messages
daterange:*startdate-enddate*	Searches for pages indexed within a specified date range (requires Julian dates)
define: *or* define	Displays definitions of the specified word or phrase
filename:	GMAIL—Searches for file attachments with the specified filename
filetype:	Finds documents with the specified extension
from:	GMAIL and GOOGLE DESKTOP—Restricts search to the From: lines of email messages
groups:	GOOGLE GROUPS—Searches for messages in the specified group(s)
has:attachment	GMAIL—Restricts search to emails with file attachments
in:	GMAIL—Restricts search to emails stored in a specific location: **anywhere**, **inbox**, **trash**, or **spam**
inanchor:	Restricts search to the anchor text (link text) of web pages; used with a single keyword
inblogtitle:	GOOGLE BLOG SEARCH—Restricts search to blog titles
info:	Displays information about the specified URL
inpostauthor:	GOOGLE BLOG SEARCH—Restricts search to blog postings by the specified author
inposttitle:	GOOGLE BLOG SEARCH—Restricts search to the titles of individual blog posts
insubject:	GOOGLE GROUPS—Restricts search to the subject line of messages
intext:	Restricts search to the body text of web pages; used with a single keyword
intitle:	Restricts search to the titles of web pages; used with a single keyword
inurl:	Restricts search to the URLs of web pages; used with a single keyword
is:	GMAIL—Restricts search to emails that are **starred**, **read**, or **unread**

Operator	Description[1]
label:	GMAIL—Restricts search to emails with the specified label
link:	Finds pages that link to the specified URL
location:	GOOGLE NEWS—Finds news articles from sources in the specified location
machine:	GOOGLE DESKTOP—When the Search Across Computers feature is enabled, restricts search to the specified computer
movie:	Searches for information about the specified movie, including show times
OR	Searches for pages that contain one or another keyword, but not necessarily both
phonebook:	Displays phonebook listings
related:	Displays web pages that are similar to the specified URL
rphonebook:	Displays residential phone book listings
safesearch:	Enables SafeSearch content filtering
site:	Restricts search to a particular domain or website
source:	GOOGLE NEWS—Finds news articles from the specified source(s)
stocks:	Displays current stock price for the specified stock symbol
store:	FROOGLE—Searches for products offered by the specified online store
subject:	GMAIL and GOOGLE DESKTOP—Restricts search to the Subject lines of email messages
to:	GMAIL and GOOGLE DESKTOP—Restricts search to the To: lines of email messages
under:	GOOGLE DESKTOP—Restricts search to subfolders located under the specified folder
weather	Displays the current weather conditions and forecast for the specified location
what is *or* what are	Same as **define**; displays definitions of the specified word or phrase

[1]Search operators that only work on a specific search service are so noted in the description.

Index

Symbols

! operator, 198

% operator, 198

( ) operator, 366, 737

" operator, 366

"" operator, 737

~ operator, 34, 737

^ operator, 198

* (whole-word wildcard), 36

* operator, 737

** operator, 198

+ operator, 196, 737

- operator, 196, 737

. . operator, 737

/ operator, 196

&as_filetype=xxx URL parameter, 48

&as_qdr=m# URL parameter, 47

&num=x URL parameter, 48

Numbers

1-week stock charts (company/security pages), 85

3D buildings (Earth), 328, 339

3D modeling (SketchUp), 671-672

3D terrain option (Earth), 328

52-week high, 86

52-week low, 86

1001 Secret Fishing Holes, 310

A

ABC News website, 516

academic information searches (Scholar), 118

  accessing, 118

  adding to websites, 128

  advanced searches, 124-126

  benefits, 120

  content

    adding, 130

    identifying, 119

  invisible web information, 121

  libraries

    access, 129

    links, 126

  non-public information, 119

  Preferences page, 126

  print-only content, 120

  publishers, 130

results, 121-123
searches, 124

Account Properties dialog box, 397

Ad-Aware SE Personal, 613

Add a Feed button, 111

Add a Placemark button, 343

Add button, 562

Add It Now button, 166

Add Web Sitemap button, 624

Add/Remove Gadgets dialog box, 562

adding
advertisements to websites, 640-644, 647
    AdSense for Content, 640-641
    AdSense for Search, 641-642
    AdSense Referrals, 650-652
    earnings potential, increasing, 654-658
    joining AdSense, 643-644
    performance, monitoring, 653
    revenues, 642
businesses to Maps, 290
comments to Google Answers, 470
contacts (Gmail), 372-374
content
    Book Search, 476-477
    Personalized Homepage, 165

Scholar, 130
custom buttons to Toolbar, 541
events to Calendar, 577-579
gadgets to sidebar, 562
Google searches to websites
    customizable Google Free WebSearch, 678-680
    Free SafeSearch, 676-677
    Free WebSearch, 675-676
    Free WebSearch with SiteSearch, 677-678
    Site-Flavored Google Search, 681-682
guests to Calendar events, 581
items to Shopping list (Froogle), 235
numbers, 196
products to Froogle, 232
RSS feeds to web pages, 115-116
search boxes to websites, 647, 650
signatures to Gmail, 382-383
websites
    Scholar, 128
    Sitemap, 622-623
    web index, 620

addition operator, 196

Adobe
Photoshop CS, 605
Photoshop Elements, 605
Reader, 614

AdSense, 15
adding ads to websites, 640-644, 647
    AdSense for Content, 640-641
    AdSense for Search, 641-642
blogs, 418
for Content, 640-641
content-sensitive, 658
earnings potential, increasing, 654-658
joining, 643-644
performance, monitoring, 653
Referrals, 650-652
revenues, 642
for Search, 641-642

advanced mathematic functions, 198

Advanced Search page, 26, 44-46
alternatives, 49
SafeSearch filtering, 177

advanced searches
blogs, 103-105
books, 478-479
Froogle, 226-228
Groups, 495-497
hard disks, 553-554
images, 436-437
Scholar, 124-126

advertising. *See also* **AdSense**
adding to websites, 640-644, 647
    AdSense for Content, 640-641
    AdSense for Search, 641-642

AdSense Referrals,
650-652

earnings potential,
increasing, 654-658

joining AdSense,
643-644

performance, monitoring,
653

revenues, 642

Blogger, 417-418

Calendar, 569

revenues, 14-15

search results pages, 659

across Google Network,
659

ads, creating, 660, 663

costs, 660

performance, monitoring,
664

third-party sites, 659

AdWords, 15, 659

across Google Network,
659

ads, creating, 660, 663

API, 685

costs, 660

performance, monitoring,
664

third-party sites, 659

Afghanistan Google site,
731

after: operator, 737

after:year/month/day
operator, 366

Agenda view (Calendar),
574

airport conditions, 149

airports/transportation
layer (Earth), 339

alerts, 211-213

deleting, 216

groups, 212

managing, 215-216

news, 212, 515-516

signing up, 213-214

web, 212

algebraic operators, 196

Alkemis Local website, 304

allinanchor: operator, 40,
46, 737

allintext: operator, 40, 46,
737

allintitle: operator, 39, 46,
738

allinurl: operator, 39, 46,
738

Alta Vista Babel Fish web-
site, 193

alternate advanced search
forms, 49

alternative place names
layer (Earth), 339

American Heritage
Dictionary of the English
***Language* website, 143**

American Samoa Google
site, 731

and searches, 32

Anguilla Google site, 731

animated maps, 697

Answers, 465

comments, adding, 470

cost, 467

previously answered ques-
tions, viewing, 467, 470

questions

asking, 470-472

clarifying, 473

types, 466

viewing, 472

rating answers, 474

researchers, 466

Answers.com, 140

Antigua and Barbuda
Google site, 731

Apartment Ratings web-
site, 301

APIs (Application
Programming Interfaces),
683

AdWords, 685

Blogger Atom, 685

Calendar Data, 685

Data, 685

Gadgets, 685

Maps, 685, 693-698

Search Appliance, 685

Toolbar, 685

Web, 685-687

Apple

Dashboard, 564

iTunes Video Store web-
site, 449

Macintosh Google search,
134

arccotangent operator, 199

arccsc operator, 199

archive Blogger tags, 428

archiving

Gmail messages, 368-369

usenet, 492

arcos operator, 199

arcsec operator, 199

arcsin operator, 199

arctan operator, 199

area, 205

Area 51 mashups, 315

Area 51 Satellite and Aerial Photos website, 315

Argaili White & Yellow website, 72

Argentina Google site, 731

Armenia Google site, 731

articles (News), searching, 513-514

Ask Question button, 470

asking questions (Google Answers), 470-472

Associated Press News Mashup, 297

Atom syndication, 416

attachments (Gmail)
    adding, 361-362
    saving, 362
    scanning for viruses, 371
    viewing, 362

Australia Google site, 731

Austria Google site, 731

author: operator, 124, 495, 738

Auto Color button, 592

Auto Contrast button, 591

AutoFill button (Toolbar), 537

AutoLink button (Toolbar), 536

automatic word stemming, 34

average volume, 86

Azerbaijan Google site, 731

B

BackRub search engine, 12

Bahamas Google site, 731

Bahrain Google site, 731

Bangladesh Google site, 731

banks/ATMs layer (Earth), 339

bargains, searching (Froogle), 222-223
    adding products to, 232
    advanced searches, 226-228
    best bargains, 234
    buying items, 228
    cell phones, 526
    functions, 222
    local bargains, 229-230
    main page, 223
    merchant reviews, 232-234
    product detail pages, 225-226
    results, 224-225
    searching, 223
    Shopping list feature, 235-236
    store inventories, uploading, 262
    Wish list, 236

bars/clubs layer (Earth), 339

BART Map/Schedule, 304

Base
    attributes, 246
    eBay, compared, 263-264
    items
        browsing, 251-253
        bulk uploads, 261-262
        buying, 253-254
        prohibited items, 247-248
        searching, 248-251
        selling, 256-260
    labels, 246
    overview, 246

BBC News website, 516

bcc (blind carbon copy), 360

bcc: operator, 366, 738

Bechtolsheim, Andy, 12

BeenMapped.com, 314

Beermapping.com, 302

before: operator, 738

before:year/month/day operator, 366

Belgium Google site, 731

Belize Google site, 731

Berkeley Software Distribution (BSD), 134

best bargains, 234

Best Google Videos website, 448

Best of the Web website, 58

beta, 87

The Big One website, 315

bird flu mashups, 315

bird-watching mashups, 314

BizRate, 222

blind carbon copy, 360

blocking Google Chat users, 390

Blog button, 411

blog posts (company/ security pages), 85

Blog Search
Advanced Search page, 103-105
listing blogs with, 99
results, evaluating, 102
searches, 98-100

Blog Templates website, 422

Blog This! button, 588

Blogger
advertisements, 417-418
Atom API, 685
Blog Search page, 100
blogs
accounts, 405
creating, 405-408
syndicating, 416-417
viewing, 408
comments, 414
Dashboard, 100
Google Toolbar, 411-412
hit counters, 431
hosts, changing, 419-421
overview, 404
posts, 409-412
templates, 421
choosing, 406, 421
coding, 425

HTML tags, 425-429
third-party, 421, 424
website, 422

blogosphere, 99

blogs (web logs), 97
advanced searches, 103-105
Blogger
accounts, 405
advertisements, 417-418
comments, managing, 414
creating blogs, 405-408
editing posts, 412
entries, posting, 409-411
Google Toolbar, 411-412
hit counters, 431
hosts, changing, 419-421
overview, 404
syndication, 416-417
templates. See Blogger, templates
viewing blogs, 408
feeds
adding to web pages, 115-116
finding, 110
importing, 112
sharing, 113-114
URLs, 111
finding, 98-100
Google Video Blog, 448
High Fiber Content, 403
hosting communities, 401
listing with Google Blog Search, 99
overview, 402
reading, 108-109

reasons for, 403
results, evaluating, 102
site URLs, 111
subscriptions, 106-107, 112
Tech Blog, 403

BlogSkins website, 422

blogurl: operator, 103, 738

Bloomberg website, 79

body text searches, 40

Bolivia Google site, 731

Book Search, 476
additional book information, 484
advanced book searches, 478-479
content
adding, 476-477
viewing, 479-480
Google Books Library Project, 477
Google Books Partner Program, 476
publishing community conflict, 484-487
searching, 478
standard web search, 477

book: operator, 738

Bookmark button (Toolbar), 535

Books Library Project, 477

Books Partner Program, 476

borders layer (Earth), 339

Bosnia and Herzegovina Google site, 731

Boston Globe website, 517

Botswana Google site, 732

bphonebook: operator, 738

Bravenet Counter Site Stats website, 431

Brazil Google site, 732

Brin, Sergey, 11

British Virgin Islands Google site, 732

broadcast news websites, 516

Broadway plays/shows, 300

BroadwayZone, 300

browsers
   buttons, installing, 544
   Google as home page, 172-173

browsing
   Directory categories, 62-64
   Groups, 493
   items (Google Base), 251-253

BSD (Berkeley Software Distribution), 134

Bulgaria Google site, 732

bulk items, uploading (Google Base), 261-262

BunkerShot.com Golf Course Explorer, 310

burning photos, 604

Burundi Google site, 732

Business Week website, 517

businesses
   adding to Maps, 290
   finding, 288-290
   location data, 262

Button Gallery button, 541

buttons
   Add, 562
   Add a Feed, 111
   Add a Placemark, 343
   Add It Now, 166
   Add Web Sitemap, 624
   Ask Question, 470
   Auto Color, 592
   Auto Contrast, 591
   Blog, 411
   Blog This!, 588
   browser, installing, 544
   Button Gallery, 541
   Clear, 588
   Collage, 588
   continue, 650
   Continue to Payment Information, 472
   Create Alert, 516
   Create Calendar, 570
   Create Filter, 370
   Create My Google Answers Account, 472
   Create My Group, 502
   Crop, 595
   Customize Google for Your Site, 678
   Download Gmail Notifier, 384
   Download Google Pack, 609
   Email, 588, 602
   Export, 588, 598
   Generate HTML, 681

Get Code Now!, 116
   Get Started Now!, 647
   Gift CD, 604
   Hold, 588
   I'm Feeling Lucky, 25
   Import Contacts, 374
   Label, 588
   Order prints, 588
   Pay Listing Fee and Post Question, 472
   Picasa function, 587-588
   Play Tour, 337
   Post Message, 95
   Print, 599
   Publish Posts, 412
   Redeye, 594
   Republish, 421
   Reset North, 323
   Rotate clockwise, 588
   Rotate counter-clockwise, 588
   Rotate Right, 323
   Satellite, 276
   Save Changes, 378
   Save Preferences, 162
   Search, 26
   Search for New Content, 111
   Search Homepage Content, 166
   Search Mail, 364
   Search Video, 447
   Send Email, 114
   Send Pictures, 601
   Star, 588
   Start a New Discussion, 95
   Tilt Down, 326
   Toolbar, 532

adding/deleting, 540
AutoFill, 537
AutoLink, 536
Bookmarks, 535
custom, adding, 541
Desktop, 534
Gmail, 535
Highlight, 539
News, 534
optional, 541
PageRank, 536
pop-up blocker, 536
search box, 532-533
Send To, 538
SpellCheck, 536
Weather, 534
word find, 539
Translate, 189
Upload Video, 459
Use This Template, 421
buying items
Base, 253-254
Froogle, 228

C

cache: operator, 43, 738
cached link (search result page), 27
calculations, 195
addition, 196
advanced functions, 198
algebraic operators, 196
division, 196
hyperbolic functions, 199
inverse trigonometry, 199
logarithmic functions, 199

multiple operations, 197
nesting equations, 197
Soople, 208-209
trigonometry, 198
Calendar, 567-569
advertising, 569
calendars
friends, 571
holiday, 571
multiple, 570
personal, 570
public, 570, 583
searching, 584
Data API, 685
events
adding, 577-579
importing, 579-581
inviting guests, 581
Quick Add, 579
setting up, 570
views, 572-575
Agenda, 574
Day, 572
Month, 573
multiple calendars, 575
Next 4 Days, 574
other applications, 575-576
Week, 573
Canada Google site, 732
capitalization searches, 29
carbon copy (cc), 360
Catalogs, 237
product categories, 239
searching, 238
viewing, 239, 242

categories
Directory, 62-64
Video, 444
CBS News website, 516
cc (carbon copy), 360
cc: operator, 366, 738
celebrity-sighting mashups, 312
Cell Phone Reception and Tower Search website, 305
cell phones
Froogle for Mobile, 526, 711
Gmail, 354, 525
home page, 526
image searches, 522
local searches, 522
Maps
downloading, 524
Maps for Mobile application, 293-294
querying via text messaging, 292
sending, 291
Mobile Sitemaps, 622
News, 516, 525
specialized web searches, 521
text messaging searches, 523-524
web searches, 520-521
cellular mashups, 305
census layer (Earth), 339
charts (Finance), 87-89
chatting
Chat, 390-391
Gmail, 393-395

Talk, 387
  connecting with other IM networks, 396-399
  customizing, 391-392
  disadvantages, 395
  status, changing, 391
  text-based, 388
  users, 388-390
  voice-based, 391

checking spelling, 687

Chicago
  Hot Dog Stands website, 302
  Transit Authority, 303
  Tribune website, 517

child Internet safety (SafeSearch content filter), 176
  Advanced Search page, 177
  disabling, 179
  levels, 176
  Preferences page, 177
  search results page URLs, editing, 178
  standard search box, 177

Chile Google site, 732

Chompster, 302

Choose File dialog box, 362

churches/cemeteries layer (Earth), 339

city boundaries layer (Earth), 339

CityRanks website, 306

clarifying questions (Answers), 473

Clear button, 588

cloaking, 635

ClubFly website, 303

CNET news website, 42

Co-op, 706

Code, 684-685

code swapping, 635

coffee shops layer (Earth), 339

Collage button, 588

College Life, 133

college/university mashups, 307

Colombia Google site, 732

comments
  Answers, 470
  blogs, 414, 427

community showcase layer (Earth), 339

CommunityWalk website, 692

company information (company/security pages), 83-85

composing Gmail messages, 360

conditional Blogger tags, 428

configuring
  AdSense ads, 644, 647
  Calendar, 570
  Earth view options, 332-333
  Google as homepage, 172-173
  preferences, 161-163
    content filtering, 163
    languages, 162-163

new results window, 163
    results per page, 163
    Screensaver, 611

contacts (Gmail), 371
  adding, 372-374
  groups, 375-377
  importing, 374
  searching, 375
  sending messages to, 377
  viewing, 374

content filtering
  images, 440
  SafeSearch, 176
    Advanced Search page, 177
    disabling, 179
    levels, 176
    Preferences page, 177
    search results page URLs, editing, 178
    standard search box, 177

content modules (Personalized Homepage)
  adding, 165
  customizing, 167-168
  deleting, 169
  gadgets, 562-564
  rearranging, 169
  unofficial, 169-170

content-sensitive advertising, 658

contextual targeting, 641

Continue button, 650

Continue to Payment Information button, 472

conversations (Gmail), 356-358

converting units of measure, 202-206
  area, 205
  cups into teaspoons, 203
  currency, 205
  data, 205
  degrees, 204
  distance, 205
  electricity, 205
  energy, 205
  hexadecimal, 206
  mass, 205
  meters to feet, 203
  miles per hour into kilometers per hour, 206
  nautical miles, 206
  numbering systems, 205
  pounds to kilograms, 204
  power, 205
  quantity, 205
  speed, 205
  temperature, 205
  time, 205
  U.S. dollars to Euros, 203
  volume, 205
  years into seconds, 204
  years to Roman numerals, 205

Cook Islands Google site, 732

Corel Paint Shop Pro, 605

corporate networks
  Desktop for Enterprise, 668-669
  Earth Enterprise, 671
  Mini, 669-670
  Search Appliance, 670-671

SketchUp, 671-672
  Toolbar for Enterprise, 667-668

cos operator, 198

cosecant operator, 198

cosh operator, 199

cosine operator, 198

cost per click (CPC), 223

cost-per-thousand-impressions (CPM), 660

Costa Rica Google site, 732

costs
  AdWords, 660
  Answers, 467
  price comparison sites, 222

cotangent operator, 198

Cote D'Ivoire Google site, 732

country-specific searches, 183

country-specific sites, 186, 731-735

CPC (cost per click), 223

CPM (cost-per-thousand-impressions), 660

Create Alert button, 516

Create Calendar button, 570

Create Filter button, 370

Create My Google Answers Account button, 472

Create My Group button, 502

crime stats layer (Earth), 339

Croatia/Hrvatska Google site, 732

Crop button, 595

cropping pictures, 595-596

cross-posting, 505

csc operator, 198

Cuba Google site, 732

cups to teaspoons conversion, 203

currency, 205

Customize Google for Your Site button, 678

customizing
  alerts, 215-216
  content modules, 167-168
  Free WebSearch, 678-680
  main search page language, 184-185
  Mobile home page, 526
  News, 512-513
  placemarks (Earth), 343-345
  searches
    Advanced Searchpage, 44-46
    and, 32
    automatic word stemming, 34
    body text, 40
    capitalization, 29
    date ranges, 41
    domains, 38
    exact phrases, 35
    excluding words, 34
    file types, 37, 48
    highlighting keywords, 43

links to specific pages, 42

most recent results, 47

number of results per page, 48

number ranges, 41

or searches, 32

page information, 43

page titles, 39

similar pages, 42

similar words, 34

stop words, 33

URLs, 39, 46-47

whole-word wildcards, 36

word order, 29

words in links, 40

templates (Blogger), 425-429

Talk, 391-392

Toolbar, 540-541

Video views, 445-446

D

Dashboard Widgets for Mac, 712

data analysis applications, 686

Data APIs, 685

data units of measure, 205

database of web pages, 18-19

date range searches, 41

date: operator, 45

daterange: operator, 41, 738

Day view (Calendar), 572

deep web, 19, 121

defaults
Map locations, 287
Toolbar
    Bookmarks, 535
    buttons. See buttons, Toolbar
    configuration, 532
    Gmail, 535
    SpellCheck, 536

define: operator, 141, 738

definition searches
Glossary, 141-142
Sets, 143-144
what is search, 139-140

degrees conversions, 204

deleting
alerts, 216
buttons (Toolbar), 540
content modules (Personalized Homepage), 169
copyrighted images, 441
gadgets from sidebar, 563
Gmail
    labels, 368
    messages, 363
websites from web index, 621

Democratic Republic of the Congo Google site, 732

demographic mashups, 306

Denmark Google site, 732

Denver Post website, 517

designing websites, 710

deskbar (Desktop), 560

Desktop, 548
deskbar, 560
downloading, 549
for Enterprise, 668-669
hard disk searches, 550
    advanced, 553-554
    basic, 550
    results, 550-553
    Timeline view, 554
index, 549, 554
Microsoft Outlook, 556
multiple computers, 556-557
SDK, 685
sidebar, 561
    gadgets, 562-564
    viewing, 561
web searches, 558-560

Desktop button (Toolbar), 534

Detroit Free Press website, 517

developing Google-based applications
Code, 684
help, 687
programming with Webs API, 685
third-party developers, 684-685
types of applications, 686-687
Webs API, 687

DG coverage layer (Earth), 339

diagnostics (Sitemaps), 625-626

dialog boxes
Account Properties, 397
Add/Remove Gadgets, 562
Choose File, 362
Display Properties, 610
Edit Button, 534
Export to Folder, 598
File Download, 362
Google Pack Screensaver, 611
GPS Device, 347
Import Contacts, 374
iTunes, 457
Jabber Accounts, 397
Measure, 345
New Placemark, 343
Options, 330
Picasa Prints and Products, 599
Print, 599
Rename Files, 590
Select Email, 602
Service Discovery, 398

diaphaneity.com, 422

dining layer (Earth), 339

dining mashups, 302-303

directions. *See* Maps

Directory, 56
accessing, 56
advantages over search engines, 60
assembly, 58-59
categories, 62-64
searching, 61-62

directories (search engines), 56-58

disabling SafeSearch filtering, 179

Discussion Groups (Finance), 91
finding, 92
new discussions, starting, 94-95
profiles, creating, 93-94
reading/rating messages, 92
replying to messages, 94

discussions (company/security pages), 85

Display Properties dialog box, 610

distance, 205

distances along paths (Earth), 345-347

dividing numbers, 196

division operator, 196

Djibouti Google site, 732

doctor searches, 299

document servers, 17

domain searches, 38

Dominica Google site, 732

Dominican Republic Google site, 732

doorway pages, 635

Download Gmail Notifier button, 384

Download Google Pack button, 609

downloading videos, 453
iPods, 457
Sony PSPs, 458

driving directions
Earth, 336-337
Maps, 280
downloading to cell phones, 524
following, 282, 285
generating, 280-281
printing, 285
reversing, 283

dynamic content (page rankings), 632

E

earnings per share, 87

Earth
3D buildings option, 328
3D terrain option, 328
custom placemarks, 343-345
default view, 323
distances along paths, 345-347
driving directions, 336-337
Enterprise, 671
GPS devices, 347
interface, 318
KML, 685
layers, 338-340
locations, 335-336
navigating, 319
keyboard, 322-323
mouse, 321-322
onscreen controls, 320
placemarks, 325-327
points of interest, 342
versions, 317-318

views, 332
  full-screen mode, 333
  latitude/longitude grid,
    333
  Overview map, 333
  preferences, 332-333
  printing, 335
  saving, 335
  zooming, 323

earthquakes layer (Earth),
339

East Timor Google site, 732

eBay, 263-264

Ecuador Google site, 732

Edit Button dialog box, 534

editing
  alerts, 215-216
  blog posts, 412
  RSS feed subscriptions,
    112

Egypt Google site, 732

[el] operator, 41

El Salvador Google site, 732

electricity, 205

email, 351
  addresses, 355
  attachments
    adding, 361-362
    saving, 362
    scanning for viruses, 371
    viewing, 362
  blog postings, 115
  cc/bcc, 360
  composing, 360
  contacts, 371
    adding, 372-374
    groups, 375-377

importing, 374
  searching, 375
  sending messages to,
    377
  viewing, 374
conversations, viewing,
  356-358
deleting, 363
forwarding, 359
inbox, 355, 363-366
incoming mail, filtering,
  369-370
inviting other users, 354
maps, 279
messages
  archiving, 368-369
  forwarding to other
    accounts, 379
  labels, applying,
    367-368
  new, notifying, 383-384
  reading in another pro-
    gram, 378-379
  signatures, adding,
    382-383
  starring, 367
  viewing from Toolbar,
    384
photos, 602
reading, 356
replying, 358
RSS feeds, viewing,
  380-381
searching not sorting,
  352-353
sending, 361
signing up, 354
spam, blocking, 371
unique features, 352
vacation mode, 379-380

Email button, 588, 602

enabling SafeSearch filter-
ing, 177-178

energy, 205

entering search queries, 24

entertainment (Video), 444
  categories, 444
  competitors, 449
  Picks videos, 448
  searching, 447
  title searches, 447
  unofficial blogs, 448
  Video Blog, 448
  videos
    downloading, 453,
      457-458
    playing, 452-456
    previewing, 450
    Top 100, 447
    uploading, 459-461
  viewing options, 451-452
  views, changing, 445-446

entertainment mashups,
302-303

Entertainment Weekly web-
site, 517

Eris' Template Generator
website, 422

Ethiopia Google site, 732

EVDB (Events and Venues
Database), 299

event finder, 299

events (Calendar)
  adding, 577-579
  importing, 579-581
  inviting guests, 581
  Quick Add, 579

Events and Venues
Database (EVDB), 299

EVMapper, 299

exact phrase searches, 35

excluding words from
searches, 34

exponents operator, 198

Export button, 588, 598

Export to Folder dialog
box, 598

exporting photos (Picasa),
598

Extensions for Firefox, 712

F

FAA Flight Delay
Information website, 304

fact searches, 148

factorial operator, 198

fair use (images), 441-442

faulty directions, 285-286

Federal Trade Commission
website, 78

Feedburner service, 416

Fiji Google site, 732

File Download dialog box,
362

filename: operator, 366,
738

filetype searches, 37, 48

filetype: operator, 37, 45,
738

filtering
content, 163, 176-179
hard disk search results,
552-553

images, 440

incoming mail (Gmail),
369-370

Finance
accessing, 80
company/security-specific
pages, 83-85
Discussion Groups, 91
finding, 92
*new discussions, starting,
94-95*
profiles, creating, 93-94
*reading/rating messages,
92*
replying to messages, 94
financial metrics, 86
interactive charts, 87-89
Market Summary, 81
portfolio tracking, 89-91
Recent Quotes, 82
Related News, 82
Today's Headlines, 82

Find a Local Racetrack
website, 310

Find the Landmark web-
site, 311

finding. *See also* searches
Area 51, 315
bird flu cases, 315
bird watchers, 314
Broadway plays/shows,
300
celebrity-sightings, 312
colleges/universities, 307
demographics, 306
doctors, 299
events, 299
Finance Discussion
Groups, 92

first kisses, 314
food/entertainment,
302-303
games, 311-312
gas prices, 299
highest elevation points,
315
homes for sale, 301
hotels, 300
items (Google Base),
248-251
libraries, 299
local business maps, 300
location bookmarks, 314
package mappers, 314
people's atlas, 314
personals, 315
photo maps, 308
political campaign contributions, 315
registered sex offenders,
315
San Francisco earthquake,
315
spacecraft, 315
sports, 309-310
time, 315
transportation, 303-304
U.S. presidential birth-
places, 314
WiFi/cellular, 305
weather, 297

FindIt @ link, 126

findu.com, 305

Finland Google site, 732

fire/hospitals layer (Earth),
339

Firefox, 612

first kisses mashups, 314

fixing photos (Picasa)
cropping, 595-596
dark/light, 591-592
off-color, 592-594
red eye, 594
special effects, 596-597

flight status, tracking, 150

Floodwater Mapper, 298

food mashups, 302-303

forward price/earnings ratio (F P/E), 87

forwarding Gmail, 359, 379

FOX News website, 516

France Google site, 732

fraudulent SEOs, 637

Free Blogger Templates website, 422

Free SafeSearch, 676-677

FreeStats website, 431

FreeTranslation website, 193

Free WebSearch, 675-676

Free WebSearch with SiteSearch, 677-678

friends calendars, 571

from: operator, 366, 738

Froogle
adding products to, 232
advanced searches, 226-228
best bargains, 234
buying items, 228
cell phones, 526
functions, 222

local bargains, 229-230
main page, 223
merchant reviews, 232-234
Mobile, 711
product detail pages, 225-226
results, 224-225
searching, 223
Shopping list feature, 235-236
store inventories, uploading, 262
Wish List, 236

full-screen mode (Earth), 333

function buttons (Picasa), 587-588

future of Google, 719-721

FutureCrisis Avian Flu Outbreak Map, 315

G

G-Mapper website, 624

gadgets, 562-564

Gadgets API, 685

GalleryPlayer, 614

Gambia Google site, 732

games mashups, 311-312

gas prices search, 299

gas stations layer (Earth), 339

Gawker Stalker website, 312

gCensus website, 306

general Blogger tags, 426

Generate HTML button, 681

GeoBirds, 314

geographic data (Earth Enterprise), 671

geographic features layer (Earth), 339

Germany Google site, 732

Get Code Now! button, 116

Get Started Now! button, 647

Gibraltar Google site, 732

Gift CD button, 604

Global Positioning System (GPS), 347

Global Surfari, 310

Glossary, 141-142

Gmail, 351, 393
attachments, 371
calendar events, 579
cell phones, 525
chats, 393-395
contacts, 371
adding, 372-374
groups, 375-377
importing, 374
searching, 375
sending messages to, 377
viewing, 374
email address, 355
inbox, 355, 363-366
incoming mail, filtering, 369-370
inviting users, 354
messages
archiving, 368-369
attachments, 361-362

cc/bcc, 360

composing, 360

conversations, viewing, 356-358

deleting, 363

forwarding, 359, 379

labels, applying, 367-368

new, notifying, 383-384

reading, 356, 378-379

replying, 358

sending, 361

signatures, adding, 382-383

starring, 367

viewing from Toolbar, 384

Notifier, 383-384

RSS feeds, viewing, 380-381

searching not sorting, 352-353

signing up, 354

spam, blocking, 371

status, changing, 394

unique features, 352

vacation mode, 379-380

Gmail button (Toolbar), 535

GMaps Flight Tracker, 304

Gmaps Pedometer website, 309

golf layer (Earth), 339

Google

accounts, creating, 89

advertising, 14-15

business model, 10

competitors, 717-719

future, 719-721

history, 11-13

Idol website, 448

mission, 10

Modules website, 169

original home page, 12

Pack Screensaver dialog box, 611

public offering, 13

revenues, 13-14

sales-only offices, 17

stock prices, 13

technology and sales offices, 17

technology-only offices, 17

Ultimate Interface, 49

Video Latest, 448

Video of the Day, 448

Weather Maps, 298

as wireless service provider, 722-723

world headquarters, 16

Google-based applications, developing

Code, 684

help, 687

programming with Webs API, 685

third-party developers, 684-685

types of applications, 686-687

Webs API, 687

Google Earth community layer (Earth), 339

Google-Yahoo Traffic-Weather Maps, 304

Googleating, 634

GoogleBot, 18

Googleplex, 16

GoogleWidgets, 170

googol, 12

GPS (Global Positioning System), 347

GPS Device dialog box, 347

Greece Google site, 732

Greenland Google site, 733

grocery stores layer (Earth), 339

group: operator, 495

Groups (Google)

advanced searching, 495-497

browsing, 493

cross-posting, 505

inviting members to join, 503-504

managing groups, 504

messages, reading, 498

netiquette, 505

new groups, starting, 501-502

new threads, starting, 500

posting, 499

searching, 492-494

subscribing, 498

Usenet, archiving, 492

viewing, 497

groups

alerts, 212

contacts (Gmail), 375-377

groups: operator, 738

GSiteCrawler website, 624

Gsitemap website, 624

Guatemala Google site, 733

Guernsey Google site, 733

gWiFi.net, 305

GymPost website, 309

H

Haiti Google site, 733

hard disk searches, 550
  advanced, 553-554
  basic, 550
  index, viewing, 554
  multiple computers, 556-557
  results, 550-553
  Timeline view, 554

has:attachment operator, 366, 738

heading tags, 631

headlines (News), 509

Health, 714

Healthia Doctor Search, 299

Hello, 601

Hello button, 588

hexadecimal conversions, 206

hierarchies
  newsgroups, 490-491
  websites, 628

High Fiber Content, 403

High Rankings website, 636

highest elevation points mashups, 315

Highest Elevation Points website, 315

Highlight button (Toolbar), 539

highlighting keywords, 43

history
  Google, Inc., 11-13
  Usenet, 490

hit counters (Blogger), 431

HockeyCat Rink Guide, 310

Hold button, 588

holiday calendars, 571

home page (Google), 24-25, 172-173

Homepage API, 169

HomePriceMaps.com, 301

Homes Sold website, 301

Honduras Google site, 733

Hong Kong Google site, 733

hosts (Blogger), 419-421

Hot Modules, 170

hotel searches, 300

HotelMapper, 300

HotorNot + Google Maps, 315

households, searching, 69-72

housing mashups, 301

HousingMaps, 301

HTML tags
  Blogger, 425
    archive, 428
    comments, 427
    conditional, 428
    general, 426
    photos, 429
    posting, 426-427
    profile, 428
    reading/listening lists, 429
    site feed, 428
  heading, 631
  META, 630-631
  TITLE, 631

Hungary Google site, 733

hyperbolic sine operator, 199

hybrid maps, 278

hyperbolic cosine operator, 199

hyperbolic functions, 199

hyperbolic tangent operator, 199

I

I'm Feeling Lucky button, 25

Iceland Google site, 733

Image Search, 155, 435
  advanced, 436-437
  basic, 436
  copyrighted images, deleting, 441
  fair use, 441-442
  filtering, 440
  results, 438-440

images
  editing in Picasa
    burning to CDs/DVDs, 604
    cropping, 595-596
    dark/light, 591-592
    downloading, 585

emailing, 602

exporting, 598

function buttons, 587-588

moving, 589

off-color, 592-594

picture library, 587

printing, 599

red eye, 594

renaming, 590

resizing, 598

saving, 598

search box, 589

searching for pictures, 586

sharing with Hello, 601

special effects, 596-597

zoom slider control, 589

searching, 151, 435

advanced, 436-437

basic, 436

copyrighted images, deleting, 441

fair use, 441-442

filtering, 440

results, 438-440

Import and Export wizard, 580

Import Contacts button, 374

Import Contacts dialog box, 374

importing

Calendar events, 579-581

contacts (Gmail), 374

RSS feeds, 112

In Search of Google Videos website, 448

in: operator, 366, 738

inanchor: operator, 46, 738

inblogtitle: operator, 103, 738

inbox (Gmail), 355, 363-366

incoming mail (Gmail), 369-370

increasing

AdSense revenues, 654-658

page rankings, 627

code updates, 631

deliberate practices to avoid, 634-636

designs to avoid, 632-634

dynamic content, 632

formatting words, 629

fraudulent SEOs, 637

heading tags, 631

hierarchical organization, 628

keywords, 628-629

META tags, 630-631

OPML files, 632

SEO, 636-637

site links, increasing, 627

text links, 629

text not images, 629

TITLE tags, 631

indexes

Desktop, 549, 554

servers, 17

web pages, 20

India Google site, 733

Indonesia Google site, 733

info windows (map mashups), 696

info: operator, 43, 738

InfoSpace website, 72

inpostauthor: operator, 103, 738

inposttitle: operator, 103, 738

installing

browser buttons, 544

Pack, 608-609

Toolbar, 532

instant messaging, 388

Gmail, 393-395

Talk, 387

chat history, saving, 390-391

connecting with other IM networks, 396, 398-399

customizing, 391-392

disadvantages, 395

status, changing, 391

text-based chats, 388

users, 388-390

voice-based chats, 391

insubject: operator, 495, 738

IntelliMapper website, 625

international news, 510

Internet Business Promoter, 636

intext: operator, 46, 738

intitle: operator, 46, 738

inurl: operator, 46, 738

inverse cosecant operator, 199

inverse cosine operator, 199

inverse cotangent operator, 199

inverse secant operator, 199

inverse sine operator, 199

inverse tangent operator, 199

inverse trigonometric functions, 199

invisible web, 19, 121

iPod video downloads, 457

Ireland Google site, 733

IrfanView, 605

is: operator, 366, 738

Isle of Man Google site, 733

Israel Google site, 187, 733

Italy Google site, 733

items (Google Base)
   browsing, 251-253
   bulk uploads, 261-262
   buying, 253-254
   prohibited, 247-248
   searching, 248-251
   selling, 256
      Google Payments, accepting, 259-260
      listings, submitting, 256-258

iTunes
   dialog box, 457
   Video Store website, 449

J

Jabber Accounts dialog box, 397

Jabber website, 396

Jamaica Google site, 733

Japan Google site, 733

Jersey Google site, 733

JibMap, 299

JoeMap website, 308

Jordan Google site, 733

Judy's Book Maps, 300

Julian dates, 41-42

K

Kazakhstan Google site, 733

Kenya Google site, 733

key metrics (company/ security pages), 83

keywords
   selecting, 51-53
   stuffing, 635

kid Internet safety (SafeSearch content filter), 176
   Advanced Search page, 177
   disabling, 179
   levels, 176
   Preferences page, 177
   search results page URLs, editing, 178
   standard search box, 177

Kosher Food/Restaurant Maps website, 302

Kyrgyzstan Google site, 733

L

Label button, 588

label: operator, 366, 739

labels
   Base, 246
   Gmail messages, 367-368

Labs, 703-704
   Co-op, 706
   Dashboard Widgets for Mac, 712
   Extensions for Firefox, 712
   Froogle for Mobile, 711
   Links, 709
   Mars, 710
   Notebook, 706
   Page Creator, 710
   Reader, 707
   Ride Finder, 711
   Sets, 143-144, 709
   Suggest, 712
   Transit, 711
   Trends, 704-705
   Web Accelerator, 713

languages, 181
   country-specific sites, 186, 731-735
   country-specific searches, 183
   default, 182
   main search page, changing, 184-185
   preferences, 162-163

specific language
searches, 182
translating, 187-189
disadvantages, 193
Google Toolbar, 192
search results, 192
text passages, 189
web pages, 190
*words with Google
Toolbar, 192*

latitude/longitude grid
(Earth), 333

Latvia Google site, 733

layers (Earth), 338-340

Lesotho Google site, 733

lg operator, 199

Libraries411, 299

libraries
access (Scholar), 129
links, 126
searches, 299

Libyan Arab Jamahiriya
Google site, 733

Liechtenstein Google site,
733

link: operator, 42, 46, 739

links
bombing, 634
farms, 635
maps, 279
searches, 40-42

Links (Google), 709

Linux Google search, 134

Lithuania Google site, 733

ln operator, 199

Local Lush website, 303

Local News by Zip Code,
297

local searches
bargains, 229-230
business maps, 300
information/services
mashups, 299-300
Mobile, 522

location bookmark
mashups, 314

location: operator, 739

lodging layer (Earth), 339

log operator, 199

logarithm base 2 operator,
199

logarithm base 10 opera-
tor, 199

logarithm base e operator,
199

logarithmic functions, 199

LookSmart website, 58

Los Angeles Times website,
517

Luxemburg Google site,
733

M

machine: operator, 739

Macromedia Flash Player
website, 452

major retail layer (Earth),
339

Malawi Google site, 733

Malaysia Google site, 733

Malta Google site, 733

management (company/
security pages), 85

managing
alerts, 215-216
groups, 504
Shopping list (Froogle),
236

Map Attack, 311

Map Builder website, 692

Map Maker website, 692

map mashups
creating with map-builder
websites, 692-693
creating with Maps API,
693
animations, 697
basic maps, 693-695
controls, 696
info windows, 696
markers, 698
profitability, 700

MapGameDay.com, 309

Maplandia News Centre
BBC World News Map,
297

Maps
businesses
adding, 290
finding, 288-290
*location data, submit-
ting, 262*
cell phones
*Maps for Mobile applica-
tion, 293-294*
*querying via text mes-
saging, 292*
sending maps, 291

default locations, 287

downloading to cell phones, 524

driving directions, 280
  following, 282, 285
  generating, 280-281
  printing, 285
  reversing, 283

faulty directions, 285-286

Google map-builder web-sites, 692

hybrid maps, 278

mashups, 295-296
  Area 51, 315
  bird flu, 315
  bird watchers, 314
  celebrity-sightings, 312
  colleges/universities, 307
  demographics, 306
  first kisses, 314
  food/entertainment, 302-303
  games, 311-312
  highest elevation points, 315
  houses, 301
  local information/serv-ices, 299-300
  location bookmarks, 314
  news, 297
  package mappers, 314
  people's atlas, 314
  personals, 315
  photo map, 308
  political campaign con-tributions, 315
  registered sex offenders, 315
  San Francisco earth-quake, 315

spacecraft, 315

sports, 309-310

time, 315

transportation, 303-304

U.S. presidential birth-places, 314

weather, 297

WiFi/cellular, 305

navigating, 274-275

satellite images, 276-278

searching, 269
  address, 269-271
  landmarks, 271
  URLs, 272-273
  web search, 274

sharing maps, 279-280

Maps API, 685, 693
  animations, 697
  basic maps, 693-695
  controls, 696
  info windows, 696
  markers, 698

MapSexOffenders.com, 315

markers (maps), 698

market capitalization, 86

market research applica-tions, 686

Market Summary (Google Finance), 81

MarketWatch website, 79

Mars, 710

mashups, 295-296
  Area 51, 315
  bird flu, 315
  bird watchers, 314
  celebrity-sightings, 312
  colleges/universities, 307

demographics, 306

first kisses, 314

food/entertainment, 302-303

games, 311-312

highest elevation points, 315

houses, 301

local information/ services, 299-300

location bookmarks, 314

Maps, 692-693

animations, 697

basic maps, 693-695

controls, 696

info windows, 696

markers, 698-700

news, 297

package mappers, 314

people's atlas, 314

personals, 315

political campaign contri-butions, 315

registered sex offenders, 315

San Francisco earthquake, 315

spacecraft, 315

sports, 309-310

time, 315

transportation, 303-304, 308

U.S. presidential birth-places, 314

weather, 297

WiFi/cellular, 305

mass, 205

mathematics
  calculations
    addition, 196
    advanced functions, 198

algebraic operators, 196

division, 196

hyperbolic functions, 199

inverse trigonometry, 199

logarithmic functions, 199

multiple operations, 197

nesting equations, 197

Soople, 208-209

trigonometry, 198

constants, 199-202

units of measure conversions, 202-206

area, 205

cups into teaspoons, 203

currency, 205

data, 205

degrees, 204

distance, 205

electricity, 205

energy, 205

hexadecimal, 206

mass, 205

meters to feet, 203

miles per hour to kilometers per hour, 206

nautical miles, 206

numbering systems, 205

pounds to kilograms, 204

power, 205

quantity, 205

speed, 205

temperature, 205

time, 205

U.S. dollars to Euros, 203

volume, 205

years into seconds, 204

years to Roman numerals, 205

Mauritius Google site, 734

Measure dialog box, 345

Menumap, 302

merchant reviews (Froogle), 232-234

messages

Gmail

archiving, 368-369

attachments, 361-362

cc/bcc, 360

composing, 360

conversations, viewing, 356-358

deleting, 363

forwarding, 359, 379

labels, applying, 367-368

new, notifying, 383-384

reading, 356, 378-379

replying, 358

sending, 361

signatures, adding, 382-383

starring, 367

viewing from Toolbar, 384

Groups

new threads, starting, 500

posting, 499

reading, 498

meta tag stuffing, 635

META tags, 630-631

meters to feet conversion, 203

Mexico Google site, 734

***Miami Herald* website, 517**

Micronesia Google site, 734

Microsoft

Desktop searches, 556

Digital Image Suite, 605

Google

search, 134

compared, 717-718

miles per hour into kilometers per hour conversion, 206

Mini, 669-670

***Minneapolis Star Tribune* website, 517**

mirror websites, 635

mission of Google, Inc., 10

Mobile

Froogle, 526, 711

Gmail, 525

home page, 526

image searches, 522

local searches, 522

Maps,

downloading, 524

Maps for Mobile application, 293-294

querying via text messaging, 292

sending, 291

News, 516, 525

Sitemaps, 622

text messaging searches, 523-524

web searches, 520-521

mod operator, 198

modulo operator, 198

Mongolia Google site, 734

Month view (Calendar), 573

Montserrat Google site, 734

most recent results, viewing, 47

movie searches, 153-156

movie: operator, 739

movie/DVD rentals layer (Earth), 339

moving photos (Picasa), 589

Mozilla Firefox, 612

MSN Video website, 449

MSNBC website, 516

multiplication operator, 196

Music, 714

music searches, 156-157

My Way, 172

My WikiMap Cheap Gas Prices, 299

My Yahoo!, 172

myGmaps website, 692

N

names, searching, 69-72

Namibia Google site, 734

National Geographic Magazine layer (Earth), 340

National Review website, 517

Nauru Google site, 734

nautical miles conversion, 206

navigating
  Earth, 319
    keyboard, 322-323
    mouse, 321-322
    onscreen controls, 320
  Google Directory
    categories, 62-64
    searching, 61-62
  Google home page, 24
  Maps, 274-275

Nepal Google site, 734

nesting equations, 197

net income, 86

net profit margin, 87

Netherlands Google site, 734

netiquette, 505

network hard disk searches, 556-557

New Placemark dialog box, 343

new results windows, 163

New York Times website, 517

New Zealand Google site, 734

News
  alerts, 212, 515-516
  articles, searching, 513-514
  cell phones, 516
  customizing, 512-513
  default page, 508
  headlines, viewing, 509
  international, 510

news feeds, 514-515
  viewing on cell phones, 525

News button (Toolbar), 534

news
  feeds, 514-515
  magazines online, 517
  mashups, 297

Newseum website, 517

newsgroups
  advanced searching, 495-497
  browsing, 493
  cross-posting, 505
  hierarchies (Usenet), 490-491
  inviting members to join, 503-504
  managing, 504
  messages, reading, 498
  netiquette, 505
  new groups, starting, 501-502
  new threads, starting, 500
  posting, 499
  searching, 492-494
  subscribing, 498
  viewing, 497

newspapers online, 517

Newsweek website, 517

Next 4 Days view (Calendar), 574

NexTag, 222

NextBus websites, 303

NFL Stadiums website, 309

Nicaragua Google site, 734

Niue Google site, 734

Noipo.org Blogger Templates, 422

Norfolk Island Google site, 734

Norton AntiVirus, 613

Norway Google site, 734

Notebook, 706

Notifier (Gmail), 383-384

nth root of operator, 198

numbers
  calculating, 195
    addition, 196
    advanced functions, 198
    algebraic operators, 196
    dividing, 196
    hyperbolic functions, 199
    inverse trigonometry, 199
    logarithmic functions, 199
    multiple operations, 197
    nesting equations, 197
    Soople, 208-209
    trigonometry, 198
  math/science constants, 199-202
  searches, 41, 152-153
  systems, 205
  units of measure, converting, 202-206
    area, 205
    cups into teaspoons, 203
    currency, 205
    data, 205
    degrees, 204
    distance, 205
    electricity, 205
    energy, 205

hexadecimal, 206
mass, 205
meters to feet, 203
miles per hour into kilometers per hour, 206
nautical miles, 206
numbering systems, 205
pounds to kilograms, 204
power, 205
quantity, 205
speed, 205
temperature, 205
time, 205
U.S. dollars to Euros, 203
volume, 205
years into seconds, 204
years to Roman numerals, 205

NYC Beer and Music Map website, 303

NYC Trafficland, 304

NYC Transit Maps, 303

O

OCLC (Online Computer Library Center) project, 120

off-color pictures, 592-594

Oman Google site, 734

omitted results, 27

OneBox specialized results (search result page), 26

Online Computer Library Center (OCLC) project, 120

onNYTurf website, 303

Open Directory Project, 58-59

Open WorldCat database, 120

operating income, 86

operating margin, 86

operators
  !, 198
  %, 198
  ( ), 366, 737
  ", 366
  "" operator, 737
  ~ operator, 34, 737
  ^ operator, 198
  *, 36, 737
  **, 198
  +, 196, 737
  -, 196, 737
  . ., 737
  /, 196
  [el], 41
  advanced blog searches, 103
  advanced mathematic, 198
  after:, 737
  after:year/month/day, 366
  algebraic, 196
  allinanchor:, 40, 46, 737
  allintext:, 40, 46, 737
  allintitle:, 39, 46, 738
  allinurl:, 39, 46, 738
  author:, 124, 495, 738
  bcc:, 366, 738
  before:, 738

before:year/month/day, 366

blogurl:, 103, 738

book:, 738

bphonebook:, 738

cache:, 43, 738

cc:, 366, 738

date:, 45

daterange:, 41, 738

define:, 141, 738

filename:, 366, 738

filetype:, 37, 45, 738

from:, 366, 738

Froogle advanced searches, 228

Gmail, 365-366

group:, 495

groups:, 738

Groups, 495

has:attachment, 366, 738

hyperbolic, 199

in:, 366

inanchor:, 46, 738

inblogtitle:, 103, 738

info:, 43, 738

inpostauthor:, 103, 738

inposttitle:, 103, 738

insubject:, 495, 738

intext:, 46, 738

intitle:, 46, 738

inurl:, 46, 738

inverse trigonometric, 199

is:, 366

label:, 366, 739

link:, 42, 46, 739

listing of, 737-739

location:, 739

logarithmic, 199

machine:, 739

movie:, 739

om:, 738

OR, 366, 739

os:, 738

phonebook:, 74, 739

related:, 46, 739

rphonebook:, 739

safesearch:, 46, 177, 739

Scholar, 124

similar:, 42

site:, 38, 46, 739

source:, 739

stocks:, 80, 739

store:, 228, 739

subject:, 366, 739

title:, 447

to:, 366, 739

trigonometric, 198

under:, 739

weather, 739

what are, 739

what is, 739

OPML (Outline Processor Markup Language), 632

Options dialog box, 330

OptLink website, 636

OR operator, 366, 739

or searches, 32

Order Prints button, 588

original home page, 12

Orkut, 715

other relevant pages (search result page), 27

Outline Processor Markup Language (OPML), 632

Overview map (Earth), 333

The Oz Report Flight Parks, 310

P

Pack
core programs, 607-608
installing, 608-609
Screensaver, 610-611
third-party software
Ad-Aware SE Personal, 613
Adobe Reader, 614
GalleryPlayer, 614
Mozilla Firefox, 612
Norton AntiVirus, 613
RealPlayer, 614
updates, 609

package mapper mashups, 314

PackageMapper.com, 314

Page Creator, 710

page excerpts (search result page), 26

page information searches, 43

page titles, 26, 39

Page, Larry, 11

PageRank, increasing, 627
code updates, 631
deliberate practices to avoid, 634-636
designs to avoid, 632-634
dynamic content, 632
formatting words, 629
fraudulent SEOs, 637

heading tags, 631
hierarchical organization, 628
keywords, 628-629
META tags, 630-631
OPML files, 632
SEO, 636-637
site links, increasing, 627
text links, 629
text not images, 629
TITLE tags, 631

PageRank button (Toolbar), 536

Pakistan Google site, 734

Panama Google site, 734

Panorama Explorer website, 308

Panoramio website, 308

Paraguay Google site, 734

parameters (URL), 46-47

parks/recreation areas layer (Earth), 340

Pay Listing Fee and Post Question button, 472

Payments
accepting, 259-260
buying items, 253-254

pay-per-click (PPC) model, 223

People **website, 517**

people searches
names, 69-72
personal information, 75-76
phone numbers, 74

white pages directories, 72
yourself, 76-78

people's atlas mashups, 314

percent operator, 198

Perfect 10 website, 441

performance
AdSense, 653
Adwords, 664

personal calendars, 570

personal information (people), 75-78

personal preferences, 161
content filtering, 163
languages, 162-163
new results windows, 163
Personalized Homepage, 164, 171
content modules, 165-169
RSS feeds, adding, 166
start page content, 165-166
unofficial content modules, 169-170
results per page, 163

Personal Weather Stations, 298

Personalized Homepage, 164, 171
content modules
adding, 165
customizing, 167-168
deleting, 169
rearranging, 169
unofficial, 169-170

RSS feeds, adding, 166
start page content, 165-166

personals mashups, 315

Peru Google site, 734

pharmacy layer (Earth), 340

Philippines Google site, 734

phone numbers, 74

PhoneBook, searching
names, 69-72
phone numbers, 74

phonebook: operator, 74, 739

photo Blogger tags, 429

photo map mashups, 308

pi, 199

Picasa
downloading, 585
function buttons, 587-588
photos
burning to CDs/DVDs, 604
cropping, 595-596
darkness/lightness, 591-592
emailing, 602
exporting, 598
moving, 589
off-color, 592-594
printing, 599
red eye, 594
renaming, 590
resizing, 598
saving, 598
sharing with Hello, 601
special effects, 596-597

picture library, 587
Prints and Products dialog box, 599
search box, 589
searching for pictures, 586
zoom slider control, 589

Picks videos, 448

pictures
  editing in Picasa
    burning to CDs/DVDs, 604
    cropping, 595-596
    dark/light, 591-592
    downloading, 585
    emailing, 602
    exporting, 598
    function buttons, 587-588
    moving, 589
    off-color, 592-594
    picture library, 587
    printing, 599
    red eye, 594
    renaming, 590
    resizing, 598
    saving, 598
    search box, 589
    searching for pictures, 586
    sharing with Hello, 601
    special effects, 596-597
    zoom slider control, 589
  searches (Image Search)
    advanced, 436-437
    basic, 436
    copyrighted images, deleting, 441
    fair use, 441-442

    filtering, 440
    results, 438-440

Pitcairn Islands Google site, 734

Pixagogo website, 308

placemarks (Earth), 325-327, 343-345

Platial website, 314

Play Tour button, 337

playing videos, 452-453
  another computer, 456
  Google Video Player, 454-456
  other video players, 456

POI (points of interest), 342

PokerMashup, 311

Poland Google site, 734

political campaign contributions mashups, 315

pop-up blocker button (Toolbar), 536

populated places layer (Earth), 340

portfolio tracking (Finance), 89-91

Portugal Google site, 734

Post Message button, 95

postal code boundaries layer (Earth), 340

posting
  Blogger tags, 426-427
  blogs, 409-412
  Groups, 499

pounds to kilograms conversion, 204

power, 205

PPC (pay-per-click) model, 223

preferences
  personal, 162-163. *See also* Personalized Homepage
  search result page, 26

Preferences page, 161
  content filtering, 163
  languages, 162-163
  new results windows, 163
  results per page, 163
  SafeSearch filtering, 177

previewing videos, 450

previously answered questions, viewing, 467, 470

price
  AdWords, 660
  Answers, 467
  comparison sites, 222

price/earnings ratio (P/E), 87

Print button, 599

Print dialog box, 599

printing
  driving directions
    Earth, 337
    Maps, 285
  Earth views, 335
  image search results, 440
  maps, 280
  photos (Picasa), 599

Priority Submit website, 636

product detail pages (Froogle), 225-226

profiles
Blogger tags, 428
Finance, 93-94

programming
Google-based applica-
tions
help, 687
types of applications,
686-687
Webs API, 685-687
map mashups with map-
builder websites,
692-693
map mashups with Maps
API, 693
animations, 697
basic maps, 693-695
controls, 696
info windows, 696
markers, 698

prohibited items (Base),
247-248

public calendars, 570,
583-584

public offering, 13

Publish Post button, 412

Puerto Rico Google site,
734

purity of searches, 172

Q

Q&A, 148

quantity units of measure,
205

queries, entering, 24

questions and answers
searches, 465

comments, adding, 470
cost, 467
previously answered ques-
tions, viewing, 467, 470
questions
asking, 470-472
clarifying, 473
types, 466
viewing, 472
rating answers, 474
researchers, 466

Quick Add feature
(Calendar), 579

Quick Search box
(Desktop), 559-560

R

radius of earth, 199

railroads layer (Earth), 340

Rand McNally travel site,
286

ranking search results,
20-21

Reader, 707
accessing, 108
blogs, reading, 108-109
feeds
finding, 110
importing, 112
listing boxes, 115-116
sharing, 113-114
subscriptions, editing,
112
URLs, 111
site URLs, 111

reading
blogs, 108-109
Finance Discussion Group
messages, 92
messages
Gmail, 356, 378-379
Groups, 498
news feeds, 514-515

reading/listening lists
Blogger tags, 429

Real Estate Advisor, 301

Real-time Simple
Syndication. *See* RSS feeds

RealEstateAuctions.com,
301

RealPlayer, 614

rearranging content mod-
ules (Personalized
Homepage), 169

Recent Quotes (Google
Finance), 82

recent stories (company/
security pages), 85

red eye (pictures), 594

Redeye button, 594

refining searches
Advanced Searchpage,
44-46
and, 32
automatic word stem-
ming, 34
body text, 40
capitalization, 29
date ranges, 41
domains, 38
exact phrases, 35
excluding words, 34

file types, 37, 48

highlighting keywords, 43

links to specific pages, 42

most recent results, 47

number of results per page, 48

number ranges, 41

or searches, 32

page information, 43

page titles, 39

similar pages, 42

similar words, 34

stop words, 33

URLs, 39, 46-47

whole-word wildcards, 36

word order, 29

words in links, 40

registered sex offenders mashups, 315

related companies (company/security pages), 85

related: operator, 42, 46, 739

Rename Files dialog box, 590

renaming photos (Picasa), 590

repairing photos (Picasa)

cropping, 595-596

dark/light, 591-592

off-color, 592-594

red eye, 594

special effects, 596-597

Republic of Korea Google site, 734

replying to messages

Finance, 94

Gmail, 358

Republic of Congo Google site, 734

Republish button, 421

research

answers to questions (Answers), 465

asking questions, 470-472

clarifying questions, 473

comments, adding, 470

cost, 467

previously answered questions, viewing, 467, 470

rating answers, 474

researchers, 466

types of questions, 466

viewing questions, 472

Book Search, 476

additional book information, 484

advanced searches, 478-479

content, 476-480

Google Books Library Project, 477

Google Books Partner Program, 476

publishing community conflict, 484-487

searching, 478

standard web search, 477

Reset North button, 323

resizing photos (Picasa), 598

resources (company/security pages), 85

results (searches)

blogs

evaluating, 102

feeds, finding, 110

reading, 108-109

subscribing, 106-107

extending, 28

filetype restrictions, 48

Froogle, 224-225

hard disk

filtering, 552-553

viewing, 550-552

images

copyrighted, deleting, 441

fair use, 441-442

filtering, 440

printing, 440

saving, 439

viewing, 438-439

most recent, 47

new windows, 163

number per page, 48, 163

omitted, 27

PhoneBook, 70

ranking, 20-21

refining

Advanced Searchpage, 44-46

and, 32

automatic word stemming, 34

body text, 40

capitalization, 29

date ranges, 41

domains, 38

exact phrases, 35

excluding words, 34

file types, 37, 48

highlighting keywords, 43

links to specific pages, 42

most recent results, 47

number of results per page, 48

number ranges, 41

or searches, 32

page information, 43

page titles, 39

similar pages, 42

similar words, 34

stop words, 33

URLs, 39, 46-47

whole-word wildcards, 36

word order, 29

words in links, 40

saving, 53

Scholar, 121-123

translating, 192

viewing, 25-27

results page advertising, 659

across Google Network, 659

ads, creating, 660, 663

costs, 660

performance, monitoring, 664

third-party sites, 659

return on average assets, 87

return on average equity, 87

revenues, 86

AdSense, 642

Google, Inc., 13-14

Maps mashups, 700

Ride Finder, 711

Road Sign Math website, 312

roads layer (Earth), 340

Roadsideamerica.com, 304

Romance, 714

Romania Google site, 734

root operator, 198

Rotate clockwise button, 588

Rotate counter-clockwise button, 588

Rotate Right button, 323

rphonebook: operator, 74, 739

RSS (Real-time Simple Syndication) feeds, 98

adding

Personalized Homepage, 166

web pages, 115-116

dynamic content, 632

finding, 110

importing, 112

reading, 108-109

sharing, 113-114

subscriptions, 106-107, 112

URLs, 111

viewing in Gmail, 380-381

Russia Google site, 734

Rwanda Google site, 734

S

SafeSearch, 163

SafeSearch content filter, 176

disabling, 179

enabling, 177-178

levels, 176

safesearch: operator, 46, 177, 739

Saint Helena Google site, 734

Saint Vincent and the Grenadines Google site, 734

sales-only offices, 17

San Francisco Chronicle website, 517

San Francisco earthquake mashups, 315

San Marino Google site, 734

Satellite button, 276

satellite images, 276-278

Saudi Arabia Google site, 735

Save Changes button, 378

Save Preferences button, 162

saving

attachments (Gmail), 362

chat history, 390-391

driving directions (Earth), 337

Earth views, 335

image search results, 439

photos (Picasa), 598

search results, 53

Scavengeroogle, 312

Scholar, 118
  accessing, 118
  adding to websites, 128
  advanced searches, 124-126
  benefits, 120
  content
    adding, 130
    identifying, 119
  invisible web information, 121
  libraries
    access, 129
    links, 126
  non-public information, 119
  Preferences page, 126
  print-only content, 120
  publishers, 130
  results, 121-123
  searches, 124

Schoogle/Schoogling, 118

school districts layer (Earth), 340

schools layer (Earth), 340

scientific constants, 199-202

scraper sites, 636

Screensaver (Pack), 610-611

ScubaMAP website, 310

Search Appliance, 670-671

Search Appliance APIs, 685

search boxes
  adding to websites, 647, 650
  SafeSearch filtering, 177

search result pages, 26
  Toolbar, 532-533

Search button (search result page), 26

Search Engine Optimizer website, 636

search engines
  advantages, 60
  BackRub, 12
  directories, compared, 56-58
  optimization
    code updates, 631
    deliberate practices to avoid, 634-636
    designs to avoid, 632-634
    dynamic content, 632
    formatting words, 629
    fraudulent, 637
    heading tags, 631
    hierarchical organization, 628
    keywords, 628-629
    Logic website, 637
    META tags, 630-631
    OPML files, 632
    services, 636-637
    site links, increasing, 627
    software, 636
    text links, 629
    text not images, 629
    TITLE tags, 631
    Toolkit website, 636
  spamming, 634

Search for New Content button, 111

Search Homepage Content button, 166

search interface (applications), 686

Search Mail button, 364

search result pages, 25-27
  Advanced Search page, 26
  results page advertising, 659
    across Google Network, 659
    ads, creating, 660, 663
    costs, 660
    performance, monitoring, 664
    third-party sites, 659
  cached, 27
  extending searches, 28
  omitted results, 27
  OneBox specialized results, 26
  other relevant pages, 27
  page excerpt, 26
  page title, 26
  preferences, 26
  search box, 26
  Search button, 26
  Search Within Results link, 28
  similar pages, 27
  size, 27
  sponsored links, 26
  statistics bar, 26
  top links, 26
  URL, 26

Search Video button, 447

Search Within Results link (search results page), 28

searches. *See also* finding
Advanced Search page,
44-46
and, 32
answers, 465
  asking questions,
    470-472
  clarifying questions, 473
  comments, adding, 470
  cost, 467
  previously answered
    questions, viewing,
    467, 470
  types of questions, 466
  viewing questions, 472
  rating answers, 474
  researchers, 466
automatic word stem-
  ming, 34
bargains (Froogle),
  222-223
  adding products to, 232
  advanced searches,
    226-228
  best bargains, 234
  buying items, 228
  cell phones, 526
  functions, 222
  local bargains, 229-230
  main page, 223
  merchant reviews,
    232-234
  product detail pages,
    225-226
  results, 224-225
  searching, 223
  Shopping list feature,
    235-236
  store inventories, upload-
    ing, 262
  Wish List, 236

blogs, 98-100
  adding feeds to web
    pages, 115-116
  advanced options,
    103-105
  evaluating results, 102
  feeds, 110-111
  importing feeds, 112
  reading results, 108-109
  sharing feeds, 113-114
  site URLs, 111
  subscriptions, 106-107,
    112
body text, 40
books, 476
  adding content, 476-477
  additional book informa-
    tion, 484
  advanced book searches,
    478-479
  content, viewing,
    479-480
  Google Book search, 478
  Google Books Library
    Project, 477
  Google Books Partner
    Program, 476
  standard web search,
    477
capitalization, 29
date ranges, 41
deep web, 19
Directory, 61-64
domains, 38
exact phrases, 35
excluding words, 34
extending, 28
facts, 148
file types, 37
filetype, 48

financial (Finance)
  accessing, 80
  company/security-specific
    pages, 83-85
  Discussion Groups,
    91-95
  financial metrics, 86
  interactive charts, 87-89
  Market Summary, 81
  portfolio tracking, 89-91
  Recent Quotes, 82
  Related News, 82
  Today's Headlines, 82
Google, adding to web-
  sites
  customizable Google
    Free WebSearch,
    678-680
  Free SafeSearch,
    676-677
  Free WebSearch,
    675-676
  Free WebSearch with
    SiteSearch, 677-678
  Site-Flavored Google
    Search, 681-682
highlighting keywords, 43
home page, 24
I'm Feeling Lucky button,
  25
images, 435
  advanced, 436-437
  basic, 436
  copyrighted images,
    deleting, 441
  fair use, 441-442
  filtering, 440
  mobile, 522
  results, 438-440
index, 20

keyword selection, 51-53
languages, 181-183
links to specific pages, 42
maps, 269
   address, 269-271
   businesses, 288-290
   cell phones, 291-294
   default locations, 287
   downloading to cell
     phones, 524
   driving directions,
     280-285
   emailing, 279
   faulty directions,
     285-286
   Google map-builder web-
     sites, 692
   hybrid maps, 278
   landmarks, 271
   linking to, 279
   mashups, See Maps,
     mashups
   naming, 268
   navigating, 274-275
   printing, 280
   satellite images,
     276-278
   sharing maps, 279-280
   URLs, 272-273
   web search, 274
methodology, 51
mobile, 520-521
   Froogle, 526, 711
   Gmail, 525
   home page, 526
   image searches, 522
   local searches, 522
   maps, 291-294
   News, 516, 525

   Sitemaps, 622
   specialized web searches,
     521
   text messaging searches,
     523-524
   web searches, 520-521
most recent results, 47
movies, 153-156
music, 156-157
news articles, 513-514
number of results per
   page, 48
numbers, 41, 152-153
omitted results, 27
or, 32
page information, 43
page titles, 39
people
   names, 69-72
   personal information,
     75-76
   phone numbers, 74
   white pages directories,
     72
   yourself, 76-78
process, 17-18
purity, 172
queries, entering, 24
results. *See* results
satellite images, 276-278
saving results, 53
scholarly information
   (Scholar), 118, 124
   accessing, 118
   adding content, 130
   adding to websites, 128
   advanced searches,
     124-126
   benefits, 120
   identifying content, 119

   invisible web informa-
     tion, 121
   library access, 129
   library links, 126
   non-public information,
     119
   Preferences page, 126
   print-only content, 120
   publishers, 130
   results, 121-123
   searches, 124
servers, 17
similar pages, 42
similar words, 34
stop words, 33
technology, 132-135
travel, 149-150
U.S. government, 132,
   136
URL parameters, 46-47
URLs, 39
Usenet. *See* Groups
videos, 447
   categories, browsing,
     444
   competitors, 449
   downloading, 453,
     457-458
   Picks, 448
   playing, 452-456
   previewing, 450
   searching, 447
   title, 447
   Top 100 videos, 447
   unofficial blogs, 448
   Video Blog, 448
   viewing options, 451-452
   views, changing,
     445-446

weather, 149

web pages database, 18-19

whole-word wildcards, 36

word order, 29

words in links, 40

words/definitions
Glossary, 141-142
Sets, 143-144
what is search, 139-140

sec operator, 198

secant operator, 198

security-specific searches, 83-85

Select Email dialog box, 602

selecting keywords, 51-53

selling items (Base), 256
Google Payments, accepting, 259-260
listings, submitting, 256-258

Send Email button, 114

Send Pictures button, 601

Send To button (Toolbar), 538

sending Gmail messages, 361

Senegal Google site, 735

SEO (search engine optimization), 627
code updates, 631
deliberate practices to avoid, 634-636
designs to avoid, 632-634
dynamic content, 632
formatting words, 629

fraudulent, 637

heading tags, 631

hierarchical organization, 628

keywords, 628-629

Logic website, 637

META tags, 630-631

OPML files, 632

services, 636-637

site links, increasing, 627

software, 636

text links, 629

text not images, 629

TITLE tags, 631

Toolkit website, 636

servers, 17

Service Discovery dialog box, 398

Sets, 143-144, 709

Seychelles Google site, 735

Sharemywifi.com, 305

sharing
maps, 279-280
photos (Picasa)
burning to CDs/DVDs, 604
email, 602
Hello, 601
RSS feeds, 113-114

shopping
Base
attributes, 246
browsing items, 251-253
bulk uploads, 261-262
buying items, 253-254
eBay, compared, 263-264

prohibited items, 247-248
searching, 248-251
selling items, 256-260
labels, 246
overview, 246

Froogle, 222
adding products to, 232
advanced searches, 226-228
best bargains, 234
buying items, 228
cell phones, 526
functions, 222
local bargains, 229-230
main page, 223
merchant reviews, 232-234
Mobile, 711
product detail pages, 225-226
results, 224-225
searching, 223
Shopping list feature, 235-236
store inventories, uploading, 262
Wish list, 236

Catalogs, 237
product categories, 239
searching, 238
viewing, 239, 242

Shopping list (Froogle), 235-236

shopping malls layer (Earth), 340

Shopping.com, 222

sidebar (Desktop), 561
  gadgets, 562-564
  viewing, 561
  web searches, 559

signatures (Gmail), 382-383

signing up for alerts, 213-214

similar page searches, 27, 42

similar word searches, 34

sin operator, 198

sine operator, 198

Singapore Google site, 735

sinh operator, 199

site directory, 727-728

site feed Blogger tags, 428

Site Magellan website, 625

Site Meter website, 431

site: operator, 38, 46, 739

Site-Flavored Google Search, 681-682

SiteLab website, 637

Sitemaps, 621
  Crawl Stats page, 627
  creating, 623-624
  Mobile, 622
  Query Stats page, 626
  statistics/diagnostics, 625-626
  websites, submitting, 622-623

SitemapsPal website, 625

SketchUp, 671-672

SkiBonk website, 310

Slovak Republic Google site, 735

smugMaps website, 308

Solomon Islands Google site, 735

Sony PSPs video downloads, 458

Soople, 49, 208-209

source: operator, 739

South Africa Google site, 735

South Korea Google site, 186

spacecraft mashups, 315

Spacecraft Tracking website, 315

Spain Google site, 735

spam
  blogs, 414
  Gmail, 371

spamdexing, 634

special effects (pictures), 596-597

speed, 205

speed of light, 199

SpellCheck button (Toolbar), 536

spelling, checking, 687

sponsored links (search result page), 26

sports mashups, 309-310

sports venues layer (Earth), 340

Spotted.at website, 312

sqrt operator, 198

square root operator, 198

Sri Lanka Google site, 735

Star button, 588

starring Gmail messages, 367

Start a New Discussion button, 95

start page content (Personalized Homepage), 165-166

starting
  chats
    Gmail, 393-394
    Talk, 388
  groups (Groups), 501-502
  threads (Groups), 500
  voice-based chats, 391

StatCounter website, 431

statistics (Sitemaps), 625-626

statistics bar (search result page), 26

stock prices, 13

stocks: operator, 80, 739

stop words (searches), 33

store inventories, 262

store: operator, 228, 739

Storm Report Map, 298

street maps
  businesses
    adding, 290
    finding, 288-290
    location data, submitting, 262
  cell phones
    Maps for Mobile application, 293-294

querying via text mes-
saging, 292

sending maps, 291

default locations, 287

downloading to cell
phones, 524

driving directions, 280

following, 282, 285

generating, 280-281

printing, 285

reversing, 283

faulty directions, 285-286

Google map-builder web-
sites, 692

hybrid maps, 278

mashups, 295-296

Area 51, 315

bird flu, 315

bird watchers, 314

celebrity-sightings, 312

colleges/universities, 307

demographics, 306

first kisses, 314

food/entertainment,
302-303

games, 311-312

highest elevation points,
315

houses, 301

local information/serv-
ices, 299-300

location bookmarks, 314

news, 297

package mappers, 314

people's atlas, 314

personals, 315

photo map, 308

political campaign con-
tributions, 315

registered sex offenders,
315

San Francisco earth-
quake, 315

spacecraft, 315

sports, 309-310

time, 315

transportation, 303-304

U.S. presidential birth-
places, 314

weather, 297

WiFi/cellular, 305

navigating, 274-275

satellite images, 276-278

searching, 269

address, 269-271

landmarks, 271

URLs, 272-273

web search, 274

sharing maps, 279-280

Strike Up Your Google
Maps website, 692

subject: operator, 366, 739

Submit Express website,
637

Submit-It website, 637

Submitawebsite.com, 637

SubmitToday.com website,
637

subscribing

AdSense, 643-644

alerts, 213-214

blog search results,
106-107

Gmail, 354

Groups, 498

news alerts, 515-516

RSS feeds, 112

subtraction operator, 196

Suggest, 712

Sweden Google site, 735

Switchboard website, 72

Switzerland Google site,
735

syndicating blogs, 416-417

T

The T website, 304

Taiwan Google site, 735

Tajikistan Google site, 735

Talk, 387-388

chat history, saving,
390-391

connecting with other IM
networks, 396-399

customizing, 391-392

disadvantages, 395

status, changing, 391

text-based chats, 388

users, blocking, 388-390

voice-based chats, 391

tan operator, 198

tangent operator, 198

tanh operator, 199

Tech Blog, 403

technology searches,
132-135

technology-only offices, 17

technology/sales office
combinations, 17

temperature, 205

templates (Blogger), 421
  choosing, 406, 421
  coding, 425
  HTML tags, 425-429
  third-party, 421, 424

terrain layer (Earth), 340

text messaging (Mobile searches), 523-524

text passages, translating, 189

text-based chats, 388

Thailand Google site, 735

third party
  alternate advanced search forms, 49
  Blogger templates, 421, 424
  Google developers, 684-685
  software (Pack)
    Ad Aware SE Personal, 613
    Adobe Reader, 614
    GalleryPlayer, 614
    Mozilla Firefox, 612
    Norton AntiVirus, 613
    RealPlayer, 614

three-dimensional fly-bys (Earth)
  3D buildings option, 328
  3D terrain option, 328
  custom placemarks, 343-345
  default view, 323
  distances along paths, 345-347
  driving directions, 336-337

Enterprise, 671
GPS devices, 347
interface, 318
KML, 685
layers, 338-340
locations, 335-336
navigating, 319
  keyboard, 322-323
  mouse, 321-322
  onscreen controls, 320
placemarks, 325-327
points of interest, 342
versions, 317-318
views, 332
  full-screen mode, 333
  latitude/longitude grid, 333
  Overview map, 333
  preferences, 332-333
  printing, 335
  saving, 335
zooming, 323

tilde (~) operator, 34

Tilt Down button, 326

time, 205

Time website, 517

time mashups, 315

Timeline view (Desktop), 554

title searches, 39

TITLE tags, 631

title: operator, 447

to: operator, 366, 739

Today's Headlines (Google Finance), 82

toEat.com, 302

Tonga Google site, 735

Toolbar
  API, 685
  blogging, 411-412
  buttons
    adding/deleting, 540
    AutoFill, 537
    AutoLink, 536
    Bookmarks, 535
    custom, adding, 541
    Desktop, 534
    Gmail, 535
    Highlight, 539
    News, 534
    optional, 541
    PageRank, 536
    pop-up blocker, 536
    search box, 532-533
    Send To, 538
    SpellCheck, 536
    Weather, 534
    word find, 539
  customizing, 540-541
  default configuration, 532
  Enterprise, 667-668
  Gmail, viewing, 384
  installing, 532
  translating, 192

Top 100 videos, 447

Top Business Schools Map website, 307

Top Engineering Schools Map website, 307

top links (search result page), 26

Top Medical Schools Map website, 307

TopRank website, 637

trading volume, 86

Transit, 711

transit layer (Earth), 340

Translate button, 189

Translate page, 189

translating languages, 187-189
  disadvantages, 193
  Google Toolbar, 192
  search results, 192
  text passages, 189
  web pages, 190
  words with Google Toolbar, 192

transportation mashups, 303-304

travel searches, 149-150

trend analysis applications, 686

Trends, 704-705

trigonometric functions, 198

Trinidad and Tobago Google site, 735

Tripods website, 312

Trulia, 301

Turkey Google site, 735

Turkmenistand Google site, 735

U

U.K. Google site, 186

U.S.
  Congressional districts layer (Earth), 340

dollars to Euros conversion, 203

Fast Food Locations website, 302

government searches, 132, 136

News and World Report website, 517

presidential birthplace mashups, 314

Presidential History website, 314

Uganda Google site, 735

Ukraine Google site, 735

The Ultimates website, 72

under: operator, 739

United Arab Emirates Google site, 735

United Kingdom Google site, 735

units of measure, converting, 202-206
  area, 205
  cups into teaspoons, 203
  currency, 205
  data, 205
  degrees, 204
  distance, 205
  electricity, 205
  energy, 205
  hexadecimal, 206
  mass, 205
  meters to feet, 203
  miles per hour to kilometers per hour, 206
  nautical miles, 206
  numbering systems, 205
  pounds to kilograms, 204

power, 205
quantity, 205
speed, 205
temperature, 205
time, 205
U.S. dollars to Euros, 203
volume, 205
years into seconds, 204
years to Roman numerals, 205

University Search, 132
  accessing, 132
  technology searches, 134-135
  U.S. government searches, 136

Unix Google search, 134

unofficial content modules (Personalized Homepage), 169-170

updates (Pack), 609

Upload Video button, 459

uploading
  bulk items (Google Base), 261-262
  video, 459-461

URLs
  blog sites, 111
  Maps, 272-273
  parameters, 46-47
  RSS feeds, 111
  search result page, 26
  searches, 39

Uruguay Google site, 735

USATODAY website, 517

Use This Template button, 421

Usenet
archiving, 492
history, 490
newsgroup hierarchies, 490-491
overview, 490
searching. *See* Groups

Uzbekistan Google site, 735

V

vacation mode (Gmail), 379-380

Vanuatu Google site, 735

Venezuela Google site, 735

Video, 444
categories, browsing, 444
competitors, 449
Picks videos, 448
searching, 447
title searches, 447
Top 100 videos, 447
unofficial blogs, 448
Video Blog, 448
videos
  downloading, 453, 457-458
  playing, 452-456
  previewing, 450
  uploading, 459-461
  viewing options, 451-452
views, changing, 445-446

Video Player, 454-456

Vietnam Google site, 735

viewing
asked questions (Answers), 472
blogs, 408

book content (Book Search), 479-480
calendars, 572, 575
  Agenda, 574
  Day, 572
  Month, 573
  multiple calendars, 575
  Next 4 Days, 574
  other applications, 575-576
  Week, 573
Catalogs, 239, 242
Earth, 332
  full-screen mode, 333
  latitude/longitude, 333
  Overview map, 333
  preferences, 332-333
  printing, 335
  saving, 335
Gmail
  attachments, 362
  contacts, 374
  conversations, 356-358
  messages, 384
  RSS feeds, 380-381
Groups, 497
hard disk search results, 550-552
image search results, 438-439
index (Desktop), 554
News
  cell phones, 525
  headlines, 509
previously answered questions, 467, 470
search results, 25-27
Shopping list (Froogle), 235

sidebar (Desktop), 561
Sitemap statistics/ diagnostics, 625-626
Video, 445-446
Wish list (Froogle), 236

Virgin Islands Google site, 735

viruses
Gmail, 371
Norton AntiVirus, 613

voice-based chats, 391

volcanoes layer (Earth), 340

volume, 205

W

WalkJogRun website, 309

***Wall Street Journal* website, 517**

Wannadive.net, 310

***Washington Post* website, 517**

water layer (Earth), 340

Weather button (Toolbar), 534

weather
mashups, 297
operator, 739
searches, 149

Weather Underground, 149

WeatherBonk, 297

Web 2.0, 688-689

Web Accelerator, 713

web alerts, 212

web browsers

Google as default search engine, 542

Google browser buttons, 544

Web CEO website, 636

web indexes

page rankings, increasing, 627

code updates, 631

deliberate practices to avoid, 634-636

designs to avoid, 632-634

dynamic content, 632

formatting words, 629

fraudulent SEOs, 637

heading tags, 631

hierarchical organization, 628

keywords, 628-629

META tags, 630-631

OPML files, 632

SEO, 636-637

site links, increasing, 627

text links, 629

text not images, 629

TITLE tags, 631

websites, adding/deleting, 620-621

web logs. See **blogs**

web pages

Google database, 18-19

indexes, 20

ranking, increasing

code updates, 631

deliberate practices to avoid, 634-636

designs to avoid, 632-634

dynamic content, 632

formatting words, 629

fraudulent SEOs, 637

heading tags, 631

hierarchical organization, 628

keywords, 628-629

META tags, 630-631

OPML files, 632

SEO, 636-637

site links, increasing, 627

text links, 629

text not images, 629

TITLE tags, 631

RSS feeds, adding, 115-116

translating, 190-192

web servers, 17

WebPosition Gold website, 636

Webs API, 685-687

websites

1001 Secret Fishing Holes, 310

ABC News, 516

Ad-Aware, 614

Adobe, 605, 614

advertising, adding, 640, 644, 647

AdSense for Content, 640-641

AdSense for Search, 641-642

AdSense Referrals, 650-652

earnings potential, increasing, 654-658

joining AdSense, 643-644

performance, monitoring, 653

revenues, 642

Alkemmis Local, 304

Alta Vista Babel Fish, 193

American Heritage Dictionary of the English Language, 143

Answers.com, 140

Apartment Ratings, 301

Apple iTunes Video Store, 449

Area 51 Satellite and Aerial Photos, 315

Argaili White & Yellow, 72

Associated Press News Mashup, 297

BART Map/Schedule, 304

BBC News, 516

BeenMapped.com, 314

Beermapping.com, 302

Best Google Videos, 448

Best of the Web, 58

The BigOne, 315

BizRates, 222

Blogger, 404

Blogger templates, 421

Bloomberg, 79

Boston Globe, 517

Bravenet Counter Site Stats, 431

broadcast news, 516

BroadwayZone, 300

BunkerShot.com Golf Course Explorer, 310

Business Week, 517

CBS News, 516

Cell Phone Reception and
Tower Search, 305

Chicago
Hot Dog Stands, 302
Transit Authority, 303

Chicago Tribune, 517

Chompster, 302

CityRanks, 306

ClubFly, 303

CNET news, 42

CommunityWalk, 692

Corel, 605

deleting from web index,
621

Denver Post, 517

designing, 710

Detroit Free Press, 517

Entertainment Weekly, 517

EVMapper, 299

FAA Flight Delay
Information, 304

Federal Trade
Commission, 78

Feedburner service, 416

Find a Local Racetrack,
310

Find the Landmark, 311

findu.com, 305

Floodwater Mapper, 298

FOX News, 516

FreeStats, 431

FreeTranslation, 193

FutureCrisis Avian Flu
Outbreak Map, 315

G-Mapper, 624

GalleryPlayer, 614

Gawker Stalker, 312

gCensus, 306

GeoBirds, 314

Global Surfari, 310

GMaps Flight Tracker, 304

Gmaps Pedometer, 309

Google
Apple Macintosh, 134
country-specific,
731-732, 734-735
Free SafeSearch,
676-677
Free WebSearch,
675-676
Free WebSearch with
SiteSearch, 677-678
Idol, 448
Linux, 134
Map Attack, 311
Map Maker, 692
map-builders, 692
Microsoft, 134
Modules, 169
site directory, 727-728
Site-Flavored Google
Search, 681-682
Ultimate Interface, 49
Unix, 134
Video Latest, 448
Video of the Day, 448
Weather Maps, 298
Widgets, 170

Google-Yahoo Traffic-
Weather Maps, 304

GSiteCrawler, 624

Gsitemap, 624

gWiFi.net, 305

GymPost, 309

Healthia Doctor Search,
299

Hello, 601

hierarchical organization,
628

High Fiber Content, 403

High Rankings, 636

Highest Elevation Points,
315

hit counters, 431

HockeyCat Rink, 310

HomePriceMaps.com, 301

Homes Sold, 301

Hot Modules, 170

HotelMapper, 300

HotorNot + Google Maps,
315

HousingMaps, 301

In Search of Google
Videos, 448

including in web index,
620

InfoSpace, 72

IntelliMapper, 625

Internet Business
Promoter, 636

IrfanView, 605

Jabber, 396

JibMap, 299

JoeMap, 308

Judy's Book Maps, 300

Julian Date Calculator, 42

Kosher Food/Restaurant
Maps, 302

Libraries411, 299

Local Lush, 303

Local News by Zip Code,
297

LookSmart, 58

Los Angeles Times, 517

Macromedia Flash Player,
452

Map Builder, 692

MapGameDay.com, 309

Maplandia News Centre BBC World News Map, 297

MapSexOffenders.com, 315

MarketWatch, 79

Menumap, 302

Miami Herald, 517

Microsoft Digital Image Suite, 605

Minneapolis Star Tribune, 517

Mozilla Firefox, 612

MSN Video, 449

MSNBC, 516

My Way, 172

My Yahoo!, 172

myGmaps, 692

MyWikiMap Cheap Gas Prices, 299

National Review, 517

New York Times, 517

news magazines, 517

Newseum, 517

newspapers, 517

Newsweek, 517

NexTag, 222

NextBus, 303

NFL Stadiums, 309

NYC
Beer and Music, 303
Trafficland, 304
Transit Maps, 303

OCLC project, 120

onNYTurf, 303

Open Directory, 58

OPML, 632

OptLink, 636

The Oz Report Flight Parks, 310

PackageMapper.com, 314

Panorama Explorer, 308

Panoramio, 308

People, 517

Perfect 10, 441

Personal Weather Stations, 298

Pixagogo, 308

Platial, 314

PokerMashup, 311

price comparison, 222

Priority Submit, 636

Rand McNally, 286

Real Estate Advisor, 301

RealEstateAuctions.com, 301

RealPlayer, 614

Road Sign Math, 312

Roadsideamerica.com, 304

San Francisco Chronicle, 517

ScubaMAP, 310

Search Engine Optimizer, 636

SEO, 636-637

sharemywifi.com, 305

Shopping.com, 222

Site Magellan, 625

Site Meter, 431

SiteLab, 637

sitemaps
creating, 623-624
submittals, 622-623

SitemapsPal, 625

SkiBonk, 310

smugMaps, 308

Soople, 49, 208

Spacecraft Tracking, 315

spotted.at, 312

StatCounter, 431

Storm Report Map, 298

Strike Up Your Google Maps, 692

Submit Express, 637

Submit-It, 637

Submitawebsite.com, 637

SubmitToday.com, 637

Switchboard, 72

The T, 304

Tech Blog, 403

Time, 517

toEat.com, 302

Top Business Schools Map, 307

Top Engineering Schools Map, 307

Top Medical Schools Map, 307

TopRank, 637

Tripods, 312

Trulia, 301

U.S. Fast Food Locations, 302

U.S. News and World Report, 517

U.S. Presidential History, 314

The Ultimates, 72

USATODAY, 517

WalkJogRun, 309

Wall Street Journal, 517

Wannadive.net, 310

Washington Post, 517

Weather Underground, 149

WeatherBonk, 297

Web CEO, 636

WebPosition Gold, 636

What Time Is It?, 315

Where I Had My First Kiss, 314

widQ, 170

WikiBroker Real Estate Maps, 301

World Golf Map, 309

World Wide Webfoot, 306

Xbox Live Gamer Map, 311

Yahoo! Directory, 58

Yahoo! Video, 449

YouTube, 449

Zillow.com, 301

ZoomInfo, 73

Week view (Calendar), 573

Western Samoa Google site, 735

what are operator, 739

what is operator, 739

what is searches, 139-140

What Time Is It? website, 315

Where I Had My First Kiss website, 314

white pages directories, 72

whole-word wildcards, 36

widQ, 170

WiFi mashups, 305

WikiBroker Real Estate Maps, 301

wildcards, 34-36

wireless service provider, 722-723

Wish list (Froogle), 236

word find buttons (Toolbar), 539

words

links, 40

order, 29

searches

Glossary, 141-142

Sets, 143-144

what is search, 139-140

translating from Google Toolbar, 192

WordTranslator, 192

World Golf Map website, 309

world headquarters, 16

World Wide Webfoot, 306

X-Y-Z

X operator, 196

Xbox Live Gamer Map, 311

Yahoo!

Directory, 58

Google, compared, 719

Video website, 449

Widgets, 564

years into seconds conversion, 204

years to Roman numerals conversion, 205

YouTube website, 449

Zillow.com, 301

zoom slider control (Picasa), 589

ZoomInfo website, 73

zooming (Earth), 323

The How It Works series offers a unique, visual, four-color approach designed to educate curious readers. From machine code to hard-drive design to wireless communication, the How It Works series offers a clear and concise approach to understanding technology—a perfect source for those who prefer to learn visually. Check out other books in this best-selling series by Que:

How Computers Work, Eighth Edition
ISBN: 0-7897-3424-9

How Computers Work, Eighth Edition offers a unique and detailed look at the inner workings of your computer. From keyboards to virtual reality helmets, this book covers it all.

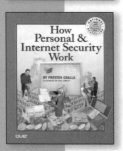

How Personal & Internet Security Work
ISBN: 0-7897-3553-9

How Personal & Internet Security Work clearly explains every aspect of security concerns that have become so important in an increasingly insecure world—everything from spyware, viruses to anti-terrorist screening systems in airports.

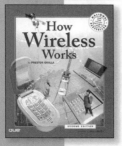

How Wireless Works, Seventh Edition
ISBN: 0-7897-3344-7

How Wireless Works gives you an insider's view on how all things wireless work, from WiFi networking, to hot spots, to wireless web surfing, to cell phones and more.

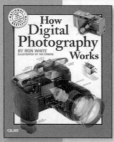

How Digital Photography Works
ISBN: 0-7897-3309-9

How Digital Photography Works offers a behind the scenes look at digital photography. You'll understand how your digital camera captures images and how your software fixes your mistakes.

www.quepublishing.com

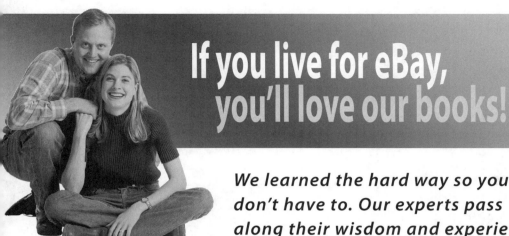

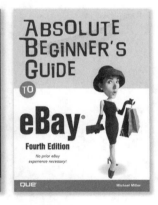